PHILADELPHIA

A NEW URBAN DIRECTION

SECOND EDITION

PHILADELPHIA

A NEW URBAN DIRECTION

SECOND EDITION

OFFICE OF THE CITY CONTROLLER
CITY OF PHILADELPHIA

FIRST EDITION
JONATHAN A. SAIDEL, City Controller
BRETT H. MANDEL, Assistant City Controller
KEVIN J. BABYAK, Assistant City Controller
DAVID A. VOLPE, First Deputy City Controller

FOREWORD BY EDMUND N. BACON

SECOND EDITION
JONATHAN A. SAIDEL, City Controller
MARISA WAXMAN, Director, Financial and Policy Analysis Unit
ANTHONY DI MARTINO, Assistant City Controller

FOREWORD BY EDWARD G. RENDELL

SAINT JOSEPH'S UNIVERSITY PRESS, PHILADELPHIA
MEMBER OF THE ASSOCIATION OF JESUIT UNIVERSITY PRESSES

The views and opinions expressed in this book are the authors'
and do not necessarily represent those of Saint Joseph's University.

LIBRARY OF CONGRESS CATALOGING-IN-PUBLICATION DATA

Philadelphia (Pa.). Office of the City Controller.
  Philadelphia : a new urban direction / Office of the City Controller, City of Philadelphia ; Jonathan A.
Saidel ... [et al.] ; foreword by Edward G. Rendell.-- 2nd ed.
     p. cm.
  Includes bibliographical references and index.
  ISBN 0-916101-53-3 (alk. paper)
  1. Urban policy--Pennsylvania--Philadelphia. 2. City planning--Pennsylvania--
Philadelphia. 3. Philadelphia (Pa.)--Politics and government. 4. Philadelphia (Pa.)--Economic policy.
5. Philadelphia (Pa.)--Forecasting. I. Saidel, Jonathan A. II. Title.
  HT168.P43P55 2006
  307.7609748'11--dc22
                              2005035874

Published by:
Saint Joseph's University Press
5600 City Avenue
Philadelphia, Pennsylvania 19131-1395
www.sju.edu/sjupress/

Saint Joseph's University Press is a member of the Association of Jesuit University Presses

THIS BOOK IS DEDICATED TO

THE CITIZENS OF PHILADELPHIA

TABLE OF CONTENTS

CHAPTER 3
FISCAL POLICY FOR PHILADELPHIA'S FUTURE 115

FIGURES

TABLES

FOREWORD TO THE SECOND EDITION

Philadelphia is a city built on layers of history. Our streets, our economy, our cultural and civic institutions have all gained strength from what has come before. Philadelphians can see and feel the history of the city and nation with each step they take through our neighborhoods. Our landmarks and civic spaces all recall specific moments in our history, some highlight progress and others our missteps. Constant, deep, and direct connections to our past, while providing stability, can promote complacency in approaching the city's challenges and opportunities. With this wealth of history at hand prompting nostalgia for the past, it may be tempting for our elected leaders and citizenry to stay the course, accept the city's failings and strive to simply manage the city's decline rather than fight for its revival. Philadelphia and all of America's cities cannot be content to live in the past, but must actively work to create a bright future for their residents and businesses.

Fortunately, Philadelphia's history is one of boldness and innovation for the common good. Our city offered citizens the nation's first public library, voluntary fire association, public school, and anti-slavery society. In 1801 on the site where City Hall sits today, the Philadelphia Water Works opened the nation's first pumping station to provide clean drinking water and resources for firefighting. This innovation transformed Philadelphia and the future of urban places from collections of individual plots of land with independent water and sewer arrangements that contributed to public health problems and filth in dense areas, to an inter-dependant system among residents, government, and businesses to collectively improve the efficiency and quality of the water supply and environment.

Today, Philadelphia remains a city of individuals and neighborhoods whose fates are intertwined. We have made great strides in improving our communities and economic vitality, but the work is not yet finished. We need to continue our pursuit of innovations that improve the quality of the city as a place to live, work, and visit. This second edition of *Philadelphia: A New Urban Direction* represents an important contribution to the ongoing process of crafting pioneering solutions to surmount the impediments to growth and improvement of the city. In updating their ground-breaking initial publication, Jonathan Saidel and the staff of the City Controller's Office have continued Philadelphia's proud tradition of seeking imaginative and effective strategies to address the trends and issues that face America's older urban jurisdictions.

Government and civic leaders can never be satisfied with their achievements, and it is incumbent upon them to rigorously reassess and refine their ideas and actions. I commend Jonathan Saidel and his staff for continuing to battle complacency and once again analyzing the current conditions of the city and developing recommendations that are appropriate to the context and the capacity of the city government to act. The ideas presented in the second edition of *Philadelphia: A New Urban Direction* will renew informed debate over the future of the city. More importantly, this work makes clear that only an ongoing focus on viable proposals for improved government performance and service delivery can bring about a more vibrant future for the city.

EDWARD G. RENDELL
GOVERNOR OF THE COMMONWEALTH OF PENNSYLVANIA

FOREWORD TO THE FIRST EDITION

We came to this beautiful, unspoiled continent from many parts of the world and thought ourselves alone because the people who were here, and their ancestors before them, managed to live for centuries without leaving evidence of their existence. In contrast, our own contribution has been to rush headlong over the continent, filling its prairies with our artifacts, abusing the land, polluting the rivers, and fouling the air.

We are rushing to our destruction and it is astounding how unconscious our supposedly rational society is about its own future. As a nation, we have two ambivalent views of it. The prevailing one is that problems projected for the future simply do not exist except in the minds of a few annoying people whom we like to dismiss as "environmental nuts." The second one is that the future is determined by some sort of statistical trend which is inevitable and beyond our power to change. And so we continue to indulge ourselves on our natural resources without discipline and to the detriment of the planet.

Over the face of our continent we have built, at enormous cost, complicated technical artifacts we call cities, where people used to live. We have paved our streets. We have burrowed into the ground and inserted an amazing complex of wires, pipes, and great concrete tubes with electrically-driven cars running through them transporting people from one place to another.

Now, we are abandoning our cities because, like the characters in Alice's Adventures in Wonderland, we have soiled our tablecloth. We are building something elsewhere which is neither city nor farm and which pollutes the land and air and threatens the very survival of life on earth. We rush headlong, developing more and more suburbs which cannot be sustained into the future as we let our cities fester. This ever-growing suburban state of mind is a great threat to our very survival.

It takes great courage to pull back the curtain and expose our folly. This is exactly what Jonathan Saidel and the City Controller's Office have done in this deeply significant book about the future of Philadelphia, and cities in general.

Philadelphia: A New Urban Direction forces us to look reality in the face, to realize that there really is a future, to lead us kicking and screaming into that future, and most importantly, to consider intelligent, sophisticated, and workable ideas on important issues which confront our cities. For these things, Jonathan Saidel and his associates deserve the highest praise.

This book charts a new direction in thought which lays the foundation for a whole new approach to what must be done for our cities if they are to survive. The danger is that one may conclude that the enormous problems and woes of the modern city are the result of inevitable trends that one person cannot do anything to change. But happily, great accomplishments are often achieved in defiance of statistical projections and "inevitable" trends. If we are really to create a better future, building on the firm foundations which Saidel has laid, we must access something much more important than numbers, namely, the untapped reserves of human energy and the amazing ability of people to revitalize their own environment and to come together to achieve wonders.

We should be very grateful to the authors of this book for having the courage to face up to the beast of our anti-city folly, for grabbing the beast by the horns, for twisting its neck in the opposite direction and giving it a good kick in its rear. Now it is up to us, individually and collectively, to follow through, to enlarge, to enrich, to simplify and to clarify, and finally to push forward the brilliant and comprehensively outlined ideas presented here for solving the problems of our cities. For we must, as a nation, pursue a vision for the future of our great cities which is clear and workable and which is so compelling that it must be accomplished.

EDMUND N. BACON
EMERITUS FELLOW, AMERICAN INSTITUTE OF ARCHITECTS

PREFACE

Not so long ago, the best place to "see" Philadelphia was from the top of City Hall, below "Billy Penn's hat." From the viewing deck, one could survey the city stretching out along the Broad and Market Street grid extending from the Delaware River to across the Schuylkill River. And not so long ago, City Hall stood at (and as) the center of Philadelphia. When it was completed in 1901, the building heralded the consolidation of governmental power, just as John Wanamaker's new department store and the banks and office buildings nearby bespoke the mass consumption culture and new information technology of the industrial age. Power radiated out from Center City, and business, shopping, and play brought people in, many arriving via the great Pennsylvania and Reading railroad train depots downtown. Today, taller buildings overshadow City Hall, crowding out a clear view of the city, and the automobile, telecommunications, and the computer culture have pulled workers and shoppers away from Center City to office complexes and shopping malls along the interstates. No mighty banking, legal, and insurance houses rule from Philadelphia as in time past; indeed, now the once proverbial "Philadelphia lawyer" or "Philadelphia banker" is likely in the employ of a firm with headquarters elsewhere. So, too, the city once known as "the workshop of the world" makes little of the textiles, carpets, glass, finished steel products, locomotives, radios, leather goods, refined sugar, or myriad other products that kept armies of workers employed for generations; even the Philadelphia Naval Shipyard closed after two centuries of service to the nation. And so the story goes.

But even as Philadelphia proper loses people and jobs to surrounding areas or places far away, a "new Philadelphia" emerges. What that "new Philadelphia" will look like remains unclear. A new convention center, hotels, entertainment complexes, and an Avenue of the Arts, all point to the new direction(s) Philadelphia might go. The conversion of the PSFS Building to a hotel and old warehouses to restaurants and clubs, and the restoration of city houses in "olde city" and elsewhere also promise to make a new Philadelphia from the old, not only in Center City but on the Delaware waterfront, along the Schuylkill River, and in neighborhoods. The new Philadelphia also will build on the bedrock of colleges and universities, museums and cultural organizations, pharmaceutical and chemical companies, and health service providers. Education, entertainment, and service promise to become the watchwords of the new Philadelphia's progress. Or so the boosters say.

Such a view, though, tells only part of the story. For the new Philadelphia cannot be seen from City Hall alone.

To get another perspective, one might climb the stairs to the Barbelin Tower, at Saint Joseph's University, on Hawk Hill. From that lofty height, one can see the city meeting the suburbs and the region growing beyond. And by looking closer at hand to the particular story of Saint Joseph's University and the Jesuits in Philadelphia, one also can see how private interest and public purpose converge(d). Stories of such confluence can be repeated—and as this book argues, must be repeated—hundreds of times in explaining how and why Philadelphia will not die.

From the days of Benjamin Franklin's *Junto*, when young artisans and mechanics worked for improved lighting, sewerage, fire safety, education, and poor relief, among other public concerns, through the Progressive era reformers, who mobilized to improve housing and health, among other crusades, to a host of faith-based social welfare and educational institutions today, which provide support to the homeless, the needy, and the disadvantaged, among other ministries, Philadelphians have sought to build community(ies) through voluntary organizations. Where government did not (or would not) go, private groups stepped in. They also lobbied government to join in public-private cooperation, which in many ways became the handmaid of progress as well as relief. To be sure, in "the private city" the pursuit of wealth often has overridden public service, and voluntarism failed to banish misery and want from Philadelphia. But in their public poses,

Philadelphians still recall the heritage of Franklin and the latter day saints, and point to William Penn's statue atop City Hall to remind themselves, and the world, that Philadelphia began as part of a "holy experiment" to build a new civil order. The authors of *Philadelphia: A New Urban Direction* invoke that same memory and mission in their call for a renewed private and public partnership.

The story of the Jesuits, and of Saint Joseph's in Philadelphia, reflects in microcosm that history (and promise) of private and public interests converging. From the time they first met in Paris in the sixteenth century and formalized their group as a religious order in Rome, the Jesuits rejected the monastic life and located their apostolates in highly-visible city locations where they taught, preached, and ministered in the context of urban culture. The Jesuits brought their vision and mission to the Americas, and in the eighteenth century to Philadelphia, which was fast developing into the vital hinge of empire and the principal port of entry linking Europe to the vast North American hinterlands. From the small chapel beginnings of Old St. Joseph's on Willing's Alley, near 4th and Walnut Streets, to the founding and staffing of churches, schools, orphanages, hospitals, and missions across Philadelphia, the Jesuits staked their claim to being city builders as well as teachers and priests. So, too, the establishment of Saint Joseph's College in 1851 gave the Jesuits the college they wanted to reach the immigrant and ethnic Catholic population. In time, the college would extend its mission outward to diverse peoples and other places, but always with a social conscience and a social contract framed in an urban context.

Neither the Jesuits nor the college (now university) ever left Philadelphia. When in the 1920s, after two moves within the city to find more space, the Jesuits decided to build a new campus, they chose a site on the city side of City Avenue. The mission was to Philadelphia, and through Philadelphia to the world. As the school grew in students, stature, and stability, it reached across City Avenue to buy properties at the "bottom" of the Main Line. It became a metropolitan institution in fact and vision. The unity of city and suburb is symbolized in the bridge over City Avenue connecting the urban and suburban sides of the campus and is promised in the forthcoming special services district along City Avenue, which will bring together city and suburbs in a common civic enterprise. Saint Joseph's boasts of itself as "Philadelphia's Jesuit University" for good reason. The city, the religious order, and the school give meaning and purpose to one another.

The future of the region, as revealed in *Philadelphia: A New Urban Direction*, rests on cooperation among city and suburban governments and institutions and on the continued growth of education, health services, communications, and small business. In its own mission and interests, Saint Joseph's stands at the intersection of both city and suburbs and regional development. Such a perspective explains why a Catholic university press chooses to publish a book on Philadelphia urban policy written by city officers.

The way one sees "the city" depends on where and how one chooses to stand. This book, drafted in City Hall and published on Hawk Hill, insists that one will be able to see the "new direction" only by adopting multiple directional angles and vantage points. It insists that "Philadelphia" no longer means the city proper. Philadelphia now embraces the region. But the book also insists that the "new" Philadelphia region cannot prosper, and might not even survive, without a vital center. The "new direction" must go both ways, toward city development, for example in such areas as education, health services, entertainment, and the arts where the infrastructure exists to sustain growth, as well as toward suburban (and beyond) regional development in small businesses, commercial and personal services, and small manufacturing where telecommunications, computers, and highways encourage growth. The "new direction" also means that no part of the Philadelphia region should try to monopolize an activity or strangle its growth elsewhere. Thus, for example, tourism, which largely has been developed by the city trading on its history, and conventions, which recently have been boosted by the construction of a new convention center and the opening of new hotels in the city, must simultaneously function as magnets drawing people and business into the city and as engines propelling them outward to places as far away as Lancaster County or as close as historic sites along the Delaware River.

Surveying the needs of the region from the perspective of City Hall and planning for the future health of the region from the perspectives of private and public institutions are the "new direction" for Philadelphia revealed in this book.

Of late, the scaffolding has come down from the restored William Penn statue and the viewing deck atop City Hall has reopened. The work on City Hall to return it to its former grandeur, amid the city's travails of adjusting to a new economic order, speaks volumes on the promise of a "new direction" for Philadelphia laid out in this book. It recalls Abraham Lincoln's words during the Civil War that work on the Capitol dome and its crowning statue of Freedom must continue because "if people see the Capitol going on, it is a symbol that we intend the union to go on." Just so for Philadelphia. One can see in City Hall, and in this book written from City Hall, the continued belief that Philadelphia must go on.

DR. RANDALL M. MILLER
PROFESSOR OF HISTORY, SAINT JOSEPH'S UNIVERSITY

PROLOGUE AND ACKNOWLEDGEMENTS
TO THE SECOND EDITION

Philadelphia has undergone a stunning and magnificent transformation in recent years. It is hard to imagine that the Philadelphia we see today, its skyline studded with construction cranes, soaring housing prices, and its residents hopeful about the future, is the same Philadelphia of 1991, a city too many people thought had seen its best days.

Our local economy continues to build upon traditional areas of expertise in education and medicine. The city schools are beginning to show improvement and many Philadelphians are healthier and wealthier than before. Philadelphia's vibrant cultural institutions, diverse dining establishments, and nightlife options are drawing people from throughout the city and beyond. The recent designation of the city as the "next great American city" by National Geographic Traveler is just one of the many recognitions of the progress that has been made.

A great deal of the credit for this transformation deservedly goes to our past two Mayors, Edward G. Rendell and John F. Street. By focusing on revitalizing our downtown and improving the daily quality of life in our neighborhoods, their back-to-back tenures have not only given hope to our residents, but saved us from sharing the fate of other older American cities.

That is not to say that Philadelphia is without problems or that more — in some cases, much more — does not need to be done. Too many neighborhoods continue to struggle with blight, are unsafe, and have unacceptable schools. Too many businesses and individuals decide to leave our city to escape burdensome taxes. Residents, buffeted by stories of corruption and cronyism, have lost faith that government is looking out for their interests rather than the special interests. All of the changes that need to be made must be considered against the backdrop of continued financial instability. These issues — and others explored in this update — must be confronted if we are going to capitalize upon the momentum we have built over the last 10 years.

The recommendations made in this update to *Philadelphia: A New Urban Direction* are built on a simple belief that that we can not allow our city to become "two Philadelphias", one of the affluent who can afford to live anywhere and the other of those who can not afford to go anywhere else. It is not an understatement to say that much as the city was standing at a crossroads in 1991 with the election of Ed Rendell, the city today stands today at another. We can build on the success of the last decade or slide back. Merely staying the course will not suffice. This book points a direction for decision makers to continue our progress.

We are one city and must work together to ensure our future.

———— • ————

In this second edition of *Philadelphia: A New Urban Direction*, we have endeavored to revisit the issues facing Philadelphia and the recommendations made to set Philadelphia on an improved path towards the future, as well as exploring new topics and proposals. This project could not have been undertaken without the assistance of many knowledgeable people, to whom I am deeply grateful.

I want to thank First Deputy City Controller Tony Radwanski, as well as my Director of the Financial and Policy Analysis Unit, Marisa G. Waxman for all their work transforming this revision from an idea to a reality. Their hard work and dedication on this project will make a tremendous contribution to the future of our city. I thank Deputy City Controller Albert Scaperotto for his efforts not only on this project but for decades of immeasurable public service to our great city. I must also acknowledge the support provided by Assistant City Controller Tony DiMartino, and interns Ryan Williams and Art Gossack, who labored tirelessly assembling the data to make this edition meaningful and substantive.

I am grateful to the many members of the current City and School District administrations who contributed their time, information, and insights to this project. Philadelphia's resurgence as a city is a tribute to their talent and dedication. Specifically, Joan Schlotterbeck, Lynda Orfanelli, Sylvester Johnson, and Kent Miller were exceptionally helpful in getting this revision complete. While many names of other City officials — along with the former officials, academics, experts, and other sources consulting for this project — are too numerous to be listed individually, they each made a substantial contribution to the ideas that form the basis for the original document and this revision.

I thank James Cuorato of Brandywine Realty Trust. Omar Blaik, John McGarry, and Anthony Sorrentino of the University of Pennsylvania were very helpful, as was Herb Wetzel from the Philadelphia Redevelopment Authority and Benjamin Ramos of the Greater Philadelphia Hispanic Chamber of Commerce. Of course, the contributions of my former Assistant City Controller Brett Mandel were most important, and I wish Brett and his organization, Philadelphia Forward all the best. Special appreciation is reserved for Kevin Babyak of Babyak Analytics and Greg Montanaro of the Foreign Policy Research Institute.

I am once again very grateful to the staff of the Saint Joseph's University Press for their faith in this project and their assistance creating such a high-quality product. Carmen Croce and Chris Foley were terrific to work with and the University is lucky to have them as part of their team. I reserve unending gratitude for Governor Edward G. Rendell, whose forward to the second edition of *Philadelphia: A New Urban Direction* enhances this endeavor and whose leadership has placed Philadelphia and Pennsylvania on a path to a brighter future.

As I prepare to step down as Controller, I owe a special thanks for the hundreds of current and former employees of this office. Our city works because these men and women make it work and I know that with the right leadership they will make Philadelphia a great place to live, work and raise a family. Serving with them and learning from them has been a privilege without compare for a rowhouse kid from Northeast Philadelphia. I want to thank my father and mother, Israel and Mildred Saidel, my four children, Hope, Nicky, Josh, and Jackie, and Carol Veneziale, my long-time secretary for all their help and understanding during my tenure in office.

Finally, I want to thank the people of Philadelphia. For 16 years, you elected me to serve you. I have traveled to every neighborhood of the city, visited with thousands of people, and attended hundreds of community meetings. These are experiences few have had and they are experiences I would never give back. In my years of serving you, I am proud of the stances I have taken, the fights I have waged, and the change I have helped bring about. During my 16 years as Controller Philadelphia has undergone a stunning transformation — but much work remains unfinished. I am very grateful for the confidence and friendship the people of Philadelphia have given to me and I wrote this book hoping the ideas within would continue to improve their lives long after my tenure as Controller is complete.

JONATHAN A. SAIDEL
CITY CONTROLLER

PROLOGUE AND ACKNOWLEDGEMENTS
TO THE FIRST EDITION

Leaving Philadelphia in 1684—two years after it was established—William Penn offered a prayer for his new city:

> *And thou, Philadelphia, the virgin settlement of this Province, named before thou wert born. What love, What care, What service, and What travail have there been to bring thee forth and preserve thee from such as would abuse and defile thee. 0 that thou mayest be kept from the evil that would overwhelm thee; that, faithful to the God of thy Mercies, in the life of right- eousness thou mayest be preserved to the end.*
>
> *My soul prays to God for thee that thou mayest stand in the day of trial that thy children may be blest of the Lord and thy people, saved by His power.*

When William Penn founded his City of Brotherly Love in 1682, it was little more than a 1,200-acre rectangle of forestland that stretched for one mile north and south between the Delaware and Schuylkill Rivers in his new colony of Pennsylvania. More than three centuries later, Philadelphia is a city of skyscrapers, industrial complexes, and neighborhoods that spans 135 square miles. During its history, Philadelphia has been one of the world's premier cities, America's largest metropolis, and the capital of the United States. Today, shaped by history and affected constantly by a changing world, Philadelphia and its nearly 1.5 million residents prepare to confront the 21st century.

As the founder of our city did more than 300 years ago, we can reflect on the care, service, and travail that has transformed Penn's "greene Country Towne" into the vibrant city it is today. Like Penn, we endeavor to preserve our city for future generations. But if Philadelphia, under the stewardship of the current generation, will be transmitted to the next generation as a city greater, better, and more beautiful than was transmitted to us, we must act now to prepare for that future.

This is the purpose of this project: to look forward, to decide where we are going as a city, and to make people think about how we can act now as we move into the future. This document provides the public and our elected and civic leadership with a blueprint describing how we can prepare Philadelphia's government to function in the future and how this city can thrive in the next century.

The City Controller's Office annually audits the financial affairs of Philadelphia government agencies and periodically analyzes agency efficiency and effectiveness by conducting performance audits. More broad in scope than a fiscal audit and more penetrating in its analysis than a performance audit, this document poses the question, "What must the government of the City of Philadelphia do to take on the challenges of the next century?" This document analyzes the performance, capabilities, and structure of City government to determine what changes—systemic, governance-based, or management-related—must occur for Philadelphia to positively confront the difficulties, challenges, and opportunities that await us in the year 2000 and beyond. Finally, this document puts forth ideas and recommendations to create a debate about the City's future. As City Controller, I am committed to using the resources of my office to conduct additional formal audits and inquiries into any of the topics raised in this document to add to the debate in the future.

The seal of the City of Philadelphia was adopted by City Council on February 14, 1874. As is customary in heraldry, each of the elements of the seal has a special significance. The plow and ship on the shield represent agriculture (very important in Philadelphia's early history) and commerce, respectively. The female figure on the left wears an olive garland, representing peace, and holds a scroll inscribed with an anchor (William Penn's chosen symbol for the County of Philadelphia), signifying hope. The woman on the right holds a cornucopia, symbolizing abundance. Above the shield, a bent arm holds the scales of justice and mercy. Below the shield is the City's motto, *Philadelphia Maneto*—"Let Brotherly Love Continue." The phrase is from the New Testament (Hebrews 13:1) and is said to have been spoken by the last of William Penn's descendants visiting Philadelphia in the 1800s. In considering the challenges that face us in the next century, it is appropriate to once again consider the words spoken by William Penn's last descendant to gaze upon our city—to renew our wish that our City of Brotherly Love continue.

Philadelphia grew from a small settlement in Penn's time to national and international prominence. Early Philadelphia dominated our country's political and governmental realm, industrial Philadelphia created goods demanded worldwide, and Philadelphia of the recent past bore the world's first computer, ushering in the information age. I grew up in an exciting Philadelphia, but some say that our best days are past. I disagree. I know that our best days are yet to come. In the past, Philadelphia has been a larger city and it has been a more prominent city, but regardless of size or stature, our city is still—at its most elemental level—a home, a marketplace, a cultural locus, an educational center, and an entertainment hub. For the millions of people like me who live, work, and play in Philadelphia, our future, not our past, is our chief concern. This document is therefore designed for us, and for posterity, as a blueprint to lead us into that future.

In recent years, Philadelphia's City government fundamentally improved operations in many ways to bring Philadelphia back from the brink of bankruptcy. Now, we must build on these improvements to meet the many challenges that confront us. As William Penn did more than three centuries ago, I pray that Philadelphia will endure our current day of trial. Like Penn's descendant, I look upon our City and repeat the simple refrain that has become our city's motto, *"Philadelphia Maneto."*

———————— · ————————

On Inauguration Day, January 3, 2000, I will greet the Mayor who will lead Philadelphia into the 21st century as I enter my tenth year as City Controller of the City of Philadelphia. When I first conceived of this document, it was designed to be a roadmap and a reference for this next Mayor based on all that I have learned during my term of service. This document represents the very best work of an office that I am proud to oversee, and I look forward to working with the next mayoral administration to implement its recommendations and make Philadelphia the city we know it can be.

Plato said, "The punishment which the wise suffer who refuse to take part in the government, is to live under the government of worse men." I am proud to be associated with the wise individuals who have chosen to take part in government by working in the City Controller's Office and toiling to produce this unique report.

I want to thank First Deputy City Controller David Volpe, Assistant City Controller Brett Mandel, and Assistant City Controller Kevin Babyak for all their work transforming this project from a vision to a reality. Their hard work and dedication resulted in a landmark report that will make a tremendous contribution to the future of our City. I thank Deputy City Controller Albert Scaperotto for his efforts guiding our professional staff; our interview team of Audit Supervisor Mary Thiel, Audit Manager Robert Oliveti, Auditor John Canal, Auditor Kenyon Dugan, and Auditor Rhonda Green; and our research staff of Auditor Robert Hurly and Auditor Trainee

Michele Kelly. I offer special thanks to Research Interns Prashant Bhuyan, Josh Dickstein, Javier Gomez, Elizabeth John, and Gina Scamby, who made important contributions to the final report, and to Meredith Jelleyman for her invaluable assistance making this document a finished product. I must also acknowledge the assistance provided by Assistant City Controller Tony Di Martino, Audit Administrator Mike Egan, Special Assistant to the Controller John Foulkes, Audit Administrator Gerry Micciulla, Director of Special Investigations Tony Radwanski, Audit Administrator Barry Weintraub, and Consultant to the Controller's Office, Howard Cain.

I am grateful to the many members of the current City and School District administrations who contributed their time, information, and insights to this project. Philadelphia's resurgence as a city is a tribute to their talent and dedication. While the names of these City officials—along with the former officials, academics, experts, and other sources consulted for this project—are too numerous to be listed individually, they each made a substantial contribution to the ideas that form the basis for this document.

I thank Greater Philadelphia First and Hal Fichandler for assistance setting up roundtable discussions with private sector leaders from: Crown Cork & Seal Co., Inc.; Dechert Price & Rhoads; Drexel University; Deloitte & Touche LLP; KPMG Peat Marwick LLP; PricewaterhouseCoopers LLP; Saul, Ewing, Remick & Saul; Sun Company, Inc.; Thomas Jefferson University; Unisys Corporation; The University of Pennsylvania; The University of Pennsylvania Health Systems; and WaWa, Inc.. I also thank AFSCME District Council 47 for its help forming a discussion group comprising members of the City's municipal workforce.

Special appreciation is reserved for the staff of the Preservation Alliance for Greater Philadelphia who provided research assistance, for Laura Weinbaum and Jefferson Moak, who helped edit the final product, and for legendary City Planner Edmund Bacon, who shared his vision of the City with my staff. Mr. Bacon's foreword improves this document just as his presence improves our City.

I am very grateful to the staff of the Saint Joseph's University Press for their faith in this project and their assistance creating such a high-quality product. By creating a partnership with a publisher, the Controller's Office was able to avoid the cost of printing the document, expand the document's reach, and benefit from the value added by the publication process. Saint Joseph's University Press will benefit from book sales. This kind of public-private partnership is emblematic of the ventures our government should embrace in the future to enhance service-delivery efforts and improve government operations.

I am similarly grateful to the firm of BDO Seidman, LLP. Under an existing quality-control-review contract with the Controller's Office, personnel from the firm proofed the text and commented on the document.

Thanks are also due to the Delaware Valley Regional Planning Commission for use of projection data from its Direction 2020 project and to the Metropolitan Area Program for use of its jurisdictional maps of the Greater Philadelphia region. Additionally, thanks are due Woods & Poole Economics, Inc. of Washington, D.C., for its population, employment, and households projections for the United States and Philadelphia, and text describing the projections and data published in 1997 (information). The information is provided for demonstration purposes only and is not intended to be relied upon in any financial or legal transaction. The use of the information, and the conclusions drawn therefrom, is solely the responsibility of the City of Philadelphia.

I owe a particular debt of gratitude to the countless City and School District employees who provided my office with much of the information and data that appear in this document. Our city works because these men and women make it work and I know that with the right leadership they will make Philadelphia a preferred place to live and work in the 21st century.

Finally, I want to thank my father and mother, Israel and Mildred Saidel, my four children, Hope, Nicky, Josh, and Jackie, and Carol Veneziale, my long-time secretary for all their help and understanding during my tenure in office.

JONATHAN A. SAIDEL
CITY CONTROLLER

INTRODUCTION TO THE SECOND EDITION
REVOLUTIONIZING THE REVOLUTIONARY CITY

Near the corner of Third and Arch Streets in Philadelphia sits a house, famous for the creation of one of the foremost symbols of our country. At the behest of George Washington in 1776, Betsy Ross designed our nation's flag as a banner behind which the newly independent country could rally. Less than a year later in June of 1777, the flag was officially adopted by Continental Congress, resolving "that the flag of the United States be thirteen stripes, alternate red and white; that the Union be thirteen stars, white in a blue field, representing a new constellation." Constellations served as guides to early sailors, providing a compass in an otherwise dark sky. The flag was a constellation, in that it signified the direction in which the United States would proceed into the future; from separate states with disparate interests to a unified nation with unified purpose.

The first edition of *Philadelphia: A New Urban Direction* was similarly a constellation for the City of Philadelphia. Created amidst a period of the city's reinvention, it indicated the best desired direction in which Philadelphia should proceed and delineated clear actions for the city's leaders to pursue. Even though thirty-seven new stars have been added to the American Flag, the thirteen stripes and blue field on which they rest remain the same. Each additional star required the reorganization and adjustment of the others, representing a symbolic change to the very real change in the country. Likewise, the second edition of *Philadelphia: A New Urban Direction* is meant to convey an addition, supplementing and updating a base that still serves as a beacon to advocates of good government and all who desire a bright future for Philadelphia.

The environment in which Philadelphia's policy choices are made has also shifted dramatically since the original publication. In 1999, the national and local economies were growing, and the city had built up an unprecedented $300 million surplus. It was clear that the city had the opportunity and the resources to make some fundamental changes. Since then, the city and nation have weathered a downturn in the economy, faced new security risks and have assumed new duties for protecting our citizens following the terrorist attacks of September 11, 2001, and the city spent the bulk of its $300 million reserve. Today, Philadelphia is struggling to avoid reverting to an untenable fiscal position. The cost of providing services to city residents continues to grow while the population and employment bases continue to shrink. The fiscal responsibility that enabled the city to amass a sizeable fund balance has given way to rampant debt issuance and missed opportunities.

The city has not been without positive advances. The Greater Philadelphia region is now one of the nation's leading centers for the life sciences and performing arts sectors. The local economy has been built upon traditional areas of expertise in education and medicine. Philadelphia is undergoing an explosion in new residential construction, both in Center City and in our neighborhoods. New skyscrapers are being built for the first time in more than a decade. The city schools show improvement and many Philadelphians are healthier and wealthier than before. Philadelphia's vibrant cultural institutions, diverse dining establishments and nightlife options are drawing people from throughout the city and beyond.

Despite these encouraging trends, there is the possibility that Philadelphia will not be able to meet the needs of current and future citizens. The work of improving Philadelphia and the lives of the people who live here is an ongoing process. The policies and programs pursued must be constantly reassessed and refined. For this reason, the City Controller's Office has chosen to revisit *Philadelphia: A New Urban Direction*. While Philadelphia is showing signs of improvement, the city is at a crossroad, poised to either revive or decline as a result of the policies implemented now and in the future. While many of the ideas presented in the original publication remain useful, the context in which decisions about governance are made in Philadelphia has changed. New opportunities have emerged as other avenues for improvement have been closed off. Each chapter in the second edition of *Philadelphia: A New Urban Direction* provides insight into reforms undertaken in the intervening years, and the reforms that still need to be implemented. The progress of recommendations from the original text is assessed, exploring the real-world impacts of the evolution of academic ideas to practical applications, while addressing issues that have grown in importance since the time of the initial publication. The updated book also offers new ideas for the betterment of the city in the context of today's changed reality. Evaluating the positive and negative effects of the changes will assist policymakers in Philadelphia and other cities as they craft governmental responses to changing needs.

The update following Chapter 1: Envisioning Philadelphia will explore the accuracy of the economic and demographic projections made in the original publication, differentiating the environment of 2005 from 1999. Each ensuing chapter re-examines Philadelphia in this context while providing new insight into the probable and potential future of the city.

The updated Chapter 2 reviews the progress being made to make government more accountable, efficient, and accessible. As personnel expenses place an ever-growing strain upon the city's fiscal resources, recommendations are offered for improved human resource management. Methods to improve the ethical standards under which the government operates are also explored, identifying shortfalls in previous reform efforts. Without the proper structure and oversight, even the most useful initiatives will be unable to generate the desired results.

With Philadelphia's financial condition once again tenuous, due in part to a tremendous expansion in the city's debt and other long-term obligations, Chapter 3 addresses the root causes of these developments while presenting recommendations for the management of the city's long-term obligations. The incremental progress towards a more competitive and fair tax structure is chronicled, and further reforms are articulated to ensure adequate financial resources to meet service needs and improve Philadelphia's economic competitiveness.

After delineating the need for proper tools for governance and fiscal discipline for the general health of the city, the second edition of *Philadelphia: A New Urban Direction* addresses specific urban challenges that Philadelphia still must overcome. The update of Chapter 4 provides a review of the major changes in the Philadelphia School District following the state takeover of city schools and the creation of the School Reform Commission and the implementation of the federal No Child Left Behind legislation. Recommendations to improve the city's economic-development strategy and implementation are proposed, with a focus on expanding opportunities for minority-owned and disadvantaged business and fostering growth of the city's arts and culture institutions. Opportunities to improve the environment through innovative land use, transportation, and energy policies are identified. The emerging need for and impacts of homeland security responsibilities of local government is covered for the first time.

Lastly, Chapter 5 will address the concept of "regionalism," detailing the difficulties in coordination while championing its relevance for key economic projects. The limited success that isolated regional partnerships and organizations have had in improving the economy and promoting tourism is explored, while remaining opportunities for cooperation are highlighted.

Together these updates are intended to provide insight into the city's progress in the past five years and offer recommendations to ensure a vibrant, thriving city in the future. As a city where history is tangible at every turn, Philadelphian can benefit from learning from its past and applying those lessons to the future. Consistent, rigorous evaluation of the policies pursued and the outcomes generated are invaluable to achieve a better Philadelphia. There is no reason that

Philadelphia cannot be the city Philadelphians believe it should be. The vision of a growing, thriving city is so compelling that it demands that Philadelphia's leaders pursue policies to make Philadelphia a preferred place to live, work, and visit.

In 1999, the Philadelphia City Controller's Office presented a vision of Philadelphia's likely future if it remained on its course at the time and proposed a comprehensive plan designed to improve Philadelphia. Contributing greatly to discussion of the issues facing an American city, the original publication provided policymakers, students, and citizens of Philadelphia and other major cities with an expanded and original look at the challenges facing an urban jurisdiction, offering recommendations to overcome those obstacles. The book identified pressing problems related to Philadelphia's public safety, governance, school district, and neighborhood deterioration, problems that continue to dominate the political discourse today. In the intervening years since its publication, some recommendations have been adopted with varying degrees of success, others have yet to receive the level of attention they deserve, and new challenges have arisen. *Philadelphia: A New Urban Direction* provides only a vision and guidance for a better Philadelphia; it is still up to the city's leaders to chart the proper course.

INTRODUCTION TO THE FIRST EDITION
REVOLUTIONIZING THE REVOLUTIONARY CITY

William Penn Proprietary & Governor of the Province of Pennsylvania &c To all to whom the presents shall come sends Greeting Know ye That at the humble Request of the Inhabitants and Setlers of this Town of Philadelphia being some of the first adventurers & purchasers within this Province For their Incouragement and for the more Immeadiate & Intire govrnment of the said Town And better Regulacion of Trade therein I Have by vertue of the Kings Letters patent under the great seal of England Erected the said Town Into a Burrough and by these presents Do Errect the said Town & Burrough of Philadelphia Into a City which said City shall Extend the Limits & Bounds as it is layd out Between Dellaware & Skoolkill

With these words from the preamble to the first charter of the City of Philadelphia, William Penn incorporated the City on October 25, 1701. Just under three centuries later, this document, the oldest document in the City's custody that relates to early municipal government, and the only charter of the City that bears the Proprietor's signature, rests, unchanged, in the City Archives. The City of Philadelphia has since changed dramatically and will continue to change into the next century. *Philadelphia: A New Urban Direction* is the result of an effort to consider likely future scenarios for Philadelphia and examine City government's current ability to prepare for the challenges of the next century. The central theme, government's fundamental ability to serve the needs of the citizenry, has confronted Philadelphia before.

Without power to tax under the first charter, the City had great difficulty paying debts and providing public services. After the American Revolution, a new municipal charter was adopted to give Philadelphia more ability as a city to maintain streets and bridges, care for the poor, and maintain public order. In *Citizenship in Philadelphia* (1919), J. Lynn Barnard and Jessie C. Evans wrote of Philadelphia's early years:

> *Philadelphia grew rapidly, and with this rapid growth in population there was increasing need for the town itself to look after all sorts of civic interests that could no longer be properly attended to by private citizens. Unfortunately, the town government proved unequal to the task. The legislative body, known as the 'Common Council,' was unbusinesslike, and there was no efficient administrative department. Precious time was wasted, and such public works as were found necessary were built extravagantly. Streets, police and fire protection, taxation, all alike suffered from lack of leadership and business ability.*[1]

At the dawn of the 1700s, Philadelphia was woefully unprepared to take on the challenge of a new century. At the dawn of the 21st century, modern Philadelphia encounters different problems—population loss, fiscal stress, and the challenges of federal devolution—but must confront the same question: Is the government of the City of Philadelphia prepared to take on the challenges of a new century? This document addresses that central question and analyzes the performance, capabilities, and structure of City government to determine what changes must occur to enable Philadelphia to move efficiently and effectively past the year 2000.

APPROACH AND METHODOLOGY

In approaching this project, the Controller's Office crafted a process that would be both inclusive and informative. Analysts and auditors spent countless hours consulting with government officials, experts from various fields, academics, and activists. The result is a document that looks forward, looks back, and constructs creative approaches as part of an attempt to design a governmental response to the challenges Philadelphia faces today—and will likely face tomorrow.

Paint a Picture of a Future Philadelphia

The Controller's Office created a composite sketch of a future Philadelphia based primarily on projections formulated with the use of a forecasting and simulation model created by Regional Economic Models, Inc. (REMI)—as modified by assumptions formulated by the Controller's Office—and corroborated by projections and data from:
- Delaware Valley Regional Planning Commission;
- Philadelphia City Planning Commission;
- Pennsylvania State Data Center;
- Woods & Poole Economics, Inc.; and
- Various other local and national organizations and experts.

While history presents no shortage of unfulfilled predictions and pronouncements, the trends identified here as part of the picture of a 21st-century Philadelphia represent the City Controller's Office's best prediction of the most likely scenarios for the City's future. If these projections are accurate and nothing occurs in the future to alter the assumptions that form the foundation for the forecasts, this composite sketch represents a correct and unsatisfying view of Philadelphia's future. The true value of the process of creating these projections, however, is not to sketch the precise economic and demographic landscape Philadelphia will have in 2015, but to identify trends that are likely to occur if the *status quo* persists. The projections, therefore, show likely future directions that indicate areas where governmental action is

---

[1] Lynn J. Barnard, Ph.D. and Jessie C. Evans. *Citizenship in Philadelphia* (Philadelphia: 1919. Arden Press of Philadelphia, 1998). <http://www.libertynet.org/ardenpop/appcitiz.html>

needed, or where governmental action or inaction would be detrimental. The projections will certainly be affected by a host of unanticipated future actions and reactions, and even the most dire future projections could be counteracted over time with the right policies. Of course, the reverse is also true: that there are no future scenarios which could not be worsened by deleterious policies and actions.

Identify Likely Implications of Projected Future Trends

With a composite sketch of Philadelphia's likely future as a guide, the Controller's Office interviewed former and current City officials, academics, and experts to determine the implications of the identified trends. Through formal questionnaires and face-to-face interviews, Controller's Office staff canvassed the heads of Philadelphia government agencies to elicit response to the forecasted projections and implications. The Controller's Office also conducted a thorough literature review to gain an understanding of the challenges facing Philadelphia and urban America.

Identify Ways to Improve Philadelphia City Government Operations

Using the projections for the future and likely implications as a foundation, the Controller's Office performed analyses designed to formulate recommendations to create a flexible, responsive, and accessible government that will be able to take advantage of the opportunities of the next century. Based on the assumptions established by the projected future trends, research focused on:

- *Creating a Government for the Future*—how the City of Philadelphia should be governed and how its government should address the challenges and opportunities of the next century.
- *Fiscal Issues for Philadelphia's Future*—how the City of Philadelphia budget and the City's system of revenues and expenditures can enable the City to move into the future.
- *Proper Governmental Responses to Current and Future Challenges*—how the City of Philadelphia can respond to the specific challenges that confront it.
- *Addressing Philadelphia's Place in the Greater Philadelphia Region*—how the City, in its role in the metropolitan area, can best interact with surrounding jurisdictions in a way that benefits the entire Greater Philadelphia region.

Present Recommendations and Fiscal Impact of Identified Action Steps

This document provides the public and the City's elected leadership with a blueprint describing how to prepare Philadelphia's government to function in the future. Accordingly, recommendations for action are highlighted in the text. Where possible, the Controller's Office has identified the fiscal impact associated with the relevant action steps.

21ST-CENTURY PHILADELPHIA—THE CITY AS A PREFERRED PLACE

In the pages ahead, the Controller's Office articulates a vision for Philadelphia government that is based on projections for the City's future. Simply put, if the City is to thrive in the future, 21st-century Philadelphia must be a preferred place to live, a preferred place to run a business, and a preferred place to visit. As a city, Philadelphia has been losing residents and employers for decades, but despite recent trends—and any projections based upon those trends—it is clear that opportunities exist to make Philadelphia such a place. While people have flocked to cities to live, work, and play for centuries, the more recent flight from cities to suburbs is proving to be an experiment that has failed. The isolation and inefficiency manifested in the sprawl that grows beyond City borders and the irresponsibility of allowing formerly cohesive neighborhoods to decay inside cities have created a backlash from economists, environmentalists, and suburbanites themselves. The City's leadership, therefore, must create a city prepared for the future, primed to be a preferred place to raise a family, run a business, and engage in recreational, cultural, and entertainment activities. Success in the future should not be based on whether the City generates a budgetary surplus, but whether it creates growth.

If Philadelphia is to be such a preferred place, its government must be:

- Led by elected leaders who shape policy directions and administered by competent managers who are encouraged to manage well;
- Able to adapt efficiently to changing times and changing demands;
- Focused to respond to incentives that demand performance and results; and
- Focused on providing customer-friendly interactions with citizens, employers, and visitors.

If Philadelphia government is to create such a preferred place, it must:

- Establish budgetary structural balance to implement fiscal discipline and keep the cost of government in check; and
- Reduce the cost of government and capitalize on the worth of the City to reduce the tax burden on residents and employers.

If Philadelphia government is to convince individuals that Philadelphia is such a preferred place, it must:

- Implement sound economic development policies to grow Philadelphia into the future;
- Create a quality educational system accessible to all families;
- Increase demand for City housing and create an outlet for Philadelphia's housing stock;
- Create a safe city in which people can live, work, and play;
- Advance efforts to better link City attractions and showcase Philadelphia to the world; and
- Make mass transportation a favored mode to best move the City's masses.

If Philadelphia government is to operate such a preferred place, it must:

- Involve other local government, state, and federal officials in an effort to strengthen the City's role in the Greater Philadelphia region;
- Work with the governments of other jurisdictions to make the entire region more competitive; and
- Work with local, state, and federal officials to confront regional fiscal disparities, sprawl, and congestion, and promote incentives for intra-regional cooperation.

Philadelphia is already the preferred place to live, run a business, and find entertainment for a great number of residents, employers, and visitors. Looking to the future, a vibrant and growing 21st-century Philadelphia can be such a preferred place for millions more. Philadelphians who embrace the City and all it has to offer know this can happen. Philadelphia's elected leaders can craft a governmental response to make it happen. This document, its concepts, and its recommendations create a direction to make success a reality.

Readers are encouraged to refer to Appendix sections for a map of Philadelphia, an organizational chart of the City government, City agency descriptions, a discussion of governance in Philadelphia, and a discussion of taxation in Philadelphia.

PHILADELPHIA'S FUTURE IN CONTEXT: A BRIEF HISTORY

More than 300 years old, Philadelphia is a city that has been shaped by history and changed by the actions of generations of residents who began to make and remake the City before America was born. That history will surely continue to shape the City's future.

Established by William Penn in 1682 and incorporated as a city in 1701, Philadelphia grew rapidly in less than 100 years into the premier English-speaking city of the New World. By 1765, Philadelphia was the largest city in what would become the United States of America with nearly 5,000 dwellings and more than 25,000 inhabitants. Early Philadelphia was primarily a trade city, despite the fact that its port on the Delaware River rested approximately 100 miles upriver from the mouth of the Delaware Bay which was approximately 200 miles farther than New York from Great Britain. But Philadelphia enjoyed a geographic advantage in its surrounding agricultural richness and its "hidden river," the Schuylkill, which served as a highway to central Pennsylvania and connected merchants to the natural resources of the Philadelphia countryside. Port activity, including shipbuilding and European and West Indian trade, drove the Philadelphia economy and was complemented by the work of small craftsmen and merchants. When the Second Continental Congress voted to declare independence from Great Britain, Philadelphia played host to the assemblage of the American Colonies' most significant citizens. Before it became known as Independence Hall, the steeple of the Pennsylvania State House—home to what would eventually be called the Liberty Bell—rose 168 feet (15 stories) to ornament the early skyline.

Captured and occupied during the Revolutionary War, liberated Philadelphia was the site of the Constitutional Convention in 1787. After the capital of the newly-formed United States of America was temporarily located in New York, Philadelphia served as the nation's capital from 1790 to 1800, before its permanent move to Washington D.C.

Despite losing its status as the nation's capital, Philadelphia continued to experience exponential growth. The first United States Census, conducted in 1790, counted 54,391 Philadelphians clustered largely along the Delaware River, but by 1830, the City had more than tripled in population and had grown to more than 188,000 inhabitants. Embargoes on the importation of European goods, resulting from ongoing tensions with both Great Britain and France, curtailed port activity, leading early 19th-century Philadelphia to develop a strong manufacturing base. Papermakers, printers, bookbinders, shoe cobblers, and foundries, spurred by the many Philadelphia inventors and skilled craftsmen, thrived along the streams surrounding Philadelphia.

To house 19th-century Philadelphia's population explosion, homes in the City were largely built in row house style. By building rows of identical units with shared common walls and limiting frontage on streets, row homes were inexpensive to build and cheap enough to allow a large percentage of the population to own their homes. Row after row was completed to house the influx of European, mainly German, immigrants flowing into the City. In stark contrast to the low, red-brick row houses, great Greek Revival structures such as the Second Bank of the United States and the Fairmount Waterworks rose to complement Philadelphia's expanding skyline and lend credence to the notion articulated by painter Gilbert Stuart that Philadelphia was the "Athens of America."

Many would argue that from the mid-1700s through the early 1800s, Philadelphia was the most cosmopolitan city in the New World. During that era, the City gave life to many institutions that survive to this day, including Pennsylvania Hospital (the first hospital in the colonies), the Walnut Street Theater (the first theater company in the United States), the Pennsylvania Academy of Fine Arts (the first art school and museum in the country), and the University of Pennsylvania (the university founded by Benjamin Franklin).

But despite the growth and prosperity, Philadelphia was soon surpassed as the largest American city. New York City's population exceeded Philadelphia's by 1810 and the construction of the Erie Canal in the 1820s established New York as the major commercial center for the East Coast. Although it was no longer the capital, and no longer the largest or busiest city, Philadelphia still enjoyed growth. But growth was not just confined to the central city, still a roughly two-square-mile rectangle between the Delaware and Schuylkill Rivers. By 1840, more people lived within the larger

Philadelphia County but outside the City limits than lived within the City's borders. In 1854, responding to the growth of the City and its suburbs and the need to bring political and social order to the area, the General Assembly of Pennsylvania (which moved its capital from Philadelphia—where it had been since 1683—in 1799) consolidated the City and County of Philadelphia, merging the City and its many surrounding boroughs and townships into a single jurisdiction. This expansion of the City gave Philadelphia the tax base necessary to provide the services—water, sewage, street paving, police, fire—necessary for a growing industrial center. Established as both a city and a county, Philadelphia's borders were fixed along lines which with the exception of one very minor early 20th-century addition of land, still define the City. Annexation of surrounding jurisdictions is technically possible, but given political realities and the stipulation that the population of any to-be-annexed jurisdiction would have to approve annexation, expansion of the City has not been a realistic option.

The expanded City, enlarged from two square miles to more than 135 square miles, incorporated surrounding districts into the City and gave Philadelphia ample room to develop within its new borders. Thus, by 1860, Philadelphia claimed a population of more than 565,000. The original city became a compact central business district (Center City) enhanced by the vitality of formerly independent townships such as Germantown and Frankford. But City-County consolidation also made possible the development of many "suburbs within the City," which allowed some neighborhoods to abandon the density of row homes and the grid street pattern to accept more spacious duplexes and detached houses complete with yards.

After serving as a hub of wartime activity during the American Civil War, Philadelphia embraced the arrival of the Industrial Revolution as industry spread throughout its neighborhoods. Clothing and textiles employed more than 40 percent of the City's workforce with most of the remainder spread in smaller amounts across a variety of types of manufacturing including machine tools and hardware, shoes and boots, and paper and printing. The tremendous industrial base expanded throughout the City, establishing specialized districts of smaller, more flexible plants than found in other cities, enabling Philadelphia to retain many small manufacturers into the 20th century. The leather and wool district spread northeast from the original City limits; garment shops spread south. Furniture and woodworking spread west, and metalworking spread northwest. Housing built up around these centers of employment, creating neighborhoods of economic opportunity. As the nation's birthplace and, according to boosters, the City where industry was found in the greatest variety and perfection, Philadelphia was the logical choice to host the Centennial Exposition of the United States in 1876.

While Philadelphia was home to well-established African-American and German communities from before the Revolutionary War, the City's diversity expanded with its population growth. As Philadelphia grew toward the 20th century, African-Americans from the American South and Irish and German immigrants poured into the City, supplemented later by Italians and Eastern Europeans, expanding the population to nearly 1.3 million by 1900 and over 1.5 million by 1910. To shelter this tremendous influx, the street grid was extended and more than 100,000 houses, mainly row houses, were constructed. With newly-created building and loan associations providing financial assistance, many new immigrants were able to purchase homes, while many established Philadelphians relocated to more luxurious mansions within the expanded City, but outside the original City limits.

This influx of residents represented the greatest population expansion in Philadelphia's history. During this time, a grand Second Empire-style City Hall was completed at the center of William Penn's original city. An indication of Philadelphia's significance and Philadelphians' sense of their city, it was conceived as the tallest building in the world, only to be surpassed by the Eiffel Tower and Washington Monument by the time of its completion. A tremendous edifice of granite and marble, it remains the tallest masonry structure without a steel frame in the world. In the building's crypt, four great columns form the base of the City Hall tower. The top of each column is crowned with carvings depicting races of the world—pillars representing Africa, Asia, Europe, and America—holding up the massive tower's weight. As an apt metaphor for a city with a history of racial and ethnic strife, the statues can still be seen as the people, segregated, either propping up their government, or being pressed down by its oppressive heaviness. Completed in 1901, built by thousands of laborers, many newly arrived, and topped by a 37-foot statue of the City's founder, City Hall's tower dominated the skyline, rising 548 feet to the top of William Penn's hat.

Called "corrupt and contented" by muckraker Lincoln Steffens, Philadelphia earned Steffens' dubious honor as "the worst-governed city in the country" in 1903. Through the Great Depression and two World Wars, Philadelphia struggled like other American cities with political reform and efforts to confront the ills of the modern metropolis. The economic crisis of the Depression established Philadelphia as a strong union city, and developed public support for subsidized housing and slum clearance. During this era, the City's diverse economy enabled it to weather the storm better than other industrial cities and left the City able to take advantage of the wartime increase in manufacturing demand.

Despite the stresses of war and depression, Philadelphia undertook major public works projects and private development during the first half of the 20th century. The City's mass transit infrastructure soon tunneled underground and along elevated tracks, linking outlying neighborhoods to Center City. The Delaware River Bridge (now, the Benjamin Franklin Bridge) connected Philadelphia to New Jersey. The majestic Benjamin Franklin Parkway and its resident museums built the "city beautiful." Numerous colossal buildings housing the burgeoning federal bureaucracy, grand railroad stations, and art deco commercial towers added to the boom. The most important construction of the era may have been America's first truly modern skyscraper, the Philadelphia Saving Fund Society building. Perhaps the best American example of the International Style, the building rose 39 stories—to a height just below the statue of William Penn atop City Hall—and suggested that Philadelphia would once again set standards of progress for the nation.

But after World War II, Philadelphia reached a significant turning point on two fronts. The 1950 Census showed Philadelphia at its peak population of 2,071,605. Though the City had grown from settlement until 1950, suburbanization, job loss, and residential flight would reduce its population in the following decades. Without the fresh lure and lower costs associated with newer Sun Belt locations, and unable to annex growing suburbs like other cities, post-1950 Philadelphia was fated to endure a constant struggle to meet the needs of its citizenry as its population—especially middle-class whites—decreased. While job and population loss were not immediately felt in the years after 1950 (many planners were still projecting growth for the City into the 1960s), a second fundamental shift totally redefined Philadelphia government in 1951.

In response to continued political scandal and corruption, a reform movement developed and succeeded in crafting and enacting a new Home Rule Charter, winning voter approval of the Charter, and ousting the City's Republican elected leadership (Philadelphians had elected Republican mayors in nearly every election from the Civil War until 1951). These shifts in power and governance structure rewrote the fundamental rules of government in Philadelphia and influence the City to this day. Since 1951, the Mayor of Philadelphia and a solid majority of City Council have been Democrats, and the 1951 Home Rule Charter (supplemented in 1965 by a Home Rule School District Charter) has been virtually unchanged as the law of the land. Only two minor amendments—one to the Charter and one to the School District Charter—have ever been approved by the electorate. Other efforts to more fundamentally reform or rewrite the Charter have been rejected by Philadelphia voters.

The new Charter was a landmark document and was widely proclaimed as an important instrument for improved government. It created a new culture of responsible municipal government in Philadelphia with a strong merit-based civil service system, a streamlined administrative organization, and a coherent financial structure. By thwarting corruption while providing the City's chief executive with extensive executive and administrative powers, the new Charter fostered effective governmental operations.

Under the current City Charter, Philadelphia is governed under the strong mayor/weak council form of government. The Mayor has vast powers: nearly unchecked appointment and removal privileges for top officials, influence over the budget including complete control over revenue estimates, extensive administrative oversight, creation of policy initiatives, and the ability to veto Council-approved legislation. Not as weak as the "weak council" label implies, City Council forms the legislative branch of the government, vested with the power to enact ordinances and make lump-sum alterations to the Mayor's budget. In this capacity, Council establishes effective taxation rates and adopts the operating and capital budgets.

While the basic structure of the City government serves the City well, including the merit-based civil service system and the overall governmental and financial structures, government under the 1951 Charter has many limits. The enabling legislation, which gave Philadelphia Home Rule, does not confer the power of eminent domain—the power to take private land with proper compensation—or the power to exceed a state-set debt limit. Under the Charter, the Mayor is only able to serve two consecutive terms. Without Charter change, the elected leadership is unable to formally create new departments to meet new needs and enter into long-term real estate leases without the use of a governmental authority. Crafted amidst a reform movement intent on banishing corruption, the Charter established stringent procurement, personnel management, and financial controls.

Philadelphia's School District, which had been led by a judicially-appointed board and funded by taxes set by Pennsylvania's General Assembly, did not come under direct local control until the 1960s. But local control is not necessarily direct control. Regarding the School District— appointment of top officials, preparation of the budget, administrative oversight, and initiation of policy—the strong Mayor is potentially impotent and Council has little direct ability to create change. Neither the Superintendent of Schools nor the nine-member Board of Education is directly accountable to the Mayor or to Council. The Board appoints the Superintendent and the Mayor appoints the members of the Board (three members every two years). The School District budget is prepared and adopted separately from the City budget. The Board of Education—which, depending on how long a Mayor is in office, may include no appointees of the current Mayor—prepares and adopts a budget. The Board has exclusive control over the preparation and adoption of the School District budget, but lacks the power or responsibility to raise revenues to balance the budget. City Council is responsible for authorizing or refusing to authorize the necessary taxes to fund the budget, but the Mayor and Council cannot directly alter the budgetary choices of the School District.

Even with its limits, the new Charter and the reform movement that created it revitalized Philadelphia's government. Unfortunately, however, government under the Home Rule Charter could not compensate for the larger economic trends that were affecting most of America's older industrial cities. As technological improvements permitted manufacturers to expand production with fewer workers, and as foreign goods gained market share in America, the percentage of the nation's labor force employed in manufacturing dropped precipitously. Although Philadelphia was still growing through 1950, many major manufacturers, employing whole neighborhoods of workers, had already left before the approval of the new Charter.

While many manufacturers closed or left Philadelphia for regions where labor was cheaper, jobs and workers also relocated within the Greater Philadelphia region to more spacious and racially segregated suburbs. Philadelphia's portion of regional population and employment was eventually overtaken by the surrounding region. Abandonment and decay, the result of the City's loss of more than 25 percent of its population during the past five decades— and more than 100,000 residents and 100,000 jobs during the past decade—had a profound effect on Philadelphia.

Philadelphia's history in recent decades can be illustrated by a series of graphs showing the changes that have occurred. Like other older American cities, Philadelphia has experienced population and job loss while economic shifts and migration patterns have changed the City's demographic makeup. Philadelphia's population has declined as jobs have disappeared. The City's population has aged as many working-age families have moved out. Inmigration and outmigration have increased the minority population both in terms of numbers and percentages while economic shifts have changed the mix of employment opportunities in the City. (See Figures 1 through 6.)

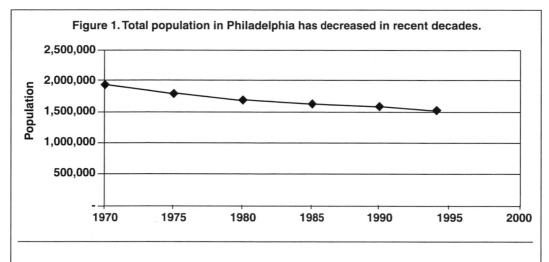

Figure 1. Total population in Philadelphia has decreased in recent decades.

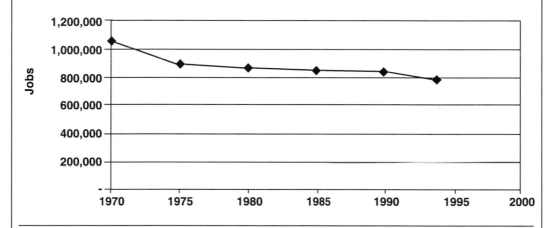

Figure 2. Total employment in Philadelphia has declined in recent decades.

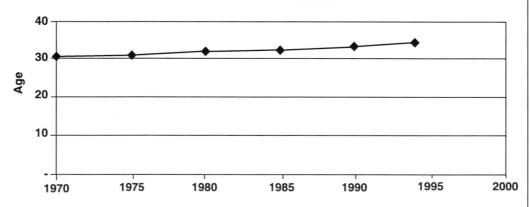

Figure 3. The median age of Philadelphia's population has increased in recent decades.

Source: U.S. Department of Commerce, Bureau of Economic Analysis

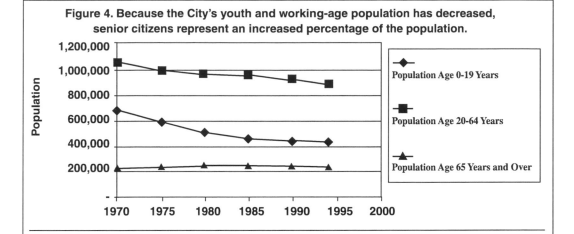

Figure 4. Because the City's youth and working-age population has decreased, senior citizens represent an increased percentage of the population.

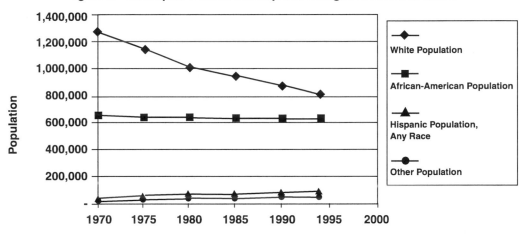

Figure 5. Philadelphia's ethnic makeup has changed in recent decades.

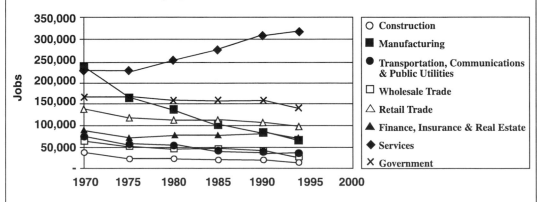

Figure 6. Manufacturing employment in Philadelphia has declined while employment in the services sector has increased.

Source: U.S. Department of Commerce, Bureau of Economic Analysis

The demographic and economic shifts of the second half of the 20th century fundamentally altered the City. While the increasing political strength of the minority population finally brought diversity to the City's elected leadership, the flight of white and middle-class Philadelphia residents has been devastating to the City. Loss of residents and jobs turned once-thriving neighborhoods into areas of concentrated poverty. Increased percentages of poor households—and the increased crime, decay, and economic dislocation associated with high poverty concentration—heightened the troubles of a city reeling from job and population loss. Philadelphia's violent crime rate and per-capita violent crime rate rose dramatically from the 1960s through the 1990s. Although the City received financial help from the federal and state governments, the unreimbursed cost of providing services to the poor pressured the City's elected officials to increase taxes, which chased more residents and jobs from Philadelphia and deepened the cycle of despair.

As is the case with many of America's older cities, the story of modern Philadelphia is a tale of two cities with many of Philadelphia's most fashionable neighborhoods located just a short walk from economically depressed areas. Urban renewal efforts have attacked decay with some success, particularly in Center City, but private development has been slow to return to many blighted neighborhoods. Notable instances of gentrification, such as the re-creation of Society Hill, which revitalized one of Philadelphia's oldest neighborhoods, have invigorated selected areas of the City. But resources to replicate that success have been limited. Despite recent Asian and Hispanic immigration, despite a vibrant Center City, and despite a highly diversified regional economy, modern Philadelphia is littered with thousands of abandoned homes and industrial "brownfields," and is home to an overwhelming majority of the region's poor.

Only years after hosting festivities for the nation's bicentennial and celebrating the 300th anniversary of the founding of the City, Philadelphia found itself in dramatic fiscal peril. By 1990, the City was beset with a cumulative budget deficit of more than $200 million and City credit was reduced to "junk bond" status. Municipal services suffered, and facilities and equipment were neglected as the City struggled against collapse. With the establishment of the Pennsylvania Intergovernmental Cooperation Authority (PICA), an authority created by the Commonwealth of Pennsylvania to provide financial assistance and oversight to Philadelphia, the City was able to avoid the immediate threat of bankruptcy. Through strong leadership and sound fiscal stewardship—augmented by a strong national economy and favorable market conditions—the City bolstered revenue collections, cut labor costs, enhanced workforce performance, and improved government operations to address longer-term problems. Philadelphia moved from fiscal crisis to record surpluses in less than a decade. But systemic problems of job erosion and aging infrastructure remain, threatening to undo the fiscal gains of the 1990s.

Nearing the beginning of the 21st century, Philadelphia is a city of contrasts. Center City is vibrant and full of activity, partially driven by a burgeoning tourism trade and a commitment by City government to make Philadelphia a destination city. Throughout the City, many neighborhoods are solid middle-class enclaves where working families raise their children. But underperforming schools chase many young residents from Philadelphia, and too many neighborhoods suffer from the effects of concentrated poverty. In the late 1980s and early 1990s, developers broke the informal height barrier of William Penn's statue, and new skyscrapers, capped by One Liberty Place, rose above City Hall's tower. These new additions brighten the evening sky with dramatic lighting, which can be seen as a beacon of hope for the future—or a showy distraction from the problems of modern Philadelphia 61 stories below.

Philadelphia's storied past can be viewed in its architecture and its infrastructure, from historic buildings such as Independence Hall and City Hall, to signs of urban decay such as abandoned homes in North Philadelphia and vacant office buildings of Center City. To preserve the successes of the past and correct current problems, Philadelphia's government must reassess its ability to lead the city forward in the face of recent developments and likely future changes. The ideas advanced in this book are intended to begin that process.

OVERVIEW

The recommendations expressed in this document will not necessarily solve the City's problems, but are put forth to enhance City government's ability to act and react to current problems, market trends, and external developments. Global economics will shape the City's future, as will federal and state policies and local developments. Local government cannot alter the international price of oil or change preferences for urban or suburban living, but it can spend its money wisely to fund tax-reduction efforts and more effectively prevent crime. The recommendations on subsequent pages are designed to address such issues and to enable Philadelphia to take on the challenges of the next century.

In 1937, the Federal Writers' Project created *Philadelphia: A Guide to the Nation's Birthplace*, which admonished:

> *[Philadelphia's] voice is the voice of a city of contrasts—a city of wealth and poverty, of turmoil and tranquility, of stern laws often mitigated by mild enforcement; a city proud of its world-molding past and sometimes slow to heed the promptings of modern thought.*[2]

The City cannot continue to repeat the same mistake. Projections for Philadelphia's future establish clear imperatives to address the problems that confront the City. This document represents a plan of action to accept the challenge of a new century—a blueprint for restructuring the City's governmental approach to its future. Mindful of its world-molding past, Philadelphia must heed these promptings of modern thought to move into a vibrant future.

---

[2] Federal Writers' Project, *Philadelphia: A Guide to the Nation's Birthplace* (Philadelphia: University of Pennsylvania Press, 1988).

CHAPTER 1
ENVISIONING PHILADELPHIA
PROJECTIONS AND IMPLICATIONS FOR THE FUTURE

SICINIUS
What is the city but the people?
PLEBEIANS
True,
The people are the city.

—Shakespeare
Coriolanus

PROJECTING THE FUTURE

In 1950, Philadelphia was home to more than two million residents. In 1990, the City was home to fewer than 1.6 million. If this simple trend continues, Philadelphia will be a ghost town by the beginning of the 22nd century. Of course, the future population will be determined by a host of factors other than recent historical trends. After all, prior to 1950, the City had experienced long-term population growth since its settlement.

As late as the 1950s, City planners were still optimistic about growth in Philadelphia and some projected that the City would grow to exceed a population of 2.75 million living in a metropolis teeming with more than 1.2 million jobs. Based on such projections, the City's 1960 Comprehensive Plan proposed a series of concentric and radial expressways designed to criss-cross the City and link its expanding neighborhoods and the region with a growing Center City. Had the plans been completed, the infrastructure would have cut through viable City neighborhoods in the name of progress to create such thoroughfares as the the 52nd Street Expressway in West Philadelphia and the Cross Town Expressway along the edge of Center City on South Street.

Citizen opposition and lack of funds ultimately doomed these projects, and many would argue that, since official projections turned out to be incorrect, the City is much better off without the intrusion of infrastructure designed to move three million residents. Philadelphia is a city that is in many ways designed for a population of two million (the Home Rule Charter and much of the City's physical infrastructure come from a time when Philadelphia's population was at its peak) yet the City currently struggles to fund expenses with a population that has fallen below 1.5 million residents. One can only imagine what it would be like to maintain a city designed for a population of three million with the resources of a still-decreasing population.

History books are filled with rosy projections and dire forecasts that turned out to be inaccurate, but one must continue to look ahead to plot a course. If the course requires correction, one can certainly adapt. Being prepared for a future scenario, regardless of whether it ever comes true, is better than facing the future with no preparation. As President Dwight Eisenhower once reportedly said, "Plans are useless, but planning is essential."

It is not important to identify an exact number of residents likely to inhabit the City of Philadelphia in the future, but it is important to plan for the future based on sound assumptions and theories, and to use these to direct the governmental response to the challenges of the next century.

For example, the implications for a city expecting population growth will be much different than the implications for a city expecting a decline in population. The growing city would have to plan to serve additional residents with a growing tax base while the shrinking city would have to plan to serve fewer residents with a declining tax base. Whether projections for the future, and the implications drawn from those projections seem rosy or bleak, the City's actions in coming years, as well as actions and events at the state, federal, or global levels, can improve or worsen future conditions. If City leaders can craft sound policies and implement them to make Philadelphia a preferred place for employers, families, and visitors, the City will be able to take advantage of opportunities for future growth and avert potential negative consequences of projected challenges. Understanding the worth and limits of projecting the future, the City Controller's Office directed its analytic efforts toward identifying likely future scenarios for Philadelphia.

CITY CONTROLLER'S OFFICE PROJECTION—PHILADELPHIA OUTLOOK 2015: A FORECAST OF THE CITY AND ITS ECONOMY

During the past two decades, powerful economic and social forces have thrown Philadelphia and many other large urban areas into economic malaise. The shift in employment from manufacturing to services, middle-class flight to the suburbs, changes in federal fiscal policy, and the urbanization of poverty have resulted in decreased population and employment levels and have placed tremendous strain on the City's budget.

In recent years, however, greater austerity in spending, combined with local tax reduction and improvements in service-delivery efforts, enabled Philadelphia to exploit the unprecedented strength of the national economy and improve its economic outlook. Indicators of this renewed strength include interest in the City's real estate market, strong private-sector job gains during the last two years, and stronger-than-average growth in City tax collections. Some treat these as signals that the City is proceeding on a long-term path of economic recovery. Others believe this improvement may merely be a temporary deviation from the longstanding downward trends, brought on by extraordinary growth in the national economy and various one-time revenue gains. They argue that as soon as the national economy slows to a more modest growth path, the City could revert to its long-term downward spiral. It is instructive to address this debate by stepping back and looking at the big picture from a long-term perspective to identify the fundamental problems that the City may face in the future. Within this context, the Controller's Office developed a long-term forecast of the City's economic and demographic landscape.

Some forecasts are based strictly on intuition. Others are based on a formal simulation model. The Controller's Office forecast methodology relies on both techniques through a three-step process. First, a long-range forecast was developed using the Regional Economic Models, Inc. (REMI) Economic and Demographic Forecasting and Policy Simulation Model. The REMI model was chosen because of its exemplary track record and the fact that it offers a particular theoretical structure that is widely accepted by economists. Despite its superiority over alternative simulation models, it is not perfect. Thus, in an effort to improve accuracy and intuitive appeal, the second step involved making adjustments to the forecast after review by Controller's Office staff. Finally, the forecast was subjected to review by economists based in the Philadelphia region.

In the most general sense, the Controller's Office forecast appears to be relatively mixed. Whether the news is good or bad depends on the viewing lens. The data suggest that compared to its 1995 level, Philadelphia should expect to enjoy some absolute growth in gross output, income, and employment through 2015. However, the data further show that, unless policy is changed at the state and federal levels, demographic trends shift dramatically, or local actions continue to create change and improve economic conditions, the City will continue to lose its share of aggregate economic activity relative to the United States as a whole. Moreover, population forecasts show that there will likely be fewer Philadelphia residents in 2015 than there were in

1995, in large part due to the flight of working-age population responding rationally to economic incentives placed before them. (See Table 1.1.)

It is important to note that this forecast falls under the realm of the time-honored *ceteris paribus* (all else equal) caveat. The Controller's Office is in no position to predict, for example, future policy actions of the federal government or dramatic developments at the local level, which may alter the future economic and demographic landscape of cities. Yet, despite the possibility for error due to exogenous events, there are two irrefutable implications that flow from the observed forecasts:

1. In the aggregate, any absolute growth observed in local economic activity is expected to emerge from continued national prosperity. The direction of the national economy has set the upper bound on the expected growth of the City of Philadelphia.
2. The projected decline in the City's share of economic activity relative to the United States as a whole is a signal that, without major policy shifts, the business and residential communities of the City of Philadelphia, on average, are expected to continue to operate at a competitive disadvantage.

Figuring out how local government should respond in terms of policy and service delivery is therefore tantamount to forging a more competitive economic and social climate in which Philadelphians will live, work, and play.

Table 1.1. Forecast Summary for the City of Philadelphia					
	1975 (actual)	1995 (actual)	2015 (forecast)	1975–1995 Change (actual)	1995–2015 Change (forecast)
Employment	898,918	777,155	780,100	-13.5%	0.4%
Percentage of Total U.S. Employment	0.91%	0.52%	0.45%	—	—
Population	1,793,257	1,499,762	1,418,409	-16.4%	-5.4%
Percentage of Total U.S. Population	0.83%	0.57%	0.46%	—	—
Output (Gross City Product) (billions of 1992 chained[1] dollars)	73.01	60.01	62.90	-17.8%	4.8%
Source: REMI model as adjusted by the City of Philadelphia Controller's Office					

FORECAST METHODOLOGY

Any forecast of the local economy must consider two very important issues: the growth expected in the U.S. economy and the implications of this growth for Philadelphia. The wide range of economic models that measure the implications of U.S. growth for the Philadelphia economy can be placed into one of two groups.

Models that simply rely on historical patterns and presume to know nothing about causal relationships that affect the variable(s) being forecasted are called time-series models.[2] For example, there may be a consistent pattern observed between national income growth and growth

---

[1] Chain-type indexes are geometric averages of the conventional fixed-weighted Laspeyres Indexes (such as the Consumer Price Index, which uses the weights of the first period in a two-period example) and a Paasche Index (which uses the weights of the second period). Changes in this measure are calculated using the weights of adjacent years. These annual changes are "chained" (multiplied) together to form a time series that allows for the effects of changes in relative prices and in the composition of output over time. Therefore, 1992 chained dollars are constructed by setting 1992 as the base year and using the percent changes in the annual chain-type indexes to extrapolate the real chained dollar estimates for Gross Domestic Product and its components from their 1992 current-dollar levels.

[2] In a sense, time-series models are not economic models at all, since they rely less on economic theory and more on the ability to pick up statistical regularities among data series. Theory only comes into play when trying to explain the observed statistical regularities.

in the level of employment in Philadelphia. A time-series model would make use of this pattern in an effort to predict future employment levels. This methodology is utilized to produce the short-term forecasts of Philadelphia economic activity as reported in the City Controller's annual "Mid-Year Economic and Financial Report."

Another class of model used widely in regional forecasting is the structural model. This technique requires the use of economic theory in an effort to develop causal relationships among different data series. For example, there are numerous theories about how consumption patterns respond to changes in personal income. Generally, the theory that is most viable is the one that best fits the data. Thus, in contrast to the time-series model, this technique establishes parameters in the hopes of explaining the data observed. Forecasts can then be made under the assumption that the behavioral relationships remain in place in the future.

Time-series and structural modeling techniques have different costs and benefits. Traditionally, because time-series techniques are useful for capturing short-term cyclical momentum, they are most appropriate for short-term forecasts, perhaps one or two years ahead. By comparison, structural models tend to smooth out cyclical patterns over the forecast period. It follows that they are better for long-range forecasting. Since this chapter will assemble long-range forecasts of the regional economy, this text employs the structural modeling approach in its use of the REMI model. (See Appendix IV for a brief discussion of the REMI model and how it works.)

The U.S. Economy Likely Will Experience Stable Growth in the Future

Because growth on the local level is, in part, a function of national growth, growth in the local economy is not likely to outpace national growth; it is instructive to display the assumed growth path of the national economy throughout the forecast horizon. Table 1.2 presents the key national growth assumptions used in the REMI model, which act as drivers for the forecast of Philadelphia's economy. The REMI model makes use of the Bureau of Labor Statistics' long-term economic projections, published annually in the November issue of the *Monthly Labor Review*.[3]

The unique feature of this forecast is the stability in output growth, despite the relatively slower growth rate projected for employment and population between 1995 and 2015. This is largely due to the assumption that there will be growth in productivity over the forecast horizon—a legitimate assumption given the heavy investments currently being made by businesses to enhance future productivity.

Table 1.2. National Growth Assumptions Used in REMI Forecast					
	1975 (actual)	1995 (actual)	2015 (forecast)	1975–1995 Change (actual)	1995–2015 Change (forecast)
Employment (In millions)	99.20	149.29	174.24	50.5%	16.7%
Population (In millions)	215.46	262.75	309.45	21.9%	17.8%
Output (billions of 1992 chained dollars)	$3,900.39	$6,742.90	$9,840.95	72.9%	45.9%
Real Disposable Personal Income (billions of chained 1992 dollars)	$13.38	$18.76	$22.49	40.2%	19.9%
Source: REMI					

The Controller's Office Adjusted the REMI Forecast for Increased Accuracy

No model can completely capture all of the structural relationships that exist in a local economy. Analysis of the REMI model shows that its particular structure failed to explain a

---

[3] REMI makes adjustments to the Bureau of Labor Statistics' forecast in an effort to extend the forecast horizon beyond the normal Bureau of Labor Statistics forecast horizon.

portion of the job loss that has plagued the City for many years. As a general rule in econometrics the expected value of any forecast error is zero. Thus, combined with the failures of the defined model structure, this assumption introduces the possibility of an upward bias in the Controller's Office forecast of City employment. There is also likely to be an upward bias in population figures since population is, in part, a function of employment opportunity—the REMI model has consistently understated Philadelphia's population decline. For example, the REMI model is not able to take into account the historical preference to live outside the City due to underperforming schools, high crime, and high taxes. Accordingly, adjustments were made to the forecast to remove this potential bias. Specifically, the average annual error between the level of industrial employment predicted by the structure of the model and the level actually observed was forced into the model over the forecast horizon. Consequently, this reduced the forecast of City employment and population.

Adjustments also were made for exogenous events that are expected with a high degree of certainty, but not accounted for by the model. For example, the structure of the model does not consider the impact that recent changes in federal reimbursements for Medicaid would have on the local hospital industry. Similarly, the model fails to capture the recent deal that was struck to revitalize the City's shipbuilding industry.

FORECAST OF OUTPUT AND EMPLOYMENT

The forecast of City output is driven by numerous supply- and demand-side disturbances. However, there are three essential steps to charting the course of industry and commerce in Philadelphia: identifying the markets that are emerging and declining in the national economy; considering how competitive the City's business environment is in the emerging markets and how concentrated it is in the declining markets; and evaluating whether, apart from the emerging markets, there are any niche industries on which the City can rely for growth.

City Growth Will Likely Occur in Industries for which the City Offers a Competitive Advantage

As described above, the Controller's Office forecast assumes that the national economy will proceed along a stable growth path over the forecast horizon. However, this stability belies the tremendous disparity in growth by sector. There is a central theme underlying this disparity: firms and households have and will continue to demand greater efficiency from both themselves and the government they elect. For example, under pressure to maintain austerity, the federal government will continue to downsize and deregulate. Likewise, under pressure to compete in the global marketplace, industry will continue to be hypersensitive to geographic cost differences and invest heavily in human and physical capital that will make appreciable gains in productivity.

Based on these patterns, the forecast of industry output should not be a surprise. According to the baseline forecast of the U.S. economy produced by REMI, growth will be concentrated in the high-tech sector, which includes communications, machinery and computers, electronic equipment manufacturing, and business services. The list of fastest-growing sectors is headed by establishments involved in the production, wholesale distribution, retail sale, and service of computer and other productivity-enhancing equipment. (See Table 1.3.) In contrast, declining industries are concentrated in sectors such as apparel manufacturing and food product manufacturing that demand labor with fewer technical skills but command a relatively high wage; and sectors such as pipelines and crude petroleum most affected by the ongoing deregulation of public utilities.

Once the level of industrial demand throughout the U.S. economy has been determined, the Controller's Office forecast considers how fit the business environment is in the City of Philadelphia. The forecast proceeds under the premise that firms in emerging markets will choose Philadelphia as a site for production or service delivery if the City offers a more fertile

Table 1.3. Major Emerging and Declining U.S. Markets				
10 Fastest-Growing Industries:	**U.S. Gross Domestic Product in Billions of Chained (1992) Dollars**		**Total Growth**	**Average Annual Growth**
Industry Description	1995 (actual)	2015 (forecast)	1995–2015 (forecast)	1995–2015 (forecast)
Credit and Finance	107.39	301.74	180.99%	9.05%
Communications	201.03	424.35	111.09%	5.55%
Machinery and Computers Manufacturing	194.19	392.85	102.30%	5.12%
Business Services	249.19	477.94	91.80%	4.59%
Other Transportation	37.74	69.44	84.02%	4.20%
Non-Profits	85.83	149.59	74.28%	3.71%
Electronic Equipment Manufacturing	133.97	232.76	73.74%	3.69%
Motion Pictures	21.90	37.36	70.57%	3.53%
Rubber Manufacturing	59.27	101.02	70.43%	3.52%
Trucking	115.93	197.02	69.94%	3.50%
10 Fastest-Declining/Slowest-Growing Industries:				
	1995 (actual)	2015 (forecast)	1995–2015 (forecast)	1995–2015 (forecast)
Tobacco Manufacturing	17.09	8.25	-51.74%	-2.59%
Banking	68.81	44.81	-34.87%	-1.74%
Primary Metals Manufacturing	40.49	28.21	-30.31%	-1.52%
Leather Manufacturing	3.54	2.49	-29.64%	-1.48%
Stone, Clay, etc. Manufacturing	36.21	35.05	-3.20%	-0.16%
Local/Interurban Transportation	14.40	14.70	2.06%	0.10%
Mining	126.45	132.53	4.81%	0.24%
Food Product Manufacturing	140.32	148.32	5.71%	0.29%
Fabricated Metals Manufacturing	82.74	90.31	9.14%	0.46%
Textiles Manufacturing	29.76	32.55	9.40%	0.47%
Source: REMI				

ground for business and commerce relative to other localities. In private industry, the precise level of national output that is produced locally is largely determined by the relative factor costs in each City industry relative to the U.S. as a whole. Figure 1.1 clearly illustrates production cost disparities showing markets where City factor costs exceed U.S. factor costs. Total factor costs include the combined costs to the firm for labor, capital, energy, and intermediate goods and services. In markets where City factor costs equal U.S. factor costs, the relative City and U.S. production costs equal one; where the number is greater than one, City factor costs are higher than U.S. factor costs. The data show that, with the exception of credit and finance and motion pictures, in all of the industries poised for expansion nationally, total factor costs are higher in the City relative to the U.S. average. This difference in factor costs suggests that the City's business environment must become more competitive if the City is to benefit from national expansion in the emerging U.S. industries.

Few of the fastest-growing City industries, displayed in Table 1.4, are consistent with the booming U.S. sectors. The credit and finance industry, which has no real cost disadvantage, the non-profit industry, and the communications industry are projected to be among the fastest-growing industries in both the City and the United States as a whole. Thus, local growth in these sectors can be attributed to broader growth in demand throughout the U.S. economy.

To determine the levels of concentration of City industries in declining U.S. markets, the Controller's Office computed a location quotient which is also called a concentration

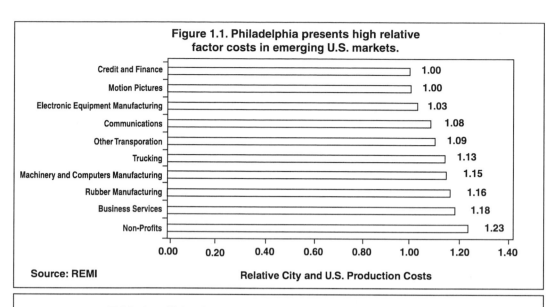

Figure 1.1. Philadelphia presents high relative factor costs in emerging U.S. markets.

Industry	Value
Credit and Finance	1.00
Motion Pictures	1.00
Electronic Equipment Manufacturing	1.03
Communications	1.08
Other Transporation	1.09
Trucking	1.13
Machinery and Computers Manufacturing	1.15
Rubber Manufacturing	1.16
Business Services	1.18
Non-Profits	1.23

Relative City and U.S. Production Costs

Source: REMI

Table 1.4. Major Emerging and Declining Philadelphia Markets

10 Fastest-Growing Industries	Industry Output in Billions of Chained (1992) Dollars		Total Growth	Average Annual Growth
Industry Description (employment level)	1995 (actual)	2015 (forecast)	% Change	1995–2015 (forecast)
Credit and Finance (10,630)	0.85	1.56	84.30%	4.21%
Communications (9,463)	2.42	4.12	70.27%	3.51%
Air Transportation (6,647)	1.03	1.75	69.46%	3.47%
Motor Vehicles (2,432)	0.50	0.84	69.31%	3.47%
Transportation Equipment (1,698)	0.33	0.54	63.73%	3.19%
Educational Services (59,102)	1.65	2.64	60.72%	3.04%
Non-Profits (40,620)	1.47	2.35	59.47%	2.97%
Hotels (5,564)	0.17	0.26	51.03%	2.55%
Auto Repair and Leasing Services (8,427)	1.06	1.60	50.10%	2.51%
Legal, Engineering, and Management Services (57,859)	3.42	4.94	44.70%	2.23%

10 Fastest-Declining Industries	Industry Output in Billions of Chained (1992) Dollars		Total Growth	Average Annual Growth
Industry Description (employment level)	1995 (actual)	2015 (forecast)	% Change	1995–2015 (forecast)
Electronic Equipment Manufacturing (2,796)	0.40	0.07	-82.59%	-4.13%
Leather Manufacturing (67)	0.01	0.002	-79.49%	-3.97%
Textiles Manufacturing (1,021)	0.10	0.02	-75.43%	-3.82%
Machine and Computers Manufacturing (2,793)	0.43	0.11	-75.17%	-3.76%
Petroleum Products Manufacturing (2,721)	3.11	1.00	-67.96%	-3.40%
Stone, Clay, etc. Manufacturing (279)	0.04	0.01	-66.87%	-3.34%
Apparel Manufacturing (6,521)	0.58	0.21	-64.06%	-3.20%
Instruments Manufacturing (1,808)	0.30	0.12	-58.74%	-2.94%
Primary Metals Manufacturing (1,020)	0.46	0.19	-58.32%	-2.92%
Fabricated Metals Manufacturing (4,903)	0.68	0.29	-57.66%	-2.88%

Source: REMI model as adjusted by the City of Philadelphia Controller's Office

index.[4] Where an industry's share of total output in the City is in the same proportion as total output on the national level, the location quotient equals one; where Philadelphia is overrepresented, the location quotient is greater than one. As shown in Figure 1.2, the City currently has an above-average concentration of output in only two of the major U.S. sectors that are expected to decline over the next decade. As a result, job losses may be expected in City businesses engaged in banking and local transportation. This output loss will have to be compensated for by growth in other areas to maintain the City's base of economic activity.

On the whole, slower output growth in the City relative to the United States will likely stem from higher costs rather than an overconcentration in declining markets. Because of the City's high-cost business environment, expected future growth must be explained by the fact that clearly defined niche markets have emerged despite apparent cost disadvantages. The major growth areas in Philadelphia, less attributable to growth in aggregate demand throughout the U.S. economy, are expected to be higher education; hospitality and tourism; motor vehicles; air transportation; auto repair and leasing; legal, engineering, and management services; and transportation equipment. These are the few instances in which higher operating costs may be offset by some revenue-raising benefit. For example, despite higher operating costs, local hoteliers are able to use Philadelphia's many historical attractions as leverage to compete in the national market for vacationers.

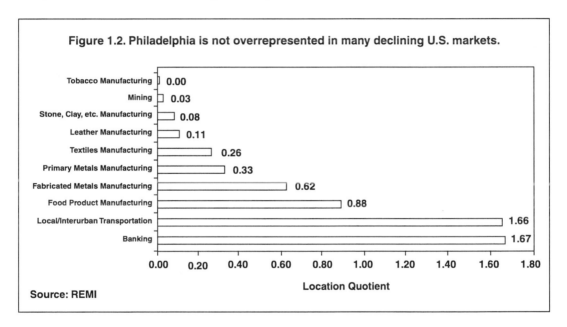

Figure 1.2. Philadelphia is not overrepresented in many declining U.S. markets.

Industry	Location Quotient
Tobacco Manufacturing	0.00
Mining	0.03
Stone, Clay, etc. Manufacturing	0.08
Leather Manufacturing	0.11
Textiles Manufacturing	0.26
Primary Metals Manufacturing	0.33
Fabricated Metals Manufacturing	0.62
Food Product Manufacturing	0.88
Local/Interurban Transportation	1.66
Banking	1.67

Location Quotient

Source: REMI

The Output Forecast Suggests Some Increased City Employment in the Future

Once the level of output (or total value added) is determined at the local level, a forecast of employment is derived easily with an assumption about value added per employee. Specifically, the level of expected future employment is simply the value added per employee multiplied by the level of output. The value added per employee by major industry division in Philadelphia is illustrated in Table 1.5. The City's continued transformation from a manufacturing economy to a service economy, as displayed in Figure 1.3, can be partially explained by the fact that for a given level of output demanded in the local economy, fewer employees are needed in industries with a

---

[4] The specific computation: the location quotient represents the concentration of City output in a particular industry relative to the U.S. as a whole. A quotient greater than one implies that the City has a greater concentration of output in these industries than found at the national level.

Table 1.5. Output per Employee in Philadelphia by Major Industry Division (thousands of 1992 chained dollars)

	1975 (actual)	1995 (actual)	2015 (forecast)	1975–1995 Change (actual)	1995–2015 Change (forecast)
Durable Manufacturing	97.98	160.17	258.37	63.5%	61.3%
Non-durable Manufacturing	272.23	281.98	356.83	3.6%	26.5%
Construction	122.43	104.67	105.30	-14.5%	0.6%
Transportation, Public Utilities	114.50	158.11	275.09	38.1%	74.0%
Finance, Insurance, and Real Estate	126.71	203.55	261.22	60.6%	28.3%
Retail Trade	36.87	37.89	52.32	2.8%	38.1%
Wholesale Trade	65.92	101.32	160.99	53.7%	58.9%
Services	47.80	48.96	51.62	2.4%	5.4%
Agriculture, Fishing, Forestry	32.71	20.63	17.16	-36.9%	-16.8%

Source: REMI model as adjusted by the City of Philadelphia Controller's Office

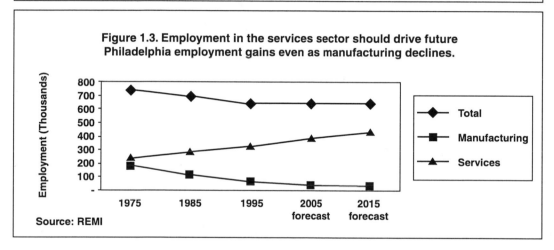

Figure 1.3. Employment in the services sector should drive future Philadelphia employment gains even as manufacturing declines.

Source: REMI

higher value added per employee. Simply put, the dramatic increase in output per employee forecasted in certain industries could suggest that in the future these industries will be able to maintain current levels of production with fewer workers.

One distinguishing feature of Philadelphia's projected future employment growth is its concentration in the services sector. While some lament the further loss of manufacturing-related jobs because such jobs are usually associated with a wage that can support a family, expansion in the services sector will create many new jobs in Philadelphia that offer a relatively high wage level.

Certainly one reason for the relative growth in service employment is that manufacturing has experienced much more intense global competition and technological advancement. It can be argued that the need to compete has driven much of the automation of plant and equipment in the manufacturing sector. Many economists assert that this same pattern will eventually bear itself out in the services sector as the industry matures. This is in line with the assumption that future U.S. employment growth will be slower due to productivity improvements.

Combined with the relative competitiveness of the City business environment and the level and composition of aggregate demand, the value added per employee defines the expected employment picture through 2015. As shown earlier, in the aggregate, the Controller's Office forecasts modest growth in City employment. Yet, the City's share of national employment will continue to fall. The industry-by-industry composition of this employment growth is generally consistent with the output growth. Table 1.6 presents employment projections by industry for the ten fastest-growing and ten fastest-declining Philadelphia industries. Consistent with changes in output, strong employment growth may be expected in the educational services, non-profits, hotels, transportation equipment manufacturing, and auto repair/leasing services industries. Strong employment growth also is expected in local/interurban transportation, legal, engineering, and management services, medical services, amusement and recreational services, and business services. This is a result of the expectation of low productivity growth in these sectors compared to other sectors. Thus, more employees will be needed to meet output demand. The ten industries expected to suffer the greatest employment losses are concentrated in the City's manufacturing sector. (See Table 1.6.)

Table 1.6. Philadelphia City Employment Projections (Ten Fastest Growing Industries)

10 Fastest-Growing Industries	Philadelphia City Employment (in thousands of people)		Total Growth	Average Annual Growth
Industry Description	1995 (actual)	2015 (forecast)	% Change	1995–2015 (forecast)
Educational Services	59.10	94.61	60.07%	3.00%
Non-Profits	40.62	64.01	57.59%	2.88%
Local/Interurban Transportation	4.47	6.86	53.62%	2.68%
Hotels	5.56	8.00	43.82%	2.19%
Transportation Equipment Manufacturing	1.70	2.38	39.93%	2.00%
Legal, Engineering, and Management Services	57.86	78.14	35.05%	1.75%
Medical Services	90.01	117.47	30.51%	1.53%
Auto Repair/Leasing Services	8.43	10.14	20.30%	1.02%
Business Services	34.72	40.01	15.24%	0.76%
Amusement and Recreational Services	7.66	8.32	8.58%	0.43%

10 Fastest-Declining Industries	Philadelphia City Employment (in thousands of people)		Total Growth	Average Annual Growth
Industry Description	1995 (actual)	2005 (forecast)	% Change	1995–2015 (forecast)
Electronic Equipment Manufacturing	2.80	0.31	-88.81%	-4.44%
Textiles Manufacturing	1.01	0.14	-86.07%	-4.30%
Petroleum Products Manufacturing	2.72	0.44	-83.68%	-4.18%
Leather Manufacturing	0.07	0.01	-83.58%	-4.18%
Stone, Clay, etc. Manufacturing	0.28	0.06	-78.14%	-3.91%
Apparel Manufacturing	6.52	1.56	-76.02%	-3.80%
Fabricated Metals Manufacturing	4.90	1.23	-74.95%	-3.75%
Rubber Manufacturing	1.12	0.30	-73.05%	-3.65%
Machine and Computers Manufacturing	2.79	0.78	-71.93%	-3.60%
Miscellaneous Manufacturing	1.54	0.49	-67.92%	-3.40%

Source: REMI model as adjusted by the City of Philadelphia Controller's Office

FORECAST OF CITY POPULATION

Perhaps no issue has commanded more attention among local policymakers than the City's long-term population slide. Between 1975 and 1995, the City population shrank by about 293,500 residents, or 16.4 percent. From the most general standpoint, there can actually be some good aspects to population decline. For example, population decline results in less strain on the public infrastructure. However, one feature of Philadelphia's population loss is the disproportionate decline of those with greater financial resources. According to the Census Bureau, the City's overall poverty rate among individuals continues to rise—from 20.6 percent in 1980 to 26.5 percent in 1993. Thus, Philadelphia can be characterized as a city that suffered a considerable loss in its tax base and a corresponding increase in poverty-related service demands.

This situation is evidenced in the long-term trend in the City's income distribution. For example, according to State Income Tax records, the number of individuals in the bottom quartile of the City's income distribution grew from roughly 28 percent in 1980 to 32 percent in 1996. With the exception of the top quartile, the average income across each group fell in real terms during the same 16-year period. (See Figure 1.4.)

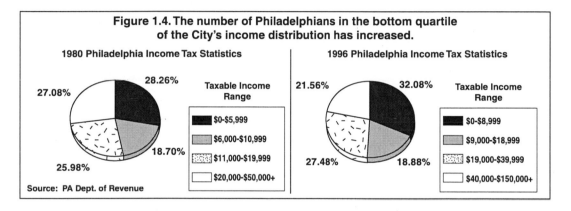

Figure 1.4. The number of Philadelphians in the bottom quartile of the City's income distribution has increased.

1980 Philadelphia Income Tax Statistics

28.26%
27.08%
18.70%
25.98%

Taxable Income Range
- $0-$5,999
- $6,000-$10,999
- $11,000-$19,999
- $20,000-$50,000+

1996 Philadelphia Income Tax Statistics

21.56%
32.08%
27.48%
18.88%

Taxable Income Range
- $0-$8,999
- $9,000-$18,999
- $19,000-$39,999
- $40,000-$150,000+

Source: PA Dept. of Revenue

Historical Job Loss Contributes to Philadelphia's Population Loss

To understand the underlying reasons for the City's population decline, calculations must account for two major sources of population change: change due to natural causes and change in net migration to and from the City. A forecast of natural population changes is based on a relationship between birth and death rates that occur in the population. Table 1.7 displays the

Table 1.7. Annual Change in Population for Selected Years by Major Component			
Natural Changes	1974–75	1984–85	1994–95
Births	+25,044	+25,279	+22,041
Deaths	-17,845	-16,350	-14,927
Total natural change in population	+7,199	+8,929	+7,114
Migrants	1974–75	1984–85	1994–95
Economic	-35,478	-27,732	-19,440
International	+2,155	+2,172	+2,568
Change in Military	+1,570	-148	+1,703
Over 65	-4,311	-4,424	-4,479
Total Migration	-36,064	-30,135	-19,648
Source: REMI			

annual change in the City's population by component for three selected years. The data show that the balance of births and deaths was positive and relatively stable each year. However, the net loss due to migration overwhelmed the positive growth stemming from natural causes.

Migration includes estimated numbers of international migrants (immigrants), retired migrants, economic migrants, and military personnel and their dependents. Economic migrants are defined as individuals under 65 who were part of the civilian U.S. population the year before and have migrated to or from Philadelphia in response to relative economic and amenity factors— anything that affects quality of life, such as the quality of the public school system, neighborhood safety, quality of infrastructure, and climate. Since research shows that individuals are actually willing to forego higher wages in exchange for a more amenable environment, the importance of such amenity factors in considering influences on migration cannot be overstated. Other things being equal, employers must offer a higher wage to attract employees to less amenable work locations. Empirical estimates from the REMI model show that Philadelphia employers must offer wages that are, on average, 20 percent higher than the U.S. average to compensate for differences in quality of life. This 20 percent includes the additional tax liability assumed by Philadelphia residents.

Given the stability of natural population changes, international migration, and changes in military personnel, projections of the City's aggregate population hinge largely on the expected flow of economic migrants. For the purposes of estimation, it is assumed that the relative amenity level is constant over the forecast horizon. If the relative amenity level increases or decreases, population numbers can be expected to respond accordingly—attracting and retaining population is based on factors the City controls. Thus relative employment opportunity drives the Controller's Office population forecast,[5] which, in turn, is a function of the relative competitiveness of the City's business environment. As described earlier, the job picture will likely improve in absolute terms, but continue to falter in relative terms through 2015. Since economic migrants respond to relative employment opportunity, the City's population will likely continue to shrink through 2005, then increase slightly through 2015 as economic opportunity increases in Philadelphia. This

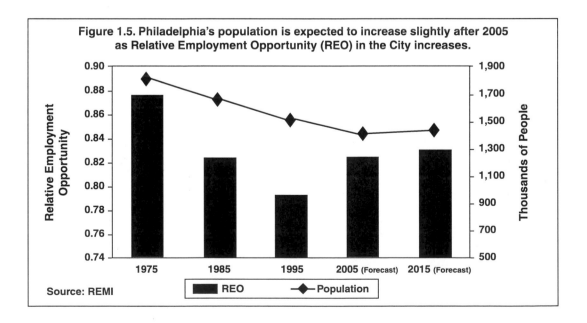

Figure 1.5. Philadelphia's population is expected to increase slightly after 2005 as Relative Employment Opportunity (REO) in the City increases.

Source: REMI

---

[5] Relative Employment Opportunity is the residence-adjusted employment divided by the labor force in the City relative to the same ratio for the U.S. as a whole. Essentially, this measure indicates the probability of being employed in the City relative to the U.S. and is a determinant of economic migrants.

projection offers a challenge and an opportunity. Since population is not expected to increase at the same rate as employment, the forecast suggests that the City could increase benefits and decrease disadvantages associated with life in Philadelphia to retain and attract additional residents. (See Figure 1.5.)

Employment Shifts Will Continue to Alter the Composition of Philadelphia's Population

In the future, Philadelphia will likely have fewer employment opportunities relative to the United States as a whole even as employment opportunity in the City increases. The economic incentives created by the differences in quality of life and diminished employment opportunities not only affect the aggregate population level, but also have implications for the expected age distribution. For example, the loss of working-age population was a singular feature of the City's population loss over the historical period studied. Traditionally, this is the most mobile segment of the population, and thus the cohort that is most responsive to the economic and amenity factors described above.

Under the assumption of a constant quality of life and limited growth in relative employment opportunity, the Controller's Office forecast shows that population in this age group should continue to leave the City through the entire forecast period. Figure 1.6 illustrates the historic and projected population breakdown by age cohorts, and indicates that Philadelphians age 30-49 are likely to decrease as a percentage of the City's total future population. This suggests that providing these individuals with job opportunities, and providing a quality system of public education for their children, is crucial to any effort to retain Philadelphia residents.

The Controller's Office forecast contemplates a broader-based decline by age cohort than in past years. Specifically, the older and younger cohorts are expected to contribute equally to the projected population loss through 2015. However, there may be some bias inherent in the REMI model structure projection of population by age cohort.[6] Table 1.8 presents population projections by age.

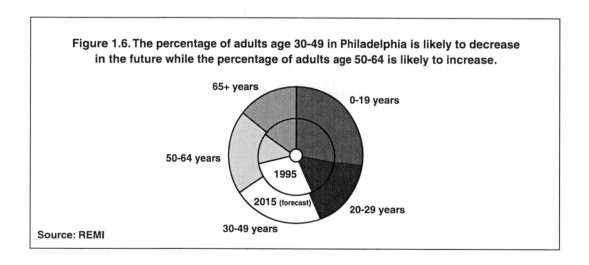

Figure 1.6. The percentage of adults age 30-49 in Philadelphia is likely to decrease in the future while the percentage of adults age 50-64 is likely to increase.

65+ years

0-19 years

50-64 years

1995

2015 (forecast)

20-29 years

30-49 years

Source: REMI

---

[6] Specifically, historical patterns suggest that income plays a role in determining fertility rates. Yet, the REMI model structure only considers fertility patterns by age. This introduces a possible bias, since there is less migration among individuals in the lower income strata. The REMI model also assumes that individuals older than 65 years of age respond to economic incentives in a similar fashion to economic migrants. However, the REMI model fails to capture the various benefits offered to senior citizens residing in the City (such as discounted utility charges and transportation) that may work to reduce outmigration or increase inmigration.

Table 1.8 — Philadelphia Population Forecast by Age (in thousands)							
	Population 1975 (actual)	Population 1995 (actual)	Population 2015 (forecast)	Net Change 1975–1995 (actual)	Net Change 1995–2015 (forecast)	Percent Change 1975–1995 (actual)	Percent Change 1995–2015 (forecast)
0-4 years	118.02	109.07	105.27	-8.95	-3.80	-7.58%	-3.49%
5-9 years	139.06	108.72	96.75	-30.34	-11.98	-21.82%	-11.02%
10-14 years	158.50	98.71	87.47	-59.80	-11.24	-37.73%	-11.39%
15-19 years	163.27	99.16	93.23	-64.11	-5.93	-39.27%	-5.98%
20-24 years	152.66	112.62	122.01	-40.05	9.39	-26.23%	8.34%
25-29 years	136.81	121.65	120.26	-15.16	-1.39	-11.08%	-1.14%
30-34 years	108.59	114.62	94.72	6.02	-19.90	5.55%	-17.36%
35-39 years	85.26	115.36	69.22	30.09	-46.13	35.30%	-39.99%
40-44 years	89.54	105.30	64.90	15.76	-40.40	17.60%	-38.37%
45-49 years	99.36	88.69	80.51	-10.67	-8.17	-10.74%	-9.21%
50-54 years	109.18	72.61	88.11	-36.57	15.49	-33.49%	21.33%
55-59 years	104.82	62.26	100.95	-42.56	38.69	-40.60%	62.14%
60-64 years	96.32	59.50	89.90	-36.82	30.40	-38.23%	51.09%
65-69 years	82.70	64.64	69.18	-18.05	4.54	-21.83%	7.02%
70-74 years	61.65	62.02	49.23	0.37	-12.79	0.59%	-20.63%
75-79 years	44.24	48.90	35.20	4.66	-13.70	10.53%	-28.01%
80-84 years	26.81	31.91	23.99	5.10	-7.93	19.02%	-24.84%
85+ years	16.46	24.04	27.54	7.58	3.50	46.05%	14.55%
Total Population	1,793.25	1,499.76	1,418.41	-293.49	-81.35	-16.37%	-5.42%

Source: REMI model as adjusted by the City of Philadelphia Controller's Office

FORECAST OF PERSONAL INCOME OF CITY RESIDENTS

Wages and salaries, interest and dividends, transfer payments, and adjustments made for the flow of income earned by place of residence largely comprise the income of City residents. Wage and salary disbursements in Philadelphia are expected to increase by 103 percent between 1995 and 2015—roughly 5 percent per year. While this growth is greater than the forecast for inflation, its rate is slower in comparison to the previous 20-year period. The data show that a portion of the wage and salary disbursements generated by City jobs will flow outside the City/County borders. Specifically, the residential adjustment, estimated from journey-to-work patterns that capture the dollar volume flowing outside the City from City jobs, is expected to grow from $8.2 billion in 1995 to an estimated $15.1 billion by 2015. However, because the value of the residential adjustment as a proportion of wage and salary disbursement is expected to decrease slightly, City residents may be expected to fill an increased number of City jobs. This change could also be explained by an increasing number of City residents filling suburban jobs. (See Table 1.9.)

Therefore, City government is presented with a two-fold challenge for the future. First, City government must ensure that Philadelphia residents are adequately prepared for the jobs that will exist in the City in the 21st century. In addition, the City government must improve quality of life in Philadelphia to retain, as residents, individuals who work outside the City. By increasing the number of City residents employed in Philadelphia jobs, the City government can help reduce the flow of money out of the City economy.

Transfer payments, which include payments for Social Security benefits and other social welfare and insurance programs, are slated for growth through 2015, albeit at a much slower pace in comparison with the previous 20 years. This is a result of two offsetting patterns. The aging of the population will result in additional federal disbursements under the Social Security program.

Table 1.9. Personal Income 1975, 1995, and 2015, Level and Percent Change (billions of nominal dollars)					
	1975 Level (actual)	1995 Level (actual)	2015 Level (forecast)	1975–1995 Change (actual)	1995–2015 Change (forecast)
Wage and Salary Disbursement	$9.290	$23.314	$47.523	150.9%	103.8%
Other Labor Income	$1.278	$5.238	$10.372	309.9%	98.0%
Tot Labor Income	$10.568	$28.552	$57.894	170.2%	102.8%
Less Soc. Insurance Contributions	$0.557	$1.980	$4.125	255.2%	108.4%
+ Residential Adjustment	-$2.954	-$8.188	-$15.089	177.2%	84.3%
+ Div, Int., Rent	$1.215	$4.073	$6.476	235.3%	59.0%
+ Transfer Payments	$2.358	$9.237	$15.051	291.6%	62.9%
Personal Income	$10.630	$31.693	$60.207	198.2%	90.0%
Less Taxes	$1.326	$4.060	$8.427	206.2%	107.6%
Disposable Personal Income	$9.304	$27.633	$51.780	197.0%	87.4%
Real Disposable Income Per Capita	$11.837	$16.272	$20.235	37.5%	24.4%
Source: REMI model as adjusted by the City of Philadelphia Controller's Office					

However, this growth will be partially offset by restraint in disbursements for welfare programs as a result of recent federal and state legislative changes. Combined with a reduction in the rate of population loss, slower increases in transfer payments and increased income flowing out of the City are expected to stunt the growth of real disposable income on a per capita basis. Between 1995 and 2015, growth in real disposable income per capita is expected to average less than 1.3 percent per year. This growth contrasts with the 1.9-percent annual growth rate observed between 1975 and 1995. If disposable personal income on a per capita basis grows at a slow rate during the next two decades, the City's future tax base will exhibit similar slow growth.

OTHER PROJECTIONS

Delaware Valley Regional Planning Commission

The Delaware Valley Regional Planning Commission (DVRPC) is a bi-state agency established in 1965 to provide comprehensive coordinated planning for the Greater Philadelphia region. DVRPC provides technical assistance and conducts research to inform the region's policymakers. In 1995, DVRPC completed work on Direction 2020, a project that quantified the needs of the region and crafted a plan for regional land use and transportation needs. As part of that effort, DVRPC created a series of forecasts for the region that focused on changing population, housing, and employment.

DVRPC predicts continued population losses for Philadelphia spread throughout the City but occurring at a slower rate than the population losses of recent years.[7] By 2020, DVRPC projects a population decrease of approximately 4.8 percent from its 1990 population level. Breaking this projection down to the neighborhood level (see Figure 1.7 for neighborhood boundaries), only Center City is projected to gain residents while areas such as Lower North Philadelphia and South Philadelphia are projected to lose 12.5 and 7.9 percent of their 1990 population, respectively. This growth in Center City is already occurring, mirrored by expansion of downtown areas in cities across the country. (See Table 1.10.)

---

[7] DVRPC predicts population loss at a slower rate than the Controller's Office. However, because recent Census Bureau estimates of the City's current population are below DVRPC's forecast for the year 2000, DVRPC's predictions may be overly optimistic.

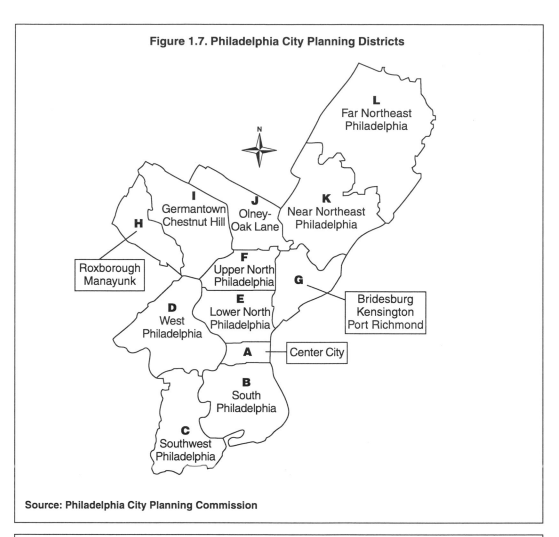

Figure 1.7. Philadelphia City Planning Districts

L
Far Northeast
Philadelphia

N

I
Germantown
Chestnut Hill

J
Olney-
Oak Lane

K
Near Northeast
Philadelphia

H
Roxborough
Manayunk

F
Upper North
Philadelphia

G

D
West
Philadelphia

E
Lower North
Philadelphia

Bridesburg
Kensington
Port Richmond

A — Center City

B
South
Philadelphia

C
Southwest
Philadelphia

Source: Philadelphia City Planning Commission

Table 1.10. DVRPC Population Forecasts by Neighborhood					
	1990 (actual)	2000 (forecast)	2010 (forecast)	2020 (forecast)	Change 1990–2020 (forecast)
Center City (A)	45,644	48,158	50,895	52,409	14.82%
South Philadelphia (B)	170,944	167,169	160,872	157,304	-7.98%
SW Philadelphia (C)	81,885	80,863	79,412	78,416	-4.24%
West Philadelphia (D)	219,713	216,689	212,401	209,468	-4.66%
Lower N. Philadelphia (E)	146,491	140,547	133,702	128,178	-12.50%
Upper N. Philadelphia (F)	106,045	103,338	99,926	98,283	-7.32%
Kensington (G)	94,715	93,340	91,393	90,063	-4.91%
Roxborough/Manayunk (H)	42,525	41,850	40,896	40,246	-5.36%
Germantown/Chestnut Hill (I)	103,266	101,649	99,363	97,804	-5.29%
Olney–Oak Lane (J)	176,550	174,798	172,299	170,575	-3.38%
Near NE Philadelphia (K)	237,252	234,625	230,887	228,316	-3.77%
Far NE Philadelphia (L)	160,547	159,839	158,814	158,092	-1.53%
Total	**1,585,577**	**1,562,865**	**1,530,860**	**1,509,154**	**-4.82%**

Source: Delaware Valley Regional Planning Commission

There will not only be fewer people in future Philadelphia as foreseen by DVRPC, but future Philadelphia residents will be older. The DVRPC forecast foresees large decreases in population age 20-44 years and increases in the population age 45-64. The DVRPC regional 1990–2020 forecasts predict only a 5.6-percent increase in children under 15; a 14.7-percent decline in those age 15-44; a 21.9-percent increase in those age 45-64; and a 20.1-percent increase in those age 65 and over.

Despite predicting decreasing population, DVRPC forecasts a slight increase in the number of occupied housing units in Philadelphia. Largely driven by divorce, decisions by young adults to postpone marriage, and an increasing population of "empty nesters," DVRPC foresees the increase in occupied housing units to be concentrated in Center City, Roxborough/Manayunk, and Far Northeast Philadelphia. Other Philadelphia neighborhoods are expected to experience little or negative growth in the number of occupied housing units.

With regard to employment in Philadelphia, DVRPC predicts some long-term growth driven by expansion of the services sector. Employment growth is forecast for Center City, Far Northeast Philadelphia, and West Philadelphia, with continued losses forecast for other City neighborhoods, including significant losses for Lower North Philadelphia, Upper North Philadelphia, and Kensington. Similarly, DVRPC forecasts increased numbers of employed residents for Center City, Far Northeast Philadelphia, and West Philadelphia, with decreased numbers of employed residents for Upper and Lower North Philadelphia.

Despite forecasts of population loss, DVRPC projects an increase in vehicle availability for the City as well as the region. By 2020, DVRPC suggests that vehicle availability could increase by as much as 9.2 percent over 1990 levels, increasing the number of cars on City streets by more than 48,000. The number of cars in the region could increase by nearly one million vehicles. Automobile trips, truck trips, and vehicle miles of travel are all expected to increase. The DVRPC forecast anticipates the vehicle miles of travel in the region to increase by 32.6 percent between 1990 and 2020.

Woods & Poole Economics, Inc.

Woods & Poole Economics, Inc. is a small, independent corporation specializing in long-term county economic and demographic projections. Through the use of a database containing more than 550 economic and demographic variables for every year from 1970 through 2020, Woods & Poole produces comprehensive proprietary economic and demographic projections. Since the Woods & Poole projections are performed simultaneously for every county in the United States, the actions and reactions occurring across the country are reflected in local projections for Philadelphia. Such a methodology is, therefore, not a simple extrapolation of recent historical trends, but an effort to capture regional flows and constrain the results to a previously determined U.S. total.

The Woods & Poole technique generally follows a standard economic "export-base" approach. With such an approach, certain industrial sectors at the regional level are considered "basic"—these sectors produce output that is not consumed locally, but is "exported" out of the region for national or international consumption. That assumption allows sectors to be linked closely to the national economy and therefore follow national trends in productivity and output growth. To account for regional variants to normal "basic"/"non-basic" industry definitions, the model has built-in corrections. For example, the traditionally "non-basic" services sector in Las Vegas, Nevada, would be considered a "basic" industry because Las Vegas' status as an enter-tainment center causes the services sector to be exported. Woods & Poole also uses exogenous information about Economic Area[8] economies to sharpen the focus of its projections. The demographic portion of the regional model follows a traditional cohort-component analysis based on calculated fertility and mortality in each county, modified by economic migration patterns as a function of employment opportunities.

---

[8] Economic Areas, defined by the U.S. Department of Commerce, Bureau of Economic Analysis, are aggregates of contiguous counties used to measure cohesive economic regions in the United States.

The Woods & Poole model projects that Philadelphia's population will continue to fall through the year 2020. Population is expected to fall 10.8 percent between 1994 and 2020 (1994 is the most recent year for which actual data exist in the 1997 Woods & Poole model). The Woods & Poole model projects that this population will age through the year 2020. The median age of Philadelphia's population is expected to increase by 6.5 percent between 1994 and 2020 since the population of those age 65 years and over is not expected to fall as quickly as the populations of younger Philadelphians. Growth is forecasted for the 50-54-year-old, 55-59-year-old, 60-64-year-old, and over 85-year-old subgroups.

Woods & Poole projects that this population will be changing in terms of ethnicity through the year 2020. The white population is expected to decrease by 29.4 percent between 1994 and 2020. Similarly, the African-American population is expected to decrease by 6.8 percent between 1994 and 2020. During the same time, Philadelphia's Hispanic population is expected to increase by 58.8, while Asian and other populations are expected to increase 219.8 percent.

As the population changes in terms of total population, age of population, and ethnicity, Woods & Poole foresees an impact on the number of households and number of persons per household in Philadelphia. Woods & Poole projects the number of households in Philadelphia to fall by 8.3 percent between 1994 and 2020. At the same time, demographic shifts including increased number of seniors living without their families or single adults living alone and lifestyle changes, including divorcees and unmarried individuals living together are projected to lower the number of persons per household by 3.1 percent between 1994 and 2020.

Finally, with regard to the City's economy, Woods & Poole foresees an economy driven by the services sector and less involved in manufacturing. Specifically, the Woods & Poole model projects the services sector to grow in terms of employment by 23.9 percent between 1994 and 2020 while manufacturing is projected to contract by 38.2 during the same period. The wholesale trade and transportation, communications, and public utilities sectors are expected to contract significantly while the finance, insurance, and real estate, construction, and retail trade sectors are expected to contract less significantly between 1994 and 2020. With continued government devolution, federal government employment is expected to decrease, but overall government employment is expected to increase between 1994 and 2020 as state and local government employment increases with their expanded roles.

With regard to overall employment, however, the Woods & Poole model forecasts a roller-coaster ride capped off by a positive outcome. Employment is expected to increase by 5.4 percent between 1994 and 2020 as the model projects job growth for Philadelphia after the year 2010. However, employment is expected to fall 3.3 percent between 1994 and 2000 and 2.6 percent between 1994 and 2010.

CONSENSUS

While the future will ultimately present itself in due time despite efforts to predict it, projections for the future provide insight about what may occur if current conditions continue. Projections performed by the City Controller's Office, the Delaware Valley Regional Planning Commission, and Woods & Poole Economics, Inc. differ at the margins, but all point to further population decline and some employment growth. Of course, external influences and actions by the City can alter the future.

The Controller's Office projection and independent forecasts foresee a future Philadelphia populated by fewer residents. The projections foresee the population of future Philadelphia to be older, more ethnically diverse, and possibly endowed with fewer financial resources. While projections foresee increased economic opportunity and an increase in the number of City jobs, many of these jobs will require above-average educational attainment, which could shut many Philadelphians out of opportunities. But the City is not powerless to affect this projected future.

As the projections also indicate, by lowering the cost of doing business in Philadelphia, the City can expand economic growth. By improving the quality of life in Philadelphia, the City can attract and retain residents.

Having created a picture of future Philadelphia, it is now possible to consider the implications of the various predictions for population shifts, demographic changes, and economic conditions. Such information will help frame recommendations designed to address the challenges of the 21st century and improve the outlook for the City's future.

IMPLICATIONS OF A CHANGING POPULATION

The City will have new issues to face as the faces of Philadelphians change. A city that is growing will have different challenges than a city that is contracting. The citizens of a city growing poorer will place different demands on government than the citizens of a city attracting more wealthy residents. The government of a city flush with incoming revenues will be presented with different opportunities than a city struggling to meet expenditures. The fact that Philadelphia is home to a changing population implies that it is a changing city—a city that must change to meet the challenges of the 21st century.

Diminishing Population

A city with a population likely to decrease by more than 5 percent during the next two decades will be a city with fewer taxpayers to fund expenditures, but also a city with fewer citizens to serve. While Philadelphia is likely to lose population, the physical area of the City is unlikely to change (annexation of adjacent municipalities or secession by current City neighborhoods are both improbable). Since the number of streets to be policed and repaired and the number of sewer and water lines to be maintained are likely to remain the same despite the flight of taxpayers, the City will be forced to consider raising taxes per capita, decreasing services, or both. Since the Controller's Office does not project a return to previous levels of population and employment any time in the foreseeable future, the City will need to improve efficiency in the delivery of municipal services to maintain a balanced budget without altering service levels or increasing revenues. Nothing in the City Controller's Office projections indicates that problems such as the high number of vacant houses in the City or declining neighborhood density will be solved through significant inmigration.

A loss of population can be expected to lead to a net decrease in demand for land and a rising housing vacancy rate. This trend may be mitigated by an increase in the number of divorcees and older citizens living alone, which could decrease the number of people per house in Philadelphia in general. It naturally follows that a decline in population density will likely mean the loss of viable density in many neighborhoods. Without sufficient concentrations of people, provision of normal municipal services becomes extremely expensive. Similarly, neighborhoods may suffer if they are home to fewer customers than necessary to support neighborhood stores, recreation facilities, or other establishments. In such cases, population loss may continue to cause communities to break down in many areas of the City.

With declining population, neighborhoods can be expected to show wear in terms of abandoned buildings, vacant lots, and deteriorated homes. According to a University of Pennsylvania Wharton Real Estate Center research paper, national surveys indicate that once more than 3 to 6 percent of a neighborhood's buildings become abandoned, the neighborhood becomes predisposed to instability as insecurity sets in, followed by decay as vacant buildings become havens for drug use, vacant lots become illegal dumping grounds, and the community suffers from a general lack of involvement. Similarly, the premise of the broken-window theory of crime holds that if a window in a building is broken and left unrepaired, more broken windows will follow because the unrepaired broken window signals that no one is vigilant. Any decay is likely to breed additional decay.

Because population levels help determine political representation, continued population loss is likely to result in a further reduction of political clout for Philadelphia. Similarly, because population is used to help determine funding levels for many state and federal programs, additional population loss is likely to result in reduced intergovernmental funding for City agencies.

As population decreases, however, the City may benefit from a diminished population. For example, fewer residents will produce less trash and therefore the City could spend less for tipping fees. Unfortunately, such decreases in expenditures are not enough to counter the loss of tax base that accompanies population loss. Money to fund City programs must therefore be found in the existing budget. Faced with inadequate revenues, the City has historically been forced to choose between needed social services and maintenance of physical infrastructure. Too often, the physical infrastructure has been neglected, causing facilities to deteriorate, but also causing the City to commit to a higher level of capital spending to fund major repairs and renovations that could have been avoided by less expensive ongoing maintenance. With population loss threatening the City's ability to maintain its current stock of physical assets, the City could have an opportunity to consider consolidating facilities to better serve the citizenry and to avoid future budgetary stress due to a lack of adequate preventive maintenance.

In many ways, Philadelphia, in terms of physical assets, is built for the population of 1950 and needs to be "rightsized" for the population of the 21st century. The City's physical infrastructure, organization, staffing levels, and staff deployment patterns will need to be addressed for the government to better respond to these changes. Agency personnel will need to be trained, retrained, and cross-trained as part of efforts to coordinate services with other agencies and increase flexibility to better respond to the changing city. Agencies will need to alter the way they interact with consumers of government services and the public to respond to new or changing challenges. Finally, to ensure that revenues are maximized in light of projected further tax base erosion, City agencies must increase efficiency and effectiveness at all levels and charge appropriate user fees, fines, and other charges to maximize revenue while minimizing barriers to participation.

Aging Population

The likelihood that the age distribution of Philadelphia's population will change in the coming decades has many implications. As the median age of a population increases, that population will tend to achieve greater representation in higher income categories and professional positions. In a vacuum, this has favorable implications since a maturing population would be expected to attain a high degree of wealth compared to the general population. However, as the City's population grows increasingly older, and as an increasing percentage of residents retire from the workforce, collections from income-based sources such as the City Wage and Net Profits Tax will suffer. Similarly, as the City experiences a decrease of working-age people, its population will hold a lower percentage of City jobs and the City will experience reduced Wage and Net Profits Tax collections because suburbanites filling jobs in the City pay a lower Wage and Net Profits Tax rate. In addition, increases in elderly residents could tax City agencies as they are forced to meet the transportation and healthcare demands of the growing elderly population.

Crime can be expected to increase also the percentage of youths in a given population increases. Because projections indicated a likely increase in the number of individuals aged 15-24, Philadelphia could witness a greater incidence of crime in the future. An increased youth population is associated with an increase in out-of-wedlock births, female-headed homes, and welfare dependency. This increasing youth population may put more pressure on the City's health and human services agencies, police, courts, truancy-enforcement programs, prisons, and probation-oversight system.

Finally, migration patterns show that Philadelphia has been losing, and may continue to lose, a significant number of young children and young adults. Combined with compelling anecdotal evidence, this helps confirm the notion that school quality is a major factor in residents' relocation decisions. Without any reason to believe that this trend will be mitigated by other factors, the need to reverse this pattern places additional pressure on City leaders to improve the quality of education in Philadelphia.

Slow Economic Growth

While the projections for the future foresee sure growth, that growth will not be sufficient to break the crushing cycle of poverty that plagues Philadelphia. Concentration of poverty, and the prospects for its increase, have been primary contributors to the ills of the American city. In 1980, 29 of the 365 census tracts in Philadelphia were labeled "extreme poverty tracts" in which 40 percent or more of resident families lived in poverty. By 1990, this number increased to 37 tracts. The number of "poverty tracts" in which at least 20 percent of families live in poverty increased from 116 to 149 (of 365) during the same period. How the population changes in terms of residents' income level can be expected to have significant consequences for Philadelphia.

According to the work of scholar William Julius Wilson and others, concentrated poverty multiplies the severity of problems faced by the residents of poor communities in terms of hastened outmigration of non-poor from a neighborhood, increased disconnection with job networks, and increased social isolation. As the concentration of poverty within a jurisdiction increases, an increase in teenage pregnancy, high school dropouts, and joblessness can be expected to follow. Similarly, an increasing concentration of poverty within a jurisdiction can be expected to result in middle-class flight, business disinvestment, declining property values, exodus of basic private services, gang activity, and loss of desire to achieve academically. More specifically, socioeconomically distressed neighborhoods tend to foster concentration of violent crime.

Joblessness, even when not associated specifically with concentrated poverty, has many implications for the City. As concentrations of unemployment increase, residents of neighborhoods experiencing high unemployment face a total isolation from the world of work. As unemployment increases in an area, that area's housing stock can be expected to suffer from deferred maintenance as residents' disposable income decreases. An increase in joblessness, racial segregation, and single parentage in a jurisdiction will likely lead to isolation from middle-class society and the private economy. Without a supply of jobs, labor quality will suffer and a general lack of skills desired by the marketplace may be expected to effectively shut many City residents out of the workforce. This skill gap, combined with the disappearance of low-skill jobs that offer family-sustaining wages and benefits, creates a caste of unemployed residents that drain the resources of the City.

As poverty in a jurisdiction increases, increased direct costs will be imposed on the local level for health, homelessness abatement, recreation, and housing programs. Since much of this increased cost is unreimbursed by the state and federal governments, this can dramatically affect a city budget. Indirectly, increased poverty will also increase expenditures for police-related services to respond to criminal and domestic disturbances and fire-related services to respond to fire and medical calls not traditionally associated with more wealthy jurisdictions.

As a city's population grows increasingly poor, it becomes home to an increasing percentage of people who are dependent on government for income, do not contribute to the tax base, and demand increasing amounts of public expenditures on services not demanded by more wealthy citizens. Therefore, according to research on the financial impact of poverty performed by the University of Pennsylvania's Wharton Real Estate Center, cities with large poor populations tend to have relatively high education-related costs and tend to spend more per capita on primary poverty functions (welfare, health and hospitals) and indirect poverty functions (police, fire protection, and the judicial system) even after substantial transfers from the state and federal governments.

Similarly, an increasing percentage of impoverished residents may be expected to further tax the City's Department of Human Services. More individuals relying on the City to meet their

Mental Health/Mental Retardation needs may be expected to further tax the Department of Public Health. An increasing population of impoverished residents, combined with increasing numbers of vacant structures, raises the risk of fire and increases the importance of preventive efforts as well as quick response. Increasing poverty may increase the number of children with risk factors that mark them as candidates for early academic failure, making it more important than ever to provide a system of public education that can truly provide residents with a bridge to opportunity. Finally, because an increased poor population may be associated with the spread of communicable disease and may be more likely to allow medical problems to deteriorate into serious conditions before seeking help, an increasing population of impoverished residents can be expected to place increased pressures on responding City agencies.

Responding to homelessness in Philadelphia, for example, does not only increase costs for the Office of Emergency Shelter and Services, the agency specifically charged with homelessness abatement. A variety of agencies, including the Mayor's Office of Housing and Community Development, the Department of Public Health, the Department of Human Services, the Police Department, the Department of Licenses and Inspections, the Philadelphia Housing Authority, and the Redevelopment Authority all directly or indirectly respond to issues surrounding homelessness.

Changing Ethnic Makeup

Philadelphia's changing ethnic composition will also have implications for the City and its agencies. A projected decrease in the white population, a smaller projected decrease in the African-American population, a sizable increase in the Hispanic population, and a major expansion of the Asian population will change the City in important and fundamental ways.

Racial tension may increase in the future as the white population decreases and as Hispanic and Asian populations assert themselves in the local economic and political system. Similarly, tensions are likely to increase as new minority groups expand into neighborhoods that are currently home to other minority communities.

Continued immigration—largely Hispanic and Asian, but also Eastern European—may be expected to result in the substitution of immigrants for native residents and can be expected to affect the City in many ways. For example, because new-immigrant groups often tend to have more children than other groups, the City may need to spend more on educational and recreational services. Similarly, immigration indirectly changes the characteristics of other residents by changing employment or housing opportunities. Historically, immigration also encourages outmigration. Indirectly, immigration may also change the price of City services as schools, for example, may increase programs such as English for Speakers of Other Languages at the cost of other programs. Immigrants can also be expected to infuse new vitality into City neighborhoods and alter the skill level of the City's workforce. Finally, as the City changes in ethnic makeup, languages other than English will be more common and the City could face increasing political pressure to make services and programs more accessible for non-English speakers.

IMPLICATIONS OF A CHANGING ECONOMY

In the global village that is the modern world, economic forces, both worldwide and local, will shape Philadelphia's future. A city overflowing with job opportunities will place different pressures on local government than a city without work. In cities undergoing economic expansion, citizens will demand a different response from government than cities in decline.

Economic Shifts

In recent years, the City of Philadelphia has lagged behind the Greater Philadelphia region and the nation at large in terms of economic growth and response to economic recovery. To deal with the fiscal side effects created by forecasted short-term economic decline, Philadelphia could be forced to reduce costs, reduce services, raise taxes, or borrow for the future. While the creation of a sufficient job and tax base is necessary to address problems of housing-stock age and deterioration, racial isolation, and lack of opportunities, many societal problems require direct remedies beyond economic growth: health and nutrition programs for poor children, employment and training for job seekers, and housing and community-development programs for declining neighborhoods. These difficulties are likely to be compounded by the requirements of welfare-reform legislation, which will force approximately 60,000 heads of households in the City to find work to maintain their government financial assistance in coming years before totally losing benefits after receiving welfare benefits for a total of five years.

The new economy is typified by national and international interdependence, which tend to disconnect structures of opportunity from City neighborhoods. Historical changes in residential and infrastructure construction patterns have shifted jobs away from older industrial neighborhoods and into suburbs. The changing nature of work has resulted in increasing feminization of the workforce, coupled with increased educational requirements for employment, while the dispersal of jobs throughout urban regions has concentrated minority populations and isolated them from higher-paying opportunities.

Continuance of current economic trends may likely result in further polarization of employment into the high- and low-wage sectors with few opportunities for displaced workers. Since many City residents simply lack the skills demanded in today's economy, many Philadelphians are effectively shut out of the economy. This poorly trained workforce will likely continue to make the City less attractive to new employers and place more pressure on the City to improve the quality of its workforce.

Changes in the workplace also have implications for the City itself. Technological advances in the workplace threaten to make the central office obsolete, but limited human contact may create a renewed demand for venues that foster effective face-to-face interactions. Anticipated increases in national and international vacation spending coupled with changes in vacation patterns, which make the three- or four-day weekend getaway popular, may increase the need for central, accessible entertainment options and make Philadelphia a more attractive destination city. Such demand for hospitality and air transportation services could help offset the likely drop in business-related travel that should accompany the recent departure of notable corporate headquarters from Philadelphia.

Similarly, economic shifts have implications for the City. Neighborhood stores may find it increasingly difficult to compete successfully with larger chains, and with free parking and tremendous buying power, large "category-killer" stores such as Home Depot are likely to continue to threaten the survival of many "mom-and-pop" stores. Losing such stores located within walking distance of neighbors not only reduces the amenity of convenience for the neighborhood, but decreases the safety of the neighborhood due to the loss of vital foot traffic.

In general, the high costs associated with business in Philadelphia contribute to its lack of competitiveness. But despite such characteristics, which deter business, cities do have certain competitive advantages. As Harvard Business School Professor Michael Porter expounds, cities—and even inner-city neighborhoods with above-average unemployment and below-average income levels—truly have an advantage in strategic location, local market demand, integration with regional clusters, and human resources. In a just-in-time economy, the central location of city neighborhoods offers a competitive edge to companies that benefit from proximity to central business districts and concentrations of companies such as food processors and business-support firms. The tremendous density of city consumers can support supermarkets and shopping centers even in low-income areas that have suffered great population loss. The potential to form integrated business clusters in cities can help start-ups prosper and provide an outlet for goods by allowing large companies access to emerging inner-city markets. Finally, the great numbers of workers and entrepreneurs that can be found in cities represent great energy that cannot be found in less densely populated suburban communities. Shackled by factors that discourage business from locating in Philadelphia, the City must capitalize upon such advantages in the future.

The changing local economy will force City leaders to continue to rethink tax policies that currently favor real estate developers and some large service firms (such as untargeted abatements that reward builders even if they are responding to market forces) to the disadvantage of small manufacturers. Similarly, because Philadelphia's City Wage and Net Profits Tax tends to raise wages and salaries (since employers feel the need to compensate for the negative effects it has on earnings and ability to attract employees), the City must persist in efforts to address such a disincentive to growth in the future. The City will also need to continue to create incentives to attract types of firms that fit into flexible manufacturing subcontracting networks and build or encourage the creation of employment programs that constantly retrain workers and match them to jobs. Finally, because many City residents lack the skills demanded by today's and tomorrow's employers, future economic development efforts must continue to address how the City can better coordinate job training efforts, from public school through worker retraining, to improve job training effectiveness and increase economic development.

Changing Regional Economy

While Philadelphia has a very diversified economy, making it less vulnerable to shocks to one particular sector of the economy, regional economic and intra-industry shifts are tremendously important to the City's future. Changes in levels of employment will have many implications for Philadelphia.

For example, the healthcare industry is undergoing market-based changes, which will cost the City thousands of jobs. In the summer of 1998, after decreasing reimbursement rates from insurance companies dramatically reduced its revenues, the non-profit Allegheny Hospital Education & Research Foundation, operator of eight hospitals and a medical school in the Philadelphia area, declared itself to be $1.3 billion in debt and filed for bankruptcy. According to the Pennsylvania Economy League, a non-profit research and consulting organization, the major shifts in the healthcare industry (managed care, emergence of for-profit hospitals, government intervention) could eventually result in the loss of 20,000 area jobs and significant hospital closings. Those same changes could also create new entrepreneurial activity that could spawn opportunities for economic growth in emerging areas of research and care provision. At the same time, managed care and other changes are altering the way the healthcare industry works, forcing the City to consider how the dictates of private medical insurers and providers will impact City agencies and the way they respond to healthcare needs.

Competition and deregulation in the gas and electric industries could have dramatic implications for Philadelphia. Hampered by the historically high cost of utility services, Philadelphia firms could save money and expand if increased competition can lower costs. Such competition will also force the City to evaluate whether it will continue to be beneficial to operate a municipally owned gas utility.

Shifts in federal and state policies should continue to place more demands on the City to provide social services to residents. The policies of the federal and state government have left counties (Philadelphia is both a city and a county) as the provider of last resort for the individuals who are unable to compete in today's economy. Services such as provision of healthcare and shelter could be demanded from local government at unprecedented levels.

Finally, the emerging dominance of the non-profit sector will have many implications for Philadelphia. The City is home to many private non-profit institutions (universities, schools, religious institutions, and museums) that add to its vibrancy but may be thought to be a drag since they are exempt from the City's Real Estate Tax. As non-profit institutions become a more significant contributor in the City economy, institutions of higher education must be seen as economic engines whose needs must be met and challenges addressed if Philadelphia is to thrive. As the

City's population and job base continue to decline while economic growth is foreseen in the non-profit sector, the City will be forced to consider whether the current tax structure can continue to support its expenditures.

IMPLICATIONS FOR A CHANGING INFRASTRUCTURE

More than 300 years of history is written on the roads, bridges, buildings, and facilities constructed publicly and privately in Philadelphia. All of the City's physical infrastructure was created in response to, or in anticipation of, the needs of residents, workers, and visitors. A city with a growing population and expanding economy will demand different levels of public investment in infrastructure improvements than a city with a declining population and contracting economy. A city with little debt and strong revenues will be able to commit a different level of funds toward maintaining its infrastructure than a city struggling to balance its budget. The challenges and opportunities of a new century will affect Philadelphia on many levels, but will be cast for posterity on the City's physical infrastructure.

Changing Pressure on Transit Infrastructure

A city with a declining population and a rebounding job base at the center of a growing region will likely see both an increased demand for spending on transit-related infrastructure in certain areas as well as diminished demand for such infrastructure in other areas. An increase in the number of privately owned vehicles in the City and region may stress its off-street parking stock as well as its on-street parking stock, which is already overtaxed in many neighborhoods.

Increased costs to maintain streets will likely place pressure on the City budget. As the City's infrastructure continues to age, roads, bridges, water mains, sewers, and other facilities will need maintenance and, in many cases, replacement. A recent history of deferred maintenance and fiscal constraints have worsened this situation.

Increased vehicle availability and usage may indicate that mass transit options are not appealing to area residents. Such a situation confounds efforts to provide a mass transit system that serves as an asset to the City and region. Unless mass transit can be provided at low cost and high convenience, individuals with other options will not leave their cars at home. Because Philadelphia is essentially a central business district confined between two rivers, connected by small streets and mediocre highways to surrounding neighborhoods and communities, mass transit is necessary to tie the Greater Philadelphia region together. If mass transit becomes transportation for only the region's low-income residents, maintaining a mass transit system will require additional public subsidy, traffic congestion will reach unbearable levels, and regional growth will be threatened.

Changing Pressure on Housing Infrastructure

Decreasing population and the aging of its homeowning population will affect the City's public and private housing stocks. Since new and abandoned housing are both such visible indicators of the health of a city, such developments will have many implications for Philadelphia.

The demand for higher-cost housing in a region traditionally increases new housing stock and causes abandonment at the lower end of the market, increasing the vacancy level. Unfortunately, while areas with large numbers of vacant properties create opportunities for gentrification, especially when such areas are close to the central business district, clashes between current and potential residents could stunt neighborhood revitalization efforts.

As discussed above, high unemployment may lead residents to save money by neglecting routine housing-maintenance expenditures. If the lack of routine maintenance causes more severe problems, houses may become structurally unsound. Once a few homes in a neighborhood become vacant, large-scale abandonment is often only a matter of time. Redevelopment has historically proven unable to redistribute job opportunities downward on a large scale, and redevelopment success has been largely confined to central business district areas where the private market has responded to government investment. Without investment from the private sector, government may be forced to deal with abandonment and vacancy at huge costs. The City's Office of Housing and Community Development (OHCD) estimates that the total cost of rehabilitating long-term vacant units in Philadelphia averages $110,000 per unit and the total cost of rehabilitating short-term vacant units averages $45,000 per unit. If, as OHCD estimates, there are approximately 19,000 long-term vacant units and 6,000 short-term vacant units in the City, the cost to rehabilitate every unit would be a staggering $2.36 billion.

As structures in the City age, unless they are maintained properly, dangerous conditions can result and government may be forced to alter the way it monitors properties to better ensure safety. Finally, the impact of vacant land is likely to erode the City's tax base, decrease property values, and increase the cost for demolition of unsafe structures and nuisance abatement.

Changing Pressure on City Facilities

As population shifts and changes, the citizenry can be expected to demand different levels of service. Areas with an expanding population may demand more services, areas with an aging population may demand different services, and areas with a diminished population may no longer exhibit the same level of demand for services. These trends will inevitably have implications for the physical assets of the City.

Inadequate City revenues have historically forced the City to choose between needed social services and maintenance of physical infrastructure. This has dire implications in terms of safety and future costs. Too often, the physical infrastructure has been neglected, causing facilities to deteriorate and also causing the City to commit to a higher level of capital spending to fund major repairs and renovations that could have been avoided by less expensive ongoing maintenance. In a city with an aging infrastructure and a declining population, decisions affecting the mix of physical assets will become extremely important.

CONCLUSION

In the face of global economic trends, national policy shifts, and ever-changing individual preferences, City government has limited ability to reverse the scenarios identified by the City Controller's Office. Growth in the national economy, a dramatic hike in crude oil prices, a change in federal tax policy creating incentives to invest in cities, or a mass movement away from leafy suburbs to vibrant urban neighborhoods would do more to improve life in the City than any shift in local policy. Similarly, anti-urban global trends, policy shifts, or preferences will eclipse the positive results of even the most brilliant local policy decisions. City government, therefore, cannot expect to have much success rowing against the tide of global shifts or national policies. But it can effectively steer its efforts to position the City to take advantage of the opportunities created by the likely future scenarios and to avoid the worst possible consequences of future challenges.

City employment growth is projected to lag national employment growth, but if government can reduce the costs of doing business in Philadelphia, the City could increase employment significantly. Employment in the service sector may offset losses in other sectors and lead to an increased number of job opportunities in Philadelphia, but if government can increase the quality of the local workforce, non-service-related job expansion could benefit residents who would otherwise be left to fight for low-skill, low-wage positions. Population loss is likely to continue, especially among young families and wage earners, but if government can increase the amenities associated with living in Philadelphia, or decrease the disamenities associated with life in the City, Philadelphia can retain a portion of residents who would otherwise migrate away. Declining population and aging housing stock are factors that will likely increase the number of vacant properties in the City, but if government can act to reduce the supply of derelict structures, foster home ownership, and encourage immigration and economic opportunity, many neighborhoods can retain vitality. Finally, the shifting population demographics and the changing profile of employment in the City will likely affect its ability to raise revenues. But if government can act to alter its tax system and improve its governmental structure, the City could generate the funds necessary to allow it to meet the changing needs of the citizenry. The future scenarios identified by the Controller's Office cannot be reversed by the actions of City government alone. But how the City acts, reacts, or fails to act, will mitigate or exacerbate the challenges presented by the future.

FORECASTS AND PHILADELPHIA'S FUTURE

Future Philadelphia will look very different from today's Philadelphia. Each of the projections discussed above has implications that go beyond the forecasts about the number of people who may reside in the City or estimates about the actual number of jobs that may exist. These forecasts tell a story of what could happen in Philadelphia. Even though the Controller's Office placed great effort into crafting reasonable assumptions to form the foundation of the projections, it is clear that they do not represent the only possible future course for Philadelphia. As described above, young adults and young children have left the City in disproportionate numbers in past years suggesting that school quality has been a driver of outmigration. The Controller's Office projections assume that this preference to leave the City rather than enroll children in the public schools will continue. If school quality—or the perception of quality in the schools—improves, it could stop the outmigration of young adults and young children.

This, then, is the measure of projections in general. Having established a range of likely scenarios for Philadelphia's future, the following chapters present recommendations for action designed to adapt to anticipated future scenarios that can be seen as inevitable, as well as present recommendations for actions designed to reverse potentially damaging trends or encourage beneficial outcomes.

Jane Jacobs titled her urban opus *The Death and Life of Great American Cities*. It is a fitting title—for great cities are not islands unto themselves, but hubs of energy and activity that will ebb and flow based on all of the outside activities that affect cities. With residents and businesses free to enter and leave, cities are at the mercy of the laws of supply and demand. With state and federal policies constantly changing the way citizens depend on local government, cities are constantly affected by ever-changing political action. Over its history, therefore, a city will experience elements of death and life many times over. As stewards of Philadelphia, elected leaders must create policies that help the City take advantage of rising tides and avoid being left behind when that tide inevitably recedes.

The changes that have occurred in Philadelphia and other American cities did not occur suddenly and, in many cases, happened as a result of rational decisions made by many individuals, families, and businesses. Anti-urban policies such as insurance and mortgage redlining and overt prejudice have certainly played a part in the decline of cities. But the decline of American cities has also been a rational choice by former city residents and employers who responded to incentives and disincentives and decided that city life was no longer attractive. Federal, state, and local actions sharpened and complicated the mix of incentives and disincentives, but the result is clear. If Philadelphia is to thrive in the future, City leaders must change the equation of incentives and disincentives for current and potential City residents and employers.

The City of Philadelphia did not achieve its current state overnight, and its decline has not occurred without help from both deliberate and well-intentioned-but-ill-advised actions from government at all levels. The long process of realigning the mix of incentives and disincentives will not occur quickly and cannot be accomplished through local action alone. Even with changes in incentives and disincentives, Philadelphia will still be at the mercy of business cycles, shifts in the global economy, and other external factors.

Colonial Philadelphia was the largest English-speaking city outside Great Britain, but was thrown into upheaval when the British captured the City during the Revolutionary War. After being revived as the capital of the United States, Philadelphia again became a virtual ghost town due to an acute yellow fever epidemic during the nation's infancy. If Philadelphia and its neighborhoods are to rebound from this latest round of decline and abandonment and accept the challenge of the 21st century, City government must act on the local level and push for action at the state and federal levels to increase incentives for residents and businesses to locate in the City and to decrease the disamenities that cause them to leave.

Philadelphia cannot solve its problems alone, nor can any city on its own correct all of the societal problems that manifest themselves in American cities. Philadelphia can only attack the problems surrounding societal decay in the most efficient and effective manner, and work with the state and federal government to address the root causes of its distress. Long-term solutions to the problems that plague American cities—poverty, crime, and social isolation—will be addressed and attacked at the local level, but must be initiated at higher levels of government. Ultimately, the resources and the commitment to change society must come from the broadest base and must be coordinated and focused at the most local level.

Philadelphia will move forward if its government encourages positive anticipated events while minimizing anticipated deleterious trends. Otherwise, Philadelphia will falter. Having put forth a best estimate of what the future may bring, and what that is likely to mean, the next chapter begins discussions surrounding a proper governmental response.

SECOND EDITION SUPPLEMENT TO CHAPTER 1
ENVISIONING PHILADELPHIA
PROJECTIONS AND IMPLICATIONS FOR THE FUTURE

PROJECTING THE FUTURE

In 1999, *Philadelphia: A New Urban Direction* painted a picture of the city's economic and social landscape through 2015 and identified a number of challenges facing Philadelphia. Assuming a continuation of a robust national economy, we forecasted that the city would achieve some modest economic growth, endure a continued loss of population, and witness the further development of an aging, poorer citizenry. The Controller's Office concluded that only a change in policies could change the city's trajectory. Recommendations were offered to alter the structure and policies of our government in an effort to change those projected outcomes into more positive trends. The initial publication of *Philadelphia: A New Urban Direction* framed discussions of the future of the city, and led to concrete changes. Further work is required, due to unimplemented proposals and the changing context in which policy decisions are made. Since 1999, numerous events occurred that have had major implications for Philadelphia's present and future:

- The bursting of the Internet stock bubble and the tragic events of September 11, 2001 sent shockwaves through the national and local economies.
- A national recession stymied economic growth during 2001.
- Astounding worker productivity growth, increasing 13.1 percent in the three years following the recession, helped spur the recovery.
- Record-low interest and mortgage rates fueled consumer and capital spending.
- Under increasing pressures to cut costs, many high wage jobs were and are continuing to be relocated to lower cost regions overseas.
- The ongoing war on terrorism and the conflict in Iraq has been reflected in significant public and private resources being devoted to security and the war effort.

For this edition of *Philadelphia: A New Urban Direction* we revisit our initial projections and have reassessed where the city is headed in the future. While the Controller's Office could not predict many of the events of the intervening years, our mixed forecast of economic growth, declining population, and an increasingly older and poorer citizenry has generally been realized. These trends are expected to continue into the future. At the same time, new trends have emerged, arising from the changing nature of the local and regional economy, and policies at the city, state, and federal levels. While the population loss may be slowing and while those industries in which Philadelphia has a competitive advantage are expected to grow, increasing poverty and an aging population is still forecasted for the future.

The fate of Philadelphia, however, is not sealed. With proper policy and governance choices, the city could alter the harmful trends and encourage the positive ones. We forecasted declining population and employment for the city's economic and demographic outlook and unfortunately those projections have been realized. Further decline is likely without strategic actions, and the recommendations of the first edition of *Philadelphia: A New Urban Direction* remain valid and vital to the future of the city. This second edition offers additional proposals to address emerging issues and utilizes new information and analysis to better manage existing problems. Understanding where the city is today and where these developments, if left unchecked, would lead can assist government, business, and civic leaders in selecting the appropriate course of action to ensure a vital and vibrant city in the coming years. While the city continues to face many challenges, instances of progress and improvement in Philadelphia in recent years demonstrates that positive change is possible, and that the actions of the city can improve the lives of citizenry.

FORECAST OF ECONOMIC ACTIVITY

National Economy Assumed To Proceed of Steady Growth Path

In 1999, the Controller's forecast was predicated on continued national economic vitality, and that this would underpin local economic performance. Although Philadelphia's economic fortunes have tended to lag behind the national condition, reacting more slowly to upturns or downturns in the US economy, the city has typically followed the same trajectory as the national economy. The original publication expected that local economic growth would be a product of the continuing national prosperity. At that time the national economy was experiencing unprecedented growth, due to a wide variety of drivers and influences. The nation slipped into recession in 2001, but has since gotten back on a path of modest economic growth. In fact, the national average annual growth rate in population, employment, and output has been stronger during 1995-2005, compared to the annual growth forecasted over the original 20-year forecast horizon, though there have been large year-over-year differences. Yet Philadelphia has not exhibited similar growth. This suggests that, despite faster-than-expected economic growth observed nationally, the local economy has produced slower economic growth than originally projected. Philadelphia's stable, diversified economy does not react as sharply as the nation overall to either boom times or recessions. The negative impact on Philadelphia during the recession in 2001 was less severe than other areas, perhaps in part because Philadelphia had not shared in the same robust level of growth in the preceding years.

Employment Dropping; City Growth Expected To Be Concentrated In Industries That Have Competitive Advantage

In 1999, the City Controller's Office forecasted employment in Philadelphia would remain virtually the same between 1995 and 2015, with average annual job growth at 0.0002 percent. Recent trends portend a less rosy employment scenario for Philadelphia, as evidenced by an average annual decline in employment of 0.3 percent between 1995 and 2004 according to the Bureau of Labor Statistics. Overall, Philadelphia can expect slower economic growth than originally predicted in 1999. Many sectors that, at one time showed great promise for growth, have faltered over the last 10 years. Yet, it will be shown that despite slower overall economic growth, there are some sectors of the economy which have expanded over the first 10 years of the forecast horizon. Indeed, the rise of the knowledge industry and health and information services has helped keep the local tax base afloat. Moreover, these sectors are likely to serve as the engine of economic growth for the entire region through the forecast horizon and perhaps many years beyond.

In 1999, it was expected that Philadelphia's growth would occur in industries for which the city offered some form of competitive advantage. That is, growth would be centered in industries for which the balance of advantages and disadvantages to operating in the city, both quality of life and economic, was relatively better than in other locations. These sectors, such as Educational Services and the Non-Profit sectors, were identified in the original publication, displayed, along with their projected annualized growth rates through 2015, in the table below. As a means of comparison we also display the annual growth observed over the last 10 years (the first 10 years of the original forecast horizon), with 1995 serving as the base year with projections at five year increments going forward.

Table 1.11. Philadelphia City Employment (Ten Fastest Growing Industries)		
Industry	1995-2005 Average Annual Growth (Actual)	1995-2015 Average Annual Growth (Original Forecast)
Educational Services	4.10%	3.00%
Non-Profits	1.40%	2.90%
Local Interurban Transportation	1.90%	2.70%
Hotels	-1.20%	2.20%
Transportation Equipment	-12.80%	2.00%
Legal, Engineering, and Management	-3.00%	1.80%
Medical Services	1.30%	1.50%
Auto Repair/Leasing	-1.20%	1.00%
Business Services	0.60%	0.80%
Amusement and Recreational Services	-0.20%	0.40%

The data show that the accuracy of the original forecasts made by the City Controller's Office has been mixed. Largely due to the impact of the terrorist attacks of September 11, 2001 and the ongoing threats to national security, there was a marked slowdown in travel and tourism employment, which, in turn, has prompted a much slower growth path for employment in local hotels, the highly complementary amusement and recreation service industry, and other related industries.

In contrast to some of the industries that have offered disappointing growth, there are industries that have displayed a faster growth path than originally projected. For example, the educational service sector has added jobs at an even faster pace than originally expected, averaging growth at an annual rate of 4.1 percent over the last 10 years. Some sectors not identified in the first edition of *Philadelphia: A New Urban Direction*, such as the local health and information service sectors, are now growth leaders. Despite the aggregate job loss, the city's tax base has been relatively stable due to the relatively high wages paid in these sectors.

Another methodology for determining industries in which Philadelphia has a strategic advantage in is to analyze which industry sectors have a greater than expected share of the city's employment when compared to the rest of the nation. Using data from the 1997 and 2002 Economic Censuses, it is possible to see that Philadelphia has captured more than its fair share of employment in certain sectors, when compared to the national and regional economies. The Controller's Office calculated the Location Quotient (LQ) of various industries with a presence in the city.

The LQ, which is expressed as a ratio, compares the employment share of an industry at the local level to the share of that industry at the national and regional level. If the location quotient for a given industry is equal to one, then Philadelphia and the larger comparison economy have an equal share of employment in that industry. A ratio greater than one reveals a concentration of an industry in Philadelphia. For example, if three percent of the nation's employees are plumbers and three percent of Philadelphia employees are plumbers, then the location quotient is one. If four percent of Philadelphia employees are plumbers, the LQ is 1.33. The greater the magnitude of the LQ, the greater the degree of concentration in an industry. It is assumed that Philadelphia will only exhibit higher degrees of concentration in industries for which there is a competitive advantage to locating here.

The LQ for 62 industries was calculated for the city in comparison to the national economy, with the 10 greatest listed in the table below. The highest level of concentration is found in the Petroleum and coal products manufacturing, though the Performing Arts, Spectator Sports and related industries retains its large competitive advantage. As exhibited in employment growth, educational services and health-related industries displayed significant, rapid expansion from 1997 to 2002. However, some of the industries reviewed that one would assume Philadelphia possesses an advantage in did not result in an LQ greater than one. Despite Philadelphia's focus on the hospitality sector, it has not resulted in a concentration of employment in either the food service or accommodation industries. Philadelphia specialization in the following areas is greater than expected given the magnitude of the city's employment.

Table 1.12. Philadelphia Employment Concentration		
Industry Description	2002 LQ	1997 LQ
Petroleum & coal products mfg	3.94122	1.68822
Apparel mfg	2.75775	1.33413
Performing art, spectator sports & related industries	2.68561	1.74120
Beverage & tobacco product mfg	2.52656	1.14863
Hospitals	2.47380	0.02769
Social assistance	2.43455	0.17751
Educational services	2.09884	0.69145
Professional, scientific, & technical services	1.58914	1.69491
Publishing	1.55336	N/A
Broadcasting	1.54498	N/A

FORECAST OF DEMOGRAPHICS

Population May Be Stabilizing

At the time of the initial projections, the Controller's Office anticipated that Philadelphia would continue its half century of population decline, forecasting that the city would experience an annualized net loss of 0.3 percent of its residents between 1995 and 2015. The 2000 US Census reported that the total population of Philadelphia stood at 1,517,550. Census population estimates in 2005 indicate that while Philadelphia is still shrinking, the city is not declining as quickly. Philadelphia's population changed at an annualized rate of -0.3 percent between 1995 and 2005.

The Delaware Valley Regional Planning Commission (DVRPC) last revised its population forecasts in March 2005. DVRPC projects that Philadelphia's population and employment will continue to decline through the end of the decade under current circumstances. The projections also anticipate that by 2030, employment and population will return to 2000 levels.

An Older And Poorer Philadelphia Is Forecasted

The original projections painted a picture of a Philadelphia population that will become older and poorer as time passes. An aging population, coupled with the city's heavy reliance on Wage Tax revenue to fund city services, would create a difficult situation. Despite the 22-percent drop in the city's population between 1970 and 2000, the cost of providing services to residents increased, even after adjusting for inflation. A continuation or acceleration of this trend cannot be supported.

Growth in population has been concentrated among the very young and older, working-age population cohorts. In particular, over the last 10 years, population declines were observed in the 21-44 and 65+ age cohorts. Growth in population was recorded in the 0-20, 45-54, and 55-64 age categories. Still, largest growth is forecasted in the 55-64 age category, a cohort expected to draw heavily on services, while the 35-44 category, generally higher-wage earners counted on to contribute heavily to an economy, is projected to decrease the most. As the cohorts continue to migrate from one to the next it is clear that the population will generally grow older as the city struggles to attract and retain families and younger workers.

After several years of declining poverty among Philadelphians, the most recent data available from the US Census Bureau indicate that one-quarter of Philadelphians were living below the poverty level in 2004, mirroring rising poverty rates at both the state and national level. This represents an increase from 20.3 percent in 2002, but remains below the 1996 rate of 26.5 percent. Census data show that the geographic concentration of poverty has changed little since 1990. In 1990, the percentage of households that were considered to be in "severe poverty" (a poverty rate above 40 percent) were concentrated in 37 of the city's 365 census tracts. By 2000, these households were concentrated in 39 census tracts. The number of total poverty tracts, tracts with a poverty rate of at least 20 percent, remained unchanged at 149 over the 10-year period.

Addressing the poverty rate among Philadelphians remains a pressing challenge. Philadelphia still has one of the highest concentrations of poverty in the United States. Census data from 2003 reveal that Philadelphia has the tenth highest concentration of poverty in the nation, fairing worse than Washington D.C., Baltimore, and other comparable cities.

Lessons Learned From The Past 10 Years

Given that the City of Philadelphia still lags the nation in economic growth, it is clear the city has not adopted sufficient policies to ensure that our residents and businesses are not at a competitive disadvantage. To correct this deficiency, bolder policies and programs are explored in subsequent chapters that can serve to boost the competitiveness of the city.

It is equally clear that Philadelphia's focus on individual economic development incentives rather than broad-based business tax reform has produced uneven results. While some firms have flourished, others have not met the employment projections used to justify the granting of an incentive; results were never demanded for receipt of breaks or incentives. It is quite clear that government should not attempt to pick "winners and losers."

It is much more efficient for local officials to assume strategies that would have a wider spectrum of beneficiaries. For example, a more cost effective and safer mechanism for government to help grow an industry sector, such as hospitality or life sciences, is to lower the cost of doing business for those industries so that Philadelphia is competitive with other locations, or to ensure that the pool of labor in the area is adequately trained for the types of jobs needed.

Philadelphia's graying population, concentrated poverty, and continued reliance on the Wage Tax as a significant source of revenue can become an ever-worsening problem if the ratio of wage earners to those demanding high levels of city services continues to shrink. With a major portion of city revenue being derived from wages, the loss of workers, either through the loss of jobs or retirement from the workforce, will hinder the city's ability to provide critical services. These are structural, but solvable, problems. While declining employment levels are being partially offset by rising wages, Philadelphia must pursue dual strategies to decrease poverty and the resultant demand for social services while also developing a workforce capable of funding government functions.

IMPLICATIONS FOR THE FUTURE

Slower than Expected Economic Growth

There is ample evidence to suggest that it takes the city an inordinate amount of time to share in the economic growth enjoyed nationally when the business cycle is on the upswing. It has been hypothesized that this stems from the city's relatively high concentration of poverty, which has, in turn, resulted in higher costs for social services. This not only keeps budgetary pressures and taxes at levels that make the city's business environment less competitive, it is also borne out in a pool of labor that is not adequately prepared for the jobs that are currently in demand. Efforts to reduce poverty and improve the workforce can contribute to local economic expansion.

Growth of the Knowledge Industry

The greater-than-expected growth in the city's knowledge industry is a very promising signal. This sector has and will continue to anchor the city's tax base and serve as the engine of economic growth throughout the entire region. Not only does this sector serve as a hub for attracting talent and educating the labor pool, it also provides fertile ground for entrepreneurship to flourish.

Despite growth of the knowledge industry, the city continues to struggle with the "brain drain" — out-migration of recent college graduates. The region's institutions of higher education have worked effectively to educate a pool of labor with a high degree of skill and intellect. They have also effectively created fertile ground for entrepreneurship. Unfortunately, many of these alumni and the businesses they create eventually leave the city. It is important to recognize that the situation is not as bleak as some presume. A report released by the Knowledge Industry Partnership reveals that 64 percent of those graduating from the region decide to stay, compared to Boston's retention rate of 50 percent. Even more positive is that 86 percent of graduates originally from the area reside in the region upon graduation compared to Boston's 42 percent. Greater Philadelphia's weak link comes in the retention of non-native students — only 29 percent choose to stay after graduation (Boston retains 42 percent of non-natives). Philadelphia can and must do a better job at retaining these graduates by providing them with economic and lifestyle opportunities that are offered in competing locations.

City Revenues and Services

If Philadelphia continues to lose population and employment remains primed for only modest growth, due in part to an uncompetitive tax structure and business environment, the city should plan for smaller future revenue growth from Business and Wage Taxes. This may be offset by an increase in higher wage jobs. If the national economy continues growing steadily, Philadelphia's competitive sectors should likewise continue to expand. With an older population expected to increase demands on the health services sector, the net impact on the city's total tax revenue will be dependant upon the size of the individual effects. Similarly, Philadelphia's future economy could be shaped, at least in part, by the composition of its elderly population and general wealth disposition. Should the 2004 increase in poverty represent a forward-going trend, Philadelphia could struggle to achieve economic growth and would be faced with increased demand for poverty-related services.

The prospects for Philadelphia's future economic and demographic trends remain fairly similar to five years ago. As such, most of the recommendations made in the original edition of *Philadelphia: A New Urban Direction* remain useful policies for improvement. New information and subtle shifts in these trends also warrant new approaches to making Philadelphia a preferred place to live, work, and visit. As Philadelphia charts a course for the city in the 21st Century, meeting the economic and social challenges will be a difficult, but possible, endeavor.

CHAPTER 2
CREATING A GOVERNMENTAL FRAMEWORK FOR THE FUTURE

*Governments, like clocks,
go from the motion men give them.*

—William Penn
Pennsylvania's Frame of Government

GOVERNMENTAL FRAMEWORK AND PHILADELPHIA'S FUTURE

Discussions surrounding recommendations for change rightly begin with a consideration of the overall framework and structure of City government. While governmental structure may seem to be a dull topic compared with the subject of crime, the municipal culture established by that structure is crucial to effective governmental operations since it sets the tone for all governmental activities. Even the most brilliant policy initiatives will be stymied by a government that is unprepared or ill equipped to carry them out. Once that framework is set and a proper municipal culture established, government—like a clock—can be set in motion.

That motion can, however, be misdirected. In the past half-century, many City residents and employers have walked away from Philadelphia. This exodus has been encouraged by federal and state policy, motivated by racial prejudice, and forced by economic conditions. It has also been inspired by the direct action of Philadelphia's government. Federal and state policies created thousands of miles of expressways and mortgage-assistance programs, facilitating the flight of City residents, but by raising taxes instead of better managing spending, local government further encouraged that flight beyond the City limits. Racial prejudice and fears motivated many former residents to move away from increasing minority populations, but government's inability to provide quality schools or fight the spread of crime encouraged them to settle in suburbia. Economic conditions forced employers to consider taking their jobs elsewhere, but the City's failure to capitalize on its competitive advantage and give employers an economic rationale to remain in Philadelphia made their relocation decisions easy.

One can readily see how City government actions have placed Philadelphia at a disadvantage. The REMI model estimates that Philadelphia employers must offer wages that are on average 20 percent higher than the U.S. mean to compensate for differences in quality of life and tax liability. But individuals are willing to forego higher wages in exchange for a more amenable environment. Even though costs associated with living and working in Philadelphia may remain comparatively high, the City's future actions can help to counteract projected population loss. Similarly, business owners consider a number of factors beyond tax rates and other costs in making location decisions. Employers consistently report labor quality, labor cost, and accessibility to markets as major factors in relocation decisions.

While the City government cannot directly alter federal policy or global economic trends to reverse the population and job losses of recent decades, City government can build a government that works to attract and retain businesses and individuals. As the City Controller's Office projections indicate, the City has many opportunities to attract and retain businesses and residents in the future. Creating a hospitable atmosphere by improving the City's infrastructure and the convenience of various permitting processes, while decreasing disamenities such as crime and a low-quality workforce can improve the City's fundamental competitiveness. With such an environment, Philadelphia can be a magnet for residents, businesses, and visitors.

In The Netherlands, the City of Tilburg fundamentally altered its governmental framework, changed its municipal culture, created a successful management plan to run the City like a business, and established itself as the best-managed city in Europe according to the results of a 1993 competition sponsored by the German Bertelsmann Association. By re-engineering the government based on what is now known as the Tilburg Model, a system that links departmental budgets with price, products, performance, and customers, the City has focused on efficiency. Since implementing the model, Tilburg streamlined its governmental organization, reducing the number of departments from 16 to six, each headed by a single director instead of four. Department heads now produce business plans, which are subject to approval by City Council, and receive managerial freedom and responsibility to realize their plans. By investing governmental savings into tax-reduction efforts and amenities for citizens and visitors, Tilburg has become a more competitive city. While only the sixth-largest city in The Netherlands, Tilburg previously had the country's third-highest tax rate. After Tilburg's transformation, its taxes now rank 31st among cities in The Netherlands.

THE TILBURG MODEL

Three basic principles define the Tilburg Model. First, all government activities are defined as products with a fixed output, a visible outcome, and an integrated cost assignment. Second, politicians address "what" questions, while administrators address "how" questions, creating a sound division of responsibilities where politicians articulate the will of the people through policy decisions and governmental managers work to make agencies achieve results. Finally, by using a sophisticated system of planning and control, government managers can measure performance to foster improvement in governmental operations while external auditing verifies the reliability of government accomplishments. Fundamentally, the Tilburg Model assumes that a city—with its wide variety of products and services—is politically and bureaucratically easier to manage if operated under a businesslike managerial structure. The following tools make the Tilburg Model work.

1. *The general policy plan*—The basic agreement for the policies for the next four years are laid down in a general policy plan articulated by the City's elected leadership shortly after they take office.

2. *The perspectives amendment*—Every spring the perspectives amendment is prepared as a report on the progression, realization, and possible adjustments of the general policy plan. This amendment outlines the expected strategic and financial developments and includes a discussion of the strategic objectives, possibilities, and the available funding for the next budget year.

3. *The City budget*—Since 1990, the budget is an output budget that clearly links funding to products, departments, and the expected level of performance.

4. T*he departmental budget*—The departmental budget furnishes a complete survey of the products that each department will provide in the next year, of the performance objectives and the activities to be carried out, and the expected income and expenditures. Each department prepares its own budget, which should have a direct relation to the City budget.

5. *The management report (marap) at the departmental level*—In the marap, the department head reports regularly (currently three times each year) about the progression and the realization of the departmental budget. The marap always

includes a financial projection and analysis of the estimated year-end actual budget spending. The departmental marap is analyzed in a report prepared and submitted for comments and approval to various political committees in the presence of the department head and the external auditor.

6. *The management report at the City level*—The management report is prepared at the City level in a consolidated form on the basis of the departmental maraps.

7. *The departmental annual report*—Within three months after the end of the budget year, each department produces an annual report accounting for departmental performance and including a departmental balance sheet and profit and loss statement.

8. *The annual report of the City*—Based on the departmental annual reports, the City creates a consolidated annual report providing a survey of the relevant income and expenditures of the previous year. It also provides a comprehensive financial analysis, consolidated balance sheet, and profit and loss statement. All departmental and City annual reports are audited and approved by the City's external auditor.

9. *The preventive investigation of the department*—Every four years, each department is investigated by an external consultant to determine whether the department is operating efficiently. The comprehensive audit addresses social matters, management quality, strategic developments, and service-delivery efforts.

10. *Market survey*—Twice each year, an external consultant performs a market survey to gauge citizen satisfaction with government services and products.

11. *Effectiveness investigation*—Since 1994, the law requires cities to submit to an investigation of the effectiveness of municipal administration performed by the City's external auditor.

The Model has been so successful that the City of Tilburg trademarked the name "Tilburg Model" and sold its components to a multinational consulting organization. City officials in The Netherlands, across Europe, and around the world are taking lessons from the Tilburg Model to make their cities work to attract residents, employers, and visitors.

A proactive governmental response can make future Philadelphia such a model city. To improve its ability to react to changing times and population demographics, the City can alter the structure of its government. To operate such an adaptable government, the City can give management the tools needed to respond flexibly to a changing environment. To help slow and reverse the outflow of residents and businesses the City can improve its interactions with citizens and employers and improve service-delivery efforts. Finally, to enable the City to keep pace with a world that is constantly changing, it can modernize governmental policy responses and promote constant governmental improvement.

ESTABLISHING A PROPER GOVERNMENTAL STRUCTURE FOR A CHANGING WORLD

Like many of Philadelphia's storied buildings, its government has stood the test of time and is basically structurally sound. But Philadelphia exists in a changing world. Communication has rapidly progressed from letter, to facsimile, to e-mail. Travel has matured from locomotive to supersonic speed and beyond. As the world changes, government must evolve. Like those old buildings, many of Philadelphia government's internal systems require modernization to make them efficient for today's—and tomorrow's—standards. If homeowners cannot make such modifications, their homes deteriorate and they end up paying more each year to live with inefficient electrical or plumbing systems. If the City's governmental systems are neglected, residents and business owners must pay higher taxes to maintain a diminished level of service.

The 1951 Philadelphia Home Rule Charter, a document that has only been amended once in the ensuing decades, established the rules that govern day-to-day governmental operations in Philadelphia. In many ways, the document adopted to eliminate corruption and prevent governmental abuse does not help government address the problems of today or tomorrow. The government designed to thwart corruption must become more flexible to meet changing needs. The City must alter its governance to allow for more creative use of government power while protecting citizens and workers from abuse. Only a flexible government will be well equipped to take on the challenges of the coming century.

Organizations must adapt to changing times to survive and the City is no exception. To best serve Philadelphia's residents and employers, the City can create a more flexible government that will be better able to respond to new and current challenges. The City can improve coordination efforts between its agencies and various quasi-governmental agencies. Finally, to make government agencies work better together, the City can alter service-delivery efforts to create more effective government operations.

Flexible Governmental Structure

In Philadelphia, the dictates of the City Charter rather than the needs or demands of the citizenry determine the City's governmental structure. It is virtually impossible for the Mayor and City Council to change the overall organization of the executive and administrative branches of the City government under the current Charter. New departments can only be created by amending the Charter, a process that requires approval by City Council and City voters. Existing departments may only be abolished by City Council if the agency no longer has any functions to perform. Council may add new powers and duties to the various agencies established by the Charter, but the intent of the framers of the Charter was that the 1951 structure of government be preserved intact for the future. Various mayoral administrations have created new offices and officers to address needs not contemplated in 1951—an Office of Housing and Community Development to address housing issues, and an Office of Transportation to address transportation issues—but no Mayor has been able to totally reorganize the government. (See Appendix II for a discussion of governance in Philadelphia, an organizational chart, and agency descriptions.)

CHANGING PHILADELPHIA

While the Mayor of Philadelphia has vast powers to alter the administration of City government, changing the way local government works often requires more than Mayoral action:

- Changing local school policy requires action by the Philadelphia Board of Education.

- Changing tax, regulatory, and other significant policies requires approval by a majority of City Council (9 of 17 votes).

- Changing the City Charter requires the approval of a majority of Philadelphia voters. A Charter amendment can be placed on the ballot by citizen action (the proper submission of a petition signed by 20,000 registered voters) or by two-thirds vote of City Council (12 of 17 votes). Alternatively, a Charter Commission empaneled by a two-thirds vote of City Council or initiated by a citizen petition (signed by 20,000 registered voters) can place proposed changes to the Charter directly on the ballot for voter approval.

Because state and national laws and regulations restrict the City's ability to alter policy at the local level, action by Congress or, more often, by the state legislature (the Pennsylvania General Assembly), is sometimes required to change local government operations.

Without the power to realign or create new departments, Philadelphia has experienced a proliferation of Mayor's Offices, each created to address a perceived need. When agencies are created to perform new functions such as the Office of Housing and Community Development, which was created to develop comprehensive strategies and programs for creating viable urban neighborhoods, the new agencies are not necessarily prepared for long-term effectiveness. While most City employees are members of the civil service system, most of the employees of these newly-created agencies are exempt from civil service and serve at the pleasure of the Mayor. This transience threatens the new agency's ability to develop institutional memory and forces members of new agency regimes to waste time familiarizing themselves with agency procedures.

When new agencies are created to facilitate effective performance of the functions of other City departments such as the Capital Program Office, which was created to oversee project management for the City's capital projects, the new agencies may be needlessly duplicating efforts if other agencies continue to perform the same functions internally. While the creation of such an agency might improve governmental operations in one area, the creation of an agency framework, often including hiring duplicative staff such as personnel officers and administrative services directors, printing new letterhead and agency stationery, and even renting and furnishing new office space, may waste City resources. This redundancy, compounded many times over as agencies proliferate, may blunt the productivity improvements associated with the new agency's creation.

Finally, when new agencies are created to address cross-governmental issues not envisioned by the Charter such as the Office of Transportation, which was created to advocate for transportation policies in the best interests of the City and to act as a focal point for all transportation-related issues, the new agencies may not be able to adequately work within the current governmental framework to achieve their missions. Agencies charged with facilitating the efforts of many other agencies have the power to suggest change, but lack the power to cause change. The necessity to generate receptivity from other agencies hampers governmental effectiveness.

To allow its elected leaders to do more than tinker at the margins of government, the City should change the Charter to allow for the routine creation and abolition of departments and the transfer of existing functions among departments. Such action should only be permitted through mayoral action with City Council approval. With the ability to create new service departments, abolish unneeded agencies, and shift responsibilities from one agency to another, Philadelphia's elected leaders would be able to make government fit the needs of the citizenry and make government form follow government function. Because the City is obligated by state law to bargain the impact of every anticipated change that would affect wages, hours, or conditions of employment with affected unions, this power could not be used as a way to unilaterally decrease wages, increase hours, or otherwise negatively alter employment conditions.

RESTRUCTURING PHILADELPHIA GOVERNMENT

Philadelphians have advocated for changing Philadelphia governance since the adoption of the Philadelphia Home Rule Charter in 1951. Despite numerous reform efforts, the basic structure of Philadelphia government is today as the framers of the Home Rule Charter established it nearly 50 years ago. If the Charter could be amended to allow for the routine creation and abolition of departments, and the transfer of existing functions among departments, City leaders would gain the ability to shape the government to efficiently and effectively meet current and future needs.

Notable suggestions put forth in recent decades for the use of this power include the following opportunities to create, delete, or merge agencies.

Reorganize Government

- Create clusters of service-delivery departments organized around central governmental themes to consolidate and focus the efforts of various City agencies. Such an effort would consolidate back-office functions to achieve savings and improve inter-agency cooperation to facilitate the operations of like agencies. A Community Services Cluster could incorporate agencies such as the Free Library of Philadelphia, the Public Health Department, the Department of Human Services, and the Recreation Department. An Administrative Services Cluster could incorporate support services such as the Procurement Department, the Personnel Office, and the Law Department to facilitate the work of service-delivery clusters.

Short of a total governmental reorganization, specific recommendations have addressed individual needs.

Service Agencies

- Create a Department of Corrections to replace the Philadelphia Prisons System, operate correctional services, and respond to all corrections-related complaints and grievances.

- Create a Department of Housing to replace the Office of Housing and Community Development and produce and implement a coordinated City housing strategy.

- Create a Department of Arts and Culture to oversee City support for cultural institutions and City-run arts-related programs and commissions.

- Create a Department of Transportation, replacing the Office of Transportation, to incorporate transportation-related functions from the Department of Streets, Department of Public Property, and Office of Transportation.

- Create a Department of Sanitation, incorporating sanitation-related functions from the Department of Streets to focus on sanitation-related activities only.

Internal Service Agencies

- Create a City Data Center to manage and disseminate the City's collection of information products.

- Create a Communications Department to provide communications services to City agencies.

- Eliminate the Office of City Treasurer (the official custodian of City funds) and merge the Treasurer's duties with those of the Director of Finance.

Liaison Agencies

- Create a liaison office for institutions of higher education to coordinate the City's interactions with Philadelphia's colleges, universities, and technical schools.

- Create a liaison office for immigrant and language services to support immigrant services and the creation of non-English City documents and service-delivery efforts.

Restructuring Government Operations

Philadelphia's governmental structure was built in many ways for the needs of its 1950 population and must be re-engineered for the needs of the City's future population. To respond to population shifts and changing service demands, the organization, staffing levels, and staff deployment of City agencies must be better tailored to suit the changing City. To function effectively under pressure to do more, and spend less, City agencies will need to improve internal performance as well as interactions with other City agencies. To fight the deleterious effects of projected future trends, the City's agencies will need to cooperate more with agencies of other levels of government.

In Philadelphia, major government re-engineering efforts have already improved operations, investing in new technology to improve productivity and analyzing work procedures to streamline operations. By continuing to change the way government works and the way its agencies interact, the City can improve service delivery and make government services a reason to locate and remain in Philadelphia. To make government work, the City can use technology to create a flexible system of support agencies focused on facilitating service-delivery efforts and improve the relationships between service agencies.

If Philadelphia's service agencies are to function well, they must be supported adequately. Personnel must be hired in a timely manner, goods and services must be procured when needed, and facilities must be kept in good repair. The Controller's Office routinely has difficulty filling vacancies for even entry-level positions. The poor condition of many Police facilities has been the focus of recent media reports. While the Personnel Office has dramatically reduced the amount of time it takes to test potential employees, service delivery suffers if the Recreation Department is unable to run after-school programs because of hiring delays. Safety is compromised if the Fire Department is unable to quickly purchase lifesaving equipment. Employee morale sags when working conditions are substandard.

The City of Stamford, Connecticut, altered the way its government works to improve service-delivery efforts. A 1995 Charter change movement reorganized the government from 22 agencies reporting directly to the Mayor into four directorships: Operations, Administration, Legal Affairs and Public Safety, and Health and Welfare. Departments of Traffic and Parking, Planning and Zoning, Parks and Recreation, and Public Works were formerly all independent agencies. After being reorganized into subsets of the Office of Operations, Stamford officials were able to create a centralized system to handle inquires and a more efficient refuse and recycling system.

In Philadelphia, decententralization efforts from past decades have hindered inter-agency communication, increased governmental costs, and diverted employees within agencies from performing functions related to agency missions. Individual agencies used different computer systems, which hampered inter-agency interactions and prevented effective data sharing. As a whole, the City wasted time and money to resolve communications difficulties. Individual agencies invested in computer hardware and maintenance, which needlessly inflated budgets. Throughout government, agencies invested in sophisticated equipment and paid for maintenance services without achieving economies of scale through citywide consolidation. Finally, individual agencies have funded positions within their budgets—personnel officials, procurement officials, Local Area Network administrators, and other administrators—that have nothing to do with the agencies' stated business functions. By taking on these administrative costs, agencies have diverted funds away from expenditures to fulfill agency missions.

By examining information technology expenditures, one can see how costs have been dispersed throughout Philadelphia's government. In 1978, City agencies combined to spend twice as much money on information technology as the City's central information technology agency. By 1998, City agencies combined to spend more than five times as much money on information technology as the City's central information technology agency. Unless the City can achieve economies of scale and other efficiencies by controlling this exponential increase, as well as similar increases occurring in other areas of administrative spending, the City will never be able to function efficiently in the future.

In recent years, the City has made strides to confront this issue. CityNet, the City's Wide Area Network, has improved inter-agency communications. The installation of building-wide network servers has saved money by eliminating the need for costly servers to support individual agencies. Ongoing database consolidation efforts have the potential to foster back-office consolidation throughout the government.

Such efforts could eliminate the inefficiency in supporting, for example, a central personnel agency as well as personnel officers in individual agencies. A 1994 Controller's Office audit of the City's 911 system recommended consolidating the separate Police and Fire Department 911 communications room operations to improve service and reduce expenses. Similarly, the City Controller's Office 1993 Deferred Maintenance Study recommended that the City consolidate the 19 different maintenance units under the Department of Public Property to achieve economies of scale and increase productivity. The Department of Public Property recently took over the responsibility for maintenance of police facilities, but overdecentralization continues throughout City agencies. For example, the Department of Public Health has 31 maintenance staff members, the Department of Human Services has 32, the Philadelphia Prisons has 95, and the Recreation Department has more than 85. These employees currently report to individual agency heads and each unit has some level of administrative support and requires its own supplies and materials, storerooms, and workers. Based on the existing structure, maintenance staff experiencing downtime in their workload cannot be accessed by units in other agencies.

To focus all governmental agencies on their distinct missions and to improve the overall effectiveness of operations, the City should expand departmental administrative reform efforts to consolidate back-office functions in centralized agencies, focus all agency operations on each agency's individual missions, and enhance inter-agency coordination. Departmental administrative reform could also evaluate ways to reconstitute City-agency organization by functional clusters as a way to help streamline processes. The effort could also focus on reorganizing the structure of government to transform support agencies from independent agencies into a single back office formally responsible to service-delivery agencies.

Demand from citizens to address quality-of-life issues provides pressure to improve governmental service-delivery efforts. Fiscal pressures provide the imperative to reduce the cost of government. Technology has provided the means to significantly consolidate the support functions of government to allow service-delivery agencies to focus on their missions. By continuing efforts to reform agency administrations, the City can improve operations and significantly reduce the cost of government.

BEYOND BACK-OFFICE CONSOLIDATION

Beyond ensuring that support agencies are focused on allowing service agencies to work for the public, making government work means eliminating needless duplication of effort. The City's Department of Recreation (created as a separate agency by the 1951 Charter to operate and manage City recreational facilities) and the Fairmount Park Commission (established by the Commonwealth of Pennsylvania in 1867 to preserve the purity of the City's water supply, and charged in the 1951 Charter with managing and maintaining Philadelphia's park system) perform many of the same functions and have missions that overlap with regard to recreation activities and park maintenance. The Department of Recreation maintains approximately 50 "passive" parks in its system, including Fitler Square, a one-block oasis of benches, trees, sculpture, and a fountain in Center City as well as Fort Mifflin, the historic Revolutionary War citadel that held the British Navy at bay while General George Washington retreated with his troops to Valley Forge. The Fairmount Park Commission operates recreation centers and swimming pools, including the swimming pool in South Philadelphia's Franklin D. Roosevelt Park.

Inter-departmental investigation of these issues concluded that the Department of Recreation's "passive" parks have suffered from lack of maintenance while Fairmount Park staff does not operate the Park's active recreation facilities to their maximum potential. While a Department of Recreation/Fairmount Park Commission committee detailing potential transfer of resources and responsibilities notes that the transfer could generate short-term costs, economies of scale and the eliminated duplication of effort should reduce costs over the long term. Improvements in service delivery for both passive and active recreation sites should be the major benefits of efforts to address coordination of recreational activity services.

Like recreation, economic development in Philadelphia involves many City agencies. City agencies, authorities, and quasi-governmental organizations all promote economic development in Philadelphia. Transportation in Philadelphia involves another conglomeration of agencies. Job training and human service delivery are similarly divided among many agencies. Another "alphabet soup" of agencies and authorities addresses housing in Philadelphia. But after a recent overhaul of the relationships among housing-related agencies and officials more clearly segregated the roles and responsibilities of housing agencies, officials indicate that efforts are better coordinated. A host of contractual obligations and relationships among agencies has more effectively divided functions, eliminating much duplication in delivery of housing-related services. While the coordination of housing activities may still require attention, efforts to more clearly delineate roles and responsibilities among agencies focusing on the same problem is clearly desirable.

Similarly, the City operates a downtown visitor shuttle dubbed the Phlash, while the region's mass transit system runs a similar service as bus route 76—the Ben Frankline. The Phlash and the Ben Frankline both serve a similar customer base and visit a nearly identical list of Philadelphia attractions. Since the City subsidizes the regional mass transit authority as well as Phlash operations, the City could combine the two services to save money as well as eliminate one cutesy nickname from the Philadelphia transit vocabulary.

City-School District Consolidation Opportunities

Many of the support services performed by the City of Philadelphia are needlessly duplicated by the School District of Philadelphia. Closer cooperation between the City and the School District can reduce expenditures and increase the effectiveness of service-delivery efforts. The framers of the 1965 Educational Supplement to the Philadelphia Home Rule Charter contemplated City-School District cooperation and even suggested potential areas for cooperation:

Section 12-402. School District-City Cooperation

(a) The Superintendent shall, in conjunction with the several departments, commissions and boards of the City, devise methods and bases of cooperation and coordination to the maximum extent practicable between the City and the District relating to joint purchasing of supplies, equipment and contractual services, use of recreational and park equipment and facilities, control and prevention of juvenile delinquency, city planning, capital programming, capital budgeting, comprehensive development planning, health services and any other phase of the District's work. The Superintendent shall recommend for the Board's approval such agreements on these subjects with the City, as well as with other governmental or non-profit agencies, as will further the efficient and effective administration of the District.

(b) The Superintendent shall also, in conjunction with City procurement officials, regularly review all possibilities for more economic operation which could result from greater cooperation and coordination between the City and the District, and which are consistent with the needs of the school system.

In the early 1980s, the City and School District attempted to consolidate print shop activities. The effort lasted for about one year and was then abandoned amid questions about lines of authority and chain of command. If consolidation is to work, either the City or the District must take full responsibility for the consolidated operations and exercise full control over all employees—District employees could become City employees or City employees could become District employees. Disparities in pay and benefits, including pensions, would have to be addressed, but past experience with similar employee transfers suggest that such issues can be successfully overcome. For example, as part of recent port-consolidation efforts, employees were transferred from a City-related port agency to a Commonwealth-related port authority.

Increased cooperation between the City and School District is not a new idea. The City and District successfully coordinate many efforts, including use of fueling sites and truancy enforcement efforts. Unfortunately, cooperation has occurred on a scattershot basis, driven by individual officials rather than the need to improve operations. In the future, cooperation efforts must be intensified, and each operational activity of every unit scrutinized for potential opportunities to save money and improve service.

The City and School District as well as the Philadelphia Parking Authority (PPA), Philadelphia Housing Authority (PHA), and Philadelphia Gas Works (PGW) all employ large vehicle fleets to perform various governmental functions. The City maintains a fleet of almost 6,000 vehicles that are serviced at approximately 17 sites located in various parts of Philadelphia. The School District has a fleet of approximately 1,100 buses, cars, and vans serviced at five sites in the City. Additionally, PGW, PPA, and PHA have large fleets that are serviced at various locations. With the exception of some cooperation in the use and operation of fuel sites, the fleet management operations of each of these governmental entities is largely autonomous.

In servicing their fleets, each governmental unit employs managers, mechanics, stores, payroll staff, and clerical and administrative personnel. Given their similar missions and the close physical proximity of their facilities, it is clear that some overlap exists in the facilities and personnel responsible for fleet management. (See Table 2.1.)

If the School District would contract with the City's Office of Fleet Management to provide required maintenance services, the District's nine administrative positions—including stores personnel, secretarial staff, and management—could be reduced or redeployed. (See Table 2.1 for City-School District fleet budgetary statistics.) Other personnel savings could be generated through cooperative buying. For example, the job of writing specifications for vehicles that both the District and City use, such as sedans, trucks, and vans, could be consolidated. Additionally, the City and District could generate true financial savings from procuring vehicles cooperatively.

Savings could also be generated through consolidation of facilities. The Office of Fleet Management has recognized the operational and economic benefit of building consolidation and is

Table 2.1. City and School District Fleet Management Budget Statistics (not including benefit costs)		
	City	School District
Fiscal year 1999 Budgeted Obligations	$76,513,586	$1,986,200*
Fiscal year 1999 Staffing Level	566	50
Number of Vehicles	5,720	1,125*
Number of Clerical, Administrative, and Management Positions	84	9*
Administrative Cost	$2,888,037	$431,900*

Source: City Controller's Office
*Fleet Management costs/personnel associated with 39 mechanics and support staff—does not include Transportation Operations (scheduling of buses and contract oversight) or vehicle purchase costs.

in the process of reducing its service facilities from the current 17 to fewer than 10, with a large state-of-the-art centralized repair facility. As Figure 2.1 illustrates, there is a great deal of overlap in the location of the fleet management facilities owned and operated by the City, School District, PGW, PPA, and PHA. By consolidating fleet management facilities, the City and other governmental entities could reduce utility, maintenance, and security costs.

As an added benefit, consolidating fleet facilities can help eliminate NIMBY—"Not In My Back Yard"—concerns. In many cases, closing facilities causes uneasy feelings for citizens because they feel services will be negatively impacted. This is not the case with fleet facilities. Residents almost universally express concern about locating a fleet facility in their neighborhood. They fret about increased truck traffic, pollution, and blight. Through a consolidation effort, fewer facilities would be required to perform the same level of service.

Another area for potential consolidation involves building services. As discussed above, the Controller's Office has consistently advocated consolidation of City building-service functions within the Department of Public Property, as originally contemplated in the City Charter. The City must also consider possible ways to consolidate efforts with School District maintenance units. The School District employs a maintenance and engineering staff of approximately 940 employees, located at schools and regional maintenance sites. Many of the maintenance staff work in specialized trades, such as plumbing, that are required in all buildings. Because many of the City and District facilities are located in close proximity to each other, consolidation efforts could reduce staff downtime and travel time between jobs. Similarly, the City and District could derive benefits from consolidated warehouse space and information systems.

Further consolidation could involve security operations. The City currently has a police force of almost 7,000 officers. The District has a security force of over 340 personnel. From a financial perspective, consolidating police forces under the purview of the Philadelphia Police Department could save money. In this case, however, money does not tell the whole story. The mission and duties of the School District police officer are markedly different than those of the Philadelphia police officer. School police officers act as disciplinarians, law enforcers, and mentors. The duties they perform probably would not be appropriate for the "regular" City police officer. Therefore, it may not make sense to consider wholesale consolidation.

One area within security operations that may need change is the relationship of non-teaching assistants (NTAs) and security officers within the District. The District employs almost 600 NTAs whose duties are to assist teachers, work with students, and maintain order. In a 1994 School District Performance Audit, the Controller's Office recommended that, based on the job description and actual duties of the NTAs, the District could move toward replacing NTA positions with security officers. Such a move could have saved up to $1.1 million annually and reduced confusion concerning each job's responsibilities. While the NTA job description has been changed to minimize the security responsibility, it is important to remember that one of the primary jobs of both NTAs and security officers is to maintain student relations and minimize conflict. Based on this common goal, the District could move toward one security officer job classification through a phased reduction of the NTA complement. In addition, savings could be generated because fewer overall security officer positions would be required. Similarly, deployment could be optimized by matching the number of security officers to the degree of security risk.

Consolidation of public health functions could further improve service-delivery efforts. Currently, the District employs approximately 300 nurses to serve more that 470 public and non-public schools. In addition to employing nurses, the District has created a Family Resource Network responsible for management and coordination of its physical and mental health programs. The Family Resource Network comprises 51 employees, plus the above-mentioned school nurses. The City's Department of Public Health is responsible for promoting and improving the health care of all City residents. While some coordination exists between the District and the Department, primarily in infectious disease diagnosis and control and immunization programs, coordination and continuity of care for school children could potentially be improved through a consolidation of District healthcare services within the Department.

The Department of Public Health is responsible for a vast array of physical and mental health activities, provided directly or through subcontractors and affiliates. A consolidation of District personnel within the Department would allow and encourage increased coordination of immunizations, doctor and dentist visits, and mental healthcare and crisis intervention. Currently, some families receive services from many of the following different government or government-sponsored service providers:

- A social worker from the Department of Human Services if abuse or neglect is suspected or found;
- A doctor or dentist through the Department of Public Health's District Health Centers;
- A therapist or social worker from a mental health-related or mental retardation-related non-profit organization, or a therapeutic staff-support person, behavioral specialist, or counselor from a non-profit organization contracting with the Department of Public Health;
- A court-appointed social worker or public defender social worker;
- A school nurse, dentist or physician; or
- An Office of Emergency Shelter and Services case worker.

A child or family will receive more benefit from the coordinated provision of mandated or needed health and social services. Having numerous different service providers at best provides confusion and at worst creates dysfunction. This potential consolidation may not save funds, but could result in better and more coordinated service delivery to a portion of the City's population that is increasingly at risk.

One area of consolidation that could generate savings involves health benefits. The School District provides health benefits directly for all of its approximately 25,000 employees. The City provides full health benefits to approximately 7,500 of its non-represented employees as well as employees who opt out of the union-negotiated health plans. The City's labor contract dictates that the City allot funds to the unions directly for represented employees' health benefits and the unions, in turn, separately contract for health coverage for their members. The 1998 City composite rate paid per employee ranged from $299.90 to $418.24 per employee, per month, depending on the type of carrier. The School District's cost per employee ranged from $232.86 to $442.10, per employee, per month. This unaudited comparison suggests that the City and School District could combine covered employee groups to negotiate better rates or coverage. While there are no guarantees that a larger group will result in lower quoted rates, the larger size of the group may allow both the City and District to leverage better coverage or better service.

Information systems management represents an area of consolidation that has been suggested by the City in recent years. Approximately three years ago, the School District rejected a proposal to have the Mayor's Office of Information Services (MOIS) take over the District's information systems in an effort to reduce hardware, software, and networking costs. While the District has reduced the size of its information technology workforce through contracting out and reducing positions, consolidating with the City's increasingly sophisticated information systems framework could generate further savings and synergies. In addition, as in virtually every consolidation opportunity discussed above, savings could be generated through staffing reductions or redeployment within the administrative ranks.

In recent years, the City has had great success in consolidating information systems personnel and contracts within MOIS. This effort has allowed MOIS to redeploy staff to fill vacancies, thereby reducing the overall staff complement. In the future, the City and School District could investigate the potential for savings and efficiencies from information systems consolidation.

Finally, purchasing is an area where consolidation efforts have a tremendous potential to save money and improve services. The City and the School District annually procure millions of

Figure 2.1. Philadelphia Fleet Facilities

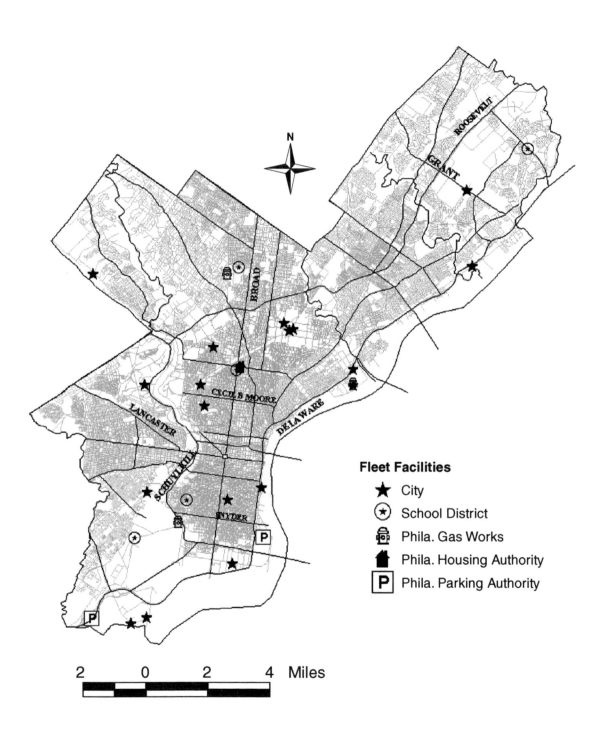

Fleet Facilities

★ City

⊛ School District

🏠 Phila. Gas Works

🏠 Phila. Housing Authority

P Phila. Parking Authority

2   0   2   4   Miles

Source: City of Philadelphia Mayor's Office of Information Services

Figure 2.2. Philadelphia Service Districts

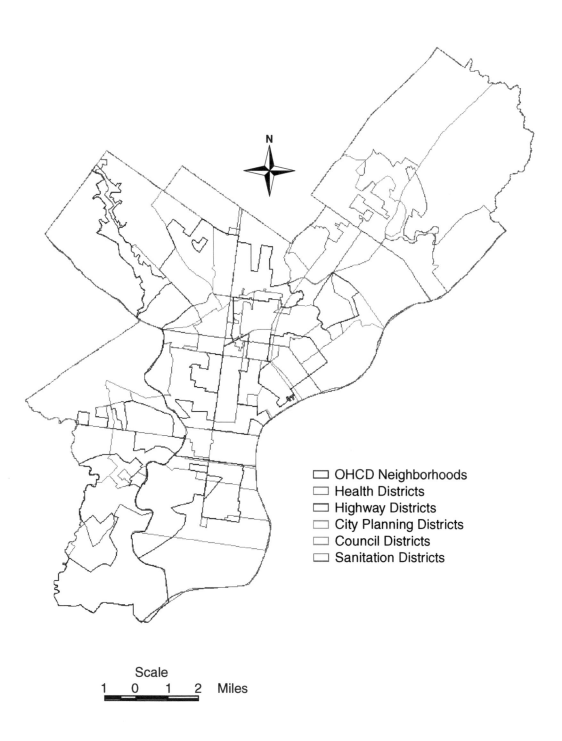

N

OHCD Neighborhoods
Health Districts
Highway Districts
City Planning Districts
Council Districts
Sanitation Districts

Scale

1   0   1   2   Miles

Source: City of Philadelphia Mayor's Office of Information Services

dollars worth of materials, supplies, equipment, and competitively bid services. Unfortunately, little cooperation exists between the City and the District in the procurement of these goods and services. The District regularly reviews the City's bids to determine if it should "piggyback" on the City's purchases. In most instances, however, because of inconsistent specifications and pricing differences, the District fails to utilize the City's bids.

While there are differences in quantities purchased, because the District and City are such large and complex institutions, there are many similarities in the types of goods and services that each entity purchases. The City and District currently purchase many like items including computers and electronic equipment; printing and copy service; vehicles; office supplies; furniture; maintenance services; food; and tools and parts. Given the need to conserve scarce taxpayer dollars, it is imperative that the City and District create joint specifications for items purchased by both parties, review each other's bids to determine if synergies can be achieved through joint purchasing, work with vendors to determine if volume discounts can be realized, and explore consolidation as a means to reduce staff and contractual costs and bid prices.

The District employs 22 persons in the Purchasing Unit and 16 in centralized warehousing and distribution. The City employs approximately 75 workers in the Procurement Department. Substantial savings could be generated from the elimination or redeployment of selected management, purchasing, and clerical workers in both entities. For example, the District employs four buyers, eight secretaries, and three supervisors. The City employs four clerks, ten buyers, and four supervisors responsible for non-public works purchasing. In addition, the Procurement Department employs another 18 clerks in its Administrative Processing unit and six employees in its Administrative Services division. Through a consolidation of purchasing operations, existing employees could be redeployed to other units or agencies as vacancies occur, thus reducing overall City expenditures. The District could channel newly-freed resources into critical instructional activities.

As large, complex, multifaceted organizations, the City and School District require many of the same support services to facilitate their distinctly different missions. Based on the current and future need to do more with less, both entities must look to coordinate services and consolidate operations in every possible area. Substantial savings could be generated by eliminating or redeploying administrative, management, and clerical employees; lowering purchasing, mainte-nance, and training costs; and reducing facility needs and storage costs. Most important, consolidation efforts could help the City and District improve the quality of service-delivery efforts. To reduce expenditures and increase the effectiveness of governmental operations, the City should explore opportunities to work with the School District and quasi-governmental organ-izations to consolidate functions such as fleet management, building services, security, public health, health benefits, information systems management, and purchasing. Other areas that could be reviewed for potential cooperation include legal services, recreation sites, and capital programming.

Coterminous Service Districts

The boundaries for service districts in Philadelphia were traditionally designed to meet specific problems and needs that differ from agency to agency, but taken together, form a nearly incomprehensible web of overlapping jurisdictions. As illustrated by Figure 2.2, displaying just a few service-delivery districts presents a confusing picture and shows how the overlap of district boundaries can add difficulty to inter-agency cooperation.

Philadelphia's service districts are based on old population configurations and overlap each other in ways that are not necessarily based on service-delivery trends. One police district may span several recreation districts. A sanitation district may roam through several fire districts. Without overall coordination at the neighborhood level, government is apt to function in nonsen-sical ways. Streets that are paved and relined may be ripped up soon afterward for water main repairs. Malfunctioning traffic signals may come to the attention of police, but not to personnel in the Department of Streets, who must ultimately make a repair. At the district level, City personnel might be focused on their agency missions, but may not be focused on overall coordination. As a result, coordination across agencies is lacking and citizens tend to view City government as unresponsive to neighborhood service needs.

Without coterminous service districts, it is difficult for the agencies of Philadelphia's bureaucracy to effectively communicate at the neighborhood level. Even with the addition of computer networks and systems that sort data on a geographic basis, because each agency of the bureaucracy divides the City differently, data-sharing efforts are limited. Data may be aggregated and prepared for various geographic areas, but because each agency divides the City differently, providing two separate agencies with the same information requires needless duplication of effort. For example, because the districts of the Police Department and the Sanitation Division of the Streets Department do not share common boundaries, any effort to provide data for each agency about the number of abandoned homes per district must be completed twice. Similarly, because the Department of Licenses and Inspections divides the City differently than the Fire Department, data about the number of dangerous structures within a specific district are not readily transferable at the neighborhood level.

New York City confronted this issue as part of its 1975 City Charter revision. As part of overall administrative decentralization, New York voters adopted measures to create community districts. City service-delivery agencies then organized local service districts to be coterminous with the new community districts. Each agency then assigned an official to be responsible for agency operations in the district. That official became part of a district service cabinet comprising the agency representatives, Council members, a representative of the Department of City Planning, and other officials. In New York City, the largest, most complicated American city, coterminality became a fact, increasing the capacity of the bureaucracy to integrate its resources across function and agency lines, and increasing the ability of government to respond to local needs.

Since 1994, the City of Philadelphia has operated a targeted neighborhood stabilization program called Partners for Progress. Through this coordinated program, a strike force comprising personnel from various service departments converges on designated neighborhoods to remove abandoned cars, clean and seal vacant properties, carry out health assessments, conduct fire-prevention outreach, and establish an intensive police presence. An oft-repeated success story recounts that, while examining a vandalized vacant property, a Department of Licenses and Inspections employee found that water was flowing into an adjacent house. Because of the program's coordination, Water Department personnel were able to shut off water service within two hours. Such a coordinated response allows agencies to improve service delivery while satisfying the citizenry with results.

Agency coordination works on a focused level in Philadelphia with Partners for Progress and should be expanded throughout the City. The City should implement coterminous districts to improve service delivery and communications between agencies and to promote the concept of employee ownership and stewardship at the neighborhood level. Such an organizational structure could increase the capacity of the City bureaucracy to integrate functions across agency lines, share data, and plan for the future. Because the service-delivery areas for some agencies are much larger than others, coterminous districts could be broken into smaller subdistricts, so, for example, each sanitation district could comprise two police districts. Districts could be based on City Council boundaries, could correspond to census tracts, or could follow more geographically significant lines. Districts could be coordinated by the Managing Director (who supervises the service departments of the government) and directed by Deputy Managing Directors who could each be responsible for a separate district. Though it would increase costs, neighborhood City Halls could be created to help root coterminous districts in the community and could include office space for each of the ten district Council members as well as agency representatives. Such offices could house mini-agencies where citizens could get licenses and permits in person or use Internet kiosks—which could be funded with the use of sponsorship and advertising agreements—to link directly to City government.

When combined with district coterminality, technological advances such as network and Geographical Information System (GIS) technology will intensify government's ability to coordinate services and respond to needs. The Philadelphia Streets Department has already utilized GIS technology to develop new time- and money-saving refuse-collection and snow-emergency routes. The Internet and inter-agency networks allow information to be shared at a universal level and make it easier for agencies to interact with each other and the outside world. The City's Wide Area Network provides agencies with e-mail, and creates the backbone necessary for future on-line communications among City agencies. Government can use these tools to make service delivery an amenity and a reason to live, work, or locate a business in the City.

For example, the use of network and communications technology allows the City to utilize non-vertical organizational structures and achieve efficiencies in service-delivery efforts through the use of more project-based teams. By using employee teams comprising personnel from different agencies to achieve a common goal, the City can improve the effectiveness of agency operations. As part of its efforts to re-engineer the Philadelphia government, the City has used inter-agency teams to analyze government operations and propose improvements. In the future, the City could expand the use of such project-based efforts to improve service. As a result, the City can capitalize on the expertise that exists in various agencies and eliminate the need to duplicate efforts by hiring specialists throughout the bureaucracy.

RECOMMENDATIONS FOR ACTION

The City should alter the Charter to allow the Mayor, with the consent of City Council, to routinely create and abolish departments and transfer existing functions among departments.

Action Steps:

- Work with City Council to amend the Charter to allow, without Charter change, the routine creation and abolition of departments and the transfer of existing functions among departments.

- Work with the City's municipal unions to reorganize the government to improve overall governmental operations.

Fiscal Impact:

- Potential one-time cost incurred as a result of governmental restructuring.

- Potential long-term savings from improved governmental flexibility.

To focus all governmental agencies on their distinct missions and to improve the overall effectiveness of operations, the City should expand departmental administrative reform efforts to consolidate back-office functions in centralized agencies, focus all agency operations on each agency's individual missions, and enhance inter-agency coordination.

Action Steps:

- Create an inter-agency departmental administrative reform task force to review City service-delivery efforts.

- Evaluate opportunities to consolidate and centralize the City's back-office functions and utilize network and other communications technology to centralize functions dispersed throughout the bureaucracy.

- Evaluate opportunities to maximize the resources that funding agencies devote to functions that contribute to accomplishing agency missions and minimize resources devoted to administrative functions.

- Evaluate opportunities to reconstitute agencies to eliminate waste and duplication of effort, and enhance quality of service-delivery efforts.

- Examine the potential to consolidate similar operations functioning in separate agencies.

- Examine the potential to utilize project-based teams to eliminate duplication of effort and improve service-delivery efforts.

Fiscal Impact:

- Potential short-term cost to conduct governmental review.

- Potential short-term cost to invest in communications technology.

- Potential long-term savings through improved operations.

- Potential to reduce personnel costs and expand service efforts by consolidating administrative functions.

- Potential to eliminate duplication of effort, reduce overhead and material use, and achieve other economies through consolidation efforts.

To reduce expenditures and increase the effectiveness of governmental operations, the City should explore opportunities to work with the School District—and other quasi-governmental organizations—to consolidate common functions.

Action Steps:

- Work with the School District and other quasi-governmental organizations to consolidate support operations to the extent permissible by law.

- Work with the City's municipal unions and represented workers in other entities to address consolidation issues.

- Examine consolidation opportunities in areas such as fleet management, building services, security, public health, health benefits, information systems management, and purchasing.

- Address pay, benefits, and pension issues, including the timing of benefit-adoption windows established for City and District employees, involved in any consolidation efforts.

- Review agency operations, contractual obligations, and purchasing-related specifications to establish opportunities for City-District cooperation and consolidation.

- Complete necessary transfer of authority and personnel to make consolidation efforts a reality.

Fiscal Impact:

- Potential short-term cost to achieve City-District consolidation.

- Potential long-term savings through improved operations and increased economies of scale.

- Potential to reduce personnel costs and expand service efforts by consolidating administrative functions.

- Potential to deaccession unneeded facilities.

- Potential to eliminate duplication of effort, reduce overhead and material use, and achieve other savings through consolidation efforts.

The City should establish coterminous service districts for agencies to promote inter-agency cooperation and improve service-delivery efforts at the neighborhood level.

Action Steps:

- Work with the City's municipal unions to address issues surrounding coterminous service districts.

- Establish a sensible network of coterminous districts for City service agencies.

- Work with City agencies to establish district cooperation protocols.

- Utilize GIS and network and other communications technology to foster the formation of coterminous service districts and coordinate service-delivery efforts.

- Examine the potential to utilize project-based teams to eliminate duplication of effort and improve service-delivery efforts.

- Consider creating mini-City Halls in each district to facilitate cooperation and service delivery.

Fiscal Impact:

- Potential short-term reorganization costs.

- Potential annual cost to establish and maintain mini-City Halls or Internet kiosks if desired.

- Potential long-term savings through improved governmental operations.

CREATING A FLEXIBLE PERSONNEL STRUCTURE

Philadelphians elect a Mayor every four years who can appoint many government officials to direct the operations of City agencies. But the actual work of these agencies is carried out by a legion of workers who may already be working for the City when the Mayor takes office and who are likely to continue working for the City after that Mayor leaves office. The vast majority of City employees are members of the civil service system, and their average tenure is approximately 11.3 years, for fire and police, the average tenure is 16.9 years and 11.9 years, respectively. The City works only if City employees make it work. Any effort to improve governmental operations for the future must inevitably involve the municipal workforce and must inevitably focus on helping City workers improve service-delivery efforts.

The City needs a workforce that can function effectively in the rapidly changing environment that will be its future. The citizenry can elect Mayors and Mayors can appoint Commissioners, or reorganize governmental agencies for years, but the City will never be able to sustain true improvement without an effective workforce, appropriate professional development, and capable workforce management.

Twenty-first-century Philadelphia should be staffed by a flexible, competent workforce, prepared to meet new challenges. The City can create a sustainable labor-management partnership to foster efforts to implement cost-saving initiatives and improve governmental operations. To create such an improved workforce, the City can focus on attracting an excellent cadre of employees to serve the citizenry. The City can manage and effectively train its workforce to create a system of constant improvement. Finally, the City can work with municipal unions to create conditions where workers are protected in a system where management has reasonable power to hire, promote, manage, and discipline employees.

69

Labor-Management Cooperation to Improve Governmental Operations

Within the City government, labor and management disagree about many issues. Management may be focused on the need to reduce the cost of government while labor may be more concerned about job security issues. But where unilateral interests intersect, management and labor can work together for mutual gains. If labor and management can work together to improve service-delivery efforts in a way that improves working conditions and saves money, then everyone, including the citizenry, wins. Similarly, both labor and management must realize that if the City cannot improve operations, costs will have to be cut through more drastic measures.

Working with the City of Fort Lauderdale, Florida, municipal unions entered into a program called the Cooperative Association of Labor and Management (CALM) to increase productivity, reduce waste, and save money. Under the program, the City and a municipal union established a labor-management committee to promote understanding between the City and its unionized employees. According to Fort Lauderdale officials, since its creation in 1993, CALM has worked to consolidate the Fort Lauderdale Public Works and Public Utilities Departments into the Department of Public Services and develop new job performance standards and measures. By underbidding private pipe-laying contractors, a CALM initiative saved the City approximately $4 million, and by reorganizing the City's beach maintenance operations, another CALM initiative resulted in a 12-percent increase in productivity. Labor and management can cooperate to save money and improve governmental services.

The City of Seattle, Washington, has used a labor-management committee to address efficiencies in equipment-sharing initiatives, schedule adjustments, and overtime review. After achieving savings by redefining overtime the City dedicated 50 percent of the savings to employee training and development. With a trust level established, Seattle's labor-management partnership is attempting to tackle broad issues such as performance pay and redefining employee classifications.

In recent years, labor-management cooperation initiatives in Philadelphia have created notable programmatic successes and have achieved significant savings. For example, under a City of Philadelphia pilot program known as the Redesigning Government Initiative, the employees and management of the City's Recreation Department have worked together to promote and improve the Department's summer meals program. Other facilitated partnerships have improved operations and created savings in the Streets Department and Water Department.

The City can build on its current labor-management cooperation successes to save taxpayer dollars, promote a work culture based on cooperation, and make the City's municipal unions part of an effort to transform Philadelphia into a city that works. Other cities have created models that have achieved success, and the City's limited experience with labor-management partnerships shows that it can work in Philadelphia. The City should establish a permanent labor-management partnership as a forum for input from labor and management to facilitate efforts to fundamentally change the way government functions. Such a sustained effort can be used to address issues from competitive contracting and agency reorganization, to workforce training and pay-for-performance. With such a partnership, the City's elected and appointed leadership could work with members of municipal unions to create the necessary consensus that will allow the City to reinvent its governmental structure, improve service-delivery efforts, and reduce the cost of government operations. With such input, the City's workforce can work proactively to improve working conditions, enhance career development initiatives, and advance job security issues.

Attracting an Excellent Workforce

As the median age of City workers increases along with the median age of the general population, large numbers of retirements will challenge the City's ability to maintain an excellent workforce. The easiest way to create an excellent workforce for the future is to recruit excellent workers. To do so, the City can expand the pool of potential employees to increase the likelihood that talented individuals will become employees, raise the qualifications for entry-level employees to help cultivate a more capable workforce, and help remove the barriers to ongoing education to provide an incentive for individuals to join the City's ranks.

By ordinance and regulation, City employees are required to be residents of the City of Philadelphia for one year prior to their appointment to a City job. Waivers may be granted for individual jobs in cases where qualified applicants cannot be found within the City, but for practical purposes Philadelphia residents comprise the talent pool for open City positions. While this provision was enacted to ensure that City residents fill City jobs, it dramatically shrinks the talent pool and clearly limits the ability to use City employment as a magnet to attract new residents. As an effort to enhance neighborhoods, requiring City employees to be neighbors in the City they serve can be a worthy policy, and the Supreme Court has affirmed that individuals may be excluded from employment by the City of Philadelphia while living elsewhere. In the interest of enlarging the City's potential talent pool, the structure of the residency requirement could be reconsidered.

Surveying residency requirements in other major cities, only Boston joins Philadelphia in requiring civil servants to reside in the City before becoming employed by the City. In other major cities, the most stringent residency requirements only demand that new hires must be City residents on their first day of employment. Employees in Philadelphia who are exempt from civil service are only required to become residents within six months of being hired. To enlarge the potential pool of candidates for City jobs, the City should alter its residency requirements to permit non-Philadelphians to apply, and be hired for, City employment. What is good for exempt administrators should be good for all employees—new hires should establish a *bona fide* residence in the City within six months of being hired.

Requiring applicants for City employment to meet higher standards can also help improve the quality of the workforce. As part of its well-publicized effort to fight crime, the New York City Police Department raised the minimum age for recruits from 20 to 22 and now requires recruits to have served in the military or earned 60 college credits. These more mature applicants received valuable training in school or in the military and have had more of an opportunity to show whether they exhibit character flaws that might exclude them from service. In Philadelphia, the City's Police Department Integrity and Accountability Office recently recommended a thorough reassessment of the Police Department's hiring criteria and standards after determining, among other findings, in recent years individuals entering the Police Academy at an age younger than 25 exhibited a higher rate of dismissals than their older counterparts. In all cases, relying on a third party to evaluate potential hires by requiring applicants to earn a college degree or alternate certification removes pressure from the City's personnel-screening system. To improve the quality of hires, the City should review all City job qualification requirements to determine which qualifications need to become more demanding for the future.

To address the difficulty in recruiting qualified paramedics, the City provides scholarships to Philadelphians for a nine-month training program. The Fire Department estimates that the City has already saved nearly $1 million since November 1994 by hiring graduates of the program. To further improve the quality of hires, the City could establish a loan program for college students who are interested in a police career to help City residents meet new standards. Loans could be forgiven in whole or in part, if a student becomes a police officer, with the extent of the forgiveness of the loan determined by length of service. The City could seek funding for such a program from private foundations or from the state or federal government.

One area where limiting the candidate pool can help the City involves the uniformed services. To provide public safety-related services in the most efficient and effective manner, the City must minimize the financial and personnel-related costs associated with injuries to police and fire personnel. The Controller's Office examined more than 2,700 injured-on-duty records dated January 1996 to October 1998 and found that injured police personnel age 35 and over recuperated for, on average, 25 days before returning to active duty. Injured police personnel under the age of 35 recuperated for, on average, 16 days before returning to active duty—nine days less than their older counterparts. Because younger police officers return to work much more quickly than older officers do, they impose fewer disability-, leave-, and overtime-related costs upon the City.

To compensate for such age-related costs, the cities of New York and Houston place an age limit on potential new police officers and firefighters. Washington D.C. places an age limit on potential new firefighters. While courts have traditionally upheld age limitations with regard to public-safety personnel so long as such limits are rationally related to furthering the public safety by assuring physical preparedness, Pennsylvania unlawful-discrimination law has not been interpreted to allow such limitations. If an age qualification is reasonably necessary to the essence of the particular business, and if age is accepted as a reasonable proxy for safety-related job qualifications, such limitations can be employed to help screen potential employees. The City should place age limits on new hires for the Police and Fire Departments to improve the quality of personnel in terms of fitness for duty and to reduce health-related costs. To enable the City to put such limits in place, the City should work to alter state unlawful-discrimination legislation. Alternatively, since age is only a proxy for fitness for duty, the City could use annual or regular fitness tests to gauge the ability of these workers to do their jobs.

Finally, after reworking the overly stringent Philadelphia residency requirement, the City could actually begin to recruit workers. Philadelphia is home to some of the nation's finest universities and colleges, and attracts students from around the globe who come to earn degrees. While many exempt positions attract recent college graduates, and while many students find internships with City agencies, active recruitment of college students is virtually unknown in Philadelphia. The City should aggressively court graduates of local universities for hire as middle-management-level employees to help attract qualified workers and use City employment as a brain magnet to help keep local college graduates in the area.

Maintaining an Excellent Workforce

Replacing talented workers costs the City money and reduces workforce productivity. Private-sector human resource officials estimate that replacement costs can run as high as one-half of salary or as much as $12,500 to replace a worker making $25,000 per year. According to a report on human resources management produced by the National Academy of Public Administration, private firms have estimated that hiring and training a new employee can cost an organization from three-quarters to one-and-one-half times the employee's annual salary. Incurred costs include recruitment, advertising, administrative efforts, hiring procedures, and training. The organizational period of adjustment in absorbing the new hire can take more than one year. Retaining and maintaining an excellent workforce is, therefore, crucial if the City is to improve productivity and overall service delivery.

Improving worker-training efforts is one way to both improve workforce quality and retain a productive workforce. Due to constant budgetary pressure, however, City training efforts have been inadequate, earning criticism from workers, managers, and agency heads. Not surprisingly, a 1997 personnel survey of 345 member municipalities conducted by the International Personnel Management Association found that, behind recruitment and selection, training and development ranked as the top human resources priority.

Under a program initiated in 1993, the Philadelphia Fire Department reimburses employees up to $500 for each course they successfully complete in any fire-science discipline offered at Community College of Philadelphia or Holy Family College. Through fiscal year 1997, 425 employees had enrolled in classes to take advantage of this offer. The City Controller's Office annually provides at least 40 hours of continuing professional education for its auditors. Human resource experts suggest that the average worker should receive about 40 hours of training each year. The City must approach this benchmark and further increase workforce productivity through ongoing training efforts. Across the country, community colleges are working to expand job-training and skill-enrichment programs in addition to their traditional associate degree programs. The City of Philadelphia and the Community College of Philadelphia collaborate on a number of degree and skill-enhancement programs. Some programs are even conducted on-site at City facilities. To increase training efforts in the future, the City could work with Community College of Philadelphia to create more programs specifically tailored to City agencies and employees. To ensure that training money is spent wisely, the City could validate such expenditures by tracking the value added by training efforts.

In the private sector, human resources officials are working to base job descriptions on required competencies and reduce the overall number of job titles into "job families" grouped by such competencies. By simplifying classifications and establishing the similar talents and skills required to perform jobs that were previously seen as distinct, corporations are able to work with potential and current employees to establish career-development plans and implement effective training programs. For example, managers in a purchasing agency require similar training as managers in a fleet management agency and, therefore, need to acquire the same competencies for future career development.

In recent years, the City has initiated an ambitious effort to analyze all of the positions in City government. When completed, the City will be able to structure positions around core competencies. By using occupational profile data compiled by the federal government, the City will be able to create legitimate and valid distinctions among job types as well as recognize similarities among various positions. Such ability will improve efforts to consolidate job classes, evaluate training curricula, create career development initiatives, and institute performance appraisal programs.

To best organize its human resources development efforts and to enable improved workforce development and compensation programs, the City should continue and expand its efforts to reorganize personnel classifications by competencies. By simplifying the number of job classes in the City of Philadelphia, and by focusing job descriptions on the skills required, the City will be able to test and promote based on competencies and create training efforts for each personnel classification to develop those competencies. If the City's personnel system could be freed from duties involved with creating and re-creating job descriptions and tests for positions, it could focus on quickly filling job openings and developing the core competencies required by all workers to perform their jobs. Similarly, if the City could work with municipal unions to establish the levels of skill and talent required to perform various jobs, the City could more effectively link pay-for-performance efforts. The City could, for example, fund union-run training efforts and then hold workers accountable for the skills they should master during their training.

To cut overtime costs and improve the flexibility of its workforce, the City Controller's Office initiated a program to cross train its account clerks to enable them to perform additional functions traditionally associated with higher-level clerks. Once trainees complete their training and demonstrate their new competencies, they receive job certifications at a higher level and earn additional pay. While some individuals may fear that cross training efforts threaten to make workers generalists, with no specific skills, organizations that are not able to cross train their employees may be forced to use layoffs to achieve savings. By cross training its employees, the Controller's Office is able to achieve savings by creating a more adaptable workforce and increasing productivity, while rewarding employees who complete training with additional pay.

By focusing on competencies and training, the City could also increase workforce productivity efforts by expanding programs that offer bonuses to workers or performance- and skill-based pay. Under such programs, employees could receive salary supplements based on competencies demonstrated, coursework and degrees completed, or on-the-job performance. For example, in San Diego, California, as part of an effort to increase the City's ability to serve non-English speakers, workers who demonstrate competency in a language other than English are eligible for a higher level of pay than other employees of the same classification. The City of Claremont, California, eliminated automatic across-the-board cost-of-living adjustments in favor of market-based range adjustments and one-time lump-sum bonuses. Bonuses are offered to line employees and managers and all employees are eligible for merit increases commensurate with their performance as rated during an annual performance appraisal process.

Promoting Management Flexibility While Preserving Worker Protection

In 1948, Philadelphia's Chief of the Amusement Tax Division, William B. Foss, committed suicide. Foss, who had embezzled from the City for years, feared scrutiny from a committee that had originally been established to look into possible new sources of revenue to fund an employee pay increase. While searching for government inefficiency, the committee uncovered scandalous practices including theft, forgery, and falsifying records. More scandals and more suicides followed Foss' death, providing the momentum for the movement that ultimately concluded with the adoption of Philadelphia's new Home Rule Charter in 1951. Therefore, it is not difficult to see how the 1951 Charter developed as a document designed to prevent corruption rather than encourage flexible use of government power. Having endured the era of the spoils system when hiring and promotions were based on patronage and bribery, the framers of the Charter established a strong and objective civil service system.

Pressures to find money to fund employee raises uncovered the corruption that ultimately helped lead to the reform that became the new rigid Charter. Similarly, pressures to make government more efficient and effective force the City to re-examine personnel issues for ways to increase the likelihood that government will work better while preserving worker protection.

Some jurisdictions seeking to improve personnel operations have reassessed the system of merit protections known as civil service and have decided that the system itself had to go. The State of Georgia effectively eliminated its civil service system in 1996. Employees hired after July 1, 1996, can be promoted, demoted, or transferred instantly. All new Georgia employees serve "at will." Alternatives to the use of a civil service system to deliver governmental service, including purchase-of-service agreements and privatization, are already widespread throughout government at all levels.

Given Philadelphia's history of management abuse and corruption, the City Controller's Office is not ready to advocate the abolition of the civil service system. With the development of strong public-sector unions and the establishment of complex collective bargaining agreements, City workers gained protection against management-by-whim that permit the City to infuse its personnel system with more flexibility without threatening to return to the days of the spoils system. Armed with this flexibility, City managers and administrators can improve service-delivery efforts. As discussed in an upcoming section focusing on providing incentives for performance, if agencies and employees are rewarded based on results, then administrators who use this additional flexibility to express prejudice or reward friends would do so at their own peril. In a roundtable discussion with members of the City's white-collar municipal union, participants expressed a strong desire to create systems in Philadelphia government that reward managerial performance based on objective criteria. By rewarding performance, the City can focus managers on using managerial flexibility to enhance productivity.

To create a more flexible personnel system, the City can conduct a thorough review of the Charter provisions and subsequently promulgated regulations that comprise the rules of civil service in Philadelphia to identify areas that can be altered to improve personnel operations. Among any other findings, such a review should address increasing the number of exempt positions in City Departments, expanding the number of candidates that can be certified for hire or promotion, and lengthening probationary periods for certain new hires.

Regardless of the size of the agency, service departments that can employ more than 7,000 workers are limited by the Charter to a total of four employees who are exempt from civil service and serve as "at will" employees: the Commissioner, two exempt deputies, and one exempt secretary or clerk. While some Mayors have appointed Deputy and Assistant Managing Directors to serve in various departments to increase the number of exempt employees managing departmental operations, the limit on additional exempt deputies is particularly troublesome in the uniformed service departments where such a maneuver is less feasible. However, such efforts create budgetary confusion because the salaries for Deputy and Assistant Managing Directors are not included in the budgets of the agencies in which they truly work. Furthermore, Mayors have added Deputy Managing Directors to managerial positions in departments such as Health and Recreation, but they cannot make a Deputy Managing Director a Police Captain or Fire Lieutenant. To allow the Mayor greater managerial authority for the operations of City departments, the City should alter the Charter to allow the Mayor and department heads to appoint additional exempt employees. Such a change could be determined on a sliding scale based on the size of the department and could establish separate rules for the uniformed service departments. After such a change, the City could stop the practice of employing Deputy and Assistant Managing Directors within individual agencies to rationalize agencies' chains of command, promote accountability, and reduce confusion in the City's budgetary and accounting systems.

The Charter-imposed "rule of two" requires that, if an appointing authority decides to fill a position, the choice is generally limited to one of the two individuals ranked highest on the list of eligible candidates. Limiting hiring and promotional opportunities to the two top candidates does not allow managers enough choice, especially since numerous excellent job candidates might only be separated by decimal places after achieving scores that are statistically equivalent. While managers might pass over qualified candidates because of prejudices or favoritism, if the citizenry demands excellent service it is clear that hiring and promotion decisions should not be so limited. Of the 20 largest U.S. cities, only Philadelphia uses a rule as restrictive as the "rule of two." The Commonwealth of Pennsylvania uses a "rule of five." A 1992 International Personnel Management Association survey of public personnel practices revealed that 90 percent of respondents use a "rule of three" or more. The City should alter the Charter to expand the "rule of two" to give managers more flexibility in hiring and promotional activities.

Finally, the Charter imposes a six-month limit on the length of probationary periods of employment to discourage officials from using lengthy probationary periods to effectively use new employees as "at will" employees. For many jobs in the civil service system, however, six months is simply not enough time to accurately judge an employee's performance. Some employees, including police officers, are still in training after six months and cannot be fairly evaluated. Once employees move past the probationary period, many managers refuse to attempt to fire anyone, since the effort becomes a drawn-out process involving a complicated set of rules and due process. The City should, therefore, alter the Charter to authorize variable-length probationary periods for different job classes so employees can be evaluated in a fair, but thorough, manner before they earn the full protection of the civil service system.

RECOMMENDATIONS FOR ACTION

The City should establish a permanent labor-management partnership as a forum for input from labor and management to facilitate efforts to fundamentally change the way government functions.

Action Steps:

- Work with the City's municipal unions to create a permanent labor-management partnership to address issues involving the municipal workforce.

- Establish protocols and decision rules for partnership operations.

- Establish the range of issue areas for which the partnership would make decisions.

- Consider the use of a facilitating organization to foster effective partnership operations.

- Negotiate the institutionalization of the labor-management partnership into collective-bargaining agreements to create permanence.

Fiscal Impact:

- Potential to create a mechanism to improve governmental operations and advance money-saving efforts involving the City workforce.

The City should alter its residency requirement to permit non-Philadelphians to apply, and be hired for, non-exempt City employment. New hires should be required to establish a *bona fide* residence in the City within six months of being hired.

Action Steps:

- Work with the City's municipal unions to address residency issues.

- Work with City Council to pass legislation to alter current residency requirements.

- Alter current civil service regulations concerning residency requirements to allow new employees to establish residency after being hired.

Fiscal Impact:

- Potential to expand City tax base by attracting new residents.

- Potential to expand the talent pool for City hires and improve the quality of the City workforce.

The City should review job qualification requirements for all City positions to determine if job requirements should be made more stringent to increase the likelihood of hiring excellent employees.

Action Steps:

- Work with the City's municipal unions to address job qualification issues.

- Review current job requirements for City positions.

- Alter current job requirements, where appropriate, to increase the likelihood that the City hires high-quality employees.

- Utilize third-party certification such as college degrees or alternate certification, where possible, as a screen for qualified applicants.

Fiscal Impact:

- Potential to increase workforce productivity and efficiency.

- Potential to reduce testing, training, and separation costs by improving the quality of new hires.

The City should place age limits on new hires for the Police and Fire Departments to improve the quality of personnel in terms of fitness for duty and to reduce health-related costs.

Action Steps:

- Work with the City's municipal unions to address age-limit issues.

- Work to alter unlawful discrimination legislation in the Pennsylvania General Assembly.

- Review job classifications for positions for which age requirements are appropriate.

- Create age requirements for selected positions.

Fiscal Impact:

- Potential to decrease disability-, leave-, and overtime-related costs.

The City should aggressively court graduates of local universities for hire as middle-management-level employees to help attract qualified workers and use City employment as a brain magnet to help keep local college graduates in the area.

Action Steps:

- Alter residency requirements and create necessary regulations to allow the City to recruit graduates directly into management-level positions.

- Establish outreach and recruitment efforts with local colleges and universities.

Fiscal Impact:

- Potential ongoing cost to operate outreach.

- Potential increase in tax base through retaining local students as City residents.

The City should continue and expand its efforts to reorganize personnel classifications by competencies to enable improved workforce development and compensation programs.

Action Steps:

- Work with the City's municipal unions to address personnel classification issues.

- Examine, reclassify, and simplify the City's many job titles and descriptions by core competencies.

- Establish necessary ongoing training efforts for each personnel classification to hone competencies and maintain an excellent workforce.

- Use personnel classification efforts to explore bonus programs for workers who complete coursework in their fields.

- Use personnel classification efforts to explore skill-based pay programs to reward excellent workers.

Fiscal Impact:

- Potential to increase annual training spending.

- Potential to increase personnel costs to maintain job classification data in a usable form.

- Potential to compress the number of City positions and decrease advertising, testing, and administrative costs.

- Potential to increase the validity of testing and decrease future liability costs.

- Potential to improve training efforts and enhance overall workforce productivity.

The City should alter the Charter to allow for the appointment of additional exempt employees.

Action Steps:

- Work with the City's municipal unions to address issues surrounding the appointment of additional exempt employees.

- Work with City Council to amend the Charter to allow for the appointment of additional exempt employees.

- Create a formula to establish the proper number of exempt employees per department, or establish additional exempt employees on a department-by-department basis.

- Stop the practice of employing Deputy and Assistant Managing Directors within individual agencies.

Fiscal Impact:

- Potential to increase personnel costs from appointment of additional exempt employees.

- Potential to improve overall agency operations.

The City should alter the Charter to expand the "rule of two" to give managers more flexibility in hiring and promotional activities.

Action Steps:

- Work with the City's municipal unions to address flexibility-in-hiring issues.

- Work with City Council to amend the Charter to expand the "rule of two."

- Alter civil service regulations accordingly.

Fiscal Impact:

- Potential to increase agency productivity by giving managers more hiring flexibility.

The City should alter the Charter to authorize variable-length probationary periods for different job classes so employees can be thoroughly evaluated before they earn the full protection of the civil service system.

Action Steps:

- Work with the City's municipal unions to address issues associated with probationary periods.

- Work with City Council to amend the Charter to authorize variable-length probationary periods for different job classes.

- Alter civil service regulations accordingly.

- Establish probationary periods for different job classes.

Fiscal Impact:

- Potential to increase agency productivity by screening employees in a more effective manner.

CREATING AN INTERACTIVE AND ACCESSIBLE GOVERNMENT

For more than two-and-a-half centuries, Philadelphia attracted a constant stream of new residents and produced jobs for hundreds of thousands of people. But in recent decades, many residents made the decision to leave Philadelphia. Since many people have the option to locate elsewhere in the region—even if the City is the reason they are in the area—the City's leadership is challenged to make Philadelphia as accessible and inviting as possible. Cities offer independence for seniors, social life for people of all ages, enlightenment for students, and immersion for immigrants. Cities offer opportunity for employers and workers and fertile marketplaces for goods, services, and human capital. Future Philadelphia must appeal to people, institutions, and enterprises naturally inclined to urban areas and it must be the City's stated mission to provide governmental services that will attract and retain residents, visitors, and employers.

Improved Government Interactivity

Citizens want some very basic improvements in government. They want to deal with one agency rather than several and use one-stop shopping to complete transactions with government. They want to interact with government at their convenience rather than at the whim of the bureaucracy—over the phone or on-line—to access government at any hour from their home or office. Finally, they want to be served by people who are focused on helping them.

Customer service must become a priority for governmental agencies that interact with the public. One-stop shopping, universal-purpose forms, and on-line interaction with government can help residents and employers avoid duplicating their efforts and wasting time dealing with multiple agencies. Streamlining interactions with government will help remove barriers to entrepreneurship and encourage business creation and expansion. To take advantage of these tools, however, agencies must make it their mission to maximize the ease with which residents and employers transact business with government. Customer-friendly government is about more than being nice. It is an important step toward showing residents and employers that they are valued.

Database and network technologies allow the City to create inter-agency information sharing on a citywide level. Individual agencies can control data entry locally, but information can be shared globally. By establishing systems that allow for inter-agency information sharing, the City can improve interaction among its agencies to improve interactions with the public.

To give entrepreneurs the ability to deal with the City with the click of a button, the City can create one-stop shopping for start-up businesses and utilize on-line technology to place all forms and procedures for applications on-line. To reduce paperwork and duplication of effort, the City can make one payment on itemized statements, one license application procedure, and one form the rule for anyone wishing to do business in the City. The City can enable all interactions with residents, businesses, and vendors that are currently accomplished over the phone or in person to be accomplished on-line. Finally, the City can make interactions with vendors and citizens "paperless," to use electronic forms, requests for proposals, and other correspondence to improve communications and save supplies and money.

The Louisville, Kentucky, Department of Inspections, Permits & Licenses acts as an umbrella agency for review of development projects, permitting, contractor licensing, and inspection processes. The Department has implemented one-stop shopping for the whole process of development review and permitting for developers, contractors, and private citizens. Where previously applicants had to visit several locations for stamps of approval from officials involved in fire prevention, surface water management, site improvements, landscaping, construction review, and building inspection, these approvals now can be accomplished through one office. Thirteen types of permits, each with specific data for the type of permit and fee calculations, are now recorded and tracked by computer. Permit status is tracked automatically and reports detailing inspection and expiration dates can be readily produced. Inspection functions, which had been performed by separate inspectors for environmental, zoning, and health and safety violations, are now checked by one code-enforcement officer, cross-trained to recognize problems in all three areas. The City of St. Paul, Minnesota, created a similar one-stop shop for licenses and permits where customers can visit a single-service counter and interact with a special project facilitator who has the experience and authority to provide answers for customers on every aspect of the project.

In recent years, Philadelphia has moved to create many customer-friendly initiatives. A Mayor's Business Action Team (MBAT) was created to assist businesses in accessing City services in various agencies. In its first four years, MBAT helped over 13,000 clients navigate a maze of agency interactions. The City launched a web site (www.phila.gov) to establish its presence on-line. A recent overhaul has increased the number of interactions with government that can now be accomplished using the Internet. However, to go into business in Philadelphia, entrepreneurs are required to seek a City Tax Number from the Department of Revenue, a Business Privilege License and Use Registration Permit from the Department of Licenses and Inspections, plus additional licenses that may be required for particular types of business running the gamut from Acetylene Cylinder Storage to Weighing & Measuring Devices. In addition, approvals could be required of new business owners from the Department of Licenses and Inspections (business compliance- and fire-related approvals), the Health Department (hygiene- and food-related approvals), the Police Department (firearm-, pool hall-, and dance hall-related approvals), the Streets Department (use of sidewalk and streets-related approvals), and the Art Commission (sign and similar fixture-related approvals). Individuals seeking to build an addition to a house could need to communicate with the Department of Licenses and Inspections, the Streets Department, the Water Department, the Art Commission, and the Historical Commission. It is currently the exception, rather than the rule, that interactions with government—zoning inquiries, initiation of utility service, tax payments—can take place on-line.

Efforts such as the creation of MBAT and the ongoing improvements to the City's web site are good models for the future, but the City's mandate must be to make all agencies work together to provide one-stop shopping; to make every agency allow individuals to accomplish on-line any interaction that can currently be accomplished with a phone call, letter, or personal visit; and to make all agencies collaborate on efforts to use databases and networking technologies to create universal forms that capture data once for use by multiple agencies. To foster improved interactions between government, citizens, and employers, the City should expand inter-agency cooperation to create one-stop shopping for residents and employers. To facilitate one-stop interactions, the City should establish universal-purpose forms and itemized bills supported by network and database systems.

In 1996, the U.S. Postal Service launched a pilot program called WINGS (Web Interactive Network of Governmental Services), a joint local, state, and federal government customer service initiative designed to present government services around life events, allowing people to complete government business on many levels in one session. According to Postal Service officials WINGS provided 24-hour, seven-day-per-week public access to government service in Charlotte, North Carolina, with one-stop shopping—a single point of access to multiple-agency service offerings. While the pilot program ended in 1997, pending an evaluation of how to use such a service in the future, the Postal Service claims that WINGS not only helped change people's perception of government service by allowing individuals to access governmental service on their own terms, but also resulted in cost savings due to reduced need to interact with citizens on a face-to-face basis.

The City of Houston, Texas, allows building contractors to apply for building permits on-line and even accepts permit-application payments through an on-line credit-card transaction. Houston's on-line permit systems also allow architects to monitor the status of drawing reviews, which helps architectural firms stick to project timetables. By reducing the number of payments and informational requests that agency personnel must process, City personnel are free to attend to other duties.

The City of Indianapolis/Marion County's web site currently allows individuals to interface directly with a permits database. This eliminates the City's need to perform data entry of permit information and allows users to search for permit information on-line. Individuals unlucky enough to receive an Indianapolis parking ticket can pay the ticket on-line. Developers and neighbors can view zoning base maps on-line. Citizens can view City-County ordinances on-line. While the site does not yet allow visitors to accomplish every single interaction with government on-line, it is clear that in the not-too-distant future it will be unthinkable to be unable to conduct business with government on-line.

The City-operated Philadelphia International Airport became the first airport in the United States to offer real-time flight information via the Internet to help travelers complete their trips. Departing businesspeople can check flight information before leaving their homes, and families preparing to pick up loved ones can make sure flights are on time before leaving for the airport.

Other Philadelphia agencies ignore this resource at their peril. Local industry officials estimate that in 1998, approximately 77,000 Philadelphia households, or approximately 192,000 individuals, are connected to the Internet. This number is increasing by 20-30 percent per year. Some surveys indicate that as many as 525,000 Philadelphians have access to the Internet in some form. The Greater Philadelphia region has approximately 1.63 million individuals on-line. Within five years, half of the City's population could live in a home that is on-line, and with recent efforts to connect schools and libraries to the Internet, every citizen will be able to access government on-line in the very near future.

To complement efforts to improve interactions with government, the City should expand efforts to enable residents, businesses, contractors, and vendors to accomplish on-line, all interactions with government that are currently accomplished over the phone or in person. The City has linked public libraries to the Internet in recent years. In the future, the City could expand such efforts to better link to the citizenry by installing computer kiosks connected to the Internet in other public buildings and public places. Taking advantage of Internet technology will make Philadelphia government more customer-friendly and make Philadelphia a place where customer service helps retain and attract residents and businesses.

Furthermore, by allowing Philadelphians to access government on their terms—with one stop and on-line where possible—the City can save money by eliminating or redeploying many of the operators and clerks who deal with citizens in person each day. The City could derive additional savings by reducing the amount of materials used to produce duplicative forms and paperwork. For example, a 1988 City Controller's Office review of unnecessary reports within the Police and Public Health Departments suggested that, by reducing redundant paperwork, the City could have saved approximately $114,000 in paper/reproduction-related costs annually and more than $4 million in personnel costs.

Creating a government that works is without value unless those who interact with government know how to make government work. Interacting with government in Philadelphia is easy, if one can reach the proper City employee who can deliver results. But without a resource to explain what number to call, dealing with City government, or any government, can be a painfully frustrating experience. It does not have to be that way. There is no reason for citizens to spend hours on the telephone being connected, reconnected, and disconnected, and no one should be forced to trudge from office to office attempting to resolve governmental transactions. If one-stop shopping and seamless interaction with Philadelphia's government is to be the norm, then residents and employers will need to know how to access one-stop shops and how to approach the systems. If no one knows which office to call or where to go, one-stop shops or on-line resources will be wasted efforts.

In recent years, the City of Philadelphia has published a number of brochures touting governmental programs. The Mayor's Business Action Team created a "Services to Business" brochure. The Department of Licenses and Inspections published a booklet called "License Requirements—A Guide to Starting a Business in Philadelphia." The Revenue Department published a "Plain Talk Tax Guide."

The City of Norfolk, Virginia, publishes "Norfolk's Business Resource Guide," a "how to" and "who to call" guide that is indexed by topics such as building permits, parking, and starting a business. The guide, which is also available via the City of Norfolk web site, provides a comprehensive directory of Norfolk's permit and regulatory processes designed to assist the business community as a point of reference.

In their minds, citizens deal with "government," not a specific governmental agency. To improve the way government works, the City should move beyond agency-specific guides and specific brochures to create a citizens' manual and business owners' manual as handbooks for all governmental interactions. The handbook, which could be part of an annual report to the citizenry, and should be available on-line and as a reference in City public libraries, would include a thumbnail sketch of the agencies of the government and their missions as well as a "who to call" reference section to better link citizens to government service. Such a resource would also be valuable for City employees in their efforts to help citizens navigate the City bureaucracy. The cost to print and distribute such a resource could be offset by a sponsorship arrangement. The private sector interacts with consumers through customer-service hotlines. The City could complement a citizens' manual and a business owners' manual by expanding efforts such as MBAT to give individuals and employers a customer-service hotline to access all agencies government through a central, customer-friendly conduit. To expand knowledge of these resources, the City could publicize the customer-service hotline number and the citizens' manual on water bills and other City communications.

To improve interactions with the citizenry at large, and make it easy to understand what government has done and is doing, the City should formally update, codify, and publish, in hard copy and on-line, all City regulations, Executive Orders, City Solicitor opinions, and Administrative Board[1] rules. These enactments have the effective force of law, but are not codified and can be difficult to find in any orderly manner. Similarly, City ordinances, both pending and enacted, and minutes of City Council meetings are published and available with the Office of the Chief Clerk of City Council, but the City should also make them available on-line. A corporate sponsor could help offset publication of such information.

Expanding Government Accessibility to All Residents

From across the globe, immigrants have flowed to Philadelphia since its settlement. Data from the REMI model show that even as Philadelphia lost tens of thousands of residents in past decades, international migration to Philadelphia has averaged more than 2,000 individuals per year. In the past, European immigrants helped populate the City. In recent years, Asian, Latin American, and Eastern European immigrants found new opportunities in Philadelphia and infused the City with new vitality.

A city's population density and diversity allows immigrants the chance to become quickly immersed in a new culture. Especially in cities with previously established ethnic enclaves, new immigrants can find the supports they require to succeed in their new land. Philadelphia should look to exploit this competitive advantage by promoting more immigration and serving new Philadelphians in a manner that encourages them to settle in the City for the long term.

The New York City Department of City Planning estimated that from 1990 to 1994, 563,000 documented immigrants settled in New York City. More people immigrated to New York City in those five years than have left Philadelphia in the past fifty years. The Department of City Planning showed that this immigration has had a substantial positive effect. Immigrants helped shore up New York's population even as the native-born population left the City. In some neighborhoods, immigrants occupy three-quarters of the housing units. Additionally, the Department of Planning noted that the youthful age distribution of immigrants, combined with high birth rates has historically led to a substantial growth of the second generation. Immigrant groups not only help stabilize population loss upon arrival, but help repopulate cities in later years.

New York City established a Mayor's Office of Immigrant Affairs and Language Services in 1989 to develop immigration and language initiatives. The Office currently works to help immigrants adapt to life in New York, offers language assistance, and publishes and distributes a "Directory of Services to Immigrants" and a "Language Bank Directory" for City agencies. In serving immigrants, the Office acts as a liaison between immigrant communities and City agencies and coordinates with non-profit organizations to provide services for immigrants. In providing language services, the Office recruits and tests City employees as volunteer translators and reviews translated City agency documents. The budget for the four-person Mayor's Office of Immigrant Affairs and Language Services was $191,742 in fiscal year 1998.[2]

---

[1] In Philadelphia, the Administrative Board comprises the Mayor, Managing Director, and Director of Finance, and is generally responsible for the determination of uniform policies to govern the administrative details of City government.

[2] Source: New York City Mayor's Office of Immigrant Affairs and Language Services.

The City of Boston, Massachusetts, established an Office of New Bostonians in July 1998 to "strengthen the ability of residents from diverse cultural and linguistic communities to play an active role in the economic, civic, social, and cultural life of the City of Boston." The new Office will conduct a public education campaign to inform immigrants about City services, coordinate a plan to advocate within City agencies to make them more user-friendly for immigrants, and analyze and report on newcomer demographics and research. In its first year, the Office seeks to complete its first public education campaign, conduct an internal survey of immigrant services, and produce five new City service brochures in five different languages. The four-person Office is budgeted to cost the City of Boston $250,000 for the 1999 fiscal year.[3]

Creating a government that works means creating a government that works for all residents of the City. The City and its residents suffer if language is a barrier that prevents the government from delivering effective service, or prevents residents from fully participating in economic and civic life. By making the City more accessible to non-English speakers, government not only becomes more user-friendly, but Philadelphia becomes a more hospitable city. By becoming a more hospitable place, the City will attract new immigrants whose energy and abilities can help it thrive. As the City's ethnic makeup changes, languages other than English will be more and more common in Philadelphia communities. To improve services to non-English speakers, help repopulate neighborhoods, and make Philadelphia an attractive immigrant destination, the City should improve accessibility for non-English-speaking residents and immigrants by formally establishing an agency charged with improving services to immigrant communities and non-English speakers. Such an agency could work within government to provide forms and outreach in a variety of languages and market Philadelphia to potential immigrants. Encouraging increased immigration and serving the City's increasingly diverse population will directly benefit some, but will indirectly benefit all the residents and employers of the City, whether new Philadelphians, children of new Philadelphians, or descendants of new Philadelphians.

RECOMMENDATIONS FOR ACTION

The City should expand inter-agency cooperation to create one-stop shopping for residents and employers to interact with government.

Action Steps:

- Create an inter-agency task force to establish how residents and employers interact with City government.
- Organize interactions by life events or economic events to form one-stop shopping opportunities.
- Establish inter-agency cooperation protocols, network and database systems, and personnel procedures to make one-stop shopping a reality.
- Use savings from reduced per-unit cost of City transactions to fund investments in necessary technology.
- Enhance customer service by shifting personnel no longer needed to process transactions into positions that foster inter-agency data sharing and cooperation.

Fiscal Impact:

- Potential short-term cost to establish new communication systems.
- Potential material and personnel savings due to reduced need to process transactions.

---

[3] Source: City of Boston Office of New Bostonians.

- Potential to reduce the per-unit cost of City transactions.

- Potential to retain and attract residents and employers to maintain and expand the City tax base over the long term.

The City should establish universal-purpose forms and itemized bills supported by network and database systems to facilitate one-stop interactions with government.

Action Steps:

- Create a cross-jurisdictional task force to establish the fields of information that would be required to create universal-purpose forms for various interactions with government.

- Establish inter-agency cooperation protocols, network and database systems, personnel procedures, and billing/accounting conventions required to enable individuals to pay multiple fees with one check.

- Evaluate the potential to use Internet and credit-card technology to facilitate bill payment.

Fiscal Impact:

- Potential short-term cost to establish new on-line transaction and security/control systems.

- Potential personnel savings due to reduced need to process transactions.

- Potential to reduce the per-unit cost of City transactions.

- Potential long-term revenue increase from improved collections of previously avoided permits or fees and long-term cost savings from reduced material use.

The City should expand efforts to enable residents, businesses, contractors, and vendors to accomplish on-line all interactions with government that are currently accomplished over the phone or in person.

Action Steps:

- Survey all City agencies to determine how individuals interact with government, factoring in one-stop shopping opportunities and universal-purpose form information.

- Complete requisite programming and utilize secure transaction systems to enable necessary interactions.

Fiscal Impact:

- Potential short-term cost to establish new communication systems.

- Potential personnel savings due to reduced need to process transactions.

- Potential to reduce the per-unit cost of City transactions.

- Potential long-term benefit from increased collections of previously avoided permits or fees and long-term cost savings from reduced material use.

- Potential long-term savings from reduced need to process governmental transactions.

The City should create a citizens' manual and a business owners' manual as handbooks for all governmental interactions.

Action Steps:

- Survey all governmental agencies to determine how individuals interact with each, factoring in one-stop shopping opportunities and universal-purpose form information.

- Create and publish comprehensive directories of governmental interactions as a reference.

- Create an on-line version of the directories.

- Create a customer-service hotline for individuals and employers to interact with government in a customer-friendly manner.

- Publicize the customer-service hotline number and the citizens' manual on water bills and other City communications.

- Solicit corporate sponsorship to defray production costs.

Fiscal Impact:

- Potential short-term cost to produce a citizens' manual that could be offset by a sponsorship agreement.

- Potential to improve governmental operations and realize savings from the creation of one-stop-shopping and on-line-interaction initiatives.

The City should update, codify, and publish regulations, Administrative Board rules, Executive Orders, and City Solicitor opinions in hard copy and on-line.

Action Steps:

- Collect and organize all City regulations, Administrative Board rules, Executive Orders, and City Solicitor opinions.

- Publish—in hard copy and on-line—and regularly update a registry of City regulations, Administrative Board rules, Executive Orders, and City Solicitor opinions.

- Solicit corporate sponsorship to defray production costs.

Fiscal Impact:

- Potential short-term cost to publish documents and establish on-line systems that could be offset by a sponsorship agreement.

The City should publish City ordinances, resolutions—both pending and enacted—and minutes from City Council meetings on-line.

Action Steps:

- Complete requisite programming and personnel training.

- Publish information on-line.

- Solicit corporate sponsor to defray production costs.

Fiscal Impact:

- Potential short-term cost that could be offset by a sponsorship agreement.

The City should establish an agency to coordinate service delivery to immigrant communities and non-English speakers, and market Philadelphia to potential immigrants.

Action Steps:

- Establish an agency that will survey City immigrant services and facilitate the creation of non-English City documents and service-delivery efforts.

- Use such an agency to facilitate service delivery to immigrant communities and non-English speakers.
- Use such an agency to market Philadelphia to potential immigrants.

Fiscal Impact:

- Potential annual cost of approximately $200,000 to operate new agency.
- Potential to encourage long-term tax-base growth through retaining residents and attracting immigrants.

PROMOTING CONSTANT GOVERNMENTAL IMPROVEMENT

Enhancing the quality of service delivery in Philadelphia is too important to be left to chance. To attract residents and retain businesses, the City must create mechanisms to encourage constant improvement. City leaders and employees want to improve conditions in Philadelphia, but absent incentives that reward performance, political pressure, and institutional inertia can too often interfere with even the most well-intentioned efforts toward improvement. Government agencies must be encouraged to perform if government is to produce results. Government employees must be rewarded for producing results if government agencies are to perform effectively. Like the City of Tilburg, Philadelphia can use a more businesslike managerial structure to utilize performance data to improve governmental operations and focus governmental agencies on creating outcomes desired by the citizenry.

In the future, to be sure that government is providing services well, citizens must know that they are receiving value for government spending and they must be confident that they are paying an appropriate price. Without mechanisms to compel government to efficiently provide excellent service, elected and appointed officials are apt to respond to political incentives, manage to avoid crisis, or react to pressures from a variety of sources. If government could be focused on service delivery through performance goals and rewards based on accomplishment, then government officials can focus on making government work. Similarly, charges of favoritism and prejudice involving efforts to increase managerial flexibility in hiring and promoting could be blunted if managers had proper incentives to make agencies work. By playing favorites or displaying prejudices instead of hiring and promoting qualified workers, managers would threaten their ability to meet performance goals.

To promote constant governmental improvement, the City can set standards for service delivery by establishing benchmarks for performance measurement. The City can link governmental performance to budgeting to improve agency accountability and make government accountable to the citizenry. Like private industry, the City can create mechanisms to encourage agencies to achieve savings and increase agency innovation. The City can reward employee performance and innovation. Finally, the City can build service delivery into long-term planning efforts to provide an institutional focus on improving service to the citizenry.

Performance Measurement

After filling 81,098 potholes in fiscal year 1996, the City of Philadelphia only repaired 36,295 potholes in fiscal year 1997. One may question what those numbers really show, since the City endured a blizzard in fiscal year 1996 and a mild winter in fiscal year 1997. In fiscal year 1997, the City reported that all reported potholes were repaired within four working days during peak pothole season. That is little consolation to anyone who had the misfortune to run into a pothole before that fourth day. The point of performance measurement is not just to track inputs and outputs. To be effective, performance measurement must measure outcomes and track quality that can be used to create more accountability.

As any coach will explain, if you do not keep score, you are only practicing, and if you do not establish a goal, you are just playing. Any City official who has heard complaints about service delivery can confirm that the residents of Philadelphia certainly keep score and expect results, not just good play. If service delivery is to be a reason to locate and stay in Philadelphia, City government must then produce results.

Too often, government creates a perverse incentive for its agencies and employees. If agencies are unable to succeed in their mission with their current budget, the City often rewards them by increasing their budget, but if agencies are able to succeed in their mission and achieve savings, the City often cuts the budget and asks them to be successful with less. If government is to produce value for the citizenry through its service-delivery efforts, the City must create proper performance measurements and proper incentives for government agencies to perform.

If residents want streets to be clean or if residents want to reduce the number of fires in the City, then residents, through the budgetary decisions of their elected officials, can reward agencies and their employees based on the cleanliness of streets and the number of fires that occur in the City. If the City articulates what is expected from governmental agencies and City employees, productivity can count. The City can then base agency budgets and employee compensation on how government serves the citizenry. Agencies could then receive the flexibility to address their missions as long as they produce desired results.

The State of Oregon is a leader in benchmarking efforts, having established a 20-year strategic plan that articulates clear goals for the state. Oregon's benchmarks do not measure progress by inputs or outputs such as dollars spent and clients served. Instead, the benchmarks focus on specific outcomes in specific areas such as reducing violent crime, raising adult literacy, or increasing the miles of waterways that meet federal water quality standards. This effort, which has involved the public as well as private entities in formulating benchmarks, provides purpose and mission for the state and its agencies. By committing to the goals articulated by the benchmarking progress, Oregon has set standards for measuring statewide progress and institutional performance.

With reasonable benchmarks and mechanisms for data collection and presentation in place, the City can create incentives for agency performance and consequences for non-performance. The City of Portland, Oregon, produces an annual "Service Efforts and Accomplishments Report" that contains information on the spending, workload, and results of the City's six major service agencies as well as information from comparable cities and results from a citizen survey. With this report, independently prepared and verified by the Portland City Auditor, Portland budget analysts and the City Council use service-delivery and performance measures to establish performance goals and to add explanatory information to budget requests and subsequent appropriations.

As part of efforts to improve quality of life in Philadelphia, the City now produces a "Mayor's Report on City Services" that presents performance measures, and the results of a citizen survey, for major City agencies. This report, first published for fiscal year 1996, is a step in the right direction. This effort has improved each year it has been published and can become an instrument that accurately gauges the performance of the government—the inputs, outputs, outcomes, efficiency, and customer satisfaction measures.

In 1993, Congress passed the Government Performance and Results Act mandating all federal departments to begin measuring performance and results. The Governmental Accounting Standards Board, the organization that creates governmental accounting rules for state and local governments, will likely require all states and localities to begin reporting on service efforts and accomplishments in coming years. In an era when local government is forced to do more with less and increase the efficiency and effectiveness of service-delivery efforts, performance measurement provides managerial tools to make government work. At a time when local governments are pressured to show results, performance measurement is an excellent way to hold government accountable for spending tax and intergovernmental revenues.

To institutionalize improvement in service-delivery efforts, measure agency performance, and create useful information tools that could help agency managers improve service-delivery efforts, the City should establish an effective performance measurement program to monitor service-delivery efforts and focus agencies on results. As part of such an effort, agencies could be compelled to refocus agency missions based on desired outcomes and efficiency targets that are in line with legislative intent as well as benchmarks—the results expected from government service—established by citizens, businesses, and other stakeholders. Citizen and employer surveys can help sharpen government's understanding of the perception of government service and help solve problems before they become reasons for residents and businesses to relocate.

Because of its independence, the City Controller's Office could be established as the agency that audits such performance measurement data in Philadelphia to ensure that such data are properly verified and presented. In 1998, for example, the Controller's Office began work on an effort to audit and independently confirm City crime statistics. After the Federal Bureau of Investigation threw out Philadelphia crime statistics for 1996 and 1997, and a 1998 *Philadelphia Inquirer* investigative series disclosed that the Philadelphia Police routinely recode crime reports to reduce their severity and artificially hold down crime statistics, it is clear that an independent verification of performance data is needed.

To improve City managers' ability to use data to improve performance, the City could invest in software packages designed to present performance data in a practical and user-friendly manner. Finally, the City could join the International City/County Management Association's Comparative Performance Measurement Consortium—an effort to provide participating jurisdictions with accurate, fair, and comparable performance information to help guide performance improvements in the areas of police, fire, neighborhood services, and internal support services—to give performance measurement efforts outside perspective and validity.

Linking Performance to Budgeting

Performance measurement can be used as more than a management tool. For performance measurement to truly be effective, the City must link governmental plans to budgets and results to create a cycle of constant improvement. In 1993, Milwaukee, Wisconsin, adopted a form of performance-based budgeting. Milwaukee's budget allocates money to departments based on policy objectives. Departmental managers are now responsible for producing results, not spending money. Planning and budgeting are now components of a single system of issue identification, objective setting, strategy development, and resource allocation. As part of this effort, Milwaukee first created a citywide strategic plan to identify and analyze key problems and develop plans to produce change. Departmental plans were then developed to focus individual agency missions on City objectives. The City then developed outcome indicators with no more than five objectives and related indicators per department to measure whether long-term objectives are being met. Departmental budget requests were simplified and focused on results. Sixty-two percent of previously required budget forms were eliminated or made optional. Forms that focused on justifying specific line items were eliminated in favor of new forms created to show links between funding, objectives, and activities. Finally, budget allocations were re-engineered by providing each department with an allocation at the beginning of budget preparation which focused agency heads on deciding how to use money to meet goals, instead of after departments had submitted their budget requests which focused agency heads on manipulating the budget process. Milwaukee budget documents now list agencies' major objectives, outcome indicators, and spending at the highest level; funding by activity at a lower level; and line items at the lowest level, retained to meet legal and accounting requirements. Milwaukee's budgeting structure now focuses agencies on achieving results within budgetary limitations.

The City of Indianapolis, Indiana, completed an ambitious effort to generate Activity-Based Costing of City Services as part of its efforts to create competition for government service delivery contracts between municipal workers and the private sector. Armed with activity-based data, Indianapolis created what is dubbed a "Popular Budget." In the Popular Budget, agency goals are established along with the accomplishments expected at the department and division level, performance measures for each division, and the cost of each performance activity. The Popular Budget facilitates debate by spelling out the outcomes and activities that each department hopes to achieve.

Under the Performance-Based Budgeting system in the State of Texas, performance targets are included in the General Appropriations Act. Agencies must then periodically report outcome, output, efficiency, and explanatory measures, which are verified or called into question by the State Auditor's office. To complete the cycle of accountability, the Governor and the State Legislature are authorized to make mid-year budgetary appropriations to punish or reward agencies based on agency performance levels.

In 1994, the City of Philadelphia City Controller's Office completed a "Pilot Project for Performance Measurement and Performance-Based Budgeting" as part of an effort to provide more accountability and better resource management for the City. After endorsing the concept of performance-based budgeting, the Controller's Office recommended a three-step process to implement performance-based budgeting in Philadelphia. First, the City would need to allocate indirect and overhead costs to the various agency service areas. Second, the City would need to develop a methodology to crosswalk the line-item budget to department service areas to link line items to service-delivery efforts. Finally, the City would need to determine performance indicators to help measure progress.

The blueprint to link performance with budgeting in Philadelphia exists. The City should use benchmarking and outcome management to make performance-based budgeting work for Philadelphia. The citizenry is not concerned with how hard government is trying to address a problem or how much money government is allocating to address a problem. People care about results. By moving beyond input and output measures to incorporate goals, outcomes, efficiency, and customer satisfaction into the budget process, the City of Philadelphia can build a government focused on performance, rather than on spending.

Performance-Based Incentives

Demanding high performance necessitates a system of rewards for that performance. Any effort to focus agencies and individual employees on outcomes must create a system of incentives to encourage managers and workers to achieve their goals. At the highest level, agencies that consistently achieve their goals or show progress toward reaching their goals should have more latitude with regard to departmental spending. Alternatively, agencies that show little progress toward reaching their goals should have significant oversight and limited discretionary spending and should be required to seek approval for all but the most basic agency decisions.

If the only consequence of agency savings or efficient operations is a reduced budget, managers will have little reason to achieve savings. The City's Fairmount Park Commission expended considerable effort to create a new concession agreement that could possibly generate millions of dollars of new revenue. While the parks should benefit from better service, the Charter dictates that the revenue that results from this initiative will go straight to the City Treasury with no guarantee that the Park Commission will ever be rewarded from its efforts.

Because of its unique status as an entity that predates the City Charter, the Free Library of Philadelphia is not required to deposit overdue fine money into the City Treasury. Instead, the Library is able to use those revenues to support Library operations. Other agencies could benefit from similar arrangements whereby non-tax revenues could be deposited in the City Treasury, but reserved for the agency that generated the revenue. The Department of Licenses and Inspections could use revenue from fees and permits to expand inspection efforts or the Records Department could use revenue from document search fees to purchase technology designed to improve access to City documents.

In Los Angeles County, as part of a countywide marketing program, agencies are encouraged to create marketing opportunities because net revenues from agency marketing programs are credited back to the agency. Institutional effort toward marketing enterprises is rewarded by allowing agencies to keep newly-generated revenues. The School District of Philadelphia rewards schools that reduce energy costs by allowing the schools to keep a percentage of savings. School leadership is encouraged to reduce overall energy costs, saving money for the District, and earning new revenue for school-based initiatives.

In 1995, Congress authorized the National Parks to increase user fees or implement new ones and keep 80 percent of what was collected instead of forwarding the money to the U.S. Treasury. In the first year, the program raised $53 million over and above the roughly $80 million that existing fees generated—a 66-percent increase. The increased revenues were directed to restorations and improvements at individual parks. Instead of driving away visitors with increased fees, the improvements made possible by higher fees increased attendance by 3.5 percent at the 100 parks that raised their fees.[4]

The City should create mechanisms to allow agencies that improve efficiency to use a portion of savings to expand their services in other areas. If an agency saves money it should not be penalized by having its budget cut by an amount that corresponds to the amount of savings. Similarly, the City could allow agencies to establish enterprise funds and keep a portion of the proceeds to encourage entrepreneurial activities in agencies looking to expand services. (See Chapter 3 for further discussion on this concept.)

Employees who are focused on improving service delivery can help create government services that serve as an amenity for citizens. Without such incentive, improving service delivery could be an afterthought. As part of its oft-publicized competitive contracting efforts, the City of Indianapolis has an Incentive Pay Program that it uses to financially reward employees for achieving cost savings and for exceeding performance goals. Employees or employee groups that meet preset performance goals are eligible for incentive pay. Performance guidelines are established with the help of the City's Performance Measures Analyst to ensure that measures are designed to achieve desired results and are not unreasonably low. Year-to-date scores allow employees to track consistent measures of their progress. At the end of the year, a previously agreed upon formula is applied to the performance measure to determine whether incentive pay is merited and the amount of bonuses due to workers.

Indianapolis City employees won a competitive contract to provide Fleet Services by agreeing to forego a scheduled 2-percent union pay raise in the third year of their agreement in favor of a plan that gave employees the incentive to generate additional savings beyond those in the proposal itself. According to City documents, in the first year of the contract, Fleet Services employees were able to exceed the savings provided for in the agreement. While the City already saved millions because the competitively won contract was far below the former cost to provide Fleet Services, the additional savings earned Indianapolis more than $568,000, and employees more than $142,000. Fleet Services' yearly incentive pay has averaged $870 per employee per year, encouraging the president of the union representing Fleet Services workers to declare, "Even though we gave up a raise for right now, we're definitely going to come out ahead in the long run."[5]

The International Personnel Management Association cites numerous examples of employee gainsharing. In Charlotte, department heads set savings goals along with the City Manager. If those goals are met, employees receive 50 percent of the savings, divided equally among employees. Sunnyvale, California, managers are eligible for bonuses based on agency productivity. New York City Probation Department employees are already sharing in $1.1 million in annual re-engineering savings.

In a 1998 survey of 646 public-sector organizations, the International Personnel Management Association found that 54 percent of respondents reported that compensation was based largely or entirely on performance. The City should develop an incentive pay system for

---

[4] Lynch, Michael W. "Public-Private Partners that Work," *Investor's Business Daily*, June 11, 1998.

[5] As quoted in "Case Study #11: Fleet Services." Prepared by the City of Indianapolis.

Philadelphia workers that takes into account both performance and customer satisfaction to foster improved service delivery and reward good work. By carefully crafting expectations and goals, the City can implement a form of gainsharing so that the City, and its municipal workforce, can both benefit.

Creating performance-based incentives in Philadelphia can also enhance the accountability that is often lacking in the City bureaucracy. For example, the Controller's Office consistently reports on the disappearance of millions of dollars of City personal property, computers, office furniture, office equipment, etc., in the various agencies of the government. Lack of timely inventory counts, poor record keeping systems, lack of sufficient accounting personnel, lax oversight, all result in the chronic failure to safeguard City assets. Because managers are rarely sanctioned when property is lost, vigilance over the personal property inventory is not a priority. If proper incentive mechanisms and/or sanctions could enhance accountability for agency operations, managers would focus on agency outcomes, agency operations, and even agency property.

Performance measurement only matters when accompanied by accountability. Many activities in government can be measured, but if employees and decision-makers are not held accountable for their success or failure, performance measurement is of little value. Government must also be accountable for the assets it purchases with taxpayer dollars. The agencies of the Philadelphia government operate under dozens of property rules and regulations, but the cumbersome systems for managing property and equipment, coupled with reduced staff to manage property make these rules difficult to enforce. To enhance governmental accountability for personal property, the City should implement systems to make it easy to track, manage, and cost personal property assets as well as materials and supplies inventories. Such systems could improve data accessibility, enhance record keeping and reconciliation, require the immediate submission of loss reports, and include sanctions against individuals and departments failing to safeguard City assets.

With a reduced number of central service agency employees available to monitor these assets, agencies must receive tools necessary to maintain an effective system of control. For example, the new Personnel Department Human Resource System that should be implemented in coming years contains a module that can track property by individual employee. This system, which contains the equivalent of a file folder showing all property and equipment assigned to each employee could be used extensively by agencies to manage City property. In addition, the City could consider consolidating inventory field points across the City and increasing operating hours to minimize the potential for theft.

Institutionalizing the Long View

The City must consistently look to the future if it is to ensure continuous governmental improvement. As part of the legislation that created the fiscal oversight agency enabling Philadelphia to emerge from crisis in the early 1990s, the City is required to produce a Five-Year Financial Plan each year. This long-view perspective has been invaluable in evaluating City budgetary issues. By expanding the traditional one-year focus, the Five-Year Plan forces City officials to consider the consequences of decisions beyond the next fiscal year. It would be wise to institutionalize such a planning tool.

The City should build the long-term planning of the Five-Year Plan into the Charter to mandate multi-year budgetary planning. Elected and appointed officials too often view the future as only as long as their term of office or the length of the current mayoral administration. Long-term planning will extend those horizons and provide the citizenry, the business community, and bond rating agencies with documentation of City intents and the satisfaction that government is planning for the future.

RECOMMENDATIONS FOR ACTION

To institutionalize improvement in City services, measure agency performance, and create useful information tools that could help agency managers improve service, the City should establish an effective performance-measurement program to monitor service-delivery efforts and focus agencies on results.

Action Steps:

- Refocus City agency missions based on desired outcomes and efficiency targets.

- Develop appropriate benchmarks and performance measures for City agencies that can be used to evaluate agency performance over time.

- Conduct citizen and employer surveys in an ongoing manner to sharpen customer satisfaction measures.

- Establish data collection procedures and train personnel to perform duties associated with data collection and assimilation.

- Establish the City Controller's Office, as an independent arbiter to audit performance measurement data in Philadelphia to ensure that such data are properly verified and presented.

- Consider purchasing software packages to improve City manager's ability to use performance data to improve operations.

- Consider joining the International City/County Management Association's (ICMA) Comparative Performance Measurement Consortium to give performance measurement efforts outside perspective and validity.

Fiscal Impact:

- Potential short-term cost to develop appropriate agency performance measures.

- Potential annual ongoing cost to conduct surveys, establish membership in the ICMA Consortium, and publish a report on government performance for the citizenry.

- Potential cost (as much as $175,000 per 100 users) to purchase performance data analysis software.

- Potential to increase agency efficiency and effectiveness and generate cost savings through attention to performance.

The City should link performance with budgeting to focus agencies on efficient and effective service delivery.

Action Steps:

- Work with agencies to establish and allocate indirect and overhead costs to the various service areas.

- Use Internet and client-server technology to improve agencies' ability to capture financial and performance information at the functional or activity level.

- Develop a methodology to crosswalk the line-item budget to department service areas to link line items to service-delivery efforts.

- Incorporate determined performance indicators in budget documents to help measure progress.

- Structure the budgetary process to allocate money to agencies based on accomplishment of policy objectives.

- Consider working with City Council to pass legislation or amend the Charter to mandate performance-based budgeting.

Fiscal Impact:

- Potential short-term cost to establish performance budgeting framework.

- Potential to increase agency efficiency and effectiveness through the focus on performance.

The City should create mechanisms to reward agency and individual performance, and encourage entrepreneurial activities.

Action Steps:

- Establish necessary accounting protocols and policies to allow agencies to retain a portion of newly-generated revenues or budgetary savings.

- Establish policies to allow agencies to establish enterprise funds and keep a portion of the proceeds of enterprise revenues.

- Work with the City's municipal unions to address issues associated with pay-for-performance programs.

- Develop an incentive-pay system for workers to reward performance.

Fiscal Impact:

- Potential to increase revenue and decrease operating expenditures at the agency level.

- Potential to improve agency service-delivery efforts.

To enhance governmental accountability for personal property, the City should implement systems to make it easy to track, manage, and cost personal property assets as well as materials and supplies inventories.

Action Steps:

- Through Executive Order or ordinance, stress the importance of safeguarding City personal property assets to agency managers and in training efforts for new employees.

- Provide agencies with technology to track supplies and property.

- Create citywide teams to perform timely inventory counts and consult with agencies concerning proper personal property management.

- Require the timely submission of loss reports and limit agency managers' ability to label items as "Cannot Locate."

- Compile citywide loss reports annually identifying those agencies failing to safeguard City assets.

- Consider consolidating the City's inventory field points.

Fiscal Impact:

- Potential short-term cost for new personal property inventory tracking and management systems.

- Potential to reduce the need for future inventory and equipment purchases and achieve future savings.

The City should build the long-term planning of the current, legally-mandated Five-Year Financial Plan into the Charter to mandate multi-year budgetary planning.

Action Steps:

- Work with City Council to amend the Charter to mandate multi-year budgetary planning.

Fiscal Impact:

- Potential to achieve long-term savings by focusing City officials on long-term planning.

KEEPING AN HISTORICAL CITY MODERN

Philadelphia is a city of postmodern skyscrapers and Colonial houses with a history spanning more than 300 years. While much of Philadelphia's charm is derived from its rich and varied history, its 21st-century government should be modern and should adhere to the best modern government thinking to fit the times. Having learned the disastrous consequences of cramped and haphazard development from the great London fire, William Penn designed Philadelphia with its now-famous grid of perpendicular streets. Modern Philadelphia should similarly learn from its past to design a better future.

To keep its historical city modern, Philadelphia's government can evaluate and modernize the legal and regulatory systems to reflect today's realities, to make the City more accessible and attractive to potential residents and employers, and to protect the City from liability. The City can also employ "sunset" requirements to ensure that new programs and agencies must prove their worth if they are to be continued.

Modernizing Legal and Regulatory Systems

In Philadelphia, it is illegal to spit on the sidewalk. In fact, the anti-spitting law is the very first entry dealing with prohibited practices in public places in the Philadelphia City Code. While spitting may be repulsive to some, even the most ardent tough-on-crime activists would be hard-pressed to justify the cost of making police officers enforce such a law. The law, therefore, remains on the books, while violators and law-enforcement officials on the streets ignore it. Law enforcement is a difficult business. Government should not overburden law-enforcement officials with the responsibility to decide which laws should be enforced.

Because of zoning laws, Philadelphians are not permitted to operate many types of businesses from their homes. No neighbor wishes to live next door to a smelt-at-home business, but with Internet and telecommunications technology allowing individuals to conduct enterprise from their dens, City zoning laws for residential areas could permit additional types of businesses to coexist in a neighborhood setting.

In many neighborhoods, residents must purchase parking permits to park cars on City streets or face the threat of a ticket. In other neighborhoods, however, enforcement officers look the other way while cars double-park at fire hydrants and stop signs. Even though many neighborhoods suffer from a lack of parking, the City exposes itself to tremendous liability when it willfully neglects enforcement of its parking laws. The City risks lawsuits from anyone injured in a motor-vehicle accident where illegally-parked cars are a contributing factor, from anyone unable to seek medical attention because a double-parked car blocks his or her way, or from anyone whose house is damaged in a fire when Fire Department vehicles cannot navigate streets due to illegally-parked cars.

Addressing the accumulated laws, regulations, and practices that govern civic behavior is a way to keep Philadelphia modern. Indianapolis, for example, empaneled a Regulatory Study

Commission in 1992 to improve the regulatory climate by eliminating burdensome and unnecessary local laws and improving the regulatory code to encourage economic activity. According to City officials early successes included taxi deregulation, which removed artificial barriers to market entry, doubling the number of new taxi companies and lowering fares by nearly 7 percent, and elimination of nuisance permits for homeowners, which had been required for such minor home improvements as replacing a door or window. The regulatory changes are now working in Indianapolis to save taxpayers money, free the bureaucracy from needless paperwork, and create a more customer-friendly atmosphere.

While individual City ordinances and regulations were adopted with the best interests of the citizenry in mind, taken as a whole they create a frustrating web of rules for citizens, employers, and developers. A recent City Controller's Office survey of Philadelphia business owners confirmed that the City's regulatory structure creates a significant burden for employers. Non-Center City business owners complained about regulations and the regulatory structure more than their Center City counterparts. This distinction suggests that smaller businesses, without personnel specifically dedicated to interacting with the City's regulatory bureaucracy, are more directly affected by the City's regulatory structure.

Philadelphia recently initiated an effort to examine ways to streamline and modernize the City's Pension Code. To improve quality of life and limit its liability concerns, the City should examine and modernize all locally-enacted ordinances and regulations to create a system of laws that can be enforced and a code of regulations that do not needlessly deter economic activity. The City's system of laws, regulations, licenses, permits, and code requirements should be as customer- and business-friendly as possible to both protect public welfare and encourage development.

Using Sunset Measures to Control Program and Agency Proliferation

Government, like a gas, seems to expand to fill the container into which it is placed. New demands beget new agencies that spawn new programs. When threatened, agencies hold favored programs hostage, threatening that any proposed budget cuts would hurt popular efforts. Endless governmental proliferation comes at a cost that government cannot afford to pay now or in the future. Citizens and City officials must be able to reign in government and its proclivity to generate new programs. Such ability could focus City agencies on tomorrow's challenges rather than yesterday's problems.

For decades, the State of Texas has used a process called Sunset Review to periodically assess agencies to determine if the policies carried out by each agency are still needed. With the advent of strategic and performance-based budgeting in Texas, the Texas Sunset Review Commission now uses performance data during its 12-year cyclical review of state agencies. If an agency is not performing its mission, it can be threatened with the ultimate sanction—full elimination. The City of Philadelphia should follow this example and place sunset provisions on its agencies and service-delivery efforts to control their proliferation and use performance as the criteria for agencies to continue operation. If a program does not accomplish its goals, it should be reevaluated and given another chance or discontinued so that its funds and personnel could go elsewhere to make a difference.

RECOMMENDATIONS FOR ACTION

The City should examine and modernize all locally-enacted ordinances and regulations to create a system of laws that can be enforced and a code of regulations that do not needlessly deter economic activity.

Action Steps:

- Establish a task force to review City ordinances and regulations.

- Work with business organizations, community groups, and advocacy organizations to design a system of ordinances and regulations that protect the citizenry while encouraging growth.

- Work with City Council to adopt any ordinances necessary to eliminate nuisance laws or regulations or create reasonable new laws or regulations.

Fiscal Impact:

- Potential one-time cost to conduct legal review.

- Potential savings from increased efficiency and potential indemnity savings from decreased liability.

- Potential to increase tax revenues from any resulting business expansion.

The City should place sunset provisions on its agencies and service-delivery efforts to control their proliferation.

Action Steps:

- Create reasonable sunset provisions on agencies and service-delivery efforts.

- Create mechanism to review programs and service-delivery efforts based on sunset criteria.

Fiscal Impact:

- Potential future savings from elimination of agency and program proliferation.

CONCLUSION

Employers and residents are free to leave Philadelphia. Projections for the future show that the City must do its part to reduce the cost of doing business and improve quality of life to attract and retain employers and residents. To create a municipal culture focused on retaining employers and residents, the City must establish a flexible governmental framework, one that will be able to adapt to new challenges and focus City agencies on performance and improvement.

To create a proper governmental framework for the future, the City must allow for periodic reorganization of the government. Elected officials must be able to routinely create and abolish departments and transfer existing functions among departments. To improve governmental efficiency and effectiveness, the City must explore efforts to restructure and consolidate government operations. Similarly, the City should explore opportunities to work with the School District and other quasi-governmental organizations to consolidate common functions. By establishing coterminous service districts for its agencies, the City could further promote inter-agency cooperation and improve service-delivery efforts at the neighborhood level. All of these initiatives must be complemented by increased overall flexibility throughout the City's personnel system. Such flexibility must be pursued in a way that utilizes labor-management cooperation to improve governmental operations, maintain and attract a superior workforce, and provide reasonable protection for the rights of City employees.

To focus governmental agencies on performance and improved service-delivery efforts, service to the citizenry must become a priority. The City must employ Internet technology and interpersonal outreach to create an accessible government that seeks to improve the ability of employers and citizens to interact with City government. The City must firmly embed performance measurement within the governmental culture and link agency performance with budgetary and compensation processes. Finally, to ensure that historical Philadelphia is able to operate as a 21st-century metropolis, the City must modernize its catalog of laws and regulations and utilize sunset measures to control program and agency proliferation.

Having focused on setting government in clockwork-like motion, the discussion of a governmental response to future challenges turns to a consideration of the fiscal policies necessary to fuel that motion.

SECOND EDITION SUPPLEMENT TO CHAPTER 2
CREATING A GOVERNMENTAL FRAMEWORK
FOR THE FUTURE

To best meet the needs of its citizens, a government must operate efficiently, be accountable for its actions, and be accessible to all those it serves. Philadelphia's government structure was organized in a different time, to meet the needs of a different population. The 1951 Charter which established the rules that govern the city's day-to-day operations could not anticipate many of the challenges and opportunities presented in the 21st Century. For example, it was impossible to foresee the role of local government in preventing terrorist attacks, or in the provision of internet access. In order to provide the highest level of service to today's residents and businesses, the city needs to be equipped with appropriate tools and management structures that allow the government to respond to the population's changing needs. In recent years, steps have been taken to streamline service-delivery efforts and pursue a more customer-oriented focus to enhance the accountability, efficiency, and accessibility of city government, but as the demands on our government evolve, so must the framework of governance.

ESTABLISHING A PROPER GOVERNMENTAL STRUCTURE FOR A CHANGING WORLD

In the first edition of *Philadelphia: A New Urban Direction*, the Controller's Office made recommendations to alter the city's governmental structure to improve its ability to meet modern challenges. In 1999, the Controller's Office proposed that the city should expand administrative reforms that promote inter-departmental cooperation and consolidation of back office functions. The suggested reforms were intended to eliminate duplication of efforts and thereby provide services to the public more efficiently and economically. To further broaden the opportunities for cost reduction, the City Controller's Office recommended that the administration explore enhanced cooperation with the Philadelphia School District and quasi-governmental agencies, such as the Philadelphia Housing Authority.

Since we called for these efforts, plans have been laid for consolidation in Streets Department Districts and survey district management, a reduction in the number of Recreation Department program districts from 10 to seven, and pooling of clerical support across units in the Department of Licenses and Inspections. The fiscal year 2006 Five-Year Financial Plan for the city also outlines plans to continue consolidation and clustering efforts with regard to administrative functions (such as budgeting and payroll), Department of Public Health labs, centralized warehousing and inventory systems, and facilities maintenance. To promote improved interdepartmental interaction among the agencies providing social services to children and families, $1.5 million has been earmarked in the fiscal year 2006 to 2010 Capital Program for the Managing Director's Office for the development of an integrated database to promote information sharing. Less progress has been made in coordinating functions and purchasing with the Philadelphia School District and quasi-government agencies, but the city has increasingly made use of state purchasing contracts that provide lower costs for goods and services through bulk buying.

While several departments are consolidating or reorganizing their service districts, Philadelphia still does not have coterminous service districts for the various city functions, as was proposed in the first edition of *Philadelphia: A New Urban Direction*. Coterminous service districts promote information exchange among city departments to guide decision making and help simplify citizens' interaction with the city. The confusing nature of Philadelphia's overlapping service districts necessitated the publication of an atlas of maps by the Philadelphia City Planning Commission (PCPC) entitled "The Political and Community Service Boundaries of Philadelphia." This publication, intended to be helpful to citizens, weighs in at a stunning 120 pages and illustrates the complexity of navigating the city's various boundaries and districts. While this document can help those both inside and outside government navigate the many service areas, Philadelphia has clearly not yet established a sensible network of coterminous service-delivery areas.

In order to allow that the form of government is dictated by the needs of the citizenry, the Controller's Office recommended that the Charter be altered to enable the routine creation and abolition of city departments by mayoral action with City Council approval. To date, such a change has not been accomplished and the proliferation of departments and offices of a transient nature continues.

The routine creation and abolition departments and the transfer of responsibilities among agencies have proved to be particularly difficult in the area of housing and community development. As altering the Charter to allow for more flexibility in government structure can only address some of the problems associated with the proliferation of housing-related agencies, the city should adopt a mechanism to coordinate the missions and activities of housing and development departments with similar or complementary objectives by appointing interlocking directorates to promote a more unified policy vision.

In Philadelphia, responsibility for the housing needs of the city is dispersed across varied departments and agencies. The Philadelphia City Planning Commission is charged with the preparation of comprehensive city plans, zoning ordinances and amendments, regulations regarding land sub-divisions, the examination of proposed development, and in the development of housing policy. The Department of Licenses and Inspections is responsible for correcting dangerous and unlawful conditions, including cleaning and sealing abandoned buildings, providing for emergency repairs, and demolishing vacant structures. The Redevelopment Authority (RDA) facilitates the development of under-utilized property, using eminent domain to take possession of vacant, tax-delinquent, and blighted structures. The RDA is also Philadelphia's lead agency for the financing of the city's affordable housing programs. The Philadelphia Housing Development Corporation (PHDC) develops new and rehabilitates existing housing for low- and moderate-income families. The agency also operates programs in joint ventures with community development corporations (CDCs). Philadelphia's Office of Housing and Community Development (OHCD) runs programs that benefit low- and moderate-income residents, including homeownership opportunities, housing repair programs, and special needs housing. OHCD funds programs implemented by the RDA, PHDC, and the Department of Commerce. The Philadelphia Housing Authority (PHA) acquires, develops, leases, and operates affordable housing options. The Philadelphia Industrial Development Corporation (PIDC) promotes economic development, including marketing and strategic sale of excess city property. While the aforementioned agencies and authorities perform slightly different functions, insufficient coordination, collaboration, and collective planning creates inefficiencies and unnecessary redundancies. In 2001, the Neighborhood Transformation Initiative (NTI) was launched to eliminate blight and improve neighborhoods. Included in the NTI plan was a proposal for much-needed reorganization and consolidation of a portion of the city's housing and community development agencies, in order to better coordinate policies and implementation, as well as reduce costly redundancies.

The complete or partial consolidation of the older agencies and authorities has not been possible, in some cases because funding and legal powers of these entities are distinct and must remain so. The RDA must remain a separate entity to retain its power of eminent domain. The PHA cannot be integrated with the RDA, though its mission was similar, because agency funding comes directly from the Federal Government. Other consolidations, however, are legally permissible but have proven difficult. To feasibly address concerns of coordination and consolidation, even absent Charter amendments to enable the routine creation and abolition of departments, the city should utilize mayoral appointment powers for the boards of the RDA, PHA, PIDC, and PHDC and coordination with mayorally-appointed leadership of the Philadelphia City Planning Commission, OHCD, and NTI to create interlocking directorates. While this would not fully address duplication of effort, a more uniform approach to policy making and program implementation could be achieved. The city could designate a single agency for housing and community development organization, and the interlocking leadership of the various agencies would then encourage consistent implementation.

RECOMMENDATION FOR ACTION

The city should form interlocking directorates of housing and development entities.

Action Step:

- Utilize mayoral appointment powers for the boards of the RDA, PHA, PIDC, and PHDC and coordination with mayorally-appointed leadership of the Philadelphia City Planning Commission, OHCD, and NTI.

- Designate a single agency for housing and community development policy formulation.

Fiscal Impacts:

- Potential to eliminate duplication of effort and reduce redundant staff, space, and equipment costs.

- Potential to maximize investments in development and revitalization efforts.

Establishing a Flexible Personnel Structure

In 1999, we recommended that a permanent labor-management partnership be created to facilitate efforts to improve government. Since the publication of *Philadelphia: A New Urban Direction*, the city has negotiated new contract agreements with each of the city's four major unions, but only limited progress has been made towards establishing a more flexible personnel structure. In all of these labor contracts there were no provisions for altering residency requirements or requirements for new hires. There have been no amendments to the Charter to give more flexibility to managers in hiring, promotion, or probationary periods.

Certain personnel practices proposed in the first edition of *Philadelphia: A New Urban Direction* have been adopted. We recommended that the city place age limits on new hires for the Police and Fire Department. In 2002, a change was secured to prevent the appointment of new police officers over the age of 40. The city has also continued to reorganize personnel classifications, as we recommended, and has also initiated "competency-based testing" as part of the hiring process.

To improve the quality of the workforce and promote equity among civil service and appointed employees, the Controller's Office had previously recommended that the city should alter its residency requirement to allow all new hires to establish a bona fide residence in the city within six months of hiring. Given that the probationary period for new hires is still one year, we now recommend that the amount of time a new hire has to establish a residence in Philadelphia should be equal to the current probationary period, one year.

RECOMMENDATION FOR ACTION

The city should alter its residency requirement to permit non-Philadelphians to apply, and be hired for, non-exempt city employment. All new employees should be required to establish a bona fide residence in the city within one year of hiring.

Action Steps:

- Work with the city's municipal unions to address residency issues.
- Work with City Council to pass legislation to alter current residency requirements.
- Alter current civil service regulations concerning residency requirements to allow all new employees to establish residency within one year of hiring.

Fiscal Impacts:

- Potential to expand city tax base by attracting new residents
- Potential to expand the talent pool for city hires and improve the quality of the city workforce.

Creating an Interactive and Accessible Government

In 1999, the Controller's Office offered a variety of recommendations to improve citizens and businesses interaction with government, and many of the proposals suggested enhanced use of information technologies for information publication and gathering. Unless citizens are able to understand or access government programs and services, even a well-planned initiative will fail to generate the desired outcome. While government must strive to become more accountable and more efficient, these efforts will not positively impact residents and businesses if communication with the municipal government is inconvenient or impossible. The city has made many strides in the past several years to serve its constituents better, but more can be done.

In recent years, local, state, and the federal government have increased the number of services offered online, incorporating new technologies into operations to lessen costs and improve access to services. The advent of "E-Government," where effectively implemented, has gradually promoted efficiency, led to better service delivery, improved services for business, and increased government transparency.

In 1999, the Controller's Office recommended that the city should expand opportunities for online interactions, such as bill payment, license and permit applications and information about city programs and services. Beginning in early 2004, the City of Philadelphia expanded the capability of its website and online applications, allowing businesses and residents to conduct some transactions through www.phila.gov. The Department of Revenue now allows individuals and businesses to apply for a tax account number and pay the Business Privilege License fee, file and pay school income tax returns, and file and pay Wage Tax annual reconciliation returns. Individuals can also find the market and assessed value and ownership for any Philadelphia property, or pay parking ticket fines through the website. However, at present, the only service residents can request online is abandoned or neglected vehicle removal.

While Philadelphia has improved its efforts and the slate of available online options, the city and its residents would benefit from expanding its offerings. Philadelphians are still not able to review proposed and enacted ordinances and resolutions, minutes from City Council meetings, and other city publications on the city's website, nor have comprehensive manuals for residents and businesses been made available on the internet or in hard copy, as we recommended in 1999. Targeted handbooks have been created, such as the Office of Housing and Neighborhood Preservations guide for developers. We continue to recommend that the city should further expand and upgrade the information and transactions available on its website.

Other cities have realized large cost savings and/or improved service delivery by allowing for 24-hour-a-day, seven-days-a-week, "one-stop-shopping" on their websites. For example, in Fairfax, Virginia developers and homeowners can check the status of a building permit or schedule an inspection online instantaneously. Philadelphia's website should be actively updated and streamlined, re-worked to improve navigability and function. Philadelphia should not, however, improve online customer service at the expense of other methods of interaction, such as via phone, in-person at mini-City Halls or central city offices. Many Philadelphians prefer non-web-based options, or lack internet access. The city's customer-service efforts should be designed to communicate with citizen in the manner they find convenient, at a reasonable cost to taxpayers. E-government initiatives have the potential to improve in-person and telephone services through a decreased overall workload. Online transactions impose a minimal cost on the city, while presenting large benefits to the public, allowing interaction with the city at a time of their choosing while reducing the number of parties involved.

The city should also embrace the potential of information technologies to not only spread information to citizens, but also to gather information from residents about issues facing the city and their satisfaction with service delivery efforts. Philadelphians are clearly eager to communicate their thoughts and ideas to city government through electronic means. A poll about a proposed smoking ban on the city's website in August 2005 was so popular that it had to be removed for fear of overwhelming the city's servers. Philadelphia's website should not only serve as a resource for citizens, but can be utilized by city management to gain insight into the wants and needs of city residents.

Another opportunity to harness the power of online interaction is in the disposition of surplus city property. Other municipalities, such as the City of Milwaukee, have used their websites for online auctions for items the city no longer has a use for, such as cars and office furniture. The online auction reaches a larger population that in person auctions, and creates the potential for more competition, higher bids, and increased revenue. Winning bidders of online auctions collect their items from the city's warehouse.

In the first edition of *Philadelphia: A New Urban Direction* we recommended that the city could make itself more accessible to foreign-born residents and potential residents by creating an agency to facilitate service delivery and communication with immigrants and non-English speakers. In order to improve access for these populations to city services, Philadelphia launched the "Global Philadelphia" initiative in the fall of 2003. Required by Presidential Executive Order 13166 to take "reasonable steps to provide meaningful access" to services, Global Philadelphia has sought to build the necessary infrastructure to develop and expand the city's language accessibility capacity for those with limited English proficiency. The initiative provides for the translation of city documents related to receiving or complaining about services, or those that facilitate the understanding or actualization of rights, as well as providing general interpretative services. Currently, Philadelphia offers translation of 170 languages through telephonic interpretation, and allows the scheduling for in-person interpretation for over 80 languages.

The Global Philadelphia initiative has improved access to the city's services, notably for the Police Department, the health centers, and emergency shelters. The initiative has been especially important for the Department of Licenses and Inspections, which estimates that a third of all in-person applicants for permits and licenses have limited English proficiency. By improving language accessibility for these individuals, Licenses and Inspections has improved output, both in revenues and in permits and licenses issued.

Philadelphia was once known as a haven for immigrants, offering both religious freedom and economic opportunity. Yet today, the immigrant population of the city represents a low share of the total population, compared with other major US cities. While other cities have grown in the past decade, Philadelphia has lost population because it has failed to attract new residents, foreign or domestic. Philadelphia must re-establish itself as friendly to immigrants.

Many of the nation's older industrial cities have benefited from attracting immigrants, and as the city strives to attract new residents we cannot afford to ignore this potential pool of new Philadelphians. Philadelphia already possesses a diverse population from diverse backgrounds, with approximately 10 percent of Philadelphians having been born outside the United States, according to the 2000 US Census. Immigrants and their descendants represent a net benefit to cities, generally paying $80,000 more in taxes than they receive in local state and federal benefits over a lifetime. Moreover, 70 percent of new immigrants are over 18 and are in their prime working years, imposing no additional burden to fund their education and costs of upbringing, according to the Welcoming Center for New Pennsylvanians. Yet, government and business services have been generally less accessible to immigrants than to the indigenous population; language and cultural barriers reduce participation in civic life from a significant and growing group.

To date, no city department or agency is charged with immigrant affairs; only the Welcoming Center for New Pennsylvanians, a private organization established in 2003, has made immigrant services its mission. Philadelphia must embrace its foreign-born population, seeking to fully engage them in the civic, social, political, and economic life of the city. The city should establish an agency equipped to provide English classes, legal consultation, and assistance in the acquisition of housing, employment, education, and healthcare, which would clearly illustrate the city's commitment to the well-being of all its residents. A Philadelphia that is more accessible to immigrants and residents alike, would attract new citizens whose energy and abilities could help to repopulate city neighborhoods, alleviate city funding concerns, and spur economic growth.

Providing better access to government information can also improve the relationships between the city, business, residents, and the media. Philadelphia's current information disclosure procedures are based upon the Commonwealth's Right-to-Know law, Right to Know Act, 65 P.S. §66.1 et seq., as amended effective December 23, 2002. The legislation stipulates what type of information the public does and does not have access to, when the public can have access, and methods of appealing a denial of access. Most states require that requests for information be responded to within seven business days, Pennsylvania requires a response within 10 days. States deemed more accessible typically allow requestors that are denied information their choice of whom to appeal to, either administrators or the courts, and sets clear timelines for the hearing of appeals. Pennsylvania only permits appeals to the head of an agency, and sets no time limit that an appeal must be responded to within. Additionally, government violators of the Right-to-Know law in Pennsylvania only face civil penalties, and there is no escalation in penalties for repeated offenses, creating little incentives for government agencies to become more open and transparent. The Philadelphia City Charter also includes reference to the disclosure of information by outlining the types of information that will not be released, such as those that would hinder law enforcement or violate an individual's right to privacy, and stating that the public should have access all other documents.

Although Pennsylvania's Right-To-Know law was amended in 2002, the city should lobby for further improvement to enhance the public's access to information. The city could press for better appeal options for requestors and a timeline for responses to appeals. The city could also seek escalating penalties for repeated violations. Alternately, the city could simply improve public access procedures without a change in state legislation. For example, it is the stated policy of the Mayor's Office of Information Services to respond to information requests in five business days, half the time allotted by the state legislation.

RECOMMENDATIONS FOR ACTION

The city should continue to expand the opportunity for online government transactions and the information available on the city website.

Action Steps

- Allow businesses and residents to track status of service requests online.

- Increase information and transactions available online as recommended in the first edition of *Philadelphia: A New Urban Direction.*

- Make use of online auctions to dispose of surplus city-owned property.

Fiscal Impacts:

- Potential short-term costs for technology.

- Potential long-term savings from reduced need to process transactions.

- Potential long-term revenue increases from improved collections.

- Potential revenue generation from online auctions.

- Potential savings from reduced storage costs for surplus items.

The city should utilize the internet to collect information about citizens' needs and priorities.

Action Step:

- Conduct online surveys about citizen priorities and satisfaction.

Fiscal Impacts:

- Potential short-term costs for technology and survey analysis.

- Potential to improve governmental operations.

The city should establish an agency to connect immigrants with opportunities for English classes, legal consultation, and assistance in the acquisition of housing, employment, education, and healthcare, in addition to marketing Philadelphia and coordinating service delivery for recent arrivals.

Action Steps:

- Collect and disseminate information about non-government services available to recent immigrants.

Fiscal Impacts:

- Potential short-term costs associated with administration and outreach.

- Potential long-term savings from recent immigrants being equipped to begin new lives in Philadelphia.

The city should improve disclosure of public information to increase transparency and citizen satisfaction.

Action Steps:

- Work with state officials to amend the Commonwealth's Right-to-Know legislation.

- Adopt procedures that exceed the standards set forth in the Commonwealth's Right-to-Know legislation.

Fiscal Impact:

• Potential costs associated with more timely information provision.

Promoting Constant Governmental Improvement

In 1999, the Controller's Office recommended that the city should establish a comprehensive performance measurement system and link performance to the annual budgeting process and change the Charter to mandate multi-year budgeting. The city first began a performance measurement program in fiscal year 1994, and began surveying citizens about their satisfaction with city services in 1996. To date, multi-year budgeting has not been added to the Charter and current performance measurement efforts still do not represent a concise method of analyzing agency goals, inputs, outputs, outcomes, efficiency, and citizen satisfaction measures.

Currently, the city's performance measures are not linked to individual employee performance. The city should continue to improve its performance measurement activities, specifically by creating links between agency missions, service outcomes, and individual job performance. For example, the City of Austin, Texas actively monitors agency performance in an effort to guide managerial decisions. Each department creates a business plan outlining a mission and goals, extending from individual employees to the department as a whole, which are then linked to the budget and measures of outcome. Included in their performance management system is the Success Strategy Performance Review (SSPR). Each city employee is evaluated with the SSPR, with supervisor and employee acting in congress to develop goals and to gauge performance. An individual's SSPR evaluation also details his/her contribution to agency outcomes, as well as performance goals to the overall business plan.

Creating mechanisms to reward agencies and individuals for excellent performance was recommended by the Controller's Office in 1999. City's employees are best positioned to identify practices and procedures with potential to improve services, reduce costs, or both. Programs directed at promoting employee innovation can not only increase productivity and efficiency, but also encourage management and staff communication. To date, the city has not adopted programs for gain sharing or performance-based pay and bonuses. To promote creative problem solving, the City Controller's Office, in conjunction with the Greater Philadelphia Chamber of Commerce, instituted the Innovative Employee Incentive Plan. City and school district employees can suggest mechanisms to improve service or increase efficiency, with the best suggestions earning up to $500 in cash and gift certificates each quarter. While not all suggestions are implemented, some ideas have yielded large benefits for Philadelphia—one has even generated over $5 million in new revenue since 1998.

Other cities have used rigorous, regular performance measurement and information gathering about citizens' needs and satisfaction levels to improve service delivery quality and efficiency. In 2000, Baltimore initiated its CitySTAT program, a tool designed to improve accountability through tracking and assessment of service activities. Evolving to encompass most service departments, CitySTAT provides Baltimore's leadership with a mechanism to focus on established priorities, developing tactics and strategies to efficiently address the city's needs.

In 2002, the CitySTAT program was augmented with the addition of CityTrak, a 311 system residents could call with any service request. The creation of a single number for all non-emergency requests consolidated calls to the city in a single source, reducing the number of non-emergency calls to Baltimore's 911 system, while enhancing citizens' communication with the city. The 311 service was later expanded to Baltimore's website, allowing residents to submit requests online. Requests, either via phone or online, are routed to the relevant department, and residents are provided with a tracking number with which they can later find the status of their inquiry. Baltimore's 311 system, coupled with coterminous service districts, has streamlined the system for managing all calls to the city and service requests, making departments accountable for the service requests they receive. Moreover, from the data provided by the call and online database, city leaders can track weekly trends and issues of concern in Baltimore.

Taken together, CitySTAT and CityTrak produced a combined $43 million in cost savings, cost avoidances, and revenue enhancements in only the program's first three years, while improving the quality of municipal services, according to the City of Baltimore. Of the roughly one million calls received, 700,000 requests were resolved, without a single lost call. By comparison, Philadelphia's call center, though not as well publicized nor as service-inclusive as Baltimore's 311 system, was only able to answer 75 percent of all calls in fiscal year 2004. Due to the success of its system, Baltimore is also able to guarantee that potholes will be filled within 48 hours of receiving a complaint.

Governments around the country and the globe have traveled to Baltimore to view the operation of CitySTAT. Many cities have implemented a version in their own jurisdictions. Philadelphia should not fail to be among the followers, as the system has real potential for this city. As of yet, Philadelphia has hesitated due to fears of costs, even though net benefits have been proven in other cities. The initial start-up cost of CitySTAT was less than $285,000, and ongoing operations are less than $400,000 annually, mostly comprising personnel costs. While the cost of operating the 311 call center has approached $4 million annually, Baltimore's leaders and residents alike believe the benefits of improved, efficient service alone have far outweighed the cost. While the city should continue to pursue implementing a 311 and CitiStat-like system to improve data collection and service delivery, short-term solutions are available. As an interim measure, Philadelphia should enhance its centralized systems for accepting, distributing, and tracking information and service requests from citizens on the city website and call center in order to better coordinate and monitor service and information requests.

In 1999, the Controller's Office recommended that the city take action to better track public property, materials, and supplies. The city is now taking steps to centralize warehousing and implement a citywide inventory system. According to the City's fiscal year 2006 Five-Year Financial Plan, this effort is expected to reduce costs by nearly $5 million through fiscal year 2010. To date, the city has not begun tracking public property by individual employee to promote accountability, although some departments may have the capability to do this internally.

RECOMMENDATIONS FOR ACTION

The city should continue exploration of implementing a system to handle non-emergency service and information requests and adopt a system of rigorous performance measurement.

Action Steps:

- Continue efforts to implement a 311 system for comprehensive handling and tracking of non-emergency calls.

- In the near term, continue to consolidate existing call centers and introduce a unified tracking system for service and information requests.

Fiscal Impacts:

- Short-term costs of training and equipment costs for a 311 system.

- Long-term costs of operating a 311 system.

- Long-term savings from eliminating duplication of effort among city call centers.

- Potential to improve government operations.

The city should adopt a system of performance measurement that creates links between agency missions, service outcomes, and individual job performance.

Action Step:

- Purchase and utilize software programs to link tracking of agency missions, service outcomes, and individual job performance.

Fiscal Impact:

- Potential short-term costs for training and software.

- Potential for long-term improvements in government operations.

Keeping a Historical City Modern

This year, Philadelphia celebrates the 300th birthday of Benjamin Franklin, a man known for his lifelong dedication to innovation for the common good. Philadelphia must continue to embrace his drive to develop products and processes to accomplish everyday tasks more efficiently and effectively. Ensuring that our government structure and regulatory system reflect modern needs and priorities should be undertaken comprehensively, as we recommended in 1999, although a piecemeal approach has continued. Additionally, no steps have yet been taken to utilize a sunset review process to determine if the city's agencies and initiatives are serving ongoing purposes.

The Controller's Office recommended that the city work with business and civic groups to design a regulatory system that protects the citizenry while promoting growth. Although no government-directed task force was formed, the Building Industry Association (BIA) of Philadelphia released a report in October 2004 that called attention to Philadelphia's outdated, unwieldy development process that serves as a barrier to new construction, employment growth and tax revenue expansion. Philadelphia's zoning and building codes do not account for today's realities, such as new building technologies and materials and the rise in telecommuting. The BIA proposed 10 fixes that would modernize and streamline the development process in Philadelphia and make the process more predictable. Chicago, New York, Pittsburgh and other major cities have recently undertaken similar efforts with great success. Since Philadelphia has not yet seen fit to establish a task force to proactively review and modernize the city's legal and regulatory systems, the city should carefully evaluate efforts put forth by non-governmental entities and speedily adopt those that are deemed utile.

RECOMMENDATION FOR ACTION

Until a comprehensive process for reviewing Philadelphia's legal and regulatory systems is undertaken, the city should speedily review and adopt appropriate measures to streamline and modernize these systems offered by business and civic groups.

Action Steps:

- Establish committee to review suggested reforms.

- Work with City Council to pass legislation for modernization of legal and regulatory systems.

Fiscal Impacts:

- Potential short-term administrative costs.

- Potential long-term savings from elimination of unnecessary government operations.

- Potential increased revenue as a result of increased business activity.

Ensuring the Public's Trust

Since the publication of the first edition of *Philadelphia: A New Urban Direction*, it has become painfully clear that the perception and reality of corruption has shaken public trust in city government. Convictions of city officials and private citizens doing business with the city have cast a pall over Philadelphia. The costs of government misconduct are more than just dollars lost; the public loses confidence and respect for those chosen to govern them and in the actual governing institutions themselves. Philadelphians deserve more than the best and most capable individuals representing them; they deserve complete and honest service from those individuals. The city should establish a mechanism for formulating and enforcing meaningful ethics reforms to improve the transparency of government operations, and restore public confidence in its actions.

It is critical that the public has faith in its government. A government structure designed to meet the needs of its constituents cannot achieve the desired outcomes if there is real or perceived corruption. A government requires the respect and faith of the people in order to be legitimate and effective. Without this support Philadelphia's leaders will not be able to make the hard choices that are needed to improve the city.

Unfortunately, Philadelphia has been far from immune from such ills. Early 20th Century author and muckraker Lincoln Steffens, noting the rampant political patronage and election fraud in the city, termed Philadelphia "corrupt and contented" in his book, *The Shame of Cities*, a characterization relevant then and, to an extent, today as well. While the enactment of the 1951 Home Rule Charter effectively curbed much patronage through the establishment of the civil service system, Philadelphia has not been able to shed itself of governing misdeeds or to ensure completely the integrity of its employees. Recent federal investigations have brought to light grave misuses of positions of authority and an ingrained culture of "pay-to-play" between city leaders and potential contractors, through which access and economic benefit can be gained through financial and political support.

Breaches in the public's trust have instigated calls for reform throughout Philadelphia's history. In June of 1961, Mayor Dilworth appointed a committee to formulate recommendations regarding the process involving procurement of goods and services by the city, the hiring and supervision of civil service employees, and the standards of ethics to which every city employee should adhere. The Mayor's Ad Hoc Committee on Improvement in Municipal Standards and Practices, known as the Fordham Committee after the committee's head, Jefferson B. Fordham, delivered a set of recommendations that led to the creation of the Philadelphia Board of Ethics.

Formally amended in 1963 to include an ethics code and the new Board of Ethics, Philadelphia's new Code provisions established rules governing the standards and conduct expected of its employees. Businesses, corporations, individuals, and organizations are prohibited from offering, and employees, elected, appointed, or otherwise, are prohibited from soliciting, accepting, or receiving any gift, loan, gratuity, favor or service of substantial economic value that may influence one in the discharge of his official duties. Employees of Philadelphia cannot have a personal or financial interest in proposed legislation, unless such interest is publicly disclosed and the individual disqualifies himself from any interaction, involvement, or official action regarding the legislation. The Board of Ethics, central to the reform efforts, was charged with providing advisory opinions to officers and employees with respect to ethical standards. The Board also issues recommendations to the Mayor and to City Council concerning methods to improve the ethical standards of municipal service, including initiatives concerning the organization, procedure, and enforcement of established standards. The Philadelphia Code was further amended in 1982 and 1995 to require city employees to file statements of financial interests each year, and also to elaborate the penalties for violation of the ethical standards. Despite the presence of ethical standards and a Board of Ethics, Philadelphia remains far short of achieving an exemplary record of municipal integrity, though reform efforts continue.

In 2003, the 21st Century Review Forum, a committee empanelled to formulate recommendations for the Mayor's second term, included a sub-committee on ethics. Finding many of the current ethics statutes and provisions inadequate, the Ethics Committee presented a series of recommendations for improving the standards of conduct in the city's municipal service. Currently, guidelines concerning proper conduct and ethical behavior are dispersed between both the Philadelphia Code and Charter, preventing easy access to or understanding of requirements. The Committee advised the creation of a single "Omnibus Code of Ethics," including the publication of a Handbook of Ethics to facilitate dissemination to employees, individuals, and companies.

The Ethics Committee recommended disbanding the current Board of Ethics in favor of a new, Charter-mandated Board. The original Board of Ethics was required to meet only four times per year and served in only an advisory capacity. The 21st Century Review Forum Ethics Committee supported expanded powers for a Chartered Ethics Board, including training, monitoring, adjudicatory and enforcement authority. It was recommended that the new Board of Ethics include a professional staff to support operations, as well as establish a "Whistleblower Hotline" to receive reports of potential ethics violations. Increased and improved employee training was deemed critical to the success of new ethics reform efforts, both to educate as to what is required and to instill a "culture" of ethical behavior. Though the original Board of Ethics was revived in 2004 in response to increasingly public ethics violations and has expressed interest in forming a new Board, the Ethics Board remains as it was in the 1960s; of limited scope and without any real abilities. The city should adopt the ethics recommendations of the 21st Century Review Forum.

Both the administration and certain members of Council favor the creation of a new, more capable board, but to date, debate over the size and structure of a new board has delayed its creation. The city should establish a Charter-mandated, able and independent Ethics Board as soon as it is possible. The Board should comprise five full-time, salaried members, with two appointed by the Mayor, two appointed by the Council, and one appointed by the City Controller. An Ethics Board of this structure would provide balance between the two main branches of Philadelphia government and avoid potential conflicts of interest by preventing any appointment to hold sway over the whole. Given the Office of the Controller's current involvement in fraud investigations and encouragement of ethical government practices, the Office should be included in the formation of any Ethics Board to promote impartiality.

The Board should be endowed with broad powers, including enforcement and investigative powers, to ensure it possesses the abilities to perform its mandated function. As with the Office of City Controller, the Board should be granted, through a Charter provision, a protected base level of funding each fiscal year, to insulate it from outside influence. The Board should provide classes upon request from city department heads in order to educate staff on appropriate conduct. The city should also follow through on the recommendation of the 21st Century Review Forum and institute a "Whistleblower Hotline," allowing for both the anonymous online and over-the-phone reporting of alleged ethical violations by city employees and citizens. Lastly, the city should enable anonymous inquiry by residents and city workers seeking to know if certain behavior is ethical or not. While the perception is that unethical behavior is usually perpetrated purposefully, in some instances an individual may just not be aware that some action may be unethical. With proper educational efforts, being uninformed about ethical obligation should no longer be an issue. For those who are found to have willfully violated ethical standards, Philadelphia needs to fairly and consistently implement meaningful penalties as a signal that the city is dedicated to earning the public's trust, and to present a deterrent to future unethical practices.

Campaign Finance Reform

Philadelphians deserve the best and most capable individuals advocating their interests and working for their benefit in city government. Ideally, elections would serve to provide the public with the opportunity to select the best person to represent them based on credentials, not the amount of money they raised or connections possessed. The city should effectively reform campaign finance practices so that individuals would campaign, and once elected, hopefully act in the interest of the city as a whole and not sectarian interests.

Historically, Philadelphia has lacked comprehensive campaign finance rules or restrictions. In 2003, new ordinances regarding campaign contributions and expenditures were added to the Philadelphia Code, placing limitations on donations and use of funds for Mayoral and City Council elections. The amendments limited individual contributions to $1,000 and political committees to $5,000 in any election year for Mayor or City Council. Beginning in the 2007 election cycle, candidates for Mayor or City Council may opt to sign a contract with the Election Reform Board, agreeing to limit expenditures and to report all contributions and outlays to the Board. Signing the contract limits Mayoral candidates to spending $2,000,000, while Council candidates can spend no more than $250,000 on election efforts. In 2005, the Code was further amended to extend the campaign finance restrictions to other elected City officials, including but not limited to the District Attorney, the City Controller, the Register of Wills, the Sheriff, the Clerk of Quarter Sessions Court, and the City Commissioners. The amendment increased permissible contribution limits to $2,500 for individuals and to $10,000 for all other contributors, as well as limiting the total amount of contributions candidates could receive. While compliance with the law can be compelled, there are no defined penalties for a candidate found to be in violation of the requirements of the law. The city should alter the legislation to provide for clear penalties for violations, and consistently enforce them.

At present, the limitations placed on campaign contributions lack adequate provisions for enforcement and transparency. Easily accessible, detailed records of political donations should be available online for public perusal. Incumbents and candidates would then be able to be held accountable for acting to the benefit of a specific interest rather than in the general public interest. In addition to improving public access to information about direct political donations, steps need to be taken to regulate other expenditures designed to gain access to and influence over city government decision making. Private entities with an interest in the awarding of contracts or outcomes of the legislative and regulatory process hire lobbyists to advance their interests. This practice is currently unregulated in Philadelphia. The city could require the registration of lobbyists and disclosures of clients so that the public can benefit from improved information about whom and what is influencing policy and hold city leaders more accountable for their actions. Elected officials and other government employees vested with the power to make policy and contracting decisions should also face more stringent disclosure requirements. Currently, financial disclosures are only required during the period of employment, but not following separation from the city. To ensure that government decisions are not influenced by promised individual future financial gains, the city could require that financial disclosure continue for at least one year after leaving public service.

Expanding Competitive Contracting

Over 10 percent of the City of Philadelphia's fiscal year 2006 general fund budget has been allocated for Professional Services contracts, such as economists, public relations consultants, and lawyers, which are not subject to the city's competitive bidding requirements. The continued reliance on non-competitively bid contracts for a vast amount of city purchases of services creates the opportunity for misuse and abuse. Too often, non-competitively bid City contracts may have been awarded on the basis of personal and political motives. These contracts did not always represent the best value for the citizens of Philadelphia or, in the very least, bypassed a more equitable system of contract distribution.

In 2005, City Council adopted legislation that seeks to further separate the influence of political contributions on governance. For city contracts or forms of financial assistance in excess of $50,000, individuals who contributed more than $2,500 and businesses that contributed more than $10,000 to a candidate or incumbent were prohibited from being granted no-bid contracts. Individuals or businesses seeking a non-competitively bid contract will be required to provide full disclosure of contributions or else be disqualified from entering into such a contract with the City.

The ordinance is set to become law on February 1, 2006 and will apply to contributions received beginning January 1, 2006, after voters approved a change to the Home Rule Charter Amendment in November 2005.

To inject additional objectivity and transparency into the city's procurement process, reliance on no-bid contracts, particularly for professional services, should be reduced. In the future, the city should be bid professional services contracts with a value in excess of $25,000, out to insure best value for the city and prevent potential conflicts of interest. While it would, in theory, be desirable to have all contacts bid, the cost and time involved to bid contracts of lower value could ultimately cost more than the contract itself and would create barriers to participation for some non-profits and smaller businesses. Many contracts are awarded to social service providers and small businesses that may not have the capacity to adequately participate in bidding processes as they are currently organized. Simplified contract proposal procedures should be devised to ensure that those entities are able to continue to vie for city work.

Moreover, the city could seek to bundle smaller contracts for common necessities across departments and authorities, minimizing, when possible, the need to issue contracts for less than $25,000. Philadelphia also must ensure than no one individual or business receives multiple no-bid contracts at a value slightly less than the $25,000 cap simply to avoid the bidding process. Any city department or authority with contracting authority should be prohibited from issuing multiple contracts for like services from the same vendor in a given fiscal year. Philadelphia already prohibits "split invoicing" to get around caps on petty cash expenditures; similar rules should be applied to non-competitively bid contracts.

Historically the justification for no-bid contracts has been that the nature of the services or supplies required was not suitable for an open bidding process, either because the need was immediate (such as immediate demolition services) or specialized (legal work related to bond issuance). Failing to require a competitive process can lead to informal price fixing among firms, limited opportunities for small business and poor value for the public dollars expended. To avoid these pitfalls in the future, the city could pre-certify firms based upon set performance criteria and compensation guidelines. Interested firms could seek approval to work under the terms stated; the city could then rotate contract awards among the certified firms. Philadelphia has already established rotational contracting for towing services to protect the public interest and safeguard against fraud, as well as to improve the functioning of the service.

RECOMMENDATIONS FOR ACTION

The city should establish a mechanism for formulating and enforcing meaningful ethics reforms to improve the transparency of government operations, and restore public confidence in its actions.

Action Steps:

- Work with City Council to adopt the recommendations of the 21st Century Review Committee on ethics.

- Establish a Charter-mandated Ethics Board, adequately funded to promulgate and consistently enforce clear ethics regulations.

- Allow city employees and residents to make anonymous inquiries about the ethicalness of various scenarios.

Fiscal Impacts:

- Potential short-term administrative cost to initiate an Ethics Board.

- Potential ongoing operating costs of Ethics Board.

- Potential long-term savings from preventing and stopping misappropriation of city resources.

The city should effectively reform campaign finance practices.

Action Steps:

- Require the registration of lobbyists.

- Require city officials continue financial disclosure for a period of time after leaving the city employ.

Fiscal Impacts:

- Potential costs associated with administration and monitoring of lobbyist registration and financial disclosures.

- Potential to improve government efficiency.

- Potential long-term savings from ensuring a purely public purpose for government decision making.

The city should bid professional services contracts in excess of $25,000 to insure best value for the city and prevent potential conflicts of interest.

Action Steps:

- Work with City Council to establish procedures for the bidding of all contracts valued at more than $25,000.

- Streamline bidding process to ensure that small and disadvantaged firms can compete for city businesses.

- Pre-certify firms under strict performance and compensation guidelines for provision of certain goods and services.

Fiscal Impacts:

- Potential costs associated with more onerous contracting procedures.

- Potential savings from enhanced competitive bidding.

Conclusion

The city can create a brighter future for Philadelphia, and make it a preferred place to live, work, and visit

To best serve its citizens, the city must be able to reorganize its government to meet the needs of current and future populations. The city must continue to explore reshaping the structure of government to better align its activities with its mission. When reorganization is not viable, the city must better coordinate policy formulation and implementation to avoid duplications of effort and leverage opportunities. Building support for change requires that the stakeholders have faith in the propriety and wisdom of the government and its leaders. Improved government accountability, through campaign financing and ethics reforms, are necessary to restore this faith. Additional support for government reforms and initiative can be achieved by increasing citizens' access to government information to promote more efficient and utile interactions between government and the residents and businesses it serves.

CHAPTER 3
FISCAL POLICY FOR PHILADELPHIA'S FUTURE

Our Constitution is in actual operation;
everything appears to promise that it will last;
but in this world nothing is certain but death and taxes.

—Benjamin Franklin
Letter to M. Leroy, 1789

FISCAL ISSUES AND PHILADELPHIA'S FUTURE

Like other local governments, the City of Philadelphia government is called upon to deliver many services. In a bustling metropolis filled with residents and visitors who are usually strangers, government must keep the peace, create conditions so that goods and services flow freely through the marketplace, and preserve the general welfare of the population. This all comes at a cost.

Some local expenditures, such as police protection, are usually viewed as essential to a municipality. Other expenditures, such as waste collection, are justified because some residents would dispose of waste in less-than-sanitary ways without such efforts and government has a compelling interest to provide the service to preserve public welfare. Still other expenditures, such as investments in cultural assets, are usually seen as undertakings to improve the quality of life in a way that encourages residents to remain part of the municipal tax base and entices visitors to contribute their discretionary spending to that tax base. Different jurisdictions make different decisions about which services must be funded by government, and all jurisdictions face the push and pull of the political system in making such decisions. Questions surrounding taxing and spending issues, therefore, will be impossible to resolve in a way that satisfies all parties. Some assumptions, however, should be articulated in a universally acceptable manner.

In the long run, the government of the City of Philadelphia cannot spend more money than it takes in. One year's deficit might be offset by a prior year's surplus, but eventually a government that spends more than it takes in will collapse into a form of quasi-bankruptcy. Similarly, the government of the City of Philadelphia cannot simply raise taxes indefinitely to fund expenditures. Given that residents and employers have already shown their willingness to leave the City, rising taxes, left unchecked, will eventually raise the cost of remaining in Philadelphia to a level that will chase all businesses and individuals out. Finally, given that City government must not spend more than it takes in over the long term, and given that raising taxes indefinitely at the City level will chase away residents and businesses and erode the tax base, it is clear that the City cannot fund the tremendous cost to correct the ills of society by itself. Efforts to fund wealth transfers and progressively attack problems such as poverty and social dislocation are properly fought at the state and federal government level. Any effort to transfer wealth at the local level must be looked at very carefully to weigh any anticipated social benefit against the budgetary stress such a move is likely to cause.

Philadelphia's government faces the challenge of funding expenditures knowing that it can neither spend more than it collects, nor raise taxes to fund expenditures indefinitely. The challenge is further compounded by the fact that if the City's population continues to decline, its tax revenues and certain intergovernmental revenues based on the level of the City's population will also decline. The City can meet that challenge. To ensure that the government lives within its means, the City can establish budgetary structural balance—the condition when the cost of services provided by local government equals the local economy's ability to fund those services—to impose fiscal discipline and reduce the likelihood of future fiscal crises. The City can increase the amount of taxes it exports and reduce its reliance on taxes that vary with economic conditions. The City can increase its ability to collect what it is owed so that all taxpayers pay their fair share to support governmental spending. The City can reduce the cost of government to reduce its need for taxes. Finally, the City can take advantage of its market to generate non-tax revenues and give it the ability to adequately confront the challenges of the 21st century.

PROMOTING STRUCTURAL BALANCE FOR FISCAL HEALTH

As anyone who prepares a budget understands, whether it involves a large corporation, a small business, or a household, revenues must keep pace with expenditures over the long run to ensure viability. If selected expenses increase, then other expenses must decrease or revenues must be increased to achieve balance. If expenses increase without a corresponding cut in other expenditures or increase in revenue, balance will be lacking. If any budget is out of balance for too long, and if options to borrow, avoid expenditures, and take other evasive maneuvers are exhausted, collapse can be the only result. Before that collapse, however, expenses will increase as borrowing costs mount, avoided expenditures will become costly problems, and maneuvers to evade collapse will be accompanied by a high price. Efforts to avoid collapse do little to improve the structural health of the budget. In the end, only by creating the conditions that make expenditures likely to meet revenues over the long run can the budget truly be healthy. (See Appendices II and III for discussions about the City budget and taxation in Philadelphia.)

Columbia University Professor Ester Fuchs has studied what she dubs the "permanent urban fiscal crisis." In her essay, "The Permanent Urban Fiscal Crisis," Professor Fuchs contends that "the structure of the American federal system forces cities to compete with one another for all tax revenues, leaving virtually every local government with insufficient resources to finance needed services." She declares that "cities can balance their budgets, but it is most often at the expense of basic services." While Fuchs argues that the fiscal problems that American cities face are structural, and that they can only be solved through the creation of a new model of urban fiscal policy at the state and federal levels, she also acknowledges that the structural characteristics of a city's fiscal policy process can be designed to make a city less likely to experience fiscal stress and crisis.

Examining New York City and Chicago, Illinois, and how both have responded to fiscal stress in this century, Fuchs shows how cities can be predisposed to fiscal crisis. She cites the fact that Chicago mayors have a structural advantage in the fiscal policy process, with greater control over the budget. Chicago's fiscal responsibility for expensive deficit-producing and redistributive services is shared with other Chicago region jurisdictions and the State of Illinois. Alternatively, New York, with its high social welfare costs and substantial contributions to mass transit, corrections, and health and hospital services may be destined to endure periodic fiscal crises. To promote fiscal stability, Fuchs advises cities to control the demands of interest groups on local revenues so that expenses can be kept low or programs and personnel can be cut if the City's resource base shrinks; and to minimize the cost of service delivery by acquiring revenue from non-local sources or by having another governmental jurisdiction fund and administer the service.

Examining the City of Philadelphia's budgets from past decades, one can see the way budgetary stress taxes the citizenry—literally. The City's General Fund has increased steadily since Philadelphia first shifted to its current June-to-July fiscal year. Even when expressed in constant dollars, the increase is clear. By fiscal year 1997, the City increased its actual General Fund expenditures by 30 percent over its fiscal year 1970 expenditure level. (See Figure 3.1.)

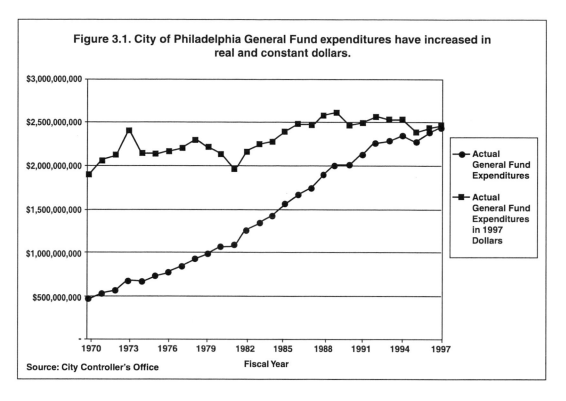

Figure 3.1. City of Philadelphia General Fund expenditures have increased in real and constant dollars.

Source: City Controller's Office

    While General Fund expenditures have decreased in constant terms in recent years, when Grants Revenue Fund expenditures—programmatic grants-in-aid from other governmental sources—are included in expenditures, one can see that City spending has even increased during the fiscal austerity years following the 1990 fiscal crisis. The money included in the Grants Revenue Fund represents money appropriated by the state and federal governments or other non-Philadelphia sources and does not directly affect locally generated revenues. However, because the City is often required to match such funding at some level, increases in the Grants Revenue Fund can force the City to increase locally-generated revenues. (Note that the City of Philadelphia established its current system of accounting for grants revenue in 1975.) (See Figure 3.2.)

    Examining budgetary increases on a per capita basis, Figure 3.3 shows the stark effect of increased spending accompanied by population loss. In constant dollars, City per capita General Fund expenditures have increased by more than 72 percent between fiscal year 1970 and fiscal year 1997. Total per capita General Fund and Grants Revenue Fund expenditures have increased by more than 57 percent between fiscal year 1975 and fiscal year 1997.

    These increased expenditures fund a variety of service efforts. City officials have responded with a variety of programs designed to meet needs and demands of Philadelphia's changing population. Additional federal and state mandates (funded and unfunded) designed to address social ills have served to further drive up City expenditures. According to a Wharton School study of the fiscal burden of unreimbursed poverty expenditures in Philadelphia, public health- and human services-related efforts have been the primary source of this increase in spending. For example, in 1985, the City provided more than $83 million to pay for poverty programs. In 1995, that figure grew by $51 million—a 15-percent increase in real terms. Note that this figure only includes direct expenditures on poverty-related programs. Indirect expenditures such as increased police and fire services are not included. Unreimbursed poverty expenditures were 6.7 percent of Philadelphia's own-source revenues in 1985, but increased to 7.6 percent in 1995.

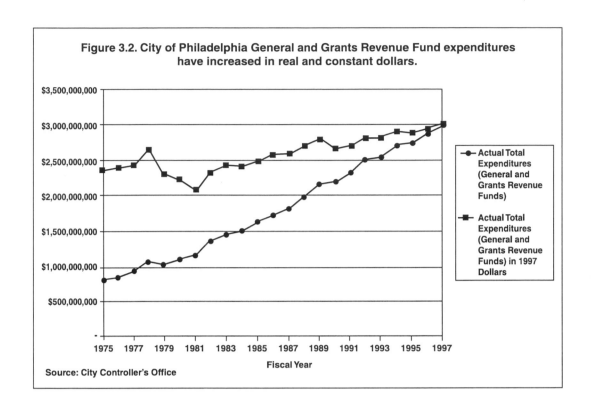

Figure 3.2. City of Philadelphia General and Grants Revenue Fund expenditures have increased in real and constant dollars.

Source: City Controller's Office

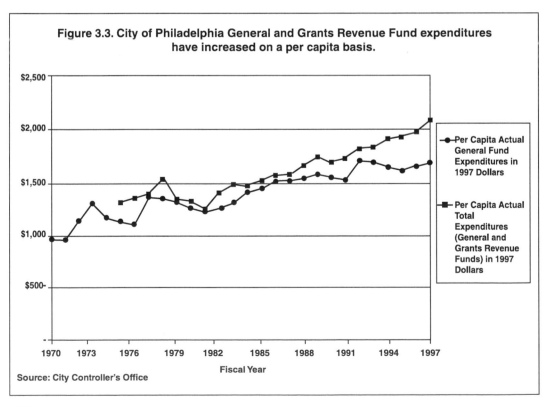

Figure 3.3. City of Philadelphia General and Grants Revenue Fund expenditures have increased on a per capita basis.

Source: City Controller's Office

As government expanded services and expenses, federal and state assistance also increased, but never in an amount sufficient to cover all expanded City services. When federal and state aid declined precipitously, the City raised taxes. There have been 30 increases in the City wage, property, and business tax rates since 1966—19 increases since 1981. Robert Inman, Professor of Finance, Economics, and Real Estate from the University of Pennsylvania's Wharton School, explained how Philadelphia's revenue need from taxation outpaced its maximum revenue potential, triggering the 1990 fiscal crisis. In "The Fiscal Future for American Cities: Lessons from Three Cities," Inman explains that when Philadelphia's lack of structural balance finally resulted in fiscal crisis, its revenue need from taxation of $1,108 per resident was significantly higher than its maximum revenue potential of $944 per resident.

Simply put, even though the City of Philadelphia budget may not be running a deficit today, there is an imbalance between the services being provided and the local economy's ability to pay for these services. Structural balance can be achieved, however, if the increase in the size of the City budget can be made to equal the rate of increase in the City's long-run economic growth. The Pennsylvania Intergovernmental Cooperation Authority, established to provide financial assistance and fiscal oversight to Philadelphia after its 1990 fiscal crisis, concluded a November 1996 white paper titled "Revenue Stress in the City of Philadelphia" by admonishing,

Philadelphia, while currently living within its means, has not achieved structural balance. Although the city has managed to balance its budget and increase its General Fund surplus balance in each of the past four years, its tax base continues to erode. Greater levels of state and federal funds for health and human services and improved revenues from fees, fines, interest, and other entities have not offset dependence on locally-generated tax revenues to provide basic services. Revenues thus remain in jeopardy of severe contraction in the eventuality of a declining national economy.

While this warning is stark, it is only premised on the City's current spending and does not take into account the need to make additional capital improvements to physical assets, expand service-delivery efforts to improve quality of life in City neighborhoods, and invest in technology to improve governmental operations at all levels. The warning also fails to note the likelihood of future pressure from municipal unions for significant wage increases, since the workforce sacrificed so much during the City's fiscal crisis. Not only must Philadelphia move toward structural balance, it must do so realizing that it faces tremendous demands to expand expenditures while it will have limited ability to further reduce costs at the expense of the workforce.

But achieving structural balance is not impossible. Cities can impose fiscal discipline and remain vibrant. Between 1992 and 1998, the City of Indianapolis actually reduced the size of its budget. According to the Indianapolis City Controller's Office, the City of Indianapolis' approved 1992 budget (adjusted to delete expenditures that are no longer the City's responsibility) equaled $459.7 million. The proposed 1999 budget (similarly adjusted to delete expenditures that were not the City's responsibility in 1992) calls for the City to spend $441.4 million. Even when examining the raw numbers, Indianapolis' 1992 approved budget equaled $481.3 million while the proposed 1999 budget is only $464.4 million. The Indianapolis budget did not just decrease after adjusting for inflation, the government is actually spending less money in real and constant dollars.

To achieve structural balance in the future, the City must ensure that its budget should not increase more than the its long-term economic growth rate, which means that the City must essentially freeze its budget at current expenditure levels, despite the demands of agencies and the citizenry to expand service. Future administrations will need to justify any expansion of spending efforts with a corresponding increase in revenue or a decrease in spending elsewhere in the budget. Agencies will face similar choices and should have opportunities to keep a percentage of agency revenues and retain savings to enable them to expand services.

Unless the City budget is in structural balance, another fiscal crisis is only a downturn in the economy away, but with structural balance the City can plan for a sound financial future. To do so, the City can create budgetary mechanisms to cushion against economic downturns. The City can ensure the ongoing maintenance of its physical assets so that the temptation to neglect routine maintenance in the short run does not turn into major expenditures in the long run. Finally, the City can rightsize its government to create a government the tax base can support.

Something for a Rainy Day

While Philadelphia currently enjoys the fruits of the ongoing national expansion, recession and decline will eventually come as part of normal fluctuations of the business cycle. The growth and production of spring fades to the inevitable winter. That is why the fabled ant stored its food for the coming cold, while the grasshopper, who played the summer away, was left unprepared to face the change in seasons.

Efforts to achieve budgetary structural balance are damaged by unwise expenditures when the City is flush with revenue, just as they are harmed by attempts to cut necessary spending when the City faces deficits. Building a lavish recreation center when money is plentiful negatively affects budgetary structural balance if the City will be unable to afford expenditures to maintain the facility into the future. Non-recurring revenues should therefore fund one-time expenses or should be placed into a pool to create endowments to maintain service levels. One-time revenues, should not be used to create facilities or programs that will necessitate ongoing City expenditures and negatively alter structural balance. Similarly, attempts to cut essential social programs or facility maintenance expenditures when budgets are tight may save a few dollars in the short run, but will likely result in the need to increase social spending and maintenance expenditures in the future. In both cases, efforts to achieve structural balance are damaged as the size of the overall budget increases in a way that is not correlated to the rate of increase of long-term growth.

Financial mechanisms are often employed to hold down spending that may accompany the rapid revenue growth characteristic of economic upswings and to stabilize spending during periods of revenue contraction associated with an economic downturn. Many states, including the Commonwealth of Pennsylvania, employ rainy-day funds to provide reserves to relieve the need to raise taxes or cut spending in times of need and to provide a way to cap expenditures in times of plenty. Such mechanisms may include legally-obligated triggers for fund contributions and formulaic methods to determine the amounts of fund withdrawals to improve long-term governmental financial conditions.

Cities such as San Antonio, Texas, and Baltimore, Maryland, maintain fund balances as a rainy-day fund to cushion against fiscal emergencies and recessions. According to Baltimore officials, the City established the City's rainy day fund in 1993 and currently have more than $8 million, approximately 0.75 percent of the City's General Fund expenditures, as a cushion against a future economic downturn that is growing by $800,000 each year during economic expansion.

Legally prohibited from carrying forward funds from one fiscal year to the next, New York City employs a budget-stabilization account to pledge excess current revenues to meet unforeseen future expenses. The budget-stabilization account is established by law and funded with revenues when revenue projections for the coming fiscal year will exceed expenditures. If at any time during the fiscal year additional revenue is recognized for that fiscal year in a budget modification, the City is required to allocate 50 percent into the budget-stabilization account. Expenditures from the budget-stabilization account must be preceded by a specific request for appropriation, identifying a particular purpose for the funds, and must be approved by a Council supermajority. Since New York City may not carry forward funds from one fiscal year to the next, expenditures from the revenue stabilization fund may be used as a source to prepay future year costs (for example, debt service costs). Thus, while unlike a true rainy-day fund, the budget-stabilization account must be fully spent each year, the City can replenish the account in the subsequent year if conditions are favorable.

By creating a rainy-day fund, Philadelphia can increase the likelihood that it will be able to sustain an acceptable level of governmental services over the long run without recurrent need for personnel layoffs, service cuts, or tax increases. Such actions could improve the City's long-run economic outlook and improve its image in the eyes of bond rating agencies, which could help reduce future borrowing costs. The City should create a rainy-day fund within the Charter-mandated budgetary structure. To enhance budgetary structural balance, such an action should be accompanied by requirements that contributions to the rainy-day fund be made when the rate of increase in revenue collections exceeds long-term economic growth rates; and that withdrawals be permitted only when revenue collections fall below long-term economic growth rates. Alternatively, a budget-stabilization account, modeled after New York City's account, could be created to achieve similar results short of restructuring the City's budgetary framework. With such a mechanism, some of the savings the City achieves in good years could be used to make a lump-sum payment against its unfunded pension liability to lower the payments of future generations. Similarly, with such a mechanism, the City could curtail its ability to spend recklessly when the economy booms and revenues soar.

Maintaining Capital Assets

In 1994, the Philadelphia City Planning Commission estimated that the City only spent capital dollars at 59 percent of the rate needed to maintain the public infrastructure in excellent condition. It is often deferred maintenance and a failure to perform the routine facility preservation chores, usually the result of budgetary cutbacks or efforts to decrease annual spending, which drive the demand for capital repairs. In 1993, a City Controller's Office Deferred Maintenance Study identified over $24 million in deferred maintenance citywide and determined that the City would be required to absorb at least $31.7 million (estimated to be at least $73.5 million when debt service is included) in capital renovation costs in the future as a result of deferring maintenance. Legal claims against the City emanating from deferred maintenance further increase costs.

Too often, as a way to cut costs, the City has neglected routine maintenance and repair of its physical assets. From recreation centers to City Hall, the City has not spent operating funds to keep assets in top condition. As a result, the City has had to increase borrowing costs to fund capital expenditures to rebuild and replace facilities that would have been much less costly to maintain with routine examinations and repairs. For example, failing to fix a leaky roof at a recreation center may lead to a need to replace a gymnasium floor. If facilities are not properly maintained, the City will incur higher utility costs where buildings are not energy efficient and risks lawsuits where facilities are dangerous. While it is convenient to save a few dollars in the operating budget by shortchanging the maintenance needs of the physical infrastructure, it is a recipe for shabby facilities in the short term and a lack of structural balance in the long term.

Philadelphia, like many other cities, has two budgets: an operating budget and a capital budget. The operating budget purchases goods and services that will be consumed in a short period of time, while the capital budget funds long-term investments in land and major construction projects with a useful life of more than five years. In the capital budget, bond issues are often used to pay for proposed projects so long as Philadelphia does not exceed its state-determined debt limit. Grants from other governments also help fund the capital budget.

In theory, the separation between the operating and capital budgets is designed to prevent the City from incurring future debt to fund recurring expenses. Thus, it is proper to incur debt that will be paid off by future generations to create an asset, such as a library, which will be enjoyed by future generations, while it is improper to incur debt to purchase basic cleaning services since such efforts must occur regularly and are therefore only enjoyed by current Philadelphians. There may, however, be flaws to this logic. Capital expenditures drive the operating budget. After a building is constructed using capital funds, the City must then maintain it using operating funds. For many buildings, this can be a tremendous burden. Philadelphia's grand City Hall, for example, is a magnificent building, but it is not energy efficient at all. With each new technological advance and safety requirement, the building must be retrofitted and adapted. At one point, Philadelphians even considered demolishing the massive building only to realize that the cost to tear down the world's tallest free-standing masonry building, complete with walls more than 22-feet thick at points, was prohibitive. Today's Philadelphians are therefore saddled with the maintenance costs imposed by the spending of previous generations. At the other end of this spectrum, if today's Philadelphians neglect routine maintenance expenditures, future generations will be burdened with the cost of replacing many assets that should have been preserved properly. If, as part of an effort to cut costs, the City defers or avoids performing maintenance, future generations will have to shoulder an increased burden.

In 1965, the City dedicated the Municipal Services Building, constructed at a cost of $20 million and designed to alleviate the need to rent commercial space for City agencies. Less than 30 years later, after allowing the building to deteriorate, the City spent an additional $45 million to modernize the offices, replace major building systems, and remove asbestos. During the nearly two-year renovation, City workers and offices were temporarily relocated to rented space, further increasing the cost of the effort. Failure to adequately maintain the Municipal Services Building, therefore, burdened current and future Philadelphians with the costs of renovating the building.

As documented in its 1998–2003 Capital Improvement Program, the City of Seattle, Washington, has made a commitment to focus its capital expenditures on major maintenance efforts. In 1994, the City established a Citizens' Capital Investment Committee to analyze the capital investment plan. The Seattle City Council incorporated the Committee's recommendations to substantially increase major maintenance funding to General Fund departments by increasing a real estate transfer tax to fund subsequent capital spending plans. With a commitment to capital maintenance and a requirement that Seattle departments now submit 20-year maintenance-need plans on a regular basis, the City is making strides to preserve its capital infrastructure for the future.

In an older city like Philadelphia, historical buildings present a particular challenge. In 1975, the City moved the house that may have been the oldest in Philadelphia from a sewage treatment plant near the International Airport to the nearby Fort Mifflin Revolutionary War historic site, at a cost to the City of $200,000. The so-called Cannonball House had endured the trials of history since before the Revolutionary War, but was demolished in 1996 after the City allowed years to pass without spending money to preserve the building. While the building was decrepit, one historic preservation activist claimed that $5,000 worth of spending could have properly preserved the building if had it been used to repair the building's roof 15 years prior to the structure's ultimate demolition. In the end, without funding maintenance efforts, the City wasted the $200,000 spent to move the house. The total cost of the loss of a building dating back to a pre-William Penn settlement in what now is Philadelphia can never be fully calculated.

The City has had notable preservation successes in recent years. The School District of Philadelphia, the Preservation Alliance for Greater Philadelphia, the Avenue of the Arts, Inc., and the Pew Charitable Trusts have collaborated in a noteworthy effort to maintain one of Philadelphia's architectural treasures. In creating the new home for the Philadelphia High School for the Creative and Performing Arts, the School District reused the Ridgway Library, an imposing temple-like structure constructed more than a century ago but left vacant in recent years after serving as a City recreation center. While the reuse of the building is a stunning victory for the school and the City, true success will only be achieved if the building is adequately supported in its refurbished state. To ensure proper maintenance, the Pew Charitable Trusts provided a maintenance endowment for the school that is distributed to the School District by the Avenue of the Arts, Inc., based upon certification by the Preservation Alliance that the District has performed required maintenance. A thick Inspection and Maintenance Manual for the building, prepared by the Preservation Alliance, outlines how and when routine maintenance must be performed, detailing everything from what kind of masking tape must be used in painting projects to how to properly install joint sealants. If the School District performs maintenance properly, it is reimbursed for its maintenance expenditures from the endowment fund. A similar endowment is planned to help preserve the City's historic Fairmount Waterworks.

Other jurisdictions have generated new revenues from tax measures or surcharges on new development and set aside funds to be used for historic preservation. Several states, including Maryland and Virginia, have a check box as part of tax returns that allows residents to donate money to such efforts. In Virginia, for example, residents may donate money to an open space recreation and conservation fund. The Commonwealth of Pennsylvania can place a check-off box on state tax returns to collect funds to maintain historic Philadelphia buildings. Alternatively, the City could place a check-off box on water bills to solicit money to fund such maintenance efforts. A not-for-profit organization could be created to accept such funds and administer a proper maintenance program.

Since Philadelphia is largely built as a city, its focus in the future must be to adequately maintain its facilities. While fixing a leaky roof might not solve all of the City's problems, if the City ensures that routine maintenance is actually the routine, it can save money and improve its physical infrastructure. With future population decline likely to negatively affect revenue collections, the City is pressured to design creative ways to use capital expenditures and proper ways to use operating funds to adequately maintain current and future physical assets.

To ensure that it adequately plans for the future of its physical assets, and to more closely link capital expenditures to operating costs, the City should create and annually update a physical assets maintenance plan. To ensure that it properly maintains its physical assets for the future, despite pressure to increase other government spending, the City should establish a separate fund within its annual budget (or within each agency's budget) dedicated to fund maintenance of physical assets. An independent entity such as the City Controller's Office could periodically certify whether the City and its agencies spent its asset maintenance funds properly and whether the City received value for its expenditures. The maintenance reserve could be mandated by a Charter amendment for an amount set each year based on the estimated cost to adequately maintain City assets as established by the City Planning Commission. Because any new capital expenditures would automatically increase the amount of this maintenance reserve, elected officials would be able to see how any capital expenditures would automatically increase future operating expenditures. With such a mechanism to impose spending discipline, the City could then use life-cycle costing to evaluate capital projects to determine the true, long-term costs of a project. Life-cycle costing can help establish the notion that purchasing value up front in creating a capital asset may be more costly, but often saves maintenance and capital costs over the life of the asset.

To help fund maintenance efforts (estimated by the City Controller's Office Deferred Maintenance Study in 1993 at an increase over then-current expenditures of over $24 million), especially for maintenance on historic structures, the City could seek grants from private foundations and other private sources. Given the historic nature of many of the City's assets the City could solicit private foundations and individual donors to create endowments to help ensure the maintenance of the City's most treasured assets, including the tremendous collection of public art created by the 1-percent-for-art set-aside as part of all public construction projects that is often left to deteriorate without proper maintenance. As discussed above, the City could solicit donations through the use of a check-off box on City water bills. Philadelphia could also follow the lead of the State of Maryland to reduce maintenance costs by leasing historic properties to tenants who agree to restore them at little or no cost to the state.[1] Under such a program, tenants for structures such as Philadelphia's many Fairmount Park houses could live in the properties rent-free for life as long as they undertake and fund renovations consistent with historic preservation standards. The properly preserved properties would revert to the City after their deaths. Alternatively, the City could allow local colleges or universities to restore historic City properties as part of historic preservation curricula. After such restorations, the colleges and universities could utilize the properties for institutional purposes, while maintaining some level of public access.

---

[1] Oldenburg, Don. "Rent-free for life," *Preservation*, September/October 1998. p. 12.

Rightsizing the City Government—Physical Assets

In 1950, the population of the City of Philadelphia was more than two million people. The year 2000 census will likely show that Philadelphia's population has fallen below 1.5 million—roughly the number of people who lived in the City in 1910. But in 1910, the vast lands of Northeast Philadelphia and Southwest Philadelphia were largely unpopulated. As late as 1930, the City was home to more than 13,500 acres of farmland. In 1950, many currently populated City neighborhoods were still undeveloped tracts of land. Thus, while compared to the City's 1950 population, Philadelphia is now a much smaller city; compared to the City's level of development in 1910 (and in 1950), Philadelphia is physically a much larger city. Philadelphia is a city designed for a higher density, currently operating at a much lower density.

While the number of Philadelphians has decreased, the City's infrastructure (sewer and water lines, streets, and street lighting) has expanded. The number of City facilities, while serving fewer people, also expanded. As density in the City has fallen, at dramatically disproportionate rates in different neighborhoods, communities have suffered in economic and social terms. Remaining Philadelphians have had to pay for the consequences in terms of vacancy, disinvestment, and the resulting concentration of poverty. Since fiscal year 1970, the City's per capita actual General Fund expenditures have increased more than 72 percent. (See Table 3.1.)

Table 3.1. Per Capita Actual General Fund Expenditures in 1997 Dollars	
Fiscal Year	**Expenditures**
1970	$969.53
1997	$1,670.68
Source: City Controllers Office	

For the future, Philadelphians can hope that 500,000 people will abruptly decide to buck the historical and projected trends and move *en masse* to the City, instantly creating a market for long-vacant housing and suddenly repopulating and reenergizing abandoned neighborhoods. But even if Philadelphia can become a city that is a magnet for families and employers, it is not reasonable to expect to see that level of inmigration, which is roughly equivalent to the population of State of Wyoming, picking up and moving to Philadelphia. Alternatively, if the City is to be able to adequately maintain its infrastructure and effectively serve residents, visitors, and businesses, it can better fit the City to its current population and then grow into the future.

Twenty-first-century Philadelphia must become a "rightsized" City endowed with an appropriate level of physical assets and served by an appropriate level of municipal employees. If Philadelphia's government is to be able to adequately serve its citizenry in the most efficient and effective manner, it must be sized to a level that can be supported by its citizenry. The City can downsize its government to help rightsize the City.

According to the Planning Commission, in the early 1980s, Philadelphia had a public infrastructure that would have cost $28.6 billion to replace while the City was rehabilitating it at an annual expenditure of $252 million, or 45 percent of the level required to maintain all facilities in excellent condition. While the Planning Commission showed that this disparity had been improved by 1994, when capital spending averaged $530 million, or 59 percent of the rate needed to maintain a public infrastructure then estimated to cost $41.6 billion to replace, it is clear that deteriorating infrastructure is a tremendous burden.

In 1995, the Philadelphia City Planning Commission examined City infrastructure investment levels and demonstrated what occurs when a city is not rightsized. According to the Planning Commission's estimate, in 1994 the City would have had to spend nearly $900 million annually, roughly equal to a 70-percent increase in capital spending, to maintain City facilities in an excellent condition. That additional funding would have represented an additional $242 for every Philadelphian in 1994. It is obviously very costly to keep a city in good repair. It is especially difficult in an old city where some physical assets are over 100 years old. Like residents on fixed incomes who have watched their children leave home to find themselves burdened with a property that has become too expensive to maintain, the City faces a very real challenge trying to preserve its urban infrastructure.

City facility levels have been altered dramatically since Philadelphia adopted its Home Rule Charter in 1951. In 1952, with a population of over two million, the City maintained 34 police facilities, 88 fire facilities, and 43 library facilities. In 1998, with a population of less than 1.5 million, the City maintains 42 police facilities, 66 fire facilities, and 54 library facilities. Similarly, the City maintained 13 Water Department facilities, two Health Department facilities, and 284 Recreation Department facilities in 1952. In 1998, the City maintains 52 Water Department facilities, 22 Health Department facilities, and 655 Recreation Department facilities. (See Table 3.2.)

Many factors drive the facility-level changes detailed in Table 3.2. After 1952, for example, the City established and constructed District Health Centers to meet the demand for community-based medical care. As the City's population moved into previously unpopulated tracts of land in Northeast and Southwest Philadelphia, the City built new recreation facilities. Interestingly, while certainly affected by changes in demand as well as changes in the geographic distribution of the City's population, the Fire Department is the only City of Philadelphia service department that has decreased its facility level during the past decades. The Fire Department has remained remarkably constant in its per capita facility level while the other departments all now have more facilities per person than in 1952.

Table 3.2. Comparison of City of Philadelphia Facility Levels						
Department*	Facilities†			Number of People Served by Each Departmental Facility		
	1952	1998	Change	1952	1998	Change
Police	34	42	24%	60,930	35,191	-42%
Fire	88	66	-25%	23,541	22,394	-5%
Water	13	52	300%	159,354	28,423	-82%
Licenses & Inspection	1	3	200%	2,071,605	492,667	-76%
Streets	4	16	300%	517,901	92,375	-82%
Records	2	2	0%	1,035,803	739,001	-29%
Recreation	284	655	131%	7,294	2,256	-69%
Public Health	2	22	1000%	1,035,803	67,182	-94%
Human Services	2	4	100%	1,035,803	369,501	-64%
Public Property	N/A††	N/A††	N/A††	N/A††	N/A††	N/A††
Library	43	54	26%	48,177	27,370	-43%

Note: **Readers are urged to exercise caution and be mindful of the changing role of government and its agencies, contracting-out initiatives, and evolving agency missions when interpreting this table. For example, in 1952, the Department of Public Health operated Philadelphia General Hospital and the Philadelphia Hospital for Contagious Diseases, but now both hospitals are defunct and the City operates numerous health centers throughout the City in addition to laboratories and other facilities. Similarly, as residents populated Northeast Philadelphia in recent decades, many recreation facilities were constructed to meet new demands.**

1998 City of Philadelphia population is represented by the Census Bureau's estimate of Philadelphia Population (1,478,002) as of 7/1/96, 1952 (selected because it is the first year of City operation under the current City Charter) population is represented by the 1950 Census count (2,071,605).

*Departments include the ten service departments created by the 1951 Philadelphia Home Rule Charter plus the Free Library of Philadelphia.

†Facilities count is taken from City of Philadelphia Site/Facility Capital User Code List and Rental Property List, and from City Archive material.

††It is not possible to compare and propererly allocate Public Property facilities because numerous departments are housed in Public Property facilities and many facilities are utilized by non-City entities.

Comparing facility levels of agencies that should be similarly constituted in other cities (Police, Fire, and Library agencies) to agencies in a group of older, industrial cities, a group of significant cities near Philadelphia, and a group of newer, growing cities, evaluations of Philadelphia facility levels are mixed. Including Philadelphia, this group of ten cities represents seven of the ten largest American cities and all of Philadelphia's largest neighbor cities. Philadelphia police facilities serve fewer residents than seven of the nine cities—only Boston and San Diego police facilities serve fewer residents. Philadelphia serves fewer residents with each of its libraries than six of the nine comparison cities. Philadelphia serves more residents with each of its fire facilities than six of the nine comparison cities. (See Figure 3.4.)

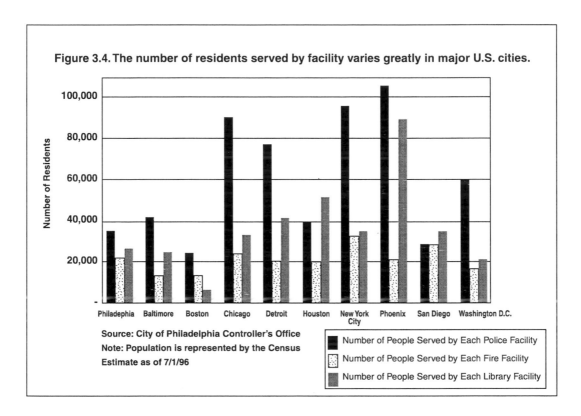

Figure 3.4. The number of residents served by facility varies greatly in major U.S. cities.

Source: City of Philadelphia Controller's Office
Note: Population is represented by the Census Estimate as of 7/1/96

■ Number of People Served by Each Police Facility
▢ Number of People Served by Each Fire Facility
▨ Number of People Served by Each Library Facility

At the most basic level, need should drive demand for facility construction. A new neighborhood may need a new library to meet demand for library services. A growing community may need a new fire station to meet growing demands for fire-protection services. Once built, however, facilities and other capital expenditures drive operating expenditures. For example, utility and maintenance costs incurred to operate a newly-constructed police station increase City expenditures. When considering facility levels, therefore, the City must examine operating costs in addition to the demand for services associated with the facilities. Philadelphia may even have fewer facilities than residents demand, but may have more facilities than it can afford to maintain, draining resources that could be better spent elsewhere. Similarly, Philadelphia may have more facilities than a comparable city, but if it can afford to maintain them, this increased number of facilities may be an amenity that improves service-delivery efforts and the quality of life in Philadelphia.

The Philadelphia City Planning Commission issued a report in the late 1980s that evaluated the City's recreational facilities and provided guidelines for recreation-related capital spending. The report found that as a whole, Philadelphia provided a quantity of active recreation facilities that compared favorably with any large American city, that Philadelphia developed recreational facilities beyond standards set by the City's 1960 Comprehensive Plan (a plan designed for a much larger population), and that when measured against industry benchmarks, Philadelphia almost always exceeded established standards. While the report noted that some City neighborhoods were served at a higher level than other areas of the City, its most significant finding was the tremendous need for facility maintenance and rehabilitation that threatened facility usefulness. For the future, the Planning Commission recommended timely maintenance and repair of neglected facilities, building new facilities as a last resort and only at new recreational sites, and closing facilities in need of a great deal of rehabilitation located in overserved areas in order to make increased personnel and capital resources available to under-served areas.

Looking to the future, the City must address its current stock of physical assets in a similar manner for opportunities to consolidate and deaccession properties. The City should re-examine the need for its current capital infrastructure to help lower the operating and capital costs that currently go toward maintaining the physical infrastructure of the City. Consolidating City facilities not used by the public—garages, warehouses, and lots—might not create much of a public outcry. However, closing facilities frequented by the citizenry will not be an easy task to accomplish and it certainly will not be popular. But, where necessary, it must occur. Certain neighborhoods may feel the pain of this action more acutely than others, but as a whole, the City is more viable with 70 well-maintained pools than 80 pools that the City must struggle to keep in good repair, or 2,000 miles of streets that are level and smooth instead of 2,400 miles that are uneven and crumbling.

Closing City facilities is not easy. Neighbors may oppose any closings that will limit their access to City services or that could be perceived as a move that would reduce the safety or desirability of their community. Community leaders will be sympathetic to neighbors' concerns and quick to use considerable influence and pressure to fight for their constituents' interests. The City's elected leadership will proceed very slowly when considering whether to close a City facility.

When making similar decisions about military bases in the late 1980s, the Department of Defense concluded that as a nation, the United States had more military bases than needed to support its nation's military forces. The United States Congress then provided the Department of Defense with the authority to conduct base realignment and closure (BRAC) reviews. An independent commission reviewed Department of Defense recommendations for base closure and realignment and submitted its final recommendations for approval by the President and the Congress. The BRAC commission was charged with judging the Department of Defense suggestions based on objective criteria and the President and Congress had the ability to either accept the BRAC recommendations in total or reject the entire package. In four rounds of cuts, the Department of Defense closed numerous facilities, generating billions of dollars of savings for the Department of Defense. While the Department of Defense asserts that many local communities have a stronger, more diverse economic base now than they did before BRAC, this effort was not painless—as a result of BRAC, the City of Philadelphia alone lost thousands of jobs and is still trying to encourage economic development at the sites of former military installations. Assuming the facilities truly did need to be closed, the BRAC process accomplished its mission, allowing the Department of Defense to close and realign bases in an effective manner, where the very idea of base closings was previously considered a political impossibility.

Closing facilities, however, is not the only way to rightsize the City. In planning new construction and renovations, the City can create facilities with multiple purposes. For example, the City recently completed a facility that houses the First Police District and the Fire Department's Engine Company 60/Ladder Company 19 in South Philadelphia. Combining police and fire facilities or health and recreation facilities in the future may allow the City to deaccession unneeded properties and consolidate the number of total buildings the City must maintain.

The City should create a BRAC-like commission, or endow the City Planning Commission with BRAC-like authority, to examine the City's inventory of physical assets to determine whether certain facilities could be deaccessioned and whether necessary new construction could consolidate two or more functions currently housed in separate facilities. The recommendations of this body could dictate the terms of the City's Capital Program (the City's six-year capital expenditure blueprint). By empowering such a commission to do its work, the elected leadership of the City could allow an expert panel to present a plan to rightsize the City in terms of its number of physical facilities, one that spreads the pain of any necessary cuts across the entire City. By using future savings to enhance service-delivery efforts and adequately maintain remaining facilities, the elected leadership of the City could ease the pain of this difficult, but necessary, action. The City can close facilities if it must. Consider that—given the opposition that can be expected from any effort to close a City Fire Station—the Fire Department is the only Philadelphia service department to reduce its facility level from 1952 to 1998.

The City should also expand the role of the City Planning Commission in creating the mandated Physical Development Plan beyond traditional physical planning to place greater emphasis on human services and economic development considerations. By expanding the City Planning Commission's responsibility for service-related planning, the City would enhance its ability to focus on the future and how future physical development plans would impact service delivery.

The City could also help rightsize its physical assets by working to reduce its maintenance obligation for streets and sidewalks. Streets and sidewalks link the City together, but at a cost. For example, in fiscal year 1999, Philadelphia plans to spend $13.1 million in capital dollars to reconstruct and resurface streets. Each year, the City routinely deaccessions certain streets, usually closing them to assemble a parcel for development or striking them from the City grid for some civic purpose. For each linear mile of street no longer maintained by the City government, the City saves more than $58,600 in foregone costs for each time the mile of street would have had to be resurfaced, and $1.2 million for each time the mile of street would have had to be reconstructed. The City would also be able to forego the costs associated with maintaining stop signs (about $22 per year) and traffic signals (about $282 per year) made unnecessary by the change. While there is a cost involved in terms of rerouting traffic or mass transportation routes, various rights-of-way questions, and issues involving utility infrastructure, removing streets from the City grid can benefit communities and institutions.

Locust Walk on the campus of the University of Pennsylvania is an example of such action where the City allowed the closing of Locust Street where it passed through the University campus. Now a leafy campus path instead of a busy city street, Locust Walk contributes to the vitality of campus life—and saves the City maintenance dollars each year. While implications for traffic patterns and transit routes would have to be considered, the City should encourage institutions and developers to take City streets "off the map" and proactively move to assemble large parcels of land for park use or future development by striking selected streets.

Some such moves will undoubtedly interfere with current commuting patterns, but could improve the vitality of university campuses and business districts or encourage development and improve neighborhood quality of life. No planner would have plunked Philadelphia's massive City Hall in the middle of the intersection of its two largest streets if minimizing traffic congestion were the only motivating factor. But for nearly 100 years, Broad and Market Street traffic has yielded each day to this edifice. Striking streets from the City grid may cause drivers to take alternate routes, but could help rightsize the City while providing life to institutions and communities across Philadelphia.

Rightsizing the City Government—Office Space

According to the City of Philadelphia Department of Public Property list of rental properties, as of October 1998, the City's annual total cost to rent office and storage space was more than $23 million. That figure includes annual rent, utility costs, and other costs associated with the various rental properties. Agency storage and office space is customarily allotted on a need basis and agencies generally receive the amount of office space requested. With the proper incentive, however, City agencies could look for ways to become more space efficient. In the future, the City should minimize the amount of office space it leases and maximize the benefit of space in City-owned buildings. To facilitate such a process, the City could allocate space costs as well as utility and telephone service costs on an agency-by-agency basis or create a charge-back system to account for agencies' use of space and utilities. City agencies would then have an incentive to reduce utility usage and office and storage space. Agencies could utilize electronic record storage technology to eliminate the need for storage space or reduce utility usage and then use proceeds from the savings to expand and improve service-delivery efforts.

If, in the future, plans for the Commonwealth of Pennsylvania to take over operations of the City's First Judicial District move forward, the City could be sure to craft a reasonable arrangement with the Commonwealth for its occupation of City-owned office space in the Criminal Justice Center, City Hall, and other buildings. Finally, as efforts to complete a renovation of City Hall are finalized, the City could plan to use unoccupied portions of City Hall to reduce the need for commercial office space rental and offsite storage. Surplus City Hall space could be provided on a fee basis to law- and media-related organizations that would benefit from establishing facilities in the heart of City government operations.

Rightsizing the City Government—Personnel

Examining data comparing Philadelphia today to Philadelphia of 1952 and to comparable cities, it is not clear that Philadelphia today employs an ideal number of workers. Demand for police services may account for the increase in the number of police personnel in Philadelphia since 1952, but while population has decreased by approximately 28 percent, library personnel has increased by 64 percent in real numbers. The number of Philadelphia residents served by employees of the Free Library of Philadelphia increased 57 percent. As was the case with facility levels, Fire Department staffing levels have remained remarkably consistent since 1952. (See Table 3.3.)

Table 3.3. Comparison of City of Philadelphia Staffing Levels						
Department*	Staffing†			Number of People Served by Each Departmental Employee		
	1952	1998	% Change	1952	1998	Change
Police	4,922	7,849	59%	421	188	-55%
Fire	3,187	2,489	-22%	650	594	-9%
Water	1,120	2,018	80%	1,850	732	-60%
Licenses & Inspection	231	460	99%	8,968	3,213	-64%
Streets	3,823	2,119	-45%	542	697	29%
Records	11	94	755%	188,328	15,723	-92%
Recreation	943	554	-41%	2,197	2,668	21%
Public Health	3,468	1,241	-64%	597	1,191	99%
Human Services	347	1,541	344%	5,970	959	-84%
Public Property	865	211	-76%	2,395	7,005	192%
Library	471	774	64%	4,398	1,910	-57%

Note: Readers are urged to exercise caution and be mindful of the changing role of government and its agencies, contracting-out initiatives, and evolving agency missions when interpreting this table. For example, the staff of the Records Department expanded when the Department was merged with the former Office of the Recorder of Deeds. Similarly, the staffing level of the Department of Public Health changed dramatically with the closings of Philadelphia General Hospital and the Philadelphia Hospital for Contagious Diseases.

1998 City of Philadelphia population is represented by the Census Bureau's estimate of Philadelphia Population (1,478,002) as of 7/1/96; 1952 (selected because it is the first year of City operation under the current City Charter) population is represented by the 1950 Census count (2,071,605).

*Departments include the ten service departments created by the 1951 Philadelphia Home Rule Charter plus the Free Library of Philadelphia.

†Staffing level is taken from the City of Philadelphia Personnel Inventory Report from March 20, 1998, and from City Archive material.

Comparing agencies in Philadelphia that should be similarly constituted in other cities, one finds that Philadelphia ranks in the middle of the pack when comparing the number of residents served by police, fire, and library employees. Each individual uniformed police officer in Philadelphia serves fewer residents than uniformed officers in five of the nine comparison cities. Each individual uniformed employee in the Philadelphia Fire Department serves fewer residents than uniformed personnel in five of the nine comparison cities. Each individual uniformed employee of the Free Library of Philadelphia serves fewer residents than library employees in four of the nine comparison cities. (See Figure 3.5.)

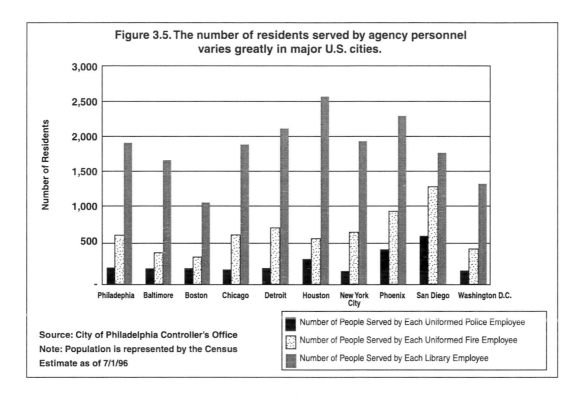

Figure 3.5. The number of residents served by agency personnel varies greatly in major U.S. cities.

Source: City of Philadelphia Controller's Office
Note: Population is represented by the Census Estimate as of 7/1/96

It is difficult to determine whether a higher staffing level is good or bad. While citizens may equate more personnel with better service, adding additional employees does not ensure improved service delivery. It is the accomplishments of the various agencies, not necessarily their staffing levels that truly matter. Agencies can and do provide more service and better service with the same number of employees or fewer. Technological improvements and productivity reforms can dramatically reduce the number of employees needed to perform the same work. With the right supports, agencies are able to improve performance and quality despite reducing personnel.

To confront rising costs associated with increasing population, the City of Virginia Beach, Virginia, converted waste-collection services from a manual operation utilizing a three-person crew to an automated waste-collection system requiring only one worker. According to City documents, including savings from a 29-percent reduction in personnel and a significant drop in Workers' Compensation claims, Virginia Beach is now saving approximately $4 million per year with automated waste collection while enjoying increased service quality. Working conditions for Waste Management Division workers have also improved dramatically. While this document does not specifically call for a reduction of personnel involved with Philadelphia waste-disposal operations, the Virginia Beach example demonstrates how technological improvements can increase productivity while reducing costs. The positive relationships between technological improvement, productivity, and cost are not likely to be reversed in the future.

In the end, reducing the cost of government may mean employing fewer people in government. Personnel costs, including benefits, comprise more than half of the City's 1999 operating budget expenditures. The City can certainly achieve savings in many areas, and there are certainly agencies that actually require more personnel to meet current demand for service, but rightsizing City government inevitably will mean addressing the size of the City workforce. The potential to reduce personnel could help generate savings to fund tax reductions or could be used to help fund expansion of the scope and quality of government services. Separation pains can be mitigated by reducing employment through attrition or through early retirement programs. Moving forward, however, Philadelphia must explore every productivity and competition initiative possible (examples will be discussed in future sections) to reduce the cost of governing the City.

Rightsizing the City Government—Pennsylvania Law and Census Undercounting

Commonwealth of Pennsylvania law considers Philadelphia a City of the First Class and a First Class County. Since Philadelphia is the only City of the First Class and the only First Class County in Pennsylvania, the laws written for Cities of the First Class and First Class Counties were all written to only apply in Philadelphia. In the future, despite its population loss, Philadelphia will still qualify as a City of the First Class because the 2000 Census will count over one million residents in the City. But because that Census count will likely count fewer than 1.5 million residents, Philadelphia will no longer qualify as a First Class County in Pennsylvania. To ensure that Philadelphia retains its current legal rights and privileges under Pennsylvania law, and that the laws written specifically for Philadelphia continue to apply to Philadelphia, the City should work with the Pennsylvania General Assembly to reduce the legally defined population necessary under the law to qualify as a First Class County.

Because current census methodology counts on respondent compliance, critics contend that it historically undercounts low-income and minority residents. Using new Census Bureau data, the National Committee for an Effective Congress determined that Philadelphia's three Congressional Districts suffered a net loss of 24,950 individuals due to the undercount. Since the year 2000 census count will be so important to Philadelphia in terms of apportioning future intergovernmental revenues and state and federal legislative representation, the City should initiate a grass-roots campaign to ensure that every Philadelphian is counted. The City could work with community leaders, block captains, political organizations, and employers to urge residents to fill out census forms. The City could create a "Stand Up and Be Counted" campaign to inform the public, target non-English-speaking communities with bilingual advertising, and use every agency that interacts with the public to encourage individuals to fill out census forms. Some estimate that the 1990 census did not count millions of city dwellers, resulting in lower levels of funding for cities. The census is not just about numbers, it is about dollars and political power. The City, and its elected representatives from every level of government, should commit to nothing less than a well-run political campaign to energize residents to be counted toward Philadelphia's future.

RECOMMENDATIONS FOR ACTION

The City should establish a rainy-day fund within the City's Charter-mandated budgetary structure.

Action Steps:

- Work with City Council to amend the Charter to create a rainy-day fund, or, as an alternative to Charter change, create a budget-stabilization account to achieve similar results short of restructuring the City's budgetary framework.

- Establish requirements for funds to be deposited in and disbursed from a rainy-day fund.

Fiscal Impact:

- Potential to improve budgetary structural balance, improve future credit ratings, and decrease future borrowing costs.

To ensure that it properly maintains its physical assets for the future, despite pressure to increase other government spending, the City should establish a separate fund within its annual budget dedicated to fund maintenance of physical assets.

Action Steps:

- Establish legal imperatives to annually create a maintenance plan for all City physical assets.

- Establish legal imperatives to set aside funds to maintain the City's physical assets before making other expenditures.

- Establish a City maintenance fund or individual maintenance funds in each City agency.

- Establish criteria to determine the amount of the maintenance fund—consider utilizing the City Planning Commission to determine the annual maintenance set-aside amount.

- Establish procedures to verify that maintenance funds are spent properly and effectively.

- Establish endowments for historic assets with contributions from foundations and individuals to aid maintenance efforts. Consider utilizing check-off boxes on City water bills to solicit funding.

- Consider establishing a not-for-profit organization to accept funds to establish maintenance endowments.

Fiscal Impact:

- Potential to increase future maintenance expenditures.

- Potential to reduce future utility costs, capital spending, and liability costs.

- Potential to improve budgetary structural balance, improve credit ratings, and decrease future borrowing costs.

The City should establish a review mechanism, through a process such as the one designed for Federal Base Military Base Closing and Realignment (BRAC), or by empowering the City Planning Commission with BRAC-like authority, to create a binding construction, maintenance, and deacquisition plan for the City's inventory of physical assets.

Action Steps:

- Authorize, by City Council ordinance, an expert panel, or the City Planning Commission, to review the City's collection of physical assets, make necessary deacquisition plans, and dictate the terms of the City's Capital Program.

- Appropriate necessary expenditures and implement recommendations.

Fiscal Impact:

- Potential one-time revenue from sale of deaccessioned property.

- Potential long-term savings from reduced asset maintenance, liability, and utility expenditures.

The City should expand the role of the City Planning Commission in creating the mandated Physical Development Plan of the City beyond traditional physical planning to place greater emphasis on human services and economic development considerations.

Action Steps:

- Expand the power of the City Planning Commission through Charter change or Executive Order.

- Create staff capacity at the City Planning Commission to accomplish expanded mission.

Fiscal Impact:

- Potential increase in annual City Planning Commission costs to perform new duties.

The City should build multi-use facilities when possible to reduce future asset maintenance costs.

Action Steps:

- Evaluate the possibility of building multi-use facilities for future City construction projects.

- Build multi-use facilities where possible.

Fiscal Impact:

- Potential long-term savings from reduced asset maintenance expenditures.

The City should work with local institutions, developers, and communities to remove streets from the City grid to enhance institutional campuses, assemble development parcels, and create neighborhood open space.

Action Steps:

- Survey communities, developers, and institutions to determine streets that could be candidates for removal from the City grid.

- Work with institutions, developers, and communities to settle ownership and rights-of-way issues.

- Work with transit agencies to mitigate traffic-flow problems.

- Authorize action by City Council ordinance.

Fiscal Impact:

- Potential long-term savings from reduced asset maintenance expenditures, $58,600 in foregone costs for each time a mile of street would have had to be

133

resurfaced and $1.2 million for each time a mile of street would have had to be reconstructed; $22 per year for each stop sign and $282 per year for each traffic signal in foregone costs for each stop sign and traffic signal made unnecessary by the change.

The City should minimize the amount of office space it leases and maximize the benefit of space in City-owned buildings.

Action Steps:

- Create incentives for City agencies to reduce office space and utility usage.

- Allocate office space and utility costs on an agency-by-agency basis to provide an incentive for agencies to achieve savings.

- Work with the Pennsylvania Judiciary to establish a reasonable arrangement for the use of City-owned office space if the Commonwealth of Pennsylvania assumes operation of City courts.

- Use the ongoing renovation of City Hall to open up new usable office and storage space.

Fiscal Impact:

- Potential long-term savings from reduced need for office space rental and reduced utility costs.

To ensure that Philadelphia retains its current legal rights and privileges under Pennsylvania law, the City should work with the Pennsylvania General Assembly to reduce the legally defined population necessary under the law to qualify as a First Class County.

Action Steps:

- Work to pass legislation altering the legal definition of a First Class County in the Pennsylvania General Assembly.

Fiscal Impact:

- Potential to maintain funding levels established by Pennsylvania Law.

The City should initiate a grass-roots campaign to ensure that every Philadelphian is counted in the year 2000 census.

Action Steps:

- Organize a grass-roots campaign to encourage Philadelphians to fill out census forms.

- Work with community leaders, block captains, political organizations, and employers to urge residents to fill out census forms.

- Create outreach efforts to low-income and non-English-speaking communities.

Fiscal Impact:

- Potential to increase intergovernmental revenues due to the City.

PRODUCING A SOUND TAXATION PLAN

Sound taxation policies designed to make Philadelphia competitive with rival jurisdictions must accompany efforts to place the City budget in structural balance. As Supreme Court Chief Justice John Marshall admonished almost two centuries ago, "the power to tax is the power to destroy." In Philadelphia, demand for tax revenues, and the system of taxation that determines what is actually taxed, places the City at a competitive disadvantage. In a very real sense, the power to tax is destroying the City's future.

Wharton Professor Robert Inman compared Philadelphia's tax burden as a percentage of income with suburban Philadelphia jurisdictions and found that in 1994–95, Philadelphia families annually paid 12.3 percent of their income in local taxes. By contrast the average suburban Philadelphia family paid approximately half that amount. But it is not just the amount of tax burden that makes the City less competitive. Its particular mix of taxes, specifically its over reliance on the Wage and Net Profits Tax, places Philadelphia at a competitive disadvantage, and serves to drive residents and employers from the City. Based on Inman's work, the City Controller's Office estimated the impact of recently enacted and proposed Wage and Net Profits Tax cuts on the number of City jobs and found that anticipated cuts should create more than 18,000 jobs.

The imperative to address the City's tax system is compounded by likely trends for Philadelphia's future. If, in the future, Philadelphia is to experience continued population loss, particularly among wage earners, Wage and Net Profits Tax collections will suffer. If growth in the non-profit sector outpaces growth in other sectors, Real Estate Tax collections may lag since such institutions pay no Real Estate Taxes. (See Appendix III for a discussion of taxation in Philadelphia.)

To create a system of taxation in Philadelphia that encourages growth and maximizes employment opportunities, the City can maximize the benefit of tax-reduction efforts. In addition, the City can make its tax policy consistent with other policies to maximize the impact of its tax effort.

Maximizing the Benefit of Tax-Reduction Efforts

In the midst of Philadelphia's 1990 fiscal crisis, City officials contemplated increasing taxes to fund the growing municipal deficit. However, research performed by Professor Inman showed that increasing taxes would have further eroded the City's tax base, potentially causing a loss of revenues. In more technical terms, Inman showed that the City was near the peak of its Wage and Net Profits Tax and Business Privilege Tax revenue hills. Sound managerial policies and state intervention allowed Philadelphia to emerge from fiscal crisis, but, despite the national economic expansion, the City continued to lose residents and jobs as its share of national product declined. In an effort to confront the high local tax burden that contributed to Philadelphia's decline, the City initiated a tax-reduction plan.

Combined with the modest effects of tax reduction, momentum generated by the robust national economy has finally generated some local growth. Yet, Philadelphia's growth still lags behind the nation as a whole, a signal that efforts to improve the City's competitive position and reduce the local tax burden must be increased.

By definition, any tax-relief plan that does not compromise services has a positive effect on the economy since it represents an injection of money into the local economy. However, tax reduction is most effective when it is steep enough to influence household and business location decisions.

Most of the literature on firm location decision shows that tax differentials traditionally were an insignificant variable in influencing business location to a particular region. However, once a business committed to a region, tax differentials played a vital role in the specific location decision. Household location decisions were quite similar, since people have a propensity to follow jobs. More contemporary literature depicts a stronger relationship between business location and inter-regional tax differentials. During the past two decades, profound technological changes have enhanced the geographic mobility of employers. This new flexibility has intensified inter-regional competition and placed a greater premium on savings from locating to lower-tax regions. Few businesses will move their entire operation in an effort to lower their tax liability. However, as noted by economist Robert Tannenwald, when locating a new plant or branch, tax differentials are likely to become a more important factor. It follows that inter-regional tax differentials do make a difference.

Although Philadelphia has reduced the tax liability on local business each year since fiscal year 1996, a recent study by Vertex, Inc. showed that Philadelphia is still the most taxing place to do business among 27 major American cities. Vertex looked at taxes on a hypothetical service company with 125 employees, $15 million in revenue, and $1.5 million in profits. That company would pay $1.39 million in federal, state, and local taxes in Philadelphia—16 percent above the median for all cities surveyed. (See Figure 3.6.)

Pennsylvania's two largest cities, Philadelphia and Pittsburgh, ranked as the cities with the highest and fourth highest tax liability in the Vertex study. While it is clear that state taxes contribute to Philadelphia's high overall business tax burden, the City's locally imposed business taxes are also much higher than other cities. Philadelphia must, therefore, continue its tax-reduction efforts to bring its tax liability into line with competitor cities. But taxes must be comparatively low, not objectively low, to encourage growth. If economic development efforts center on promoting industries that find a competitive advantage in being located in Philadelphia,

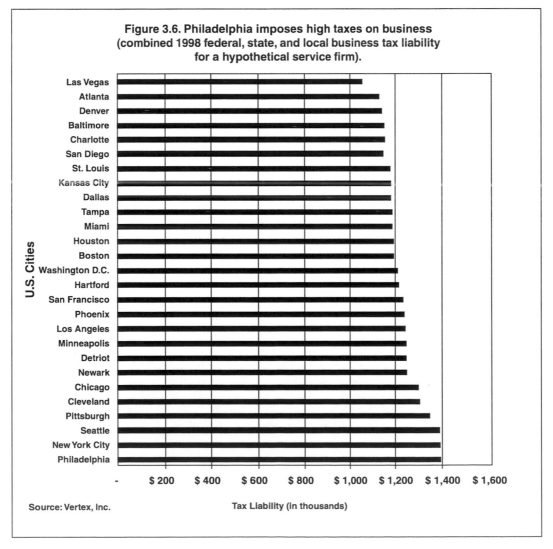

Figure 3.6. Philadelphia imposes high taxes on business (combined 1998 federal, state, and local business tax liability for a hypothetical service firm).

Source: Vertex, Inc.

the City may not have to reduce the tax burden to a level consistent with every other locality. Instead, the City must identify its true competitors, other localities that offer the same industries a competitive advantage, and then make sure the tax burden in Philadelphia (coupled with other costs of doing business) is comparatively lower.

For example, if one of the City's goals is to promote medical research and development activities, then local officials should adjust relevant taxes so that they fall in line with other medical research-intensive localities such as Boston, Baltimore, and Chicago. Likewise, in the case of efforts to promote hospitality and tourism, the City's taxes related to hotels, rental cars, and other tourist amenities should be comparable to other "destination cities." Thus, in trying to attract tourists and conventions, Philadelphia taxes are only "too high" if they are higher than taxes in rival cities. As indicated in Table 3.4, according to a 1997 National Conference of State

Table 3.4. Combined State and Local Hospitality-Related Taxes			
City	Accommodation Taxes	Restaurant Taxes	Rental Car Taxes
Baltimore, MD	State Tax 5% Local Lodging 7% **Total 12%**	State Tax 5% **Total 5%**	State Tax 11.5% **Total 11.5%**
Boston, MA	State Tax 5.7% Local Lodging 4% **Total 9.7%**	State Tax 5% **Total 5%**	State Tax 5% Plus Surcharge: $10.30 per rental **Total 5%** **Plus $10.30 per rental**
Chicago, IL	State Tax 6.2% Local Sales Tax 1.1% Metro Pier & Expo Tax 2.5% Chicago Occupancy Tax 3% Stadium Tax 2.1% **Total 14.9%**	State Tax 6.25% Local Sales Tax 1.5% Metro Pier & Expo Tax 1% Central Business Tax 1% **Total 9.75%**	State 5% Local Car Rental Tax 1% Metro Pier & Expo 6% Central Transaction Tax 6% Plus Surcharge: $2.75 per rental **Total 18%** **Plus $2.75 per rental**
Detroit, MI	State Tax 6% Local Lodging Assessment Tax 2% Stadium Tax 1% Convention Facility Tax* 6% **Total 15%**	State Tax 6% Local Tax 1% **Total 7%**	State Tax 6% Local Tax 2% **Total 8%**
Las Vegas, NV	Local Lodging Tax 6% Other Local Tax 2% **Total 8%**	State Sales Tax 7% **Total 7%**	State Tax 13% **Total†† 13%**
Los Angeles, CA	Local Lodging Tax 14% **Total 14%**	State Tax 6% Local Sales Tax 2.25% **Total 8.25%**	State Tax 6% Local Sales Tax 2.25% **Total 8.25%**
New York, NY	State Tax 4% Local Sales Tax 4.25% Local Lodging Tax 5% Plus $2 per day **Total 13.25%** **Plus $2 per day**	State Tax 4% Local Sales Tax 4.25% **Total 8.25%**	State Tax 9% Local Sales Tax 4.25% **Total 13.25%**
Philadelphia, PA	State Tax 6% Local Sales Tax 1% Local Lodging Tax 6% **Total 13%**	State Tax 6% Local Sales Tax 1% **Total† 7%**	State Tax 8% Plus $2 per day Local Sales Tax 1% **Total 9%** **Plus $2 per day**

Source: National Conference of State Legislatures
*Convention Facility Tax rate varies in Detroit from 3% to 6% according to room size.
†Philadelphia Restaurant Tax total does not include the local 10% Liquor Sales Tax.
††Las Vegas Car Rental Tax total does not include an additional off-airport car-rental fee of 8%.

Legislatures study of the combined state and local hospitality-related taxes, Philadelphia presents a competitive total hospitality-related tax burden.

Even if the City can attract and retain employers with a favorable tax structure, the City-imposed tax burden on families often encourages residents and potential residents to move outside the City limits. According to the Washington D.C. Department of Finance and Revenue, the local tax burden on a family of four with a $25,000 annual income in Philadelphia was $3,119 in 1996, higher than many notable American cities. (See Figure 3.7.)

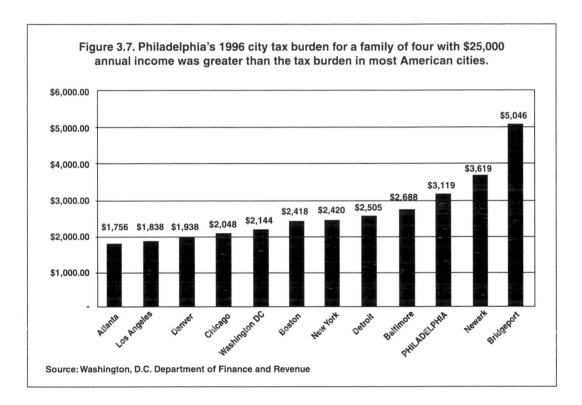

Figure 3.7. Philadelphia's 1996 city tax burden for a family of four with $25,000 annual income was greater than the tax burden in most American cities.

Source: Washington, D.C. Department of Finance and Revenue

Any effort to restructure Philadelphia's taxes must, therefore, encourage residents as well as employers to move to or remain in the City. If Philadelphia must continue to lower taxes, one must question how much the City can further lower its taxes without threatening service-delivery efforts.

HOW LOW CAN YOU GO?

To determine whether the City can further reduce taxes without compromising service in the process, the City Controller's Office used regression techniques to estimate the City's current position in relation to the peak of the revenue hill for the Wage and Net Profits Tax levied on Philadelphia workers and employers.[2] Figure 3.8

---

[2] The Controller's Office's methodology is very similar to Inman, 1992. However, the current analysis deviates in three noteworthy ways from Inman's methodology. First, the Controller's Office now has more information. Second, unlike Inman's use of only payroll employment, the Controller's Office used total wage and salary disbursements as the measure of the Wage and Net Profits Tax base. Third, the Controller's Office altered the model specification by adding the national unemployment rate to the list of independent variables. In equation form, the model was specified as follows: $base_t = B_0 + B_1 wtax_t + B_2 urate_t$, where base represents annual City wage and salary disbursements, adjusted for inflation, from time t=1969–97, $wtax_t$ and $urate_t$ represents the annual City Wage and Net Profits Tax rate and average U.S. unemployment rate, respectively over the same period.

shows that the relationship between tax rates and revenues generated from the various taxes is a nonlinear one which implies that, moving from left to right, higher and higher tax rates earn proportionately less and less revenue approaching the peak of the hill (Point B). Moving to the right of the peak, raising taxes actually produces a net loss in revenues. Point A on the graph below represents the amount of revenue (in real terms) that would be generated from levying the 1997 effective tax rate. All points on the solid-circle line are evaluated in consideration of the current stage of the business cycle, as measured by the 1997 national unemployment rate. Thus, changes in economic activity are represented by a shift in the line. (See Figure 3.8.)

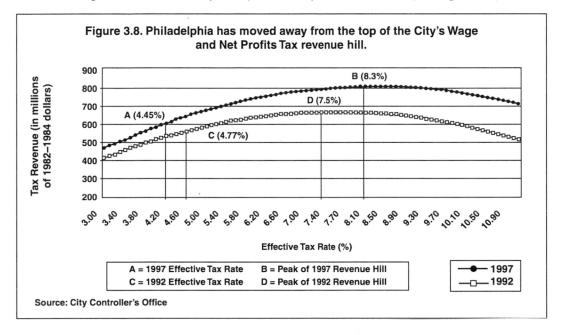

Figure 3.8. Philadelphia has moved away from the top of the City's Wage and Net Profits Tax revenue hill.

| A = 1997 Effective Tax Rate | B = Peak of 1997 Revenue Hill |
| C = 1992 Effective Tax Rate | D = Peak of 1992 Revenue Hill |

Source: City Controller's Office

For example, Points C and D on the outline-square line represent the actual and peak 1992 Wage and Net Profits Tax rates levied on Philadelphia workers, respectively, evaluated at the 1992 national rate of unemployment. Clearly, the data show that because of improvement in the local economy, brought on by a robust national economic performance and tax rate reduction, the City has moved further away from the peak of the revenue hill since 1992.

From the estimates the Controller's Office derived the relationship between economic activity, as measured by the national unemployment rate, and the effective tax rates. The line in Figure 3.9 represents the *locus* of unemployment rates, a proxy for the national business cycle, and effective Wage and Net Profits Tax rates that keep revenues constant.

For the purposes of analysis, this curve is divided into three sections. Section I depicts a situation in which the economy is close to the peak of the business cycle (unemployment is low), yet far away from the peak of the revenue hill. In this section the slope is very steep. Because the economy is strong, tax reduction must also be steep to create a market response that will maintain revenue levels.

This contrasts with the situation in Section II, in which the economy is at or near the trough of the business cycle (unemployment is high) and the peak of the revenue hill. In this case, because the economy is weak, any tax reduction will help stimulate growth. Thus, tax reduction in its own right is a very effective means of generating revenues. In Section III, beyond the apex of the revenue hill, the tax burden has become so intrusive that, regardless of the stage of the business cycle, tax reduction is required to maintain revenues.

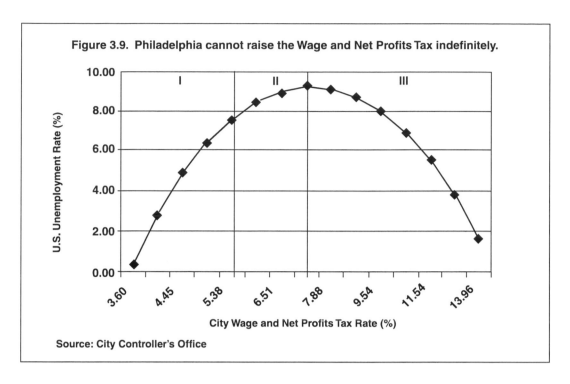

Figure 3.9. Philadelphia cannot raise the Wage and Net Profits Tax indefinitely.

Source: City Controller's Office

The implications of the nonlinear relationship between tax rates and general economic conditions are profound. In 1992, when the national economy was just beginning to pick up momentum, any revenue lost from tax reduction could easily have been offset by the robust growth in the national economy. However, the economy is currently near the peak of the business cycle, as indicated by the historically low national unemployment rate of 4.6 percent in October 1998. Any future reduction of taxes must, therefore, be met by significant improvement in the national economy to maintain constant revenues—something that is highly unlikely given the tightness of current market conditions. It follows that if the City reduces taxes to improve its competitive position—which it clearly must do to promote certain industries—foregone revenues must be balanced with commensurate productivity gains and/or other efforts to grow the local economy.

To this point, the argument that steeper tax reductions are required to increase the City's competitiveness and grow the local economy assumed a fixed level of governmental obligations. However, there clearly is a relationship between the growth in the City economy and the need to fund services. If tax reduction and other economic development efforts are successful at growing the economy, by definition there will be less need to subsidize business in an effort to compensate for the burden of the tax. Similarly, there is a close association between City spending and economic performance in other areas as well. For example, there is a positive relationship between the City's Fire Department expenditures and the local unemployment rate between fiscal years 1980 and 1997.[3] This positive relationship is also consistent with the findings of a recent Controller's Office audit of the City's Fire Department, which presented evidence showing that there was a high correlation between the incidence of fire emergencies and the economic state of City neighborhoods. Economic growth, therefore, should reduce service costs to the City.

---

[3] The correlation coefficient between the two variables was +0.5. As a general rule, coefficients between 0.3 and 0.6 indicate at least moderate statistical significance.

The inverse relationship between City agency expenditures and the City's economic performance shows that City expenditures are directly related to the state of the economy and should offer some evidence that steeper tax reduction, combined with other policies to promote growth, may be less risky than budget estimates predict. Indeed, if City officials do not reduce taxes to be more in line with competing regions, the City will necessarily forego a substantial amount of revenue and incur additional costs associated with a weaker local economy.

It is clear that, as a city, Philadelphia taxes its businesses and residents too much. The City, therefore, must commit to an effort to analyze its tax structure to determine which taxes should be lowered, and which could be raised, to improve Philadelphia's competitiveness. To maximize the benefit of tax-reduction efforts, the City should review its taxes and tax rates in comparison with rival cities, and then reduce taxes accordingly to retain and attract employers and residents. For example, the City's Wage and Net Profits Tax ranked as the most onerous of major City taxes according to respondents to the Controller's Office survey of Philadelphia employers. The Business Privilege Tax ranked a close second.[4] A discussion in the following section presents analysis suggesting tax-reduction policies to maximize employment growth. Because the City cannot count on continued national prosperity to maintain revenues, the City must fund such tax-reduction efforts by achieving savings in governmental operations. Many initiatives to reduce the cost of government are described in this chapter. As noted above, decreasing the City's tax burden should result in additional savings from a reduced need to subsidize business and a reduced need to meet social costs.

Making Tax Policy Consistent with Other City Policy

In recent years, the City has reduced its Wage and Net Profits Tax and Business Privilege Tax. If it must reduce taxes further to be competitive, the City must reduce the right taxes, given its economic development policy objective of maximizing employment opportunity in Philadelphia.

As part of the most recent City Controller's Survey of Business Establishments, business owners rated the City's tax structure as excellent, good, fair, or poor. Not surprisingly, over 75 percent of the respondents gave it a poor or fair rating. The disdain for the City's tax structure was also evident in the responses to another tax-related question. Asked to rank various policies in terms of how beneficial they would be to their individual business, respondents overwhelmingly indicated that tax reduction would provide the greatest benefit—in lieu of improving labor quality, reducing crime, improving quality of sidewalks and roadways, and improving the public school system. When asked which, among the five major City taxes, if reduced, would be the most beneficial to their individual business, respondents indicated that the Wage and Net Profits Tax and the Business Privilege Tax ranked as the most onerous.[5] This should be some indication that the current City administration has been reducing the right taxes.

Using the REMI model, the City Controller's Office ran through three separate simulation exercises to compare the taxes in terms of the respective employment effects stemming from a dollar of reduction in tax liability.

Simulation #1: What is the effect on aggregate City employment through 2010 from a permanent reduction of $50 million in the gross receipts portion (the portion of the Business Privilege Tax levied on gross receipts of businesses carrying on or exercising for profit any trade, business, profession, vocation, or commercial activity) of the City's Business Privilege Tax in 1999? (See Table 3.5 and Figure 3.10.)

The reduction in the Business Privilege Tax liability was treated simply as a reduction in the cost of doing business in the City of Philadelphia. The $50 million was distributed among the

---

[4] Office of the City Controller, City of Philadelphia, Pennsylvania. "Controller's Mid-Year Economic Survey 1998–1999." December, 1998.

[5] Ibid.

industries in proportion to their respective level of taxable gross receipts, as per the 1997 Business Privilege Tax return files.

The vehicle by which a reduction in the cost of doing business influences employment depends largely upon how competitive the industry is. Due to competitive pressures, industries that serve primarily export demand (have a positive net export ratio) are in no position to influence the price of their product. These industries are "price takers." Thus, the reduction in costs serves to raise profitability, which encourages new suppliers to enter the Philadelphia market.

By contrast, industries that primarily serve local demand have greater control over their product prices. Thus, cost reduction is quickly born out in lower prices as an effort to gain local market share. In turn, price reduction raises the demand for products or services. Employment is then increased in an effort to fill new orders.

It should not be surprising that the industries affected most by the reduction are those that have a greater sales presence in the City of Philadelphia. In particular, restaurant and retail establishments, legal, engineering, and management services, and business services are poised to generate the greatest number of jobs from the reduction. In the aggregate, the Controller's

Table 3.5. Employment Effects of a $50 Million Tax Reduction in 1999 by Major Tax Type and Industry					
Wage And Net Profits Tax Reduction		**Business Privilege Tax (Gross Receipts) Reduction**		**Business Privilege Tax (Net Income) Reduction**	
Industry	Predicted City Employment Growth by 2010	**Industry**	Predicted City Employment Growth by 2010	**Industry**	Predicted City Employment Growth by 2010
Restaurant/Retail Trade	109	Restaurant/Retail Trade	214	Legal, Eng., & Mgt. Services	176
Non-Profit	68	Legal, Eng., & Mgt. Services	133	Restaurant/Retail Trade	160
Medical Services	62	Business Services	120	Medical Services	114
Educational Services	52	Eating/Drinking Places	90	Eating/Drinking Places	80
Legal, Eng., & Mgt. Services	50	Non-Profit	86	Business Services	75
Other	449	Other	840	Other	652
Total	**790**	**Total**	**1,483**	**Total**	**1,257**
Source: REMI					

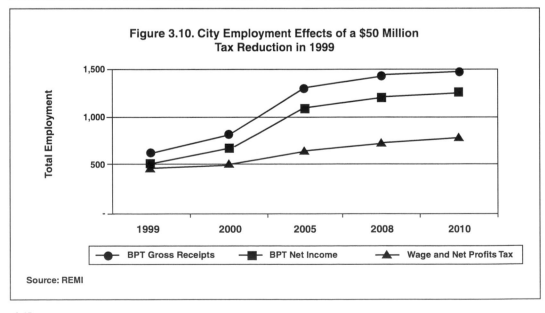

Figure 3.10. City Employment Effects of a $50 Million Tax Reduction in 1999

Source: REMI

Office estimates that over 1,483 jobs will be generated across all City industries by 2010 from a $50 million reduction in the Gross Receipts portion of the Business Privilege Tax.

Simulation #2: *What is the effect on aggregate City employment through 2010 from a permanent reduction of $50 million in the net income portion (the portion of the Business Privilege Tax levied on the net income of businesses carrying on or exercising for profit any trade, business, profession, vocation, or commercial activity) of the City's Business Privilege Tax in 1999? (See Table 3.5 and Figure 3.10.)*

The dynamic generating employment in this simulation is identical to the case of reduction in the Gross Receipts portion of the Business Privilege Tax, with one notable exception. In this case, the $50 million reduction in the cost of doing business in the City of Philadelphia is distributed in conformity with the dispersion of net income held across City industries, as per the 1997 Business Privilege Tax return files.

In this simulation exercise, the Controller's Office estimated that legal, engineering, and management services, restaurant and retail establishments, and medical services would generate the greatest amount of employment opportunities for the City by 2010. The aggregate effect from a $50 million reduction in the Net Income portion of the Business Privilege Tax by 2010 is a net addition of 1,257 jobs compared to a baseline forecast.

Simulation #3: *What is the effect on aggregate City employment through 2010 from a permanent reduction of $50 million in the resident and nonresident City Wage and Net Profits Tax in 1999? (See Table 3.5 and Figure 3.10.)*

The direct impact from a Wage and Net Profits Tax reduction is initiated on both the supply and demand sides of the labor market. On the supply side, there is an increase in the real after-tax wages, resulting in additional spending and labor force participation in the City labor market. Since the City Wage and Net Profits Tax is levied on both residents and nonresidents, the $50 million in reduced taxes is apportioned to residents and non-residents based on their share of the tax base—60 percent Philadelphia residents and 40 percent non-residents.

The reduction will also benefit the demand side of the market. Since the Wage and Net Profits Tax is capitalized into the employers' wage offering, a reduction in the tax also serves to reduce the cost of doing business in the City. The amount of cost reduction depends on the degree of capitalization. Using econometric techniques, the Controller's Office identified industries that have historically been most affected by changes in the tax—industries that have a highly elastic labor demand curve with respect to changes in the tax.[6] The elasticity estimates are used in the simulation exercise. Specifically, a portion of the $50 million reduction in the Wage and Net Profits Tax is assumed to accrue to business by an amount equivalent to the elastic industry's share of all wage and salary disbursements in the City.

Since much of the direct savings to taxpayers flows to non-City residents, it should not be surprising that a reduction in the Wage and Net Profits Tax offers less benefit to the City, in terms of employment growth, relative to a commensurate reduction in the Business Privilege Tax. By 2010, a $50 million reduction in the City's Wage and Net Profits Tax will produce a net gain of 790 jobs in the City of Philadelphia. The simulation exercise shows that the Philadelphia suburbs will gain nearly 540 jobs from a tax cut originating in the City. A reduction in the Wage and Net Profits Tax will clearly have a greater impact on the City economy if the reduction could be constrained to the

---

[6] The Controller's Office computed elasticity measures for every two-digit industry in the City of Philadelphia through estimation of the following regression equation: $(PHBASE_{it}/USBASE_{it})=B_0+B_1TIME_t+B_2ETAX_t$, where $PHBASE_{it}$ represents annual average wage and salary disbursements for the City of Philadelphia for industry i at time t, $USBASE_{it}$ represents annual average wage and salary disbursements for the U.S. as a whole for industry i at time t. The Controller's Office expresses the City's tax base in relation to the U.S. base to properly control for each industry's unique sensitivity to structural change and national business cycle. $TIME_t$ represents a time series dummy, which accounts for long-term structural changes in the base over time, and $ETAX_t$ represents the effective Wage and Net Profits Tax rate at time t.

resident portion of the tax.[7] In this case, roughly 1,100 City jobs would be generated from a $50 million reduction in the resident portion of the City's Wage and Net Profits Tax.

It should be noted that these estimates may be biased downward to the extent that they did not properly capture the degree to which the Wage and Net Profits Tax is capitalized into wages. When labor has more bargaining power, the tax is more likely to be capitalized into wages. Because there is currently a shortage of skilled labor nationally, wages are already inflated. Reducing the Wage and Net Profits Tax could help promote employers seeking to fill such high-skill jobs.

Given that tax relief works directly through disposable income, the simulation exercise further shows that most employment activity will be concentrated in local industries with high concentrations of local consumption, restaurant and retail, legal, engineering, and management services, and educational services. A summary of the simulation results is displayed in Table 3.5 and Figure 3.10.

The data clearly show that a dollar of tax reduction affecting the Business Privilege Tax generates larger employment effects compared to a similar reduction in the Wage and Net Profits Tax. In particular, reducing the gross receipts portion of the tax would offer the greatest benefit. Although reducing the net income portion of the tax would offer a slightly lower return from a dollar of tax reduction, it would generate significant growth in the for-profit sectors and would be consistent with a strategy of targeting for-profit industries for economic development.

To maximize the impact of tax-reduction efforts, in terms of job growth, the City should continue to reduce the gross receipts portion of the City's Business Privilege Tax. A reduction of the gross receipts portion of the Business Privilege Tax offers a greater return to the City from a dollar of tax reduction compared to the net income portion of the Business Privilege Tax or the Wage and Net Profits Tax. While a reduction of the net income portion of the Business Privilege Tax would offer less of a return, such an action is consistent with other economic development efforts to promote growth in the for-profit sectors of the economy. (See discussion on Economic Development in chapter 4.) Reductions in the Wage and Net Profits Tax or other City tax will increase residents' disposable income but will stimulate job growth to a lesser extent.

RECOMMENDATIONS FOR ACTION

To maximize the benefit of tax-reduction efforts, the City should review its taxes and tax rates in comparison with rival cities and then reduce taxes accordingly to retain and attract employers and residents. This review should focus on industries for which the City presents a competitive advantage, but for the onerous tax burden.

Action Steps:

- Conduct independent comparison analysis of City taxes compared with specific taxes and tax rates in rival cities.

- Establish required changes in the current tax structure to enable the City to take advantage of its competitive advantages.

- Work with City Council to pass tax-reduction legislation.

Fiscal Impact:

- Potential to reduce City tax revenues by an amount that must be met with reduced governmental expenditures.

---

[7] The current rate of taxation for the Wage and Net Profits Tax is 4.6869 percent of wages, earnings, and net profits of Philadelphia residents and 4.075 percent of wages, earnings, and net profits of non-residents. By law, the non-resident rate is capped at 4.3125 or 75 perecent of the resident rate, whichever is higher. However, as part of future tax-reduction efforts, the City may reduce the Wage and Net Profits Tax on residents—without reducing the tax on non-residents.

- Potential to increase City tax revenues in areas where the City's tax burden is comparatively low to offset tax reductions.

- Potential to expand the City's tax base in the long term.

To maximize the impact of tax-reduction efforts, in terms of City job growth, the City should place a priority on reducing the City's Business Privilege Tax rates.

Action Steps:

- Work with City Council to pass tax-reduction legislation.

Fiscal Impact:

- Potential to reduce City tax revenues by an amount that must be met with reduced governmental expenditures.

- Potential to expand the City's tax base in the long term.

INCREASING COLLECTIONS TO HOLD DOWN TAX INCREASES

Most Philadelphia residents and employers pay their taxes. While such payments may be accompanied by considerable grumbling about the level of taxes in Philadelphia, the vast majority of Philadelphians pay their fair share. Too many, however, do not; requiring the City to demand more taxes than necessary from those who do pay. To decrease pressure on the City to raise taxes in the future, 21st-century Philadelphia must improve the way it collects taxes.

Tax avoiders and evaders generally do not pay taxes for one of two reasons: they cannot afford to pay taxes or they can afford to not pay taxes. While some individuals find that their tax burden outweighs their ability to pay, others are able to rationalize that the City's collection efforts are lax enough to provide an incentive to avoid paying taxes. In 1997, for example, the City increased the interest rate applied to delinquent business and wage taxes from 6 percent to 12 percent annually, and increased the interest on property taxes from 6 percent to 9 percent annually. Until this change, delinquent taxpayers effectively had an incentive to avoid paying taxes, place the avoided tax payments into an investment vehicle, earn a rate of return greater than the percentage of the City's penalty, and then wait for the City's collection efforts to catch up with them. By the time the City took action, many avoiders were able to make a handsome profit.

Another example of the collection problem was illustrated by the City's 1997 tax lien sale. In 1997, the City and the School District used over $100 million of delinquent Real Estate Tax liens to securitize a bond issue. The liens were sold to a governmental authority that employed collection agents to collect the liens to pay off the bonds. Faced with the real consequence of collection agents knocking on their doors looking for back taxes, many delinquent taxpayers suddenly found the ability to pay. In the weeks preceding the lien sale, more than three times the typical number of taxpayers entered into payment agreements with the City to avoid having their property included in the sale. When faced with real consequences, many avoiders decide that they no longer can afford to not pay taxes. By collecting more from those who previously decided they could afford to not pay taxes, the City may be able to lower taxes enough to enable others to make a contribution who currently cannot afford to pay taxes. Similarly, by increasing collections from tax avoiders and tax evaders, the City would send the message to the citizenry that taxes are required from all Philadelphians. This message should make paying taxes more palatable in general in a city where many believe that favored individuals and businesses do not pay their fair share.

To improve collections, the City can refrain from subsidizing residents and businesses through government inaction. The City can develop more customer-friendly collections efforts and use technology to improve collections. Finally, the City can improve intergovernmental cooperation to enhance its ability to collect taxes and enforce collections.

Collecting Revenue and Avoiding Subsidization

Government often provides subsidies to encourage or enable certain actions. In Philadelphia, however, City government often subsidizes individuals and companies through inaction. If the City wishes to subsidize individuals or organizations, the subsidy should be based on need or designed to encourage certain actions. Lax tax collection subsidizes those who choose not to pay at the expense of those who do pay.

In general, the City is encouraged to take distinct action to ensure that any government subsidies are offered through government action—not through government inaction. If taxes are too high, taxes should be cut across the board. Tacitly allowing some individuals to not pay taxes is no solution. If some Philadelphians need assistance paying utility bills, government can provide grants or loans. Allowing some individuals to not pay utility bills is not an answer.

MAKING COLLECTIONS MAKE SENSE

Two examples illustrate the folly of subsidization through governmental inaction. In the first example, non-collection of taxes favors certain businesses at the expense of competitors, while in the second, a legislated preference reduces utility rates for some while grant programs for the truly needy cannot meet demand. In both examples, the City loses revenue.

Maximize Liquor Sales Tax collections: A recent City Controller's Office Audit found that the City of Philadelphia does not collect the total Liquor Sales Tax due the School District. According to the Pennsylvania Liquor Control Board, Philadelphia has 2,112 establishments subject to the 10-percent tax on the sale of liquor, malt, and brewed beverages, but only 1,430 establishments (about two-thirds) are currently filing tax returns. In November 1996, the Revenue Department referred approximately 800 non-filer cases to the City's Law Department for enforcement action. As of April 1998, the Law Department collected from approximately 100 of these non-filers an average of $3,000 each. These results suggest that the School District could be due an additional $2.1 million in uncollected Liquor Sales Tax.

Consider a means test for the senior citizen discount for gas service: The City-owned gas utility grants all senior citizens a 20-percent discount on their utility bills regardless of need. In 1982, the Philadelphia Water Department changed its age-based senior citizen discount to a means-tested discount. At that time, the Water Department provided a senior citizen discount to more than 92,000 households. Today, the Department provides a means-tested discount (household earnings cannot exceed $20,900 to qualify) to approximately 50,000 households of all ages. The Philadelphia Gas Works (PGW) currently offers a non-means-tested senior citizen discount to approximately 102,000 households. If PGW applied a means test for gas bills similar to the one applied by the Water Department for water bills, the utility could generate revenue from at least 50,000 additional households to help lower gas rates across the board, or help fund assistance efforts for those who cannot afford utility service. It is important to note that a higher income limit could be used or the income limit could be phased in over time to minimize any impact on middle-income seniors. Because a large percentage of seniors live on fixed income, many would qualify for a means-tested discount. New revenues would only be generated from the City's more prosperous seniors.

Customer-Friendly Collections

Not many Philadelphians enjoy paying taxes. There is no reason to compound that natural animosity by complicating the tax-paying process. The City should make collections more taxpayer-focused to increase customer service and the efficiency of collection efforts.

Because the City has a variety of taxes, it is possible for an individual to have multiple tax liabilities and filing requirements. The City's Department of Revenue currently sends taxpayers separate returns and separate bills for each tax, and taxpayers make separate payment agreements to discharge delinquency for each tax. This tax-focused administration is costly, inefficient, and less convenient for the taxpayer. Under a tax-focused system, an individual may have a payment agreement for one tax but not others, multiple mailings to the same individual are common, and duplicative agency effort is required to administer dealings with the same person. Since 1994, the City's Revenue Department has invested more than $9.3 million in computer systems that have improved the Department's ability to coordinate billing and enforcement of City taxes. Additional systemic improvements are planned for coming years to move to a more taxpayer-focused system of administration to simplify mailings and allow the City to forge one payment agreement for all delinquent balances.

Beyond making collections more taxpayer-based, the City can improve taxpayers' ease of payment by using new technology. With the use of telephone and on-line filing, the City can make paying taxes more customer-friendly while making collections more certain. The Commonwealth of Massachusetts installed a telephone-filing system to enable taxpayers to file their returns from their homes or offices. As documented in the Controller's Office 1998 "Department of Revenue Tax Enforcement Performance Audit," through paper savings and improved efficiency, Massachusetts was able to make back the $700,000 start-up cost and begin to generate savings after only two years of telephone filing. Commonwealth of Pennsylvania residents filed taxes by phone for the first time in 1998. The "TeleFile" system not only improves the ease of paying taxes—the 15-minute process prompts users to answer questions while a computer handles the major calculations and reports how much residents owe—but also helps reduce the need to store paper returns, saving the Pennsylvania Department of Revenue processing and supply expenses. Similarly, the Pennsylvania Tax Information Data Exchange System was developed by the Department of Revenue to allow businesses to use Electronic Data Interchange and Electronic Funds Transfers to pay taxes. By downloading free filing software from the Department's Internet home page, businesses can save time and effort while the Department of Revenue increases the certainty and efficiency of collection efforts.

Certain Philadelphia taxes such as the Business Privilege Tax require information that may be too complex to submit effectively over the phone. However, because of the ease with which other taxes can be collected using communications technology, the City could consider abandoning such an intricate tax structure in favor of a less-complicated tax, which would be easier for the government to collect—and easier for citizens to understand.

Other jurisdictions have used credit-card technology to make interactions with governmental collections agencies more user-friendly. Approximately 10 percent of county taxpayers in Arlington County, Virginia, used credit cards to pay their taxes in 1997.[8] In Pennsylvania, the Pittsburgh-area municipality of Cranberry Township accepts charge payments for taxes and other fees. Other jurisdictions are following suit as part of a project promoted by the Pennsylvania Local Government Investment Trust. The Philadelphia-area jurisdictions of Upper Dublin and Warminster Townships allow residents to use credit cards to pay for park-and-recreation fees such as public golf course greens fees.[9] The Internal Revenue Service announced that, beginning in 1999, taxpayers will be able to use credit cards to pay their federal taxes. Philadelphia officials concluded that the cost of using credit cards as part of collection efforts outweighed potential

---

[8] Anderson, Curt. "New for '99: Some can tell the taxman to charge it," *Philadelphia Inquirer*, August 21, 1998. p C1.

[9] Murawski, John. "Citizens can swipe away taxes, fees," *Philadelphia Inquirer*, August 8, 1997. p B1.

benefits. In the future, demand from the citizenry to increase the ease with which they pay City taxes and fees could cause officials to reconsider that analysis.

The City should invest in the technology necessary to improve the ease with which taxpayers pay their obligations. The City could use on-line technology and telecommunications technology to make paying taxes more customer-friendly while making collections more certain. The City could save costs by creating the systems necessary to allow residents and businesses to conduct business with government with credit and debit cards. Finally, the City could expand efforts to offer citizens and businesses the option to file tax returns by phone or on-line through the use of electronic data interchanges and electronic funds transfers.

Improving Intergovernmental Cooperation for Improved Collections

Since 1990, when the City of Philadelphia Revenue Department entered into a data-sharing program with the Internal Revenue Service, the City has added nearly 16,000 new accounts and $15.9 million in assessments. Inter-jurisdictional cooperation can be very effective in tax enforcement, but historically, there has been limited cooperation between the City and the Commonwealth of Pennsylvania. As of the publication of the City Controller's Office "Tax Enforcement Performance Audit" in June 1998, neither the City nor the Commonwealth had designated a tax-enforcement liaison, and the Commonwealth was not attending periodic tax/economic meetings between the City and federal government even though they were invited. Poor cooperation can lead to lost revenue.

The City should pursue the creation of a formal agreement to share tax information to improve cooperation between the City and the Commonwealth. To complement such an effort, the City could establish a liaison with state collections agencies to increase cooperation in the area of tax enforcement. The City should also pursue additional opportunities to match City tax files to state and federal income tax data (which it already has) to enhance collections. To enhance such matches, the City could replace internal tax identification numbers with the federal employer identification number issued by the IRS. The City could further integrate its tax databases to allow for more matching to increase collections. The City could then use its enhanced matching ability to make sure that businesses seeking City tax abatements, City economic development funding, or special legislation from City Council pay back taxes before receiving governmental assistance.

RECOMMENDATIONS FOR ACTION

The City should make collections more taxpayer-focused to increase customer service and the efficiency of collection efforts.

Action Steps:

- Continue efforts to re-engineer tax systems to permit the City to simplify mailings and to forge one payment agreement for all delinquent taxes.

- Use any future efforts to address Philadelphia's menu of taxes as a way to simplify filing and collection procedures.

- Consider redesigning current taxes and design future taxes in ways that foster on-line filing of tax returns.

Fiscal Impact:

- Potential to reduce costs and generate additional tax revenue.

The City should invest in the technology necessary to improve the ease with which taxpayers pay their obligations.

Action Steps:

- Investigate the potential uses for telecommunications and Internet technology in revenue collections efforts.

- Explore efforts to allow residents and businesses to conduct business with government with credit and debit cards.

- Expand efforts to offer citizens and businesses the option to file tax returns by phone or on-line through the use electronic data interchanges and electronic funds transfers.

- Work with City Council to pass legislation to enable the City to accept "personal identification" numbers or "electronic" signatures so that the City can accept tax returns over the phone or via the Internet.

- Implement necessary systems to complement new technology.

Fiscal Impact:

- Potential short-term cost to fund acquisition of new technology.

- Potential to decrease transaction and other administrative costs.

- Potential to increase collections.

To improve cooperation between the City and the Commonwealth of Pennsylvania, the City should pursue the creation of a formal agreement to share tax information.

Action Steps:

- Work with Commonwealth of Pennsylvania officials to create a formal agreement to share tax information.

Fiscal Impact:

- Potential to increase City tax revenue.

The City should pursue additional opportunities to match City tax files to state and federal income tax data to enhance collections.

Action Steps:

- Acquire Commonwealth of Pennsylvania tax data.

- Utilize state and federal tax data in matches with City tax filers.

Fiscal Impact:

- Potential to increase City tax revenues.

REDUCING THE COST OF GOVERNMENT—NON-PERSONNEL RELATED

The challenges facing the City of Philadelphia—both today and in the future—are daunting. The demands placed on government are infinite and the needs of the citizenry are limitless. This document calls for better performance from government that could create savings, but many improvements will require increased governmental expenditures. It is incumbent on the City's governmental leadership, therefore, to reduce the cost of providing government services in an effort to better meet the demands of Philadelphia residents, visitors, and employers.

As demonstrated above, Philadelphia government spending has increased in nominal terms, in real terms, and per capita in past decades. While mandates from other levels of government and new demands from citizens and employers have undeniably placed more pressure on government to do more, because the level of support the City receives from other governments has decreased and the City's tax base has declined, the City is challenged to do more with less. There are many opportunities for the City to reduce the cost of government, and even though some savings may only be realized after an initial investment, such opportunities must be pursued if the City is to be able to meet the challenges of the next century.

To reduce the cost of government, the City can improve construction procedures to increase the buying power of City capital dollars and it can spend less to procure goods and services. Additionally, the City can invest in technology to reduce operating costs in many agencies. Finally, the City can alter legal prohibitions to enable future savings.

Construction, Contracting, and the City

Government construction projects are often derided for what critics charge are higher-than-reasonable costs and longer-than-reasonable periods of construction. Many Philadelphia agency heads apparently agree. In 1996, the Free Library of Philadelphia, the agency that operates the City's libraries, entered into a unique lease arrangement with a governmental authority and a foundation that is allowed to spend City capital funds to renovate City libraries. Rationalizing that a private project-management firm could complete construction faster, at less cost, and at a higher quality, the Free Library now skirts various government-imposed rules and regulations, designed to improve governmental accountability and reduce corruption, that may increase construction costs and the length of construction projects.

Also in 1996, responding to concerns that the City is not as efficient as it could be in managing capital projects, the City created a Capital Program Office to increase the managerial efficiency of the City's Capital Program by consolidating the project management functions of the Architecture, Engineering, and Facility Planning Divisions of the Department of Public Property with the financial management and oversight functions of the Managing Director's Office and the Finance Department. But, apparently unsatisfied by this development, the City's Commerce Department, Division of Aviation recently entered into a deal similar to the library lease to allow a commercial airline to build a new terminal and avoid governmental construction project regulations.

The Capital Program Office has made substantive improvements to the City's project management process, completing long-delayed projects while reducing average project duration and decreasing professional services design fees. The City must now work to change state law and internal City operations to complement these improvements and allow the City to get the most for its construction dollar.

The construction regulation mentioned most often by internal and external critics of the cost of government construction is the multiple-contractor requirement. Like only a handful other states, the Commonwealth of Pennsylvania employs a four-part bidding law to require government agencies embarking on public construction projects to solicit separate bids for general construction; heating, ventilation, and air conditioning; plumbing; and electrical work. Multiple-contractor requirements were originally intended to lower costs based on the theory that, even with additional administrative costs, four low bids from separate bidders each attempting to minimize costs would be less costly than one low bid by a general contractor. But those administrative costs, coupled with coordination problems and resulting delays, may increase the cost and length of construction for projects built under multiple-contractor laws.

According to Princeton University Professor Orley Ashenfelter in "Contract Form and Procurement Costs: The Impact of Compulsory Multiple Contractor Laws in Construction," a paper published by the National Bureau of Economic Research Inc., New York State's multiple-contractor law increases public construction costs in New York City by about 8 percent on average, but by far more for small projects. The same report declares that the law also doubles construction time, while providing no measurable improvement in the quality of public buildings.

While, by law, the City must award contracts to the lowest responsible bidder, the City often incurs increased costs during construction because bidders intentionally bid low, knowing that by using inevitable change orders involved with construction, they can increase the costs later. Furthermore, because of four-part bidding, the general contractor has no contractual authority to coordinate or direct the progress of the other selected contractors. The poor coordination that often results can increase the cost and time of public sector construction projects.

But law is not the only factor driving construction costs. While the private sector routinely pays contractors for construction services within 30 days, the City often cannot complete the required approval process to authorize payments within 45 days. Because of this delay, many contractors who require a more regular cash flow decide not to bid on City construction projects. Since the supply of bidders is therefore diminished, the City cannot take advantage of competition to hold down construction costs. Because bidders realize that they will wait 45 days for payment, they often increase their costs to the City to cover their own increased borrowing expenses. Similarly, because private companies pay on a more certain schedule, many builders will give low priority to City projects, compromising efforts to speed up construction projects.

To reduce the cost and time involved with public construction projects, the City should work to repeal the state's four-part bidding law. To increase competition for construction contracts and improve the City's leverage with builders, the City should firmly commit to paying contractors for construction services within 30 days. Finally, because some bidders have won contracts with a low bid only to charge the City a great deal as part of change orders, the City could demand that, as part of the bidding process, contractors break down their bids based on the individual elements of the contract—labor, particular materials, and distinct equipment. By doing so, the City could better evaluate bids to determine if they are truly responsible and minimize "surprise" costs in change orders since all the costs that could be involved with a change order would be detailed in the original bid.

The City can also reduce the cost involved with everyday purchasing. While City procurement issues traditionally surround efforts to make sure that the City purchases value at the lowest possible cost, the City must redefine how it procures goods and services and interacts with vendors and contractors to reduce the actual cost of purchasing. Private-sector firms are reducing their numbers of suppliers, relying on suppliers to add value in addition to supplies, and lowering the cost to pay an invoice to below $3. Because the City may not receive data about purchases in a manner compatible with City systems, managers often lack the information necessary to make informed purchasing decisions. City government can change the work of the purchasing agency from monitoring the purchasing process to working strategically with agencies and vendors to improve customer service and the quality of supplies—and to reduce the cost to purchase goods and services. Private-sector purchasers and an increasing number of governments are utilizing on-line purchasing, electronic data interchanges, and electronic funds transfers to reduce the need for procurement agencies to administer the procurement process and increase the time spent proactively working with vendors to reduce purchasing costs.

San Diego County, California, uses what officials have dubbed "BuyNet" to do business with vendors when purchasing goods totaling less than $100,000. Competitive bids totaling less than $100,000 are accomplished via e-mail or through the County's interactive electronic commerce system. This system makes it easy to do business with government since suppliers can be notified of opportunities and the results of bidding automatically, and it removes much of the buyers' workload, allowing procurement officials to concentrate on making decisions rather than shaping the process.[10] Increasing the amount of electronic or on-line interaction also saves money by reducing paper consumption and the need for filing space.

---

[10] "The Paper Prohibition," *Governing*, November 1997. p. 58.

Procurement agencies add value when they are working with customers and vendors to purchase quality goods and services at the best possible cost, but add little value processing paperwork and forms and administering the oversight of the procurement process. The City should improve the overall procurement processes to reduce vendor payment processing costs. By requiring vendors to provide detailed supply information in a form compatible with its systems, the City could eliminate invoice processing and use postaudit functions to verify that the City received value for its payment. By utilizing client-server-based technology, electronic data interchanges, and electronic funds transfers, the City could eliminate much of the paperwork-oversight functions associated with procurement. By working with vendors to increase vendor-managed inventory, the City could reduce handling and warehousing costs.

City employees would then be able to simply check a box on a computer screen to indicate delivery of supplies while all the information about the types and quantities of supplies would be automatically entered into City computer systems. Such efforts would also allow the City to increase the amount of just-in-time inventory it purchases and reduce storage costs associated with warehousing supplies. Similarly, managers would be able to improve performance measurement and overall agency operations because such efforts would give managers better information about how agencies use supplies.

Utilizing Technology to Create Savings

Technology continues to shape the world and all institutional and interpersonal interactions. From the Geographic Information Systems that pinpoint criminal activity to help fight crime, to smart cards that allow governmental aid recipients to access their accounts with debit cards, technology is improving the way government performs. Technology can also help government save money.

In Philadelphia, for example, the Office of Fleet Management installed a Fleet Accounting Computer Tracking System at a cost of just under $2 million to better track fleet information. According to the City's fiscal year 1998 five-year plan, the system has generated nearly $3.9 million in savings in four years through reductions in overtime costs, emergency repair contracts, fuel use, and parts purchases. Similarly, as documented in the five-year plan, energy-efficient light bulbs in City offices, installed at a cost of $350,000, now save the City $470,000 annually. By redesigning storage space, investing in new shelving technology, and utilizing letter-sized filing instead of legal-sized filing, the City of Philadelphia Prothonotary was able to eliminate $100,000 in outside storage-space rental fees.

TECHNOLOGY AND GOVERNMENTAL SAVINGS

While the use of technology has saved Philadelphia money and improved service-delivery efforts, other jurisdictions are also improving governmental operations with the use of emerging and established technology.

- Knoxville, Tennessee, developed a Municipal Modular Equipment System (MMES) for citywide collection of curbside yard waste, trash deposits, and snow and ice removal from City streets that utilizes a modular truck platform from which specialized equipment can be easily and quickly interchanged. Compared to traditional equipment, MMES saves approximately $1.16 million in equipment costs and reduces annual operating costs by more than 52 percent. (Documented in *Public Works*, June 1996.)

- Pittsburgh, Pennsylvania, became the first City to auction municipal debt on a maturity-by-maturity basis exclusively through the Internet. Pittsburgh was able to save approximately $150,000 in insurance costs and was able to reduce the anticipated true-interest costs due to the elevated level of competition the Internet auction provided. (Documented in *The Bond Buyer*, November 19, 1997.)

- The Massachusetts Department of Revenue purchased a state-of-the-art imaging system to help automate tax return processing. Massachusetts recouped its investment in four years while nearly doubling productivity from 350 returns per day to 628. Savings from paper reduction and the elimination of storage fees helped offset costs. The Philadelphia Department of Revenue is working to introduce the implementation of a similar imaging system for the future. (Documented in *civic.com*, September, 1997.)

- Numerous Chicago-area municipalities including Tinley Park, Illinois, increased the miles of annual streets repaved by approximately 20-25 percent by switching from the grind-and-pave method to Hot-In-Place Recycling. Hot-In-Place Recycling, which is already being utilized in a pilot program in Philadelphia, saves time and money by heating, removing, and mixing the asphalt pavement surface with a recycling agent, then replacing the asphalt on the pavement without removing the material from the original site. (Documented by Robinson Engineering, Ltd. of South Holland, Illinois.)

With the use of imaging technology, Philadelphia can reduce storage costs by reducing the need for voluminous filing systems. With network and Internet technology, Philadelphia can save supply costs by working to make all City interactions "paperless." With energy-consumption-reduction technology, the City can replace inefficient energy systems, light fixtures, and light bulbs to save utility costs. The challenge is not necessarily figuring out how technology can help government save money, but how to fund the investment in technology to achieve the savings.

In 1992, Philadelphia established a Productivity Bank as a revolving fund to stimulate project-specific investments to achieve cost savings, revenue gains, and service improvements; promote the strategic development of productivity initiatives across City government; and change the way City government conducts its business by encouraging innovation, accountability, and entrepreneurship in service to the public. Established with $20 million in capital derived from a 1992 bond issue, the Productivity Bank has already loaned $20.2 million for 14 projects that are forecast to provide financial benefits to the City of more than $56 million in the near future.

In 1992, the Commonwealth of Massachusetts issued a $109 million general-obligation bond to fund 24 technology-related projects, marking the first time a state financed an information technology project with long-term borrowing.[11] The City of Pittsburgh entered into a partnership with a manufacturer to install energy-efficient streetlights throughout the City. Under the terms of the partnership, the manufacturer paid the up-front costs and the City repaid the manufacturer through the energy-cost savings.[12] A similar deal in Texas was used to establish public information kiosks in the state. The vendor provided the kiosks and the Texas Employment Commission repaid the vendor with the savings generated by the reduced need for user visits, which were rendered unnecessary by the more user-friendly kiosks.[13] The City of Milwaukee Assessor's Office markets data products to help cover database development costs. While access to property ownership and assessment data can be viewed on the City's Internet site, the City sells a CD-ROM product to buyers who intend to do business with the data. Milwaukee's marketing program allowed the City to cover the bulk of Milwaukee's costs to develop the CD interface.[14] The City of Honolulu, Hawaii, maintains GIS data including land use, permit, infrastructure, and environmental data in over 70 layers covering more than 600 square miles. Honolulu currently generates

---

[11] Harris, Blake. "How to Finance 'Service to the Citizen' Projects,"
<http://www.govtech.net/publication/servicecitizen/financing.shtm>

[12] Ibid.

[13] Ibid.

[14] Ammerman, Peggy. "Sharing the wealth: Taking GIS data to the public," *American City & County*, October, 1997. p. 32.

approximately $50,000 annually through data sales efforts and expects to be able to generate enough money from sales of data products to fund yearly data maintenance efforts.[15]

Technology has already made a tremendous impact on governmental operations. In the future, Philadelphia must be positioned to take advantage of technological improvements in order to be able to best serve its residents and employers at the lowest possible cost. Furthermore, as the City reviews its computer systems to ensure that they are Year 2000 compliant and able to function properly past the year 2000, the City has the opportunity to determine which systems need to be modified to better serve agency missions. The City should utilize innovative efforts to fund acquisition of technology that can help improve the efficiency and effectiveness of governmental operations. The City can expand the capitalization of its Productivity Bank, or create a similarly structured Technology Bank dedicated specifically to the purchase of new technology, to give agencies the ability to tap into new technologies and improve service. Alternatively, the City can explore issuing bonds to fund technology projects. Partnerships with the private sector can also help offset the costs involved with investments in technology; lease arrangements, for example, can help reduce the City's ongoing maintenance costs and allow the City to keep its technology investment up to date. Finally, the City could sell information products and access to anonymous versions of the City's tax data, perhaps facilitated through the creation of a City data center not unlike Pennsylvania's State Data Center, to help fund the acquisition of new technology.

Achieving Savings Through Charter Change

Certain areas of the City Charter could be altered to improve governmental flexibility and create savings. For example, the Charter currently requires the Revenue Department to read all water meters, collect water and sewer rents, and bill customers. The City could save money by allowing the Water Department to read meters or contract out meter reading to another entity, such as the City-owned gas utility, and have Gas Works personnel read water meters simultaneously with gas meters. To enable future savings, the City should change the Charter to allow agencies other than the Revenue Department to bill for, and collect, water and sewer rents due the City.

The Charter also requires that City real estate leases for more than four years must include a clause reserving the City the right to terminate the lease without liability. Because this four-year termination clause effectively means that, from the point of view of the contractor, there is no guarantee that the City will continue any lease agreement beyond the fourth year, the City has a limited ability to enter into legitimate long-term leases and qualify for lower-rate, long-term financing. To get around this Charter provision, the City often uses a governmental authority to enter into the long-term lease, but the City must then pay the authority legal fees each month for their administration services. This decreases governmental accountability since such arrangements obscure what the City truly owns and leases and complicates City financial statements. To enable the City to reduce costs and simplify transactions, the City should change the Charter to permit the City to enter into long-term real estate leases.

RECOMMENDATIONS FOR ACTION

To reduce construction project cost and time, the City should work to repeal the state's four-part bidding law.

Action Steps:

- Work to pass legislation repealing the state's four-part bidding law in the Pennsylvania General Assembly.

---

[15] Ammerman, Peggy. "Sharing the wealth: Taking GIS data to the public," *American City & County*, October, 1997. p. 32.

Fiscal Impact:

- Potential to decrease future construction costs.

To increase competition for construction contracts and improve the City's leverage with builders the City should firmly commit to paying contractors for construction services within 30 days.

Action Steps:

- Utilize network technology to accelerate intra-agency and inter-agency payment approval processes to decrease the amount of time before the City pays contractors.

- Create imperatives for agencies to complete inter-agency approval processes. Consider reducing agency capital budgets based on the number of times an agency cannot complete internal approvals on time.

Fiscal Impact:

- Potential to decrease future construction costs by increasing competition on construction projects and reducing contractors' borrowing costs.

The City should re-engineer overall procurement processes to reduce vendor payment processing costs, allow better tracking of individual purchases, and reduce payment delays.

Action Steps:

- Establish information-tracking systems that can be used by vendors to enable the City to eliminate invoice processing functions, better collect and track purchase data, and increase the use of vendor-managed inventory.

- Work with vendors to allow the City to better collect purchasing data with software and systems.

- Utilize Internet technology to allow for on-line advertising and electronic bidding.

- Utilize new systems and software to better collect purchase and payment data.

- Utilize electronic data interchanges and electronic funds transfers to reduce vendor payment processing costs.

Fiscal Impact:

- Potential to decrease City vendor payment processing costs.

- Potential to reduce City handling and warehousing costs.

The City should utilize innovative efforts to fund acquisition of technology that can help improve the efficiency and effectiveness of governmental operations.

Action Steps:

- Evaluate the use of bonding, public-private partnerships, user fees, and a "Technology Bank" to fund the acquisition of technology necessary to improve governmental efficiency.

- Utilize proper funding mechanism to purchase new technology.

- Utilize lease arrangements to help reduce the City's ongoing maintenance costs and allow the City to keep its technology investment up to date.

Fiscal Impact:

- Potential short-term costs for technology acquisition.

- Potential to reduce service-delivery costs.

The City should alter the Charter to allow agencies other than the Revenue Department to bill for and collect water and sewer rents due the City.

Action Steps:

- Work with City Council to amend the Charter to allow agencies other than the Revenue Department to bill for and collect water and sewer rents due the City.

Fiscal Impact:

- Potential long-term savings from elimination of duplication of billing and collection efforts.

The City should alter the Charter to permit the government to enter into long-term real estate leases.

Action Steps:

- Work with City Council to amend the Charter to permit the government to enter into long-term real estate leases.

Fiscal Impact:

- Potential long-term savings from reduced borrowing and administrative costs.

- Potential long-term savings from reduced costs to the City due to the increased contractor confidence that should accompany true long-term contracts.

REDUCING THE COST OF GOVERNMENT—PERSONNEL RELATED

In Philadelphia, total personnel costs: payroll, pension, and employee benefits, represent approximately 57 percent of the General Fund budget. For government to do more with less, the City must cooperate with its municipal workforce to reduce the cost of government by addressing personnel-related costs.

To reduce the cost of government, the City can create more flexible personnel practices to reduce overtime and sick time costs. The City can address pension costs sensibly and can make payments on future obligations while times are good to reduce future costs. Finally, the City can increase competitive contracting to make government as efficient as possible.

Flexible Personnel Practices to Reduce Costs

By altering personnel practices, many private companies and government agencies have increased productivity, decreased absenteeism, and cut overtime costs. The City can explore alternative benefit plans and work schedules to cut costs, improve employee morale, and enhance the overall working environment.

Other jurisdictions have adopted short- and long-term disability plans in lieu of sick leave to help cut sick leave abuse and save money. In Los Angeles, California, a city that already had a noncontributory long-term disability plan in place, the City replaced five 50-percent-pay sick days per year with a noncontributory short-term disability insurance plan in an effort to reduce sick-time abuse. Employees in Los Angeles gave up some sick time, but know that their short- and long-term disability plans can protect them in case of a prolonged medically-necessary absence from work. The City should explore adopting a short- and long-term disability plan to reduce sick time abuse and generate significant savings. If Philadelphia could utilize short- and long-term disability plans to reduce annual sick leave, or bargain with municipal unions to reduce the number of sick days in exchange for the creation of such plans, the City could generate savings in reduced sick time and overtime costs each year.

A 1997 International Personnel Management Association survey of public personnel practices revealed that more than 43 percent of responding governmental agencies have work schedules that include a workweek compressed into four days. Many City of Philadelphia agencies already permit some measure of flex time so that workers can establish their own arrival and departure times within certain parameters. The City of Pittsburgh allows employees to submit compressed work schedules, which allow one day off per two-week pay periods or one-half day off per week. The State of Colorado allows workers to schedule a four-day workweek of ten-hour days. By expanding the workday to ten hours and compressing the workweek to four days, employers are able to give employees a day of liberty each week, which reduces employees' use of other leave time and saves money. The City should explore efforts to allow agencies to create compressed workweeks for employees. If a four-day workweek in Philadelphia could reduce the need for employees to use leave to deal with personal matters, the City could generate additional personnel savings.

Alternatively, to reduce overtime, the City could negotiate with bargaining units to allow every member of a work unit to leave work early (but be paid for a full shift) if the unit has successfully completed its work for the day. By creating an initiative for work units to complete their task in a timely manner, the City could save money as its workers leave work early. In task-oriented areas such as trash collections and field maintenance, such a system—backed by proper oversight to verify the quality of work—could hold down City overtime costs.

Further cooperation between labor and management can create additional savings. Largely by hiring an outside agency to organize and monitor the care and maintenance of City workers injured on duty, Philadelphia has reduced the number of workdays lost to injury by 45 percent between fiscal year 1996 and fiscal year 1998. Total City indemnity costs, however, remain in excess of $33 million. From cases of police brutality to employees neglecting to repair dangerous conditions, many of the City's liabilities are absolutely preventable. For example, the failure to replace a missing stop sign at an intersection cost the City $360,000 to settle a lawsuit after a woman was killed in a traffic accident at that intersection. By providing workers with the proper incentives, the City can reduce its liability costs. The City should reduce liability costs by creating an incentive program with municipal workers that would split future liability savings. For example, the City and its workers could split savings above and beyond the City's average liability costs over the previous five years—savings could fund safety training efforts and could be shared with employees on a bargaining unit basis, by agency, by division, or by an alternative method negotiated with municipal unions.

Pension Liability and Responsibility

Because of its unfunded pension liability, the City of Philadelphia must make large payments to the Pension Fund beyond the amount required to fund the pensions of current employees. In fiscal year 1998, unfunded liability payments cost the City approximately $159.3 million, approximately 7.25 percent of the City's General Fund. Recent changes in state legislation will allow the City to reduce its unfunded liability payments through the adoption of a ten-year rolling amortization, but even with the change, unfunded liability payments are expected to consume more and more of the City's General Fund revenues. While the City has already adopted a policy of making payments to the pension fund that are over and above the minimum obligation required by law, the City could reduce future costs by using some of the savings it has been able to achieve in past years to make a lump-sum payment against the City's large unfunded actuarial accrued pension liability. If, as an alternative to a rainy-day fund, the City adopts a budget-stabilization account, stabilization funds could be used to prepay pension liability to reduce future costs.

Simply funding the Pension Fund fully, however, is not enough. Pensioners actually lose money in real terms each year because their pension payments are fixed. For example, a pensioner receiving $1,000 per month upon retirement in 1983 received the same $1,000 per month in 1997, but as a result of inflation, the buying power equaled a $597-per-month pension. For the more than 32,000 City pensioners, approximately 68 percent of whom live in Philadelphia, this means a real decrease in disposable income and a real decrease in quality of life. The City can do more for these individuals, who gave their years of service to Philadelphia and its citizenry, as it works to lower the amount of its unfunded liability.

Many cities have issued pension obligation bonds to reduce unfunded pension liability. By taking advantage of low interest rates, such a bond could generate a large amount of cash, which could be invested at a rate to both pay bond debt service and generate additional investment revenues. At the time of the writing of this document, the City was pursuing such a measure. With proper measures in place to reduce risk, such a bond issue could not only fund a reduction of unfunded pension liability, it could fund a reasonable cost-of-living adjustment for pensioners to ensure that the buying power of their pension remains constant in years to come. Recognizing the need to stabilize pensioners' purchasing power, the federal government provides pensioners with an annual cost-of-living adjustment. Additionally, to help pensioners, the City could adopt a policy similar to the City of Miami, Florida, where investment returns above and beyond an actuarially determined assumed-interest rate could be split between a contribution to pensioners to help make up for the loss of their pension's buying power and contributions toward unfunded liability.

To reduce future costs, the City should reduce the unfunded liability of the City's Pension Fund. If the City has the choice of using additional funds to make payments against unfunded liability or provide a cost-of-living adjustment or bonus to pensioners, it should be remembered that, because so many pensioners live in Philadelphia, every extra dollar in pensioner pockets creates a real economic impact in the City. With mechanisms such as pension bonds and pensioner bonuses issued based on investment performance, the City can reduce future obligations, increase the buying power of pensioners, and improve its economy in the process.

Competitive Contracting

If competitive contracting can improve service-delivery efforts and reduce the cost of government, the City of Philadelphia has an obligation to its citizenry to fully explore such options. In 1992, the City of Philadelphia established its Competitive Contracting Program and has already contracted out 43 different City services, saving more than $36.2 million each year. Monitored by a special oversight committee that identifies competitive contracting opportunities and reviews required economic analyses developed by City agencies, the City has contracted out such services as security at the Philadelphia Museum of Art and Prison Health Services. Services such as Police Horseshoeing and Sludge Processing Center operations were retained as City-performed services after City employees re-engineered operations to create significant savings. While contracting out work will affect staffing levels, under Philadelphia's Competitive Contracting Program, no employees have been involuntarily separated from City service without first being offered alternative employment by the new service provider or the City.

The City of Indianapolis is often recognized as a leader in managed competition efforts. In 1993, the City contracted out management and operation of the Indianapolis Advanced Wastewater Treatment facilities—the largest privately managed municipal wastewater operation in the United States. A consortium of private companies promised to cut costs by 40 percent and save the City $65 million in the five years of the contract, while matching or exceeding the previous environmental performance. Two years into the contract, the City had already realized $22.6 million in savings. Accidents were down 80 percent, lost workdays were down 91 percent, and employee wages and benefits rose 4.1 percent. Employee grievances dropped to zero.[16]

---

[16] Eggers, William D. Cutting Local Government Costs Through Competitive Privatization. California: California Chamber of Commerce and the Reason Public Policy Institute.

Indianapolis used its managed competition process to open refuse-collection services to competition. The City's Department of Public Works actually won three of the ten contracts open for competition, helped lower the cost-per-household for trash pickup from $85 to $68, and earned its employees bonuses averaging $1,750 per worker for their efforts. The City of Phoenix, Arizona, has contracted out refuse collection, decreasing refuse collection costs nearly 20 percent on a per-household basis over the first 13 years of the program. Other jurisdictions have opened to competition formerly City-operated services such as Parking Enforcement, Airport Operations, Library Operations, and even Fire Services.

According to a publication produced by the California-based Reason Public Policy Institute titled "Cost Savings from Privatization: A Compilation of Study Findings," based on reviews of over 100 independent studies of increased competition in specific government services, increased governmental competition and privatization efforts typically demonstrate cost savings of 20 percent to 50 percent. While Philadelphia has accomplished much with its competitive contracting efforts, it can further reduce governmental costs with additional competitive contracting efforts.

Contracting out City-owned utility operations is one potential area for future competitive contracting efforts. The collection of assets known as the Philadelphia Gas Works (PGW) is owned by the City of Philadelphia and managed by a non-profit corporation led by a seven-member Board of Directors appointed by the Mayor. The City receives a payment as a "return on its investment" from PGW that is set by City Council, currently equal to $18 million per year. According to a 1995 Pennsylvania Economy League report, that payment has decreased as a percentage of the City's overall operating budget from 2.27 percent in 1973, the first year of operation under the current management structure (the City previously contracted with a private company to operate PGW), to 0.76 percent in 1995. Had that payment kept pace with the percentage of PGW's gross revenue that the payment to the City represented when the City severed its ties with the private company, PGW would have returned $70 million to the City in 1994. Alternatively, if the payment had returned the same percentage of PGW's gross revenue to the City when it was raised to an $18 million payment in 1980, PGW could have earned $31 million for the City in 1994. While the collection of assets known as PGW is, by far, the largest municipally owned gas utility in the United States, every other municipally owned gas utility with more than 100,000 customers returns a payment to its owner City that is significantly larger than Philadelphia's return from PGW. By contracting out the operation of PGW, the City could explore whether a private operator could operate the utility efficiently and earn the City a proper return.

To reduce the cost of government and improve service-delivery efforts, the City should aggressively explore additional opportunities to open service-delivery efforts to competition from private-sector providers. In all such cases, the City must work with its municipal unions, through the processes set forth by any established labor-management partnership, to give municipal employees a chance to bid on and win contracts through a fair, competitive process. With proper oversight and a fair process, competition can continue to save money for the City and improve services for the citizenry. However, all costs and benefits must be considered as part of any effort to evaluate the expansion of competitive contracting in Philadelphia. The City must be careful to factor in any lost revenues that may result from wages and salaries paid to workers who reside beyond the City limits insofar as they would be replacing wages and salaries that currently remain in Philadelphia.

Alternatively, in areas where government can effectively compete, the City could encourage agencies to expand service-delivery efforts. The City of Philadelphia Office of Fleet Management (OFM) was established to centralize responsibility for the acquisition, assignment, maintenance, rehabilitation, and disposal of City vehicles. Since its establishment, OFM raised the availability of City vehicles from 70 percent at the end of fiscal year 1993 to 91 percent at the end of 1997 while reducing the overall size of the City fleet. Agencies, which are able to perform as well, should be encouraged to expand their service. For example, Fleet Management could similarly serve the fleet needs of quasi-governmental agencies, or even surrounding governmental jurisdictions.

Half a world away from Philadelphia, the Auckland, New Zealand, Fleet Services Department is part of a directorate called City Enterprises. Many of the agencies in the City Enterprises directorate market their services to jurisdictions outside Auckland City. In addition to serving the other agencies of the Auckland City government, these agencies occasionally even serve the private sector. City Design, the Auckland engineering and architectural agency, generates approximately 15 percent of their NZ$11 million budget (approximately $5.8 million in U.S. dollars) from activities performed for other local authorities or from the private sector. Auckland's Fleet Services and City Design agencies not only perform their missions to serve the agencies of Auckland's government, they perform their tasks well enough to generate revenue by marketing their services in competitive situations.

In Indianapolis, after the City's fleet maintenance department was challenged through competitive contracting, City workers managed to reduce costs, in part by outsourcing some formerly in-house functions, to earn incentive pay. According to City documents, overall annual savings to the City of Indianapolis equaled $8.5 million over the course of a three-year contract from 1995 to 1997. With such a strong reputation in vehicle maintenance, Indianapolis Fleet Services was able to expand service and revenues to other customers including a local hospital, a local university, private utilities, and public safety departments outside of City government.

By contracting out the City Print Shop, Philadelphia has saved more than $2.7 million since fiscal year 1993. The City could open all internal services to competition to encourage improvements in service-delivery efforts and, where legally permissible, allow successful agencies to supplement their budgets through marketing excess service capacity to other governmental, or private, entities. With such a balanced approach, agencies can generate savings by becoming more efficient, but can avoid the need for dramatic employment-level cuts by expanding their efficient service to other consumers.

RECOMMENDATIONS FOR ACTION

To reduce personnel costs, the City should explore adopting a short- and long-term disability plan.

Action Steps:

- Work with collective bargaining units to establish short- and long-term disability plans.

- Work with insurance providers to procure new short- and long-term disability plans.

- Establish policies and procedures related to new short- and long-term disability plans.

Fiscal Impact:

- Potential to decrease costs associated with sick-leave abuse.

To reduce personnel costs, the City should explore efforts to allow agencies to create a four-day workweek for employees.

Action Steps:

- Work with collective bargaining units to establish four-day workweeks.

- Establish policies and procedures related to new four-day workweeks.

Fiscal Impact:

- Potential to decrease overtime costs.
- Potential to decrease costs associated with sick-leave abuse.
- Potential to increase overall government productivity.

To reduce liability costs, the City should create an incentive program for municipal workers that would reward workers based on decreased liability costs.

Action Steps:

- Work with collective bargaining units to establish a liability-reduction incentive program.
- Establish policies and procedures related to new liability-reduction program.
- Establish accounting and dispersal system to track savings and payments.

Fiscal Impact:

- Potential to decrease liability costs.

To reduce future costs, the City should reduce the unfunded liability in the City Pension Fund.

Action Steps:

- Utilize pension bonds and year-end fund balance surpluses to reduce unfunded liability in the City's Pension Fund.
- Examine the potential to use pension-bond revenue and higher-than-average Pension Fund earnings to fund a reasonable cost-of-living adjustment.

Fiscal Impact:

- Potential to decrease future pension-related costs by exceeding the City's required contribution to the Pension Fund.
- Potential to expand economic activity in the City by increasing the buying power of pensioners with a cost-of-living adjustment.

To reduce the cost of government, the City should aggressively explore additional opportunities to open service-delivery efforts to competition from private-sector providers.

Action Steps:

- Work with collective bargaining units and labor-management partnerships to evaluate additional opportunities to open City services to competitive contracting.
- Evaluate current City procedures for competitive contracting to determine if they are adequate for future competitive efforts.
- Implement any necessary changes to City competitive contracting procedures.
- Competitively contract City services.

Fiscal Impact:

- Potential to reduce service-delivery costs.
- Potential to increase overall government productivity.

GETTING WORTH FOR THE CITY—GENERATING REVENUE

From the ancient settlements that constructed walls and provided safe havens to trading caravans to the present-day metropolis that establishes a telecommunications infrastructure to facilitate modern business practices, cities have always thrived by creating a marketplace and exacting a toll from those who profit from market interaction. Cities establish a forum for free trade and voluntary exchanges that creates wealth. In such a voluntary exchange of goods or services, there is not only an exchange, but also mutual benefit. If one individual has cheese steaks but no soft pretzels, and another has soft pretzels but no cheese steaks, then according to the laws of supply and demand, soft pretzels will be more valuable to the first individual while cheese steaks will be more valuable to the second. If they trade a soft pretzel for cheese steak, because each individual values the item received more than the item traded, they not only make a fair exchange, they are both increasing their individual wealth and utility.

City leaders must understand the value the City creates as a marketplace. Despite population loss, millions of individuals use Philadelphia as a place to live, work, and play. By taxing those who profit from the marketplace created in Philadelphia, the City benefits and is able to increase the amenities of the marketplace to stimulate additional market activity.

City leaders must similarly understand the City's value in the marketplace. If, in the cheese steak and soft pretzel example, the individual with soft pretzels is willing to exchange more than one soft pretzel for a single cheese steak, then the second individual is not maximizing his or her individual benefit by exchanging a cheese steak for a single soft pretzel. By capitalizing on such disparate values, television networks charge more to advertise during the Super Bowl than during the overnight rebroadcast of the evening news. By taking advantage of its true value in the marketplace, the City can further increase marketplace amenities or reduce the costs of entry into the marketplace.

To enhance revenues and receive worth for the City's role in the marketplace, 21st-century Philadelphia can capitalize on the worth of the goods it provides and the services it performs and can better enforce local laws and regulations. The City can take advantage of the value of its place in the market. The City can enter the market itself to find value in the marketplace. Finally, the City can tap into the largesse of Philadelphians to enhance its assets.

Establishing the Worth of City Services

The free-rider problem plagues efforts to establish appropriate charges for goods and services produced by government. Some number of individuals will always decide not to pay for their consumption of goods where it is difficult to exclude people from consuming the good and where one person's consumption of the good does not necessarily limit another person's consumption. Therefore it is nearly impossible to truly assess an individual's elasticity of demand for such a good. Unable to establish the true worth of such goods, and faced with free riders that see no imperative to pay a price for such goods, government inevitably provides them in an inefficient manner. By increasing the excludability of such goods, the City can better establish the worth of such goods to the public. If the City can better establish the worth of such goods, it can set a price for consumption that will allow it to provide goods in a more efficient manner—and at a higher quality.

The City can design appropriate user fees for individuals who take advantage of its amenities. Ideally, the City should design user fees and other charges to maximize revenue while minimizing barriers to participation in a way that does not prevent Philadelphians from taking advantage of what their City has to offer. Recreation, Fairmount Park, and Library facilities are heavily patronized by the public but in constant need of resources to maintain them in a usable manner. In a citizen survey completed by the City in June 1997, only 52.6 percent of respondents reported that they were very or somewhat satisfied with the physical condition of neighborhood recreation centers. Only 51.6 percent of respondents reported that they were very or somewhat satisfied with the physical condition of neighborhood parks. While 68.4 percent of respondents reported that they were very or somewhat satisfied with Library Services, this total could certainly be higher. One way to help improve those percentages is to invest in facilities and programs, and one way to fund such investments is by collecting reasonable user charges.

The latest Commonwealth of Pennsylvania Department of Conservation and Natural Resources Local Government Recreation Services Survey (1990) addressed the use of user fees and charges. Of 119 respondent local jurisdictions, the average percentage of yearly recreation programs with a fee charged was 72 percent and 58 percent of respondent jurisdictions charged a greater fee for non-resident participants than for resident participants. While Philadelphia's high concentration of residents living below the federal poverty line reduces the likelihood that significant revenue could be generated through recreational facility user fees on a per-person basis, some level of support can help offset City costs and improve services.

People value goods and services with a price and undervalue the same goods and services when they are provided free of charge. The City provides free summer concerts while some suburban jurisdictions charge admission to similar events. The City opens pools to residents for free while State Parks charge visitors an entrance fee. While the City may decide such service should remain free, to help offset service-delivery costs and to ensure that participants value City facilities, the City should evaluate its current menu of programs and activities enjoyed by the public to determine appropriate user charges, even if such a payment represents only a token contribution. The Free Library prides itself on providing materials at no cost, but small fees for loans of best-selling novels and videotape rental, where the library competes with private bookstores and video rental stores, could help expand library services. For example Portland residents who visit libraries in larger Multnomah County, Oregon can "rent" bestsellers for about $2 per week. The Recreation Department and Fairmount Park administer many much-demanded and much-used sports fields, but fees (many groups are currently asked to make donations to local sports organizations) from groups that monopolize sports fields for non-City-organized league games could help keep facilities in the best shape possible. As mentioned in Chapter 2, the City could establish separate funds to allow revenue from such efforts to be channeled back to agencies that generate them.

Because many users of recreational community services are non-Philadelphians, the City should implement higher non-resident fees to ensure that non-City residents pay their fair share to use City facilities. While a beach-tag-like system for the much-used jogging and bicycle paths along the Schuylkill River (similar to those employed to charge users of public beaches) may be impractical, for activities at facilities with greater excludability, higher non-resident fees should help tap into the resources of non-Philadelphians who use recreational facilities. It is wonderful that area residents flock to the City's libraries to do research and it is encouraging that so many residents of neighboring jurisdictions enjoy City ice rinks, but it would be nicer still to see them pay a reasonable non-resident user fee to fund resources they obviously do not find in their own communities.

THE FREE LIBRARY OF PHILADELPHIA—UNDERVALUED?

The Free Library of Philadelphia lends out more than six million items each year at no cost, but the Library is also home to many rare and unique treasures that attract visitors and researchers from Philadelphia and around the world. From the Patent Collection containing a copy of every patent the U.S. has ever issued to a Rare Book Collection boasting museum-quality tomes and artifacts, the Free Library is home to resources of tremendous value. In 1998, for example, the Free Library exhibited a fraction of its incredible Print and Picture Collection in the foyer of the main library building, but the entire collection, home to prints by luminaries such as Andy Warhol, Roy Lichtenstein, Pablo Picasso, and Alexander Calder, is always available for public reference to any visitor. In the future, the Free Library could charge visitors, or more specifically, non-resident visitors, a fee to access specialty collections or charge admission to special displays of the Library's unique holdings. By charging visitors who wish to take advantage of its rare treasures, the Free Library can increase revenues that could be used to expand its services to Philadelphia taxpayers that support all Library services.

In addition to licenses and fees, the City also imposes fines and penalties for many activities that it wishes to discourage. Some penalties, such as those imposed for parking next to a fire hydrant or those imposed on skateboarding in public squares, are designed to foster public safety. Other penalties, such as those imposed on dog owners who do not clean up after their pets or those imposed for littering, are designed to improve quality of life in the City. But penalties will only be effective if individuals feel that the consequences imposed by the penalty and the likelihood that they would actually have to pay that price outweigh the benefit those individuals derive from performing a prohibited action. Too often, however, individuals in Philadelphia become aware that the price they would pay for non-compliance—the penalty, multiplied by the likelihood that offenders would actually pay the price if caught—is minimal. Their actions, however small, add up to cost the City.

Skateboarders generally avoid the plazas surrounding City Hall and the City's Municipal Services Building where anti-skateboarding laws are usually enforced, but they flock to John F. Kennedy Plaza Park (Love Park), just across the street, where their activities are rarely challenged. In fiscal year 1998, the City spent approximately $3,100 to repair damage to the park's granite pavers that was caused by skateboarders. This project represented approximately 100 hours of labor that could have been devoted to other park needs and was necessary even though the City created a facility in South Philadelphia's Franklin D. Roosevelt Park specifically designed for skateboarders. In addition, according to Fairmount Park officials, the City may have to spend approximately $50,000 in the near future to repair granite capping in the park damaged by skateboarders.

To avoid tipping fees that can equal up to $65 per ton, many individuals and professional contractors decide to illegally deposit debris in empty neighborhood lots. A 1995 Pennsylvania Economy League survey of the costs associated with illegal dumping in Philadelphia determined that the direct costs involved with removal and disposal of illegal dumping, enforcement of illegal dumping laws, and prosecution of illegal dumpers take more than a $5 million bite out of the City budget each year. Indirect expenses, including increased costs to private entities for removal and disposal of illegal dumping on private property, lost tax revenues from avoided legal dumping activities, and devaluation of properties in affected neighborhoods, further increases the toll of illegal dumping in Philadelphia.

To avoid the cost of private waste disposal, which is required by law in Philadelphia for properties that house more than six apartments, many property owners violate the law and allow tenants to place their trash on the curb for City collection. This costs the City in real terms. First, the City must pay sanitation workers to collect this extra trash. Then, the City must pay the cost to dispose of this extra trash. Finally, the City loses the taxes, and any resulting multiplier effect, that could have been generated by the economic activity created by the private waste disposal that should have resulted from compliance with the law.

The City's Department of Streets implemented a program called Streets & Walkways Education & Enforcement Program (SWEEP) to educate Philadelphia citizens about their responsibilities under the City's Sanitation Code. Streets Department officials indicate that voluntary compliance with the law has increased and that SWEEP focus areas have become visibly cleaner. The Streets Department has received requests from community groups to expand SWEEP into additional areas. SWEEP has worked to decrease non-compliance because residents and employers realize that abiding by the law not only improves the appearance of the City, but that their failure to abide by the law will result in their paying a high price.

The City should make enforcement of City laws and regulations a priority. After a proper regulatory review in consultation with business and neighborhood groups, the City should hire more inspectors where there is a compelling public interest to enforce quality-of-life regulations: safety of structures, trash regulations, parking regulations, valet regulations, etc. The City could expand the use of SWEEP-like programs to help improve the quality of life in its neighborhoods. Because inspectors would only cite violators, citizens and business owners who comply with the law should never have to pay a fine. Alternatively, the City could change the dynamic for such enforcement efforts by charging all owners of multiple unit dwellings a per-unit charge for trash disposal on a yearly basis until property owners produce proof that they are utilizing the services of a private hauler to remove weekly trash. Similarly, as part of licensing procedures, the City could charge contractors a per-ton fee for to-be-disposed-of waste from projects that could be held until the contractor produces proof that waste was disposed of properly. Since the City receives a much more favorable rate for waste disposal, the City could reduce the costs to contractors and multiple-unit property owners by picking up and disposing of their waste at the cost to the City plus a reasonable fee. Finally, because the highest fine the City may impose by law was established decades ago at $300, the City could work with the Pennsylvania General Assembly to increase that amount and increase the City's ability to use fines as a deterrent.

Capitalizing on the City's Role in Establishing a Marketplace

The City of Philadelphia is a marketplace where many individuals and businesses make their fortunes. The City's role in fostering market operations extends from its role in protecting public safety, to its role in maintaining the City infrastructure, to the City's own purchase of goods and services. In the future, the City can use its role in establishing a marketplace to improve its ability to provide essential City services.

In surveying selected charges and fees for various cities, the Controller's Office found great disparities in the fees charged by other major cities. An annual license to operate a barber shop in Philadelphia costs $25 per year while in Detroit, Michigan, a similar license costs $70. Philadelphia charges vendors $250 per year for a Center City food vending license while Washington D.C. only charges $130. Different cities have obviously come to different conclusions about fair and appropriate fees and charges. (See Table 3.6.)

Ideally, licenses and fees should be directly linked to the administrative and oversight costs associated with providing the oversight necessary to comply with the legislation establishing such licensing. Additional charges are added in an effort to compensate society for any "losses," such as the loss of an unobstructed view when a billboard is erected. The City, therefore, must regularly reevaluate whether its licenses and fees are adequate to cover costs and properly related to the activities they address.

The City should evaluate its license charges and fees on a regular basis to determine whether the City generates enough revenues to adequately cover administration expenses, whether charges are unreasonably high and should be lowered to increase entry into the marketplace, or whether charges are a nuisance to collect and administer and should be abolished. Street-opening charges, for example, could be based on square footage instead of a flat fee and a higher fee could be charged for newly-resurfaced streets. The City could examine charges to ensure that the City charges an appropriate fee for companies that use City rights-of-ways.

Alternatively, some fees in Philadelphia may already be too high or of such little value that they should be eliminated. A fiscal year 1996 Controller's Office audit analyzed the accounting system codes for the 245 different licenses, permits, and fees administered by the City's Department of Licenses and Inspections and discovered that 49 codes had no activity in fiscal year 1996. Half of the 195 codes with positive revenue, taken as a whole, generated less than 1 percent of the Department's total license, permit, and fee revenue. One asbestos-related license actually yielded

City	Table 3.6. Selected Charges and Fees for Various Cities			
	Annual Barber Shop	Annual Central City Food Vendor (3' x 6')	Permit to Break Street (5 square yards)	Annual Outdoor Advertising Business License (14' x 48' billboard)
Philadelphia	$ 25.00 (last altered 1988)	$250.00 (last altered 1990)	$300.00 (last altered 1990)	$150.00* (last altered 1991)
Baltimore, MD†	$ 50.00	$ 375.00	$ 300.00	$ 1,290.00
Boston, MA	$ 30.00	$ 270.00	$ 155.25	$ 100.00
Chicago, IL	$ 125.00	$ 125.00	$ 138.00	$ 1,636.00
Detroit, MI††	$ 70.00	$ 115.00	$ 392.00	$ 88.00
Houston, TX	$ 25.00	$ 100.00	$ 180.00	$ 15.00
New York City, NY†††	$ 15.00	$ 262.50	$ 135.00	—
Phoenix, AZ	$ 40.00	$ 75.00	$ 50.00	$ 365.00
San Diego, CA††††	$ 34.00	—	$ 75.00	$ 210.00
Washington, D.C.†††††	$ 30.00	$ 130.00	$ 350.00	$ 672.00

Source: City of Philadelphia Controller's Office

*While the fee for an annual outdoor advertising business license is set by law, pending the result of ongoing litigation, and responding to court direction, Philadelphia only charged $100 for an Outdoor Advertising Business License as of November, 1998.

†For outdoor advertising in Baltimore, $1.80/sq. ft. is the maximum charge.

††For permits to break streets in Detroit, $392 is a charge per day.

†††New York charges a percentage of the gross negotiated price for outdoor advertising.

††††San Diego does not permit central city vending.

†††††For Permits to break streets in Washington, $300 is the maximum charge plus a $50 inspection fee.

negative revenues. Where revenue generation is minimal, administrative costs could actually exceed revenues collected. If licensing is necessary, then the ensuing charge must be substantial enough to cover administrative costs associated with license oversight. If licensing is not necessary, it should be eliminated to remove one more inconvenience to City residents and business owners.

Changes in telecommunications law have encouraged many cities to reevaluate rights-of-way charges levied on the companies that run power lines, wires, and cables through cities to conduct their business. Most cities are still struggling to understand the total ramifications of recent legislative changes that allow localities to recover reasonable costs associated with oversight and inspection of rights-of-way use. However, according to officials from New Orleans, Louisiana, the City was able to raise its per-foot charge for telecommunications rights-of-ways from about $.30 to $2.60 based on a review of the true cost to the City to maintain rights-of-ways. The per-foot charge is now tied to the Consumer Price Index so it will increase with inflation. In Philadelphia, where the City charges rights-of-way users a minimal per-pole tax, and extracts commitments by conduit owners to move their conduits at no cost to the City during major construction projects, the City could be able to recover a larger amount for the value of its rights-of-ways. The City is currently working on a master ordinance to address such issues, and could use the effort to gain greater control of the management of the rights-of-way permitting process and to address the recovery of the actual costs associated with rights-of-ways management in Philadelphia.

Since so many residents, workers, and visitors pass through the City each day, advertisers are naturally eager to try to reach them. While many residents consider any level of outdoor advertising a blight on the cityscape, most accept some level of visual promotion as part of the urban fabric. The Supreme Court has ruled that governmental regulation cannot control the content of expression unless it serves a "compelling state interest, and is narrowly tailored to fulfill the government's objective." However, the Court has held that if the government seeks to regulate only time, manner, and place of expression, such a regulation will withstand Constitutional scrutiny unless it "unduly impedes the normal flow of expression." Therefore, as long as the City does not single out specific advertising content, and so long as the City does not unduly limit alternative channels for information communication, it may regulate advertising in many ways. For example, because billboards affect City aesthetics, the City may specifically charge high license fees on billboards. Similarly, because honor boxes (newspaper vending machines) affect the appearance of the streetscape and can interfere with public mobility, the City may regulate the size, shape, appearance, and placement of honor boxes. Finally, because there is no First Amendment right that guarantees an advertiser the ability to place messages on another's property, the City may prohibit advertising on utility poles, trees, or streetlights, or prohibit vendors from chaining honor boxes to City property.

The City could increase license fees for billboards to better reflect their value in the urban market. The City may also regulate emerging forms of advertising not contemplated in current City ordinances. As advertisers begin targeting the urban market with "mobile" billboards that clog traffic, blimp and airplane advertising across the sky, and virtual ads broadcast for home viewers on City-owned sports facilities, the City could re-examine advertising licensing to be sure to regulate and collect fees related to these new promotional avenues. The City could license and regulate the appearance and placement of honor boxes to better manage the streetscape. To eliminate illegal signage, both commercial and non-commercial, that litters its neighborhoods, the City can raise advertising license fees to cover the cost of more thorough inspection and enforcement efforts. To capitalize on advertisers' desire to find inexpensive ways to reach Philadelphia residents, workers, and visitors, the City could establish corrals for honor boxes and advertising kiosks in neighborhoods to serve as free forums for community advertising messages. Corrals and kiosks could be purchased and maintained with revenue from permanent advertisements on the corrals and kiosks themselves. Similar arrangements (the use of advertising kiosks and advertising messages) have been proposed to fund the acquisition and maintenance of self-cleaning public toilets throughout Philadelphia.

By embracing advertisers' desire to reach the Philadelphia market, the City can improve its appearance, increase its revenues, and even provide public toilets for its streets. New York City is currently negotiating a comprehensive franchise deal to allow one company to build, maintain, and operate at least 3,300 bus shelters, 430 newsstands, and 30 public toilets. Advertising panels on these structures would generate more than $1 billion over 20 years.[17] In Philadelphia, combining such elements with public trash cans, benches, honor box corrals, free neighborhood advertising kiosks, and other street furniture could create an attractive package for an enterprising marketing company.

The City can also use its purchasing power in the marketplace to increase the value of being a Philadelphia establishment. The City spends hundreds of millions of dollars purchasing goods and services each year yet much of that money goes to firms and individuals from outside the City. In general, City purchases other than those for professional services must be awarded to the lowest responsible bidder. According to the Procurement Department, the City made more than $227 million in competitive bid awards for public works and service, supplies, and equipment in fiscal year 1997. Of that amount 46.6 percent flowed to Philadelphia companies. Non-Philadelphia companies won more than half the contracts, worth $121 million. Because the contracts to Philadelphia companies include many national and international companies with local sales offices in Philadelphia, many more contracting dollars leave the City even though they may be paid to entities listed as Philadelphia companies.

Given the wage and business taxes recovered by the City from local firms, as well as the subsequent multiplier effect, some bids that may appear higher from local bidders are actually less costly to the City than lower bids from non-local firms. If, in determining the lowest responsible

---

[17] Dunlap, David W. "Rethinking a City's Street Furniture," *New York Times*, January 18, 1998. p. 1.

bidder, the City considered the tax revenues that would flow back to the City in determining the lowest responsible bidder, the City could increase the number of contracts that are awarded to companies headquartered in Philadelphia.

To improve the local economy, other jurisdictions have enacted local-preference legislation to afford local firms an advantage over non-local firms. The City of Albuquerque, New Mexico, for example, provides businesses in the Albuquerque Metropolitan Area with a set preference factor in bids for goods and services. San Francisco, California, grants locally owned businesses a preference to reduce the burden on local businesses due to the high costs of doing business in the City and to encourage businesses to locate and remain in San Francisco. In upholding San Francisco's local-preference law, a Ninth Circuit Judge ruled that "a city may rationally allocate its own funds to ameliorate disadvantages suffered by local businesses."[18] The court held that the preference did not impose a discriminatory burden on non-residents solely because of their residency status, but was an attempt to lighten the burden that San Francisco businesses must bear that is not shared by non-residents.

To evaluate the use of a local preference in Philadelphia, the City Controller's Office utilized the REMI model to compare a forecast of the City and suburban economies with and without local preference in the City of Philadelphia. Assuming a $50 million increase in local demand in the personal services/repair, business services, and construction industries and an increased marginal cost of the local-preference program of $10 million, the REMI model suggests that such a program would result in a net gain of almost 400 jobs in Philadelphia and $12 million in additional real Gross City Product by 2015. By contrast, because the exercise would also create a subsequent decrease in suburban demand in the above-listed industries, the suburban communities as a whole could be expected to experience a loss of over 760 jobs and 1,400 residents as a result of a local-preference program in the City. While the City would benefit from such a program, unless the likely reduction in social costs that may arise from any net gain to the City offsets the suburban decline associated with such a local-preference program, such a program could represent a net loss for the Greater Philadelphia region. (See Chapter 6 for a more thorough description about regional cooperation and regional competitiveness.)

To use the City's purchasing power as an economic development tool and to reduce the burden on local businesses, the City should explore the use of a local preference for City businesses as part of the procurement process. To enact local-preference legislation in Philadelphia, most informed officials agree that the Charter requirement that contracts shall be awarded to the lowest responsible bidder would have to be altered to permit the City to factor in a local preference.

Taking Advantage of the City's Market

The City is not just a vehicle for establishing a marketplace, it is a marketplace itself. With approximately 25,000 City workers, Philadelphia as an employer is larger than many municipalities. Philadelphia operates a fleet of vehicles that crisscross the City each day and a collection of facilities frequented by millions of visitors each year. Information produced by City government as part of its normal operations is coveted by marketers and researchers and unserviceable City property is desired by souvenir seekers. Philadelphia can capitalize on this value by establishing advertising venues, marketing City resources, and cashing in on its ability to offer marketers exclusivity in promotional efforts.

The City of Philadelphia currently contracts with an outside firm to place advertisements on bus shelters. In exchange for contracting the right to sell advertising on bus shelters, the City receives a floating fee of $66.12 per month per shelter or 20 percent of ad revenue, whichever is higher. The leasing firm is responsible for everything from constructing and maintaining the shelters to selling the advertisements and mailing a check to the City. According to the Mayor's Office of Transportation, in fiscal year 1996 this initiative included advertising on 254 shelters, which generated $415,978 in new revenues.

Some have raised concern about controlling the content of such advertising, but the Supreme Court has affirmed and reaffirmed the notion that such facilities are not "public forums" and that

---

[18] Associated General Contractors v. City & County of San Francisco, 813F.2d 922 (9th Circuit 1987).

governmental entities can therefore restrict speech as long as the criteria for restriction are reasonable in light of the purpose served by the forum as well as viewpoint neutral. The bus shelter deal in Philadelphia provides for a City veto over ads.

The City of New Orleans experimented with a pilot program where civic notices, sponsored by business and community organizations, were placed on the trunk panels of police cars. The St. Clair County, Illinois, Sheriff's Department has accepted money to place ads on the front fenders above the wheel wells of department vehicles.[19] Public transportation agencies in Portland, Charlotte, and Philadelphia have been able to raise significant revenues through advertising on transit vehicles. The Cherry Creek School District, a district of 36,500 students located just southeast of Denver, Colorado, sells advertising space on school buses, "time and temperature" signs placed on school grounds, and on district athletic facilities. In Texas, the Grapeville-Colleyville School District, near the Dallas/Fort Worth Airport, sells advertising space on school roofs to generate revenue as part of efforts to market to air travelers. Howard County, Maryland, and the Washington D.C. School District have entered into rooftop leasing arrangements with telecommunications companies to capitalize on the growing demand for tower and antennae sites and to generate new revenues.

To help raise revenue, expand services, and offset its need to raise taxes, the City should expand advertisement leasing efforts to high-visibility City venues. By taking advantage of the market in this manner, the City could be able to generate new revenue with minimal effort. As with other initiatives, a percentage of the revenue from such activities could be returned to the agency that hosts new City advertising to create an incentive for agencies to pursue such activities.

POTENTIAL FUTURE ADVERTISING AVENUES FOR THE CITY

The City of Philadelphia offers many advertising venues that could represent opportunities for the City to raise revenue and for advertisers to reach their market. The City's day-to-day involvement could be minimized through a contract with a private firm that would solicit advertisers, sell advertisement space, install artwork, maintain advertisement-related equipment, change advertisements when necessary, and forward revenue to the City. In all cases, advertisements could be blatantly commercial ("buy XYZ Company's product") or tempered as a civic-awareness message ("XYZ Company reminds you that smoke detectors save lives"). Potential future advertising avenues for the City include, but are by no means limited to the following suggestions. The City could:

- Sell advertising in and on municipal buildings. Community bulletin boards in health and recreation centers could contain an advertising message, advertisements on the roofs of City buildings near airports could target departing and arriving flights.

- Lease rooftop space on City buildings for telecommunications towers and antennae.

- Sell advertisements to be hung on the fences of municipal baseball fields and stenciled onto the grass of municipal soccer fields.

- Sell advertising on City vehicles including Streets Department waste-disposal trucks and Water Department vans.

- Sell the right to place advertising messages in employee payroll envelopes or on internal City e-mail.

- Sell advertising on street furniture including honor box corrals, the envisioned public toilets, trash cans, and benches.

---

[19] "...Just Don't Call 911 to Order a Pizza," *Governing*, March 1996. p. 17.

- Expand the sale of sponsorship of City events.

Faced with critical revenue shortages and a need to provide and maintain vital public services, some jurisdictions have actually entered the marketplace to help make ends meet. By marketing services, expertise, and even souvenirs, these jurisdictions have been able to raise revenues and enhance service-delivery efforts without seeking new funds from taxpayers. As previously noted, the City of Milwaukee Assessor's Office sells a CD-ROM product with property ownership and assessment data to marketers. The library system in Multnomah County, rents space to a nationwide coffee bar chain, leases library space for banquets, and sells discarded books at its own used bookstore. The City of Chicago sells surplus municipal property in a City store. By allowing agency creativity to blossom, these jurisdictions have created a culture that encourages agency heads to think of ways to enhance revenues beyond additional requests from the General Fund.

Los Angeles County is a leader in such entrepreneurial efforts. Empowered by state enabling legislation that allows jurisdictions to market employee expertise or services, and to license and market jurisdiction names, logos, depictions of county property, and other intellectual property, Los Angeles County has embraced a countywide marketing program. In addition to advertising on County property, corporate sponsorship opportunities, and sales of surplus County property, Los Angeles County has actually licensed a new County logo and sells County- and agency-related merchandise to the public. The County operates a mail-order company that sells items such as shirts, pins, and hats with the LA County logo. The Coroner's office sells toe-tag key chains and beach towels designed with the police-chalk outline of a body. Sales of these items were substantial enough to fund an anti-drinking and driving program as well as an extra Coroner's vehicle and an emergency radio. Specific agencies also provide expertise and services. The County's human relations agency offers ethnic diversity training and consulting while the County library offers specialized research services for business at a price. According to County documents, in fiscal year 1995–96, Los Angeles County realized approximately $4.7 million in total countywide marketing revenues, an amount that is expected to approach $20 million by the year 2000.

To expand revenue potential and to let loose the creative power of City government—and provide consumers with unique holiday gift ideas, the City should pursue state enabling legislation to allow the City and its agencies to market expertise and services as well as the City name and other real and intellectual property. As with other initiatives, a percentage of the revenue from such activities could be returned to the agencies that offer marketing opportunities to create an incentive for agencies to pursue such activities.

POTENTIAL FUTURE CITY MARKETING AVENUES

The City of Philadelphia offers many marketing venues that could represent opportunities for the City to raise revenue and provide value for consumers. The City's day-to-day involvement with such efforts could be minimized through a contract with a private firm or the creation of a non-profit corporation that could operate City marketing activities. Potential future marketing avenues for the City include, but are by no means limited, to the following suggestions. The City could:

- Establish through the Procurement Department, which has the authority to dispose of unserviceable personal property, or through the creation of a non-profit corporation, a boutique to sell used City property, including old street signs, parking meters, demo voting machines, and memorabilia from the City's defunct Civic Center. A branch store could sell disposable library books to the public.

- Establish leases for concessionaires in City facilities including cappuccino bars in libraries and juice bars at recreation centers.

- Aggressively expand efforts to market the excess capacity of the Water Department's Water Systems to surrounding jurisdictions. The City currently provides water services to many non-Philadelphia jurisdictions, but could provide additional services since the system's peak daily treated water delivery in fiscal year 1997 was only approximately 79 percent of the system's total rated capacity.

- Sell information products produced to marketers and anonymous tax data to researchers.

- Contract with an outside firm to market, promote, and manage the private use of public spaces in City Hall and other City facilities for meetings, affairs, and parties.

- Market its expertise in public safety training, diversity training, laboratory services, and legal research to private entities to raise revenues.

- Enter into moneymaking enterprises such as souvenir sales to sell everything from models of City Hall to replica City police cars and fire engines to Fairmount Park tee shirts.

- Trademark an official logo and market novelty items such as official City of Philadelphia key chains, baseball hats, and tote bags.

- Explore legal options to create exclusive licenses for merchandising of City-owned property such as the Liberty Bell and Independence Hall. The City can explore legally trademarking and copyrighting images and representations of these much-reproduced icons, or it could issue licenses to vendors to sell "official City of Philadelphia" Liberty Bell and Independence Hall souvenirs.

Selling exclusivity is a way that the City can further capitalize on marketing efforts. By offering companies the right to be the exclusive providers of a product in Philadelphia, the City can multiply the value of its concessionaire-type contracts. Companies have demonstrated their desire to pay private and public entities a premium for arrangements that create official sponsors, vendors, or suppliers.

Philadelphia's Fairmount Park Commission recently executed a contract for parkwide food, non-alcoholic beverages, merchandise, concession rental and management. While the Park Commission realized minimal revenues from prior deals, this new parkwide concession contract should reduce Park Commission oversight costs and generate millions of dollars in new income. The City recently entered into an exclusive contract with a telecommunications company for cellular phone usage that allows the City to deduct $10,000 each month from its bills as compensation for the potential to use the City's name in company advertisements.

In 1992, the Pennsylvania State University entered into an exclusive brand contract agreement with Pepsi-Cola worth $14 million. In 1996, the University of Minnesota signed a deal with Coca-Cola worth $28.5 million.[20] While Colorado's 33,000-student Colorado Springs School District 11 had earned a percentage of sales from school vending machines, it was able to dramatically increase revenues by establishing a deal with a soft drink manufacturer that—according to District officials—will bring the district between $8 and $11 million over ten years in exchange for exclusive district-wide vending rights.

Multnomah County's library system raises $40,000 per year by offering a VISA card option for paying fines.[21] The Commonwealth of Pennsylvania capitalized on exclusivity by contracting to make Microsoft the exclusive provider of e-mail and business-application software for every

---

[20] Schuster, Karolyn. "Exclusive Brand Contracts," *Food Management*, February, 1998. p. 34.

[21] Multnomah County Library. "The Official Website for Entrepreneurial Libraries," <http://www.multnomah.lib.or.us/lib/entre>

[22] Dilanian, Ken. "Pa. signs deal with Microsoft," *Philadelphia Inquirer*, July 14, 1998. p 1.

desktop computer in state government. State officials claim that the deal allowed the state to save at least $8 million on the cost of updating and standardizing its software and was worth enough to Microsoft that the software giant donated nearly $13 million in software and in-kind support to state education and economic development programs.[22] Companies pay millions to be the exclusive car of the Olympics or the official sports drink of Major League Baseball. In Philadelphia, and across the country, corporations have spent millions to "name" sports and entertainment venues. The City of Sacramento, California, has announced that it will sell sponsorships and naming rights to many City facilities.[23] Similarly, officials in Allegheny County, Pennsylvania, have proposed selling the naming rights to various county-owned buildings and facilities. New York City is working with the world's largest sports management and marketing agency to develop opportunities for City Parks, Transportation, and Sanitation departments to sell licensing rights to corporate sponsors.[24] Los Angeles County entered into an agreement with an automaker that calls for the company to donate vehicles for lifeguard operations in exchange for exclusivity—no other vehicle manufacturer can have signage at events on Los Angeles County beaches.[25]

To multiply the value of City marketing efforts, the City should develop exclusive-rights contracts with vendors and concessionaires. For a city looking to grow revenues and for companies looking to sell products, exclusivity can be a win-win situation.

POTENTIAL FUTURE CITY EXCLUSIVITY AVENUES

The City of Philadelphia offers many exclusivity opportunities that could raise revenues and provide value for companies looking to capture market share. Potential future City exclusivity avenues for the City include, but are by no means limited to, the following suggestions. The City could:

- Sell exclusive vending and pouring rights at City facilities and functions to beverage companies. The worth of such a contract could be increased exponentially by including the School District, the Philadelphia Zoo, and other institutions in an exclusive package.

- Sell the "naming rights" for City-owned sports and entertainment venues and other City-owned facilities.

- Sell exclusive rights to telephone companies that look to place public phones in City facilities and on City streets.

- Establish an exclusive arrangement with a credit card company to be the only company from which that the City would accept payments for City taxes, fines, and other fees.

- Explore exclusive contracts to reduce the cost of purchases of telecommunications technology, information technology, and maintenance supplies.

- Contract with a private company to operate restaurant facilities and provide maintenance services in John F. Kennedy Plaza Park (Love Park). The park, which often suffers from neglect and poor maintenance, is much traversed because of its location at the foot of the Benjamin Franklin Parkway just to the north and west of City Hall. The park is also home to a visitors' center that may soon be vacated and could be transformed into a restaurant facility.

---

[23] Suellentrop, Chris. "This Government Brought to You By...," *Governing*, November 1998. p. 43.

[24] Hurt, Harry III. "Parks brought to you by...," *U.S. News & World Report*, August 11, 1997. p. 45.

[25] Lemov, Penelope. "Balancing the Budget with Billboards and Souvenirs," *Governing*, October 1994. p. 50.

Capitalizing on Philadelphia's Largesse

Philadelphians can be very generous people. Many of the institutions that define Philadelphia to this day were initiated by private donors. The Free Library of Philadelphia, the nation's first public non-profit library, began as an effort by determined citizens to open a subscription library beyond the reach of the cultural elite. Pennsylvania Hospital, the first public hospital in what would become America, was originally funded through private donations matched by public funds. The City can capitalize on this ethic to improve Philadelphia facilities and the overall quality of life in the City.

The Fairmount Park Commission operates a "Gifts for all Seasons" program through which contributors can donate a bench or tree to the park system. Contributors can be recognized with plaques or certificates. The Free Library of Philadelphia Foundation solicits contributions to improve the library system. Salt Lake City, Utah, recognizes corporate donations that fund curb cuts by placing a gold medallion in curb cement noting, "Access provided by . . . ."[26] Colleges and universities and other non-profit institutions, of course, thrive on donations and customarily offer naming rights to buildings, rooms, and furnishings to encourage and recognize contributions.

The City should create a "legacy" program to aggressively market the concept of donating funds to the City. The administration of such a program could be contracted out to a private company or accomplished through the establishment of a non-profit corporation. Facility naming rights, plaques, and other recognition opportunities could be used to court donors from individuals looking to commemorate the birth of a child by planting a tree to groups looking to memorialize the passing of a loved one by having a recreation center named for them. The City could capitalize on the generosity of Philadelphians through grand gestures like naming the Municipal Services Building for a favored Philadelphian in exchange for a substantial contribution from supporters, to more modest efforts such as a "buy-a-brick" program to help fund City Hall renovations through the sale of engraved bricks in the City Hall courtyard. The City could follow the lead of Napa, California, and allow residents to check a box on their monthly water bills to donate funds toward specific City causes such as park development. In addition, the City could create a brochure describing recognition opportunities and specific worthy City causes to publicize citizens' ability to make charitable, tax-deductible donations to the City at holiday time and throughout the year. Opportunities could similarly be advertised on the City's web site.

RECOMMENDATIONS FOR ACTION

The City should evaluate its current menu of programs and activities enjoyed by the public to determine appropriate user fees. Fees should maximize revenue while minimizing barriers to participation in a way that does not prevent Philadelphians from taking advantage of what their City has to offer.

Action Steps:

- Establish a task force or mandate agency self-review to determine the true cost of City programs and activities.

- Complete efforts to assess the impact that fees and related regulations have on business creation and expansion.

- Design appropriate user charges and fees on an agency-by-agency basis to offset operating costs.

- Implement necessary controls to enable user-fee collections.

---

[26] Perlman, Ellen. "Disability Dilemmas," *Governing*, April, 1998. p. 33.

- Where possible, design user fees and charges to tax non-residents at a higher level than Philadelphians.

Fiscal Impact:

- Potential to raise additional revenue to offset City operating costs.

The City should evaluate its license charges on a regular basis to determine whether the City generates enough revenues to adequately cover administration expenses, or whether charges are unreasonably high and should be lowered to increase entry into the marketplace.

Action Steps:

- Establish a task force or mandate agency self-review to determine the true cost of administering inspections and other oversight procedures.

- Design appropriate user charges and fees on an agency-by-agency basis to offset administration costs.

- Eliminate those fees that do not generate enough revenues to adequately cover administration expenses.

- Eliminate unreasonably high fees that prevent entry into the marketplace.

- Implement necessary enforcement procedures to discourage non-compliance and increase the likelihood that consequences for violators will be swift and sure.

Fiscal Impact:

- Potential to raise additional revenue to offset City operating costs.

To use the City's purchasing power as an economic development tool and to reduce the burden on local businesses, the City should explore amending the Charter to allow a "local preference" to be granted for City bidders as part of the procurement process.

Action Steps:

- Work with City Council to amend the Charter to allow, where legally permissible, for the adoption of reasonable local-preference legislation.

- Work with City Council to adopt local-preference legislation.

- Establish policies and procedures for implementation of local preference in the City's competitive bidding rules.

Fiscal Impact:

- Potential increase in City revenue from expansion of local tax base.

To help raise revenue, expand services, and offset the City's need to raise taxes, the City should expand advertisement-leasing efforts to high-visibility City venues.

Action Steps:

- Establish an inventory of City properties that could be included in advertisement-leasing efforts.

- Contract with a private company to lease advertising space, construct and maintain advertisement receptacles, and oversee all phases of advertisement-leasing efforts.

Fiscal Impact:

- Potential to expand City revenues.

To expand revenue potential, the City should market expertise and services as well as the City name and other real and intellectual property.

Action Steps:

- Work to pass legislation in the Pennsylvania General Assembly to enable the City to market its expertise, services, and real and intellectual property.

- Alternatively, establish a not-for-profit organization or use a governmental authority to implement such a program.

- Create guidelines for permissible City and agency marketing efforts.

- Establish proper internal structures or work with a private company to create mail-order catalogues, a store to sell City wares, and other marketing outlets.

- Establish necessary financial and accounting protocols to enable such activities and to dedicate incoming revenues to specific agencies and programs.

- Market City and agency expertise, services, and real and intellectual property.

- Develop exclusive-rights contracts with City vendors and concessionaires to multiply value of City marketing efforts.

Fiscal Impact:

- Potential short-term cost to establish marketing infrastructure for City services and property.

- Potential to expand City revenues.

The City should create a "legacy" program to aggressively market the concept of donating funds to the City.

Action Steps:

- Establish proper approvals to receive donations from the state and federal governments.

- Create a "legacy" program to encourage individuals and organizations to donate funds to the City, its agencies, or specific programs.

- Alternatively, establish a not-for-profit organization or use a governmental authority to implement such a program.

- Establish necessary financial and accounting protocols to enable such activities and to dedicate incoming revenues to specific agencies and programs.

Fiscal Impact:

- Potential short-term cost to advertise "legacy" program.

- Potential to expand City revenues.

CONCLUSION

It is clear that the City cannot rely on tax increases to fund expansion of governmental services. It is equally clear that government is being asked to fund improvements in service-delivery efforts while reducing the cost of living and doing business in Philadelphia. Therefore, strict fiscal discipline must drive taxing and spending decisions as the City accepts the challenge of simultaneously reducing costs and improving services. To enforce that fiscal discipline, the City must impose overall budgetary structural balance to ensure that the cost of services does not exceed the ability of the local economy to fund those services. In addition, the City must reduce expenditures and increase revenues to fund future service improvements and tax cuts.

To achieve budgetary structural balance, the City can enact measures to link future spending to the City's economic growth. By establishing a rainy-day fund or budget-stabilization account, the City can prevent lavish spending in times of economic expansion while saving funds for future economic downturns. By creating appropriate asset-maintenance plans and rightsizing the government, the City can better ensure that future Philadelphia will be able to afford the cost of government over the long term. Finally, the City can maximize the impact of tax-reduction efforts by reducing the gross receipts portion of the City's Business Privilege Tax. By concentrating tax-reduction efforts on this particular tax, the City can generate the highest number of jobs for each dollar of tax reduction and make its tax policy consistent with the overall goal of creating jobs.

To fund future government expenditures and tax cuts, the City can reduce the cost of government, better collect what it is owed, and generate new revenues through entrepreneurial activities. By making collections more customer-friendly and improving intergovernmental cooperation, the City can increase tax collections. The City could generate savings by investing in upgraded technology and altering legal restrictions to improve governmental flexibility with regard to capital spending and long-term contracts. Additional savings could be realized through efforts to work with municipal unions to decrease the personnel-related cost of government. Finally, the City could generate new revenues by imposing reasonable user fees for currently undervalued governmental services, pursuing entrepreneurial ventures such as advertising revenues and exclusive-provider pacts, and tapping into the generosity of the citizenry.

To complement a government focused on improved service-delivery and stringent policies providing fiscal discipline, future Philadelphia must look toward proper governmental responses to specific urban challenges. The next chapter moves the discussion in that direction.

SECOND EDITION SUPPLEMENT TO CHAPTER 3
FISCAL POLICY FOR PHILADELPHIA'S FUTURE

FISCAL ISSUES AND PHILADELPHIA'S FUTURE

When the first edition of *Philadelphia: A New Urban Direction* was published, the city was returning to financial health. The scars of the fiscal crisis of the early 1990s were fading — tax rates were declining, tax revenues were growing, and the city accrued a comfortable fund balance, peaking at nearly $300 million in fiscal year 2000. With this comfortable financial cushion in place, the original recommendations made in *Philadelphia: A New Urban Direction* focused on ways to allocate our resources to have the maximum positive impact. Today Philadelphia's fiscal condition is precarious, as growth in expenditures outpaces revenue growth year after year, causing the city to once again flirt with red ink. Given this state of affairs, charting the correct course for the city will require innovative solutions to curb expenses and generate revenues.

The late 1990s were marked by an expanding national economy, and a strategic attempt in Philadelphia to adopt and implement policies to enhance local economic vitality and government efficiency. It was from this position of relative financial strength that many of the initial proposals were made. In the intervening years much has changed, and Philadelphia is once again struggling to maintain sound financial footing. Subsequent market and policy shifts at the local, state, and federal level have changed the framework in which the city's budget priorities are determined.

Today, the city's tax rates are still declining, creating a more conducive environment for private economic activity, and tax revenues continue to grow. Despite this, the city has suffered consecutive years of structural deficits, eating through the accumulated surplus. Failure to maintain a surplus jeopardizes the city's ability to handle unforeseen expenses and can undermine the city's debt ratings, leading to higher interest rates and issuance costs; and thus increasing future expenses. A diminished surplus can only be caused by either a shortfall in revenues, an expansion in costs, or a combination of both. In Philadelphia, much of the blame can be placed upon the city's ballooning obligations, rather than declines in revenue.

Between fiscal years 1998 and 2004, general fund revenues grew by 24 percent, with substantial increases in the Revenue from Other Governments and Locally Generated Tax Revenues. Over the same time period, the city's obligations grew by over 30 percent. Annual budgets have cautiously estimated revenues, particularly with respect to tax revenues, and contained wildly optimistic expenditure projections. Unfortunately, the growth in revenues has not been able to keep pace with growth in expenditures, driven by new programs and expenses, such as funding for new professional sports stadia, a bailout of the city-owned gas utility, and new blight- and crime-reduction initiatives, and the fund surplus has been depleted.

Philadelphia's General Fund obligations expanded at an average annual rate of 4.6 percent, outpacing inflation and further stressing the city's finances. Beyond the expected growth in expenditures indicated in the annual budgets, spending exceeded budgeted amounts annually from fiscal year 2000 through fiscal year 2004. The city's labor costs, including wages, healthcare, and pensions, accounted for 58 percent of the city's General Fund budget in fiscal year 2004. The city's expenditures on personnel expanded by 50 percent between fiscal years 1998 and 2004, in constant year 2000 dollars.

The fiscal year 2006 to 2010 Five-Year Financial Plan does not anticipate a return to the robust fund balances of the late 1990s. Without the substantial cushion provided by the positive fund balances of the late 1990s, managing expenditure growth becomes essential to meeting future fiscal challenges. Philadelphia has paid a significant price for its high tax rates, which helped chase firms and families out of the city. Raising tax rates in the future to cover expenditure growth would be counterproductive, and only serve to further shrink the tax base. Given current federal policies and budgetary stress at the state level, greatly enhanced revenues for Philadelphia from those sources is unlikely. The city must adopt a multi-pronged strategy to ensure a return to healthy fund balances and fiscal stability. This approach must focus on efforts to enhance the efficiency of service delivery and expansion of the tax base.

In this environment of fiscal stress, expensive labor contracts, and a shrinking tax base, the city must focus on doing a better, more efficient job of providing core services, rather than assuming additional burdens. Long-term strategies to address the diminished fund balance include reversing long-standing contributors to the city's decline, such as low educational attainment and crime. The city can meet these challenges in a manner that both produces improved outcomes and maintains fiscal stability. In the short term, it is essential that the city control costs, stem revenue reductions, and identify untapped alternative revenue sources.

Promoting Structural Balance for Fiscal Health

Given the changes in the city's financial condition since the original publication of *Philadelphia: A New Urban Direction*, maintaining structural balance and fiscal responsibility has become even more important. Unfortunately, Philadelphia continues to spend beyond its means and has not enacted necessary reforms to prevent future fiscal stress. Although legislation has twice been introduced to establish a Rainy Day Fund, no law has been enacted and Philadelphia still lacks a legal mechanism for socking away extra resources in case of unforeseen expenditures or an economic downturn in the future. As New Orleans and the Gulf Coast rebuilds in the wake of Hurricane Katrina and New York continues to contend with the physical and economic impacts of the terrorist attacks of September 11, 2001, it is clear that American cities cannot always predict their future needs. Philadelphia must provide itself with adequate funds for emergencies to ensure the ongoing viability of the city.

Maintaining Philadelphia's physical assets in peak condition remains a managerial and financial challenge. As yet, the city has not created a specific fund for maintenance of capital assets nor established a transparent process to assess the ongoing need for assorted city-owned or operated properties. The Philadelphia City Planning Commission has promulgated benchmarks for the appropriate nature and number of physical assets, such as parks, recreation centers, and libraries, given the city's current and future demographics, but a comprehensive strategy to right-size through strategic downsizing and introduction of multi-use facilities, and maintain the city's inventory of capital assets remains elusive. The City Controller's Office conducted an audit of the Department of Recreation that found unsafe conditions and significant deterioration, caused in part due to an oversupply of facilities. In addition to the recommendations in the original book to address the city's capital assets, the city should require that significant capital projects also project future maintenance and operations costs to better gauge the true costs associated with new physical developments.

Given that the city has not been able to adequately maintain existing facilities, Philadelphia needs to fully assess the costs and service needs generated by additional developments. Currently, the vast majority of capital projects that the city undertakes are funded with borrowed money that will have to be repaid with interest overtime. In addition to the costs associated with bond issuance, and principal and interest repayment, new facilities will require ongoing maintenance and other operating costs, such as utility charges and staffing. The affordability of new facilities can be better understood if all costs associated with a project are considered. This information should be made available to elected officials and the general public to better inform discussions regarding proposed capital projects.

Maintaining the appropriate number of public facilities is contingent upon a clear understanding of the nature and magnitude of the population to be served. Tracking Philadelphia's population accurately is essential to enable adequate planning for future needs and maintaining funding from state and federal sources that is allocated based on population. The 2000 US Census was conducted with an effort to correct a history of undercounting in urban areas, and resulted in a higher than expected population for Philadelphia and other major cities. The Philadelphia City Planning Commission utilized their Geographic Information System to supply the US Census Bureau with a comprehensive list of addresses which identified locations that the Census Bureau had not. Additionally, the city contracted with the United Way to do outreach to community groups and traditionally undercounted populations. The declining rate of population loss and improved counting procedures make the need to alter the definition of a first class city in the Commonwealth of Pennsylvania, recommended in first edition of *Philadelphia: A New Urban Direction*, less pressing.

As Philadelphia's population continues to shrink, fewer and fewer people will have to support the growing cost of local government. To ensure that future generations of Philadelphians can maintain fiscal health of the city, it is essential that today's leaders do not saddle them with an onerous debt burden. Like any homeowner with a mortgage, the City of Philadelphia has financial obligations to repay borrowed money. Debt repayment takes precedence in allocating the city's resources, before a single dollar can be used to pay a police officer or repave a road. As the amount of the annual budget allocated to debt repayment grows, it means a smaller proportion of funds are available for direct service delivery efforts. The city should adopt a comprehensive policy for debt issuance and management, and implement cost-saving recommendations, to prevent future fiscal peril.

There are already controls in place to guarantee that borrowing today will not overwhelm the taxpayers' capacity for repayment in the future. As far back as 1874, Article IX of the Pennsylvania Constitution established debt limits for Pennsylvania municipalities. In the beginning, the state constitution established a limit of seven percent of the assessed value of taxable property, both real and personal. Following several intermediate adjustments, the Pennsylvania Constitution was further amended in 1951 to base the debt limit on a 10-year average of assessed real estate valuations. The limit was increased to 13.5 percent of assessments and personal property was removed from the calculation of the debt limit's base. In addition, the 1951 changes included a distinction between electoral and non-electoral debt. Non-electoral debt allows Philadelphia's City Council to authorize up to 3.0 percent of the 10-year average of assessed real property for capital purposes without voter approval. The voters of the municipality must specifically authorize all other debt. However, in no case can the total of electoral and non-electoral debt exceed the 13.5 percent maximum.

Despite this limit, Philadelphia's debt service and long-term obligations continue to represent a growing portion of the annual budget and is a threat to Philadelphia's fiscal stability. Changes in the city's borrowing patterns, anticipated future borrowings, reduced credit ratings, and national economic forces signal that the city may once again be on a path to fiscal instability. The city is inching towards its debt limit, and at the same time is expanding the long-term obligations that do not count against its debt limit but the repayment of which is secured by the city.

In fiscal year 2006 more than 15 percent of every general fund revenue dollar will fund long-term obligations. Before any other obligation is paid, the first 15 cents must be spent on long-term obligations, thus leaving only 85 cents of every general fund dollar to deliver city services. As this ratio increases, less and less money will be available to fund vital services for the citizens of Philadelphia. Rarely is there any public debate surrounding the affordability of a new borrowing, unlike the scrutiny that tax reduction and new initiatives face. A dollar spent on debt service is a dollar that cannot be spent on other priorities, and it is important that the costs and benefits of each spending initiative be analyzed.

Borrowing is not necessarily harmful, and in many instances can provide a net benefit to the citizens of Philadelphia. Borrowing money allows the city to undertake projects and initiatives that could not be funded through the operating budget. For projects that have benefits that will be accrued for years, costs can be allocated over the same time horizon.

In 1992, Philadelphia was on the brink of bankruptcy. The city was unable to fund capital projects and infrastructure repairs, and if started projects were often unfinished. Budget deficits were mounting with projections in the $200 to $300 million range. Pension obligation payments went unpaid in favor of operating expenses. In short the city was "robbing Peter to pay Paul." With the creation of the Pennsylvania Intergovernmental Cooperation Authority (PICA) and the enactment of the PICA legislation, sound fiscal initiatives, sane spending polices, and a strong national economy, the city was able to begin the ascent back to safe financial ground.

Before the inception of PICA, Philadelphia's long-term obligations were near the maximum of its legal debt limit. When PICA was established in late fiscal year 1992, the remaining debt margin, the amount of money the city can borrow before reaching its limit, was a mere $82 million out of the over $1 billion the city was authorized to borrow. From fiscal years 1993 to 1995, the city did little borrowing on its own. During this time, city Capital Budgets were funded through PICA. As a result, the city lowered its gross bonded debt and expanded its debt margin. However, with recent borrowings and continued bonded debt authorization, the debt margin has once again narrowed. The city is again approaching a situation similar to the early 1990s.

As of February 1, 2005 the city's legal debt limit was approximately $1.3 billion with a legal debt incurring capacity remaining of $98.5 million. Thus, the city cannot seek authorization for more than this amount in new debt without first repaying some of its existing debt. The city currently has over $4.1 billion in total long-term obligations. However, only 20 percent of this total is actually attributed to the city's own bonded debt. The remaining 80 percent consists of other long-term obligations – quasi-governmental – and PICA debt.

One of the most striking aspects about debt in Philadelphia in recent years is the expansion of city debt obligations through the use of quasi-public agencies to circumvent the state-mandated limits on borrowing. Even though this debt does not count against the city's debt limit, it is a burden on city taxpayers and creates the potential for undermining the city's ability to provide services in the future. In these instances, quasi-governmental agencies issue debt for city projects, and the city makes lease payments to the agencies in an amount equal to the debt service. Projects and initiatives financed in this manner include the Neighborhood Transformation Initiative, for which bonds were issued by the Redevelopment Authority to reduce blight, the construction of the Criminal Justice Center and the Curran-Fromhold Correctional Facility, financed through the Philadelphia Municipal Authority in the 1990s, and new professional sports stadia supported by bonds issued by the Philadelphia Authority for Industrial Development.

Philadelphia may soon see relief for some of its obligations for the Pennsylvania Convention Center, as a result of state legislation authorizing slots facilities in the Commonwealth of Pennsylvania. The Pennsylvania Convention Center Authority (PCCA) was established in November 1986 to develop and promote a convention center facility in the Philadelphia metropolitan area. The authority is responsible for maintaining, furnishing, and operating the Pennsylvania Convention Center. Under a lease-and-service agreement between the city and PCCA, the city is required to pay an annual service fee to PCCA. In practice, a tax on hotel occupancy generates revenue to pay much of this debt. But, because the hotel taxes do not generate enough money to pay the full amount, the city must spend additional general fund dollars to pay the annual service fee. So long as there are any bonds outstanding, the service agreement cannot be terminated by the city, but tax revenues from gaming may eventually be used to reimburse the city for this expense. City obligations for the Pennsylvania Convention Center should be reduced in the future. The gaming-enabling legislation allocates a portion of the tax revenues for the expansion and operations of the Center.

The magnitude of the city's debt service and long-term obligations is not the only troubling aspect of the city's debt management. Choices the city makes today about the nature of the debt will have financial repercussions in the years to come. While there is little that can be done to lessen the weight of the city's past borrowing, strategic decision making can ensure that future generations of Philadelphians are not saddled with a crushing level of debt.

The city's debt policy should ensure that debt incurred today does not place such a burden on future Philadelphians that it will be more difficult to avoid fiscal peril in the future. To achieve this, the city should review new borrowing and lease and service agreements within the context of the city's overall long-term obligations and other budget priorities. While individual projects often appear useful and represent a tiny portion of annual spending, the compounded impact of numerous borrowings significantly constrains opportunities for spending on other priorities. Current practice is to debate these projects individually, outside of the annual budget setting process. Rather than approving these projects and initiatives on an ad hoc basis over the course of the fiscal year the Mayor could annually make a recommendation of how much additional annual debt service payment can be afforded, during the budget setting process. This could then be linked to the amount of funds that can be leveraged, given interest rates and borrowing costs. Once a total amount that could be borrowed is determined, potential projects can be prioritized and funded. For example, it could be determined that the city can afford an additional annual payment of $20 million in the future for debt service, and any new operating and maintenance costs that the new projects generate. A $20 million annual payment could support a $275 million in investment. The city would then review the total costs associated with proposed projects, prioritize them, and fund as many as possible until the aggregate costs equals $275 million.

Reducing the costs associated with Philadelphia's debt can also protect the future fiscal stability of the city, while making more funds available for to meet current needs. For the first time in recent history, the city issued two types of bonds, $50 million of fixed-rate bonds, and $200 million of variable-rate bonds. Now 25 percent of the city's outstanding general obligation bonds are variable rate. As a reference point, Boston has $803.8 million in general obligation bonds outstanding, all of which are fixed-rate bonds. The theory behind issuing variable rate bonds was that the rating agencies like to see the mix of fixed and variable rate bonds. However, Boston with all fixed rate bonds has a much higher credit rating by the three major rating agencies. Fitch, Moody's and Standard & Poor's have assigned ratings of "AA-," "Aa2'" and "AA'" respectively to these bonds reflecting Boston's capacity to pay debt service. Whereas Philadelphia latest rating as reported in the fiscal year 2004 financial statements for General Obligation Bonds were "A-," "Baa1," and "BBB," respectively from the same rating agencies.

The Controller's Office questions the wisdom of the issuance of bonds with variable-rate interest provisions. While this may save the city money presently, there is no guarantee that interest rates will not increase dramatically over the life of the bonds and rise above the current fixed rates. In fact, the Federal Reserve recently raised interest rates for the eighth time in the last year. While the current rate is still not threatening the city's variable rate bonds, continued rate hikes could be a further burden upon the citizens and taxpayers of Philadelphia. The city does have the option of refinancing these bonds at some future date but there are costs associated with any refinancing. The city should review its policy on variable rate debt given the rising interest rate environment.

Interest rates and the amount of principal are not the only factors influencing the total costs of debt issuance in Philadelphia. Arranging these financial transactions has typically required a significant number of professional services providers, such as legal counsel and financial advisors for all parties involved. These costs are paid out of the amount borrowed, and thus are repaid with interest over the life of the debt. To minimize the debt burden on future generations of Philadelphians, the city should look for ways to reduce costs associated with the issuance of debt.

Philadelphia uses a flat fee structure for professional services, under which firms are paid an individually negotiated amount plus reimbursement for out-of-pocket costs and no detailed record of performance is required. The city should change its procedures regarding professional services associated with bond issuance to ensure that it is receiving the best possible value. The city could pre-certify professional service providers who meet the city's performance and payment criteria, and then award contracts on a rotating basis. All professional service providers could also be required to submit detailed invoices. Philadelphia may also achieve savings by funding debt issuance costs out of the operating budget rather than bond proceeds, as the City of Boston does.

RECOMMENDATIONS FOR ACTION

The city should project all costs associated with capital projects, including principal and interest repayment and ongoing operations and maintenance costs, prior to committing funding.

Action Step:

- Create mechanism to forecast all costs associated with capital projects over their useful lifetime.

Fiscal Impacts:

- Potential to improve future budgeting through enhanced information about future needs.

- Potential increased expenses from new administrative activities.

The city should review new borrowing and lease and service agreements within the context of the city's overall long-term obligations and other budget priorities.

Action Steps:

- Determine the city's willingness and ability to support additional annual long-term obligations.

- Identify the amount of funding that can be leveraged with that amount.

- Work with City Council to prioritize and fund projects and initiatives.

Fiscal Impact:

- Long-term improved fiscal stability.

The city should review its policy on variable-rate debt.

Action Steps:

- Assess other cities' use of variable rate debt and the reaction of the rating agencies.

- Consult economists on the likelihood and impact of rising interest rates.

- Apply conclusions to future borrowings.

Fiscal Impact:

- Potential decrease in future debt service obligations.

The city should reduce the costs associated with debt issuance.

Action Steps:

- Pre-certify professional service providers who meet the city's performance and payment criteria, and then award contracts on a rotating basis.
- Require additional performance documentation from service providers.
- Pay debt issuance costs with operating rather than borrowed funds.

Fiscal Impacts:

- Elimination of interest costs for professional services.
- Saving from increased competition and monitoring.

PRODUCING A SOUND TAXATION PLAN

Efforts to craft a more sound taxation plan for Philadelphia have produced concrete results in the past five years. Since the initial publication of *Philadelphia: A New Urban Direction*, when we called for a comparison of Philadelphia's tax structure with rival jurisdictions, and a focus on reducing the job-killing Business Privilege Tax, the nature of the debate around Philadelphia's taxes has been transformed. Already, the city has reviewed Philadelphia's tax structure in relation to other jurisdictions, and incremental reductions to the gross receipts portion of the Business Privilege Tax have been enacted. No longer do civic, government, and business leaders question whether the city needs tax reform. Without a fair and competitive tax structure, investments in public infrastructure, programs and amenities will have limited impact in reversing decades of population and job loss. Conversely, tax reductions that lead to a decline in services will also confound attempts to improve the city, both socially and economically. A proper balance between the two can be established, while still ensuring the fiscal stability of the city budget. The positive impact of steady Wage Tax rate reductions, as well as continued evidence of the devastating impact of the city's high tax burden on local economic activity, are broadly understood. Current discussions focus on what form the reductions should take, their magnitude, and their timing.

Much of the current policy activity with regard to taxation in Philadelphia had its genesis in a fall 2001 report issued by the City Controller's Office. The *Tax Structure Analysis Report* reviewed the role city taxes play in driving residents and employers from Philadelphia and evaluated the city's taxes in comparison with rival cities and surrounding jurisdictions. It examined what the city should do, in theory, and analyzed what it could implement, given legal and other barriers, and crafted recommendations based on what the city can accomplish within its current constraints.

According to research performed for the Controller's report, despite positive growth in the U.S. economy since 1992, and positive growth in the regional economy since 1993, it was not until after the city reduced taxes that it finally experienced some limited job growth. In fiscal year 1996, the city began a series of cuts to the Wage Tax and the gross receipts portion of the Business Privilege Tax. According to the Bureau of Labor Statistics, employment in Philadelphia finally increased — after nine straight years of decline — between 1997 and 2000 by more than 30,000 jobs. More important, city tax revenue increased significantly even after the tax cuts. Despite the cut in the Wage Tax rate, total Wage Tax collections increased by 18.8 percent between fiscal year 1995 and fiscal year 2001 — an increase greater than the rate of inflation. Similarly, despite cuts in the gross receipts portion of the Business Privilege Tax that represented a 10.7 percent reduction to the overall Business Privilege Tax rate between fiscal year 1995 and fiscal year 2001, total Business Privilege Tax collections increased by 33.2 percent during the same period — also greater than the rate of inflation.

It was determined that to improve the city's competitiveness Philadelphia needed to accomplish the following:

- Significantly reduce business taxes;
- Shift taxes to cut Wage Tax and encourage development through a shift to Land Value Taxation;
- Accelerate the pace of Wage Tax reductions;
- Eliminate confusing/unfair elements of the tax structure; and
- Improve business-friendliness of the tax structure.

Despite the clear call to action in the City Controller's *Tax Structure Analysis Report* and other publications, in the winter of 2001 Mayor Street announced a policy shift that would have halted the incremental reductions in the city's Wage Tax in place since 1996, while increasing the pace of reduction to the gross receipts portion of the Business Privilege Tax. Taken together, these changes would have diminished the tax reductions, as compared to the tax rate declines embodied in the prior year's Five-Year Financial Plan. The City Controller convened a group of influential citizens that spawned a broad coalition of community, government, media, and business leaders that demanded that the reductions continue as scheduled, culminating in a march on City Hall with over 1,000 participants. The efforts were successful and the Wage Tax rate reductions were restored.

The alliance built to preserve the Wage Tax rate reductions enhanced the momentum for tax reform in Philadelphia. In the following months, Controller Saidel continued to lead efforts to promote business tax reforms and exploration of Land-Value Taxation (LVT), as was called for in the first edition of *Philadelphia: A New Urban Direction*. Through implementation of LVT, the tax burden on structures would be reduced and the portion of Real Estate taxes on land would be increased. This shift could help combat the city's spreading scourge of blight by encouraging development and reducing the incentives for allowing properties to decay or remain underutilized. It would also reduce the tax burdens for more than 80 percent of city homeowners. While these and other efforts helped educate government officials and the public about the need and opportunities for tax reform, it became clear that a more comprehensive approach would be needed to ensure that Philadelphia could create a competitive tax structure and lessen the tax burden.

A resolution was introduced to amend the City Charter to authorize the formation of a commission to examine tax related issues. In November 2002, by an overwhelming four-to-one margin, the voters of Philadelphia endorsed the creation of the Tax Reform Commission. The Commission set out to create a fiscally responsible blueprint for tax reform and reduction in January 2003. The Commission comprised 15 appointees selected by the Mayor, the City Controller, the City Council President, and representatives of various business organizations. Despite initial concerns that the Commission would simply slow the momentum of tax reform in Philadelphia, a package of recommendations was put forth in less than one year.

The Tax Reform Commission found, as many had expected, that Philadelphia's tax burden was much higher than the surrounding suburbs and other cities with which we compete for economic activity. Additionally, the Commission discovered that the distribution of taxes among certain groups of taxpayers was far from equitable. To improve the fairness of the city's tax structure and enhance Philadelphia's economic competitiveness the Commission included recommendations to:

- Eliminate the Business Privilege Tax to make Philadelphia a more competitive location for businesses;
- Reduce the Wage Tax to attract and retain firms and families;
- Implement Land-Value Taxation to encourage development and discourage speculation;
- Improve the accuracy and fairness of the city's real estate assessment system;

- Improve fairness in the way the city taxes incorporated and unincorporated firms so that sole proprietors and partnerships no longer pay a higher tax burden than their corporate competitors; and
- Adopt single-sales factor apportionment based on Philadelphia sales to remove the disincentive for firms with few Philadelphia sales to remain in the city.

The blueprint was bold in its goals, but adopted a modest and incremental approach to implementation to ensure that the changes were fiscally responsible and did not create a shock to the city budget. While the work of the Tax Reform Commission was heartily endorsed by a broad array of community and business organizations, including the 21st Century Review Forum and the Economic Development Summit, both convened by the Mayor, City Council and the Administration held that the work of the Commission required additional study. Commission members urged the adoption of the 28 specific recommendations as a package, as the success of some were dependent of the implementation of others. This was not the tactic embraced by the Administration and City Council and a piecemeal approach to tax reform continued.

The debate on tax reform has taken place during a period of fiscal uncertainty for Philadelphia. A nearly $300 million surplus has been all but eliminated, and despite years of increased spending and borrowing, Philadelphia's municipal services' quality continues to fall short in many areas. Concerns arose that continuing tax reductions would hamstring efforts to improve the quality of life in Philadelphia by diverting much needed resources away from the public sector. To date, this supposition has not been borne out, based on a review of tax revenue collections since the city's rate reductions began in 1996. Each year, revenues rose despite the rate reductions.

Many of the recommendations proposed by the City Controller's Office and the Tax Reform Commission have been adopted, yet much more remains to be done to ensure that Philadelphia has a fair and competitive tax structure. These efforts have been focused in three main categories: the Wage Tax; the Real Estate Tax; and business taxes. These are the areas in which the city taxes more than competitor jurisdictions, with institutionalized inequalities. The Board of Revision of Taxes is overhauling the method of property assessment to increase fairness and transparency. Incremental cuts to the gross receipts portion of the Business Privilege Tax are planned. Technical changes to the Real Estate Transfer Tax have been made to close loopholes that have been exploited by certain commercial entities and a schedule of Wage Tax rate reduction is in place through 2015 to reduce the rate to 3.25 percent, the lowest rate since 1969.

Additional Wage Tax rate reductions are scheduled to occur as a result of a redistribution of state tax revenues from slots facilities. The enabling legislation for gaming in the Commonwealth envisions that a portion of the taxes on these facilities will be used to offset local revenue losses as a result of Wage Tax rate reduction in Philadelphia. Philadelphia's receipt of these funds is contingent upon the city continuing planned rate reductions, in addition to the steeper cuts made possible from the receipt of gaming revenues until 2010. The gaming-funded Wage Tax rate reductions can spur economic development without reducing revenues received by the City of Philadelphia from this source. The combination of the already legislated Wage Tax rate reductions and the steeper reductions enabled by the transfer of gaming tax revenues can result in a supply side effect. The share of the funds that will be available from the Commonwealth for Philadelphia cannot yet be determined as fewer than expected taxing jurisdictions have opted to participate in the revenue sharing. There are ongoing discussions about altering the mechanism for disbursement of gaming revenues to local taxing jurisdictions for tax reduction. Furthermore, the amount of revenues will also be dependent upon the timing and success of the introduction of this industry into the Commonwealth.

Given the uncertainty of the receipt of these funds and the requirement to continue Wage Tax reductions in the coming years, currently recommended improvements to the tax structure, such as the gradual elimination of the Business Privilege Tax, should not be abandoned or altered. These tax reform recommendations represent an affordable means of creating a less onerous, fairer and more competitive tax structure without sacrificing the city's ability to deliver services.

RECOMMENDATIONS FOR ACTION

The city should reform its business taxes to encourage economic expansion and improve fairness.

Action Steps:

• Work with City Council to enact legislation to gradually eliminate both the net income and gross receipts portions of the Business Privilege Tax.

• Adopt single-factor apportionment to remove a disincentive for businesses with the majority of their sales outside Philadelphia from locating here.

• Eliminate disparities in the city's business taxes that place unequal burdens on different types of business entities.

Fiscal Impacts:

• Potential short term costs from revenue reductions.

• Potential long-term revenue growth from increased economic activity.

The city should reform its real estate taxes to discourage speculation and neglect and improve budgeting and fairness.

Action Steps:

• Work with City Council to implement Land-Value Taxation by shifting a greater portion of the tax burden to the land, and lessen the burden on structures to encourage development and remove incentives for allowing properties to deteriorate.

• Make the imposition of the Real Estate Tax more fair by separating the assessment and appeals functions,

• Create a taxpayer advocate.

• Address issues of people's ability to pay to protect vulnerable homeowners.

• Institute a system of budget-based rate setting after the assessments are completed each year.

Fiscal Impacts:

• Potential costs associated with new positions and procedures.

• Potential revenue growth from reduced property decline and neglect.

• Potential tax expenditures to address people's ability to pay.

INCREASING COLLECTIONS TO HOLD DOWN TAX INCREASES

In 1999, the Controller's Office offered recommendations to improve the city's tax collection efforts. Then, as now, we believe that one of the best ways to fairly generate revenue to support city services is to ensure that all taxpayers can and do pay the amounts owed. Through the use of online forms and payment options, the city has improved customer service and efficiency. The Revenue Department has also been working to improve collection rates for a variety taxes. The city has been matching city records with Internal Revenue Service data to better identify individuals who are liable for Philadelphia Wage Taxes but had previously not being making payments. The efforts of the Tax Reform Commission included recommendations to simplify the filing and collection procedures for some taxes. The embrace of proposals from the first edition of *Philadelphia: A New Urban Direction* represents progress, but further improvements remain. The city still has not yet enacted a formal agreement with the Commonwealth for tax information sharing, and tax filing and collection could be further simplified to promote greater compliance and improve customer service as was originally recommended.

REDUCING THE COST OF GOVERNMENT — NON-PERSONNEL RELATED

Philadelphia's expenditures continue to expand at a greater pace than revenue receipts. One mechanism to address this imbalance is to reduce the resources needed to complete various government tasks. In the first edition of *Philadelphia: A New Urban Direction* we identified numerous ways that the city could reduce the cost of government. With respect to contracting for goods and services, the Controller's Office stated that savings could be achieved by reducing the period of time it takes to process invoices and committing to paying vendors within 30 days. The City Controller's Office has reduced the amount of time it requires to approve payment voucher from approximately two weeks to three days as a result of reorganization and cross-training of personnel. Other technological enhancements to reduce costs associated with procurement have been implemented, such as making bid documents available online.

Other methods of reducing that the costs of government, such as repealing the state's four part bidding law, altering the Charter to allow agencies other than the Revenue Department to bill water and sewer rents and to allow long-term real estate leases, have not been implemented to date. Although the city has neither expanded the Productivity Bank nor created a separate Technology Bank, funding of technological enhancements with funds to be repaid with the savings enabled by the technological improvements continues. Productivity Bank loans have recently been authorized for website creation and improvement, electronic bill payment over the Internet, and a computerized system to monitor the attendance of Police personnel in city courtrooms.

REDUCING THE COST OF GOVERNMENT — PERSONNEL RELATED

Given that personnel costs represent a large portion of the annual General Fund budget and that these costs continue to grow, managing the expense of the city's workforce is an essential element of fiscal stability, as it is necessary that the city provide high quality services at a price the citizens can afford. The workforce of Philadelphia's government—its police, sanitation workers, librarians, health service providers, elected officials and many others—are the greatest asset of the city, ensuring the delivery of vital services. At nearly 58 percent of the budget, personnel costs are by far the largest expenditure from the city's General Fund. Despite the city's difficult financial situation over the past few years, personnel costs continue to grow. Improved human resource management structures would enable improved quality and quantity of services through enhanced workforce efficiency, without further burdening city taxpayers. Reducing the cost of Philadelphia's workforce by a modest one percent could save the city almost $20 million annually, freeing funds for higher employee wages, increased or diversified services, or lower taxes for all Philadelphians.

In 1999, the Controller's Office presents recommendations to both lower costs and improve the quality of Philadelphia's workforce and the services it provides to the public. We had proposed that the city open more opportunities for competitive bidding in service delivery. Although competitive contracting continues, it has not been aggressively pursued and we continue to recommend that the city pursue these opportunities. In particular, the city should explore contracting out the operations of the Philadelphia Gas Works (PGW). In 1999, we noted that the city could receive a greater return on its investment than the $18 million annual payment set by City Council under an alternative management structure. As of fiscal year 2005, these payments and repayment of a $45 million loan made to PGW by the city have been suspended. At the same time, rising natural gas rates and other factors have led the management of PGW to request and receive approval for increased rates for customers. We strongly suggest that alternative management structures be explored to address these issues.

The Controller's Office also recommended that the city explore creating a four-day workweek and we continue to support this recommendation. In addition to proposal's cost-reduction potential, this recommendation could contribute to improved air quality and reduced traffic congestion by diminishing the number of commuters on the city's roads on a given day. We also recommended the city implement short-and long-term disability plans to lessen sick leave abuse and save money. Although the city indicated a intent to enact such a program, no labor contract has been negotiated to include this personnel management practice.

In 1999, the Controller's Office recommended that an incentive program be created to help reduce the city's liability costs. In this new edition of *Philadelphia: A New Urban Direction* we propose an expanded version of this idea. The city should encourage innovation among city workers to generate revenues, reduce expenses, and improve service. In order to further promote cooperation and to encourage a sentiment of stakeholdership among the workforce, Philadelphia should actively encourage and utilize creativity and innovation from its employees. As the center of operations and service provision, the city's employees are best positioned to identify practices and procedures with potential to improve services, reduce costs, or both. Programs directed at promoting employee innovation can not only increase productivity and efficiency, but also encourage management and staff communication.

While encouraging innovation among employees may produce innovative ideas and suggestions, employees will have little incentive to think and act creatively or implement new ideas unless provided with some tangible benefit. By allowing employees or a department as a whole to receive a portion of generated savings, management and employees will have motivation to find and implement cost saving mechanisms. As such, Philadelphia should seek to implement a system of gain sharing, enhancing employee participation in and benefit from the successful savings initiatives.

Baltimore County's gain-sharing system provides a concrete illustration of a program that, in only its first year, saved the county more than $600,000. Working under employees voluntarily trained as "Team Facilitators," groups of employees team together to identify, evaluate, and market cost-saving proposals to the Personnel Department and the County Executive. If approved and savings are realized, individual employee bonuses are determined by the proposing team, a task typically reserved for management.

To further motivate employee excellence, the city could institute a system of financial rewards for outstanding work. In the private sector, employees are routinely awarded bonuses for high achievement, a system that public institutions have been slow to adopt. Monetary bonuses or salary increases create incentives for employee diligence, while concurrently demonstrating recognition and appreciation of effort. In order to create a viable system of performance pay, Philadelphia must first create an equitable performance measurement system and train management in performance measurement and evaluation.

The City of Claremont, California was one of the first cities to institute a performance-pay program, initially in an effort to retain employees. Based on the recommendation of supervisors responsible for regular employee evaluations, city employees can become eligible to receive bonuses up to 10 percent of their annual salaries. Additionally, each month three or four employees are nominated by their peers to receive the Recognition Award of up to $750. To ensure that performance-based incentives are fairly awarded the city would need a reliable method of assessing employees' contributions to government operations. Without an effective, comprehensive performance management system for individuals, agencies, and the governing entity as a whole, improving compensation and training programs will arguably yield lesser returns than could otherwise be achieved if the active gauging operations was a priority. Granted sufficient flexibility in hiring and operational practices, management can be held accountable for the performance of their staff and department. By incorporating goal setting, benchmarking, and by linking budgets to performance measures, budget and management decisions would more aptly reflect the priorities of the government while facilitating quantifiable improvements to service delivery.

The City of Austin, Texas actively monitors agency performance in an effort to guide managerial decisions. Each department creates a business plan outlining a mission and goals, extending from individual employees to the department as a whole, which are then linked to the budget and measures of outcome. Included in their performance management system is the Success Strategy Performance Review (SSPR). Each city employee is evaluated with the SSPR, with supervisor and employee acting in congress to develop goals and to gauge performance. An individual's SSPR evaluation also details his/her contribution to agency outcomes, as well as performance goals to the overall business plan.

While bonuses and performance pay may alleviate some of the public versus private sector compensation disparity, cities struggle to attract and retain the most talented individuals, due to generally lower salary levels for similar jobs. Salaries are assigned by job class, leaving management little leeway to adjust offered salaries based on the skills and experiences of potential employees. Moreover, allocating salary by job class is typically unresponsive to market demand, preventing municipalities from competing with the private sector for high quality individuals with in-demand skills. Frequently, a raise in salary is only possible through an increase in job classification, irrespective of the work actually being performed.

The city could adopt a "broad-banding" system to be more flexible and manageable, allowing for some decentralization of human resources to the departmental or agency level. The number of job classes would be reduced and generalized, while expanding the range of acceptable salaries for each position. In cities that have introduced significant flexibility into human resource operations, government salaries have become more competitive with the private sector and enabled salary levels to respond to market pressures for individuals with in-demand abilities. Moreover, broad-banding systems have allowed management to raise employee salaries periodically or for exceptional performance, without necessitating a change in job classification.

In 1999, the Controller's Office recommended that the city reduce the pension fund's unfunded liability and that opportunities to provide pensioners with cost of living increases should be explored. The city issued approximately $1.3 billion in pension obligation bonds in fiscal year 1999 to reduce the unfunded liability, but is now pursuing a strategy that pushes costs onto the future taxpayers. Beginning in fiscal year 2004, the city began to fund the pension using the minimum municipal obligation payment, which calls for lower payments than the city had been making previously. While this saves the city money in the short term, it increased the unfunded liability in the out years.

Although the city has not yet implemented all of the Controller's recommendations for reduced costs and improved quality of personnel, Philadelphia has embarked on new initiatives to improve human resource management. Philadelphia introduced a retirement incentive, the Deferred Retirement Option Plan (DROP), to improve the quality of the city workforce in October 1999. The city instituted this program to try to keep the more-experienced employee, especially in the uniformed forces, from leaving the payroll. This retains institutional knowledge while providing a date certain for experienced employees to leave city employment. With the more-experienced employee still on the job, the city can plan to train younger employees for promotional opportunities within the department. Thus, DROP could be viewed not only as a retirement incentive, but also as a way to facilitate on-the-job training throughout the government.

Under this program, the city is relieved of its obligation to contribute to the pension fund for an employee in the DROP, and the administration knows that regardless of all other factors, any employee who enrolls in DROP must separate from the payroll in a maximum of 48 months. By having a definitive period, the administration maintains flexibility in planning future budgets and future personnel levels. Thus, the framework for right-sizing the government takes shape. The DROP affords the city the opportunity to re-evaluate departmental staffing levels, as well as cross train new and current employees. It allows the city to hire additional employees in areas where needed and re-deploy employees within departments.

Participants in the DROP accumulate pension payments as if retired, but still remain on the active city payroll. Active DROP participants' accumulated pension payments are guaranteed to earn 4.5 percent annually. The payments, while credited to the individual DROP participant, remain with the pension fund. There is no separation or segregation of dollars; the pension fund keeps control of the money. The advantage here is that the city has the opportunity to reinvest these pension dollars in hopes of having a return on their investments greater than the guaranteed 4.5 percent for DROP participants. Any return greater than the guaranteed rate is kept in the pension fund and used for further reinvestment of pension dollars. When the DROP originated, the stock market — which historically has averaged a return of approximately 11 percent per year — was performing well and the fund enjoyed returns of 15 percent in fiscal year 1998, 11 percent in fiscal year 1999, and 9.5 percent in fiscal year 2000, well above the 9.0 percent return rate set by the actuary. As the stock market started to decline, the fund absorbed losses of 5.5 percent and 5.2 percent in fiscal year 2001 and fiscal year 2002, respectively. In spite of this fact, the city was obligated to pay the DROP participants the guaranteed rate even though the fund was not performing at an equivalent level. If the pension fund continues to earn less than 4.5 percent over the long term, the DROP's 4.5 percent guarantee will create a significant cost to the city in future years.

Due to action by the Board of Pensions and Retirement, this program will continue into the future. The Controller's Office is pleased to see the continuation of the DROP, but suggests that, with some adjustment to the guaranteed earning rate, the program can be improved. Rather than a guaranteed return of 4.5 percent, the city should offer DROP participants a variable rate of return tied to the performance of the pension fund. This return could be a combination of a guaranteed return of at least 1.5 percent plus a calculated percentage of the annual return on the pension investments. The annual review of the funds performance would determine the return for each successive year.

RECOMMENDATIONS FOR ACTION

The city should explore alternative management for the Philadelphia Gas Works.

Action Steps:

- Identify alternative management structures for PGW.
- Assess costs and benefits various alternatives.
- Pursue most positive alternative.

Fiscal Impacts:

- Potential short-term costs associated with evaluation of alternatives.
- Potential long-term revenue increases from loan repayment and expanded annual payments.

- Potential long-term tax revenues from gas works operations if new management is a for-profit entity.

The city should use financial compensation to encourage innovation among city employees to reduce costs, generate revenue, and improve service.

Action Steps:

- Initiate program to solicit and evaluate employee recommendations for improvement to government operations and establish procedures for implementing recommendations.
- Establish performance measurement system linking employee actions to overall goals.
- Institute a system of financial rewards for outstanding work.
- Adopt a "broad-banding" system to be more flexible and manageable, allowing for some decentralization of human resources to the departmental or agency level.

Fiscal Impacts:

- Potential operational costs for suggestion program administration and rewards.
- Potential revenue generation and cost reductions from suggestion implementation.
- Potential short-term costs associated with implementing personnel performance measurement.
- Potential costs associated with performance payments.
- Potential savings from improved worker productivity and retention.

The city should offer DROP participants a variable rate of return tied to the performance of the pension fund.

Action Steps:

- Work with the Pension Board to alter the rate of return for DROP participants.

Fiscal Impacts:

- Potential reduced cost of DROP payments

GETTING THE WORTH FOR THE CITY — GENERATING REVENUE

In 1999, the Controller's Office proposed that Philadelphia would be better equipped to provide amenities to residents and visitors if it accurately recouped the costs of services through user fees and permitting costs. These recommendations have been implemented in some areas. To better reflect the cost of issuance, the city increased various city fees, including ditch permits and copies of Police Incident Reports. The city also found that the cost of issuing a gun permit far exceeds the state-regulated fee, and has lobbied state legislators to have the permit cost increased. While this represents important progress, the city should implement a regular procedure for the evaluation of permit fees and the costs of issuance to ensure that costs are recovered without unnecessarily creating barriers to participation for business and personal activities regulated by the city.

To offset the need to raise taxes and to help generate revenue and expand services, the first edition of *Philadelphia: A New Urban Direction* recommended that the city pursue more advertising and sponsorship opportunities. Since then, the city has also announced its intention to create a comprehensive strategic marketing program to generate revenue. Some piecemeal efforts have been achieved, such as the placement of trash receptacles with advertising space on city sidewalks and leasing city rooftops for the placement of telecommunications equipments. Although the city's comprehensive effort has yet to be completed, other cities and the Philadelphia School District have developed programs for corporate sponsorships and naming rights. Philadelphia should continue its efforts in this area and integrate opportunities for corporate and private legacy programs to support city activities.

As the Controller's Office recommended in the original publication of *Philadelphia: A New Urban Direction*, the Charter was amended to provide for a local preference in the awarding of city contracts. Effective since July 2004, local firms meeting certain criteria have their bid price discounted by five percent during the evaluation process. Progress has also been achieved in marketing the city's expertise and services. The Philadelphia City Planning Commission began to market its unique expertise by charging private citizens and developers for the maps it produces. This effort is anticipated to generate $60,000 annually. The city has also developed an improved system for right-of-way management, which charges fees based on the surface area of the street being opened, and the age of the street.

CONCLUSION

Continuing dedication to ensuring that our workers work better, smarter, and safer can transform the city's human resources into a model of efficiency and equity. Pursing opportunities to reduce costs and generate revenues are essential to maintaining the fiscal health of the city and ensuring that the service needs of Philadelphians can be met. Capable management should seek to inspire a sense of purpose and mission within agencies, allowing employees to see the results of their actions and the effect on the city and its people—recognizing outstanding performance and rewarding it, monetarily and otherwise. Through active assessment and accountability mechanisms, Philadelphia's leadership can demonstrate the value government offers, providing effective and efficient service at the lowest possible cost to its taxpayers.

While it is addressing the needs of current citizens, it is also imperative that the city protect the resources needed to serve the next generation of Philadelphians. Careful consideration of the debt issued by the city is essential to ensure that Philadelphia's infrastructure is maintained without leaving inadequate resources to meet other obligations in the future. The city must also ensure that the costs of living and doing business in Philadelphia are not so high that firms and families continue to leave Philadelphia. Fiscally responsible, comprehensive tax reforms can improve the city's competitive economic position, without undermining the city's ability to provide needed services. With sound fiscal policies, the city will be able to meet the needs of its populace today and in the future.

CHAPTER 4
RESPONDING TO SPECIFIC URBAN CHALLENGES

States, like other things, have a function to perform;
and the state which shows the highest capacity
for performing the function of a state
is therefore the one which should be counted greatest.

—Aristotle
The Politics

PHILADELPHIA'S SPECIFIC GOVERNMENTAL CHALLENGES

Until this point, this document has focused on ways to fundamentally change the City of Philadelphia's approach to governing in the 21st century. Previous sections have addressed appropriate governmental structure and sound fiscal policies to enable government to better prepare for Philadelphia's future. Such subjects are crucial to governmental operations, just as changing the rules of any game will dramatically affect the way the game is played. Altering the size of baseball's strike zone would favor some players and hurt others. Allowing the king to move more than one square per turn in chess would change players' strategic thinking process. But, ultimately, the skill of individual players and the tactics they employ will determine the outcome of the game. City governance and fiscal policies can foster or inhibit effective and efficient governmental operations. But such changes only enable improvement in actual governmental operations. Altering governance can only create conditions that can lead to better service delivery. Changing fiscal policies can only promote growth, not ensure it.

Therefore, the emphasis of this document now shifts away from macro-level discussions about the structure and policies of Philadelphia's government, toward more specific discussions of the governmental challenges that confront the City and its agencies. How Philadelphia deals with specific problems—encouraging economic development, educating its children, making the City safe—will determine how Philadelphia residents, employers, and visitors respond. A city with reasonable regulatory policies encourages business formation. A city with excellent schools retains residents. A city with safe streets attracts visitors. Having set forth policy recommendations designed to create a government that works and fiscal policies crafted to design a sustainable system for Philadelphia to live within its means, the following sections detail proper governmental responses to specific future challenges.

ECONOMIC DEVELOPMENT—GROWING PHILADELPHIA INTO THE FUTURE

Like many other urban centers across the United States, Philadelphia has fallen into a state of economic distress. The extraordinary growth in the national economy during the last business expansion has done very little to break the crushing cycle of poverty and related social problems. Local efforts to capitalize on tourism as a growth industry are simply not enough to provide the

City with a solid economic foundation for the next century. Recent changes in federal and state welfare laws have added a new dimension to the City's socioeconomic problems. Soon, roughly 60,000 heads of households in the City of Philadelphia will be forced to find work in an economy that has just maneuvered out of a recession-like state.[1] As the welfare-reform clock ticks, the pressure to expand the local economy mounts and local officials continue to search for answers.

Harvard economist Michael Porter may indeed have an answer. He has vociferously argued that it is time to put away the social model of delivering government services in favor of an economic model. The emphasis under the social model was to redistribute wealth in an effort to fund the necessary social services and income supports to lift City residents out of poverty and subsidize selected businesses (in favor of others). Though well intentioned, these policies have been a failure for two reasons.

First, the social model fails to address the underlying problems associated with a significant underinvestment in skills and infrastructure that are now necessary for individuals and businesses to compete in the global economy. Often due to lack of funds and/or the inefficient use of existing funds, training programs fall short in providing trainees with the high level of general skills that are demanded by employers in today's economy.[2] As compensation for the City's debilitating tax structure, subsidies designed to temporarily increase business and personal incomes are offered to businesses without consideration for the true long-term costs or benefits to the local economy. However, because the tax structure is still debilitating, and residents still lack the requisite skills demanded by employers, government persists in using subsidies to compensate for problems without addressing them directly.

Second, as competition in the global marketplace intensified, businesses and residents became more reluctant to pay the higher taxes required to support business subsidies and anti-poverty programs. Partially due to the technological advances that enable businesses to locate anywhere, attempts to redistribute wealth within the City encouraged a massive outmigration of jobs and people following those jobs.

Alternatively, an economic model addresses the problems inherent in the social model by altering the general focus of local policymaking from the redistribution of wealth to the creation of wealth. In considering public investment, the most efficient means of creating wealth is to ensure that the citizens of Philadelphia have the opportunity to be gainfully employed. It follows that government taxing and spending decisions must be guided by an economic paradigm centered on maximizing employment opportunities.

In addition to tax cuts, many of the City's recent business attraction and retention initiatives have been designed to lower the tax burden on selected employers. To do so, the City has used Tax Increment Financing (financial instruments designed to set aside future property tax gains to fund current real estate developments), designated portions of the City as areas where employers receive certain tax breaks, and created tax abatements for selected projects. Unless the City is to be forever at the mercy of employers requesting tax breaks, it must complement such initiatives with efforts that capitalize on the City's competitive advantage and reduce the disadvantages that employers associate with operating a business in the City. Sustainable growth will only occur when employers want to locate in Philadelphia—ultimately this will be determined by the fitness level of the City's business environment.

---

[1] In the "1996–1997 Mid-Year Economic and Financial Update" the Controller's Office introduced a measure of the local business cycle—the coincident index for the City of Philadelphia. According to this measure of the aggregate state of the local economy, the City of Philadelphia was in a recession-like state from April, 1988 through June, 1996.

[2] Nobel Prize-winning economist Gary Becker was credited with being the first to draw a distinction between general and specific skills. General skills are basic educational abilities (reading, math, and the sciences)—skills that can be carried from employer to employer. Specific skill refers to those skills that are unique to one particular employer. Becker's research showed that employers are generally willing to pay to teach employees specific skills. However, they are not willing to pay for employees to aquire general skills.

THE COMPETITIVE ADVANTAGES AND DISADVANTAGES OF CITIES—
AN ECONOMIC DEVELOPMENT POLICY FRAMEWORK
FOR PHILADELPHIA

The goal of City economic development policy should be to maximize employment opportunities for the citizenry. Businesses thrive when they operate with a competitive advantage. Michael Porter argues that "only attributes that are unique to the inner-city will support viable business." Essentially these are the features of the City's business environment that provide it with a competitive advantage in producing a particular good or service. Through his ongoing research, Porter has found that the unique features providing cities such as Philadelphia with a competitive advantage include:

- **Strategic Location**—Perhaps the most favorable aspect of doing business in any large urban area such as Philadelphia is its proximity to markets. This should be no surprise, as the City can offer a competitive advantage to any business that relies on a high concentration of people and companies, entertainment and cultural attractions, some of the nation's finest universities, and easy access to all major modes of transportation.

- **Local Demand**—Though the average household income in Philadelphia is quite low, its high population density translates into an immense market with substantial purchasing power. Because of the sheer density of the City's population, even low-income neighborhoods have purchasing power that exceeds less densely populated suburban communities when examined on a per-square-mile basis. For example, income per square mile in Philadelphia as of 1996—$239.2 million—far exceeded the average of the other Southeastern Pennsylvania counties: Bucks County, $28.3 million; Chester County $20.0 million; Delaware County, $88.7 million; Montgomery County, $58.2 million. After massive business disinvestment in urban areas during recent decades, this immense market is left poorly served. Many City residents travel great distances to shop for necessities—or shop in their neighborhoods at high-priced "convenience" stores—wasting money that could be spent purchasing additional goods and services.

- **Integration with Regional Clusters**—The City may not offer a competitive advantage to every industry, but can capitalize on gains made by other local jurisdictions through the development of regional clusters (collections of related companies that are competitive nationally or even globally). For example, though the software company SAP America chose to locate its U.S. headquarters outside the City along an established suburban business corridor, the move creates indirect benefits to the City economy since a number of SAP support services and suppliers are based in the City of Philadelphia.

- **Human Resources**—The oft-cited mismatch that exists between the skills currently demanded by employers and those currently supplied by the labor pool stretches well beyond the City borders. The shortage of skilled labor is a national problem. The City's high density of labor creates advantages for potential employers as it is endowed with a large pool of low to moderately skilled labor available to work at a relatively low wage. Additionally, the City's universities and colleges produce a wealth of young, well-educated talent poised to fill jobs. While suburban employers are acutely affected by this problem, the sheer volume of potential employees mitigates the skills mismatch for City employers.

Porter has also identified several negative aspects of doing business, which are common across most large urban areas across the United States. The City must address these deterrents to starting and maintaining a profitable operation if it is to capitalize on its competitive advantage. In Philadelphia, these areas include:

- **Tax and Regulatory Costs**—Despite efforts to reduce local wage and business taxes, the tax burden in Philadelphia remains considerably high compared to competing localities. Considerable resources are devoted to subsidizing business in an effort to compensate for high taxes. In the future, to reduce the cost of doing business in Philadelphia, the City could directly act to reduce taxes, rather than continue to spend the resources to compensate for them. Similarly, the City must foster real economic growth and avoid the precedent of City government making investment decisions in the private marketplace by transferring tax revenues from some businesses to other businesses (often competitors) through subsidy. Beyond the tax structure, the zoning, permitting, and licensing structures are much more costly and cumbersome in the City than in the suburbs. In addition to focusing on the tax structure, the City could reduce this burden by directly addressing its zoning, permitting, and licensing structure and utilizing one-stop shopping and Internet technology to improve the ease with which employers interact with City agencies. (See Chapter 2 for a more thorough discussion of this subject.)

- **Security**—The perception and reality of crime in the City are significant barriers to economic development. According to a recent Controller's Office survey of Philadelphia business establishments, crime ranked just behind taxes as the most troubling aspect of doing business in the City. Indeed, crime against property adds to operating costs as firms in the City incur costs for security guards, extra lighting, and other crime-prevention-related expenditures. Additionally, the threat of crime against employees and customers discourages individuals from working and conducting business in the City.

- **Quality of Land**—While vacant land is abundant in the City of Philadelphia, it is often not seen as economically viable for businesses making location decisions. For example, though well intentioned, Enterprise and Empowerment Zones have been located in the City's most disadvantaged areas with the hope that tax relief and other benefits associated with the Zones could encourage development. To date, the success of the Zones has been limited as developers and employers continue to choose to forego benefits associated with the Zones for locations with greater amenities and potential to generate profit. In the future, the City could focus its efforts on improving the physical appearance and overall safety of disadvantaged areas to capitalize on the interest of potential tenants who are attracted by the low cost of land in such areas. Similarly, the City could direct subsidy efforts toward land requiring environmental remediation to encourage reuse of urban "brownfields."

- **Access to Capital**—While various governmental and quasi-governmental loan pools have provided local business establishments several outlets for lending, growing businesses lack equity capital. For example, according to officials at the University City Science Center (UCSC)—the largest Philadelphia incubator of high-tech business—many UCSC businesses would expand but lack capital to finance growth. In the future, the City could directly invest in venture capital funds or direct pension fund dollars toward such investments to provide resources for growing Philadelphia firms.

- **Quality of Labor**—As noted above, the City is home to a large supply of low-skilled laborers who are willing to work. However, because many lack basic education and soft skills, their prospects of becoming gainfully employed are slim. Nobel Prize-winning economist Gary Becker found that businesses are willing to pay for specific training (training that is unique to the particular firm), but they are not willing to pay for general education (the basic skills that carry from one employer to another). Thus, any shortcoming in the City's system of public education is likely to be a significant deterrent to economic growth. This supports research presented in the City Controller's Office "1997 Mid-Year Economic and Financial Report," which shows that there has been a significant correlation between the economic growth of regions and the educational attainment of the respective urban centers of those regions. As discussed below, the City could work with School District officials to improve public education in Philadelphia and link students to careers and higher education to improve the overall quality of the City workforce.

In a major city, everything can be directly related to economic development. While tax and regulatory policies are clearly connected to economic development, issues ranging from policies toward homeless persons sleeping on City streets to maintenance efforts at recreational facilities affect employers' location decisions and individuals' market preferences. Everything the City does—from collecting trash to providing mental health services—ultimately helps or hurts City efforts to encourage employers to create family-sustaining jobs.

If efforts to foster economic development in Philadelphia can continue to expand the local economy, it will become fundamentally clear that the growth feeds on itself. New businesses will spawn new ideas, concepts, and other new businesses. Ultimately, this will lead to significant revenue generation for the City. Additional economic activity will also ease pressures on City expenditures. Every person who comes off the unemployment rolls and moves into a job reduces the City's need to spend in such areas as health and human services and police and fire protection, and reduces the City's need to offer subsidies to employers to compensate for the excessive tax burden. By encouraging economic expansion and promoting job creation, the City can clearly define areas that should be the center of its economic development efforts and capitalize on its competitive advantages to create growth.

Targeting Economic Development Efforts

City officials have a wide array of tools available to them to attract and retain business. Some tools such as low-interest loans, tax breaks, and subsidies for worker training are very specific in nature and can be packaged to proactively engage a specific establishment to expand within, or relocate to, the City. Other tools are more indirect. For example, general improvement in the City's cultural attractions can help spur demand for hotels through an impact on travel and tourism. Similarly, general income tax reduction benefits all local businesses to a varying degree since it removes distortions in the labor market and raises the buying power of consumers. Whether the City should be allocating its scarce economic development dollars to direct or indirect policy efforts has been a matter of considerable debate.

Many argue that the City should invest very little in direct economic development activity on the grounds that such efforts are neither equitable nor efficient. The equity argument stems from the fact that any direct subsidy to a particular business runs the risk of giving one firm in a particular industry an unfair advantage over other competing local firms. The efficiency argument arises from the fact that efforts to support a given business may not be cost-effective. Simply put, subsidies may be going to industries that have few prospects for growth or create little or no impact on the economy when they expand.

Nearly a decade has passed since the publication of *Post-Industrial Philadelphia*—an effort by the Greater Philadelphia Economic Monitoring Project to lay a foundation for regional economic development. By evaluating the purchase and sale linkages of local industry, the authors were able to develop criteria that could be used by policy makers to target industries for economic development. In particular, the Monitoring Project developed estimates of the impact an industry's expansion has on the Philadelphia regional economy (industry multipliers) and the degree to which an industry exports goods and services beyond the region's boarders (net export ratios).

During the last decade, the economy has undergone a period of major structural change. As a result, there has been considerable change in the patterns of inter-regional trade and change in industry multipliers and net export ratios. By using REMI to update the analysis performed by the Greater Philadelphia Economic Monitoring Project—constraining the analysis to the City of Philadelphia rather than for the greater Philadelphia region as a whole and evaluating industrial employment forecasts to introduce an additional criterion to be considered when targeting industries for economic development—the Controller's Office was able to:

- Evaluate the long-term prospects for growth by forecasting industrial employment growth through 2015;

- Evaluate the competitive position of each industry by estimating how much each industry exports beyond the City's borders; and
- Estimate the economic impact from the expansion of a particular industry by computing a labor and employment multiplier.

The first factor to consider when targeting industries for development is the long-term expectation for growth. The City will be much more successful in its attempts to grow the City economy by targeting industries that are slated for strong growth over the long term. Though the City may have a competitive advantage in some areas, these areas may decline as a result of either a shift in regional or world demand or broad structural change. The Controller's Office was able to project prospects for growth by evaluating a forecast of U.S. industrial employment. Table 4.1 displays the ten U.S. industries that are expected to post the fastest employment growth through 2015.

Table 4.1. Top Ten U.S. Fastest-Growing Industries (thousands of employees)		
Industry	Level Change 1995–2015 (forecast)	% Change 1995–2015 (forecast)
Business Services	6,498.95	70.86%
Non-Profits	2,920.08	61.85%
Amusement and Recreational Services	1,314.95	56.72%
Educational Services	1,402.16	53.43%
Medical Services	5,227.41	49.27%
Credit and Finance	961.89	49.17%
Auto Repair/Leasing Services	727.59	45.92%
Legal, Engineering, and Management Services	2,386.75	35.74%
Personal Services	1,178.88	34.96%
Hotels	519.14	27.73%
Source: REMI		

It is interesting to note that the fastest-growing U.S. industries are generally concentrated in high-tech goods and services—business services and legal, engineering, and management services are part of the "high-tech" sector.[3] In short, the prediction is that the nation as a whole has a competitive advantage in the high tech trades.

The second factor to consider when targeting industries for development is the competitive position of the industry in Philadelphia. Local industry produces goods and services for the purpose of serving consumers and other industries. The production of goods and services for consumers and industries beyond the City borders is referred to as export demand. Estimates of the degree to which an industry serves export demand have often been used as a proxy for competitive advantage. The theory supporting this is quite simple. To be chosen as a production site for a particular good or service for export, the City must offer a special attraction—or competitive advantage—for that type of production. The firm must foresee some overriding benefit to producing goods in the City as opposed to any other area. Thus, an economic development strategy based on promoting areas where the City has been deemed to have a competitive advantage would be commensurate with encouraging growth in industries that primarily serve export demand. Table 4.2 (column 2)

---

[3] Also included in the high-tech sector, but missing from the list of the ten fastest-growing industries, is the engineering and management industry.

Table 4.2. Characteristics of Philadelphia's Competitive Position

(SIC) Industry	Net Export Ratio	Relative Factor Cost (City/U.S. Average)
ALL CONSTRUCTION	-0.39	1.12
MANUFACTURING		
Food and Kindred Products	0.26	1.06
Textile Mill Products	-0.74	1.09
Apparel and Other Textile Products	-0.12	1.15
Lumber and Wood Products	-0.85	1.05
Furniture and Fixtures	-0.27	1.01
Paper and Allied Products	-0.03	1.23
Printing and Publishing	0.04	1.09
Chemicals and Allied Products	0.28	1.14
Petroleum and Coal Products	1.77	1.03
Rubber and Misc. Plastic Products	-0.81	1.16
Leather and Leather Products	-0.96	1.40
Stone, Clay, and Glass Products	-0.88	1.00
Primary Metal Industries	-0.55	1.31
Fabricated Metal Products	0.10	1.00
Industrial Machinery and Equipment	-0.54	1.15
Electronic and Other Electric Equipment	-0.55	1.03
Transportation Equipment	-0.50	0.99
Instrument and Related Products	-0.63	1.15
Misc. Manufacturing Industries	-0.60	1.13
TRANSPORTATION AND PUBLIC UTILITIES		
Railroad	1.11	1.11
Local and Interburban Passenger Transit	0.86	1.03
Trucking and Warehousing	-0.29	1.13
Other Transportation	0.42	1.09
Transportation by Air	0.60	1.22
Communication	0.51	1.08
Public Utilities	-0.07	1.13
ALL WHOLESALE TRADE	0.04	1.13
RETAIL TRADE		
Restaurant Retail	-0.22	1.05
Eating and Drinking Places	-0.26	1.03
FINANCE, INSURANCE, AND REAL ESTATE		
Depository Institutions	0.76	1.34
Credit and Finance	-0.17	1.00
Insurance	0.26	1.58
Real Estate	0.56	1.05
SERVICES		
Hotels and Other Lodging Places	-0.50	1.10
Personnel Service/Repair	-0.08	1.25
Business Services	-0.26	1.18
Auto Repair, Leasing Services, and Parking	0.82	1.21
Motion Pictures	-0.61	1.00
Amusement and Recreation Services	-0.33	1.02
Health Services	0.72	1.33
Legal, Engineering, and Management Services	0.67	1.32
Educational Services	2.71	1.53
Non-Profits	0.88	1.23
Private Households	0.13	1.32

Source: REMI

displays estimates of the net export ratio—the proportion of each industry's output that is exported beyond the City's borders.[4]

When deciding where to produce a good or service for export, businesses consider the balance of all costs and benefits that affect the profitability of their operations. Data from Table 4.2 (column 3) offer some statistical insight regarding the cost side of the equation. In particular, the data reflect total factor costs, which represent the combined cost of the major areas of production (labor, capital, energy, and intermediate goods) in the City relative to the United States as a whole. The data show that with the exception of fabricated metal products, transportation equipment, credit and finance, and motion pictures, total factor costs in Philadelphia are higher across all industries relative to the U.S. average. For example, the leather industry (the largest net importer) accepts costs that are 40 percent higher in Philadelphia relative to the U.S. average.[5]

The data also show that some industries have maintained a high net export ratio despite tremendous cost disadvantages. For example, despite factor costs that were almost 53 percent higher than the U.S. average, the local educational services industry has benefited from tax-exempt status and close proximity to institutions that make use of college and university research and development activities. But the reverse can also be true. An industry can be a net importer in areas where the City has a competitive advantage. In such a case, one can conclude that the City's competitive advantage may not have been effectively exploited. For example, apparently missing from the list of net export industries is the local hotel sector. Many have argued that the City has a tremendous competitive advantage in this area, given its rich historical and cultural attractions. Until recently, however, the hotel sector has been unable to take advantage of these assets.

Finally, when targeting industries for development, it is critical to estimate the impact of industry expansion on the local economy. Using REMI, two separate measures were developed to estimate the impact of an expansion in each City two-digit Standard Industrial Classification (SIC): an employment multiplier and labor multiplier. The employment multiplier is defined as the number of jobs generated throughout the entire City economy from a given increase in employment in a particular industry. The employment multipliers reported in Table 4.3 (column 2) reflect the aggregate job gains in the year 2010 from a one-time employment increase of 1,000 jobs in the industry in question.[6] For example, the employment multiplier for the City's hotel industry (1.28) implies that for every 1,000 new hotel jobs gained in 1999, an additional 280 jobs are generated elsewhere in the local economy by 2010. Similarly, for every 1,000 new private metal manufacturing jobs gained in 1999, an additional 2,840 jobs are generated elsewhere in the local economy by 2010. The data show that, all else equal, the City economy will benefit most from an expansion of employment in primary metals manufacturing, petroleum products manufacturing, banking, public utilities, and air transportation.

The labor multiplier, which reflects the aggregate number of jobs gained in the year 2010 from a one-time increase of $1 billion in year 1999 real industry sales volume, is displayed in Table 4.3 (column 4). For example, because the estimated multiplier for the Philadelphia hotel industry is 37.75, an exogenous $1 billion stimulus to industry sales in 1999 would create 37,750 jobs throughout the entire City economy by 2010. The multipliers reveal that, all else equal, the City economy would benefit most from an expansion of output in private household services, educational services, local/interurban transportation, hotels, and amusement and recreational services.

When identifying industries to target for economic development policy, the multiplier itself is not the primary indicator. Rather, it is the relative rank of the multiplier that matters. In general,

---

[4] The specific computation for each industry is (X-M)/(Y+M), where X is the value of exports, M is the value of imports to the City, and Y is the value of gross City product. Note that this computation is generally consistent with location quotients, a measure of the concentration of the City's employment in a particular industry relative to the U.S. average.

[5] Note that due to the very low presence of business activity in the City, agriculture, mining, and the tobacco manufacturing industries were excluded from the analysis. It is safe to presume that the City is a net importer of these goods and services.

[6] Note that these multipliers were originally reported in the City Controller's Office's 1998 Mid-Year Economic Update.

Table 4.3. Philadelphia's Industry Multipliers and Average Wage Level and Rank

(SIC) Industry	Employment Multiplier		Labor Multiplier		Local Demand Multiplier		Average Wage	
	Level	Rank	Level	Rank	Level	Rank	Level	Rank
ALL CONSTRUCTION	1.23	37	11.33	18	0.14	42	25.41	30
MANUFACTURING								
Food and Kindred Products	1.70	12	3.95	42	0.17	37	36.61	16
Textile Mill Products	1.34	27	8.12	28	0.18	35	28.34	28
Apparel and Other Textile Products	1.29	30	10.71	21	0.20	33	20.42	34
Lumber and Wood Products	1.38	24	7.22	31	0.22	30	20.04	36
Furniture and Fixtures	1.24	35	15.11	13	0.25	24	21.76	32
Paper and Allied Products	1.64	13	4.97	38	0.21	31	45.19	9
Printing and Publishing	1.42	26	8.57	27	0.23	27	33.89	23
Chemicals and Allied Products	1.97	6	4.62	41	0.23	29	61.20	3
Petroleum and Coal Products	3.16	2	1.49	45	0.16	39	63.36	1
Rubber and Misc. Plastic Products	1.44	20	7.67	30	0.24	26	34.80	21
Leather and Leather Products	1.25	33	8.71	26	0.20	32	25.19	31
Stone, Clay, and Glass Products	1.59	15	8.71	25	0.31	17	34.55	22
Primary Metal Industries	3.84	1	5.99	36	0.48	7	41.89	12
Fabricated Metal Products	1.35	26	6.16	34	0.17	38	31.91	24
Industrial Machinery and Equipment	1.54	16	11.11	20	0.27	20	36.95	15
Electronic and Other Electric Equipment	1.42	21	7.04	32	0.19	34	35.05	20
Transportation Equipment	1.17	40	6.00	35	0.15	41	44.27	10
Instrument and Related Products	1.40	23	6.94	33	0.16	40	37.00	14
Misc. Manufacturing Industries	1.45	18	10.58	22	0.26	23	28.62	27
TRANSPORTATION & PUBLIC UTILITIES								
Railroad	1.84	9	5.57	37	0.27	21	62.11	2
Local and Interburban Passenger Transit	1.08	43	41.19	3	0.23	28	16.22	39
Trucking and Warehousing	1.64	14	9.15	24	0.37	13	25.98	29
Other Transportation	1.81	10	12.17	17	0.51	5	30.11	25
Transportation by Air	2.13	5	7.91	29	0.46	9	50.46	6
Communication	1.45	19	3.16	44	0.10	43	47.89	8
Public Utilities	2.17	4	4.84	39	0.26	22	58.44	4
ALL WHOLESALE TRADE	1.40	22	9.80	23	0.24	25	36.00	18
RETAIL TRADE								
Restaurant Retail	1.19	39	20.70	11	0.29	19	14.86	41
Eating and Drinking Places	1.17	41	33.18	7	0.32	15	10.40	46
FINANCE, INSURANCE &, REAL ESTATE								
Depository Institutions	2.38	3	14.25	14	0.74	2	42.83	11
Credit and Finance	0.94	44	4.82	40	0.05	45	54.67	5
Insurance	1.86	8	12.91	16	0.48	8	48.06	7
Real Estate	1.90	7	3.73	43	0.18	36	12.16	43
SERVICES								
Hotels and Other Lodging Places	1.28	31	37.75	4	0.54	4	19.32	37
Personnel Service/Repair	1.25	34	35.20	6	0.46	10	11.00	44
Business Services	1.23	36	25.22	9	0.32	16	21.20	33
Auto Repair, Leasing Services, and Parking	1.79	11	11.29	19	0.44	12	18.04	38
Motion Pictures	0.89	45	13.94	15	0.09	44	14.37	42
Amusement and Recreation Services	1.30	29	35.78	5	0.60	3	15.31	40
Health Services	1.26	32	18.39	12	0.35	14	36.09	17
Legal, Engineering, and Management Services	1.47	17	21.52	10	0.44	11	37.32	13
Educational Services	1.31	28	45.04	2	0.83	1	29.15	26
Non-Profits	1.21	38	32.63	8	0.49	6	20.26	35
Private Households	1.12	42	89.80	1	0.30	18	10.78	45

Source: REMI

two factors explain the variation that exists between the labor and employment multiplier for a given industry as well as the variation in each multiplier across industries: average industry wages and the amount of locally produced goods and services used by that industry.

The rank data show that the labor and employment multipliers are inversely related.[7] While at first glance this appears to be a contradiction, closer inspection reveals that it is quite intuitive. Industries with high employment multipliers generally employ high-value-added labor—each employee adds significant value to the firm's output. Subsequently, these individuals are paid a higher wage. All other things being equal, higher wages have greater secondary spending effects on the economy. For the same reasons, the low-wage sectors tend to have significantly larger labor multipliers.[8] That is, for a given increase in output demand, the low-wage sectors require a greater number of employees relative to the sectors that employ high-value-added labor. For example, because the average wage paid in the hotel sector is among the lowest across the City industries, increasing hotel employment creates a small secondary spending effect on the local economy. But because the hotel sector offers relatively low wages, more employees are required to respond to new demand for hotels. Therefore, because increasing employment in the hotel sector only creates a minor ripple in the local economy while increasing demand for hotels creates a significant number of jobs, the hotel sector will have a low employment multiplier and a high labor multiplier.

The role of the value added of each employee is by no means the only determinant of the variation in employment and labor multipliers across industries. The degree to which a particular industry makes use of other local industries for support is another factor in determining multipliers. An increase in demand in a particular industry requires an increase in input usage to meet this demand. Industries can either make use of goods and services that are imported from outside the City, or they can make use of locally produced goods and services. Clearly, expansion of an industry that predominantly uses locally produced inputs has a greater impact on the local economy compared to those that make extensive use of imported goods for inputs. The cumulative effect of an increase in demand for locally produced inputs across all City industries resulting from a given increase in demand in a particular industry is quantified by the local demand multiplier, displayed in Table 4.3 (column 6).

Not surprisingly, most of the industries that employed local producers for goods as inputs are concentrated in the service sector. In particular, the data suggest that educational services, banking, amusement and recreational services, and hotels all make extensive use of locally produced goods as inputs. The data also depict a very close association between the labor multiplier and the local demand multiplier.[9] This occurs because firms that use the goods and services of other local firms generate increased local demand and increased local employment.

In an effort to identify the industries to target for economic development, it is instructive to provide a summary rank of the industries based on ability to stimulate the local economy, existence of a competitive advantage, and recent industry growth experience. In assigning this ranking, a distinction is made between the impact of expansion from a given increase in the industry's employment versus an increase in its final demand. This is a very important distinction, since the employment multiplier shows which industries would generate the greatest benefit—or return on investment—from a dollar spent on economic development efforts to increase employment. By contrast, the labor multiplier shows which industries would generate the greatest benefit to the City from a dollar spent on economic development efforts to increase output

---

[7] The correlation coefficient between the two variables was -0.52. As a general rule, correlation coefficients between 0.3 and 0.6, in absolute value, reflect moderate association between two variables. Coefficients between 0.6 and 1.0 and between 0.0 and 0.3 reflect high and low association, respectively.

[8] This is borne out by the fact that the correlation coefficient between the average wage for each industry and the labor multiplier was -0.63.

[9] The correlation coefficient between the labor multiplier and the local demand multiplier across the industries was 0.64.

(demand for industry goods and services). Following the Convention of the Greater Philadelphia Economic Project, the Controller's Office uses the labor multiplier in creating summary rankings. Table 4.4 shows industry rankings as calculated by summing the individual rank of each industry's net export ratio, labor multiplier, and projected employment growth.

Table 4.4. Top Ten Two-Digit Industries for City Economic Development Policy					
Industry	Net export ratio rank	Labor Multiplier rank	Projected Job Growth rank	Summary Rank	Overall Rank
Educational Services	1	2	2	5	1
Legal, Eng., & Mgt. Services	9	10	4	23	2
Auto Repair/Leasing Services	6	19	1	26	3
Non-Profits	4	8	15	27	4
Medical Services	8	12	9	29	5
Local/Interurban Transportation	5	3	24	32	6
Insurance	15	16	6	37	7
Business Services	27	9	3	39	8
Banking	7	14	19	40	9
Hotels	33	4	10	47	10
Source: REMI					

A unique feature of the industries that appear high on the list is the degree to which they trade with each other. For example, all of the industries mentioned in Table 4.4 above rely heavily on the educational services sector for producing a talented pool of labor and its research and development services. Similarly, the local hotel sector relies heavily on the growth of the City's cultural and historical institutions (all of which are classified under the non-profit industry) for its own development. Because of this high degree of trade, it is clear that targeted economic development should center on promotion of clusters of industries rather than an individual firm or industry. For example, for the purposes of crafting policies for development based on their unique trading patterns, most of the industries from the top ten list can be clustered into three functional areas:

- Hospitality and tourism—including hotels, non-profits (museums, zoos, and gardens), and auto leasing services;
- Financial services—including insurance and banking; and
- Medical and technology-based producer support—including educational services, legal, engineering, and management services, medical services, and business services (advertising and computer and data processing).

To maximize the impact of the City's economic development efforts, the City should target activities toward industries that are able to stimulate local economic activity, exhibit a competitive advantage, and have significant prospects for growth. Targeting should take place in such a way that best utilizes the City's competitive advantages created by its strategic location, high market demand, possibilities for integration with regional clusters, and ample supply of human resources. This must be coupled with a firm commitment by government to address the weaknesses of a cumbersome tax and regulatory system, poor access to capital, ongoing concerns about security, and the quality of land and labor. The impediments to local economic growth must be addressed directly instead of through subsidies to businesses and individuals designed to compensate for these impediments. For example, the City should ensure that the areas of Philadelphia which offer certain location advantages, such as their nearness to the City's universities or major transportation thoroughfares, are given the highest priority for environmental cleanup, infrastructure improvements, and crime reduction efforts. Similarly, the City's tax and regulatory burden should be adjusted to be more consistent with localities that offer a similar competitive advantage to the industry clusters that are the basis of City business attraction and retention efforts. Such a strategy would create the best possible return on the City's limited economic development resources.

LET'S MAKE A DEAL—
PUBLIC INVESTMENT IN PRIVATE ENTERPRISE

Government is often asked to subsidize private enterprises through direct governmental grants, tax abatements, infrastructure improvements, and other expenditures. In theory, government benefits if investments produce a positive, sustained, and widespread private market reaction. The test for whether public investment should be used to encourage private investment must then compare the cost asked of the public with the benefit the public can expect to derive from that project.

In the recent past, the citizens of Philadelphia have helped construct the Pennsylvania Convention Center in part to spur private hotel development. City of Philadelphia infrastructure improvements facilitated the development of a privately funded sports arena. City government created a tax abatement to encourage developers to convert commercial office space to residential apartments. Many other deals, big and small, move forward every day.

Because its resources are limited, it is very important that the City invests wisely in any effort to promote economic development. Looking to the future, the City can create mechanisms to ensure that the public truly benefits from public investment in private enterprise.

In the City of Indianapolis, a Metropolitan Development Commission (comprising individuals appointed by the Mayor of Indianapolis, Marion County Commissioners, and the City-County Council) serves as an independent review board for all requests for tax abatements, and is responsible for approving or denying such requests. In addition, the City requires all recipients of tax abatements to execute a Memorandum of Agreement that outlines the agreed-upon level of investment, employment, and wages for the project, and sets forth a time frame in which the commitments must be reached. The Memorandum indicates the conditions under which the City shall terminate a tax abatement or request repayment of all or a portion of tax savings received. With such an independent review and a provision to "clawback" abatements if developers fail to meet agreed-upon levels of investment and employment, Indianapolis is able to invest wisely and protect the City's interests.

In the future, the elected leaders of Philadelphia will be asked to invest in many projects, from a new sports stadium (or two) to new tourist attractions, to a host of other private ventures. Clearly, the public should only make an investment toward projects that create a benefit that equals or exceeds that investment—otherwise that same investment could be used elsewhere to create a proper benefit.

To best protect the public's interest, an independent agency such as the City Controller's Office could formally review cost/benefit analyses to determine whether public investment above a certain amount truly creates a benefit large enough to justify the expenditure. Similarly, the City could include "clawback" clauses as part of any large public investment to create a legal mechanism to recover public expenditures if private development does not meet promised economic impact or job-creation goals.

Public investment in private enterprise can benefit the public as well as individual entrepreneurs. In the future, the City's task is to make sure its public investment creates an appropriate benefit and create consequences for entrepreneurs when the benefits fail to meet expectations.

Should the City Play Ball?—Public Funding for a New Sports Stadium

City-owned Veterans Stadium is a functional if unglamorous home for Philadelphia's professional baseball and football teams. Leases with the respective teams commit them to play in Veterans Stadium until 2011. Because the need for a new home for the teams is questionable, public funding for a new stadium (or two) only makes sense if such development will create economic benefits for the City equal to or greater than the City's share of stadium development costs. Benefits would include direct jobs, increased tax revenues, and any subsequent multiplier effect. Costs would include direct costs, any publicly funded investments to improve infrastructure surrounding a new stadium, and any resulting need to demolish Veterans Stadium. As discussed above, an independent agency could verify any cost/benefit analyses used to justify proposed investments in sports venues.

The City could work toward a true partnership between the City and its professional sports teams. In return for a public investment in the creation of a new stadium (or two), Philadelphia and its teams can maximize return on investment:

- If the City provides funds for a new stadium, which will only have a marginal effect on recreational consumption patterns (a new stadium will only shift spending within the region, not create sufficient new economic activity to justify public subsidy), the decision of where to locate the stadium should be the City's. In order to maximize the economic impact of a new stadium, the City—not the team(s)—should select the location based on the City's priorities for creating revitalization and growth.

- Because the costs to fund construction of a new stadium will most likely outweigh future benefits, for its contribution to development costs, the City should be entitled to receive a proportionate share in the profits from all revenue-generating activities connected with a new stadium.

- Because new venues will increase the value of the franchises, the City could insist on sharing that increased value if a team is sold.

- Because the teams are currently committed to playing in Veterans Stadium until 2011, the City would be doing its sports teams a service in helping to create new facilities. Philadelphia could, therefore, follow the lead of the City of Indianapolis and insist that teams commit to the City in the future. In exchange for public funding for the current basketball arena in Indianapolis, the National Basketball Association's Indiana Pacers must remain in Indianapolis or else forfeit a cash payment equal to one-half the value of the franchise. As part of a deal for a new arena in Indianapolis, the team must pay off the balance of the arena mortgage if it chooses to leave the City.

- Despite the fact that teams operate with local monopoly control, team owners often claim that they require a new stadium to compete with other franchises. If, after benefiting from the new revenues and other benefits associated with a new stadium, a team is consistently unable to produce winning results on the field, the public may deserve compensation. If the public is to invest in a stadium under the pretense that new stadium revenues will improve a team's performance then those new revenues should be directed toward putting a winning team on the field—not toward a team owner's bank account. As a "clawback," the City could require that if teams exhibit consistent poor performance over an extended period of time (despite the additional revenues and associated benefits created by a new facility) they should reimburse the City for part of its investment in a new stadium. Alternatively, instead of a "clawback," the teams could grant the City a larger portion of stadium revenues as compensation.

The City can work with professional sports team owners to create a partnership where fans can watch teams in beautiful facilities, owners can satisfy their need to enhance their bottom line, and the City can realize a substantial return on its reasonable investment. The City might just have to play a little hardball to make it happen.

Capitalizing on the City's Competitive Advantages

By focusing on areas where it has demonstrated strengths, the City can maximize the impact of economic development efforts. While the City must continue to reduce its high tax rates, improve the quality of its workforce, and reduce disamenities such as crime, 21st-century Philadelphia is challenged to exploit untapped markets where the City offers a competitive advantage. Even though most economic development resources should be devoted to addressing the City's liabilities—high tax rates, low-quality workforce, and quality-of-life deficiencies—the City should pursue specific policies to promote the three major functional areas (hospitality and tourism, financial services, and medical and technology-based producer support).

The City can fine-tune methods of promoting hotel growth. Research performed by the Controller's Office shows that, due to its low wage offering, hospitality industry employment multipliers are very low in comparison to the labor multipliers. Thus, for a given dollar of economic development spending, stimulating the output demand for hospitality and tourism has a greater impact on the local economy than direct efforts to expand employment. As a result, City economic development efforts should focus less on direct subsidy to hoteliers and more on the means of stimulating the demand for the industries' output. Perhaps the most effective way of accomplishing this would be to focus more attention on complementary goods and services. For example, rejuvenating the City's cultural and historic assets would, in turn, raise the demand for travel to the area, thereby raising demand for hotel space. Thus, making these traditional cultural and historical possessions more attractive while luring new entertainment facilities will inevitably promote the growth of the City's hotel market.

The City could also stimulate the market for hotels by placing additional emphasis on the expansion of other sectors of the economy that rely heavily on travel, adding complimentary goods (expanding the Pennsylvania Convention Center or creating the proposed National Constitution Center in Independence National Historical Park), improving support services such as rail and air transportation, and expanding and better coordinating marketing campaigns for the City as a tourist destination. An additional feature of this method of developing the hospitality sector is that the "market" decides exactly how many hotels are needed in the City. Direct subsidies to certain hoteliers risks simply displacing other hoteliers within the industry. Conversely, rising attendance at tourist attractions would subsequently stimulate hotel growth.

Direct subsidy could be reserved for specific properties with historic significance. In "The Economic Benefits of Preserving Philadelphia's Past," the Preservation Alliance for Greater Philadelphia estimated that in the past two decades, more than $1.5 billion has been invested in the rehabilitation of historic commercial properties, creating 55,000 jobs and generating more than $1.3 billion in household income. As the City competes for tourists, and as industries such as the motion picture industry compete for new business and new projects, the City's historic structures and locations represent competitive advantages. The City could stimulate expansion in those industries by continuing assistance and abatement initiatives that encourage reuse and preservation of historic buildings.

Additionally, the City can put promotion of for-profit institutions on equal footing with hospitality and tourism. In their "Report on Regional Benchmarks," the civic leadership organization Greater Philadelphia First identified proximity to the City's universities and technical training institutions as the primary source of competitive advantage for profit-making businesses. The for-profit institutions are able to both take advantage of the pool of talent and research and development services produced by the City's academic institutions. Thus, an efficient method of promotion would be to make educational institutions the foundation of economic development efforts.

In 1998, the City declared Market Street West—the corridor stretching west from City Hall through the Central Business District and a number of major Philadelphia universities—as the "Avenue of Technology" to advertise the synergy created by the area's dense concentration of technology companies. Since technology companies depend on the graduates and resources of local colleges and universities, this move will help promote Philadelphia's educational institutions. In the future, the City could further stimulate growth in this area by addressing capital constraints facing high-tech organizations with grants and loans, giving priority to urban-renewal efforts that would improve the geographic environment surrounding universities, and offering business establishments grant assistance to expand investment in worker training and increase demand for continuing education at universities.

PROMOTING EDUCATIONAL INSTITUTIONS

The City of Philadelphia is home to 12 traditional colleges and universities plus many additional professional schools, academies, and institutes. Dozens of additional institutions are located in surrounding jurisdictions. Higher education is the City's second-largest employer. According to the Commission for Independent Colleges and Universities, colleges and universities in the Philadelphia area contribute $3.95 billion in direct purchases and indirect impact to the local economy. Clearly, higher education in Philadelphia means more to the City than student spending and Big Five basketball. Cooperative efforts to encourage graduates to remain in the City and innovative partnerships between universities and City schools will benefit the City as well as its institutions. These recently announced efforts to connect the City to its schools are a step in the right direction, but more can be done to capitalize on Philadelphia's educational institutions as economic development engines. While all of the City's efforts to reduce the cost of living and improve quality of life in the City help its institutions, in the future the City could expand efforts to promote its educational institutions by:

- Working with colleges and universities to create an "Institute of Philadelphia Metropolitan Studies" to encourage further cooperation between colleges and universities, their communities, and the City. A similar program between the City of Portland and Portland State University provides access to the resources of higher education for Portland communities, generates information about the metropolitan area for local officials, and creates substantive partnerships between the University and City agencies.

- Working with colleges and universities to incorporate into curricula internships with the City and opportunities to work with City government agencies. With such an effort, the City could benefit from student input while students could gain exposure to the City—and develop a connection with Philadelphia that could extend past graduation. In New York City, a Public Service Corps, an Urban Fellows program, and a Government Scholars program attract students and graduates to the City and City government.

- Using City colleges and universities as the foundation for tourism-promotion and immigrant-attraction efforts. Because the City's institutions of higher learning draw students from around the world, aggressive outreach to prospective students and their families could encourage new visitors and new residents to come to Philadelphia.

- Creating a liaison office in the City bureaucracy for colleges and universities to better coordinate interactions between the City and its institutions of higher education. A central office could effectively work with local institutions to confront specific concerns and general town/gown issues.

- Creating programs to encourage City employees to pursue college and post-graduate degrees at local institutions. With such a program, the City could improve the quality of the municipal workforce while increasing the demand for educational services at local institutions.

- Allowing colleges and universities to improve campus atmosphere by closing off City streets running through their campuses. While such an initiative would have to take neighbors' concerns and traffic patterns into account, it could enhance campus vitality throughout the City.

- Working with colleges and universities to enhance their surroundings by expanding mortgage-assistance programs for faculty and students who purchase homes in the neighborhoods surrounding campuses. A successful mortgage-assistance program operated by the University of Pennsylvania provides a model that shows that investing in neighborhoods surrounding institutions benefits schools and the community alike.

The City can roll with the punches from restructuring in the financial services sectors. While industry restructuring has adversely affected the City, the financial services sector offers high-value-added employment opportunities, exports a significant portion of its output, and makes significant use of other local industry. Thus, promotion of this sector would be of tremendous benefit to the City's economy. While the City cannot affect the wave of deregulation and technological progress, which has prompted structural change within the financial services sector, it can mitigate some of its negative consequences. For example, the City's recent effort to provide an exemption from taxes on net profits for business trusts represents a step in the right direction.

The City could further minimize negative effects of restructuring in the financial services sector by working with industry leaders to identify untapped market potential in the City. By adjusting the overall tax structure to make it more profitable for banks to operate in Philadelphia, the City could continue to create a more fertile business environment for the industry to grow.

Finally, the City could expand outreach efforts to neighborhood business. After surveying City employers, the Controller's Office found that business establishments not located in the Central Business District are generally more unhappy with their interaction with government than their Central Business District counterparts.[10] This may be some indication that neighborhood businesses are in need of a "collective voice" to interact with government for them. As a result, it is worth considering expanding the role of the Mayor's Business Action Team.

The City could also enhance connections by regularly reaching out to business owners and operators for feedback focused on improving specific governmental operations. By conducting a telephone survey of business owners, operators, and chief executive officers, the City of Tacoma, Washington, was able to identify impediments to economic growth from the perspective of the people who actually do business in the City. The Tacoma City Council then unanimously approved a package of license and tax reforms based on the feedback.

RECOMMENDATIONS FOR ACTION

The City should maximize the benefits of its economic development efforts by targeting its limited economic development resources.

Action Steps:

- Encourage development of industry clusters that make extensive use of other local industries for support, have significant prospects for growth, and are projected to generate a significant multiplier effect on the City economy (hospitality and tourism, financial services, and medical and technology-based producer support).

- Maximize efficiency by focusing economic development efforts on policies that cut across industries through initiatives that benefit industry clusters as opposed to initiatives that meet the needs of individual businesses.

---

[10] Office of the City Controller, City of Philadelphia, Pennsylvania. "Controller's Mid-Year Economic Survey 1998–1999." December, 1998.

Fiscal Impact:

- Potential to maximize the use of economic development expenditures to expand the City's tax base.

The City should pursue specific policies to promote growth in industries for which the City offers a competitive advantage.

Action Steps:

- Promote growth in the hospitality industry by enhancing the City's cultural and historic assets; and stimulate the market for hotels by placing additional emphasis on the expansion of other sectors of the economy that rely heavily on travel, adding quality complementary goods, and expanding and better coordinating marketing campaigns for the City as a tourist destination.

- Promote for-profit institutions by making educational institutions the foundation of economic development efforts and encouraging business expansion into under-served markets.

- Promote the financial services sector by working with industry leaders to identify untapped market potential in the City and by adjusting the overall tax structure to make it more profitable for banks to operate in the City.

- Promote neighborhood businesses by expanding outreach efforts to neighborhood businesses and using feedback to drive regulatory reform efforts.

Fiscal Impact:

- Potential to maximize the use of economic development expenditures to expand the City's tax base.

EDUCATION—CREATING A SYSTEM OF PUBLIC EDUCATION FOR ALL PHILADELPHIA FAMILIES

Migration patterns show that while individuals of all ages have left the City, Philadelphia has lost a disproportionate number of young adults in recent years. Examining U.S. Commerce Department data, it is clear that in recent years individuals age 20 to 34 have migrated from the City in disproportionately high numbers. These individuals are either young parents or young people considering parenting. While issues like crime and taxes affect every age group and encourage many individuals to leave the City, the disproportionate outmigration of young adults confirms what surveys consistently show: the quality of schools is a major determining factor in Philadelphia residents' relocation decisions. If educational options in Philadelphia do not improve, the flight of young adults and families with young children will continue. The City is therefore challenged to make public schools an option for Philadelphia's families—or create another mechanism to keep families with school-age children in the City.

Improving public schools in Philadelphia would not just allow the City to retain residents, it would encourage economic development, increase overall economic growth, and improve the life chances of even the most disadvantaged students. Because worker quality is a major factor in firm relocation decisions, improving public education in Philadelphia would increase the likelihood that employers will relocate to Philadelphia and be able to find quality workers in the City. The City Controller's "1997 Mid-Year Economic and Financial Report" showed that if educational attainment in Philadelphia had matched the average of the nation's largest 25 urban areas, regional mean employment from 1969–94 would have been 15 percent higher and regional average earnings would have been 10 percent higher. Improving public education in Philadelphia, therefore, increases the likelihood that the City and its suburbs will experience economic growth.

Increased educational attainment also serves to raise an individual's median earnings. Data from the Census Bureau show that in 1996, for workers age 25 and older, median income increased with each additional level of educational attainment—men with less than a ninth-grade education earned a median of $14,319, women earned $9,181; men with a high school diploma earned a median of $26,313, women earned $15,489; men with an associate degree earned a median of $33,067, women earned $21,671; men with a bachelor's degree earned a median of $44,511, women earned $29,640; men with a professional degree earned a median of $72,052; women earned $44,905. Over time, these earnings are increasing in current and constant dollars. Improving public education increases the likelihood that all Philadelphians will be able to reap the benefits that a quality education can provide.

The failure of urban public education hurts cities and their residents in different ways. Many individuals with resources feel compelled to leave cities for a jurisdiction with a better system of public education for their children, or are forced to pay a premium to send their children to non-public schools while remaining within the urban environment. Individuals who are unable to move, unable to pay non-public school tuition, or unable to access non-public schools through other means are stuck with little choice than to leave their children at the mercy of the system of public education. In Philadelphia, and across the country, urban school districts have responded by creating magnet schools and other special programs to provide an atmosphere more conducive to learning for children with special abilities or talents. While such Philadelphia public schools represent perhaps the best schools in Pennsylvania and rival any schools—public or private—in the nation, the vast majority of urban public schools are underperforming.

Approximately 80 percent of Philadelphia school children qualify for free or reduced-priced lunches. Much of Philadelphia's non-poverty population opts for private or parochial education (approximately 25 percent of Philadelphia school children are enrolled in non-public schools), or qualifies for one of Philadelphia's magnet schools or special programs. Neighborhood schools are, therefore, left with the task of educating students who face tremendous poverty-related pressures at home and in their communities. These students may have little, if any, educational support from their families and few role models in their communities who can attest to the power of education to improve life chances. The difficulty of effectively making education a bridge to opportunity in such an environment can be illustrated by the experience of the Belmont 112.

THE BELMONT 112 AND PUBLIC EDUCATION IN PHILADELPHIA

In 1987, George and Diane Weiss were inspired to make an extraordinary deal. They made a promise to the 112 sixth graders at Philadelphia's Belmont Elementary School during the students' graduation ceremony. The couple promised to pay for the college education of all students upon their graduation from high school. In addition, the Weisses established a "Say Yes to Education" program with a full-time staff to provide extra tutoring, mentoring, and direction for the students. In a school where two-thirds of the students' families received welfare benefits, and few of the students' parents finished high school, the opportunity of a free college education was unique. In an environment where education experts predicted that perhaps 10 percent of the children would ever go on to college, the extra support and incentive was remarkable.

The so-called Belmont 112 students not only continued their traditional education, they met regularly with private tutors and received the attention of Say Yes staffers—and the Weisses themselves—to complement and supplement parental involvement. But the challenges faced by the Belmont 112, and other at-risk students, go far beyond the ability to pay for college. One year after the extraordinary announcement at the Belmont graduation, eight students were not promoted to the eighth grade and one student was dead at age 13, killed during a knife fight between two men. After only one year from the much-publicized graduation ceremony where hope and opportunity came together, it was clear that the Belmont 112 did not win the lottery; they received a challenge to beat the odds.

As the Belmont 112 continued their schooling, the Say Yes to Education program continued its support. The Weisses fought to place many of the students into an alternative high school where they could receive the benefits of programs coordinated with the University of Pennsylvania. The challenge to beat the odds also continued. One student went to jail for murder. Another died as a result of injuries suffered in the wreck of a stolen car. By the time the first of the Belmont 112 graduated high school—early—in 1992, two of the Belmont 112 were dead, one boy was in state prison, 12 other boys had served time in residential placements for crimes committed, 15 of the girls had babies, and only 51 students were on the normal track for graduation.

When the first two students of the Belmont 112 fulfilled the Weisses' vision and graduated college in 1997, the Say Yes to Education program had already cost approximately $5 million—roughly $4,500 per student per year. In addition to the two college graduates, of the 112 who graduated in 1987, 19 were on track to receive four-year degrees, and 23 more received or were on track to receive two-year degrees. In total, 62 had received their high-school diplomas. Four of the remaining students were dead including one young man who committed suicide, leaving behind a note that read in part, "Believe me, I did my best."[11]

If experts predicted that, without extra support, only 11 of the Belmont 112 would have graduated from high school and gone to college, the assistance provided by the Weisses involvement and the Say Yes to Education program increased the likelihood that a child from the Belmont Elementary School would move on to post-high school education by 464 percent. But even with all the support of the Say Yes to Education program and the extraordinary involvement of their benefactors, many students met tragic ends, made terrible mistakes, or succumbed to pressures most children never face. More than ten years after hearing that their college education would be free and that additional support would help them reach college, 44 percent of the Belmont 112 failed to graduate high school.

To an optimist, the lesson of the Belmont 112 is that with the right resources—presumably more than the additional $4,500 per student per year spent to achieve the success rate of the Belmont 112—government can help at-risk students overcome societal disadvantages by making public education a way to a better life. An additional $4,500 per student would increase School District of Philadelphia spending by more than $900 million each year if Philadelphia were to provide Say-Yes-to-Education-like supports for every single school child. If one takes a less rosy view of the lesson of the Belmont 112, one concludes that the disadvantages faced by certain students are too great to overcome no matter how willing society is to commit resources and effort toward making public education a bridge to opportunity. While the true answer lies somewhere between the two extremes, it is clear that the City and School District can do better. The question becomes whether the City and District can ever do enough.

To respond to the challenge of improving public education in Philadelphia, the City can alter School District governance to provide an incentive for elected leaders to focus on educational issues. The City can follow the lead of other jurisdictions and implement programs that have proven ability to increase educational attainment. The City can increase the District's ability to fund efforts to create change. Finally, if the City cannot improve education by improving the public schools, it can consider ways to increase the other-than-traditional public school options available to its families.

---

[11] Mezzacappa, Dale. "Under a cloud of despair, he ended a life of promise," *Philadelphia Inquirer*, July 19, 1996. p. B1.

Governance and the School District

One overriding factor inhibits the implementation of policy recommendations desired or demanded by the citizens of Philadelphia. The complicated governance structure of the School District of Philadelphia provides no ability for elected leaders to directly influence District performance, offers no incentive for political actors to focus their attentions on education in Philadelphia, and promotes no accountability to the citizenry for the provision of such a significant governmental function. Altering School District governance will not automatically improve public education in Philadelphia, but it could give the City's elected officials the incentive and the power to directly promote change.

Philadelphia is governed under the strong mayor/weak council form of government. The Mayor has vast powers and Council plays an instrumental role in forming City policy. But when considering the Philadelphia School District—appointment of top officials, preparation of the budget, administrative oversight, and initiation of policy—Philadelphia's strong Mayor and activist Council both have little opportunity to create change.

Neither the Superintendent of Schools nor the nine-member Board of Education is directly accountable to the Mayor or Council. While the Mayor appoints Board members from lists provided by a nominating panel, the Mayor is limited to three appointments every other year. Because Board appointments are scheduled to be made at the end of the Mayor's second year of office, and because Board members are appointed to six-year terms, any given Mayor will not appoint the full membership of the Board unless he or she is reelected and finishes the sixth year in office. Even further from direct mayoral influence, the District Superintendent is appointed—and, if necessary, removed—by the Board of Education.

The School District budget is prepared and adopted separately from the City budget. The Board of Education—which, depending on how long a Mayor has been in office, may contain no appointees by the current Mayor—prepares and adopts a budget. The Board has exclusive control over the preparation and adoption of the School District budget, but lacks the power or responsibility to raise the revenues to balance the budget. City Council is responsible for authorizing (or refusing to authorize) the necessary taxes to fund the budget, but the Mayor and Council cannot directly alter the budgetary choices of the School District. Because of the tenuous connections between Philadelphia's elected leaders and the operations of the School District, the Mayor and City Council may have little political incentive to work for improvement.

During the past decades, many local voices have called for governance changes to improve district performance. Notably, the Committee of Seventy, a Philadelphia-based non-partisan, good-government organization, has long advocated increased mayoral control over public education. The Committee of Seventy recommends that the Mayor be authorized and required to appoint a School Board and a Superintendent to terms concurrent with the Mayor's, that the School District budget be formulated in conjunction with the budgets of other City departments (in consultation with the Mayor and subject to City Council changes in lump-sum appropriations), that a separate fund within the budget be established to protect education funds, that the City Controller exercise the same preaudit authority over District expenditures currently applicable to City expenditures, and that the Mayor approve all collective bargaining agreements with labor unions affiliated with the School District.

Other governance-related proposals advanced by local state legislators would decentralize the School District by creating more neighborhood-based control over schools. Still other voices call for the Commonwealth of Pennsylvania to take control of the School District of Philadelphia. While critics contend that changes in governance do not necessarily result in any difference in student achievement—that the surest determinants of student achievement are parental education and occupation—there is a definite nationwide trend toward firmly connecting school district governance to cities' highest elected officials.

In 1995, the Illinois legislature granted the Mayor of Chicago control over the operations of the City's schools and the School District budget. With the City's elected School Board replaced by a Board appointed by the Mayor, the Mayor was suddenly accountable for school performance and able directly to affect district policies and procedures. Early indications suggest that this change has been successful. Administratively, the Mayor—through his handpicked School Board—has reworked labor contracts, funded an $806 million capital improvement plan, and is on target to eliminate a $1.3 billion deficit. Academically, achievement test scores have increased across the district and, with a substantial decrease in "social promotion," students are forced to attend summer school to achieve a true passing grade.[12]

In Boston, the Mayor now has the power to appoint the formerly elected school board. In New York City, the City Chancellor of Education received more control over hiring and the authority to take over failing schools. In Sacramento, voters approved a change from an elected school board to a board appointed by the Mayor.

But changes in governance do not guarantee success. In Baltimore, where the Mayor has long had the authority, control, and accountability that other mayors now have, City schools still exhibit the underperformance of other urban districts. The Maryland legislature recently moved to reorganize school governance by giving the Governor more influence over School Board appointments. Failed experiments in decentralization and neighborhood control undertaken in Chicago and New York City reinforced what Philadelphia learned a full century ago—decentralization results in politicization and inefficiency. In the long run, unless the City, surrounding jurisdictions, and the Commonwealth of Pennsylvania address funding inequities, concentration of poverty, and socioeconomic decline, it is unclear at best that governance reform alone can improve student achievement in any large urban district.

With respect to public education, Philadelphia's elected officials already have all the power that they choose to exercise and all the responsibility they choose to accept. But under the current governance structure, they also have the ability to evade responsibility and use governance as an excuse for inaction. With little ability to directly influence district policy, achieve management reforms, produce budgetary efficiencies, or otherwise affect student achievement, Philadelphia's elected leadership has limited capability or incentive to pursue recommendations to save money, enhance revenues, or improve the system of public schools. To more closely vest responsibility for the administration of the Philadelphia School District with the City's elected leadership, the City should work with the Pennsylvania General Assembly for School District governance reform.[13] The Mayor could approve all collective bargaining agreements with labor unions affiliated with the School District. The Mayor could directly appoint the School Superintendent. The Mayor could appoint the Board of Education to terms concurrent with the Mayor's or the Board could be eliminated. The School District budget could be formulated in conjunction with the budgets of other City agencies (in consultation with the Mayor and subject to City Council changes in lump sum appropriations), and a separate fund within the City budget could protect education funds. The City Controller could exercise the same preaudit authority over District expenditures currently applicable to City expenditures. Governance reform is not a panacea, but should be viewed as a necessary step toward providing elected officials with the ability to implement reforms through increased control over the appointment and budgetary processes and the incentive to act through increased accountability.

Implementing Programs That Work

Armed with a governance structure that gives them true power to create change at the School District, Philadelphia's elected leadership could focus on improving public education by imple-

---

[12] Mahtesian, Charles "Handing the Schools to City Hall," *Governing*, October 1996. p. 38.

[13] The First Class City Public Education Home Rule Act (1963) gives Philadelphians limited authority to alter school governance. Specifically, any alteration of school governance designed to expand the City's role in the School District's budgetary process beyond its current role (authorizing the School District to levy sufficient taxes to balance the District budget), could only come as a result of action by the Pennsylvania General Assembly. If Philadelphia's elected officials are to wield significant managerial authority over School District operations, the state legislature must act to make it possible.

menting programs that work. As the example of the Belmont 112 illustrates, efforts to improve student achievement by providing students with the supports they may not receive at home are accompanied by tremendous costs and mixed results. More troubling for attempts to replicate similar programs on a district-wide basis is the fact that such efforts utilize scarce funds that could be spent on programs that benefit all students. If parents with other options do not believe that their children are benefiting from public education in Philadelphia, they will remove their children from the public school system, increasing the percentage of students in the schools who require extra supports.

Some efforts, however, do improve educational attainment for all students and could be employed to improve public education in Philadelphia. Longer school days can make education a bigger part of students' lives. Smaller classes—especially in low grades and at ratios of fewer than 20 students per teacher—can allow teachers to focus on individual students. Linking school to the work world or higher education can help students move on to worthwhile careers.

In 1994, the National Education Commission on Time and Learning issued the results of its two-year investigation. "Learning in America is a prisoner of time," said the Commission, arguing that the time available is the unacknowledged design flaw in American education.

To fix the design flaw, the Commission asserted that any school reform that includes higher standards and accountability should be met by additional time for teaching and learning. Their argument centered on dispelling the myths that are inherent in the current structure of school time: that students arrive at school ready to learn in the same way, on the same schedule, all in rhythm with each other; that academic time can be used for non-academic purposes with no effect on learning; that because yesterday's calendar was good enough for today's parents, it should be good enough for today's children (despite major changes in the larger society); that schools can be transformed without giving teachers the time they need to retool themselves and reorganize their work; and that it is reasonable to expect students to meet world-class standards within the time-bound system that is already failing them.

The recommendations issued by the Commission included the need to keep schools open longer to meet the needs of students and communities and preserving the time that teachers need for their own professional development. These recommendations were echoed in the School District of Philadelphia's recent Children Achieving reform program. Specifically, the Children Achieving Action Plan calls for an extended day program for at-risk children, additional professional development for teachers, and keeping schools open three additional hours for community access. However, implementation has taken shape in an *ad hoc* fashion and on a much smaller scale than initially intended.

Research confirms common sense. Some students simply take more time to learn. The evidence further suggests that students at risk of failure benefit most from any additional time. Poverty is the most often-used indicator of the at-risk population. By this criterion, virtually 80 percent of the Philadelphia School District's student population needs additional time. Research points to the lack of child care as one of the most significant barriers to welfare recipients' entry into the labor force. It follows that extending the school day may offer additional flexibility to the work schedule of parents. Finally, crime reports show that most violent crimes committed by juveniles occur during the hour immediately following school. Criminologists argue that this is primarily the result of the lack of supervision during this time (the latchkey effect). Extending the day would reduce the likelihood of youth being unsupervised.

Local policymakers have already considered the issue of additional time. Nineteen minutes were added to the length of the teacher's workday as part of the latest labor agreement. As part of a ruling in a School District desegregation case, a Pennsylvania judge mandated a limited amount of extra instructional time for a portion of the student population.

EXTENDING THE SCHOOL DAY IN PHILADELPHIA

The Philadelphia School District has essentially integrated two separate programs to lengthen the school day to meet a variety of needs for selected students. The purpose of the first program, the extended school hours program, is to offer academic enrichment activities, life skills training, arts and cultural initiatives, and recreational activities. This has been integrated with a second program, which simply provides extra time for instruction to address the needs of at-risk students.

Due to budget constraints this program has only been fully implemented in two groupings of Philadelphia schools referred to as "clusters" (groupings of feeder schools and high schools within a geographic area). The 16-school Martin Luther King Cluster has implemented an extra instructional time/extended school hours program in each of its schools. The program is funded with support from a private foundation, matched by funds from the Cluster's operating budget. A total of more than $700,000 (more than $500,000 from the foundation plus more than $200,000 from the operating budget) supports programs designed by each of the Cluster's schools. Funding is based on enrollment plus a formula that provides extra support for high schools, schools that contract with a non-profit educational agency, and a school's status as a "Title One" or "Desegregation" school. For $18 to $45 per student, the schools of the Martin Luther King Cluster enjoy an extended school day and provide extra instructional support for their most at-risk students.

Each of the Martin Luther King schools, with approval from the Cluster leadership, designs and implements its own program. Some schools have chosen to provide after-school tutoring while others have created Saturday schools, extended day activities, or before-school programs.

Also with support from a private foundation, the 13 schools of the West Philadelphia Cluster have created similar programs. While the programs do not reach all children (they are designed to reach the most at-risk students), they represent a sustainable effort to improve academic improvement. It is still too early to judge any empirical results from the extended instructional time, but the additional foundation support and innovation from principals provide an example that could become a model for the District.

The School District can extend the school day for all Philadelphia students. Based on expenditures to extend the teaching day, pay for extra utility usage, and provide additional custodial and security support, the cost of implementing a one-hour extension of the school day for all students using the existing teaching force and support staff would be approximately $52 million.

This cost estimate is likely to be overstated by several million dollars. First, several schools are already required to be open past the normal length of day. Thus, no additional utility costs are incurred. Second, a number of after-school programs already exist, such as the extended day programs mentioned above and the day care programs at selected schools. Thus, funding for these existing programs could be rolled into the new extended day program.

This cost estimate assumes an increase for all children. If this increase were constrained to elementary schools (where research shows it would be most effective), the cost is estimated to be $28.8 million. (See Funding Efforts to Improve Public Education in Philadelphia below for a discussion of some ways to fund this initiative.)

To enhance the impact of education on students' lives, the City should work with the District to extend the school day. Such a move will come at a cost, but the in- and out-of-school benefits of a longer school day are substantial. Providing students and teachers more time on task, alleviating parents' need to find after-school child care, and reducing the unsupervised after-school hours that too often turn into an invitation to wrongdoing will not only help public school students and their families, but improve the City itself.

In addition to a longer school day, the City should push for smaller classes in City schools. By contract, the maximum size of Philadelphia classes is set at 30 students in kindergarten through third grade and 33 students for all other grades. In surrounding suburban school districts, classes generally contain fewer than 25 students. Researchers consistently cite accelerated student achievement as class sizes fall to about 15 students. The most oft-quoted research involving class size surrounds Tennessee's Student/Teacher Achievement Ratio (STAR) Project that ran from 1985 to 1989. In 1994, Tennessee State University's Center of Excellence for Research in Basic Skills concluded that small class size resulted in clear and consistent achievement benefits for kindergarten through third-grade students in small classes (one teacher per 15 students) versus students in regular classes (one teacher per 25 students) or regular classes with a full-time teacher's aide. Even at the end of the seventh grade, four full years after their last small-class experience, students from Project STAR small classes showed clear, consistent, and statistically significant advantages over students from non-small classes. More important, the smaller class size benefited students of all races, in all locales (rural, suburban, urban, and inner city), and at all income levels. Indeed, some of the most compelling research indicates that the reduced class size is most effective in the inner-city setting.

Two significant factors inhibit efforts to reduce class size in Philadelphia: cost and space. Hiring extra teachers would require a large pool of new funding. Providing rooms for these new, smaller classes in buildings that currently bulge to fit the larger classes would require significant investment. The two factors, then, boil down to cost and more cost. Researchers estimate that reducing class size to Project STAR levels would cost approximately $1,000 per student. While external reviews have disagreed with School District assumptions, the School District of Philadelphia estimated it would require $15.6 million per year to reduce kindergarten classes to 20 students per class and $71.9 million per year to reduce average first-, second-, and third-grade classes to 17 students. The same estimate indicated that the District would require an additional $39.4 million to provide additional classrooms to accommodate such efforts until building capacity is expanded through capital expenditures.

Given the demonstrated ability of smaller classes to improve student achievement, the City should work with the District to reduce class size in Philadelphia schools. Dramatic size-reduction efforts could be limited to lower grades to reduce costs. Keeping schools open year round, with students attending on alternative schedules, could also help alleviate the need to build extra classroom space. Despite the costs, however, the research supporting class-size reduction is too compelling to delay its implementation. Smaller classes can improve student achievement and help build a more competitive Philadelphia.

Longer days and smaller classes, however, cannot work without quality instruction. Demanding excellence from students requires a commitment from government to provide the resources necessary to afford an environment more conducive to learning. It also requires an insistence that instructors meet high standards to make public education work.

Teacher accountability systems are at the center of ongoing controversy between those who suggest that teachers should be punished and rewarded based on the performance of their students and those who contend that outside-the-classroom factors (such as parental non-support and poor attendance) make it impossible to hold teachers responsible for student achievement. Actual student achievement is a combination of classroom experience, education in the home, students' innate abilities, and many other non-school related factors. Without compelling evidence that it is possible to truly gauge the value added of an individual teacher, the City must support efforts that increase the likelihood that quality teachers will stand before students in the classroom to complement other initiatives.

The National Commission on Teaching and America's Future cites Pennsylvania's complex process to remove incompetent teachers, its lifetime teacher certification that does not require training to update teaching skills, and minimal requirements for retaining teacher tenure as barriers to quality teaching. The City should work with teachers' union representatives, state education officials, and the School District of Philadelphia to push for efforts to promote teaching excellence. In recent years, Pennsylvania increased the amount of time required for new teachers to be eligible for tenure from two to three years. Additional legislative effort to raise minimum standards for teachers, require ongoing teacher training, and implement more stringent teacher evaluation can make a difference by placing better teachers in the classroom.

With Philadelphia teachers earning low salaries in comparison with other area districts, increasing compensation is crucial to attracting and retaining good teachers. To help improve teacher quality at the School District level, the District could explore mortgage assistance to compensate for the District's low salary and residency requirements for teachers—or follow the lead of the Dallas, Texas, School District and offer signing bonuses to new teachers.[14] The District could provide incentives for teachers to work in selected schools to help ensure that quality teachers gravitate to the schools that need them most. The District could alter hiring and promotion procedures to ensure that the School District is able to offer positions to prospective teachers in the spring when students receive degrees instead of later in the season, when top graduates have already accepted jobs. Similarly, the City could work with the teachers' union to create more certainty in the assignment process and make reasonable adjustments in seniority rules to make School District employment more hospitable for new hires. Finally, the City can create better working conditions by lowering class size and working with the teachers' union to trade productivity initiatives for salary increases and funding to improve building conditions.

To maximize the input of all reforms, the City should work with School District officials to link more closely public school education with post-secondary education and careers. Philadelphia's School-to-Career programs partner Philadelphia employers with schools that provide students with educational and employment experiences designed to prepare them for career success. The Philadelphia High School Academies—the nation's oldest and largest program linking work and scholarship—structure students' learning and working experience around a central theme to provide an interdisciplinary approach to career education. Philadelphia's magnet schools and programs are designed to offer specialized instruction for students who meet certain academic and performance standards. Area Vocational Technical Schools provide academic and vocational-technical education in a setting that stresses career training. These programs have effectively linked public school learning with post-school careers and ongoing education at colleges and universities, but are out of reach for some students. By rewarding achievement, behavior, attendance, and interest, these programs show students a true link between school performance and post-school life. The City could increase the reach of these educational experiences by offering "second-chance" initiatives that would give interested students additional opportunities for admission.

The City of Providence, Rhode Island, established Public Service Academies as small-learning communities within City high schools to educate future civic leaders, police officers, fire fighters, and teachers. Students who complete a special curriculum that encourages meaningful service to the community are offered partial scholarships to a local college. To enhance the linkage between schools, careers, and ongoing education, Philadelphia can follow the lead of Providence and offer scholarships to students who plan to attend a local college. As previously noted in discussions about economic development, this would benefit the City by increasing demand for post-secondary educational services in Philadelphia and encouraging expansion throughout the educational services industry.

---

14 Bradley, Ann. "New Teachers Are Hot Commodity," *Education Week*, September 9, 1998.

Additionally, to help make sure that a Philadelphia public school education means that a student can read, write, and do math at an acceptable level, the City can guarantee its graduates. In Prince George's County, Maryland, a Guaranteed Employability Program backs up each graduate with a one-year guarantee that the public school system will provide skill strengthening through adult education or counseling if an employer finds deficiencies in the skill level of public school graduates. The Los Angeles Unified School District issues a warranty affirming the quality and appropriateness of each student's preparation based on the U.S. Department of Labor Secretary's Commission on Achieving Necessary Skills (SCANS). Graduates who are not satisfactorily competent can be returned to the School District, Division of Adult and Career Education for no-cost additional training for up to one year from their graduation date. By so clearly linking educational attainment to employability for both students and employers, a guarantee can send a powerful message that school performance has true consequences.

Funding Efforts to Improve Public Education in Philadelphia

While many internal efforts and external reviews have focused on reducing costs at the School District, the costs required to reduce class size or extend the length of the school day will require additional supports. To fund such efforts, the City should continue to pressure the Commonwealth of Pennsylvania to create a more equitable school-funding system and increase cooperation between City agencies and the School District.

Many describe the current method of financing public education, which provides an incentive for wealthier communities to devote more resources to the delivery of education, as grossly unfair. The primary motivation for this claim is the tremendous spending differences observed across local school districts. For example, spending per pupil in the Philadelphia School District was substantially less than surrounding counties. During the 1995–96 school year, Philadelphia's spending per pupil was $5,782 per student. By contrast, the average spending per pupil in the City's more wealthy surrounding county Districts ranged from an average of $6,822 in Delaware County to $7,811 in Montgomery County.

However, experts argue that it is not spending per pupil that should be equalized to achieve equity. Rather, equity should be based on spending per unit of education. The distinction lies in the tremendous differences in the buying power of the educational dollar from one locality to the next. A recent research report issued by the National Center for Education Statistics found that these differences in the buying power of the educational dollar are largely a function of two factors. First, there is the need of a child that accounts for spending differences resulting from additional resources required to provide an education for children with special needs. For example, the Philadelphia School District spends considerably more than wealthier districts on programs related to school readiness and community services and supports. Second, there is the actual cost-of-living difference that must be considered. For instance, per-unit costs for utilities are generally higher in urban areas than more rural areas. Within this framework, the data suggest that the buying power of the educational dollar in Philadelphia—a high-cost urban center endowed with a significant concentration of poverty—is substantially less than other districts throughout the Commonwealth.

Many researchers and policymakers argue that a truly equitable system of financing public education would include a mechanism to adjust for these differences in buying power. This implies that, all else equal, spending per pupil should be substantially higher in Philadelphia relative to suburban and rural counties to achieve equity—quite the opposite of what exists under the current system.

Most of the state funding to the District comprises a Basic Education Subsidy. In its original form, the subsidy worked as an equalization grant, whereby each district was funded according to its relative need. Need was determined by a formula which considered such factors as a local district's level of poverty and ability to generate own-source revenues. That is, the formula made some adjustment for differences in the relative buying power of the educational dollar among the districts in the Commonwealth. However, beginning with the 1991–92 school year, the state abandoned its use of the Equalization Subsidy for Basic Education (ESBE) formula. Had the equalization formula been used, the District estimates it would have received $425.8 million over and above its actual allocation between the 1991–92 school year and the 1997–98 school year.

Commonwealth officials have made the claim that the District's tax effort, the level of locally generated tax collections as a percentage of its total market value, is too low. At first glance this appears to be a valid argument. Philadelphia School District tax effort is below suburban districts. Upon closer inspection, it can be argued that the District will have difficulty raising tax effort, given the overall tax burden. Despite recent reductions in City business and income taxes, the overall tax burden on City residents and establishments remains substantially higher than on its suburban counterparts. If the research is correct, the City's well-intentioned attempt to strike a delicate balance between raising the District's tax effort and reducing overall tax burden may be to no avail. It follows that the burden of raising the essential revenues to create a more equitable system of finance lies entirely on the Commonwealth.

In 1994, Michigan voters passed a constitutional amendment shifting most of the burden for school funding from local property taxes to a combination of statewide sales and use taxes. Vermont recently abolished its local property-tax-based school funding system, replacing it with a newly-created statewide property tax for elementary and secondary schools. The Vermont plan allows localities to levy a new local property tax, which is distributed by the state using an equalization formula. Other states are working to bring increased equity to statewide educational spending. The City must continue to place pressure on the Commonwealth to increase the equity of statewide educational spending, and to erase at least a portion of the total amount of the Commonwealth's education subsidy, under-funded since fiscal year 1992.

But the Commonwealth does not have to appropriate additional funding to the School District to increase the amount of educational spending in Philadelphia. By reducing the financial impact of certain school mandates, the Commonwealth could allow the District to achieve remarkable savings. For example, the School Code requires the District to employ attendance officers, school physicians, school nurses, and school dentists, but the District estimates that it could save $3 million annually by outsourcing those services. Similarly, the District is required by the School Code to pay for the transportation of any non-public school child—even students who attend a school up to ten miles beyond the City limits. If that mandate could be relaxed just to eliminate the requirement that the District must pay to transport students beyond the City borders (the District would still have to pay for transportation to non-public schools within the City), the District could save nearly $3 million per year. The costs imposed by these major mandates, plus additional costs imposed by other minor ones, create a very real impact on the District budget. By working with state officials and legislators to alter the Pennsylvania School Code, the City could reduce the monetary impact of school mandates and redirect savings toward educational expenditures.

Because the economic health of the City is directly tied to the future of public education in Philadelphia, the City must also use every tool at its disposal to increase investments in public education and to ensure that District funds are directed toward educational expenses. During fiscal year 1997, a one-time sale of City Real Estate Tax liens earned the School District $38.6 million. In recent years, the City of Philadelphia has provided $15 million to the School District above and beyond the tax contributions of City businesses and residents. In addition to potential savings through City-School District consolidation of internal services discussed in Chapter 2, the City can alter policies that have worked to hold down District revenues. Such efforts could reduce the negative impact of City programs on the District and increase District revenues on a permanent basis.

To spur recent real estate development in Philadelphia, City officials have employed tax abatements and Tax Increment Financing (TIF). The City, and to a much lesser extent the School District, which is legally required to approve TIF projects, benefits from this new development through increases in non-Real Estate Tax revenues. However, Real Estate Taxes for properties developed in TIF districts, or for properties benefiting from tax abatements, are foregone during the abatement period or for the life of the TIF. Since more than 30 percent of School District revenue is derived from the District's 55-percent share of City Real Estate Taxes, the School District loses a significant source of revenue when TIFs and abatements are used.

Proponents declare that, if not for these abatements or TIFs, projects would not move forward, so there is no real loss of revenue. But clearly the School District would realize a much larger increase in revenues if loans, grants, or other subsidies could be substituted for abatements or TIFs to make the same projects possible. An examination of one TIF deal, the development of the Naval Business Center, illustrates the loss to the School District. Projections performed by the City Controller's Office, using data supplied by the Philadelphia Industrial Development Corporation, indicate that the total revenue foregone by the School District for the duration of the TIF (1998 to 2017) is estimated in present dollars to equal $18,770,453.[15]

Realizing that TIFs and abatements inhibit School District revenue growth, the State of Michigan has moved to compensate affected districts. Recent legislation has mandated that for new TIF developments, tax increment revenues must be solely derived from non-school property taxes. For past TIFs, tax increment revenues derived from school property taxes will be made up to the schools by the state through higher school aid payments. On the municipal level, the Akron, Ohio, City Council recently voted unanimously in favor of a 96-year deal to reimburse schools whenever property tax breaks are offered.

Similarly, as part of the legislation creating "Renaissance Zones" (economic development zones in which businesses and residents will receive certain tax exemptions or credits and property will be exempt from property taxes for up to 15 years), the State of Michigan is required to reimburse school districts each year for all tax revenue lost as the result of the tax exemptions. In 1998, the Commonwealth of Pennsylvania created "Keystone Opportunity Zones" patterned after the Renaissance Zones as virtually tax-free geographic areas. Unfortunately, the legislation creating the Keystone Opportunity Zones does not reimburse school districts for lost tax revenues.

Where possible, the City could avoid the use of TIFs and abatements in favor of low-interest loans, direct governmental grants, and other incentives that do not affect the School District's tax base to encourage development. When it uses TIFs and abatements, the City, or the Commonwealth, since the Commonwealth enables such economic development tools, could reimburse the District for revenues lost to abatements and TIFs or exempt School District Real Estate Taxes from inclusion in TIF projects. If the City is unwilling to compensate the School District for its unrealized revenues, the District could seriously consider exercising its right to opt School District Real Estate Taxes out of any future TIF activities. Additionally, the City could work to alter the Keystone Opportunity Zone legislation in the Pennsylvania General Assembly to allow for a reimbursement to school districts each year for tax revenues lost as the result of the tax exemptions associated with the creation of the Zones.

Other City programs more immediately impact the District. The Department of Recreation runs numerous programs in and on School District facilities throughout the City. Especially in the Northeast section of the City, where development of recreation and school facilities was closely coordinated, City leaders have consistently envisioned that school facilities would be utilized for Department of Recreation programs.

The coordination makes sense, but the Department of Recreation does not reimburse the School District for the use of District facilities. For the 1995–96 school year, the School District estimated that Department of Recreation facility usage costs equaled $3.9 million. For the 1996–97 school year, that figure equaled $3.4 million. In addition to these amounts, while the School District does not charge the Department for use of playing fields (charges for athletic fields are only levied when a field attendant is required to be on hand), substantial costs are incurred for maintenance due to wear and tear from Department of Recreation programs conducted on playing fields.

---

[15] This figure is a net figure—$18,770,453 includes all revenues foregone by the School District ($61,471,916), less revenues anticipated to be generated for the School District by the TIF ($42,701,463) which includes a partial rebate to the School District already built into the TIF deal.

If the Department of Recreation were to pay for its programs conducted in and on School District facilities, the District could have more than $3 million available annually to fund educational expenses. For example, one non-City organization paid the School District $936.32 for use of the Greenfield School gym for a basketball league for eight dates in the winter of 1996. For similar activities, the Department of Recreation pays nothing.

The City could also improve tax-collection efforts to increase District revenue. As noted in the previous chapter, a recent Controller's Office audit of the Revenue Department found that the City is only collecting the Liquor Sales Tax from about two-thirds of the establishments currently subject to the tax. The report estimates that the School District could be due an additional $2.1 million in uncollected Liquor Sales Tax. Additional moneys to fund proven educational programs could come from recommendations the Controller's Office has made in various performance audits including: reducing administrative costs, reforming the workers' compensation program, implementing alternates to proposed School District budget cuts, creating advertising and sponsorship programs, investigating Health and Welfare Fund savings and reforming the sabbatical program. Funds could also be generated through savings from City-School District consolidation efforts discussed in Chapter 2.

Solving the Public Education Problem

While many of its schools and programs are exceptional, the School District of Philadelphia is clearly underperforming in its efforts to educate children and prepare them for college or the world of work. But despite the District's failure, many parents have already solved the public education problem. They send their children to private schools or to recently created charter schools that are authorized by local school boards, but free from many of the legal and contractual constraints that critics suggest hamper educational efforts in traditional public schools. Approximately 70,000 Philadelphia students are enrolled in non-public schools while about 3,000 more are enrolled in public charter schools. Since about 210,000 Philadelphia children attend traditional public schools, approximately 26 percent of all City students are removed from the public schools operated by the School District of Philadelphia.

The challenge for Philadelphia's future is not to make it more likely that some children can receive an excellent education. The real challenge is to improve the overall competitiveness of the City by improving educational experiences for all Philadelphians. In a household where children do not attend public school, the problem of public education may be solved, but next door, in the larger neighborhood and throughout the City, the problem continues. If overall educational attainment remains low, even a child who receives a private school education will live in a region with diminished economic growth. If public schools cannot increase the skill level of the entire workforce, even a child who receives a charter school education will experience diminished wage growth.

Voucher programs could expand parents' ability to afford non-public education for their children. Efforts to increase the number of charter schools could work at the micro level for families who have the means or the will to take advantage of these options. However, it is unclear if charter schools or vouchers have any power to force a school district as a whole to radically change its approach to public education and improve overall student achievement. If all the parents with means or motivation remove their children from the public school system, then public schools will be left with only children from the poorest households and children with the least-motivated parents. Unless a voucher program could cover the complete cost of education including transportation, supplies, uniforms, etc. for every child; unless enough charter schools could be created to serve every single student; and unless voucher and charter programs could prohibit non-public and charter schools from "creaming" only the best students, the School District of Philadelphia would still be left with the task of educating the City's most disadvantaged students. Under such a situation, the City and region would still suffer if the public schools fail to improve overall educational attainment in Philadelphia.

To solve the problem of public education in Philadelphia for some families, the City can push for systemic change to alter the role of government with respect to education. Charters make government a consumer of educational services rather than a provider of educational services. Vouchers make government a financier of education and a competitor in the education market-place. But the worth of a voucher program or an expansion of the charter school experiment must be based on how such efforts increase the overall educational attainment level in the City. Vouchers and charters can help individual Philadelphians, but will not likely make the City more competitive by increasing the overall educational attainment of the Philadelphia workforce and decreasing the percentage of Philadelphians who are unfit for employment. Any support of such initiatives should be based on whether per-pupil-funding mechanisms for vouchers and charters allow the School District to retain funding necessary to reduce class size and implement other proven programs throughout the system. Essentially, support for any voucher program or expansion of the use of charter schools should only accompany a full recognition of the failure of the system of public education and a complete reorganization of the education delivery system.

RECOMMENDATIONS FOR ACTION

The City should work with the Pennsylvania General Assembly for School District governance reform to more closely vest responsibility for the administration of the Philadelphia School District with the City's elected leadership.

Action Steps:

- Work with the Pennsylvania General Assembly to pass legislation to alter School District governance.

- Work with the School District, City Council, and the City Controller's Office to delineate new areas of responsibility related to appointment of District officials, District budget formulation and adoption, and preaudit oversight of District expenditures.

Fiscal Impact:

- Potential to generate savings through City-School District consolidation efforts and increased operational efficiencies.

The City should work with the School District to push to extend the length of the school day to enhance the impact of education on students' lives.

Action Steps:

- Work with School District officials to extend the length of the school day.

- Work with bargaining units to enable school-day extension.

Fiscal Impact:

- Potential cost of $29-$168 million annually, depending on amount of added time and reach of additional-time program. Costs could be offset by previously-discussed revenue-raising/expenditure-reduction initiatives and foundation support.

- Potential long-term economic benefit from increase in overall educational attainment levels in the City.

The City should work with the School District to reduce class size to below 20 students per class in the early grades in Philadelphia schools.

Action Steps:

- Work with School District officials to reduce class size in Philadelphia schools.

- Work with bargaining units to enable class-size reduction.

- Construct facilities necessary to house additional classes.

Fiscal Impact:

- Potential short-term cost of approximately $40 million to provide extra facilities to enable class-size reduction. Costs could be offset by previously-discussed revenue-raising/expenditure-reduction initiatives and foundation support.

- Potential cost of $87.5 million annually.

- Potential long-term economic benefit from increase in overall educational attainment levels in the City.

The City should work with teachers' union representatives, state education officials, and the School District of Philadelphia to promote teaching excellence.

Action Steps:

- Work with the Pennsylvania General Assembly to pass legislation to promote higher standards for teacher certification and add requirements for ongoing training to ensure teacher quality.

- Work with School District officials to improve the timing and certainty of hiring procedures at the District level.

- Work with the School District and teachers' union to create hiring bonuses, mortgage assistance, incentives for teachers to work in selected schools, and more certainty in the hiring process to make employment at the District more attractive to new hires.

Fiscal Impact:

- Potential to increase annual School District administrative costs.

- Potential to increase personnel costs through signing bonuses, mortgage assistance, and incentives to teach in selected schools.

- Potential long-term economic benefit from increase in overall educational attainment levels in the City.

The City should work with School District officials to more closely link public school education with post-secondary education and careers.

Action Steps:

- Work with the School District to enhance and expand programs that link school performance to post-secondary education and careers.

- Consider efforts to offer students higher-education stipends for outstanding academic performance.

- Consider efforts to "guarantee" the quality of Philadelphia public school graduates.

Fiscal Impact:

- Potential to increase annual cost of School District Programs.

- Potential to increase District costs through the implementation of a stipend or graduate-guarantee program.

- Potential long-term economic benefit from increase in overall educational attainment levels in the City.

To fund efforts to improve public education in Philadelphia, the City should increase pressure on the Commonwealth of Pennsylvania to create a more equitable school funding system and increase cooperation efforts between City agencies and the School District.

Action Steps:

- Work with state officials to increase the equity of statewide educational funding.

- Work with state officials to compensate the District for the underfunding of the Commonwealth education subsidy.

- Work with state officials and the Pennsylvania General Assembly to alter the Pennsylvania School Code to reduce the financial impact of non-educational school mandates.

- Compensate the District for revenues lost in Tax Increment Financing deals—work with state officials to provide compensation from state sources.

- Work to alter the Keystone Opportunity Zone legislation in the Pennsylvania General Assembly to reimburse school districts each year for tax revenues lost as the result of the tax exemptions associated with the creation of the Zones.

- Reimburse the District for use of District facilities by City agencies.

- Improve tax-collection efforts to increase District revenues.

Fiscal Impact:

- Potential to increase District revenues.

HOUSING—CREATING A MARKET FOR PHILADELPHIA'S VACANT HOUSING STOCK

As the natural by-product of population loss in recent decades, Philadelphia is endowed with an overabundance of vacant homes. According to official City of Philadelphia estimates, approximately 27,000 vacant residential structures are scattered across the City, not including properties being actively marketed for sale or rent and not including properties in move-in condition and not sealed or boarded up. Of these structures, the City's Office of Housing and Community Development (OHCD) counts only 2,000 houses that are in move-in condition. The remaining 25,000 houses would require some or significant rehabilitation before they could be ready for occupancy. Using an alternative methodology, the 1990 census counted 71,824 vacant housing units in Philadelphia, including 15,774 vacant, boarded-up houses and 56,050 vacant houses that were not boarded up. The census number indicates that more than 10 percent of Philadelphia's 1990 housing units were vacant. Projections do not foresee a sudden surge in demand for housing in the City.

In 1995, the Greater Philadelphia Urban Affairs Coalition (GPUAC) published, "Housing Philadelphia: Low and Moderate Income Home Ownership—Opportunities and Constraints." According to GPUAC and its Home Ownership Task Force, because nearly half of present

Philadelphia homeowners are over age 55 (representing about 184,000 homes), and two-thirds of those are over age 65 (representing about 117,000 homes), a significant number of homes will be on the market in coming years as current owners move or die. The report concludes—based on a series of conditional estimates of the size of the ownership stock and the demand for that stock—an excess of owner-occupied housing supply over current demand levels will exist in Philadelphia from between 2,500 and 7,500 units per year.[16] The bulk of this excess demand would be located in areas of the City with the largest number of elderly owner-occupied units: Lower Northeast, West, South, North, and Northwest Philadelphia.

For the future, therefore, Philadelphia really has two significant problems related to housing. First, it must confront the fact that in many Philadelphia neighborhoods, there is simply no market for housing. Without significant inmigration, housing demand in many neighborhoods will continue to lag and property abandonment and increased vacancy will likely continue. With no market response likely to correct the surplus of vacancies, government must intervene in the marketplace to prevent the externalities associated with abandonment—decay, crime, and flight—from increasing the likelihood of total neighborhood breakdown. Second, the City must address the deterioration of large numbers of structures and properties. Because of the high number of houses owned by Philadelphia seniors and low-income residents, the City may expect its housing supply to deteriorate into an uninhabitable state, necessitating a governmental response that can shore up the housing markets in many communities.

In 1998, OHCD provided a true "snapshot" of neighborhood vacancy in Philadelphia. With a neighborhood-specific, vacant-property inventory that combined on-site photographs and field survey data with information from City agency records, one can see a property-by-property view of vacancy in one Philadelphia neighborhood. Through research performed using this data by the City Controller's Office, one can gain additional perspective on the causes and implications of vacancy.

VACANCY IN SOUTHWEST CENTER CITY PHILADELPHIA

For the City's door-to-door vacancy survey, the area defined as Southwest Center City runs approximately one mile west from Broad Street—the City's main north-south thoroughfare—to Grays Ferry Avenue between South Street and Washington Avenue. Less than one mile from City Hall, this neighborhood borders trendy Center City enclaves and hardscrabble inner-city areas and provides an interesting representation of the vacancy problem in Philadelphia. According to the real estate information system, Realist, Philadelphia's median home sale price for 1997 was $49,900. While the median sale price in the zip code containing Southwest Center City was $26,000 in 1997, 34 percent of area homes sold for more than $50,000. Some of the blocks of this neighborhood are untouched by vacancy or burdened with a lone vacant property while vacant properties and lots represent the majority of properties in other blocks. In all, approximately 16 percent of the houses in Southwest Center City are vacant and the neighborhood is burdened with 552 vacant houses and 362 vacant lots. (See Figure 4.1.)

---

[16] The authors of the GPUAC report arrive at thier estimate by suggesting that 150,000 housing units will enter the market from the current ownership pool of older households between 1990 and 2010. Using an even distribution over 20 years, they estimate that between 10,000 and 15,000 units per year will enter the supply stream from this source alone. If half of current sales come from the first wave of older residents' homes (about 7,000 units entering the market whose current owners do not plan to purchase a new home), and that supply increases at the lower estimate of 10,000 units per year, housing sales would need to increase by about 2,500 units (from the average 14,500 sales per year in Philadelphia to 17,000) to retain a balance between demand levels and supply. If, however, the supply increases at the higher rate of 15,000 units per year, or if the supply represents a smaller proportion of current sales than they have assumed, then the authors estimate that the gap between current levels and the projected supply (22,000 units) will increase significantly, to 7,500 units or higher. (See Bartelt and Shlay, "Housing Philadelphia: Low and Moderate Income Home Ownership—Opportunities and Constraints," 1995.)

Why did the houses of Southwest Center City become vacant? The research performed by the City Controller's Office suggests the following:

- *Low demand causes vacancy.* As Figure 4.1 illustrates, there are no vacant properties in thriving parts of Southwest Center City. In less vibrant parts, many vacant properties litter neighboring blocks. In the parts of Southwest Center City that are nearer to Center City proper, housing demand is adequate to prevent vacancy. Closer to Washington Avenue, many blocks are filled with vacancies and demand is insufficient to reduce their numbers. Many individuals have moved from Southwest Center City, but are unable to sell their properties. Nearly 60 percent of vacant houses in Southwest Center City are owned by individuals who own no other property in the area. Of those houses, more than 22 percent were purchased before 1971.

- *Death compounds vacancy.* As discussed above with regard to GPUAC's findings, many homeowners die, leaving property to relatives who find no demand for their inherited property. Of the 552 vacant houses in Southwest Center City, nearly half (48 percent) were sold for less than $1,000 (most sold for $1), indicating that they were likely legal transfers. Of these legally transferred houses, 63 percent are owned by individuals who do not own any other Southwest Center City vacant properties and 42 percent are owned by individuals who owe taxes on their vacant property.

- *Speculation perpetuates vacancy.* Many properties are owned by absentee speculators who are holding onto vacant properties and waiting for the market to turn in their favor. Less than 6 percent of Southwest Center City's vacant houses were posted for sale or for rent, while tax payments are current for nearly 65 percent of vacant houses. An additional 31 percent of Southwest Center City vacant houses are tax delinquent for fewer than five years. More than half of the vacant houses of Southwest Center City were purchased since 1981 and more than 20 percent were purchased since 1991—73 percent of Southwest Center City vacant houses purchased since 1991 owe no taxes. More than 18 percent of vacant Southwest Center City houses are owned by individuals who own other vacant properties in Southwest Center City.

As illustrated by the case of Southwest Center City, since properties are vacant for different reasons, the City cannot pursue one single policy to reduce the number of vacant properties in Philadelphia. The City can, however, pursue policies to increase demand for housing and increase the disincentives to speculators to encourage owners of vacant houses to make their properties productive.

Increasing Demand for Housing in Philadelphia

Every recommendation included in this document is designed to increase demand for housing in Philadelphia. From making government work to creating a budgetary framework that allows the City to live within its means, recommendations are put forth to create a government that runs the City well. From improving public education to reducing crime, recommendations are advanced to make Philadelphia a city that generates jobs and attracts residents. Specifically related to housing, however, the City can take direct action to increase demand for housing. While the City has many programs to acquire, rehabilitate, and demolish vacant homes spread throughout the City, Philadelphia continues to decay. A much more dramatic program is necessary to fundamentally change the demand for housing in the City.

If the City acquired and demolished 35 football fields worth of City housing and relocated the residents of nearly 1,000 houses to vacant houses in other parts of Philadelphia, the City could decrease the overall housing supply in the City and thereby increase demand in the neighborhoods with vacancies. At the same time, the City could assemble a large tract of land and create a unique development opportunity that could be sold to the highest bidder. Perhaps the notion sounds too draconian to even contemplate. It is happening, however, in Philadelphia today.

Figure 4.1. Southwest Center City Vacant Properties

Legend
City Owned
Vacant Lot
Vacant house

Scale
500   0   500   1000   Feet

Map produced by City of Philadelphia Mayor's Office of Information Services
Map illustrates summary results and may contain some errors and omissions.
Data Source: City of Philadelphia Office of Housing and Community Development

Figure 4.2. Vacant Properties in Philadelphia

N

· = One Vacant Property

Scale
1   0   1   2   Miles

Map produced by City of Philadelphia Mayor's Office of Information Services
Data Sources: City of Philadelphia Board of Revision of Taxes,
Department of Licenses and Inspections, and Bureau of Water Revenue

THE LOGAN SINKING HOMES

During the decade preceding 1920, homes were constructed on ash and cinder fill in the valley of the old Wingohocking Creek approximately five miles northeast of City Hall along Roosevelt Boulevard, the thoroughfare that helps connect Northeast Philadelphia to Center City. Over time, the cinder and ash fill deteriorated and damaged the structural integrity of the homes above. The homes of the Logan neighborhood were sinking.

Though it had no legal obligation to do so, in 1987 the City of Philadelphia took the unprecedented step of creating a private, non-profit agency to voluntarily relocate the area's nearly 1,000 homeowners. Mismanagement and scandal have plagued the agency, and more than ten years after its creation, the agency is still in the process of removing the remaining homeowners and demolishing the last of the Logan sinking homes. But for the record of poor administration of the program, the Logan experience is educational for efforts to help foster housing demand in the City.

Most former Logan residents have relocated within the City of Philadelphia, populating other neighborhoods that had vacancies. As the project nears completion, the City has all but assembled a 35-acre piece of land adjacent to a major transportation thoroughfare. Instead of gap-toothed blocks of decay and blight owned by numerous absentee landlords and speculators, the City owns block after block of cleared property. Despite the land's obvious need for remediation efforts, developers have expressed interest in building housing and commercial properties on the site of the Logan sinking homes. Development plans are stalled, however, pending resolution of how to fund necessary site-remediation efforts to prevent future construction from sinking back into the former Wingohocking Creek.

Through fiscal year 1996, the City spent approximately $18.7 million to relocate 351 households and additional millions to demolish houses. Including the costs to acquire homes, relocate residents, and demolish properties, OHCD officials estimate the City spent approximately $57,000 per Logan house.

Philadelphia is home to many neighborhoods that have experienced extreme population losses, and one can reasonably question the very viability of some Philadelphia neighborhoods. In 1950, Philadelphia's person per square mile density was 16,307. In 1990, that figure had dropped to 11,748. The City has already made strides to reduce the density in City neighborhoods and create detached, suburban-style housing on land that had formerly been occupied by row homes, but such efforts are not sufficient to increase demand for housing in the City. The City is funding the acquisition and razing of the 35-acre Logan area because the houses have become unstable. The City could fund the acquisition and razing of significant areas of the City because the neighborhoods have become uninhabitable. While the City acted to relocate the residents of Logan and assemble the properties because houses were sinking into the Wingohocking Creek bed, a similar effort to assemble properties in a blighted part of Philadelphia could be undertaken to relocate residents from sure ruin because their houses are sinking into decay. The step is admittedly drastic, but taking no action may be far more cruel.

Examining a map of Philadelphia with vacant properties highlighted, one can see that many areas are beset by large numbers of vacant properties while other areas are home to smaller numbers of scattered vacancies. (See Figure 4.2.)

While the City currently demolishes more than 1,000 buildings each year, the efforts are scattered throughout the City, and are generally constrained to buildings that are considered imminently dangerous. After this scattered demolition, City blocks are left "gap-toothed." In the future, the City should commit to a policy of acquiring and demolishing large (50 acres or more), sparsely populated areas of the City to maximize the effect of its demolition policy, spur demand for housing in other struggling neighborhoods, and create an asset that could be land-banked and sold for development at a later date. The City could follow the model of Logan and create a voluntary program to purchase homes, or work through a governmental authority to use the power of eminent domain to assemble the land. Given the mistakes of past urban renewal initiatives, such a policy would certainly raise potential objections of preservationists and neighborhood activists. In carrying out this policy, the City's leaders will have to stress inclusion and involve community leaders to ensure that the acquisition of land, relocation of residents, and future development are all designed with community interests in mind. Simply put, assembling the will to rightsize the City will require tremendous political skill and a large commitment of resources.

Even if the City establishes the will to acquire houses, relocate residents, and assemble more than 50 acres of City real estate, it must overcome the significant hurdle of cost to carry out such a project. Assuming the selected neighborhood is identical to Logan, costs could run as high as $80.4 million to purchase more than 1,400 homes, relocate residents to other homes in the City, and demolish 50 acres worth of houses. But the median sale price for houses in the area including Logan was $36,300 in 1997 and demolition efforts in Logan have often been piecemeal. Median 1997 sale prices in other City neighborhoods were as low as $15,000. Property owners' tax liabilities could reduce the cost of property acquisition. Widespread vacancies in such neighborhoods would further reduce the cost of relocating families. Expanding the scope of demolition efforts could reduce demolition costs, as could the high number of previously demolished properties found in any largely depopulated neighborhood. Costs would be reduced further because the City will already own many properties in targeted neighborhoods. If the City chose an area where house values are closer to $15,000, where the City or a governmental agency owns 10 percent of the homes, and where the vacancy rate nears 25 percent, the City could clear 50 acres of houses for $30 to $35 million. Such a figure would be reduced by the delinquent taxes owed to the City by property owners in the 50-acre neighborhood. High tax delinquency could reduce the cost to the City to clear 50 acres of houses by more than $1.6 million. (See Table 4.5.)

To pay for such an effort, the City could pursue various sources for funding based on the location of the to-be-cleared area and its intentions for reuse. The City could pursue funding from the U.S. Fish and Wildlife Service or the Pennsylvania Department of Conservation and Natural Resources to clear areas that could be used as wildlife and permanent open space areas; or seek funding from the U.S. Department of Housing and Urban Development to reclaim vacant and blighted properties; or apply for private foundation grants designed to support the development of urban greenways and parks. Alternatively, the City could utilize Tax Increment Financing to fund current demolition efforts with anticipated tax revenues from future development.

If history is a lesson, Philadelphia's Yorktown development shows how the clearance of a large tract of residential land can lead to private sector interest and development. In the 1950s, the City spent the equivalent of approximately $28 million in 1996 dollars to acquire and raze 153 acres of land near Temple University, which had been populated with dilapidated tenement housing, just over two miles north of City Hall in North Philadelphia. The land was sold to a private developer who built more than 600 single-family homes, with lawns, that sold to working-class African-American families and created a community that continues to thrive in the heart of the inner city.

That interest is clear today. In August, 1998 a private developer announced intentions to build a golf course on a 214-acre mothballed industrial site in Northeast Philadelphia. In 1998 a private developer announced plans for the largest post-World War II housing development in Philadelphia—a private, 20-acre gated community in Southwest Center City. Both efforts will create jobs in Philadelphia and expand the tax base.

By carefully choosing discrete areas to be cleared, the City can avoid the mistakes of past urban renewal efforts. Efforts to clear a substantial area of City land should, therefore, focus on tracts that are geographically isolated, adjacent to parkland, or abutting highways or railways so as not to create "holes" in the fabric of the City. If the City can create the correct opportunities, it can capitalize on the possibilities that private developers see in Philadelphia. If, given the chance to build on a 50-acre site in the heart of the City, a developer wants to create housing, the City benefits. If, given the surplus of vacancies spread throughout the City, a developer wants to shun housing to build a golf course, a shopping center, or an amusement park, the City still benefits. If no developer surfaces to undertake a project that could redevelop all of a 50-acre area, tracts can be subdivided into manageable plots where a number of smaller projects can move forward. If no developer is interested in the land, the City can hold it until a future time when it could be more attractive as a development site or the City could spend additional funds on an environmental reclamation effort to make the land part of the park system.

Even if the true expense involved with this effort is twice that estimated above, the benefits from such a move to consolidate the City could still outweigh costs. By "unbuilding" some Philadelphia neighborhoods that have suffered significant outmigration, the City could help rightsize the City for its current population. By adequately compensating displaced residents, the City can spur housing demand and increase vitality in other neighborhoods that have suffered decline. By acquiring and clearing a substantial area of the City—or two or three—the City can create unique development opportunities for Philadelphia's future. As part of such an effort, the City could ease the burden created by welfare reform and employ and train hundreds of welfare recipients in positions involved with the demolition effort that do not require a high level of educational attainment. Furthermore, by consolidating the area of populated land in Philadelphia, the City would be able to achieve savings by reducing neighborhood service expenditures. For example, there would be less land for the Police and Fire Departments to patrol and protect and fewer structures for the Department of Licenses and Inspections to monitor.

Table 4.5. Clearing 50 Acres of City Houses	
Action	**Cost**
Cost to purchase 918 properties for $15,000 per property	$13,770,000
Cost to compensate and relocate 918 families at a cost of $6,750 per family	$6,196,500
Cost to purchase 352 vacant properties for $15,000 per property	$5,280,000
Cost to purchase 141 properties owned by the City or a governmental agency	$0
Cost to demolish 1,170 houses for $5,000 per house	$5,850,000
Total estimated cost to clear 50 acres of City houses	**$31,096,500**
Likely tax delinquency of 352 vacant house owners	($1,268,256)
Likely tax delinquency of 241 vacant lot owners	($393,553)
Total estimated cost to clear 50 acres of City houses less tax delinquency owed to City	**$29,434,691**

This exercise assumes:

- that a 50-acre area in the City contains 1411 homes;
- that 25 percent of the homes in the 50-acre area are vacant;
- that median house value in the 50-acre area is $15,000;
- that the City or a governmental agency already owns 10 percent of area properties;
- that 241 homes would already have been reduced to vacant lots (this is the ratio of vacant properties to vacant lots found by the OHCD in Southwest Center City);
- that compensation and moving costs for families would equal approximately 45 percent of the value of their home (the approximate percentage paid to move the families in the Logan homes);
- that economies of scale would decrease demolition costs to $5,000 per home;
- that the owners of the 241 vacant lots would owe an average of $1,633 to the City due to tax delinquency (this is the same relationship between average tax delinquency of non-government-agency-owned vacant lots to median home sale prices found by the OHCD in Southwest Center City); and
- that the owners of the 352 vacant houses would owe an average of $3,603 to the City due to tax delinquency (this is the same relationship between average tax delinquency of non-government-agency-owned vacant houses to median home sale prices found by the OHCD in Southwest Center City).

Of course, Philadelphia's vacant structures themselves are not the cause of the blight that the City seeks to eliminate. In fostering demand for housing, the drastic step of wholesale neighborhood clearance can only work in the most blighted areas where rehabilitation costs outweigh the City's ability and desire to preserve the individual buildings of a neighborhood.

In other areas, the City should proactively acquire and promote the reuse of blighted structures by providing assistance and incentives to individuals who would preserve and repopulate sound structures. The City already actively acquires properties for individuals and community groups who initiate an interest in a blighted structure. In the future, the City could establish a set of criteria and initiate the acquisition process to take ownership of significant blighted properties.

The City could follow the lead of the City of Jamestown, New York, and create a residential homesteading program to proactively acquire and sell tax-delinquent properties to qualified buyers who are then eligible to receive up to $30,000 in grants to bring their new home up to code. Similarly, the City could expand the reach of programs that aid purchasers with down payments for these properties by increasing the amount of grants to new homebuyers. Such programs could be costly, but by providing purchase assistance to new homebuyers—and by acquiring properties with value, marketing them to individuals who can commit to a rehabilitation effort, and helping to remove barriers of cost—the City can complement dramatic efforts to consolidate blighted neighborhoods and spur housing demand in Philadelphia.

Creating Disincentives to Vacancy

Examining data from vacancies in Southwest Center City one can gain insight into the real estate speculation that keeps so many homes vacant in the City. Of the 552 vacant houses in Southwest Center City, more than 18 percent are owned by individuals who own other vacant houses in the area. Of those 101 properties, less than 4 percent are tax delinquent for more than five years, and more than 46 percent owe no taxes at all. Consider the case of Mr. Franklin,[17] a speculator in Southwest Center City.

In July 1981, Mr. Franklin, a Philadelphian who lives in another part of the City, purchased two Southwest Center City row houses one block apart from each other on Kimball Street for $16,000 and $5,000 respectively. In 1985, he acquired another row house for $3,300. In 1986, he acquired another row house for $6,500 and another for $3,300. In 1987, he acquired two more row houses for $5,000 and $22,400 respectively. In total, Mr. Franklin owned seven Southwest Center City properties in 1998, four along three separate blocks of Kimball Street, two on separate blocks of Montrose Way, and one on South 17th Street. All of Mr. Franklin's taxes are paid in full and his buildings sit, with most openings sealed, to await future development. None of Mr. Franklin's houses is posted for sale or rent.

If Mr. Franklin is a rational actor, he will hold onto those vacant properties until he is offered enough compensation to earn him what he considers to be a fair return on his investment or until he perceives that the cost of holding onto those vacant properties outweighs his anticipated future benefit from those properties. If the City can increase demand for housing in Philadelphia, it can increase the likelihood that some individual will offer sufficient compensation to speculators like Mr. Franklin to bring those houses back to life. If the City can increase the cost to Mr. Franklin of maintaining those houses in a vacant state, it can increase the likelihood that he will try to find a positive use for the properties and increase the likelihood that he will accept purchase offers for his houses.

Mr. Franklin's case shows how speculation can hurt the City. By holding properties vacant—often in disrepair—speculators create blight in neighborhoods. By purchasing homes that could be occupied by other buyers, speculators prevent new residents from removing blight from neighborhoods. As they wait for market conditions to change and generate worth for their properties, speculators can threaten the vitality of entire neighborhoods.

---

[17] The actual name has been changed to protect the true person's identity.

TAXING LAND TO DISCOURAGE SPECULATION

A tax on buildings discourages individuals from constructing buildings. A tax on land discourages speculation by raising the cost of holding land unused and increasing the likelihood that the owners would do something with the land to generate revenue. Economic theory would therefore suggest that removing a tax from buildings would encourage people to build more valuable buildings, while placing a tax on land would encourage people to make that land more productive.

To encourage development and discourage speculation, many jurisdictions have altered their taxation policy to place a higher tax on land than property. By shifting the tax burden from buildings to land by taxing land assessments at a higher percentage rate than building assessments, these jurisdictions have changed incentives for property usage. Because a property tax penalizes property owners who improve their properties (if the value of the property increases, the amount of taxes owed increase), speculators are encouraged to allow buildings to deteriorate and then ask for a lower property assessment. Because the cost of maintaining a vacant property—in terms of taxes—will decline as buildings decay, property owners are encouraged to speculate by sitting on properties until a developer wants to build on the site. A two-rate property tax system that taxes land at a high rate and property at a lower rate encourages property owners to develop their properties more fully since the actual value of the property is taxed at a lower rate than the land upon which it sits.

Many Pennsylvania cities including Pittsburgh, Scranton, Allentown, and Harrisburg employ such a split-rate tax. Under such a system, owners of vacant lots and blighted buildings pay substantially higher taxes because the system places a premium on the value of land. Essentially, any property owner whose land is worth much more than the property upon it would pay more under a split-rate system. Because the value of the land, not the deteriorated condition of the property, would determine tax liability, owners of vacant properties would have an incentive to do something productive with that property or sell it to someone else who will do something productive with it. In Harrisburg, for example, which has employed a split-rate tax since 1975, officials note a decline in the number of vacant structures from more than 4,200 in 1982 to fewer than 500 in 1998.

Studying the effect of two-rate property taxes on construction in Pennsylvania in 1997, Virginia Polytechnic Institute and State University Economics Professors Florenze Plassmann and T. Nicolaus Tideman show that cities that have adopted a two-rate property tax actually enjoy significantly higher levels of construction activity than they would with one-rate taxes. Projecting the impact of a building-to-land tax shift in Philadelphia in 1987, Steven Cord, President of the Center for the Study of Economics, concluded that while most Philadelphia homeowners would pay less under such a system, owners of vacant land would pay significantly more. While any shift in tax policy ultimately creates winners and losers, the split-rate tax has consistently passed popular scrutiny. Allentown voters approved the split-rate tax as part of a Home Rule Charter initiative and Pittsburgh's downtown improvement district voted to fund its own efforts through a land-tax assessment.

To spur development and to tax speculation, the City should explore the use of a split-rate property tax in Philadelphia. To implement a split-rate tax, the City would first have to conduct a uniform assessment of the buildings and land in the City. With such an assessment, the City could implement a split-rate property tax system in a revenue-neutral manner. Alternatively, a split-rate tax could be used as a way to increase tax revenues from the Real Estate Tax and reduce the City's Wage and Net Profits Tax, or as a way to reduce overall tax revenues if City leaders are confident that the resulting expanded economic activity in the City could make up for the lost property tax revenue.

Other, more direct efforts could also discourage speculation. While the City of Philadelphia attempts to dissuade property vacancy and foster public safety with a $25 Vacant Property License, in fiscal year 1998, the City only collected $65,132 in Vacant Property License fees. That amount is enough to license just 2,605 vacant properties, far below the estimated and actual number of vacancies in Philadelphia. Other cities impose more stringent requirements on vacant property owners. To help maintain vacant buildings and foster their rehabilitation, the City of Cincinnati, Ohio, requires building owners to tend to their properties. Owners of vacant buildings must annually obtain a $300 vacant building maintenance license and bring the premises into compliance with its terms which detail how properties must be protected from intrusion by trespassers and from deterioration by the weather in accordance with standards promulgated in City legislation. Failure to comply with the Cincinnati vacant building maintenance license law results in civil and criminal penalties. Similar legislation in St. Paul, Minnesota, requires owners of vacant buildings to register their properties as vacant and pay an annual fee of $200 to fund the City's efforts in monitoring the vacant building site.

As the data from Southwest Center City show, the owners of more than 64 percent of Southwest Center City vacant properties owe no taxes. But of those houses that owe no taxes, more than 31 percent have visible roof problems and more than 30 percent do not have most windows and doorways sealed. Houses with visible roof problems or unsealed entranceways quickly deteriorate. Unless roofs are properly protected, water damage from rain and snow will erode ceilings, walls, and flooring. Unless entranceways are sealed, vandals will strip properties of wiring, pipes, and fixtures. By licensing vacant properties—and enforcing more stringent rules in issuing the licenses and punishing violators—the City could help ensure that vacant houses do not deteriorate into an uninhabitable state. The City could also use this effort to raise revenue to fund vacant-property inspection efforts and increase the cost to speculators of keeping buildings vacant. The City should strengthen license requirements for vacant properties, charge a sufficient fee, and create and enforce sufficient regulations to ensure that vacant properties are maintained in a secure and safe manner. If such measures increase the incentive for vacant-property owners to sell vacant houses to others who are either willing to maintain the house properly in a vacant state or willing to maintain the house as a residence, the City benefits. If owners find no buyers, the City could acquire the houses. The City would then be in a position to sell the house to a private developer, offer it to a community development corporation, or properly seal the property until it can be developed at a future date. Alternatively, the City could employ a private property-management company to help manage and sell properties in its property inventory.

Similarly, the City should focus on better overseeing the condition of its occupied housing stock. The 1990 census shows that 1939 was the median year during which Philadelphia housing structures were built. More than 186,000 Philadelphia housing units were built between 1940 and 1959. Fewer than 150,000 units have been constructed since 1960. As a whole, Philadelphia's housing stock, and its building stock in general, is aging. While the City has a remarkable collection of structures spanning more than three centuries, 21st-century Philadelphia will be challenged to ensure that these structures remain standing and safe.

But aging buildings do not necessarily mean trouble if the population has sufficient resources to maintain them. More ominous is the fact that, because the population is aging, and because the income level of the population is likely to decrease, housing maintenance will be a major concern for Philadelphia's future. If elderly and low-income Philadelphians are unable to properly maintain their homes, their properties will retain little future value. Further neighborhood deterioration will be inevitable.

Philadelphia, therefore, must respond to two distinct challenges: ensuring that its collection of structures and buildings is maintained in a proper manner and enabling their owners to maintain their properties in a proper manner. To ensure that structures are maintained properly, the City can alter its inspection procedures to create a system where property owners would have the burden of proving that their structure is safe. Additionally, the City can expand funding and loan streams to enable property owners to best maintain their structures.

In October 1997, during a street festival celebrating the Avenue of the Arts along Broad Street, a sign attached to the facade of a privately owned parking garage fell to the street, raining bricks and cinder blocks on to the sidewalk below. The 20-foot section of wall that fell from the building killed Philadelphia Common Pleas Court Judge Berel Caesar and injured other festival attendees. While the parking garage had actually been cited by the City's Department of Licenses and Inspections for structural problems, the collapse of the building and death of Judge Caesar shows just how deadly failure to adequately ensure the safety of the City's structures can be.

If people are determined to break the law, even the most efficient government operating the most well-designed program will be powerless to do anything other than attempt to prosecute wrongdoers. Government can, however, increase the likelihood of catching violators and increase the severity of punishments for violators once caught, but inevitably some individuals will go out of their way to do bad. To improve its ability to inspect and monitor the condition of Philadelphia structures, therefore, the City can place the onus of inspection on property owners and free City personnel to pursue violators.

Car owners are required by the Commonwealth of Pennsylvania to have their vehicles inspected each year by a certified mechanic. Those who do not have proper documentation to certify the safety of their vehicle face penalties. While some individuals drive uninspected and dangerous vehicles, the vast majority of Pennsylvanians comply with the law and annually submit to a vehicle inspection. The rationale for such an inspection is simple—to protect the public safety. Such a notion makes sense for buildings as well.

In reaction to crumbling building facades in New York City, the City passed legislation requiring the inspection, every five years, of the front wall of buildings greater than six stories in height. The legislation mandates that such inspection must be conducted or witnessed by a licensed architect or engineer, and must be reported to the City's Department of Buildings. In 1991, the City of Paris, France, even went so far as to mandate the restoration and cleaning of all building facades every ten years.

The City of St. Paul requires building owners periodically to renew Certificates of Occupancy. Owners of high-hazard occupancies are required to renew their Certificates of Occupancy every year while owners of all other buildings are required to renew Certificates once every two years. By combining housing and fire inspections, St. Paul is able to increase the efficiency of operations. By charging building owners a fee, St. Paul is able to offset the cost of the combined inspection program. St. Paul officials report that the renewable Certificates of Occupancy have successfully reduced building code violations. Since individuals cannot legally operate a building without a Certificate of Occupancy, building owners are serious about making sure that their structures pass renewal inspections.

In Philadelphia, the City's Department of Licenses and Inspections regularly inspects high rise and apartment buildings for conformity with Fire Prevention and Property Maintenance Codes, but relies on complaints to drive inspections of most other buildings in the City. Without regular inspections, many of those buildings fall out of compliance with City safety ordinances. In theory, property owners have an incentive to keep their properties in good repair, especially if they occupy the property themselves. In reality, people will cut costs where they can and, too often, place themselves and the public in danger. In a city filled with blocks of row houses, a fire does not just threaten a single, poorly maintained property; it threatens many neighbors. In a City of tall buildings, falling bricks put innocent pedestrians at great risk.

To better ensure that its structures remain safe, the City should adopt a programmatic building inspection effort that will compel property owners to maintain their structures. Such a program could follow the lead of St. Paul and create a renewable Certificate of Occupancy that could be placed in jeopardy by a failed inspection and could set different standards for owner-occupied structures, multistory structures, commercial structures, and multiple-resident structures. To offset the cost of inspections, the City could fund such a program with fees payable by property owners. Alternatively, the City could follow the lead of New York City's facade inspection legislation and allow property owners to hire a licensed architect or engineer to perform the inspection and submit results to the City. As the City considers expanding requirements that structures be equipped with fire-suppressant systems and hard-wired smoke detectors to better protect against the risk of fire, the City could cross-train inspectors to perform both structural and fire inspections as is done in St. Paul and build such requirements into renewable Certificate-of-Occupancy-like programs.

In a city of row houses, dangerous conditions in one house can threaten an entire block. A November 1998 fire that started in an abandoned house burned six Southwest Philadelphia row houses and left 19 Philadelphians homeless. In densely populated areas, just a few vacant houses can cause an entire community to decline. By allowing a single property to decay, the City places neighborhoods in jeopardy. Just as Philadelphia should not subsidize individuals by not effectively collecting taxes, the City should not subsidize individuals by not enforcing laws designed to ensure that the buildings of the City are properly maintained. But because the ability to properly maintain structures is often a function of an ability to pay for required upkeep, the City cannot just focus on monitoring the condition of the City's buildings.

With many Philadelphia homeowners living on fixed or low incomes, any effort to encourage property owners to better maintain their property must be complemented with an effort to improve property owners' ability to better maintain their property. With future projections indicating likely increases in both the senior citizen and low-income populations in the City, making sure that homeowners are able to maintain their houses will become even more crucial.

The City has already established a number of programs to address such issues. Since 1992, the City of Philadelphia has operated a Basic Systems Repair Program to give the City an emergency-response capability through which preapproved contractors complete up to $2,000 of needed basic systems and heater repairs for qualified low-income homeowners. The City has also created a weatherization program for low-income homes and supports a program that provides essential repairs to the homes of Philadelphia seniors. For fiscal year 1998, the City of Philadelphia budgeted more than $18 million to provide repair, home preservation, and weatherization assistance.

To augment current assistance programs, the City should expand the reach of programs designed to help Philadelphians pay for required property repairs. To help ensure that repairs are done properly, the City could create a Coordinated Home Repair Service administered by the City as a contractor referral program to provide a reliable option for seniors seeking to make repairs on their homes. The City could contract with an outside agency experienced in such programs such as the American Automotive Association, to perform similar services. To better enable seniors to access money for needed home repairs, the City could work with lenders to utilize "reverse mortgages"—a special type of home loan that allows homeowners to convert the equity in their homes into cash—to give seniors a stream of income that could be used to maintain properties. Such a program would give the City, or financial institutions, possession of seniors' homes after their deaths so that some entity has an incentive to do something with the property. By providing low-interest loans and grants to help Philadelphians keep their properties in good repair, the City can help maintain property values across the City to stabilize the tax base and discourage flight from neighborhoods that would otherwise deteriorate.

RECOMMENDATIONS FOR ACTION

The City should commit to a policy of acquiring and demolishing large (50 acres or more), sparsely populated areas of the City to maximize the effect of its demolition policy, spur demand for housing in other struggling neighborhoods, and create an asset that could be land-banked and sold for development at a later date.

Action Steps:

- In general, alter City structure demolition policies to achieve economies of scale and avoid scattered demolition efforts.

- Establish a voluntary neighborhood reclamation project or use eminent domain to relocate residents of sparsely populated neighborhoods, repopulate struggling neighborhoods, and assemble a large area of City land for future development.

- Assemble necessary funding through a combination of local, federal, state, and private funding or through the establishment of a TIF District.

- Work with neighbors, community leaders, and elected officials to ease relocation anxieties and effectively carry out this policy.

Fiscal Impact:

- Potential cost of $30-$55 million to acquire 50 acres of blighted properties, relocate residents, and demolish houses. This funding could represent a reprioritization of current spending and/or a one-time grant from a government or private source.

- Potential to create significant one-time revenues through sale of resulting development parcel.

- Potential to expand the City tax base through future development of development parcel.

- Potential to reduce City neighborhood service expenditures until parcel is redeveloped.

In addition to current programs where the City acquires properties on behalf of interested individuals and groups, the City should proactively acquire and promote the reuse of blighted structures by providing assistance and incentives to individuals who would preserve and repopulate sound structures.

Action Steps:

- Establish policy and procedures to proactively acquire and market desirable vacant, tax-delinquent buildings in City neighborhoods.

- Establish criteria for determining which structures the City should purchase.

- Initiate acquisition procedures.

- Market properties to potential buyers and sell properties to purchasers who can commit to rehabilitation efforts—consider the use of a private marketer to enhance sales.

- Establish a loan or grant program to aid rehabilitation efforts.

Fiscal Impact:

- Potential cost to provide grants and loans for building rehabilitation.

- Potential administrative cost that could be offset by reduced tax liability.

- Potential to expand the City tax base.

To spur development and tax speculation, the City should explore the use of a split-rate property tax in Philadelphia.

Action Steps:

- Evaluate the impact of a split-rate tax on City taxpayers.
- Work with City Council to pass split-rate property tax legislation.
- Conduct a uniform assessment of the buildings and land in the City.
- Establish split-rate property tax rates.

Fiscal Impact:

- Potential one-time cost to perform uniform citywide property assessment.
- Potential to reduce the number of vacant properties in the City.
- Potential to increase economic activity in the City.
- Potential to expand the City tax base through future development.

The City should strengthen license requirements for vacant properties.

Action Steps:

- Work with City Council to pass stringent vacant property license legislation.
- Establish sufficient fees to fund vacant property inspection efforts.
- Create and enforce sufficient regulations to ensure that vacant properties are maintained in a secure and safe manner.

Fiscal Impact:

- Potential to raise revenues necessary to fund vacant property inspections.
- Potential to stabilize City Real Estate Tax base for the future.

To better ensure that its structures remain safe, the City should adopt a programmatic building inspection effort that will compel property owners to maintain their structures.

Action Steps:

- Establish a periodic inspection program for all City structures.
- Establish requirements for self-inspection and fees to offset the costs of City inspection.
- Hire and train appropriate personnel.

Fiscal Impact:

- Potential cost to expand the City's inspection capabilities to be offset by inspection revenue.
- Potential to stabilize City Real Estate Tax base for the future.

The City should expand the reach of programs designed to help Philadelphians pay for required property repairs.

Action Steps:

- Assess the need for additional property-repair assistance programs in Philadelphia.
- Work with community leaders to ensure that residents are able to access assistance programs.

- Work with lenders and seniors organizations to utilize reverse mortgages to provide seniors with an income stream to fund home repairs.

Fiscal Impact:

- Potential increase in property-repair assistance.

- Potential to stabilize City Real Estate Tax base for the future.

LAW ENFORCEMENT—CREATING A SAFER PHILADELPHIA

In the recent past, crime was often seen as just another part of "life in the big city." In Philadelphia, for decades one of the safest of America's big cities, residents and the elected leadership could rightfully point to crime statistics and rationalize that it was safe, for a big city. But stunning reductions in major crimes (murder, rape, robbery, assault, burglary, auto theft, and other thefts) in other cities have raised questions about the effectiveness of Philadelphia's crime-fighting efforts. According to the Federal Bureau of Investigation, major crimes in New York City dropped 39 percent between 1992 and 1996. In San Diego, major crimes dropped 34 percent between 1992 and 1996. In Los Angeles, major crimes dropped 29 percent between 1992 and 1996. Between 1992 and 1996 major crimes in Philadelphia increased by 2 percent.[18] Even though recent local crime statistics indicate reductions in major crimes in Philadelphia, Philadelphia still lags behind the dramatic decreases in crime experienced by other big cities. More ominously, the percentage of homicides involving guns has increased over the past decade. More than eight out of ten Philadelphia murders are the result of gun violence, the highest rate among America's largest cities.

Criminologists debate the causes of the nationwide decrease in crime and point to diverse factors from demographic shifts to policing efforts. Philadelphia must create a safe city if it is to be a successful city. As the City moves into the 21st century, citizens can expect the likelihood of the occurrence of crime to increase with the projected increase in the percentage of young adults in the City's population. The schools, health and human service agencies, police, courts, prisons, and probation-oversight system must all work together to prevent demographics from spawning an increase in crime. Additionally, as citizens demand a focus on the "quality-of-life" crimes that affect their daily lives, the City's law enforcement agencies must not only work to apprehend, prosecute, and adjudicate criminals, but must also work to make Philadelphia a more civil City.

Philadelphia's elected leadership is committed to combating crime. By the end of 1998, 753 new on-street officers will have been added to the police force with the help of federal funding provided through the 1994 federal Crime Bill. New Police Department leadership has infused the agency with new vitality. A massive, coordinated assault on neighborhoods associated with the drug trade has signaled the City's willingness to commit the personnel and resources necessary to effectively combat drug-related crimes in areas of the City that many have considered beyond the rule of law. New police helicopters, mobile data terminals, and vehicle recovery systems utilize technology to improve the City's ability to fight crime.

But if Philadelphia is to effectively reduce crime, it must respond better to persistent problems. To help reduce the amount of gun violence, the City can work with state and federal officials to reduce access to illegal weapons and create severe consequences for the illegal use of a firearm. To make the criminal justice system a more effective force for crime prevention, the City can better coordinate law enforcement and adjudication-related responses to crime. To target quality-of-life crimes without overburdening the prison system, the City can expand the use of alternatives to traditional prison sentences. Finally, to improve quality of life in Philadelphia, the City can expand the use of passive systems (defined below) to target illegal activities.

---

[18] Given the recent questions raised about crime statistics in Philadelphia (See discussion about the need to verify performance-measurement efforts in Chapter 2), readers are urged to use caution when considering these figures.

Preventing Gun Violence

When the leaders of the fledgling American nation gathered in Philadelphia to draft the Constitution more than 200 years ago, the arms that the population sought the right to bear were weapons resembling the flintlock musket that weighed approximately nine pounds, measured five feet long, and fired a single round lead ball. When the second amendment to the Constitution was adopted in 1791, the citizenry could sensibly articulate the rationale that, because a well-regulated militia is necessary to the security of a free state, the government should not infringe upon the people's right to keep and bear arms. Just years earlier, various colonial militias helped General Washington's Continentals win the Revolutionary War. But today, in an age where handguns are used with devastating killing power by unregulated criminals, and war is waged with weapons that flatten buildings and destroy whole cities, Americans can surely reconcile proper modern gun control with the ideals espoused by the men who drafted the Bill of Rights.

Including spending on prison space to hold shooting suspects for trial, conducting and administering trials, investigating shootings, and performing autopsies on shooting victims, the City of Philadelphia estimates that gun violence costs taxpayers more than $58 million each year. This estimate does not include the costs absorbed by society for hospitals and medical facilities to treat uninsured victims of shooting violence or costs to incarcerate convicted gun-using criminals. Tragically, there is no way to fully calculate the colossal value of the senseless loss of life incurred by the families and communities that fall victim to gun violence. In a nation where flintlock muskets could be used to repel foreign invaders, the right to bear arms made sense. In a nation where any kid with an attitude and a few dollars can stuff a gun in his waistband to become a danger to the community, a serious reconsideration of the freedom to use such a deadly tool is in order.

Philadelphia's elected leadership, joined by City officials from across the United States, is pursuing legal options to make gun makers liable for the public nuisance caused by their product. City, state, and federal officials are working to coordinate more effective enforcement of existing gun laws to reduce gun violence. While the citizenry should pursue such efforts as steps in the right direction, government can make gun-related, product-liability and gun-control laws more effective.

The Attorney General of the Commonwealth of Massachusetts has established regulations that make it illegal to sell handguns without tamper-resistant serial numbers, to sell handguns made from inferior materials, or to sell handguns without childproofing or safety devices. While opponents who believe that such measures must be legislated are challenging these regulations, the Massachusetts legislature is considering more stringent action. Pending manufacturer-liability legislation would hold gun manufacturers liable for injury or death resulting from the use of handguns. Advocates hope that gun manufacturers would then take steps—similar to the creation of childproof pill containers to prevent children from ingesting harmful medications—to ensure that their products could only be used by their lawful owners. New York City lawmakers passed a law requiring safety locks on newly-purchased handguns and are considering legislation that would require the 250,000 New York City gun owners to buy trigger locks for their weapons.

The City can pursue measures short of legislation infringing upon Constitutional rights to combat gun violence. To make handguns safer, and to help keep them out of the hands of those who would use them to injure or kill others, the City should push for state and federal legislation to force gun manufacturers to use currently available technology to enable guns to be used only by their owners. Further, the City should push for state and federal legislation that would hold gun manufacturers liable for injuries resulting from their failure to take action that could prevent the improper or illegal use of their product. Finally, the City should pursue local legislation to compel Philadelphian gun owners to own gun-safety devices and compel local gun merchants to sell only guns that have childproofing and safety devices.

Coordinating Law Enforcement Efforts

Effective law enforcement involves more than just a vigilant local police force. Effective prosecution and fair adjudication will remove criminals from the streets, and effective incarceration, rehabilitation, and oversight will prevent individuals convicted of a crime from victimizing others once they rejoin society. All levels of government—federal, state, and local—must work together or law enforcement cannot work to make Philadelphia safe.

In 1998, the City of Philadelphia, along with numerous state, federal, and neighborhood agencies, launched an unprecedented anti-crime initiative dubbed "Operation Sunrise" to attack drug-dealing and violent crime in one of the City's most crime-ridden neighborhoods. Under Operation Sunrise, local law enforcement agencies agreed to work with state and federal authorities to concentrate their efforts on narcotics gangs throughout the City's Fairhill and Kensington neighborhoods, approximately three miles northeast of City Hall. Just months into the initiative, violent crime in the neighborhood is down and area residents are thrilled that the City is helping them take back their community.

Three notable coordinated programs in Boston have helped cut the number of City homicides from 152 in 1990 to 43 in 1997—a 72-percent decrease highlighted by a 28-month period during which not one juvenile was killed by gun violence. "Operation Nite Lite" is a partnership between police and probation that provides courts with a tool to enforce probation terms. Capitalizing on probation officers' ability to search probationers' residences and arrest them without a warrant, police and probation officials initiated a program of joint nighttime visits to high-risk probationers. By making probation more proactive and by jointly enforcing conditions of parole such as nighttime curfews, Boston officials increased the effectiveness of probation, increasing the numbers of youthful offenders in compliance with the terms of their probation from 17 percent to 60 percent in just two years from 1992 to 1994.

From Operation Nite Lite, "Operation Cease Fire" was born as an alliance between police and criminal justice agencies that targeted the small number of juvenile offenders who were disproportionately overrepresented as both the offenders and victims of violent crime. Again, police and probation officials, working together with state and federal authorities, were able to convince youthful offenders that violence, especially when conducted with guns or knives, would bring a severe response. Enforcing federal gun-crime laws, sharing intelligence, and communicating with community leaders, law enforcement officials helped reduce the homicide rate among 12- to 24-year olds by 76 percent over a two-year period.

Boston's recently created "No 'Next Time'" project targets repeat domestic violence victimization with a coordinated effort between police, probation, state and federal officials, and the victim service community. By better coordinating intervention and enforcement of Abuse Prevention Orders, the No "Next Time" program uses more effective enforcement tactics and higher-quality arrests to target the 70 percent of Civil Restraining Order recipients who have previous criminal histories. By utilizing probation and federal officials, Boston law enforcement officials hope to create more serious consequences for offenders.

Following this theme, officials in Richmond, Virginia, initiated "Project Exile" to remove gun users from the community. Federal officials there now treat routine gun cases as federal weapons offenses so offenders receive swift prosecutions and longer sentences where local enforcement might have resulted in no prison sentence at all. During the first six months of 1998, Richmond endured only 22 gun homicides under Project Exile, down from 62 gun homicides over the same six-month period from 1997.

To improve the effectiveness of its law enforcement efforts, the City should improve agency interaction and cooperation with state and federal officials. The Philadelphia Police Department is not alone in its fight against crime and early results from experiments with increased truancy enforcement, increased cooperation between Philadelphia police and probation officials, and anti-domestic violence initiatives are encouraging. The City could better target outreach to past offenders and help prevent recidivism by better coordinating the work of probation officers and police. The City could focus on truancy and help nudge students back into the classroom by better coordinating the work of School District officials and police. Finally, the City could follow the lead of New York City and create a police agency without borders that can focus on crime throughout the City by combining City policing agencies (Philadelphia Police Department, Philadelphia Housing Authority police, and Southeastern Pennsylvania Transportation Authority police) into one force.

Courts and Crime

Crime meets punishment in the court system. Philadelphia's courts, and the judges who preside over them, will have a tremendous influence in determining whether society's response to crime will deter others from committing crime and reduce the likelihood of recidivism. Philadelphia jails are consistently operating at or over maximum capacity. The City's efforts to crack down on quality-of-life crimes could be hampered by an inability to hold defendants for trial or jail convicted offenders. Therefore, the operation of the City's criminal justice system will largely determine the effectiveness of law enforcement efforts. According to a report prepared for the Philadelphia Prisons System and the City of Philadelphia by the National Council on Crime and Delinquency, based on arrest projections and accounting for the use of special releases to ease overcrowding, the Philadelphia prison population will likely climb from its current total of about 5,600 to reach 5,835 by the year 2000 and approach 6,000 by 2005. Since Philadelphia's prison population already often exceeds 6,000—above and beyond its budgeted capacity—projections for an increase in the prison population create a serious situation. Faced with the demand to crack down on crime, but needing to avoid the tremendous expense of creating additional prison space, the City must pursue more efficient means of adjudicating individuals charged with crimes and alternative means of sentencing individuals convicted of crimes.

The State of Rhode Island created the nation's first court exclusively devoted to firearm-related cases to increase the speed of disposing such cases and the severity of the penalties associated with gun-related crimes. The "gun court" has reduced the amount of time necessary to dispose of a gun-related case from 418 days to 92 days, and resulted in offenders being sentenced to jail terms of two or more years in nearly one-third of cases, according to a recently completed government study.

Judges in Philadelphia have created a community night court system throughout the City to adjudicate quality-of-life crimes in neighborhoods. A court modeled on Manhattan's Midtown Community Court is being developed in Philadelphia to adjudicate quality-of-life offenders in Philadelphia's Center City. By providing swift and responsive justice, these courts can create consequences for even minor crimes where defendants previously may have ignored their scheduled court appearances and police may have ignored minor infractions of the law, knowing that there was little chance that violators would ever appear before a judge or receive any punishment. In community courts, sentences may consist of community service that can be coordinated by Business Improvement Districts or other community organizations. Community leaders credit such quality-of-life courts with reducing crime in City neighborhoods and court officials note that the instant adjudication reduces court backlogs and reduces the number of outstanding warrants for failure to appear in court or failure to pay fines. The Philadelphia Center City Community Court, which, based on other models, may cost between $1.3 and $2 million, could be operational in 1999.

In response to the flood of defendants appearing for drug-related offenses, the City of Philadelphia created a drug-treatment court to give defendants an opportunity to avoid jail by entering into a treatment program to become clean and sober. Defendants before the drug-treatment court waive their rights to a trial, accepting the conditions of the court and any sanctions the judge imposes, in exchange for a chance to receive drug treatment and have their record expunged. Proponents claim that preliminary studies show that drug court treatment is much cheaper than jail at approximately one-tenth the price of incarceration. Positive early indicators suggest that drug-treatment courts across the country are reducing recidivism among former addicts.

If the City is unable to reduce its prison population, it will be forced to build additional prison facilities—the City already has voter authorization to sell bonds to finance construction of a new prison. Alternatively, the City would be forced to pay other jurisdictions and utilize temporary measures such as the purchase or rental of a prison barge to house Philadelphia prisoners.

When courts work, law enforcement efforts work better. The City should explore ways to improve adjudication efforts and expand alternatives to incarceration by increasing the growing number of specialized courts in the City's court system. The City could help reduce its prison population and decrease recidivism by increasing the number of drug-treatment courts. The City could further crack down on quality-of-life crimes by expanding community night courts. Finally, the City could create real consequences for the illegal use of firearms by creating a gun court to more effectively adjudicate weapons violations.

The City can also work with state officials to address other court-related issues. Judges in Philadelphia who impose a maximum sentence of at least two years but less than five years currently have the option of sending defendants to a state or county facility. While the number of individuals serving "state" sentences in a Philadelphia County facility has decreased to fewer than 50, in the recent past, more than 600 Philadelphia County inmates—approximately 10 percent of the total inmate population—were individuals sentenced to two- to five-year terms. To help reduce over-crowded prison conditions and create room in the prison system that can be used to remove criminals from the streets, the City should push to alter Pennsylvania's sentencing law to mandate that any defendant sentenced to more than two years must serve that time in a state prison.

Because some judges may wish to reduce the hardship on inmates' families by sentencing their loved ones to a nearby county facility rather than a distant state prison, the City could push for the establishment of a state prison in Philadelphia. The City has no shortage of old industrial sites that could be reborn as a state prison and no shortage of individuals who could be employed in the new facility. If the City can reduce county prison overcrowding, open up new space for convicted criminals, and promote economic development in the City, a state prison in Philadelphia could create a win-win-win situation.

Passive Crime Fighting for a More Civil City

The City faces a dilemma in its efforts to address quality-of-life crime. By cracking down on what may have once been seen as minor crimes—graffiti, petty vandalism, prostitution—the City affirms the premise of the broken-window theory of crime. Cities across the country have demonstrated that targeting minor crimes not only reduces minor crimes, but helps reduce major crimes as well. While the citizenry may be happy to see the focus on minor crimes, and while neighbors may endorse the notion of the broken-window theory, there still exists an insistent demand that law enforcement focus on responding to serious crimes. The demand for more police on the streets is not necessarily a demand for more police to enforce anti-jaywalking laws, and any crackdown on quality-of-life crime is likely to be met with the question, "With all the crime in this city, you have nothing to do but give a jaywalking ticket?"

Many cities have turned to surveillance cameras to deter crime and help arrest and convict criminals. From Baltimore to London, England, surveillance cameras are used to improve safety in business districts, mass transportation facilities, and public recreation centers. In one public housing facility in New York City, crime dropped 44 percent in one year after 39 surveillance cameras improved the ability of police to maintain order.[19] To

---

[19] Halbfinger, David M. "As Surveillance Cameras Peer, Some Wonder if They Also Pry," *New York Times*, February 22, 1998. p. 1.

combat vandalism at public recreation centers, Lehighton, Pennsylvania, recently decided to invest in surveillance cameras. Lehighton officials report that installation—including camera, fiber-optic cable, monitors, and labor—will cost approximately $3,000, plus $300 for each additional camera. In Philadelphia, where one public pool suffered more than $30,000 worth of damage in two separate vandalism incidents in the spring of 1998, such an investment could be wise indeed.

Video surveillance can also be used to improve traffic safety and save lives. In Philadelphia, during the ten-month period from October 1997 to August 1998, a major expressway was closed for an hour or more 17 times due to tractor trailer accidents caused by vehicles travelling at excessive speed. With 3.2 deaths per 100,000 residents from 1992 to 1996 caused by red-light runners, Philadelphia ranked as the 23rd most dangerous of 78 big cities. According to the Insurance Institute for Highway Safety (IIHS), the number of fatal crashes involving red-light runners nationwide has increased 15 percent from 1992 to 1996.

But speeders and red-light runners can be stopped with passive means. In Los Angeles, New York, and a growing number of other cities, red-light cameras snap photographs of drivers running red lights. Red-light runners receive a picture of their car running a light by mail, attached to a pricey ticket. These efforts have proven their worth as a deterrent. Since New York began its red-light camera program in 1993, the number of camera-issued tickets per camera has fallen by nearly one-third. According to the IIHS, which notes that signal-running and failure to heed other traffic controls is the most frequent cause of urban crashes, after just months of enforcement using red-light cameras, Oxnard, California, reduced the overall red-light violation rate by approximately 42 percent. Some jurisdictions even employ decoy cameras to take advantage of their ability to cut down on red-light running. Scottsdale, Arizona, officials claim significant decreases in accident rates in places where photo-radar cameras—speed-clocking devices that photograph speeding cars, along with their license plates and drivers, as they whiz by—have been installed. To take advantage of red-light camera and photo-radar technology, the City would have to work to change state law to allow certain moving violations (speeding, running red lights) to be ticketed like parking violations where tickets are issued to the vehicle, not the driver, and where violators are not necessarily physically served with a ticket by a law enforcement official.

In addition to their worth as a deterrent, red-light and photo-radar camera systems raise revenue. The cameras themselves, which can cost as much as $50,000, can be leased from manufacturers who do the actual ticket processing, funded from the proceeds from fines paid by violators. To fund its red-light camera efforts, New York City established a turn-key operation with a company that installs and operates the red-light camera system, keeps a percentage of fines, and advances the remainder of fines to the City.

To help crack down on quality-of-life crime, the City should invest in passive crime-fighting measures that can aid law enforcement efforts without dramatically increasing personnel resources. The City could install surveillance cameras in transit and recreational facilities, business districts, and other public spaces to deter crime. The City could install red-light cameras and photo-radar cameras—and work to pass legislation that would allow moving violations to be ticketed like parking violations—to target speeders and red-light runners and improve safety on City streets and highways. Additionally, traffic-calming tools such as speed humps, which allow cars obeying the speed limit to run smoothly over a gentle asphalt rise, but jar vehicles travelling at excessive speeds, can help cut down on drag racing and rampant speeding. Improved street lighting can illuminate sidewalks to enliven communities and increase both pedestrian traffic and security. Graffiti-removal efforts can allow communities to take ownership of neighborhoods away from petty vandals. Philadelphia can become a more civil city with passive efforts aimed at fighting real crime.

RECOMMENDATIONS FOR ACTION

The City should push for legislation at the state and federal levels to force gun manufacturers to use available technology to enable guns to be used only by their owners and to hold gun manufacturers liable for any injuries resulting from their failure to take action that could prevent the improper or illegal use of their product.

Action Steps:

- Advocate for passage of gun-safety measures and gun-manufacturer liability legislation in the Pennsylvania General Assembly and the United States Congress.

Fiscal Impact:

- Potential to reduce the cost of gun violence to the City and its agencies.

The City should pursue local legislation to compel Philadelphia gun owners to own gun safety devices and compel Philadelphia gun merchants to sell guns only when accompanied by childproofing and safety devices.

Action Steps:

- Work with City Council to implement local gun-safety legislation.
- Establish necessary regulations as well as inspection and enforcement mechanisms to implement new laws.

Fiscal Impact:

- Potential to reduce the cost of gun violence to the City and its agencies.

To improve the effectiveness of its law enforcement efforts, the City should improve inter-agency interaction and cooperation with state and federal officials.

Action Steps:

- Convene a summit with all of the City, State and Federal law enforcement agencies operating in Philadelphia to determine potential avenues for improved cooperative efforts.
- Draft and adopt agreements or memoranda of understanding necessary to implement inter-agency and intergovernmental cooperation.
- Establish necessary systems and protocols to implement agreements.
- Consider consolidating the PHA and SEPTA police forces into the Philadelphia Police Department.

Fiscal Impact:

- Potential to reduce the cost of crime to the City and its agencies.

The City should foster efforts to improve adjudication and expand alternatives to incarceration by increasing the growing number of specialized courts in the City's court system.

Action Steps:

- Work with the Philadelphia judiciary and Commonwealth officials to expand the use of drug courts and explore the use of other specialized courts in Philadelphia.

- Work with the Philadelphia judiciary and Commonwealth officials to explore the use of a gun court in Philadelphia to improve adjudication of gun-related offenses.
- Work with the Philadelphia judiciary and State Court officials to expand the use of monitored community service and other alternatives to incarceration offered by courts operating in Philadelphia.

Fiscal Impact:

- Potential to reduce the cost of prison services in Philadelphia.

To help reduce overcrowded prison conditions and create room in the prison system that can be used to remove criminals from the streets, the City should work to alter Pennsylvania's sentencing law to mandate that any defendant sentenced to more than a two-year sentence must serve that time in a state prison.

Action Steps:

- Work to pass appropriate sentencing legislation in the Pennsylvania General Assembly.

Fiscal Impact:

- Potential to reduce the cost of prison services in Philadelphia.

To help crack down on quality-of-life crime, the City should invest in passive crime-fighting measures such as surveillance, red-light, and photo-radar cameras that can aide law enforcement efforts without dramatically increasing personnel resources.

Action Steps:

- Invest in passive crime-fighting measures to combat quality-of-life crimes.
- Work to pass appropriate legislation in the Pennsylvania General Assembly to enable the implementation of red-light and photo-radar cameras.
- Work with vendors to install and implement systems to utilize red-light and photo-radar cameras throughout Philadelphia.
- Work with community leaders and law enforcement officials to implement passive crime-fighting measures.

Fiscal Impact:

- Potential cost to implement passive crime-fighting measures, which could be offset by increased revenue from fines.
- Potential to reduce the cost of crime to the City and its agencies.

TOURISM-RELATED ACTIVITIES—SHOWCASING PHILADELPHIA TO THE WORLD

In 1842, Charles Dickens visited the United States and expressed interest in seeing two sites: Niagara Falls and Philadelphia's Eastern State Penitentiary. While in Philadelphia, he marveled at the Fairmount Waterworks and its tremendous engineering that efficiently supplied the growing city with clean water. According to Philadelphia Water Department officials, in the first half of the 19th century, the Fairmount Waterworks was the second most reproduced attraction in America—behind only Niagara Falls. The Penitentiary and the Waterworks were marvels of their time, drawing professional and mass curiosity. The

Penitentiary, which adopted a radial floor plan to house inmates in solitary confinement and was copied in prisons all over the world, drew as many as 10,000 visitors in 1858. The Waterworks, which was the heart of America's first major urban water-delivery system, was used as a pumping station until 1909 and has been the target of renovation and reuse efforts since 1974. Both attractions have long outlived their original use, fallen into disrepair, and only recently have been reborn as tourist sites. As renovations and improvements continue at both sites, enthusiasts bank on tourism to breathe life into these unique assets. The City's elected leadership and civic boosters have similarly committed to making Philadelphia a destination city, but as the experience with Eastern State Penitentiary and the Fairmount Waterworks shows, Philadelphia does not lack spectacular attractions, it lacks the ability to present these attractions in the best possible manner and lacks the ability to show its attractions off to the world.

Tourism is big business in America and across the globe. The Travel Industry Association of America reported that travelers visiting historic sites or museums typically spend about $200 more per trip than other travelers. According to the World Tourism Organization, 20 years ago, when the world's population was 4.4 billion, 287 million people took international trips. By 1996, when the world's population had increased to 5.7 billion, 595 million people took international trips. The number is expected to grow to 1.6 billion by 2020.

The economic stakes are significant. Philadelphia currently draws approximately five million tourists per year. But smaller cities without as many significant tourist sites such as Boston and Baltimore outdraw Philadelphia in terms of tourism each year, attracting nearly ten million and 7.5 million tourists respectively. In Philadelphia, tourists often spend an afternoon at Independence Hall and in the historic area before moving on to another destination, denying the City of further economic benefit from their visit. The Travel Industry Association of America estimates that tourism generates $2.8 billion in visitor spending in Philadelphia each year. Bearing in mind the tourism numbers generated in Boston and Baltimore, City officials suggest that doubling the number of Philadelphia visitors to ten million could result in an additional $2.8 billion in visitor spending, an additional $130 million in City tax revenues, and an additional 50,000 City jobs.

As discussed above, an increase in the number of visitors to the City stimulates growth in the hospitality sector. Therefore, attracting more visitors to the City's cultural and historic sites spurs demand for expansion of the number of hotels, restaurants, and entertainment venues in Philadelphia. To capitalize on its commitment to "Destination Philadelphia," the City must invest in its assets—and promote them to the world. To do so, the City can better coordinate the myriad tourism-related institutions and agencies to focus a central visitor-attraction effort and best link the City's tourist assets. The City can also establish a permanent source of funding to enable local institutions to enhance their attractions and pay for a permanent advertising and marketing campaign touting Philadelphia.

Focusing and Linking Tourism-Promotion Efforts

In Philadelphia, the Charter formally vests the power to promote the City with the Mayor and creates a City Representative (who also serves as the Director of the Department of Commerce) to publicize the City. A Philadelphia Convention and Visitors Bureau was later established as the central agency for information on visiting and meeting in Philadelphia. A Greater Philadelphia Tourism Marketing Corporation was created more recently to create and implement a marketing effort for the region. A Convention Center Authority maintains and operates the City's convention facility. More focused agencies like the International Visitors Council, the Greater Philadelphia Hotel Association, and Historic Philadelphia, Inc. promote more specified interests while the Center City District and the Delaware River Port Authority promote more concentrated geographic areas. Other agencies run and promote City festivals, conduct tours, and conduct other special events.

Because many groups promote tourism in Philadelphia, duplication and fragmentation of effort waste money and blunt their collective effectiveness. A Hospitality Cabinet has been established to provide more direction for the City's hospitality efforts, but additional consolidation is required. The City should consolidate its tourism-related agencies and provide a focus for efforts to improve Philadelphia as a destination city. Such an effort could be centered in the City Representative's Office which could be separated from the Department of Commerce[20], which could lead a consolidated and redefined collection of hospitality agencies to formally direct the City's hospitality initiatives. As part of the effort to consolidate tourism-related agencies, the City could consider ways to combine entities with similar missions to eliminate duplication of efforts, formalize and adopt a master plan for tourism-related initiatives that is acceptable to the various agencies, and establish mechanisms to ensure future collegial interactions among the agencies that promote Philadelphia.

In recent months, the Center City District, Philadelphia's downtown business improvement district, installed a comprehensive pedestrian sign system comprised of disk maps and directional signs that effectively guide visitors to the City's historic and cultural sites. With a more consolidated approach to tourism-related activities in Philadelphia, the City could further link its unique menu of attractions. Multi-attraction tickets, as well as tours and brochures packaging attractions of similar interest such as art attractions, science attractions, music attractions, etc., could better link the City's assets. By better coordinating a unified outreach to visitors and better linking its attractions, the City can grow its hospitality sector and improve Philadelphia as a destination city.

USING CITY ASSETS TO PROMOTE TOURISM

The City has many opportunities to use its assets in efforts to promote Philadelphia as a destination city. In addition to preparing and promoting City-owned assets such as the Fairmount Waterworks and Fort Mifflin as tourist destinations, the City has many opportunities to use its assets to enhance the tourist experience and lure future visitors.

City Hall—The Center of All Things Public and Private

The City could use future renovations of City Hall to create a proper flow of tourists to link Philadelphia's major attractions. Because of City Hall's central location—a short walk from the Convention Center, the Avenue of the Arts, the museums along the Benjamin Franklin Parkway, and the City's historic district—it is the ideal place for facilities aimed at orienting visitors and encouraging them to explore the City's attractions. (See Figure 4.3.) The ground floor of City Hall could house facilities to help enhance efforts to highlight all that Philadelphia has to show:

- A formal visitors' center could help familiarize tourists with Philadelphia and lead them to the City's attractions.

- Exhibit space and classroom facilities could enhance tours of City Hall itself and encourage visitors to begin their explorations of the City with a tour of its grandest building.

- A venue to sell half-price tickets to Center City theaters could lead visitors from the Convention Center to the Avenue of the Arts.

- A store selling tickets, souvenirs, and combination passes from local cultural institutions could lead visitors from the Convention Center to the Parkway museums.

- Additional exhibit space could house a City Archives Museum displaying exhibits on the history of Philadelphia government.

---

[20] Under the 1951 Home Rule Charter, the City Representative is also designated as the Director of Commerce. In practice, however, Mayoral adminsitrations have treated the office as two separate entities.

- Accessible, walk-in space could be used to house a boutique store to sell collectible used City property.
- Wide sidewalks surrounding City Hall could support sidewalk cafes to attract visitors.
- Wide sidewalks could support self-cleaning public toilets without interfering with pedestrians.

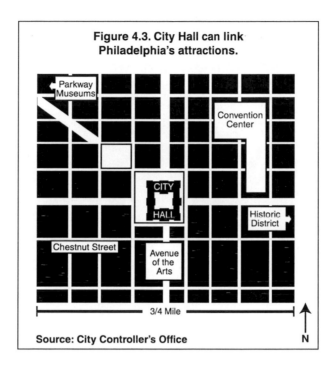

Figure 4.3. City Hall can link Philadelphia's attractions.

Parkway Museums

Convention Center

CITY HALL

Historic District

Chestnut Street

Avenue of the Arts

3/4 Mile

Source: City Controller's Office

N

Veterans Stadium—Free Advertising for Philadelphia

Major League Baseball's Philadelphia Phillies and the National Football League's Philadelphia Eagles both play their home games in City-owned Veterans Stadium. Because the live broadcast and replays from these games are viewed by millions of individuals across the country, the City could showcase Philadelphia as a tourist destination by advertising itself directly on the Veterans Stadium playing fields or their surroundings (these advertisements could even be virtual ads, seen only on television):

- On the left-centerfield wall for baseball and on the wall behind the home end zone for football, an advertisement could tempt viewers to "Visit Historic Philadelphia" and feature images of Independence Hall and the Liberty Bell.
- On the right-centerfield wall for baseball and on the wall behind the away end zone for football an advertisement could tempt visitors to "Visit Modern Philadelphia" and feature images of the City's striking new skyline and the soon-to-be completed Regional Performing Arts Center.

Chestnut Street—From Transit Mall to Cross-City Tourist Conduit

As the City moves forward with plans to renovate Chestnut Street—which has existed as a transit mall, excluding passenger-vehicle traffic, for more than 20 years—the City could make this underutilized street into the thoroughfare used by tourists. (See Figure 4.3.) Crossing Center City, Chestnut Street runs through the

Central Business District, across the Avenue of the Arts, and directly past Independence Hall. While current plans envision a return of traditional automobile traffic, the City still has the opportunity to dedicate a lane of traffic, or the entire street, as a trolley or tram route that would loop through Center City and connect its many attractions for visitors.

From the Convention Center to Independence National Historical Park—Easing into the Urban Experience

Many visitors are intimidated by the urban environment and, despite any efforts to make Philadelphia more hospitable, some visitors may need to ease into the urban experience. Even though the Pennsylvania Convention Center is located just more than five blocks from Independence National Historical Park, many visitors do not make the trip. To encourage visitors to make excursions beyond meeting rooms and ballrooms, the City could create a completely enclosed walkway from the Convention Center to the Park area. Such a connection could remove pedestrians from the streetscape. But, because the buildings along the route include department stores and The Gallery mall, a connection from the Convention Center to the adjacent building and the construction of two pedestrian bridges could link visitors from the Convention Center—through major Center City retail establishments—directly to the nation's most historic square mile.

Funding to Promote Tourism

To promote the remarkable 1996 Cezanne exhibition at the Philadelphia Museum of Art, promoters funded a major press junket, partnered with sponsors, and blanketed the East Coast with advertisements. The reward was more than 500,000 visitors and more than $86 million of visitor spending in Philadelphia.

If Philadelphia is to be a destination city, it must make its investment in tourism pay off by marketing the City and its attractions and enhancing the visitor experience. Marketing investments should be rewarded with increased visits and increased economic impact to the City. Additionally, by encouraging all of the City's tourism-related entities to enhance the experience they present to visitors, to open their attics to expand the collections on view, and to show the world all there is to see and do in Philadelphia, the City's world-class attractions can rival any others.

Many Philadelphians—let alone visitors and tourists—are unaware of the cultural and historic treasures spread throughout the City. Attractions such as the Rodin Museum, home to the largest public collection of Rodin's work outside Paris, or the Cathedral Basilica of Saints Peter and Paul, the grand Italian-Renaissance edifice designed by Napoleon LeBrun, do not draw nearly the attention they should. The Rodin Museum draws less than 10 percent of the attendance of the Philadelphia Museum of Art even though it is just blocks away along the Benjamin Franklin Parkway. The Cathedral is not even marked on the Philadelphia City Planning Commission's map of attractions in Center City created for its 1993 "Destination Philadelphia" report. Attractions such as Philadelphia's Masonic Temple, one of the world's greatest Masonic temples (located across the street from City Hall) or the Powel House, the Georgian row house formerly occupied by the first mayor of Philadelphia after the Revolution (located just blocks from the Liberty Bell), remain almost totally anonymous despite their significance and potential interest to visitors.

While many Center City sites draw steady streams of visitors, off-the-beaten-path attractions such as North Philadelphia's Wagner Free Institute of Science, the City's perfectly preserved 19th-century science museum, and South Philadelphia's Mummers Museum, the City's salute to its unique New Year's Day celebration, rarely make the agenda for Philadelphia tours. Similarly, historic Germantown and attractions throughout the Fairmount Park system are missed by most visitors.

Other sites and potential exhibits that are now inaccessible to most visitors, await the resources and leadership necessary to turn them into proper attractions. Hidden gems such as the botanical specimens and artifacts from the Lewis and Clark expedition, which rest in the archives of the Academy of Natural Sciences, and elaborate tile murals depicting early 20th-century modes of transportation, which remain tucked away in unused trolley stations at the Benjamin Franklin Bridge, remain out of public view.

In 1996, a unique partnership between the City, the state, and a private foundation established the Greater Philadelphia Tourism and Marketing Corporation (GPTMC) to build the City's image as a tourist destination and to create and monitor the success of an advertising plan for the five-county Southeastern Pennsylvania region. Public and foundation support for the agency's $4 million annual operating budget to fund advertising and marketing efforts is set to expire in the summer of 1999. According to research performed for GPTMC, the agency's $1.7 million advertising budget helped generate over one million trips to the Greater Philadelphia area in 1997. Furthermore, the advertising produced a significant improvement in image perception among likely travelers.

But, as GPTMC's research indicated, Philadelphia is only scratching the surface in terms of its share of overnight marketable trips to the region and is behind such neighboring competitor cities. If the City is to continue to promote Philadelphia as a destination city, it must continue and expand marketing efforts. The $4 million GPTMC annual budget only funds advertising efforts that reach areas of nearby states. Similarly, because Philadelphia is unable to host many touring exhibits or special events due to a lack of capital available to invest in hosting activities, the potential economic impact flows to alternate cities. To encourage its attractions to better serve visitors and improve the tourist experience in Philadelphia, the City must expand sources of funding for its historic and cultural institutions.

To fund ongoing advertising efforts and to support the City's institutions in their efforts to improve their attractions, the City should create a permanent source of funding to support tourism-related expenditures. The City could establish a fund to support advertising efforts, establish a revolving loan fund to provide resources to fund expansion and embellishment of City attractions, and provide grants to support worthy institutions and special events. Additionally, such funding can help the City turn its own underembellished tourist destinations—Philadelphia's historic City Hall, the historic houses of Fairmount Park, the City's remarkable collection of public art throughout the City—into proper attractions. A central agency or board comprised of government and tourism officials could make fund-disbursement decisions to provide proper oversight and to create another mechanism to foster enhanced coordination of tourism-promotion activities.

FUNDING TOURISM-RELATED EFFORTS IN PHILADELPHIA

By creating a pool of money to promote and enhance tourism in Philadelphia, the City could foster advertising efforts to let the world know that Philadelphia is home to more than the Liberty Bell, and to encourage institutions like the Academy of Music—one of the world's finest acoustical halls—to make themselves into proper tourist site. After eliminating duplication and fragmentation of effort by focusing and reorganizing its tourism-related agencies, the City can address permanent efforts to promote Philadelphia and its attractions. The City could continue and expand current marketing efforts with a $10 million annual budget, which could allow Philadelphia advertising to reach a nationwide or even international audience. The City could capitalize a $10 million revolving-loan fund, which could allow Philadelphia attractions to expand and enhance exhibits. Finally, the City could create a mechanism to give $5 million in annual discretionary grants, which could help institutions attract, host, and promote special events and exhibits. To do all of the above, the City could pursue one, or some combination, of the following options. The City could:

- Seek support from private foundations.

- Work to create a Regional Assets District (to be discussed further in the next chapter) to tap into regional support for its tourist-related assets.

- Increase the Hotel Tax (currently 6 percent of the cost to rent a room). A 1-percent increase could raise approximately $3 million per year.

- Seek enabling legislation from the Pennsylvania General Assembly to create a local Vehicle Rental Tax, above and beyond the current state tax of 2 percent plus $2 per vehicle per day. A 4-percent local Vehicle Rental Tax could raise approximately $1 million per year.

- Seek legislation from the Pennsylvania General Assembly to allow the City to extend its Amusement Tax (currently 5 percent of the price of event admission) to museums and other tourism-related institutions. By just extending the tax to Philadelphia's five most popular for-a-fee attractions, the City could generate approximately $1 million per year.

In its 1993 "Destination Philadelphia" report, the Philadelphia City Planning Commission notes that Barcelona, Spain, a city smaller than Philadelphia set in Europe, the world's most competitive tourist market, transformed itself from Spain's "second city" into one of Europe's great tourist attractions. By supporting, packaging, and promoting its unique collection of historic, cultural, and entertainment attractions, Philadelphia can show the world that it is truly a world-class destination.

RECOMMENDATIONS FOR ACTION

The City should consolidate its tourism-related agencies and provide a focus for efforts to improve Philadelphia as a destination city.

Action Steps:

- Work with agencies, funding providers, and institutions to consolidate tourism-related entities in Philadelphia.

- Provide incentives for tourism-related agency cooperation and consolidation.

- Alter the power, duties, and mission of City tourism-related agencies.

Fiscal Impact:

- Potential to increase tourism in Philadelphia and expand the economic benefit Philadelphia derives from hospitality-related activities.

To fund ongoing advertising efforts and support the City's institutions in their efforts to improve, the City should create a permanent source of funding to support tourism-related expenditures.

Action Steps:

- Establish a permanent source of funding to support City tourism and tourism-promotion efforts.

- Work with City Council, the Pennsylvania General Assembly, and civic and regional leaders to create the proper revenue-generation mechanisms to set aside such a funding stream.

Fiscal Impact:

- Potential short-term cost to capitalize a $10 million revolving-loan fund.

- Potential ongoing cost to generate approximately $15 million per year to promote tourism in Philadelphia.

- Potential to expand the economic benefit Philadelphia derives from hospitality-related activities.

TRANSPORTATION—MOVING PHILADELPHIA'S MASSES

The City of Philadelphia has grown as transportation progressed from horses and buggies that plodded through muddy City streets to air travel that whisks passengers from around the world to Philadelphia's airports. In the state that served as the keystone for the young American nation and nestled at the center of the busy Eastern Seaboard, Philadelphia has always thrived as a crossroads and as a transportation hub.

Richard Voith, Senior Economist and Research Adviser in the Urban and Regional Section of the Philadelphia Federal Reserve Bank's Research Department, has done extensive research on the value of transportation. In "The Downtown Parking Syndrome: Does Curing the Illness Kill the Patient?" which appeared in the Federal Reserve Bank of Philadelphia's *Business Review*, Voith explains that agglomeration, access, and congestion contribute to the value of a city's central business district. Cities and central business districts thrive by enhancing the density of the concentration of social, recreational, and business activity; by providing easy access for individuals traveling to and throughout the area; and by minimizing the congestion that would negate the advantages of agglomeration and access. Unlike cities such as Los Angeles or Atlanta, Georgia, that are essentially collections of communities surrounding freeway interchanges, Philadelphia is a central business district linked to surrounding neighborhoods and communities like a hub and spokes. Mass transportation is therefore particularly important to the City's future.

To thrive in the global marketplace, 21st-century Philadelphia must be a city where goods and services flow freely. As the world focuses on improving air-quality standards, Philadelphia must embrace the technology and transportation systems that reduce air pollution. As vehicle availability in the region and in the City increases, Philadelphia must work to ensure that congestion is minimized, pedestrian safety is accounted for, and reasonable parking options exist throughout the City. To best move its masses, aid efforts to improve air quality, and improve parking accessibility, the City can make mass transit the preferred option for regional trips, the City can work as an employer and vehicle operator to reduce pollution, and the City can alter its parking regulation scheme and create neighborhood parking options and regulations that allow residents to store their vehicles close to home.

Sensible Approaches to Transportation in Philadelphia

Local government has a limited role in creating transportation policy in Philadelphia. The City's Department of Streets is responsible for maintenance of streets and highways. The City's Department of Commerce is responsible for operating airports, docks, and wharves. The City Planning Commission coordinates transportation-related capital planning. The City's Office of Transportation is responsible for advocating transportation policies in the City's best interests. The Philadelphia Parking Authority, which is closely tied to the City, constructs and operates off-street parking facilities and manages on-street parking. Less closely tied to the City, the Southeastern Pennsylvania Transportation Authority (SEPTA) maintains a public transportation system in the five-county Southeastern Pennsylvania region and the Delaware River Port Authority (DRPA) maintains and operates

Philadelphia-area river crossings between Pennsylvania and New Jersey and a bi-state high-speed rapid-transit system. The state and federal governments, of course, have a significant say in transportation issues in Philadelphia.

Within this context, the City must coordinate the efforts of many actors within its government and work collegially with other governmental actors to actually affect transportation policy in Philadelphia. Recent and planned improvements for the Philadelphia International Airport, major mass transportation routes, and highway infrastructure contribute to the ongoing effort to increase the ease with which residents and visitors move throughout the region. While major future initiatives such as mass transit rail links to the City's Northeast neighborhoods or light rail connections to the City's distant northwestern suburbs may represent sound investments for the City's future, their completion would require significant input from the state and federal government in terms of desire, design, and funding. At the local level, however, the City can act to affect transportation in Philadelphia.

The City should commit to undertaking a single task which would reduce the stress on the City's roads and bridges, increase the citizenry's ease of mobility throughout the region, and minimize vehicle emissions to improve the region's air quality—to make mass transit the preferred mode of transportation in Philadelphia. After enduring crippling labor strife that disaffected many riders, mass transit ridership in Philadelphia has almost nowhere to go but up. Other big cities prove it can be done.

While mass transit ridership in Philadelphia declined 21 percent between 1988 and 1996, major investments in mass transit facilities and in technology enabled cities such as Denver and St. Louis, Missouri, to dramatically increase transit use. Free bus-to-subway transfers, the use of debit cards to pay fares, and unlimited trips for fixed prices in New York City have improved mass transit ridership after it had fallen by 14 percent from 1990 to 1995. Allowing the public to pay fares using a credit card has helped the City of Phoenix improve ridership.

MAKING MASS TRANSIT THE PREFERRED MODE IN PHILADELPHIA

In addition to working with SEPTA to improve the overall safety, reliability, and cleanliness of the mass transit system, the City can push for many specific improvements to help make mass transit the preferred mode of transportation in Philadelphia:

- Work with SEPTA to implement debit-card technology throughout the mass transit system to improve the accessibility of the SEPTA system.

- Work with SEPTA to alter fare structures (free transfers, unlimited trips for a set price) to encourage ridership.

- Work with SEPTA officials to equip stations with dynamic signs that can provide "next-train" and other mass transit schedule information.

- Work with DRPA to implement variable bridge tolls to reduce volume during peak hours and encourage riders to use transit alternatives.

- Work with tourism-promotion agencies and SEPTA to promote visitors' knowledge of, and use of, the mass transit system.

- Enforce uninsured driver regulations to force car owners to pay the true cost of driving or give up their cars to use mass transit.

- Advocate for the creation of new light-rail projects linking Philadelphia with its suburbs.

- Alter City parking regulations (see below) to discourage commuters from driving into Center City.

As an employer and a fleet operator, the City could further help encourage mass transit use and reduce air pollution by promoting the use of mass transit as a fringe benefit for City workers and by exploring the use of alternative fuels for City vehicles. Similarly, the City could work to limit the number of City vehicles that are provided to City officials to encourage officials to use mass transit for their commute. The City could provide TransitChek mass transit vouchers to City and School District workers as a pre-tax benefit to encourage the use of mass transit among the approximately 50,000 City and School District employees. While TransitChek is tax deductible to increase its appeal to for-profit employers, many governmental agencies in Philadelphia offer the vouchers, including the U.S. Mint and the U.S. Environmental Protection Agency.

Since the City operates a fleet of approximately 5,800 vehicles, it is responsible for a good deal of automobile emissions. While some jurisdictions that have experimented with the use of alternative fuels have found them overly costly, as the costs of alternate fuels come down, the City could consider using biodiesel and other low-pollution fuels to reduce vehicle emissions and improve air quality.

The City can also alter parking policies to encourage transit use, increase the availability of parking for downtown shoppers, and increase parking options for neighborhood residents. As in many cities, parking in Philadelphia presents many problems. To encourage business, many owners of Center City parking lots offer "early bird" specials, some charging less than $7 for all-day parking. Many parking lot owners then charge more than $7 per hour for mid-day parkers. Since monthly rail transportation from a Philadelphia suburb to Center City can cost more than $6 per day, all-day Center City parking rates make driving a competitively priced option. Mid-day visitors—who confront the fact that buses and trains are less convenient after rush hour because many run less frequently during off-peak hours—are then frustrated to find high short-term parking fees.

In "The Downtown Parking Syndrome: Does Curing the Illness Kill the Patient?" Richard Voith reports that in a survey of Center City retailers conducted by the Federal Reserve Bank of Philadelphia, 37 percent of respondents indicated that improving parking would be the most important change that could help their business. But the overall amount of Center City parking itself may not necessarily be the problem. The scarcity of low-cost short-term parking is what truly frustrates retailers.

The City of San Francisco discourages long-term commuter parking by law. Private, off-street parking spaces provided for a structure or use other than residential or hotel must maintain a fee structure so that the rate charge for four hours of parking is no more than four times the rate charge for the first hour and so that the rate charge for eight or more hours of parking is no less than ten times the rate charge for the first hour. San Francisco further prohibits such parking lots from providing discounted weekly, monthly, or other time-specific period parking. With such a measure in place, a parking lot that charges $1 per hour for parking must charge no more than $4 for four hours and no less than $10 for eight hours. Thus, lot operators are encouraged to charge less for short stays and more for long stays. Because all-day parkers are discouraged from monopolizing parking, adequate parking exists at a low enough price to meet demand. In Philadelphia, where Center City parking for eight hours can cost about $7 for workday-long parking, and where Center City parking for a one-hour lunch can equal or exceed that $7 amount, the incentives are clearly misplaced.

Policies to discourage all-day parking and encourage short-term parking should increase the economic vitality of Center City and improve the City's mass transit system, which should improve the vitality of the region. To improve the availability and affordability of Center City parking, and to further encourage mass transit use, the City should consider altering parking regulations to establish a fee structure that sets a maximum per-hour charge for short-term parking and a minimum per-hour charge for all-day parking. Such a policy should be considered based on consultation with the Philadelphia Parking Authority and Center City parking operators. Alternatively, because the Parking Authority directly sets rates for nearly 6,000 Center City off-street parking spaces—approximately 12 percent of the public off-street parking in Center City—the City can follow the lead of the City of Portland and encourage short-term parking by adopting such short-term-friendly parking policies at City-owned lots.

Another parking-related problem exists in certain areas of the City. In some Philadelphia neighborhoods, double parking on City streets, parking on cement medians, and angle parking along the curb are quaint traditions that create dangerous conditions for drivers left with limited visibility at intersections. Because emergency vehicles have difficulty navigating City streets in these neighborhoods, failure to resolve the parking problem also creates dangerous conditions for victims of medical and fire emergencies and opens the City to future liability in cases of catastrophic loss.

Philadelphia already offers long-term permit parking in many residential neighborhoods. Other cities, such as Boston, provide permit-only parking in certain neighborhoods. Providing adequate neighborhood parking to create an amenity to improve the attractiveness of city life is sound economic development policy.

To improve the availability of adequate neighborhood parking, the City should expand the use of neighborhood permit parking and resident-only parking and, where necessary, create neighborhood off-street parking to reduce the demand for curbside parking. While the cost to purchase and clear land and create parking facilities may be substantial in certain neighborhoods, costs could be subsidized by the proceeds of the sale of neighborhood parking permits. The savings in terms of reduced exposure to liability from tacitly allowing illegal parking certainly provides a compelling rationale for such an expense.

RECOMMENDATIONS FOR ACTION

The City should commit to efforts to make mass transit the preferred mode of transportation in Philadelphia.

Action Steps:

- Work with transit agencies and federal, state, and regional officials to fund investments in regional mass transit improvement.

- Work with SEPTA to improve the attractiveness of the mass transit system.

- Work with DRPA officials to alter rush hour bridge pricing.

- Provide City employees with mass transit fare as a pre-tax benefit.

- Alter City parking regulation policy.

Fiscal Impact:

- Potential increased cost for mass transit funding.

- Potential to improve the economic vitality of the City.

The City should consider altering parking regulations to establish a fee structure that sets a maximum per-hour charge for short-term parking and a minimum per-hour charge for all-day parking.

Action Steps:

- Work with City Council to pass new parking regulations.

- Implement oversight and regulatory procedures for new parking regulations.

Fiscal Impact:

- Potential to improve the economic vitality of the City.

To improve the availability of adequate neighborhood parking, the City should expand the use of neighborhood permit parking and resident-only parking and, where necessary, create neighborhood off-street parking to reduce the demand for curbside parking by increasing the overall parking supply.

Action Steps:

- Work with Parking Authority officials and community leaders to implement additional neighborhood permit parking and resident-only parking programs.

- Work with Parking Authority officials, redevelopment agencies, and community leaders to plan for, acquire, and create off-street parking in over-parked neighborhoods.

Fiscal Impact:

- Potential cost to create neighborhood off-street parking which could be offset by residential permit parking fees.

CONCLUSION

To thrive as a city in the future, Philadelphia must address the problems of a modern metropolis. To attract and retain employers, the City must capitalize on its competitive advantages, minimize disamenities for businesses, improve the quality of the workforce, reduce the impact of crime on businesses, and foster a system of transportation that allows goods to flow freely through the marketplace. To attract and retain residents, the City must improve overall quality of life by reducing crime, improving educational opportunities, and addressing the decay associated with vacant properties. By focusing on each of the specific governmental challenges outlined above, Philadelphia can confront the woes that beset cities.

Everything the City does, from collecting trash to maintaining City recreation centers, promotes or impedes economic development efforts. In addition to generally decreasing the cost of doing business, the City can target economic development activities toward businesses that gain a competitive advantage from locating in Philadelphia. By working to meet the needs of firms that benefit from a high density of local demand, high concentration of human resources, and proximity to markets, the City can maximize the effectiveness of economic development initiatives.

Because improving the system of public education in Philadelphia can help increase the quality of the City workforce, education is directly related to economic development and business-attraction efforts. But the City must also address public education to attract and retain families who, too often, see an underperforming system of public education as a reason to leave or avoid Philadelphia. By altering the governance structure associated with public schools, the City can provide local elected officials with the ability to directly affect education in Philadelphia. With that power, they could focus on reducing class size, extending the school day, and increasing the reach of effective programs to create a system of public education that works for all Philadelphia families.

After years of population decline and neighborhood decay, vacant properties and lots now scar many City neighborhoods. Projections for the future do not foresee a sudden influx of population sufficient to create a demand for properties that could eliminate the blight of vacancy throughout the City. Given this market failure, the City must stimulate demand for Philadelphia's vacant housing stock. To help rightsize Philadelphia, the City can commit to a policy of acquiring and demolishing large, sparsely populated areas of the City to increase demand for housing in other struggling neighborhoods, and create an asset for future development. Similarly, because vacancy breeds further vacancy and decay, the City can enforce disincentives to speculation and explore the use of taxation tools to encourage vacant property owners to do something productive with their holdings.

To retain and attract businesses and residents, Philadelphia must be—in perception and reality—a safe city. By targeting gun violence and effectively coordinating law enforcement efforts, and expanding specialized courts and alternatives to incarceration, the City can address one of its more vexing challenges. In addition, by utilizing passive crime-fighting measures like red-light and surveillance cameras, the City can improve civility and safety without dramatically increasing police personnel.

Philadelphia's historical and cultural attractions create a competitive advantage that can be exploited to expand employment in the hospitality and tourism industry. The City is committed to exploiting this advantage and increasing its ability to draw visitors. By uniting the efforts of tourism-related entities and organizations, the City can showcase Philadelphia to the world. By establishing permanent, dedicated funding to promote Philadelphia and its attractions, the City can become the destination for millions of additional visitors each year.

Finally, to ensure that goods and individuals are able to move easily throughout Philadelphia, the City must work to effectively move its masses. By pursuing every available avenue to make mass transit the preferred mode, the City can reduce congestion and limit the wear and tear on its roads and bridges. By specifically addressing parking policies, the City can improve the accessibility and convenience of Center City and other dense Philadelphia neighborhoods.

Given the daunting challenges faced by the modern city, Philadelphia cannot be expected to reverse its decline without outside help. Given the established interdependence between the City and its suburbs, regional cooperation is required to foster sustainable growth. The discussion surrounding Philadelphia's response to future challenges, therefore, concludes with a consideration of regional efforts to address regional challenges.

SECOND EDITION SUPPLEMENT TO CHAPTER 4
RESPONDING TO SPECIFIC URBAN CHALLENGES

Sound fiscal policies and appropriate governance structures are the necessary tools a city requires to meet the specific needs of its citizenry. These provide a government with the resources to protect the lives and property of its businesses and residents, to shelter and gainfully employee its population, to educate its children, move its travelers and goods, protect its natural and built environment, and entertain its visitors. Meeting these challenges has long been the task of local governments, but the context and capacity of city to act are constantly evolving. This second edition of *Philadelphia: A New Urban Direction* reviews the city's most recent efforts to improve the social, physical, and economic systems that determine the quality of life in the city and offers new insights into how the city can best meet the challenges that Philadelphia faces in the 21st Century.

ECONOMIC DEVELOPMENT — GROWING PHILADELPHIA INTO THE FUTURE

Philadelphia continues to chase the dream of job growth and economic vitality. Summits were held, sweeping programs have been initiated, and isolated successes have been touted, but still Philadelphia continues to lose jobs — nearly 30,000 of them between 1999 and 2004, according to the Bureau of Labor Statistics. Even when the city has seen short periods of job growth, Philadelphia tends to lag behind competitors. A variety of factors influence the rate of business formation and expansion in Philadelphia, including the quality of the labor pool; the physical environment; the relative costs of doing business here versus competitor jurisdictions; and the condition of the national and global economies. While many of these factors are beyond the control of local policy makers, the city has initiated interventions into the private market to stimulate economic growth.

Tax and Regulatory Reform

In the first edition of *Philadelphia: A New Urban Direction*, we recommend that the city target its resources for economic development on specific industries in which the city has a clear competitive advantages and are poised for growth and avoid targeting individual companies. We identified hospitality, financial services and arts and cultures as industry clusters on which the city should focus. Since that time, the city has targeted some strategic industries, while continuing to offer incentives to individual firms and projects. Tax and regulatory reform were recommended as necessary for economic growth. While incremental tax and regulatory reforms have been implemented, additional efforts are still warranted. To improve Philadelphia's economic climate, the city should reform Philadelphia's business taxes. Competitor cities and surrounding suburbs do not place this onerous burden on firms, and given an increasingly high-tech, mobile economy, the Business Privilege Tax creates a disincentive for firms that could locate anywhere from choosing Philadelphia. While revamping the city's business taxes is the critical ingredient to growing jobs and wealth in our region, combining an effective and efficient economic development strategy with a competitive tax structure will serve to enhance the diversity and strength of the local economy.

Philadelphia must also have transparent and easy procedures for enterprises seeking to do business in the city. A Controller's Office survey of small business owners found that they were dissatisfied with the service they received from the city's regulatory agencies. The license and permit fees did not reflect the quality of service and their daily business activities were obstructed by the time consumed during the application and approval processes. The results suggest that inefficiency and complex regulatory requirements are significant concerns of small business owners.

The city should streamline its regulatory processes and make them user friendly. New technologies can allow the city to do things faster with less manpower; we owe it to our residents and businesses to harness this power. The Philadelphia Chapter of the Building Industry of America has offered recommendations to improve the city's regulatory processes. As key customers for this city service, their calls for increased transparency, predictability, one-stop shopping, and modernization should be heeded to stimulate further development and improve service delivery. Particular attention should be paid to Philadelphia's small businesses, which often struggle with regulatory requirements and have difficulty accessing the city's economic development incentives. The city could take into account the needs and capacity of small businesses in the development of regulations, processes, and fees. Dedicated incentive programs, with criteria based on number of employees or revenues, should be developed to ensure that small firms are not forced to compete with the city's largest businesses for assistance.

Zoning and Planning Modernization

The cumbersome nature of doing business in Philadelphia is particularly visible in the area of real estate development. Philadelphia is undergoing many developmental changes, including the introduction of gaming, redevelopment of the Navy Yard and other waterfront locations, new skyscrapers, and new residential construction in Center City and the neighborhoods — each with environmental, economic, social, and physical impacts. Development is slowed and made more costly as a result of our outdated zoning code. The city could seek to reduce the number of projects that require variances by adopting a modern zoning code and comprehensive plan. The last comprehensive plan was produced in the 1960s and contained many assumptions that have not come to pass. Plans have been developed for individual neighborhoods since then, but the time has come to reassess the needs of the city as a whole, otherwise the city risks competing priorities and projects in different sections of Philadelphia.

Comprehensive plans provide predictability to the development process and encourage investment. Rather than nearly every new project seeking a variance or zoning change as a result of outdated plans, a new comprehensive plan would illustrate to developers what types of projects the city wants, and in which locations. Additionally, planning provides a rational process for reviewing the city's infrastructure and transportation network. An updated zoning code and comprehensive plan serve as tools to promote public goods, such as mass transit usage, affordable housing, economic development, and high-quality urban design. As the city makes new capital investments it is imperative that they meet the needs of present day Philadelphia, not the Philadelphia of the 1960s.

Although regulatory and tax reform, and modern zoning codes and plans can have a significant impact on lowering the costs of doing business in Philadelphia, the city has implemented, and will likely continue to pursue, additional strategies to create jobs. The city has employed numerous tools to create and retain jobs, falling into two general categories — negotiated and as-of-right. Negotiated incentives, in the form of loans, grants, and tax abatements are awarded to individual firms at the discretion of the Administration, while as-of-right incentives are available to any entity meeting the program's criteria.

One of the most successful as-of-right incentives offered by the city has been the 10-year Real Estate Tax abatements on 100 percent of the value added as a result of improvements. Coupled with historically low interest rates, the tax abatements have spurred significant residential, and to a lesser extent, commercial construction and conversion, since the abatements were introduced. Philadelphia also offers firms that expand employment a $1,000 credit per new job against Business Privilege Tax liabilities, as was proposed by the City Controller. Although various programs have been introduced, the city still lacks a comprehensive, clearly articulated strategy for economic development, despite several summits, committees and other efforts tasked with generating one.

Comprehensive Economic Development Strategy

Once Philadelphia has established a baseline of business friendliness through tax and regulatory reform, the city should develop a clear approach to economic development and have the appropriate tools to implement its strategy. For any program to have the desired effect measurable policy objectives must be articulated — Are we going to focus on encouraging specific industries? Supporting individual companies? Reducing regulatory hurdles to business formation and expansion? Depending on growth from companies already in the city? Or the relocation of firms currently beyond the city limits? There are an endless number of approaches to intervening into a local economy to promote growth. Selecting those strategies that would best serve Philadelphia's particular economic structure and can be implemented by Philadelphia's economic development agencies is essential.

Philadelphia has given loans, grants and tax abatements to individual firms in the heart of Center City, and has zones in less advantaged areas that allow a business that relocate there to avoid most state and local taxes for a period of time. To maximize the benefits of both these strategies, the city could designate zones with incentives tailored to specific industries that the city deems to be growth sectors. For example, the City of Chicago provides grants in designated neighborhoods for the construction of laboratory facilities for nanotechnology, biotechnology, and other related fields.

The city should rigorously review the array of economic development programs offered, and eliminate any that duplicate efforts or provide a poor value for each dollar invested. For example, if one program spends $50,000 for every job created, and another creates equivalent jobs for $25,000, the first program should either be eliminated or improved. Currently, little information is available on the performance of the city's economic development programs, especially since a significant number of departments and agencies are charged with program management. Enhanced performance measurement can guide policy decisions and resource allocation. Ongoing evaluation of the city's economic development efforts is essential.

Once careful analysis reveals the relative efficiency and effectiveness of the city's economic development programs, the focus should turn to the most skillful application of these tools. To achieve transparency and ensure efficiency and effectiveness of incentives that are not available as-of-right, the city should adopt guidelines to evaluate requests for public money to support private sector economic expansion. Each project seeking funding should be reviewed based upon the priorities of the city, and these reviews should be made public. Evaluations could consider the efficiency of the project, in terms of cost per job created and the ratio of public funds requested to dollars being provided privately, as compared to other economic development initiatives. Projects that represent a poor value for public funds should not be approved. Assessment of public amenities to be provided, and the number and quality (wage level, provision of healthcare benefits, etc.) of jobs created is warranted. Preference should be given to projects that create high-quality jobs and/or public improvements such as parks, or services currently unavailable in the project area. Proposed projects should also be evaluated for compatibility with other development projects that are underway and the overall economic development strategy. Subsidized projects should not compete with each other. By strategically deploying city funds for private development, linked to other plans and projects, the city could generate a bigger bang for the public buck spent. Finally, projects should be assessed based on their viability. A clear market demand for the project and the readiness of the developer to proceed should be considered to ensure that taxpayer money is not unnecessarily spent on doomed endeavors.

Arts and Culture

In 1999, the Controller's Office identified the hospitality, arts and culture as a key group of industry sectors that had the potential to generate wealth and create jobs in Philadelphia. Increasing Philadelphia's tourism and hospitality activity has remained a primary focus since the first edition of *Philadelphia: A New Urban Direction*. Earlier phases of this effort entailed increasing the city's supply of hotel rooms. This push, encouraged by Real Estate Tax abatements, Tax Increment Financing, and US Department of Housing and Urban Development Section 108 loans, strove to add an additional 2,000 rooms by the year 2000 to meet the demands of hosting the 2000 Republican Convention and to attract other major conventions. Following the terrorist attacks of September 11, 2001, Philadelphia, like most other cities, saw a reduction in hotel occupancy and room rates, but the future of Philadelphia's tourism remains bright. The recent terminal expansions and introduction of new low-cost carriers at the Philadelphia International Airport has contributed to a 55-percent increase in total passengers between 1995 and 2004 and a significant drop in average one-way fares. The Greater Philadelphia Tourism Marketing Corporation reports public dollars invested in marketing the hospitality sector in the past several years yielded significant returns, with a 40-percent increase in overnight leisure visitors between 1998 and 2003.

Efforts to support hospitality sector continue. Expansion of the Pennsylvania Convention Center is planned and predicated upon being able to host larger conventions or simultaneous smaller conventions. Expansion and realignment of Philadelphia International Airport runways are being explored to enable better on time service and simultaneous landings and takeoffs. Hospitality and tourism are poised to remain drivers of the local economy and failure to support this sector would waste the public dollars already invested in infrastructure and marketing efforts. Much of the success of Philadelphia's hospitality sector is supported by the arts and culture establishments that draw regional, national, and international visitors to the city.

Recent reductions in public funding of arts and cultural venues and programs, and the elimination of the Office of Arts and Culture in the city's Commerce Department have the potential to negate prior public investment in this sector and could hinder other economic development initiatives. The arts are typically viewed as a luxury, one of the first items to get cut during times of budgetary stress, but it is possible that the costs of cutting the funding will be greater than continued support for these organizations. Continued support for the city's arts and culture organizations is substantiated by the enormous social and economic benefits these institutions generate for the city and region. Arts and culture contribute to the success of other economic development strategies pursued in Philadelphia, including hospitality and tourism, as well as efforts to retain recent graduates.

Investments in arts and culture may provide a better return on investment than many other programs — particularly because of the social benefits. Not only do the arts generate jobs and tax revenue, but studies show that arts programs are linked to lower juvenile delinquency and higher student achievement. Increased spending on the arts may lead to declines in spending on social services, the courts, public safety, and the prisons. A clear understanding of the impact of spending on the arts, as compared to other economic development initiatives can provide guidance on appropriate spending levels.

While the largest 10 percent of arts and culture institutions generate 80 percent of the spending, we cannot neglect smaller organizations throughout the region. They contribute to the economic and social vitality of our neighborhoods, and can help build a broad constituency for arts and culture generally. Philadelphia could develop disbursement criteria that ensure that funds reach areas underserved by arts and culture organizations. Additionally, swings in funding levels can have a devastating impact, much as they have had for mass transit throughout the Commonwealth. Public funding for the arts needs to be predictable and reliable. The city should identify creative revenue sources to fund the Philadelphia's arts and cultural establishments. Support for the arts should be linked to other city programs and initiatives. For example, municipal arts grants could leverage other expenditures for community revitalization efforts.

As we recommended in the first edition of *Philadelphia: A New Urban Direction*, the city could explore authorization of a regional dedicated tax for the arts. The benefits of arts and cultural organizations are spread throughout the region, and so should the burden be borne regionally. Miami, St. Louis, Austin and other cities dedicate a portion of hotel taxes for cultural funding. Broward County dedicates a portion of amusement taxes to the arts. Oakland added additional millage to their real estate tax to support an Artist in Residence program at city libraries. There are precedents for regional sales tax increases dedicated to arts funding — metro Denver increased the sales tax one-tenth of a percent to fund arts and science. Arts Trust Funds and Endowments could also be seeded with public money to attract private and corporate contributions. The interest earnings on the funds could be used to make annual grants to arts and culture institutions.

Private sector support of arts and culture could be further encouraged with incentives for corporate giving. The city could enact a tax credit for corporations against the Business Privilege Tax for donations to arts and culture organizations. This could be modeled on the credit available to firms that make donations to Community Development Corporations. To expand regionally, the credit could be set against state business taxes. The city could also reorganize existing programs and initiatives to generate additional funds for arts and culture. In 1959, Philadelphia pioneered the Percent-for-Art Program, which mandates that one percent of construction costs for municipal projects be spent on art. The city should once again be on the forefront of supporting the arts. By allocating 0.5 percent to go to on-site art, and the other 0.5 percent to a fund that makes grants to arts and culture organizations the benefits can be spread throughout the city. The city should seek to expand utilization of this program, so that this change does not simply translate into less public art. For example, under state law, Tax Increment Financing (TIF) projects are considered as "public works projects," but in Philadelphia, TIF projects have not been required to incorporate the Percent for Arts requirement. In the future, authorization of Tax Increment Financing should be contingent upon participation in the Percent-for-Art Program.

Minority Participation

It has become clear that Philadelphia cannot expect to achieve a vital, thriving economy if large segments of its population do not participate in the creation of wealth, jobs, and business opportunities. Demographic changes underway in the city, region, and nation, including a growing share of city residents with Hispanic, Caribbean, Asian. and Eastern European ancestry, implies that failure to economically engage these groups will have dire consequences in the future. It is essential that the City of Philadelphia ensure that minorities, women, and the disabled have equal access to economic opportunities in both the public and private sectors. The city has developed programs to achieve this goal.

In 1982, the Minority Business Enterprise Council (MBEC) was established to assist disadvantaged firms to compete for city contracts. By certifying disadvantaged firms and providing guidance to the businesses and city departments, MBEC seeks to increase the share of city contracts awarded to such firms. Despite MBEC's more than 20 years of existence, Philadelphia falls far short of being a model for minority participation, as evidenced by the findings of an audit of MBEC activities conducted by the City Controller's Office in 2004 and recent federal investigations of malfeasance within the organization. Among the Controller's audit's major findings was that 75 percent of the 91 MBEC certification files in the Controller's Office randomly selected statistical file sample were either missing or contained insufficient documentation to support the certification decisions made by MBEC.

The audit also found that the amount of time that it has taken for businesses to become certified by MBEC varies widely, and has taken over 200 days in some cases. During the wait to become certified, firms may be missing valuable business opportunities. Based on observations and inspections, it also appears that some firms received preferential treatment. This is in direct conflict with MBEC's goal of avoiding discrimination.

Now under new leadership, MBEC is taking steps to correct the problems identified in the Controller's audit. The city should implement the recommendations made by the Controller's Office for MBEC. Key recommendations include increased collection of performance data, and that information be used to hold individuals responsible for the program functions. Specific goals should be crafted with a focus on measurable results. MBEC should also be provided with the resources necessary to effectively accomplish its mandate.

The city would be able to award a more significant share of city contracts to minority and disadvantaged businesses if there was a larger pool of certified vendors and service providers. To broaden the number of women-, minority-, and disabled-owned businesses that have an opportunity to participate, the city should turn to the region's impressive network of business alliances and chambers of commerce. These organizations are already working with firms that could qualify for MBEC certification, and may have better resources for outreach efforts. Currently, the Philadelphia School District partners with the Greater Philadelphia Hispanic Chamber of Commerce to develop a database of potential vendors, providing outreach and pre-screening. Similar partnerships with MBEC should be explored for public education and recruitment, with the organizations assisting businesses navigate the certification process.

Efforts have been made to ensure minority participation in private projects receiving public support. For example, firms seeking Tax Increment Financing assistance must prepare Economic Opportunity Plans, outlining how minorities will be included in the construction phase of the development project. Projects and firms that receive tax abatements or other incentives geared towards stimulating the economy should not only be required to offer benchmarks for minority and disadvantaged involvement out the programs outset, but also be required to document inclusion on an ongoing basis. To spread the benefit of these incentives throughout the economy, the city should implement rigorous monitoring of these performance goals. By implementing performance monitoring, the city clearly demonstrates its commitment to expanded economic opportunities and to holding incentive recipients accountable.

Supporting Small Business

In addition to MBEC, other programs seek to create opportunities for a broad spectrum of firms to participate in the local economy, but these programs are not easily accessed by those entities that could most benefit from them. Minority and disadvantaged businesses are not alone when it comes to difficulty accessing the city's economic development programs. Currently, many of the city's grant and loan programs are too cumbersome, creating a barrier to enterprises ill equipped to deal with lengthy and onerous application procedures. While larger companies may have the resources to complete the process, for many smaller firms, including minority and disadvantaged businesses, simply figuring out which agency to contact can be overwhelming.

The city's Commerce Department, the Philadelphia Industrial Development Corporation and the Philadelphia Commercial Development Corporation each offer economic development programs that could assist small and minority firms. While the Mayor's Business Action Team seeks to coordinate the city's economic development activity, "one-stop shopping" remains elusive. Additionally, the application process for these programs should be streamlined and simplified, taking into account the capacity of firms applying. The city should charge a single entity with serving smaller firms so that they have equal access to city business opportunities and programs. By having a dedicated program for these firms, it would ensure that larger companies do not squeeze out smaller firms seeking assistance.

Gaming

Philadelphia will soon face a change in the economic landscape of the city that was not anticipated at the time of the initial publication of *Philadelphia: A New Urban Direction*. The Pennsylvania General Assembly enacted legislation in July 2004 that will allow a limited number of slot parlors to operate in the Commonwealth. The passage was driven by the desire for a new revenue source. Tax revenue generated from gaming venues will be used in part to lower Property Taxes throughout the state, except in Philadelphia, where proceeds will be used to lower the Wage Tax. Many have debated the wisdom of legalized gambling, spanning several years, but the time to debate the merits of gaming has passed. Attention should now be focused on ensuring that Philadelphia reaps the largest amount of benefits while minimizing any negative impacts.

The new law provides for 14 slot machine facilities to operate throughout Pennsylvania, including non-racetrack, freestanding facilities, two of which are to be in Philadelphia. Once all the facilities are up and running, they are expected to generate $3 billion in tax revenue annually. One third of the gaming revenues will go to the Commonwealth for tax relief, five percent will be used to repay loans for capital projects, and four percent will be remitted to the communities that host the slot facilities. Other beneficiaries of gaming revenue include the horse racing industry and the expansion of the Pennsylvania Convention Center in Philadelphia.

The introduction of slots gaming will have a variety of impacts — social, physical, and economic — on Philadelphia. Therefore, careful management of the implementation and oversight of gaming is essential. A commission comprising individuals selected by the Governor and state legislative leaders will oversee this new industry as the Gaming Control Board. The Gaming Control Board will award licenses to operate slot facilities and participate in selecting locations, with some involvement of local authorities, as mandated by a recent Pennsylvania Supreme Court decision. Given the potentially large scale of the slot parlors in Philadelphia — up to 5,000 slot machines in each — the crowds they are expected to draw will place new demands on the city's services and infrastructure. In comparison, not one of Mississippi's 29 facilities has more than 2,700 slot machines.

Applicants for a slot machine license are required to provide a site plan for their proposed facility. It is imperative that the members of the Gaming Control Board and the city itself consider how these proposed facilities would fit into the surrounding neighborhood, architecturally and socially. Like many proposed large projects in Philadelphia, such as stadia and the Pennsylvania Convention Center, proper review of its impact is warranted, as once these facilities are built there is little opportunity to make changes. Ensuring the continued vibrancy and diversity of the city's neighborhoods is essential to maintaining the quality of life that residents and visitors demand. Philadelphia is too complex and diverse to ever be defined by the presence of gaming, unlike Atlantic City and Las Vegas, where gaming is the dominant industry. The gaming venues should be designed to compliment the city's array of business, cultural, institutional, and residential assets.

Furthermore, it is imperative that the facilities be evaluated on the basis of their impact on city services. Key to the success of these venues is drawing a crowd. While Philadelphia has embraced the tourism and hospitality industry, anytime a new mass of people are attracted to an area, new needs are created. This new market will impact on traffic, mass transit, parking, sanitation, public safety, and other service and quality of life issues.

To ensure that the sites finally selected maximize the economic benefit to the city, a proactive approach on the part of the local government is vital. Active analysis of potential locations has been undertaken by the to determine which sites are the most desirable. By presenting well-reasoned recommendations, the city can influence the decisions of developers and policy makers in Harrisburg.

While it remains to be seen what sites will be chosen for Philadelphia's slot parlors and who will be making the various decisions, elected, business, and civic leaders must use this as an opportunity to plan for the future. The city should champion potential sites for their suitability for hosting slot venues and complementary uses, as well as future expansion. Design and use guide-lines should be promulgated to encourage a smooth integration into the urban fabric.

The introduction of gaming in Philadelphia should also be viewed as an economic devel-opment opportunity for the entire city. Potential gaming operators' applications for licenses should address more than the physical features, but should also include plans for local hiring and contracting to enhance the Philadelphia economy. Philadelphians must possess the skills needed for casino operations. For the City of Philadelphia to receive the largest possible economic and budgetary benefit, it is important the share of employees that are Philadelphians be maximized. The city should help coordinate the local hospitality industry and education sector to provide appropriate training to give citizens the tools needed to succeed. In addition to the jobs created directly in the slots facilities, opportunities will be created for providers of supplies and services to the casinos, and it would be desirable for much of this business to flow into our neighborhoods. The city should advocate for local purchasing by the gaming facility operators. The University of Pennsylvania's Supplier Diversity Program can serve as a model for supporting local businesses. The University is committed to identifying local minority, disadvantaged, and small businesses to add economic and social vitality to both Penn and the surrounding community. By following a similar course, gaming venues can maximize the positive economic impact upon Philadelphia.

By planning ahead and anticipating costs, we can ensure that the revenue Philadelphia receives as a result of the introduction of legalized slot machines has the greatest positive impact possible on the lives of Philadelphians. Although the revenues from gambling are several years off, and the actual amount of money Philadelphia will receive remains unknown, careful preparation for the impacts of gambling on Philadelphia can help us hit the jackpot.

RECOMMENDATIONS FOR ACTION

The city should streamline its regulatory processes and make them user friendly.

Action Steps

- Adopt a modern zoning code and comprehensive plan.
- Review and implement the recommendations of the Building Industry of America.

Fiscal Impact

- Short-term operating costs for plan formulation and regulatory changes.
- Potential long-term revenue growth from increased business activity.

The city should develop a clear approach to and a comprehensive strategy for economic development.

Action Steps:

- Rigorously review the array of economic development programs offered, and eliminate any that duplicate efforts or provide a poor value for each dollar invested.
- Adopt guidelines to evaluate requests for public money to support private sector economic expansion
- Identify creative revenue sources to fund the Philadelphia's arts and cultural establishments.

Fiscal Impacts:

- Potential short-term costs associated with performance reviews and policy development and implementation
- Potential long-term savings from more efficient use of economic development resources.

- Potential revenue increases from expanded economic activity.
- Potential revenue increases for arts and culture institutions.

The city should engage all segments of Philadelphia's population in economic development activities.

Action Steps:

- Implement the recommendations made by the Controller's Office for Minority Business Enterprise Council, including the development of goals and collection of performance data, to ensure minority and disadvantaged firms participate in wealth creation and job growth.
- Establish rigorous monitoring of minority participation performance goals.
- Designate a single entity with serving smaller firms so that they have equal access to city business opportunities and programs.

Fiscal Impacts:

- Potential new operating costs associated with dedicated programs for small businesses.
- Potential new expenses for administrative improvements at MBEC.
- Potential revenue increases from increased economic activity.

The city should prepare for the introduction of gaming to maximize positive outcomes.

Action Steps:

- Champion potential sites for their suitability for hosting slot venues and complementary uses, as well as future expansion opportunities.
- Coordinate with the local hospitality industry and education sectors to provide appropriate training to give citizens the tools needed to succeed in the gaming industry.
- Advocate for local purchasing by the gaming facility operators.

Fiscal Impacts:

- Potential increased administrative costs.
- Potential increased revenue from job creation and gaming activities.

EDUCATION — CREATING A SYSTEM OF PUBLIC EDUCATION FOR ALL PHILADELPHIA FAMILIES.

Philadelphia can provide every child with an opportunity. Education is about opportunity, an opportunity for personal growth and development. It can provide a city with a more informed population, able to make more knowledgeable life choices and to more intensely participate in the life of the city. It can provide businesses with an intelligent and well-developed workforce, attracting new firms to the region. It can provide each person with the knowledge and skills needed to progress toward a more promising future.

In the first edition of *Philadelphia: A New Urban Direction*, the Controller's Office called for significant changes to the management, funding and classroom environments of the Philadelphia School District. Since then, the city and state's elected leaders came to a consensus about the need for sweeping changes to the manner in which the city educates its children. While the form of change has not been what the Controller's Office envisioned in 1999, the methods and objectives pursued, such as increasing instruction quality and amount of instruction, share the same goals.

The School Reform Commission

In 2000, citing constant and non-improving poor performance on the Pennsylvania System of School Assessment and Scholastic Aptitude tests, the Commonwealth named Philadelphia one of eleven school districts in the Pennsylvania's Education Empowerment Act for potential state takeover. In the summer of 2001, Edison, Inc. was hired to evaluate the condition of the Philadelphia School District and make recommendations for takeover. Edison recommended that 100 of the district's under-performing schools be placed under private management, that a five-member School Reform Commission (SRC) to replace the school board, and the central administration of the district be contracted out. In December of 2001, Pennsylvania's Education Secretary signed a Declaration of Distress for the district, transferring control of the Philadelphia School District to the newly-created School Reform Commission. Philadelphia agreed to submit to a "friendly takeover," in exchange for retaining management of the District's Central Office, gaining more state funding for the district and the ability to appoint one of the new Commission's five members. By 2002, the SRC had concluded that 70 of the 265 Philadelphia schools would be managed by private, for-profit providers, non-profit providers, or in conjunction with Temple University and the University of Pennsylvania, representing the largest experiment in the use of private and charter schools in the United States. Twenty-one of the 70 were also reconstituted under the district's new management model, to be implemented by the Office of Restructured Schools.

The School Reform Commission articulated goals, manifested in its Declaration of Education, to be achieved by June of 2008. The School District planned to increase early literacy, aiming for at least 85 percent of all students entering kindergarten to have attended preschool and at least 80 percent of third graders to read on grade level. Academic achievement across the district will improve from being among the worst performers in the state to at least meet average performance levels. The SRC declared that the district will meet the standards of the federal No Child Left Behind legislation, and that 80 percent of all students in grades three through 11 will perform at or above the proficient level in reading, mathematics, and science. College aptitude test scores will rise to meet or exceed the national average. Eighty-five percent of the district's high school students will graduate, and 80 percent of graduates will enroll in some form of post-secondary education. The Philadelphia School District also aimed to decrease disparities based on race, ethnicity, gender, and socioeconomic status to less than 10 percent across all academic measures. Generally, the SRC has committed the district to providing students with safer and more orderly environments in which to learn, increased partnerships with parents and community organizations, sought to provide equitable access to the district's resources to all students, and to create efficient, effective district support services. A zero-tolerance discipline policy was implemented, with alternate schools for violators, a transition to K-8 schools, facility improvements, and a greater focus on academic standards and accountability. "Content coaches" were hired for each school to assist in the district's core curricula in math and literacy, and New Teacher Coaches were hired to assist the assimilation and professional development of beginning teachers.

Philadelphia's schools have shown improvement since the School Reform Commission took control of the district. The SRC's moves to standardize the curriculum and increase the amount of instructional time through summer, after-school, and Saturday programs appear to have been successful. In early 2005, the District's independent Accountability Review Council recognized strong improvements in the district. In 2002, only 22 of the district's school attained Adequate Yearly Progress, as defined by the federal No Child Left Behind legislation. Yet by 2004, 160 of Philadelphia's 265 public schools had improved performance on PSSA exams to meet Adequate Yearly Progress standards. A longitudinal study measuring the academic progression of a single class across different years also revealed marked improvement in students' standardized test achievements. From 2002 to 2005, students improved in 23 of 26 academic categories, including by more than 10 percent in 12 categories and over 20 percent in three categories. Just over 30 percent of the second-grade class of 2002 scored at or above the national average on the exam, but by 2005 as fifth graders, 40.6 percent of the class scored at or above the national average.

In 1999, the Controller's Office also recommended that funding for the District be enhanced, through more equitable funding from the Commonwealth and compensation for revenues lost as a result of tax abatements and incentives given to stimulate economic activity. While additional state funding accompanied the formation of the SRC, to date, the Commonwealth has not fundamentally altered its formula for distribution for education fund. To mitigate the negative impact of economic development incentives on the District, recent TIF projects have partially or fully omitted Use and Occupancy Tax revenues, allowing those to accrue to the District as normal. Under the school reform legislation the city pledged to allocate an additional $45 million to the schools annually, $20 million and a millage shift in the Real Estate Tax to generate an addition $25 million from that revenue source for the schools. Given increasing Real Estate Tax collections, the city's contribution will continue to grow in future years.

While recent improvements should be lauded, the District has clearly not improved enough to be content in their progress and must fervently continue in its efforts to improve the opportunities for its students. The School Reform Commission must continue to seek out and employ methods to improve the district. However, the CEO of Schools and the School Reform Commission must be given adequate time to implement their complete plan for the school district and to allow for reforms to take effect. Summary evaluation of the success of the takeover before June of 2008 would be premature. Given the extraordinary progress made, it would be detrimental to alter the School District's management. The city should refrain from seeking to governance changes before all the reforms are implemented and given time to take root.

While it may be too soon to evaluate the overall success of the School Reform Commission's efforts, active monitoring, and assessment of all aspects of the school district — financial, administrative, academic and otherwise — is critical. The school district, as with the city itself, needs to be fiscally responsible, engaging in active performance measurement and management to ensure the most effective and efficient use of financial resources. The School Reform Commission needs to dedicate itself to keeping outstanding debt to manageable levels to prevent the costs of servicing the debt from impeding present spending initiatives. The city should encourage constant and rigorous evaluation of the impacts of the reforms to better target the use of funds, preventing expenditure on programs that are proving ineffectual and increasing spending on those that are proving successful. Philadelphia's School District must employ all possible means to guarantee that they are receiving the maximum return on each dollar spent; failing to do so would be a large disservice to our children and our city.

Formal control and influence over the operations of the school district is removed from the hands of Philadelphia's government. The city lacks the ability to directly create policy for the district or to direct the creation of its budget. However, Philadelphia can influence the environment in which the school district operates. A study conducted for the Office of the Controller's *2005 Mid-Year Economic and Financial Report* found that a key factor influencing educational performance was poverty, and that the safety of schools also appears to affect students' academic performance. Despite the connection between poverty and proficiency, the federal No Child Left Behind legislation does not account for socioeconomic conditions faced by a school district when allocating funds. As poverty reduction is beyond the control of any one school, the mandates of federal legislation could feasibly result in the School District losing considerable funding if the economic conditions deteriorate and more people fall into poverty. Given the relationship between test scores and the percentage of students who are economically disadvantaged, the city should therefore consider economic growth and development in areas stricken by poverty a priority, as well as lobbying for changes to the No Child Left Behind legislation to account for socioeconomic conditions when calculating funding levels. Moreover, the Philadelphia Police Department should seek to increase connectivity with the school district, engaging in information and resource sharing to prevent, as much as possible, violence in and around the city's schools.

High-quality education is more than achieving a certain average test score; improvement on standardized tests may not be indicative of a school's level of quality and performance, or its lack thereof. The School Reform Commission must assure that Philadelphia's children experience in the classroom translates to abilities for college and beyond. It is and will be a challenge, but the Philadelphia School District must ensure that its students are prepared to succeed in the world—a task essential to the future economic vitality and social well-being of the city.

RECOMMENDATIONS FOR ACTION

The city should refrain from altering the management structure of the Philadelphia School District until reforms are fully implemented and evaluated.

The City should work with the Philadelphia School District to address safety and poverty issues in and around schools.

Action Steps:

- Coordinate public safety resources and strategies in and around schools.

- Develop and implement programs in concert with all areas of city government to reduce poverty.

Fiscal Impacts:

- Potential costs associated with increased policing.

- Potential costs associated with poverty reduction programs.

- Potential savings in criminal justice costs from reduced crime.

- Potential savings from decreased service demands as a result of declining poverty.

- Potential increased revenues from expanded business activity made possible by improved workforce quality.

The city should encourage continued and increased performance evaluation of the School Reform Commission's efforts.

Action Step:

- Work with City Council for greater disclosure of academic statistics and benchmarks during the annual budget appropriation process.

Fiscal Impacts:

- Potential increased costs for data collection and analysis.

- Potential savings from improved efficiency.

HOUSING — CREATING A MARKET FOR PHILADELPHIA'S VACANT HOUSING STOCK

In the original edition of *Philadelphia: A New Urban Direction*, the Controller's Office offered recommendations to increase the demand for housing in our neighborhoods to combat the physical manifestations of decades of population loss. We stated that the city needed to marshal resources to strategically target abandoned properties for demolition and stimulate the market for real estate through calculated acquisition and incentive programs for redevelopment. The Controller's Office also recommended that programs to assist homeowners maintain their properties to prevent blight. A comprehensive program of property demolition and acquisition was called for, and in 2001 an initiative that incorporated those recommendations was unveiled, called the Neighborhood Transformation Initiative.

Neighborhood Transformation

The Neighborhood Transformation Initiative (NTI) included many of the actions proposed in the first edition of *Philadelphia: A New Urban Direction* for dealing with the city's vacant properties. At that time, Philadelphia had nearly 30,000 vacant buildings, a quarter of which had been deemed dangerous. Previously, annual demolition and revitalization efforts had not been able to make a dent into the city's vast stock of vacant land and structures, many of which were classified as imminently dangerous by the Department of Licenses and Inspections. The NTI program sought to address this problem by completing 14,000 demolitions, including all dangerous buildings, over five years, as well as attacking the root causes of blight and disinvestment. It was hoped that by concentrating the city's efforts and resources in this area the ongoing need for demolition could be reduced. City Council authorized a bond issue to obtain as much funding as annual $20 million debt service payments could support. The funding, eventually totaling nearly $300 million, was allocated to support the demolition, land assembly, redevelopment, as well as loan and grant programs and technology investments.

In addition to the bond proceeds, which are projected to be completely spent by fiscal year 2007, the NTI Program is supplemented by other activities funded with operating expenditures aimed at improving the city's neighborhoods, leveraging an array of public and private funding sources, as the Controller's Office initially recommended. Strategies include greening and tree pruning, mural painting and graffiti removal, encouraging minority business opportunities, and financial education. The associated initiatives utilize resources provided by the city's general fund, the state and federal government, recycled acquisition funds, the newly created Housing Trust Fund, partnerships with private sector entities, and the Philadelphia Housing Authority.

According to the most recent NTI program statement and budget, the allocation of resources was to be guided by several key principles:
- Using planning as an investment tool
- Balancing affordable and market rate housing
- Investing public funds to stimulate private market activity
- Maximizing private capital and minimizing public dollars
- Linking housing with other public and private investments

Given the ongoing nature of the program, the degree of success achieved by NTI in rebuilding neighborhoods cannot yet be fully assessed. NTI and other factors, such as the city's 10-year tax abatement program, historically low mortgage interest rates, and a nationwide trend of a return to downtown living have combined to spur reinvestment in parts of Philadelphia. NTI has played a significant supporting role in revitalizing certain sections of the city, but has fallen short of meeting all of its initial goals. Although literature about the NTI program emphasizes planning to guide revitalizations efforts, of the 34 NTI Planning Areas throughout the city, only four plans had been completed as of August 2005. Also, the computer system that will allow the city to track properties as they wend their way through the process of acquisition, assembly, and disposition has yet to be completed. The original projections of how many vacant properties could be demolished was overly optimistic, with rising costs and other factors leading to lower revised projections. Clearly, the NTI bond proceeds will not be sufficient to eliminate the city's vast stock of vacant structures.

With NTI demolition expenditures exhausted, operating dollars are once again being allocated to fund demolition activities, the city simply does not have the resources to demolish or rehabilitate all of the underutilized buildings in Philadelphia. The ultimate success of NTI hinges upon the program's ability to engender a sustained private market response to the public inter- vention. To achieve the goal of high-quality neighborhoods throughout Philadelphia once the demolition resources are exhausted, the city should continue programs that prevent structures from becoming blighted and abandoned and encourage new development. Programs to prevent blight currently include financial education and counseling, low-interest loans and grants for home repair and modification, and support for the construction of affordable housing.

The recent surge in property conversion and construction has not been equally spread throughout the city, and neighborhoods that could most benefit from the injection of jobs and activity continue to be passed over. To steer development to disadvantaged locations the city has typically offered monetary incentives and tax abatements. While at times a successful strategy, there is the potential that these inducements that lower the cost of doing business are simply moving economic activity to less efficient locations in the city. As discussed elsewhere in this chapter, outdated zoning and incompatible land programs slow the development process and increase costs. An alternative mechanism that may prove more useful and effective would be the completion of the neighborhood plans to inspire potential investors, coupled with clear zoning and design guidelines. The city should offer modernized zoning and plans to guide redevelopment in all target areas.

Under NTI, nearly $90 million will be spent to purchase land to be held for future devel- opment, rather than immediate resale or redevelopment. This represents over 60 percent of the total land-acquisition budget. The absence of neighborhood plans to guide the decision making about what properties to acquire and the slow process of acquisition hinder the ability of the city to capitalize on the surge in real estate values and frenzy for development.

Buying and Selling City Property

The city needs to be better equipped to rapidly respond to ever changing market conditions. This can be accomplished through changes in state legislation. To reduce the costs and time required to acquire property in Philadelphia, the city should lobby for enabling legislation that would permit the city to take ownership of properties more quickly in certain cases, such as when a neighborhood organization initiates court action to take over and improve blighted properties or when the tax liens exceed more than one and a half times the market value.

Once the city has successfully acquired properties and has a plan for the appropriate reuse, rapid disposition that allows sale proceeds to be reinvested in other neighborhood revitalization efforts should be a priority. Unfortunately, our fragmented government structure creates a barrier to speedy disposition. There is a seemingly endless array of local government entities with property to sell, including the Department of Public Property, the Redevelopment Authority, the Sheriff's Office, the Office of Housing and Community Development, the Philadelphia Housing Development Corporation, and the Philadelphia Industrial Development Corporation. While there seems to be no end of agencies with properties to sell, there is no single source that interested buyers can turn to in order to find information about all available land and buildings.

To get the best prices for our properties, we need to reach the widest universe of possible buyers. In addition to reaching many potential purchasers, Philadelphia must strive to make it easy to learn about what we have for sale, rather than having to contact numerous agencies. Since the Administration has not yet been able to realign its housing agencies, as called for at the outset of its blight elimination efforts, perhaps another approach is warranted to quickly move these properties into private ownership. The city should partner with the private sector to designate a single entity for the efficient sale of surplus properties.

The City of Baltimore has achieved success in transferring properties into private ownership in disadvantaged neighborhoods through an innovative program that is a partnership between public and private entities. Project SCOPE — Selling City-Owned Properties Efficiently — is a joint venture between the Baltimore Efficiency and Economy Foundation and the Greater Baltimore Board of Realtors. Realtors, earning a commission on the sales, could market and sell the city's abandoned properties quickly. To ensure that the sales generate not only revenue for the city, but also a positive impact on neighborhoods, many of the properties must be rehabilitated and owner-occupied within 18 months. Through partnering with the private sector to market and sell city-owned properties NTI could more quickly direct investment to neighborhoods in need.

RECOMMENDATIONS FOR ACTION:

The city should continue programs that prevent blight and abandonment.

Action Steps:

- Analyze the performance of existing programs.
- Identify the most efficient and effectives of preventing blight.
- Allocate adequate resources for those programs.

Fiscal Impacts:

- Potential costs associated with program administration and grants.
- Potential savings from reduced blight.

The city should complete plans and modernize zoning to guide revitalization and acquisition efforts.

Action Steps:

- Review and update zoning code.
- Complete neighborhood plans for NTI target areas.
- Coordinate neighborhood plans with comprehensive plan for the city.

Fiscal Impacts:

- Potential costs associated with plan formulation and review.
- Potential revenue increases from private investment

The city should lobby for legislation to speed the property acquisition process.

Action Step:

- Work with state officials to pass legislation to reduce barriers to strategic property acquisition.

Fiscal Impacts:

- Potential costs associated with lobbying efforts.
- Potential savings from streamlined property acquisition.

The city should partner with the private sector to speed the sale of properties for redevelopment.

Action Steps:

- Designate a single city agency for the sale of surplus property, including parcels owned by quasi-governmental agencies.

- Partner with private realtors to market and sell public-owned real estate.

Fiscal Impacts:

- Potential savings from elimination of duplication of effort.

- Potential revenue increases from higher sale values.

LAW ENFORCEMENT — CREATING A SAFER PHILADELPHIA

In the first edition of *Philadelphia: A New Urban Direction*, the Controller's Office made a series of recommendations aimed at removing the threat of gun violence from Philadelphia, including requirements for gun-safety technology. Crime and threats to public safety, particularly violence involving hand guns, continue to plague Philadelphia. In 2005, the city's homicide rate has increased, despite a nationwide trend in the reduction of gun violence. Important steps have been taken to address the problem. Still, over 80 percent of homicides in the city involve a hand gun. Philadelphia is not alone in this plight. Boston, while recording only about 20 percent of the murders that occurred in Philadelphia, had the same ratio of fatalities caused by a hand gun. Reducing gun violence remains an imperative in order to improve the quality of life in Philadelphia.

Although the city has not yet been able to compel mandatory gun safety devices, the city has employed new strategies in crime fighting. In response to the public outcry for greater security and less crime, Philadelphia instituted the Safe Streets Program in April 2002, which sought to disrupt the city's drug trade and thus reduced the associated violence. This program built upon on the earlier "Operation Sunrise" initiative, which was an unprecedented anti-crime program coordinated among city, state, and federal law enforcement agencies to attack drug-dealing and violent crime in one of the city's most crime-ridden neighborhoods. Safe Streets was aimed at not only drug dealers, but also at ridding the city of open air drug markets and corners. Police officers were stationed at high crime locations on a continuous basis. The Philadelphia Police Department states that this effort was successful in improving the safety of previously dangerous neighborhoods, but it appears that drug dealing activities moved from open air markets to indoor locations. It is not yet clear whether this evolution is an improvement. While the program may have had a modicum of success, it was not without expense. According to figures available to the Controller's Office, police overtime more than doubled to over $70 million in the first full fiscal year the program was in existence. Other costs associated with the Safe Streets initiative, such as increased obligations associated with prosecution, probation, and incarceration has been less readily quantifiable. As Philadelphia continues to address safety and quality-of-life issues, additional efforts are necessary.

Coordinated Crime Fighting

As the Controller's Office had recommended in the first edition of *Philadelphia: A New Urban Direction*, recently a broad cross section of government and law enforcement officials came together to improve their strategies and coordination for reducing violent crime in this city. This effort produced a legislative action plan entitled "Blueprint for a Safer Philadelphia." Many of the proposals in the document have already been implemented, including a new law that imposes a mandatory five-year sentence for people convicted of drug dealing while in possession of a firearm, and educational programs about juvenile justice.

Unlike many summits and panels convened to address the city's ills, the interdisciplinary approach and coordinated effort of the "Blueprint for a Safer Philadelphia" has swiftly been translated into legislation and crime fighting programs. The city should utilize a similar approach to address other public safety issues. The process and success of this approach should be duplicated to comprehensively address quality-of-life crimes without unnecessarily diverting resources away from violent crime fighting and prevention efforts. As we had recommended in 1999, the city has invested in red-light cameras at some locations as a means of reducing quality-of-life crimes using passive crime-fighting techniques.

Specialized Courts

In 1999, the Controller's Office recommended increasing specialized courts to improve adjudication efforts in Philadelphia. In 2005, the city introduced "Gun Court" in response to the growing number of crimes committed using hand guns or the illegal possession of a hand gun, as well as the growing danger to the communities when illegal guns are on the street. It is hoped that Gun Court will provide a measure of prevention before shots are fired. Every year, Philadelphia police recover some 5,000 guns — most of them semiautomatic handguns, and many from murder scenes. There are thought to be thousands more illegal guns on city streets, turning petty feuds and arguments into deadly violence. Gun Court requires a partnering of pretrial services, probation and the trial court. It is designed to handle all cases where the most serious charge is a violation of the uniform firearms act. The intention is that the trial judge assigned to these cases will be able to hold 10 bench trials a day; this includes all pretrial motions, other than motions to quash and bail motions, to be heard by the motions judge. Currently, there are about 400 cases in the active inventory that qualify for Gun Court. The life cycle of a Gun Court case is approximately 120 days to disposition, compared to 180 days when the charges were heard in Municipal Court. The new court has been in operation since January 10, 2005 and is scheduled to conclude on June 30, 2006 unless otherwise extended. The city should carefully track the outcomes and costs of this initiative to determine whether it is successful in removing guns from the streets before violence occurs.

Gun Control

As we had recommended, the city continued its effort to bolster gun control laws in Philadelphia with the introduction of several restrictive ordinances. The intention is to control the number of guns purchased or transferred in a month to one per applicant, and to make it illegal for persons to act as straw purchasers of firearms, in to evade the one gun per month purchase limitation. In addition, legislation has been introduced making it illegal for anyone to possess a firearm if that person is subject to a protection against abuse order. However, without passage of authorizing legislation by the Pennsylvania General Assembly, the city is powerless to enact any of these ordinances.

The Philadelphia Police Department's mission is to ensure the best quality of life for the citizens of Philadelphia. To help achieve this goal, the Philadelphia Police Department recently announced the formation of a new division specifically targeting gun violence in Philadelphia. This division will be under the command of a new Deputy Commissioner with the goal of being proactive in crime fighting through combining problem analysis and strategy development with manpower. The head of this division will also coordinate and act as a liaison between the communities, politicians, the clergy, and other law enforcement agencies. This new unit will have the ability to draw on any and all resources available within the Department. The hope is that this unit will take a more holistic approach to crime fighting rather than concentrate on just making arrests and instead prevent the crime before it is committed. The success or failure of this initiative will be measured not only by arrest statistics, but also by citizen satisfaction and gun confiscations.

RECOMMENDATIONS FOR ACTION

The city should monitor the costs and benefits of Gun Court to determine whether the program should be extended or expanded.

Action Steps:

- Identify, collect, and analyze performance data for Gun Court.

- Utilize information to guide policymaking on specialized courts.

Fiscal Impacts:

- Potential increased costs for data collection and analysis.

- Potential savings from streamlined procedures and reduced crime.

The city should convene a summit of law enforcement, government and community representatives to craft a legislative action plan to reduce quality-of-life crime.

Action Steps:

- Coordinate stakeholders to craft strategies for reducing quality-of-life crime.

- Work with state and local legislators to swiftly enact necessary legislation.

- Implement coordinated strategies.

Fiscal Impacts:

- Potential costs associated with policy formulation and implementation.

- Potential savings in criminal justice expenses through elimination of duplication of effort and reduced crime.

HOMELAND SECURITY — PREPARING PHILADELPHIA FOR EMERGENCIES

In the first edition of *Philadelphia: A New Urban Direction* we could not anticipate the terrorist attacks of September 11, 2001 and the increased responsibilities of local government in protecting the lives and property of Philadelphians. Hurricane Katrina, which devastated the Gulf Coast in August 2005, further illustrated the immense task cities have in preparing for, responding to, and recovering from emergency situations. While Philadelphia has always acknowledged its role in emergency management and planned for both natural and man-made disasters, recent events have made clear that local governments can be overwhelmed in the face of an emergency and cannot rely on comprehensive, immediate assistance. As the nation's security professionals and government agencies have repeatedly pointed out, it is impossible to protect everything. It is possible, however, to protect those "somethings" that are vital to the lives of Americans and the continuity of our economy and our society. Decisions must be made about how to allocate the nation's resources and set priorities in our domestic counter-terrorism and homeland-security programs and operations, given the uncertainties related to the nature, timing, and location of terrorist attacks. Given our new awareness of the importance of homeland security and emergency preparedness and the role of local governments, the Controller's Office offers recommendations to ensure that Philadelphians are adequately and efficiently protected.

It has been a widespread misconception that state and federal government resources will be available to respond to major disasters, but recent events reveal that this is not the case. Addressing state and local authorities, Department of Homeland Security (DHS) Secretary Chertoff made the situation poignantly clear, stating "You are the front line of defense." Though state and local governments have received substantial amounts of funding for homeland security programs and projects in the four years since the attacks of September 11, 2001, procedures and standards for federal communication and cooperation with sub-national homeland security offices and for identifying effective security measures have yet to be established. From the perspective of America's cities, DHS remains only in the early stages of its efforts to coordinate its work with state and local governments and the private sector. The lack of clear guidelines for preventing and managing terrorist attacks and other emergencies poses a serious problem for the state and local governments that have been delegated this responsibility.

Benchmarks for Preparedness

Philadelphia's resources for counter-terrorism, homeland security, and emergency management may be inadequate or misallocated since there are no guidelines for what "prepared" means. DHS is only now developing the clear standards and principles that are relevant to evaluating the likelihood of terrorist attacks and their expected consequences, four years after the attacks of September 11, 2001. The city should work with other local governments to demand guidelines and benchmarks from the federal government for emergency preparation activities. Currently, some federal funding is awarded to localities on a competitive basis, but without a clear assessment of the likely threats and the existing preparedness level, allocations are less likely to be driven by true need.

The lack of coordination and clear operating standards is illustrated by the now-familiar DHS color-coded Threat Advisory, introduced in March 2002. As it is currently set up, the DHS Threat Advisory is intended to function in much the same way as the Defense Department's DEFCON (DEFense CONdition) System. At the federal level, coordination and analysis of information on potential terrorist actions that could affect domestic safety and security is managed by the DHS. DHS then reviews the information and, where there is a "clear and present danger," alerts state and local homeland security offices, as well as any private firms that are likely to be directly affected by the terrorist attacks projected by DHS analysts. The result is the now familiar color—coded terrorism Threat Advisory warning indicator with the five colors ranging from green ("Low Risk") to red ("Severe Risk").

The DHS Threat Advisory conditions do not provide state and local governments with information or direction on actions to be taken. Whereas the DEFCON System has established links between threat levels and the detailed action "scripts" to be followed by the Unified Commands of the military, the "on the ground" responsibilities for identifying and implementing responses to changes in the DHS Threat Advisory color codes — protecting assets such as transportation, utilities, and healthcare systems — is treated as the direct, independent responsibility of each state and local government and their homeland security and public safety departments.

Philadelphia cannot address preparedness issues alone, even if the city anticipates being primarily responsible in the event of a catastrophe. Federal and state resources, in addition to the cooperation of regional governments and the participation of key private sector interests, will be required for any comprehensive security planning effort to be successful. The City of Philadelphia is far too important and far too central to the overall economic viability of the nation to rely simply on ad hoc judgments based on out-dated security information, standards, and guidelines. What the 9/11 Commission, empanelled in late 2002 to provide a bipartisan account of the circumstances surrounding the terrorist attacks, termed "a failure of imagination" that led to an inability to foresee the events of September 11, 2001 could easily become the status quo if the nation's cities and smaller municipalities do not recognize that they, not the federal government, are "the front line of defense."

Coordinated Emergency Planning

The city should develop and implement effective and efficient counter-terrorism, homeland security, and emergency management programs and measures for Philadelphia's citizens, civic institutions, and businesses. Planning for government actors and functions alone will severely hamper response and recovery efforts. Partnerships with the non-profit and private sectors in planning will yield a more comprehensive approach to emergency management. Philadelphia must coordinate political, civic, and business leadership to ensure that local public and private service providers — police, fire, transportation, water, healthcare, sanitation, food, and so on — are equipped to manage the city's operations and services in the disasters to those previously witnessed at home and abroad.

The City of Philadelphia has already improved the capabilities of its first line of defense through the training and equipment of its first responders, but this is only a first step. It is evident that what is needed in order to respond to the types of terrorist attacks and emergency situations that are now occurring throughout the world are not just fire engines and ambulances, but a full range of coordinated public and private services. The city should develop and implement innovative counter-terrorism and homeland security programs and measures through the application of new procedures for developing detailed, updated due diligence assessments that reflect the significant changes in terrorism, the sources of terrorist threats, and the potential impacts of the kinds of terrorist attacks seen since September 11, 2001.

Assessing Risks

In the past, most organizations — public and private — have approached risk management using much the same type of actuarial methods and standards employed by the insurance industry. Regrettably, actuarially based insurance methods and standards are of little value with respect to preventing terrorist attacks, or for that matter, in planning for the mitigation of the impacts of major attacks on civilian populations and public and private infrastructure. To protect against attacks by terrorists, the city could adopt the same procedures and methods now used by experts in terrorism intelligence: assessments of the potential impacts of terrorist actions through the identification of the objectives, capabilities, and resources of each of the terrorist groups capable of operating in the US; and identification of the ways in which specific actions can exploit the gaps and vulnerabilities in our current security systems and procedures. While there is never certainty on either side, as with venture capital investments, informed planning and execution can substantially lower risks.

Although many security experts have assumed that the likely targets in Philadelphia would be symbolic locations — Independence Hall, the Liberty Bell, or even 30th Street Station — these are far less likely targets than the region's many key utilities, intra-urban and inter-regional transportation lines, and the chemical and pharmaceutical industries. As with security organizations, terrorist groups also have relatively limited resources to carry forward their objectives, and targets will undoubtedly be selected based on the kind of "leverage" that their operations can achieve with respect to their overall objectives. The Philadelphia region clearly has a variety of critical targets that could lead to such disruption and is unquestionably a target rich location for the kinds of terrorist groups now operating internationally and domestically. As such, the most likely objectives in the Greater Philadelphia region will be the social and economic disruption of the area's civilian population and, ultimately, the disruption of a critical sector of the US economy.

To guide future decision making in its homeland security planning, the city could establish a comprehensive Security Impact Assessment (SIA) to serve as a "security due diligence process" to support the development of workable standards for allocating resources and setting the priorities for investments in the city's and the region's security. Such a process should include well-documented, comprehensive standards and procedures that employ up-to-date, detailed intelligence data, expert-driven scenario generation methods, priority setting methods, and financial analysis tools to provide evaluations of the likelihood of attacks and determine the net benefit of specific recommendations for all governmental and private sector investments in security. Federal and state security agencies, research institutions, and private sector organizations should be included in the development of the SIA.

Without a formal due diligence process, Philadelphia may find it difficult to identify the secondary effects of terrorist attacks and, therefore, recognize the specific needs of first-responders, the equipment needed to maintain public utilities, sanitation, communications, and transportation — or even provide the region's citizens with the manuals and materials required for family protection. While the security standards will likely be developed and institutionalized by federal agencies, only the city and the private sector possesses the requisite detail of knowledge and experience to produce meaningful security recommendations for the region and to put operational recommendations into practice.

To keep its citizens safe, Philadelphia must employ the best available risk-management and risk-mitigation tools and procedures in order to develop appropriate security measures for the city and the region. The city should institute regular review and updating of emergency plans. The changing nature of potential threats and the city's staffing and resources make this essential. For example, following the inadequate evacuation of New Orleans before, during, and after Hurricane Katrina, the Controller's Office reviewed emergency management plans for Philadelphia. We found that the document, updated in 2002, designated the Deputy Mayor of Transportation as the key coordinator and planner for evacuations of the city. We noted that the position of Deputy Mayor of Transportation had not been filled since September 1999. Although such updates are already conducted, they are clearly not sufficient. The city could separate the plan creation and review functions to make sure that problems are not overlooked.

Emergency Plan Review and Revision

It is not enough however to simply make plans, the city, its residents and partners should all be capable of implementing them. While public release of certain homeland security and emergency planning is unnecessary and perhaps dangerous, many Philadelphians wish to have some basic information about how to respond in various hazardous situations. The city could improve its communication of emergency preparedness to residents by providing pamphlets or enhanced online resources.

Philadelphia has thus far been fortunate that it has not suffered a devastating natural or man-made disaster, but this cannot lead the city to shirk its responsibility to prepare for future emergencies. With preparedness planning based on relevant information and clear review procedures and standards, hopefully catastrophic events can be avoided. At a minimum, however, the City of Philadelphia must be fully prepared to accept its responsibility for coordinating the allocation and prioritization of security and emergency management resources.

RECOMMENDATIONS FOR ACTION:

The city should work with other local governments to demand guidelines and benchmarks from the federal government for emergency preparation activities.

Action Steps:

- Lobby for federal performance standards for emergency preparedness.

- Lobby for federal and state assistance based on potential threats and actual needs.

Fiscal Impacts:

- Potential costs associated with lobbying efforts.

- Potential savings from enhanced preparedness.

- Potential increased assistance for preparedness initiatives.

The city should develop and implement emergency management programs and measures for Philadelphia's citizens, civic institutions, and businesses.

Action Steps:

- Coordinate planning efforts of public, private, and non-profit entities to ensure a unified response to an emergency.

- Develop a Security Impact Assessment to identify likely threats and allocate resources efficiently and effectively.

- Communicate basic emergency preparedness information to the public.

Fiscal Impacts:

- Potential costs for plan development and information dissemination.

- Potential savings from improved efficiency.

The city should rigorously and regularly review and update emergency plans.

Action Steps:

- Establish policies for regular review of emergency plans.

- Separate plan creation and evaluation functions.

Fiscal Impacts:

- Potential costs for plan review.

- Potential savings from increased efficiency.

Tourism-Related Activities — Showcasing Philadelphia To The World

A new phrase has been imprinted on the minds of people throughout the Philadelphia region and beyond — "Philly's more fun when you sleepover." After a barrage of ads, it is clear that tourists agree — Philly IS more fun when you sleep over. According to the Greater Philadelphia Tourism Corporation, overnight visitorship in the region grew 41 percent between 1998 and 2003. Tourism promotion activities in the city have grown substantially since the initial publication of *Philadelphia: A New Urban Direction*, and new attractions and events, such as the National Constitution Center and Dali exhibit at the Philadelphia Museum of Art, have helped elevate the city to the highest ranks of tourist destinations. Public and private tourist attraction efforts continue to expand and evolve, with innovative efforts such as niche campaigns targeted to specific segments of the market, such as African-American, College Students, Gays, and Lesbians.

In 1999, we recommended that the various marketing efforts be consolidated to provide one-stop shopping for visitors and potential visitors, and to eliminate costly duplication of efforts. Although the various entities have not been combined, cooperation among the tourism promoters has led to coordinated advertising efforts and resources for visitors. The first edition of *Philadelphia: A New Urban Direction* also identified several potential sources for dedicated funding to support increased advertising and other tourism-related spending. Despite the well-documented positive impact of the promotion efforts, increased dedicated funding has not been secured. Ensuring that the tourism promotion agencies have adequate resources, either from increased revenues or elimination of duplicative efforts, remains a priority.

The Controller's Office also recommended that city assets should be utilized for tourism promotion. We proposed creating a Visitors' Center in City Hall, and adding a city store, exhibit space, cafes and public toilets. With the construction of the high-tech Independence Visitors Center at 5th and Chestnut, an additional site could now represent a duplication of effort, but cafes and public toilets remain desirable amenities for visitors, residents, and workers in the area, and represent an opportunity for revenue generation. Art exhibit programs in City Hall were expanded in 2003 to include the Student Exhibition, the National Arts Program Exhibition, and exhibitions devoted to community arts organizations, nonprofits, and other city agencies. While the city does not yet have a location to purchase half-price tickets to performing arts events, as the Controller's Office suggested, an online entity, the Philly Fun Guide, offers weekly discounts on performances, announced via email and on its website.

Tourist Transportation

Once Philadelphia attracts tourists, it has long been challenged with finding the right mechanism for moving then around the city. Allowing visitors easy access to a wide variety attractions and destinations promotes longer visits and higher spending. The first edition of *Philadelphia: A New Urban Direction* proposed a trolley route along Chestnut Street in Center City to link tourist destinations. Since then, there has been a virtual explosion in the number of tourist transportation options. There are two companies operating amphibious vehicles that travel on land and on water, a London-style double-decker tour bus, and the Phlash, which began as a Septa-run, city-subsidized tourist loop that is now privately-run and funded a mixture of fares, other revenues, and state subsidy. It is a testament to the success of the city's tourism attraction efforts that many of the tourist loops are private, for-profit ventures. Following the Controller's Office recommendation to eliminate duplication of effort, there are no longer multiple publicly-funded tourist loops with overlapping routes. We also recommended that visitors may be more comfortable making their way through the city in an enclosed walkway from the Pennsylvania Convention Center to Independence National Park, thereby removing pedestrians from the streets. The restored vibrancy of our city streets is dependent upon high pedestrian traffic, and the Controller's Office now recommends that rather than investing in infrastructure to remove tourists from our sidewalks, the city should continue efforts to upgrade the streetscape, with improved signage, lighting, cleanliness, and street furniture, to make it more inviting to pedestrians.

RECOMMENDATION FOR ACTION

The city should invest in improving the pedestrian environments linking tourist attractions.

Action Steps:

• Regularly assess the quality of the public environment in tourist areas.

• Continue working with other organizations to improve signage, lighting and the over character of the streetscape.

Fiscal Impacts:

• Capital costs associated with streetscape enhancements.

• Potential increased revenues from expanded tourist spending.

TRANSPORTATION — MOVING PHILADELPHIA'S MASSES

If the residents of the Greater Philadelphia Region are the area's lifeblood, then its transportation systems are the arteries, moving people and goods around the area to social and economic ends. The roads, highways, trains, and planes are vital for the maintenance, growth, and development of greater Philadelphia. An efficient and effective multi-modal transportation system can facilitate development, lessen environmental stress, and provide a boost to the region's economy. Selecting the correct mixture of transportation modes also affects air quality and safety. Philadelphia's transportation infrastructure forms a complex system of roads, rails, ports, mass transit, and airports, and this system requires both long-range planning and day-to-day operations management. While many of the issues surrounding transportation infrastructure and planning are regional in scope, the city can act strategically to meet the transportation needs for both people and goods.

Unfortunately, greater Philadelphia's transportation systems have not kept pace with the changing residential development and economic climate in the region. The system can be labeled as, at best, mature, and its radial design is insufficient to meet the intra-suburban transportation needs that comprise much of greater Philadelphia's total miles traveled. Moreover, people are commuting further than they once did; the lack of effective land use planning and continued sprawl has placed greater demands on the capacity of the system to transport people and freight further than originally envisioned.

In the first edition of *Philadelphia: A New Urban Direction*, we noted that an array of city and non-city agencies must coordinate their efforts to affect transportation policy and operations. The universe of actors in this arena has become more fragmented since that time. The Mayor's Office of Transportation, which through the 1990s coordinated policies on transportation operations and planning, has been absorbed into the Office of Strategic Planning within the Philadelphia City Planning Commission. This creates the potential for a disconnect between the operational and long-term policy formulation. Another recent change that has further decentralized transportation policy in Philadelphia has been the transfer of control of the Philadelphia Parking Authority to the Commonwealth. Given that so many actors outside the city also have influence over our transportation systems, to best meet the needs of Philadelphians, a comprehensive approach to transportation policy within city government is warranted. To improve the coordination of those aspects of transportation policy that the city directly controls, the city should amend the Charter to reorganize all responsibilities for transportation under a single department of agency. This would include consolidating duties related to streets maintenance, airports, docks, wharves, and long-term transportation planning. A consolidated transportation department could be more influential in working with state and federal partners, as well as other regional transportation stakeholders, such as the Delaware River Port Authority and PATCO. To further ensure that Philadelphia's vision for transportation is linked to the efforts other stakeholders, such SEPTA and the Delaware Valley Regional Planning Commission, the Mayor could use his appointment powers to create interlocking leadership to advance the city's goals.

A unified approach to transportation management and policy will enhance the city's ability to implement programs to reduce stress on Philadelphia's roads and bridges. In the first edition of *Philadelphia: A New Urban Direction*, we recommended that the city take steps to make mass transit the preferred mode of travel in Philadelphia to ease congestion and air pollution. The Controller's Office identified a number of service enhancements that could be made by SEPTA to make it a more efficient and attractive option for improving mobility in the region. Financial stress and other factors have been barriers to implementing many the suggestions, such as introduction of debit-card technology for fare collection and intelligent transportation technologies. Currently efforts are being made at the state-level to finding adequate, reliable funding for mass transit throughout the Commonwealth. It is hoped that a solution to SEPTA's fiscal woes will enable additional service enhancements.

In 1999, we suggested that the city offer its employees tax deductible mass transit vouchers, and in 2004 the city began a program to do so. To further encourage mass transit usage, we recommended policies to discourage all-day parking by setting a minimum charge, and encouraging short-term parking by setting maximum per hour fees, this has not yet been enacted. Residential parking permit areas have been expanded since 1999, as a result of resident requests, as we had proposed. The city has taken steps to reduce the air pollution produced by its fleet by purchase of hybrid vehicles, as the Controller's Office proposed.

As a major metropolis, Philadelphia's transportation network includes more than roads and mass transit, and the Controller's Office believes that maintaining alternative transportation infrastructures is essential to the economic health of the city and region. Adequate port, rail and airport facilities are necessary for regional growth and prosperity. Recent capital improvements and efforts to expand the number of carriers and destinations at the Philadelphia International Airport have contributed to an impressive 55-percent increase in passengers between 1995 and 2004 and lower average one-way fares, despite the high rate of flight delays. With this new traffic, congestion at the Philadelphia International Airport has become a threat to this vital economic engine. To sustain the airport's important impact upon regional economic development, the city should assure that the airport continues to run effectively and efficiently. The city could pursue securing the resources for needed updating and expansion of facilities to allow better on time service and the capacity for even more flights and passengers.

William Penn chose to locate Philadelphia at the narrowest point between the Delaware and Schuylkill Rivers, understanding the tremendous benefits to be derived from proximity to navigable waters. Today Philadelphia's Port, managed by the Philadelphia Regional Port Authority, remains a center of commerce and employment, but must be properly maintained to stay competitive. Since its designation as a Strategic Military Seaport in 2002, there has been an increase in activity, but the potential remains to capture a greater share of the shipping market. Although the Philadelphia Regional Port Authority is an independent agency of the Commonwealth, its economic and physical impacts upon the city make its viability an area of concern for local government. The city should support the dredging of the Delaware River to improve the city and region's economic vitality. The project, which will cost approximately $300 million, will be funded primarily with federal funds, but will require roughly $100 million in local marching funds from the states of New Jersey, Delaware, and Pennsylvania, as well as from the Delaware River Port Authority. Dredging of the Delaware River to add an additional 5 feet of depth should be deemed a priority, in order to compete with deeper nearby ports, as the additional depth is needed to accommodate today's larger ships. Failure to keep out waterways free and clear can limit the size and number of ships the port can accommodate and can result in decreased shipping activity.

RECOMMENDATION FOR ACTION

The city should reorganize all responsibilities for transportation under a single department of agency.

Action Steps:

- Amend the Charter to transfer all transportation-related duties to a single agency.

- Use mayoral appointments to transportation entities to create interlocking leadership.

Fiscal Impacts:

- Potential short-term costs associated with reorganization.

- Potential long-term savings from elimination of duplication of effort and improved governmental efficiency.

The city should pursue expansion of the Philadelphia International Airport.

Action Steps:

- Work with neighboring communities to mitigate any negative impacts associated with expansion.

- Secure necessary funding to complete currently proposed projects.

Fiscal Impacts:

- Potential costs associated with airport expansion.

- Potential revenue growth associate with increased capacity.

The city should support the dredging of the Delaware River to accommodate larger ships.

Action Step:

- Lobby state officials to ensure funding for channel deepening.

Fiscal Impacts:

- Potential short-term revenue increases from construction of project.

- Potential long-term revenue increases from expanded port activities.

SUSTAINABILITY — PROTECTING THE NATURAL AND BUILT ENVIRONMENT IN PHILADELPHIA

When William Penn founded Philadelphia in the 17th century, he had a vision of "a Greene Country Towne, which will never be burnt, and always wholesome." In the 21st century, the term "green" has a new connotation, but it is one that mirrors Penn's original intent. Penn wanted a city with lush plantings and a development plan that subscribed to the highest ideals in aesthetics and public safety. Philadelphia will not be a location of choice for residents and business in the future if we fail to uphold Penn's vision and the environment is allowed to deteriorate. The aesthetic, economic, and environmental health of our city must be sustained and improved. In order to pass on a livable city to future generations of Philadelphians, it is imperative that we pursue policies that meet the needs of today's citizens while protecting the resources needed for economic, social, and environmental well-being in the years to come. Ensuring global and local sustainability will require commitment and coordination from all segments of government and business, but individual jurisdictions can adopt transportation, energy, and land use policies to preserve and protect our communities.

Since the initial publication of *Philadelphia: A New Urban Direction*, environmental sustainability has increasingly become the purview of local governments. An erosion of federal standards and resources for maintaining environmental integrity has engendered an increase in the need for municipalities to take control over environmental policies. City mayors across the nation are taking leadership in this area, in part due to a lack of leadership at the federal level. In 2005, nearly 200 mayors, including Philadelphia's, endorsed the US Climate Protection Agreement. The need for the agreement arose from the failure of the United States to ratify the Kyoto Protocols, an international agreement designed to address climate disruption. Under the Climate Protection Agreement, participating cities commit to working towards the targets set forth in the Kyoto Protocols and urging other levels of government to enact policies to reduce greenhouse gas emission standards. Participating cities are implementing public education, anti-sprawl, and other programs to promote sustainability.

The City of Philadelphia has long had programs and policies intended to protect and preserve the city's environment. The city has worked with SEPTA to promote mass transit usage, to ease congestion, improve air quality and ensure efficient and affordable transportation for the city's residents, workers, and visitors. The Division of Air Management Services monitors air quality in the city and has completed an inventory of the city's global-warming emissions. Since 1994, the city has had a Municipal Energy Office charged with reducing energy usage in city-owned properties and lowering utility costs. In 1987, Philadelphia became the first major city in the nation to mandate recycling of refuse and garbage. Although Philadelphia has not yet achieved the rate of recycling that the original ordinance envisioned, these and other efforts can contribute to preserving the sustainability of Philadelphia's built and natural environments. Additional and expanded efforts can enable us to leave a cleaner, more livable city to our children. In a 2005 audit of the city's recycling program, the Controller's Office presented recommendations to achieve dramatic costs savings. Specific improvements recommended included expanding educational and incentive programs, increasing the scope of materials subject to mandatory recycling as soon as it becomes economically feasible to do so, and issuance of a detailed implementation plan and regular performance reports.

Innovative Energy Policy

The costs and negative environmental impacts of certain forms of energy consumption pose a threat to Philadelphia's economy and quality of life. Despite deregulation of electricity and natural gas provision in Pennsylvania, motivated in part to reduce customer rates through competition, Philadelphia residents and businesses face growing energy costs. Global concerns about the sustainability of energy resources require innovative solutions to maintain an adequate and affordable supply. Philadelphia will face negative economic and environmental impacts stemming from the increasing expense and scarcity of fossil fuels. Inadequate access to affordable energy can stifle economic growth, and the burning of fossil fuels creates air pollution, leading to environmental and personal health deterioration. Employing alternative energy sources and encouraging cost effective and environmentally sustainable energy usage can ensure that Philadelphia is well positioned to withstand any future disruptions in energy delivery. By proactively seeking renewable energy sources and encouraging energy efficiency on a grand scale, Philadelphia can potentially reduce the future costs of living and doing business here, while addressing issues of environmental quality.

Technological advances have made available numerous alternative fuel and renewable energy sources, but viability in Philadelphia is dependant on cost and potential for widespread application. One option currently being explored by the Philadelphia Gas Works (PGW) to reduce fuel costs and enhance supplies is increased usage of Liquefied Natural Gas (LNG). Through liquification, transportation, and storage of natural gas becomes possible over long distances where pipeline transport is neither feasible nor desirable. Once liquefied, natural gas requires 1/260 of the space necessary for storage. Natural gas can be liquefied in a refrigeration process and is then stored at a temperature of -260 F. For international transport, LNG is shipped in double hulled tankers and delivered to receiving terminals, where it is stored in specially built, heavily-insulated tanks.

Demand for natural gas continues to grow, and those enterprises with the capacity to fulfill the nation's demand for this energy source will reap economic benefits. The Philadelphia Gas Works is among several entities vying for a LNG terminal in the region, and there are approximately 50 proposals for new or expanded LNG plants nationwide. PGW expects significant financial benefits and employment growth from expanding its current facilities in Port Richmond, where two storage tanks currently hold nearly 50 million gallons of LNG. The fiscal health of PGW matters not only to its customers who may face rising gas rates, but to the City of

Philadelphia, to whom PGW is deeply indebted, owing $45 million, as well as annual rental payments of $18 million which are currently being waived.

President George W. Bush has indicated that LNG will be a key component of the strategy to meet the nation's energy needs, and envisions that the federal government will direct the site selection process for new facilities. As the site selection process will not be governed solely by market forces, Philadelphia may find itself at a disadvantage. While LNG may present an opportunity for PGW and the City of Philadelphia economically, there are safety concerns associated with LNG transport and storage. Political and community opposition, and competition from less dense locations will be barriers to developing LNG facilities in the region. Given the intense competition to develop LNG facilities, the city cannot rely solely upon expanded access to natural gas to meet Philadelphia's future energy, economic, and environmental needs and should pursue alternative policies and programs.

An alternative power source that is gaining prominence in the Commonwealth is wind energy. Today wind is the fastest growing energy source in the world, with average annual usage increasing 34 percent over the past five years, but it still represents only 0.54 percent of electricity consumed. Wind turbines are capable of harnessing the kinetic energy generated by wind, and converting that energy into a mechanical energy. A wind generator can then convert the mechanical energy into electricity that can be distributed and utilized in the same manner as conventionally generated electricity, but with reduced environmental repercussions.

While the United States ranks fourth in the world in wind power production, several European nations are more advanced in the use of wind power. Denmark, Ireland, and Germany have invested the most in trying to harness wind power to generate electricity. Denmark is the leader in production and use of turbines with a commitment made more than 30 years ago to eventually generate half of the country's power by wind. The Irish government recently constructed the largest off shore wind farm and has plans to construct additional facilities. Germany, the world leader in wind energy production with approximately 40 percent of the entire world's wind power, hopes that by 2010 it will be producing over 12 percent of its country's electrical power needs through wind farms. Scotland has recently introduced new planning rules to allow residents to place wind turbines on their roofs. These turbines will generate approximately 1.5 kilowatts of power, enough electricity to power most domestic appliances and provide up to a third of all power needs.

Production and utilization of wind energy in Pennsylvania has been increasing in recent years. Pennsylvania schools are increasing their commitments to wind energy as part of the Pennsylvania Consortium for Interdisciplinary Environmental Policy's "Getting to 10 percent Wind" campaign. The Consortium, made up of environmental policy makers and educational institutions, launched the program with the goal of encouraging Pennsylvania schools to commit to at least 10 percent of their energy needs being provided by wind. Thirty four schools are participating in the campaign with nine having already attained the 10 percent goal.

The educational community is not the only group opting to supplement their energy needs with wind power. The state, the Philadelphia Eagles, the Pennsylvania Turnpike Commission, and others purchase wind energy. PECO Energy has a plan available to residential customers that allows, for a small monthly fee, PECO to purchase wind generated electricity and integrate it into Pennsylvania's electric grid, thus reducing the need for energy produced from other sources. Conspicuously absent from the list of Pennsylvania wind energy purchasers is the City of Philadelphia. To reduce the negative environmental impacts associated with the city's energy consumption, the city should purchase wind energy to meet some or all of its needs.

Supporting Sustainable Building Practices

Reducing reliance upon scarce energy sources through increased efficiency should be encouraged among residential, commercial, and institutional users to lower utility costs and preserve the environment. The US Green Building Council (USGBC) offers standards for the design and construction of environmentally sustainable and energy efficient buildings with clear measures to evaluate what a "green building" is and to provide guidance. The USGBC created the Leadership in Energy and Environmental Design (LEED) rating system to promote and provide guidance for the development of high performance, environmentally sustainable buildings. LEED standards address not only energy issues, but also building materials, stormwater management, and other aspects of structures that have an impact on the environment.

The City of Philadelphia's Municipal Energy Office (MEO) is a member of USGBC and works to incorporate LEED standards into municipal projects. The LEED standards are designed for new construction, and thus are not easily applicable to majority of Philadelphia's capital projects. Most of the city's capital expenditures are directed towards existing buildings and infra-structure. In 2004, the MEO developed guidelines for introducing sustainable design into building renovations.

While progress towards reduced energy consumption and enhanced sustainability in city-owned buildings is laudable, the city should take steps to encourage additional environmentally friendly design throughout the city. The city could require that public-private ventures and devel-opments seeking city assistance in the form of loans, grants, or land be design to meet LEED certification standards. In projects with both public and private participation, LEED-certified design can be required. For example, as sites and developers for Philadelphia's gaming facilities are reviewed, those with LEED-certified designs can be given preference.

Opportunities exist to integrate LEED standards into private development through government intervention. The City of Chicago has green-building requirements in place for projects receiving public assistance (such as Tax Increment Financing), as well as for private projects that are on the Lakefront or in planned developments. Philadelphia already requires that affordable housing projects built in the city meet the standards of the Energy Star Program, estab-lished by the US Environmental Protection Agency, which promotes energy-efficient products and practices. By adopting the Energy Star guidelines, economic and environmental benefits are achieved. Residents see savings in their utility costs, and it helps reduce consumption of fossil fuels that create air pollution.

While incorporating LEED and Energy Star standards into the requirements of the Philadelphia building code for all new construction may place an onerous financial burden on builders and developers that would deter construction, incentives for green building practices can be built into the city's zoning code and encouraged through planning grants and information resources for builders. Options include allowing preferential permit review for energy efficient projects and the provision of density bonuses for environmentally friendly designs.

Educational efforts should also be undertaken to promote green buildings. Cost concerns are typically cited by builders hesitant to incorporate green building technologies, but this may be a product of misinformation. A USGBC publication indicates that the premium associated with LEED certification is only two percent and is recouped through lower building operating costs in the future and potentially higher resale values. Eliminating confusion about the costs and benefits of energy efficient, sustainable construction can have a positive economic and environmental impact on the city.

Philadelphia is replete with expertise in the design and construction of innovative energy efficient buildings, and the city should seek to enhance and market this strategic advantage to achieve both economic and environmental goals. Establishing environmentally friendly design and construction as a hallmark of Philadelphia could be an economic development tool in a number of ways. First, Philadelphia has struggled to create and retain jobs in part due to the high costs of doing business here. Energy efficient buildings result in lower operating costs. By reducing one of the contributing factors to Philadelphia's costs of doing business, more firms may be tempted to remain or relocate here.

Secondly, by developing and marketing Philadelphia firms' expertise in sustainable construction and design, the city can develop a new strategic advantage that builds on our existing assets — well-trained construction and design professionals. Already, local electricians are being trained in solar technologies. By promoting cutting edge expertise in our vocational programs, and supporting green building training among the city's building trades, while attracting and training architects, engineers, and planners with the education needed to design these buildings, Philadelphia can not only provide green buildings within the city, but also export this expertise, drawing wealth into the city. A survey of the city's design and construction capacity for green buildings should be undertaken to identify any gaps in expertise that could jeopardize Philadelphia's potential to become a national center for sustainable building. Development of educational and training programs can ensure that we have a workforce with the necessary expertise in green building design and construction.

Integrated Land Use and Transportation Planning

Beyond sustainable buildings, Philadelphia needs sustainable neighborhoods. The viability of Philadelphia as a center for business, entertainment, and residential location is dependent on the provision of affordable and efficient transportation. Development of the region's roads and railways in the middle part of the twentieth century paralleled the new settlement patterns, as numerous residential suburban developments were built. As the century drew to a close, businesses followed their workers to the area's hinterlands, and the region was decentralized. The hub and spoke networks that brought people from their bedroom communities to their Center City jobs were no longer adequate to meet the region's transportation needs.

As land use patterns change, the city's transportation options must be reassessed. According to the 1997 National Resources inventory, the Philadelphia area developed land at eleven times the rate of residential growth between 1982 and 1997. The Greater Philadelphia region continues to sprawl, with the pace of land development far outstripping the pace of population growth. As this pattern continues, it creates significant challenges for the region's mature transportation network.

The city has limited power to act unilaterally on matters of transportation policy, and must work in collaboration with the various stakeholders to ensure that people and goods can move efficiently and effectively throughout the region. There are, however, some areas in which the city can be proactive in improving the quality and capabilities of our mass transit and road networks.

Emerging trends in land-use patterns in the nine-county region, including the continued relocation of jobs to suburban areas, and the recent surge in Center City residential development, could essentially reverse the traffic patterns that our mass transit and highway infrastructure was predicated upon, creating an opportunity to re-embrace elements of our hub-and-spoke transportation network, particularly our mass transit system, SEPTA.

Today, SEPTA faces a variety of challenges, from its aging infrastructure to deficient financial resources. While the solutions to these problems require involvement of regional and state actors, the City of Philadelphia can take steps independently to encourage increased mass transit usage, which will in turn generate additional revenues, relieve congestion and parking problems in the city, address air quality concerns, and create a broader constituency to advocate on behalf of the system.

Through its zoning and planning functions, the city should encourage mass transit usage by promoting denser mixed-use development around transportation stations and hubs throughout the city. When selecting or approving sites for large development projects, such as stadia and schools, the city could consider the proximity to mass transit facilities as a necessary precondition for development. This can reduce travelers' reliance on automobiles, by providing more people with easy connections between home, work, and retail locations. People are more likely to choose mass transit when it is closer to their home and destinations. Much of Philadelphia's mass transit infrastructure is in a fixed location. Since it is improbable that we will relocate subway and trolley lines to where people are currently located, we must promote opportunities for people to live and work near existing transit infrastructure.

Known as Transit-Oriented Design (TOD), this style of development supports mass transit usage by clustering numerous land uses around stations, complemented by a pedestrian-friendly environment. This pattern of land use is already evident in many areas of the city, and should be further encouraged. In addition to zoning these areas for mixed-use development, the city can offer developers increased zoning bonuses in these areas in return for partnership in completing streetscape and public space enhancement in the surrounding zone. The city could also reduce requirements for developers to provide parking at location adjacent to mass transit. This would lower costs and thus increase development activity. For projects receiving public financial support, TOD principles should be mandated in locations adjacent to existing and planned transit services.

RECOMMENDATIONS FOR ACTION:

The city should purchase wind energy to meet some or all of its energy needs.

Action Step:

- Review current energy purchases to identify opportunities for wind energy usage.

Fiscal Impact:

- Potential costs associated with premium paid for wind energy.

The city should take steps to encourage additional environmentally friendly design throughout the city.

Action Steps:

- Require LEED certification of city, public-private, and city-assisted development projects.
- Coordinate with educational institutions and the building trades to encourage professional skill development for LEED-certified design and construction.

Fiscal Impacts:

- Potential increased design and construction costs.
- Potential savings from lower building operating costs.
- Potential increased revenues from expanded economic activity.

The city should integrate transportation and land use planning to encourage mass transit usage.

Action Steps:

- Adopt zoning code regulations that allow and encourage dense, mixed-use development in and around transportation hubs.
- Review all significant development projects for proximity to transit facilities.

Fiscal Impacts:

- Potential short-term costs associated with code changes.
- Potential opportunities for private provision of public amenities.
- Potential revenue increases from expanded development activity.

CONCLUSION

In 2006, Philadelphia celebrates the three-hundredth birthday of Benjamin Franklin, who contributed greatly to the development of this city and the entire nation. Benjamin Franklin was an inventor, a diplomat, an entrepreneur, and a true statesman dedicated to improving the lives of others. As Philadelphia celebrates his many contributions to the city and nation, the city should commit to embodying his spirit of innovation for the common good. Like Benjamin Franklin, who sought solutions to everyday problems, it is imperative that today's leaders of Philadelphia continue to address the challenges facing Philadelphia with a spirit of creativity and passion for improvement.

Many of the challenges that the city faces today are the same as when Benjamin Franklin first arrived here looking for work. The city remains a location for employment, a center for learning, a place where people and goods need to move around, and a metropolis where the lives and property of residents still need protection. While the challenges remain the same, the city's leaders should constantly seek new ways to combat these problems. Philadelphia has many strategic advantages that can be harnessed to improve the physical, social and economic strength of the city. By focusing our economic-development policies on industries in which the city has a competitive advantages, and employing programs with measurable success and tailored to meet the needs of all segments of our economy, Philadelphia can create jobs for and expand wealth among its citizens. Continuing to bolster the hospitality and tourism sectors can ensure that the public investment made in the past decade will continue to provide increasing returns in the years to come.

The city can continue to improve educational quality and opportunities by supporting and evaluating reform efforts. Philadelphia can protect its residents from violent and quality-of-life crime, as well as natural and man-made disasters, with carefully planning and coordinated responses. The free flow of people and goods can be ensured while we take steps to ease air pollution, and the sustainability of the city's natural and built environments can be promoted with policies and programs to reduce energy and land consumption. By pursuing the strategies outlined in this chapter, the city can continue the Philadelphia's centuries-long tradition of innovation for the public good, in the spirit of Benjamin Franklin, one of the most creative and civic-minded Philadelphians ever to walk our cobblestone streets.

CHAPTER 5

THE CITY IN THE REGION
A DECLARATION OF INTERDEPENDENCE

We must all hang together,
or assuredly we shall all hang separately.

—Benjamin Franklin

PHILADELPHIA'S PLACE IN THE GREATER PHILADELPHIA REGION

The City's historical role as the hub and economic engine of the region has been greatly diminished in past decades. The City, therefore, must reevaluate how it fits into the future of the Greater Philadelphia region. While Philadelphia once was home to a majority of the region's population and jobs, now a majority of the region's population and a majority of the region's jobs are found outside the City limits. According to census data, the percentage of residents in the metropolitan area living in Philadelphia was less than 30 percent in 1996, down from more than 56 percent in 1950. Mirroring a national trend, regional population and job growth have been strongest in the suburban portion of the metropolitan area. Some thinkers have even suggested that Philadelphia, and cities in general, are irrelevant to the lives and well being of most Americans. Nothing could be further from the truth. Ignoring the problems of the central city must be done at the peril of the surrounding suburbs. Suburban growth is directly linked to urban viability—suburban growth is enhanced by urban growth and limited by urban decay.

In "City and Suburban Growth: Substitutes or Complements," Richard Voith reported on a study of 28 Metropolitan Statistical Areas in the Northeast and North Central United States. He found that city and suburban population, per capita real income, and employment growth are positively correlated, suggesting that cities and suburbs are complementary. If the central city declines, that decline is likely to be associated with slow-growing suburbs. Urban decline is a drain on the economic and social vitality of a region. Even in growing suburbs that surround cities in decline, Voith concludes that growth would be more robust—income and housing values would be higher—if the central city's decline could be alleviated. Analyzing how much more people were willing to pay for a house with good access to downtown Philadelphia compared with similar houses with poor downtown access, Voith concluded that increasing Philadelphia employment resulted in an increase in the value of City-accessible suburban housing while the premium paid for accessibility fell when Philadelphia employment decreased.

After analyzing the effects of City and suburban job growth on the suburban housing market, Voith concluded that while employment growth increases the value of real estate assets, all suburban communities do not share equally in the increase. Specifically, Voith noted that decentralized growth increases the value of land on the urban fringe, which benefits owners of agricultural land and developers, while centralized job growth enhances property values in existing communities. Similarly, he concluded, a decline in centralized jobs reduces the property values in existing communities.

In 1994, Charles Adams and his Ohio State University colleagues completed a study titled "Flight from Blight Revisited" and reported that suburbs surrounding cities with more socioeconomic problems had less population growth—mostly due to the fact that people from outside the region were not attracted to the area.

Nancy Brooks and Anita Summers, of the Wharton School of the University of Pennsylvania, completed an econometric analysis of the interdependencies between cities and suburbs and concluded that there is clear evidence that suburban employment growth was greater if central city employment growth was larger. The City Controller's "1997 Mid-Year Economic and Financial Report," showed how educational attainment in Philadelphia directly affected employment and average earnings throughout the Greater Philadelphia region.

The National League of Cities has published numerous reports about the relationships between central cities and their suburbs. Examining the disparities between cities and suburbs in a 1992 report, the League found that metropolitan areas with lower per-capita income disparities tend to have higher rates of employment change and that areas with smaller disparities tend to be more prosperous. Suburban communities that fail to address the problems of their core city undermine their own economic prosperity.

In its 1993 report, "All in it Together," the National League of Cities' conclusions sharpened this notion of interdependence between cities and their suburbs. Analysis of income changes showed that for every increase in central city income, there is an even larger increase in suburban income—and that for every increase in suburban income, there is a smaller increase in central city income. Similarly, the League found that when central city incomes are decreasing, suburban incomes decrease. The League's research suggests a mutual, interactive, and interdependent inter-twining of the economic fortunes of cities and suburbs—concluding that this interconnection has become stronger over time.

In addition to the economic link, opening a newspaper on any given morning will show how the stresses that many wrongly assume to be confined to urban areas—crime, poverty, drugs, decay, and fear—are a reality in the suburbs as well as the city. Minnesota State Legislator Myron Orfield has performed exhaustive research on the woes that beset urban neighborhoods and suburban communities. Orfield shows that the Philadelphia region, like many other metropolitan areas, is dramatically affected by the concentration of poverty in its central city and surrounding suburbs. This concentration of poverty destabilizes schools and neighborhoods and is associated with increasing crime and flight of middle-class residents and businesses. Orfield, who was able to spearhead regional initiatives for the Minneapolis-St. Paul area, concludes that unless cities and suburbs join forces, suburbs that are both ill equipped and financially unable to respond to decay will increasingly be beset with problems typically associated with urban areas.

Using the graphical simplicity of maps of the Philadelphia area outlining the region's woes by jurisdiction, Orfield shows what most regional residents know intuitively: many suburban communities are suffering from the effects of concentrated poverty, increasing crime, job loss, and residential flight. Even more ominous is the fact that, without institutions like universities and museums that attract visitors and vitality, without the political clout of a powerful mayor and congressional delegation that push for funds, and without the energy that even a declining city generates, these suffering suburban communities are more at risk than their central city. As illustrated in figures 5.1 through 5.4—prepared by Orfield's Metropolitan Area Project—decline has not been halted at the City line.

From head hunters for suburban employers who find it difficult to lure talent to a region with a central city in decline, to suburban business owners who are unable to find enough skilled workers because the region is full of underperforming graduates of underperforming city schools, it is clear that urban problems affect the suburban economy. From the suburban sprawl that creates traffic and pollution to the drive for new suburban development that consumes open space, it is clear that the movement of residents from the central city to the surrounding areas affects the suburban environment. Increasing suburban crime rates show

Figure 5.1. Percentage Change in Jobs per Capita by Municipality, 1980–1990

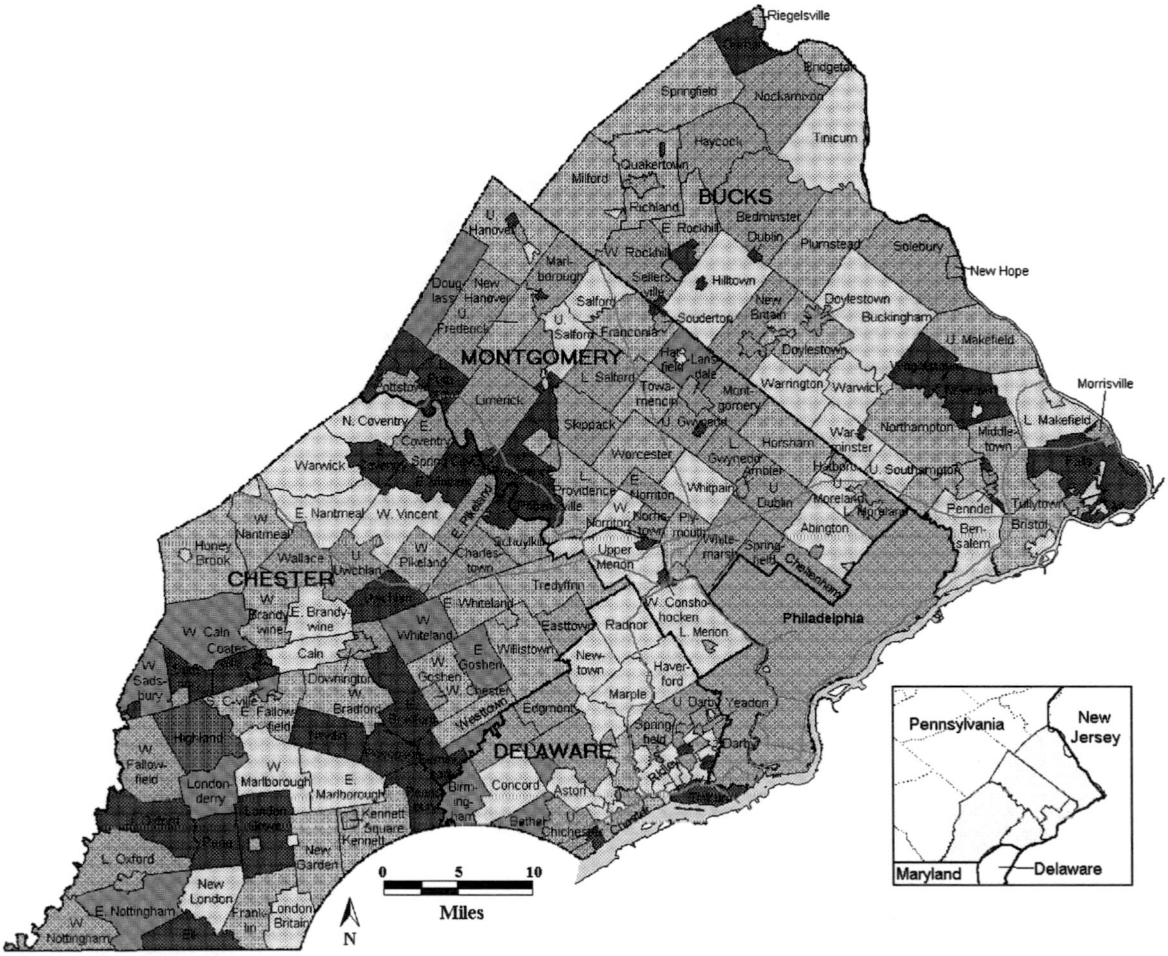

— ·· — ·· — County
———— Municipality

Percentage Change
Regional Median: 17.9%

■	-93.8	to -21.6%	(45)
▨	-19.9	to 17.3%	(74)
□	17.9	to 65.6%	(60)
▨	68.6	to 182.7%	(43)
▦	212.5	to 867.7%	(15)
▓	2,619.6%		(1)

Prepared by the Metropolitan Area Program (MAP)

DATA SOURCES: Delaware Valley Reg. Planning Commission, *1980 Data Bank for Transportation Planning & Travel Simulation*, Table 2: "1980 Demographic Data by Municipality for the Delaware Valley Region" (1980 pop.), Table 5: 1980 employment data by Municipality for the Delaware Valley Region" (1980 jobs), *Year 2020 County & Municipal Interim Population and Employment Forecasts*, Table: "DVRPC Employment Forecasts by County, 1990-2020", pp. 66-78 (1990 jobs); 1990 Census of Population STF3A (1990 population).

293

Figure 5.2. Percentage of Children Under Five Years in Poverty by Municipality, 1990

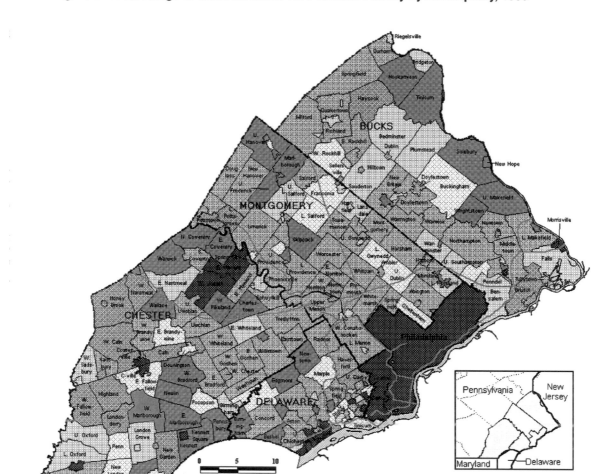

− ··− ··− County
————— Municipality

Municipalities with
"No data" had fewer than
50 children under five.

Percentage Change in Poverty		
Regional Median: 3.0%		
0%		(38)
0.3 to 3.0%		(76)
3.2 to 4.7%		(28)
5.0 to 9.1%		(40)
9.4 to 18.3%		(33)
19.0% or more		(16)
No data		(7)

Prepared by the Metropolitan Area Program (MAP)

DATA SOURCES: 1000 Census of Population & Housing Summary Tape File 3A

Figure 5.3. Change in Percentage Points Children Under Five Years in Poverty by Municipality, 1980–1990

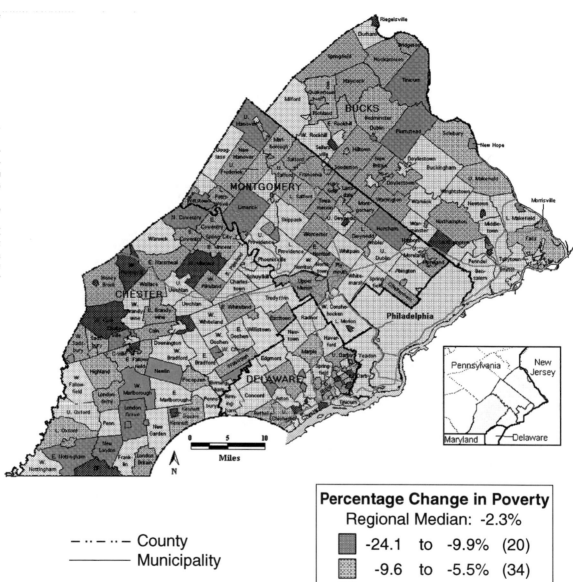

– ·· – ·· – County
————— Municipality

Municipalities with "No data" had fewer than 50 children under five in 1980 and/or 1990.

Percentage Change in Poverty
Regional Median: -2.3%

	-24.1 to -9.9%	(20)
	-9.6 to -5.5%	(34)
	-5.3 to -2.4%	(53)
	-2.3 to -0.5%	(40)
	-0.2 to +4.4%	(57)
	+5.3% or more	(21)
	No data	(13)

Prepared by the Metropolitan Area Program (MAP)

DATA SOURCES: 1980 & 1990 Census of Population & Housing Summary Tape File 3A.

Figure 5.4. Part I Crimes per 100,000 Persons by Municipality, 1993

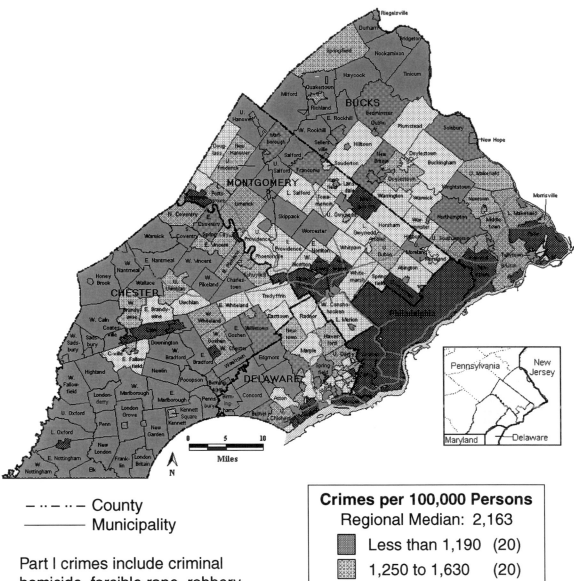

– ·· – ·· – County
——————— Municipality

Part I crimes include criminal
homicide, forcible rape, robbery,
aggravated assault, burglary, larceny,
vehicle theft, and arson.
Municipalities with "No data" did not
have individual police departmens,
but rather were under the jurisdiction
of the State Police

Crimes per 100,000 Persons
Regional Median: 2,163

▨	Less than 1,190	(20)
▦	1,250 to 1,630	(20)
▫	1,690 to 2,160	(27)
▨	2,163 to 3,060	(23)
▩	3,180 to 4,110	(21)
■	4,270 or more	(23)
▓	No data	(104)

Prepared by the Metropolitan Area Program (MAP)

DATA SOURCES: Pennsylvania State Police, Bureau of Research & Development

that fear cannot be confined to inner-city neighborhoods while increasing numbers of suburban students receiving free or reduced lunch confirm that need cannot be checked by jurisdictional boundaries.

The health of the region is intimately related to the health of its central city. The City's place of prominence in the Greater Philadelphia region may be diminished, but the future of the areas surrounding Philadelphia is clearly dependent on the future of the City itself.

The term "regionalism" often elicits strong reactions from leaders and residents of jurisdictions fearful of losing local autonomy and independence. Many leaders and individuals are therefore willing to rationally trade the potential benefits from efforts such as regional policing for the perceived benefits of local control of the local police force. Similarly, minority and low-income communities are often wary of perceived threats that regional efforts could pose toward their political influence and ability to make decisions about the future of their communities.

But efforts to work together to solve the region's problems must be seen as an investment in local economic growth, property values, and real wages. A growing body of research clearly shows that cities and suburbs are all in this together. The challenge, therefore, is to first find the point where the perceived benefit of local autonomy and independence is offset by actual economic growth. Then, any regional initiative must include an effort to ensure that small jurisdictions and minority and low-income communities are not marginalized. The benefits of regional initiatives, in terms of the potential to create cost savings for small jurisdictions and revitalize inner-city neighborhoods, are too substantial to squander by failing to include all parties in the decision-making process. Making Philadelphia into a city where government operates effectively is one step toward making that equation balance, because too many leaders and individuals are convinced that the City is inefficient in how it attacks its problems. Only when leaders and residents make the rational determination that the potential benefits of individual "regional" efforts outweigh the costs of diminished local control, will such efforts move forward.

This is not to suggest that the Greater Philadelphia region is without any regional cooperation. On the contrary, "creeping regionalism" has swept across the metropolitan area in past decades. Led by political muscle and necessity (sometimes independent of each other), issues such as revenue sharing, planning, and transportation have all been the subject of Philadelphia-area regional solutions.

State taxes in Pennsylvania have long been collected across jurisdictions to be redeployed in areas of greater need. Since 1932, the Sterling Act has allowed the City of Philadelphia to collect a tax on the wages of non-City residents who work in Philadelphia while prohibiting those residents' home jurisdictions from taxing that same income.

Cooperative agreements among cities, counties, and states have been forged to create bridges to span the Delaware River between Philadelphia in Pennsylvania and municipalities in New Jersey. The Southeastern Pennsylvania Transportation Authority was established in 1964 with state and regional funding to maintain and operate mass transportation in the five-county Southeastern Pennsylvania region. The Delaware River Port Authority was established in 1951 to maintain and operate Philadelphia-area river crossings between Pennsylvania and New Jersey and a bi-state high-speed rapid transit system. The Delaware Valley Regional Planning Commission was established in 1965 to provide comprehensive, coordinated planning for the orderly growth and development of the bi-state Philadelphia region.

Other notable efforts such as the creation of the Greater Philadelphia Tourism and Marketing Corporation and the City Avenue Special Services District show that regionalism can work on a smaller scale. The former is a non-profit organization dedicated to promoting tourism in the Southeastern Pennsylvania region. The latter is a business-improvement district established under the leadership of Saint Joseph's University as the first bi-jurisdictional special services district in the nation. The City Avenue Special Services District encompasses a 2.5-mile commercial and educational strip which crosses from Philadelphia neighborhoods into suburban Lower Merion, Pennsylvania, and illustrates that regionalism can work when local officials and residents see genuine benefits to regional cooperation.

REGIONAL EFFORTS TO MOVE TOWARD A MORE COMPETITIVE REGION

Twenty-first-century Philadelphia must foster regional cooperation to enable the Greater Philadelphia region to compete in the global market for residents, businesses, and visitors. To promote the advancement of the region as a whole, the City can encourage efforts to provide regional support for significant assets, save tax dollars and improve effectiveness through expanding cross-jurisdictional service-delivery efforts, and reduce intra-regional competition.

Regional Funding for Regional Assets

In 1988, the voters of metropolitan Denver established a Scientific and Cultural Facilities District to fund arts and cultural organizations in the Denver area through a 0.1-percent sales tax on retail sales in the six-county region. The District currently provides approximately $26 million in regionally generated funds each year to organizations and institutions in the City of Denver and surrounding jurisdictions. In 1993, Allegheny County voters created the Allegheny Regional Asset District to fund regional civic assets from half the proceeds of a countywide 1-percent sales tax. The District now disburses more than $64 million to organizations and institutions in the City of Pittsburgh and surrounding Allegheny County. Both efforts represent successful attempts to channel regional revenues to assets located in central cities and surrounding jurisdictions.

The Greater Philadelphia Cultural Alliance estimates that cultural organizations and institutions add more than $1 billion to the regional economy each year. In 1998, the Pennsylvania Economy League estimated that cultural assets generate $564 million in regional spending and more than 11,000 regional jobs. Regional funding for the region's assets could create a dramatic positive effect throughout the region. While legislation has been introduced in the Pennsylvania General Assembly to authorize the creation of such an asset district in the Philadelphia region (such legislation would allow the participant jurisdictions to determine funding mechanisms and levels), it has never come to a vote.

Even without action from the state legislature, however, Philadelphia and surrounding jurisdictions are currently able to create an asset district or establish regional asset funding. Without enabling legislation from the General Assembly, however, participating jurisdictions would be unable to set aside tax revenues as an income source and would need to rely on direct appropriations from local budgets to assemble funding.

One unresolved issue with efforts to create a regional asset district deals with whether the City of Philadelphia would be credited for its current level of culture-related funding in any revenue-collection mechanism. City leaders must be willing to increase the City's commitment to regional assets to leverage additional support and create greater regional support for those assets. To increase the likelihood of suburban support for such an asset district, district funding could also be directed to preserve the region's supply of open space.

Advocates for an asset district in Southeastern Pennsylvania suggest that funding for such a district would require approximately $25 million annually, and a contribution of approximately $10 million from the City of Philadelphia. To move this effort forward, the City should work with surrounding jurisdictions to create a logical and acceptable funding mechanism for a regional asset district.

Regional assets funding could be generated in a variety of ways. For example, a portion of a new local sales tax in the counties surrounding Philadelphia, plus a portion of the existing local sales tax in Philadelphia could fund a regional asset district. Alternatively, since regional assets can attract visitors and increase attendance at local arts venues, a portion of local hotel or amusement taxes could be dedicated to fund the creation of a regional asset district.

In addition to regional institutions and organizations dedicated to arts and culture, funding to support assets such as airports could be candidates for regional funding. An excellent transportation infrastructure is crucial to the success of a metropolitan region. Since most scenarios for a bright future for Philadelphia include a thriving central business district, mass transportation is necessary to efficiently connect Center City to the region. The Greater Philadelphia region already funds mass transit and port facilities through regional partnerships in an effort to better move people and goods. Increased regional support of air and transportation facilities could similarly benefit the entire region. A variation on the Commonwealth of Pennsylvania's Public Utility Realty Tax Act (PURTA) legislation could be created to provide funding for such assets. The PURTA tax allows local taxing authorities to receive monies lost because the local jurisdictions cannot assess real estate tax on public utility real estate. The utility companies pay the tax to the state and the state pay distributes the funds to localities based on foregone taxes. A tax on suburban jurisdictions could be assembled at the state level and reapportioned to jurisdictions that host transportation assets to improve facilities.

Finally, since they benefit the entire region, new sports arenas, visitors' centers, and other spectator facilities should also be candidates for regional support. Visitors to Philadelphia who, after viewing Independence Hall, leave the City to visit Revolutionary War battle sites, see the region as a whole, as do advertisers who purchase television commercials on Philadelphia stations that broadcast throughout the region. The City and its suburban neighbors must see the region's numerous interdependent jurisdictions the same way and provide regional support for local assets.

Regional Collaboration for Efficient and Effective Local Service Delivery

While many worry about the loss of local autonomy when the notion of cross-jurisdictional service delivery is raised, the undeniable efficiencies that can be achieved must be part of serious discussions aimed at decreasing the cost and increasing the productivity of local service-delivery efforts. The five-county Southeastern Pennsylvania region contains 238 independent local jurisdictions. It is simply impractical and inefficient for every local jurisdiction to endure the capital expense involved with construction of wastewater treatment facilities. It is, therefore, sensible that the City of Philadelphia provides wastewater treatment for many surrounding jurisdictions. Similarly, the City maintains the region's bomb squad, as it would be foolish for each local jurisdiction to fund such a low-demand service.

The University of Pennsylvania's Wharton School examined major regionalization efforts among cities and suburbs in the United States and found that regional sharing of park and recreational services, wastewater and solid waste disposal costs, and water treatment charges are relatively common in the nation's 27 largest metropolitan areas. The effort concludes, however, that many avenues to cross-jurisdictional cooperation remain unexplored. In the Philadelphia area, solid waste disposal is just one area that could be vastly improved through regional cooperation.

The City of Philadelphia Streets Department found that recycling-related manufacturing jobs in Philadelphia increased by 58.1 percent between December, 1995 and June, 1997. The same survey indicated that approximately 100 new recycling jobs have been created in Philadelphia each year since 1991. Creating a market for recyclers can make a real contribution to economic development efforts. By working together to collect and pool recyclables, the jurisdictions of the Greater Philadelphia region could increase the amount of available recycled material and create a powerful economic development tool to attract recyclers and reuse industries. To reduce duplication of efforts and promote efficiencies in service-delivery efforts across the region, the City should, where legally permissible, work with state and regional leaders to establish and expand cross-jurisdictional service-delivery efforts.

Deciding Not to Compete to Enhance Regional Competitiveness

While many local jurisdictions report significant growth, the Greater Philadelphia region as a whole is experiencing slow growth. According to the Bureau of Labor Statistics, while Philadelphia-area private industry payrolls increased by about 20,000 workers between the second quarter of 1997 and the second quarter of 1998, that 1.2-percent gain was the second lowest growth rate among the nation's largest 23 municipal areas. Only Pennsylvania's other major city, Pittsburgh, had a lower growth rate. Recent job gains in the City have mirrored gains in the suburbs after a long-term trend of Philadelphia employment being outpaced by suburban growth.

While according to the Census Bureau the number of jobs in Southeastern Pennsylvania increased by 13.6 percent between 1980 and 1990, 43 suburban municipalities lost more than 21 percent of their jobs and Philadelphia only gained 0.1 percent of its jobs during that period. As a region, Greater Philadelphia is shifting jobs and residents around, not expanding. While some localities are obviously faring better than others, and some are clearly winners in this local shell game, every locality would benefit from increased regional growth. Because jurisdictions too often waste institutional effort competing against other regional jurisdictions for employers and residents, such exertions are unproductive. These efforts often result in zero positive effect if one regional jurisdiction lures jobs from another. They can result in an overall negative effect if luring jurisdictions provide financial incentives to induce a move—if the total number of regional jobs remains constant while jurisdictions waste governmental resources providing subsidies, then total regional revenues actually decreases.

Milwaukee County, Wisconsin, has created a pact with surrounding counties that recognizes that the key to economic development is not to seek to relocate a business across jurisdictional boundaries, but to improve the overall regional conditions that sustain economic growth. The pact, entered into by Milwaukee and three neighboring counties, declares that counties receiving inquiries from businesses looking to locate from one county in the region to another will inform the county from which the business intends to move and that participating counties will not aggressively seek to attract businesses that are already located in the region. The pact also commits participating counties to encourage communities within the counties to refrain from aggressive attraction activities. Similarly, as part of an intergovernmental understanding, the City of Indianapolis will not consider granting a tax abatement to a business relocating from another Indiana community to Marion County (home to Indianapolis) unless the affected community provides a request, in writing, that the City provide such assistance.

When businesses are attracted to a region by factors such as workforce quality, geographic location, and the presence of a regional market, they make an economic decision that their move will be beneficial. When local jurisdictions use tax abatements and other financial incentives to compete for employers already located in the region, they encourage those employers to minimize their costs—thereby driving down the aggregate cost of doing business and raising the average amount of assistance all jurisdictions must provide. A non-aggression compact can begin to minimize such unproductive cross-jurisdictional infighting. The City should work with surrounding jurisdictions to establish a regional non-aggression compact to reduce regional economic infighting. As a region, Greater Philadelphia should compete with other regions for jobs and residents. Intraregional, inter-jurisdictional competition weakens the region's ability to effectively compete with the many regions of the world that would be pleased to capitalize on this weakness and lure away Greater Philadelphia area employers. As a good-faith effort, if the jurisdictions of the Greater Philadelphia region commit to non-aggression and non-competition initiatives, the City could opt not to use local preference in purchasing decisions (see Chapter 3 for a discussion of local preference), because such a move would spur an increase in City employment while hurting regional growth.

RECOMMENDATIONS FOR ACTION

The City should work with state and regional leaders to establish regional funding mechanisms for regional assets.

Action Steps:

- Work with leaders of local jurisdictions to provide dedicated funding streams for regional assets.

- Determine whether to pursue legislation in the Pennsylvania General Assembly to authorize new tax structures to raise funding.

- Establish governance, funding mechanism, recipient assets, and methods to determine fund disbursement along with other participating regional jurisdictions.

Fiscal Impact:

- Potential increase in annual City expenditures—estimated in some models as a $10 million annual contribution above and beyond current City support of regional assets.

- Potential to improve local assets and foster economic development in the City.

The City should work with state and regional leaders to establish and expand cross-jurisdictional service-delivery efforts.

Action Steps:

- Work with leaders of local jurisdictions to establish cross-jurisdictional service-delivery efforts where legally permissible.

- Establish governance, funding mechanism, and service-delivery protocols with participating regional jurisdictions.

Fiscal Impact:

- Potential increase in City revenue from contracting with surrounding jurisdictions.

- Potential savings from reduction of duplication of efforts as part of cooperative efforts.

The City should work with leaders of local jurisdictions to establish non-competition compacts.

Action Steps:

- Establish non-aggression compacts with participating regional jurisdictions.

Fiscal Impact:

- Potential savings from retaining employers and tax base.

- Potential savings from reduced need to offer specialized incentives to employers.

REGIONAL COOPERATION TO CONFRONT FISCAL DISPARITIES, SPRAWL, AND CONGESTION

From a striking new skyline in Center City to pristine housing developments in growing new suburban communities, many areas of the Greater Philadelphia region seem to be thriving. But many major corporations have left the region, moving out of City high rises. At the same time, every new suburban housing development destroys the region's dwindling supply of open space. The region as a whole is struggling in many ways.

Recent patterns of growth have resulted in sprawl, congestion, pollution, and isolation in newer suburban communities and disinvestment and economic hardship in Philadelphia and many of the older surrounding cities and boroughs. While the developed area in the metropolitan region expands, individuals spend more time in their cars, open space disappears, air pollution increases, traffic congestion worsens, and taxes increase to pay for it all. Decay, crime, poverty, and racial tensions spread beyond the City border. These "city" problems and suburban growing pains must be addressed in the near future if the region is to be able to compete for the future.

Crime rates are higher in suburban communities such as Chester and Pottstown than in Philadelphia. Bucks County's prison population has doubled since 1985 and Montgomery County's prison population has tripled since 1986. The 1990 census reported that childhood poverty in four suburban Pennsylvania communities was greater than in Philadelphia (31.9 percent). In fact, census data showed that childhood poverty is greater than 20 percent in 13 suburban Pennsylvania communities and greater than 10 percent in 42 more. Thirty-six suburban Pennsylvania communities saw increases in the percentages of pre-school children in poverty from 1980 to 1990 while Philadelphia's percentage remained roughly stable. Thirty-six suburban Pennsylvania school districts experienced more rapid "white flight" than Philadelphia between 1980 and 1990.

The region's problems are not just expressed in human terms. According to census data, from 1980 to 1990 the population of the Southeastern Pennsylvania portion of the Greater Philadelphia region increased by only .22 percent, but the size of the urbanized area actually grew by 12 percent. The population density of the Southeastern Pennsylvania area decreased 10.5 percent between 1980 and 1990. Regional sprawl cost billions in water, sewer, and highway infrastructure investment while traffic congestion has increased and resulting climate-changing greenhouse gas emissions have contributed to poor regional air quality. Loss of open space and addition of more parking lots and highways contributes to the "urban heat island" effect, raising temperatures in the area and increasing likelihood of flooding.

In 1998, the 21st Century Environment Commission, a gubernatorial commission appointed to set Pennsylvania's environmental priorities, declared that suburban sprawl is Pennsylvania's most pressing environmental problem. A graphical presentation illustrates how the regional population is sprawling. While regional population expanded by one million people between 1930 and 1960, the dramatic increase in regional development occurred between 1960 and 1990 when the population only expanded by 100,000. (See Figure 5.5.)

As the toll on people and land increases, regional taxpayers foot the bill to confront increasing social need along with new infrastructure and capital expenditures. Every community that experiences increasing poverty must direct resources toward deteriorating neighborhoods and away from other areas. As new communities grow farther from the region's hub, new roads, sewers, and schools must be constructed to meet demand. Residents in the City and in other jurisdictions in decline must not only fund programs to meet social needs in their communities, but must subsidize sprawl through tax dollars that fund infrastructure needed for new development. This combination of increased spending for social needs in deteriorating areas, combined with increased spending for new infrastructure in growing communities is clearly inefficient on a regionwide basis. If Greater Philadelphia does not address these problems, its jurisdictions will be forced to waste energies fighting today's problems and will be unable to take on tomorrow's challenges.

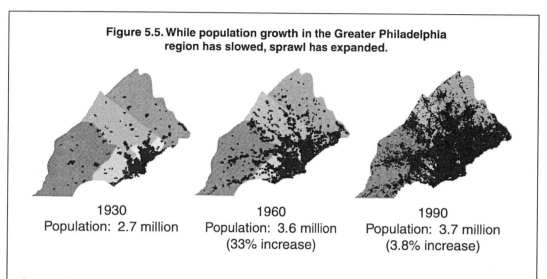

Figure 5.5. While population growth in the Greater Philadelphia region has slowed, sprawl has expanded.

1930
Population: 2.7 million

1960
Population: 3.6 million
(33% increase)

1990
Population: 3.7 million
(3.8% increase)

Source: Pennsylvania Environmental Council based on data from the Institute of the City Parks Association (1992), the University of Pennsylvania (1970), the National Park Service and the Delaware Valley Regional Planning Commission (1990)

In the future, Philadelphia must work toward regional solutions to confront fiscal disparities, sprawl, and congestion to help stabilize the region's communities, preserve regional open space, and ensure the unimpeded flow of goods and people through the region. The City can encourage efforts to focus regional resources on reducing the concentration of poverty that threatens to consume municipalities as it encourages inefficient regional growth. While such efforts could produce increased resources to fight urban problems, they may also necessitate the creation of additional regional decision-making structures to oversee the use of regional resources like the one currently in place to manage mass transit in Philadelphia.

Regional Problems Require Regional Solutions

The Greater Philadelphia region faces challenges from global economic shifts, and changes in national and state policies. If the resources of the jurisdictions of the region are occupied with efforts to build new communities as well as to stabilize older communities, then the region as a whole will be unable to compete with other metropolitan areas that focus those same resources on improving their regional workforce and infrastructure. The University of Pennsylvania's Wharton School estimates that in 1995 alone, the City of Philadelphia spent $134 million (beyond federal and state aid to the City) on what can be described as direct poverty-related expenditures. If Philadelphia, which is home to a disproportionate amount of the region's poor, had regional help to pay for its poverty-related expenditures, more City dollars could have been directed toward making the City more competitive by lowering the Wage and Net Profits Tax by more than 10 percent. Other communities would not have had to pay to fund infrastructure improvements to absorb new residents who fled deteriorating City neighborhoods for suburban jurisdictions and economic growth would have occurred across the region.

The economic health of the region is threatened by disconnects in the workforce development system. As the region decentralizes, the spatial mismatch between jobs and potential employees affects businesses and workers in all jurisdictions. Suburban employers, unable to find skilled workers, must increase wages to attract workers from farther and farther away. Urban workers find public transportation largely unable to efficiently connect them with suburban jobs. As mass transit agencies attempt to create "reverse commuting" routes, higher prices and increased mass transit costs result throughout the area.

The environmental result of regional sprawl has a variety of effects from increased bad-air days, loss of open space, rising temperatures from urban-heat-island effect, and more suburban flooding. Pollution abatement expenditures, increased climate-control costs, and rising insurance rates affect taxpayers across the region and reduce discretionary spending on goods and services.

While critical funding is diverted to deal with regional problems, the region is unable to fund needed major investments in infrastructure and the quality of the workforce. Without an excellent infrastructure, including a world-class information technology infrastructure, and without a skilled workforce, the Greater Philadelphia region will be unable to compete for the employers and residents of the 21st century.

In the Portland metropolitan area, the Greater Portland Metropolitan Service District (METRO)—the first and only elected regional government body in the country—has wide latitude to shape regional policies. The District uses tax-shared revenues to fund and operate regional mass transit, park and recreational facilities, and other regional assets. Beyond support for regional assets, METRO prepares regional transportation plans, adopts regional housing opportunity plans, develops solid waste treatment plans, and coordinates land use plans of the 27 jurisdictions within District borders. The District has developed an Urban Growth Containment Boundary to restrain urban sprawl and preserve open space, and is working to implement a fair-housing plan, and coordinated sewer and treatment plant construction.

In Minnesota, a coalition of urban and suburban legislators created a series of unique and wide-ranging solutions to the Minneapolis-St. Paul region's problems. The Minneapolis-St. Paul region has addressed property tax-base sharing, reinvestment in older communities, and fair housing issues in an effort to deconcentrate poverty, provide resource equity, and support the physical rebuilding to attract the middle class. These measures have been backed up by land planning and growth management coordinated with infrastructure, welfare reform, public works, and transportation and transit reform to promote efficiency and sustainability. The coalition has succeeded in efforts to promote regional tax-base sharing (the original Minneapolis-St. Paul regional tax-base sharing actually dates back to 1971), fair housing, transportation/transit reform, land-use planning, and a stronger metropolitan government for the Twin Cities. The Minneapolis-St. Paul region currently shares nearly $400 million (approximately 20 percent) of the regional tax base. This not only redistributes resources from growing communities toward communities with additional needs, but also discourages inter-jurisdictional competition because any regional growth now benefits the entire region instead of just one community. Other legislation placed all regional sewer, transit, and land-use planning under the authority of the Metropolitan Council of the Twin Cities—a regional planning agency. Fair housing legislation and land-use reform to preserve open space have also passed.

TAX-BASE SHARING IN PHILADELPHIA

In 1997, the Pennsylvania Environmental Council published a report prepared by the Metropolitan Area Program of the National Growth Management Leadership Project titled, "Philadelphia Metropolitics: A Regional Agenda for Community and Stability." The report argues that initiatives similar to those at work in Minneapolis-St. Paul could help reverse the social and economic polarization that weakens communities in the Greater Philadelphia region. In addressing tax-base[1] equity, the report

---

[1] Tax base refers to the value of assets subject to taxation, not the amount derived from taxation. It is therefore important to note that tax-base sharing does not actually redistribute a defined level of revenues, but a defined level of tax base from which to derive tax revenues.

offered several models of possible tax-base sharing scenarios for Greater Philadelphia designed to redistribute incremental tax-base growth in an effort to address the needs of declining communities.

In one model, the Metropolitan Area Program based regional tax-base redistribution on sharing the tax base derived from high-value residential properties (similar to the program in place in the Minneapolis-St. Paul area). If the communities of the Greater Philadelphia region contributed their 1993 residential property tax base for housing valued at greater than $200,000 into a tax-base sharing pool, and redistributed the pooled tax base back out to communities based on a formula giving preference to those communities with a low per capita tax base, the City of Philadelphia would have added more than $18 billion to its tax base. Based on the City's 1993 Real Estate Tax rates, taxing this additional base would annually generate approximately $223 million for Philadelphia and approximately $273 for the Philadelphia School District. Under this scenario, 105 Southeastern Pennsylvania jurisdictions would receive additional tax base and 133 jurisdictions would contribute tax base—four jurisdictions would receive more tax base per capita than Philadelphia.

Under a second scenario, which would place 15 percent of each community's tax base into a tax-base sharing pool and cap Philadelphia's additional tax base at $5 billion, the additional tax base would annually generate approximately $60 million for Philadelphia and approximately $73 for the Philadelphia School District. Under this scenario, 87 Southeastern Pennsylvania jurisdictions would receive additional tax base and 151 jurisdictions would contribute tax base—50 jurisdictions would receive more tax base per capita than Philadelphia.

While these tax-base sharing schemes may appear politically unpalatable, in both scenarios, a larger number of state legislative districts would gain tax base than would lose tax base.

In the Greater Philadelphia region, tax-base sharing would ease the fiscal crisis in declining communities, remove pressure from growing communities to spread local debt costs through growth, and discourage low-density sprawl. In addition it would discourage competition for tax base so the region could compete as a whole to attract employers instead of competing among jurisdictions to steal employers.

If, based on the modes put forth by the Metropolitan Area Program, Philadelphia could generate an additional $133 to $496 million in revenue, the extra funding could be used to address poverty-related expenditures, improve ailing schools, and lower taxes. Interestingly, the lower $133 million figure is nearly identical to the $134 million the Wharton School estimated that Philadelphia spent in 1995 in unreimbursed poverty-related costs. Any form of tax-base sharing could be predicated on a condition that jurisdictions receiving regionally generated funds use that new revenue in part to lower taxes and should be tied to some measure of performance to encourage effective effort management.

Seeking to address issues of school funding disparities and jurisdictional over-reliance on property tax, many Pennsylvanians look to the General Assembly for tax reform. Advocates would focus reform efforts on shifting the burden for certain governmental responsibilities to the state while expanding the tax options for local jurisdictions. Any tax reform effort must address Philadelphia's Wage and Net Profits Tax, and Philadelphia's significant burden of a disproportionately high percentage of the region's poor residents.

Some Philadelphia-area leaders have advocated for the Commonwealth of Pennsylvania to assume the responsibility to fund all education-, court-, and prison-related costs to allow local jurisdictions to use the savings to address local needs or cut taxes. Such a plan would then alter the legislation that enables Philadelphia to tax non-resident workers to allow suburban jurisdictions to tax the income of residents who work in Philadelphia. Such a move would ease the burden of suburban property owners by giving communities new tax options and force the City of

Philadelphia to reduce its reliance on the Wage and Net Profits Tax. State funding of local courts and prisons may soon become a reality as the Commonwealth of Pennsylvania complies with legal decisions directing the General Assembly to provide such funding. If Philadelphia could be unburdened of the responsibility to fund schools and courts, it would be able to reallocate approximately $650 million each year to other efforts or cut the Wage and Net Profits Tax by 60 percent. Fair housing efforts and increased regional land-use planning would complement tax-base sharing, or revenue redistribution efforts. Such measures would help deconcentrate poverty, prevent sprawl, and help the region achieve sustainable growth.

Philadelphia and ailing suburban communities suffer from problems too massive for any individual city or township to confront alone. While many suburban areas are experiencing unprecedented growth, suburban communities are not monolithic and many ailing suburbs—without world-class universities, cultural attractions, and prominent civic boosters—are more troubled, and more at risk of collapse, than Philadelphia. Unless the jurisdictions of the Greater Philadelphia region concentrate efforts on finding new solutions, further regional decline may be expected even if isolated areas continue to prosper. Just as recent urban decline has held the region back, reversing urban and suburban woes should exponentially expand regional economic growth.

Responding to an Incentive for Regional Cooperation

While the imperatives for regional cooperation are clearly in place, the incentives are often missing. Even though the interdependence of metropolitan regions is demonstrated and the necessity of regional cooperation compelling, local control is cherished by many residents and elected leaders. A mixture of "carrots" and "sticks" could promote regional cooperation.

The University of Pennsylvania's Wharton School has advanced the notion of an Urban Audit that could be used to help determine aid levels for cities. Such a tool, which would critically analyze cities' service efforts and accomplishments, could be used to apportion intergovernmental transfers or intra-regional tax-base sharing based not only on need, but also on how effectively cities use aid to address problems. In this way, the perverse incentive to fail—when a city actually receives aid based on the amount of misery found within its borders, there is a clear incentive to allow misery to continue to maintain aid levels—can be altered to create an incentive to succeed in eliminating misery.

Similarly, federal and state funding for cities and suburban jurisdictions should promote regional cooperation. Just as existing laws effectively force regional planning by mandating the creation of regional planning bodies in order to be eligible to receive certain funding, future aid and funding could be tied to the creation of regional tax-base sharing, regional land-use planning, regional service delivery, and regional fair housing efforts. It is easy to make a rational case for regional solutions to regional problems, but incentives may be required to encourage jurisdictions to follow through with action and overcome reluctance toward cooperation efforts. Assurances that any additional funding will create results could help. Much of that resistance could be overcome if federal and state aid and grants or regional funding efforts came with rewards for regional cooperation and efficient uses of shared funding, or punishments for the lack of regional cooperation and inefficient use of such funding.

When Katharine Lee Bates was inspired to pen "America the Beautiful," she wrote lovingly about spacious skies and amber waves of grain. In a later verse, she declares, "Thine alabaster cities gleam/Undimmed by human tears!" Philadelphians know that American cities have been dimmed and that, without assistance, local governments alone cannot solve all of the societal problems that are manifested in cities. Cities require additional help to address problems like concentration of poverty and deteriorating communities. But surrounding jurisdictions and the state and federal governments cannot be expected to give additional funds to the City without an assurance that the money will make a positive difference.

RECOMMENDATIONS FOR ACTION

The City should work with state and regional leaders to address regional problems.

Action Steps:

- Work to pass tax sharing or tax reform legislation in the Pennsylvania General Assembly.

- Work to address land-use, fair housing, and regional growth management issues in the Pennsylvania General Assembly.

- Work with local leaders to address regional governance and funding issues.

- Establish any necessary regional decision-making protocols and governance structures.

Fiscal Impact:

- Potential increase in City revenue or decrease in City expenditures from regional tax-base sharing or tax reform.

The City should work with state and federal leaders to create incentives for regional cooperation.

Action Steps:

- Work to ensure that state and federal legislation creating regional cooperation efforts bases any resource distribution on performance as well as need.

- Work to ensure that state and federal legislation encourages regional cooperation efforts.

Fiscal Impact:

- Potential increase in City revenues or decrease in City expenditures from tax-base sharing, tax reform, and other regional cooperation efforts.

CONCLUSION

In the end, Philadelphia's place in the region's future, like cities' places in the nation's future, must be central. Cities have consistently been the hallmark of a society's greatness. The commerce, culture, and interpersonal contact afforded by a city serve to enhance personal creativity and expand societal horizons. Eventually, the cost and folly of sprawl, and the reality that it is in the region's collective interest to strengthen its hub, will force government officials, residents, and businesses to turn attention back to the center. Other parts of the region may, and should, thrive. But for the entire region to realize its potential, all concerned must resolve that while Philadelphia may never again dominate the region as it once did, it must be a viable and vibrant core for the area.

The City government, therefore, must make Philadelphia as accessible and inviting as possible in order to spur growth. To make the City accessible, government must lower the barrier of high taxes on individuals and employers, improve the urban infrastructure to promote the effective movement of goods and services, and focus City government on customer relations. To make the City inviting, government must improve safety and the perception of safety, create a system of public education that attracts students from all communities, and produce neighborhoods that will serve as magnets for a thriving population. Elected and appointed officials must now make the City the best possible hub for a growing city-suburban area. If this region is to thrive and compete with other regions of the world, a strong Philadelphia must be its center. In a region where other jurisdictions offer families and employers inviting alternatives to life in the City, Philadelphia must exert effort to retain and attract population and jobs.

Many of the recommendations on preceding pages address ways in which the City can create a government for the future and effectively respond to future challenges. By working with surrounding jurisdictions to establish regional funding for regional assets and regional collaboration for efficient and effective service-delivery efforts, the City can improve the overall competitiveness of the region. By taking advantage of regional interconnections and avoiding energy-draining intra-regional competition, the City and its neighboring jurisdictions can confront regional fiscal disparities, sprawl, and congestion and move into the future as a united region.

SECOND EDITION SUPPLEMENT TO CHAPTER 5
CITY IN THE REGION
A DECLARATION OF INTERDEPENDENCE

PHILADELPHIA'S PLACE IN THE GREATER PHILADELPHIA REGION

No city is an island; it is a part of its surrounding environment and region, interdependently linked. The Greater Philadelphia Region shares regional amenities and labor market, one in three commuters in the region travels between counties each day, and nearly one in 12 travels between states, representing a significant flow of people and wages across borders. Local governments cooperate on some road maintenance and snow removal. They are part of mutual-aid pacts, agreeing to provide additional fire and police protection if a neighbor requires it. Examples of cross-jurisdictional cooperation on transportation projects abound. Yet while such initiatives are beneficial, they only serve to scratch the surface of the potential gains in efficiency and effectiveness if greater inter-municipal planning and development were to occur.

In 1999, the Controller's Office explored the linkages between the City of Philadelphia and its surrounding region. We noted that the economic success or failure of the central city has ripple effect through neighboring jurisdictions, and that there are shared challenges of crime, poverty and residential flight in both Philadelphia and some of its suburbs. A 2001 report by the Metropolitan Philadelphia Policy Center, entitled *Flight or Fight*, tells the story of the Greater Philadelphia Region. The study reveals that while Center City saw resurgence, the region as a whole was not competing with top tier metropolitan areas around the nation and the globe, losing ground in population and job growth, as well as real estate appreciation. While *Flight or Fight* outlined the many challenges the region faces, it offered an optimistic vision for how the region capitalize on its regional assets and fight for a better future. The recommendations echoed many of the proposals in the original edition of *Philadelphia: A New Urban Direction*, and included suggestions for improving tax and land use policies to curb sprawl and promote economic growth on a regional scale. *Flight or Fight* and other reports continue to highlight the need for a regional approach to solving the problems of urban decline, sprawl, poverty, crime and other societal ills.

Still, regionalism cannot be perceived as a cure-all or a course of action that can be easily implemented. Cities, boroughs, and towns, including Philadelphia, are reluctant to divest themselves of power and authority, even with the potential of net gains. Inability to surmount fears of negative consequences and difficulties in coordination have, to date, quashed most attempts for comprehensive regional action, although the "creeping" regionalism identified in the first edition of *Philadelphia: A New Urban Direction* continues. City leaders can only attempt to work with other regional leaders and the state to identify and forward the interests of the area. The local governments of greater Philadelphia need not clash and compete to grow and prosper; with pooled resources and abilities, there is vast potential for regional development.

REGIONAL EFFORTS TO MOVE TOWARD A MORE COMPETITIVE REGION

In 1999, the Controller's Office recommended that state and regional leaders establish regional funding mechanisms for support assets that benefit the entire Greater Philadelphia area, such as stadia and arts centers. While the Mayor has convened a panel to explore regional funding mechanisms for the arts, little progress has been made in this area. *Philadelphia: A New Urban Direction* also called for an end to competition within the region for economic activity. Greater Philadelphia jurisdictions face mounting costs and tax expenditures from incentives to lure companies from one local municipality to another, simply moving economic activity around the region rather than growing it.

In 1999, we proposed non-aggression pacts to halt the onslaught of tax breaks wars between communities. Since that time significant strides have been made in taking a regional approach to economic development. Competition drives innovation and efficiency, enabling the strongest and best organizations to prosper in the market. Yet, competition between neighboring states can often be counter-productive, especially when the competition is confined to a sub-region of the state. For years, Pennsylvania, New Jersey, and Delaware were engaged in such a competition in the Greater Philadelphia region, each offering packages of incentives to entice firms to relocate to their states to the loss of another. Not only was this process often costly, the gains each state hoped to realize were often over estimated. While the host state and local governments may realize a boost in tax revenue and potential some jobs, the region as a whole experiences no net gain in new jobs or economic benefit.

In late 2004, the governors of Pennsylvania, New Jersey, and Delaware worked together to overcome the territorial mindset and regional competition that had resulted in little economic growth for southeastern Pennsylvania, southern New Jersey, and northern Delaware. The three governors agreed to a non-competition pact, effectively declaring a truce in the competition to "steal" businesses from one state to another. Instead, the trio agreed to explore opportunities for cooperation and coordination to help establish the Greater Philadelphia region as a top location for businesses to locate or become established.

New combined ventures of public and private stakeholders have been initiated to advance the region's economic agenda have also begun since the first edition of *Philadelphia: A New Urban Direction*. To present a uniform face for the region's business attraction efforts, reduce duplication of efforts, and damper intra-regional poaching of firms, the Greater Philadelphia Chamber of Commerce created a sub-group — Select Greater Philadelphia — with the sole mission of facilitating the expansion or relocation of businesses to the region. This public-private partnership, financially supported by the City of Philadelphia, other local jurisdictions and private funds, is essentially a business development team, packaging and presenting the assets of the region and creating proposals tailored to each potential new individual firm or business. Select Greater Philadelphia's team provides clients with general market and industry specific research, site tours, and connections to established local executives to entice new business to the region. Other regional efforts to address other issues in the region have also been formed, such as the Knowledge Industry Partnership (KIP). KIP, a joint effort of Philadelphia business, civic, educational, and government entities, seeks to retain local college graduates and promote the knowledge industry in the region.

While these efforts represent positive partnerships in across jurisdictional and among business, nonprofits, and government stakeholders, more can be achieved. In 2005, civic, political, nonprofit, academic, and business leaders from Philadelphia traveled to Chicago to learn about the strategies for economic growth in that region, as part of the Pennsylvania Economy League's Leadership Exchange. Attendees were struck by the high degree of cooperation between the central city and the outlying municipalities, and the significant leadership of the City of Chicago. Central to this success is a regional vision for the future that focuses not only on economic growth, but also infrastructure and arts and culture. The Greater Philadelphia Region currently has the opportunity to rally around a specific vision for the future, namely hosting the summer Olympics in 2016. The city should lead an effort to plan and campaign for hosting this event. Simply the act of planning for the Olympics could engender cooperation among regional business, civic, and political leaders and provide the impetus for undertaken regional projects. Such an effort could provide a catalyst to reexamine the regions infrastructure needs for the coming years and could be a catalyst for setting priorities and securing funding.

RECOMMENDATION FOR ACTION

The city should take an active role in leading a bid for the 2016 Olympics

Action Steps:

- Support current planning efforts.
- Take leadership in seeking support from other jurisdictions in the region.

Fiscal Impacts:

- Potential costs associated with planning and infrastructure.
- Potential savings from increased regional cooperation and efficiency.

REGIONAL COOPERATION TO CONFRONT FISCAL DISPARITIES, SPRAWL AND CONGESTION

Philadelphia's recent revitalization has been primarily contained in specific pockets of the city. This same pattern is echoed on the regional scale, as the Greater Philadelphia Region presents isolated areas of both extreme growth and extreme decline. In 1999, the Controller's Office noted that problems associated with environmental integrity, transportation, housing, crime, poverty, and educational inequality do not end at the city's borders, and that in order to address these issues of disparity state action and regional cooperation is necessary. To date, there has been minimal progress in addressing these problems through state and federal incentives for cooperation or changes to state law to enable regional taxation and governance.

One of the clearest hurdles is the region's astounding number of local governments tht would need to be coordinated. The City of Philadelphia's government is the closest and most immediate governing body for over 1.4 million Pennsylvanians. The other 10 million plus residents fall under the jurisdiction of one or a few of Pennsylvania's over 2500 governmental units — township, borough, county, or otherwise — incorporating virtually a different governing unit for every 4670 residents in the state. Only Illinois's and Minnesota's local governance is more fragmented, though unlike Pennsylvania, townships are able to be annexed by cities or boroughs in those states, creating at least the possibility for greater coordination and planning. The five-county Greater Philadelphia region alone is home to nearly four million people in almost 250 separate municipalities, with few mandated areas of coordination in existence.

The fragmentation creates more than difficulties in coordination; it represents lost opportunities and wasted resources. Instead of working cooperatively toward common goals, more directed development and better land use strategies, the extreme fragmentation of municipalities can foster a competitive climate leading to inefficient, ineffective outcomes. Service delivery efforts and public projects may be unnecessarily duplicated and tax rates may be higher than need be if efforts could be consolidated. Local government fragmentation makes it extremely difficult for local and regional economies to adequately respond and adapt to the modern economic, social, and political climate. Growth and development are impeded, detracting from the overall economic viability and competitiveness of the region. Compared with other metropolitan regions, Greater Philadelphia has experienced slower population, employment, and general economic growth. According to a report by the Brookings Institution, the lack of growth can partially be attributed to fragmentation; the shear number of governments necessitates greater economic performance just to be on par with national and regional growth in other areas of the country.

The severe fragmentation of Pennsylvania's and greater Philadelphia's local government also exacerbates suburban sprawl and threatens the economic, social and environmental sustainability of the region. With towns and cities unable to alter their borders or effectively direct land use and re-use, new development often occurs on "greenfields," those areas that have never been developed, lessening the region's stock of valuable farm land and general open spaces. At the same time, older buildings and infrastructure in the region become abandoned or underutilized, discarding the investments of prior generations, wasting resources to maintain and operate little used facilities or to reproduce them for new development. That this results in net costs to the region municipalities is clear. Urban and inner ring areas find themselves with a surplus of infrastructure and a declining tax base that hinders their ability to maintain those assets, while newly developed areas are face fiscal strain as the try to provide adequate transportation, education and recreation infrastructure for the influx of new residents and businesses.

Pennsylvania's legal system allows for little formal regional determination for planned new construction and development. Currently, there exist only voluntary systems for cross-municipal planning, with no suburban areas cooperating with any of the state's six major metropolitan areas. Merger, consolidation, or annexation efforts have been attempted only in Pennsylvania's rural areas, and are unlikely to occur in the Philadelphia area in the near future. To overcome the impacts of fragmentation and to mitigate the negative impacts of sprawl upon both areas of disinvestment and those that are seeing an influx of development, the city should partner with surrounding jurisdictions to lobby the Pennsylvania General Assembly to enact concurrency laws.

Under concurrency laws, such as those in place in Florida, permission for development is contingent upon adequate capacity of local infrastructure, such as roads, sewers, and schools, to serve the new development, or financial resources and plans to construct such infrastructure must be in place. If applicable on a regional or state-wide scale, concurrency laws channel development to locations that can support it. Smaller suburban jurisdictions will not find themselves overwhelmed with new service demands, while building in urbanized areas would be encouraged.

Even with concurrency laws, all the regional issues of inefficient development will not be addressed. Without multi-municipality and regional planning and development review, the environmental effects of new development are often not considered or mediations under-planned. For example, over-development without adequate consideration and improvement of sewer systems could increase the likelihood that the system would become overwhelmed and flooding ensue. With development in one municipality impacting another, whether through increased or altered traffic patterns or increases in wastes, but potential new revenue accumulating only to the hosting community, concerted efforts are required to mitigate the negatives while more equitably distributing the positives. The city should work with surrounding jurisdictions to establish a system to review projects with negative spillover effects and devise a fair mechanism to reallocate municipal costs and benefits.

RECOMMENDATIONS FOR ACTION

The city should support enactment of concurrency laws by the Pennsylvania General Assembly.

Action Steps:

- Coordinate policy recommendations for concurrency law with other jurisdictions.

- Lobby the General Assembly to enact concurrency laws.

Fiscal Impacts:

- Potential short-term costs associated with lobbying efforts.

- Potential long-term revenue from increased and more efficient development.

The city should work with state and regional leaders to address spillover negative impacts from development projects.

Action Steps:

- Work to address governance and funding of regional impact reviews of development projects.

- Establish mechanism to fairly redistribute the costs and benefits of development activity.

Fiscal Impacts:

- Potential short-term expenses associated with operations of regional project reviews.

- Potential costs or revenues from reallocation of impacts.

CONCLUSION

Philadelphia and its region are forever linked in their quest to provide high-quality housing, recreational, and economic opportunities to residents, businesses, and visitors. For too long, individual jurisdictions have pursued their individual goals without concern for the impacts on their neighbors, despite the inefficient programs, policies, and initiatives that resulted. While there are some actions that can be taken by the city and other local governments, comprehensive regional cooperation will have to be supported with state legislation for regional governance and tax sharing. The Greater Philadelphia Region will be better able to lobby for these changes once we have proven that the governments can come together with shared goals and strategies for regional improvement. To achieve this, the leaders of Philadelphia, the region's economic engine and central city, must lead the charge for cooperation and coordination. The possibility of hosting the Olympics provides a central vision for public and private leaders to rally around. This effort would give the region the opportunity to not only show the world what it is capable of achieving, but to prove to itself that cooperation is feasible and possible.

CHAPTER 6
CONCLUSION

We will transmit this City,
not only not less, but greater and more beautiful
than it was transmitted to us.

—The Oath of the Athenian Citizen

TOWARD A FUTURE PHILADELPHIA

In 1682, William Penn set sail from England on a ship named *Welcome* to view his City of Brotherly Love. As Philadelphia prepares to welcome the 21st century more than 300 years later, Penn's statue atop City Hall looks over the City he founded, keeping silent vigil. Penn would scarcely recognize the municipality first rendered by Thomas Holme as an advertisement, *Portraiture of the City of Philadelphia*, displaying Penn's symmetrical gridiron pattern of wide streets and large plots. Penn's "greene Country Towne" has been transformed into a modern metropolis during the past centuries. Philadelphia has expanded beyond the City's original acreage, experienced tremendous growth, spawned monumental works of art and architecture, and fallen victim to the distress of the modern city.

As it approaches the 21st century, Philadelphia is a city of contrasts. In some ways, even the City's beautiful, thriving neighborhoods show some sign of decay. Graffiti may be scrawled on the back of a stop sign or a neighbor might wake to find shattered glass in place of a car window. But in some other ways, all of the City's blighted neighborhoods show some sign of hope. Well-tended gardens contrast with boarded-up homes and renovated houses show off the architectural gems found in even the most neglected areas. Whether the perspective is from an upscale, leafy suburb-within-the-city community, or a hardscrabble, brick and asphalt inner-city neighborhood, Philadelphia is full of vigor. By tapping into this spirit, Philadelphians can capitalize on their ability to revitalize their own environment and enter a bright future.

There is an undeniable energy in Philadelphia as the millennium draws near. Fueled by a lengthy national economic expansion and infused with the optimism of collegial political leadership, Philadelphia is moving in the right direction. While many Philadelphians consistently view the City as a place with tremendous potential, it is clear that much of that potential has already been realized and more excitement is on the horizon. From public investment in the Independence National Historical Park, to private investment in the Center City housing market, to unprecedented investment in the long-dormant U.S. shipbuilding industry, to efforts across the City to revitalize neighborhood commercial strips, Philadelphia is pulsating with activity. New investment in tourist and cultural attractions, expanded university involvement in surrounding neighborhoods, and promising private-sector responses show that this activity is spreading in a positive manner.

Philadelphia's turnaround from the brink of bankruptcy to record budgetary surpluses has generated national attention. The City's positive energy has attracted favorable notice from such diverse organizations as the Republican National Committee, which selected Philadelphia as the site of the 2000 Republican National Convention, and the Walt Disney Company, which selected

Philadelphia as the site of the world's third DisneyQuest interactive theme park. This positive momentum is slated to continue. In the near future, eye-popping waterfront development, dramatic airport expansion, and the largest post-World War II private housing development in the City, should add to Philadelphia's evolution.

The vitality that fueled the City's fiscal turnaround and stimulates development can be channeled toward continued improvements for the future. By using this momentum to energize efforts to fundamentally alter the way the City government operates, Philadelphia can prepare for the future. By capitalizing on this activity and channeling this energy toward attacking underlying decay, Philadelphia can improve quality of life in all its neighborhoods and reduce the high costs associated with doing business in the City.

One hundred years from now, William Penn will look down from his City Hall perch upon a City that today's Philadelphians will scarcely recognize. By committing to efforts to prepare City government for the future and attacking the woes confronting the modern metropolis, Philadelphians can make 21st-century Philadelphia a truly great city.

21ST-CENTURY PHILADELPHIA

Consensus projections for the future may indicate continued population losses, demographic shifts, and economic threats, but they also forecast opportunities for growth. Philadelphia's job and population loss did not begin because of one factor, and the City's elected and appointed leaders will not be able to create growth by simply addressing one issue. Philadelphia has weathered its recent fiscal crisis and, with the help of a strong economy and energetic governmental administration, is poised to take on the challenge of the new millennium. The City must now enact policies designed to reverse the downward trends of past decades, capitalize on competitive advantages, and lessen the disamenities associated with living and working in Philadelphia. If City government can do its part to reduce the cost of doing business in the City and reduce the reasons individuals choose to leave—crime, taxes, underperforming schools—Philadelphia can retain and attract residents, employers, and visitors.

The Controller's Office projections foresee growth in the national economy. But, because Philadelphia presents high relative factor costs for industries projected to experience strong growth on the national level, City economic growth can be expected to continue to lag behind national growth unless the City is able to do its part to reduce those factor costs or capitalize on growth in niche markets like higher education and hospitality and tourism. Because population growth is closely associated with employment growth, increased employment opportunity in Philadelphia should result in some population growth in the future. This increase in population is projected to lag behind employment increases due to perceived and real disamenities associated with City residency. Therefore, population levels will remain somewhat unresponsive to employment growth unless the City can improve the overall quality of life in Philadelphia. Similarly, while Philadelphia's future population may comprise a higher percentage of low-income and older individuals, by preparing City residents for future jobs and improving quality of life in Philadelphia, the City can retain and attract working-class residents to maintain and increase the vitality of its communities.

Cities have always prospered by becoming places where people want to live, transact business, recreate, and visit. Great cities attract residents by fostering vibrant neighborhoods where families can grow, entice employers by establishing a marketplace where fortunes can be made, and lure visitors by supporting attractions that draw travelers. Philadelphia's recent employment growth, a booming market for converting office buildings into apartments, and dramatic hospitality-related developments all affirm that the City is such a place for many families, employers, and visitors today. Philadelphia can become such a place for many more in the future.

While Philadelphia's fate is dependent upon the global economy, federal and state policy shifts, and changing individual preferences, Philadelphia's elected and appointed leaders can position the City to maximize opportunities to grow in the future by pursuing sound policies and administering governmental operations in a sensible manner. Each of the projections for Philadelphia's future presents challenges and opportunities. Just as poor decisions in past decades hastened Philadelphia's decline, wise decisions in the future can foster resurgence.

Without wise and determined action, the City could be fated to meet the growing needs of growing aged and low-income populations and deteriorating physical infrastructure. Faced with increasing social needs and a declining tax base, the City could be forced to consider raising taxes, cutting services, or engaging in short-term financial maneuvers which could jeopardize long-term budgetary stability. Each of these choices would serve to reverse the progress the City has made in recent years.

However, with sound policy directions, the City can avoid this scenario and capitalize on the momentum developed in recent years. The City will fully enjoy that resurgence when it creates a government focused on performance and evaluated by the results it delivers; when the City is able to reduce the tax burden on residents and employers to a level that makes Philadelphia competitive with rival jurisdictions; and when individuals view Philadelphia as a preferred place to raise a family and start a business. To fully accomplish that resurgence in the future, the City must act today.

First and foremost, the City must create a proper governmental framework and proper municipal culture for the future, which will drive all governmental operations. Everything that government does flows from its overall organization and structure. Therefore, City government must be organized and structured to meet new and changing challenges. A governmental framework designed to meet the challenges of the 1950s cannot effectively and efficiently confront the problems of the 21st century. Similarly, City government must be focused on performance to meet service-delivery demands of citizens who are free to move elsewhere. Without incentives to focus the governmental bureaucracy on results, agencies are apt to respond to political or internal pressures, which do little to improve service to the general population.

In the future, the City must be administered under a flexible governmental structure focused on making service a priority through proper incentives that foster constant service-delivery improvement while enhancing government's accountability to the citizenry. Philadelphia may not be able to alter individuals' preference for city life, but government can work to improve service-delivery efforts. By creating a streamlined governmental organization and an adaptable personnel structure, Philadelphia's government can prepare for the future. By emphasizing constant governmental improvement, Philadelphia's government can focus on the needs of its citizenry. By stressing improved government interactivity and accessibility and a commitment to keep the City's legal and regulatory systems modern, Philadelphia government can work as a magnet for residents, employers, and visitors.

With a proper governmental framework in place, the City must focus on sound fiscal policies for the future. Simply put, the government cannot tax or spend now in ways that jeopardize the City's future fiscal health. While the demands of the citizenry have no limit, City government will have to spend less to be able to fund tax cuts that are crucial to reducing the high cost of doing business in Philadelphia. With a properly flexible government and a similarly adaptable personnel system, the City can improve service-delivery efforts while reducing spending.

In the future, the City must tax effectively and spend efficiently to reduce the cost of government and craft fiscal policies designed to promote overall budgetary structural balance. Philadelphia may not be able to alter global economics, but it can enforce overall fiscal discipline to ensure that the City lives within its means. By maintaining a balance between the cost of City services and the local economy's ability to fund those services, Philadelphia can budget effectively for the future. By maximizing the benefit of tax-reduction efforts, increasing the effectiveness of tax collections, and reducing the cost of government, Philadelphia can lower the cost of living and doing business in the City. By generating revenue through entrepreneurial activities and capitalizing on the value of the City's marketplace, Philadelphia can increase its ability to fund future expenditures and tax cuts.

Grounded in fiscal discipline, a proper governmental framework that enhances performance and focuses agencies on results will permit the City to confront specific future challenges. A flexible governmental structure may enable the City to operate effectively, but unless its government provides quality schools and safe streets, the City will be unable to attract and retain residents. Fiscal discipline may encourage the City to operate efficiently, but unless government addresses the true costs of doing business in Philadelphia and improves the ease with which goods move through the marketplace, the City will be unable to attract and retain employers.

In the future, the City must convince individuals, business owners, and visitors, through its actions involving economic development, education, housing, public safety, tourist attraction, and transportation, that Philadelphia is an excellent place to live, work, and play. Philadelphia may not be able to alter local government's role in the American federal system, but it can craft more effective policies to address specific urban challenges. By targeting economic development efforts and capitalizing on the City's competitive advantages, Philadelphia can grow into the future. By stressing programs that work and altering the education-related governance structure to provide City elected officials with a more direct role in public education, Philadelphia can create a system of public education to benefit all families. By increasing demand for housing and creating disincentives to vacancy, Philadelphia can create a market for the City's vacant housing stock. By preventing gun violence, coordinating law enforcement efforts, and utilizing passive crime-fighting measures, Philadelphia can create a safer city. By focusing and linking tourism-promotion efforts and creating dedicated funding for tourism-related efforts, Philadelphia can showcase its attractions for the world. By working to make mass transit the preferred mode for residents, commuters, and visitors, Philadelphia can improve accessibility and mobility throughout the region.

In the end, the City can only do so much by itself and cannot effectively attack all future challenges without assistance. The problems associated with concentrated poverty—joblessness, crime, and decay—are manifested in the City, but are not just City problems. Economic, sociologic, and anecdotal evidence all confirm that the City and its suburban communities are inextricably linked. If suburban jurisdictions are to prosper to their potential, the City must grow.

In the future, the City must work with the leaders of the Commonwealth of Pennsylvania and neighboring suburban jurisdictions to confront the challenges that face the City and the Greater Philadelphia region—together. Philadelphia may not be able to change the Commonwealth of Pennsylvania's policies related to its largest City, but it can work more effectively with surrounding suburban communities to contend in the global marketplace. By working toward regional funding for regional assets and regional service-delivery collaboration and against intra-regional competition, Philadelphia can improve the region's ability to compete with other economic regions of the world. By working toward increased regional cooperation and regional solutions to local problems, Philadelphia can improve the region's ability to confront fiscal disparities, sprawl, and congestion.

Taken as a whole, these recommendations create a plan of action for the future that can fuel debate about Philadelphia's future. While the City's challenge to make Philadelphia a preferred place is clear, the resources to create change are scarce. Enacting the recommendations contained in this document does not have to increase the cost of government in Philadelphia. By improving overall productivity, budgeting effectively, and growing the local economy, City leaders can expand services while reducing the cost of government. In many ways, balancing the budget after Philadelphia's fiscal crisis was only a prelude to the challenge ahead—enhancing the effectiveness and efficiency of City government to improve service-delivery efforts while funding future tax cuts to promote growth.

PHILADELPHIA MANETO—ACCEPTING THE CHALLENGE

This document represents the City Controller's Office's best estimate as to what the future might hold for Philadelphia and contains recommendations for how to structure a proper governmental response to the problems and opportunities posed by that future. The projections, analyses, concepts, and recommendations contained in this document are put forth to help guide efforts to lead Philadelphia into the 21st century.

In 1916, *Harper's* magazine declared, "The one thing unforgivable in Philadelphia is to be new—to be different from what has been." In the future, however, Philadelphia must be different from what has been. By creating a city that works, supported by sound fiscal polices, Philadelphia can become a magnet for residents and employers. By acting to address specific areas of concern with resolve and purpose, Philadelphia can reverse decades of decline. By firmly establishing regional efforts to foster regional growth, Philadelphia can be a source of strength for the entire metropolitan area.

Over the course of more than three centuries, Philadelphia has been shaped by world events and host to events that have shaped the world. The arrival of a new century can be the dawn of a new era for Philadelphia and its government. By anticipating and responding to trends it cannot change and acting to improve conditions that it can affect, City government can accept the challenge of the 21st century and create a bright future for Philadelphia.

CONCLUSION TO THE SECOND EDITION

Three centuries have past since William Penn created the original plan for Philadelphia. Penn's design showed great foresight, creating a layout that would serve as the base for the growth and development of a modern metropolis. Yet no matter how thoughtfully or carefully Penn may have envisioned the maturation of Philadelphia, he could not have imagined the city becoming what it has today. Penn's successors have been charged with managing the modern Philadelphia, building upon his plan but adapting it to the demands of the present.

Though only five, and not hundreds, of years have passed since the initial publication of *Philadelphia: A New Urban Direction*, a changing and evolving city demands a re-evaluation of this plan for Philadelphia. As with Penn's plan, much of *Philadelphia: A New Urban Direction* remains relevant today. Some prescriptions made for an ailing city have improved its condition, some remain to be filled, while others have been supplanted by newer, more appropriate solutions. Philadelphia must continuously examine and re-examine the manner in which it interacts with its residents, businesses, and visitors, ensuring that the city is providing the most efficient and effective delivery of service that can be achieved; that which is best for 1995 may not be optimal for 2005. The recommendations presented in this edition of *Philadelphia: A New Urban Direction* are meant to provide a review of past and a panel of new recommendations for the present context.

Philadelphia can become a location of choice, or remain a city that struggles to retain businesses and residents. To progress towards a brighter future, Philadelphia must confront many long-standing challenges; inaction is not an option. While the task is daunting, Philadelphia must be resolute in its efforts. The city must not be content to be below average or ordinary; it must dare to be great, implementing innovative policies and programs that can deliver real benefits to the city and its people. Philadelphia can establish itself as a place where people want to start a business or raise a family, a city without peer. With determined steps toward change and reform, Philadelphia can become a preferred place to live, work, and visit.

There are opportunities to reform the government structure to make it more flexible to respond to the changing needs of our population. Confidence in local government can be restored through the enactment of comprehensive campaign finance and ethics reforms, to ensure that the citizens of the city have a government worthy of them, one that is transparent and holds its officials accountable for their actions. Through continuous technological enhancement to city functions and programs designed to reach out to residents of all nationalities and backgrounds, Philadelphia can be assured that their government is accessible and responsive.

Even a responsive, attentive government with be ineffectual without sound financial practices. Maintaining city government's fiscal integrity is essential if it is to have the resources necessary to fulfill the service needs of the population. By embracing comprehensive tax reform, Philadelphia moves towards a tax structure that is more fair and less onerous, one that encourages growth as opposed to stifling it. The city must redouble its efforts to make the tax structure more accommodating to the businesses and residents that want to be in the city, but find it not cost effective to do so. Moreover, by addressing the growing costs associated with personnel services, the city can slow the rate of growth in the city expenses, which are currently outpacing our growth in revenues. Philadelphia must also adopt a rational strategy for debt issuance and other long-term obligations. The city cannot continue to try to solve today's problems without regard to costs to the next generation of Philadelphians.

Once effective financial and management practices are in place, Philadelphia must seek to offer all the elements that contribute to a high quality of life. Ensuring the public safety, either from petty crime or terrorist action, is a challenge that can be met. Philadelphia can ill afford to only react to emergencies when and if they arise, and must instead proactively plan for all foreseeable contingencies, providing methods for prevention where possible.

In order to leave a viable, vibrant city to the children of Philadelphia the city also must adopt policies to sustain the natural and built environments. Redevelopment in neighborhoods will occur with better land use planning and partnerships with the private sector to market the city's assets. The quality of the environment can be improved by pursuing policies to reduce energy consumption, congestion, and pollution. It is possible to create a business climate that is competitive with other jurisdictions and promotes participation of all Philadelphians, without wasting resources.

The fate of the Philadelphia will also be tied to the fate the region. The city no longer only competes with Conshohocken or Cherry Hill, but also Phoenix, Mexico City, and Shanghai. The public-private partnerships that span geographical boundaries can improve the future of Greater Philadelphia, enabling the region to compete in the global economy. Philadelphia must work with regional, state, and national leaders to promote its interests and achieve greater prosperity for all. In order to achieve this outcome, the city must focus attention on the regional infrastructures that support the movement of goods, people, and ideas, advocating for regional funding and planning to facilitate their development.

Although Philadelphia is confronted with the evidence that, without change, current economic and demographic trends of ongoing population and job loss will continue into the future, the city can pursue policies designed to change the trajectory of the projections where we can and adequately respond to and ameliorate the effects where we cannot. *Philadelphia: A New Urban Direction* presents recommendations to these ends; if implemented, Philadelphia will demonstrate a commitment to a brighter future for the city and its residents.

In the preface to the first edition of *Philadelphia: A New Urban Direction*, Dr. Randall M. Miller, professor of history at Saint Joseph's University, notes that the scaffolding surrounding William Penn's statue atop City Hall symbolizes a restoration of the city to its former grandeur. Now, over five years later, some scaffolding remains around City Hall and it is still very much a work in progress. Some areas gleam with a stately polish, reminiscent of the city's finest days and the promise the city's residents had for their future; yet some are still untouched, displaying the filth and scars from decades of neglect. Philadelphia is likewise a work in progress. There are still many areas of the city that require attention and assistance, but other sections have been revived and revitalized. The city is still presented with challenges, yet there is also opportunity. There are fundamental problems, but they are not insurmountable. One day, the last piece of scaffolding will be removed from City Hall, revealing the culmination of the efforts of countless Philadelphians — a majestic City Hall, renewed and transformed, that the city can be proud to hand down to its children. With resolute steps toward progress, making the choice to once again be among the great cities of the world, creating a Philadelphia as grand and enduring as our City Hall will be.

APPENDIX I
MAP OF THE CITY OF PHILADELPHIA
The map on the following page locates notable sites referred to in this document

1. 1st Police District/Engine Company 60/Ladder Company 19
2. Academy of Music
3. Academy of Natural Sciences of Philadelphia
4. American Flag House and Betsy Ross Memorial
5. Atwater Kent Museum
6. Avenue of the Arts (Broad Street)
7. Benjamin Franklin Bridge
8. Benjamin Franklin Parkway
9. Cathedral Basilica of Saints Peter and Paul
10. Community College of Philadelphia
11. Eastern State Penitentiary
12. Fairmount Waterworks
13. Fitler Square
14. Fort Mifflin
15. Frankford
16. Franklin D. Roosevelt Park
17. Germantown
18. Holy Family College
19. Kensington/Fairhill—Site of Operation Sunrise
20. Liberty Bell/Independence Hall Independence National Historical Park
21. Liberty Place
22. Logan—Site of Logan Sinking Homes
23. Market Street West (Avenue of Technology)
24. Masonic Temple
25. Mummers Museum
26. Pennsylvania Academy of Fine Arts
27. Pennsylvania Convention Center
28. Philadelphia Civic Center
29. Philadelphia High School for the Creative and Performing Arts
30. Philadelphia International Airport
31. Philadelphia Museum of Art
32. Philadelphia Saving Fund Society Building
33. Philadelphia Zoo
34. Powel House
35. Proposed gated community in Southwest Center City
36. Proposed golf course in Northeast Philadelphia
37. Regional Performing Arts Center (Proposed)
38. Rodin Museum
39. Saint Joseph's University (Location of City Avenue Special Services District)
40. Second Bank of the United States
41. Society Hill
42. Southwest Center City—Vacant Property Study Area
43. Temple University
44. University of Pennsylvania
45. Veterans Stadium
46. Wagner Free Institute of Science
47. Walnut Street Theater
48. Yorktown Development

Figure AI.1. Map of the City of Philadelphia

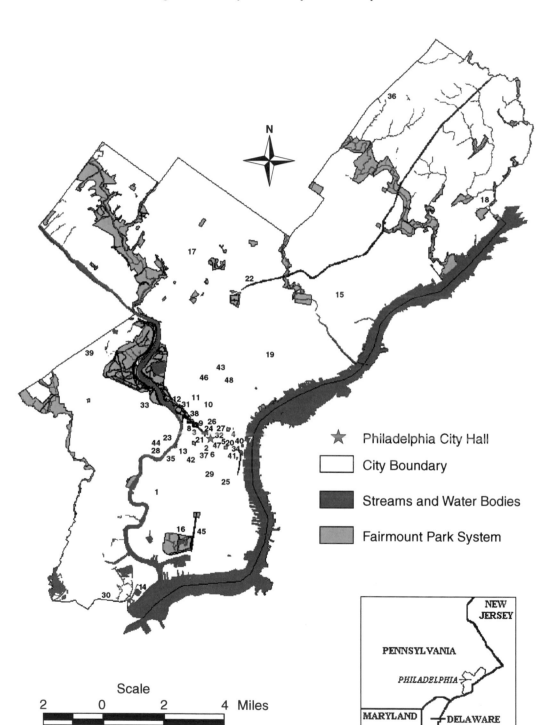

Map produced by City of Philadelphia Mayor's Office of Information Services

APPENDIX II
THE STRUCTURE OF THE
CITY OF PHILADELPHIA GOVERNMENT

GOVERNANCE IN PHILADELPHIA

The City of Philadelphia was established in 1682 and merged with Philadelphia County in 1854 to essentially form the boundaries of the 135-square-mile City today. Since 1951, the city has been governed under the Philadelphia Home Rule Charter. However, in some matters, including the issuance of short- and long-term debt, the laws of the Commonwealth of Pennsylvania govern the city.

Pennsylvania allows cities to establish "Home Rule," whereby the voters of a city may determine how their city government is organized. A "Home Rule" city may exercise any legislative power or perform any executive or administrative function that is not prohibited by its charter or forbidden by state law. The Charter divides the city government into an executive/administrative branch and a legislative branch — courts in Philadelphia are part of the Commonwealth of Pennsylvania government and are not technically a part of the city government. Philadelphia's 1951 Home Rule Charter has been amended only slighty since its adoption.

Philadelphia is the only "City of the First Class" (more than 1,000,000 residents) in the Commonwealth of Pennsylvania. As a City of the First Class, Philadelphia is subject to certain state laws that only pertain to "first class" cities. For example, as a "first class" Philadelphia is exempt from the Municipalities Planning Code, which governs zoning law in Pennsylvania, but does not apply to "first class" cities. Philadelphia, therefore, has tremendous latitude when it comes to setting local policies and administering local government functions.

The Mayor — and the offices, departments, boards, and commissions created by, or pursuant to, the Charter — exercises the executive and administrative powers of Philadelphia City government. A Mayor's Cabinet is established in the Charter to promote effective government operations and includes the Mayor, the Managing Director (who supervises the service departments of the government), the Director of Finance (who is the chief financial and budget officer), the City Solicitor (who is the city's legal advisor), and the City Representative (who is the city's ceremonial representative and the head of the Commerce Department). The legislative powers of Philadelphia city government are exercised by a City Council comprising 17 elected members.

The Charter establishes 15 city departments — additional departments may only be created by amending the Charter. The City Controller, who is an independently elected official, heads the Auditing Department. The Law Department is headed by the City Solicitor, who while appointed by the Mayor, must be confirmed by the City Council. The City Representative, who also serves as the Director of Commerce, heads the Department of Commerce. The Revenue and Procurement Departments are headed by officials who report directly to the Director of Finance. The "service departments" — Fire, Human Services, Licenses and Inspections, Police, Public Health, Public Property, Records, Recreation, Streets, and Water — are headed by officials who report directly to the Managing Director.

The executive/administrative branch of the city government includes five independent boards and commissions: the City Planning Commission, the Commission on Human Relations, the

Board of Trustees of the Free Library of Philadelphia, the Board of Pensions and Retirement, and the Civil Service Commission. The Civil Service Commission appoints the city's Personnel Director. Additional departmental boards and commissions, such as the Board of Health and the Gas Commission, are placed within the various city departments for administrative purposes.

Because — short of Charter change — city elected officials do not have the ability to create new departments to respond to new demands, the Mayor's Office has been expanded to include such agencies as the Office of Housing and Community Development and the Mayor's Office of Information Services. Other agencies such as the Office of Emergency Shelter and Services and the Philadelphia Prisons have been created and placed within the Managing Director's Office to perform specific functions.

Most city employees are members of the city's civil service system. Charter-mandated exemptions include elected officials and their deputies; certain agency heads and their deputies; Mayor's office employees; and City Council employees. School District employees and employees of the courts are not part of the city's civil service system.

In 1951, an amendment to the Pennsylvania Constitution essentially consolidated the functions of the City and the County of Philadelphia by transferring the officials and employees of county government to the city. While the status of former county agencies is complex and somewhat clouded by legal opinion, the City-County Consolidation Amendment and subsequent legislation from the Pennsylvania General Assembly incorporate former County officials including the City Commissioners, Clerk of Quarter Sessions, District Attorney, Sheriff, and Register of Wills into Philadelphia government. Even though it is not technically a formal part of the Philadelphia municipal government, the First Judicial District of Pennsylvania administers the court system in Philadelphia.

In 1965, Philadelphia voters adopted the Home Rule Charter Educational Supplement to govern public education in the city. Pursuant to the Educational Supplement, the Mayor appointed a nine-member Board of Education that appointed a Superintendent to run the School District of Philadelphia. The city authorized the Board of Education to levy taxes, but was prohibited from regulating public education or its administration.

The governing and administration of education in Philadelphia was altered in 2001. Citing consistent, non-improving performance on state and national assessment exams, the Board of Education was disbanded by the Commonwealth, in conjunction with the city, and replaced by the School Reform Commission. The School Reform Commission comprises five members, four appointed by the Governor and one by the Mayor. In turn, the Commission appoints a Chief Executive Officer of Schools, charged with overseeing and directing reform efforts.

In addition to the agencies created by or pursuant to the Charter, governmental authorities — agencies created to carry out specific, limited purposes — function independently of the city and are not subject to the Charter. Municipal authorities, such as the Hospitals and Higher Education Facilities Authority, which assists non-profit hospitals in obtaining tax-free loans for capital purposes, are authorized by City Council action. State authorities such as the Philadelphia Housing Authority, which constructs, rehabilitates, and maintains public housing in Philadelphia, are authorized by state legislation. Finally, quasi-governmental agencies, non-profit corporations established by or at the direction of the city, perform many public functions. Agencies such as the Philadelphia Facilities Management Corporation, which operates the Philadelphia Gas Works, and the Philadelphia Industrial Development Corporation, which is the official economic development agency of the city, carry out public functions not performed by the city itself.

Figures AII.1 and AII.2, Table AII.1, and the agency descriptions that follow provide more detail about the budget, staffing, and powers and duties of the individual agencies of Philadelphia's government for fiscal years 1999 and 2004. An organizational chart of the city government is included at the end of this Appendix.

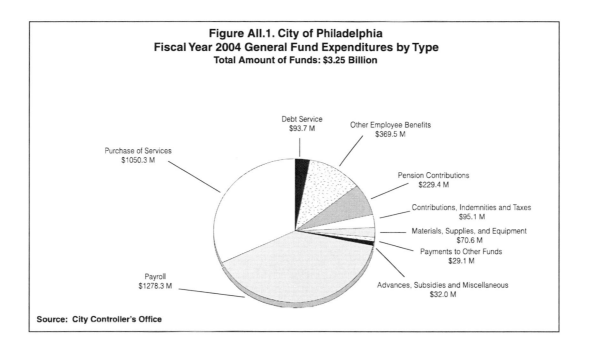

**Figure AII.1. City of Philadelphia
Fiscal Year 2004 General Fund Expenditures by Type**
Total Amount of Funds: $3.25 Billion

Debt Service
$93.7 M

Other Employee Benefits
$369.5 M

Purchase of Services
$1050.3 M

Pension Contributions
$229.4 M

Contributions, Indemnities and Taxes
$95.1 M

Materials, Supplies, and Equipment
$70.6 M

Payments to Other Funds
$29.1 M

Payroll
$1278.3 M

Advances, Subsidies and Miscellaneous
$32.0 M

Source: City Controller's Office

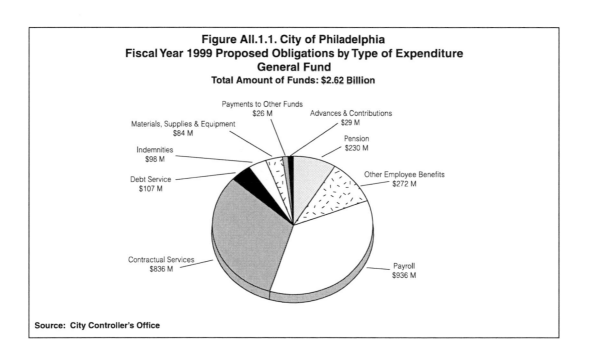

**Figure AII.1.1. City of Philadelphia
Fiscal Year 1999 Proposed Obligations by Type of Expenditure
General Fund**
Total Amount of Funds: $2.62 Billion

Payments to Other Funds
$26 M

Advances & Contributions
$29 M

Materials, Supplies & Equipment
$84 M

Pension
$230 M

Indemnities
$98 M

Other Employee Benefits
$272 M

Debt Service
$107 M

Contractual Services
$836 M

Payroll
$936 M

Source: City Controller's Office

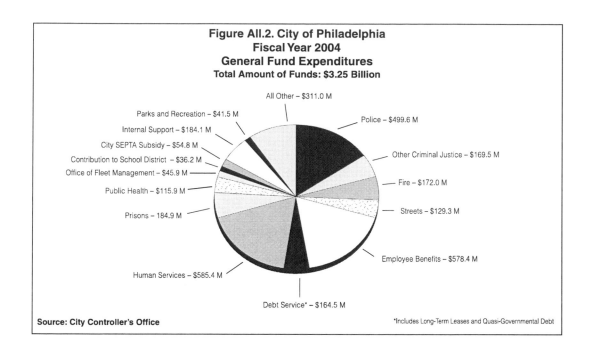

**Figure AII.2. City of Philadelphia
Fiscal Year 2004
General Fund Expenditures**
Total Amount of Funds: $3.25 Billion

All Other – $311.0 M

Parks and Recreation – $41.5 M

Internal Support – $184.1 M

City SEPTA Subsidy – $54.8 M

Contribution to School District – $36.2 M

Office of Fleet Management – $45.9 M

Public Health – $115.9 M

Prisons – 184.9 M

Human Services – $585.4 M

Police – $499.6 M

Other Criminal Justice – $169.5 M

Fire – $172.0 M

Streets – $129.3 M

Employee Benefits – $578.4 M

Debt Service* – $164.5 M

Source: City Controller's Office

*Includes Long-Term Leases and Quasi-Governmental Debt

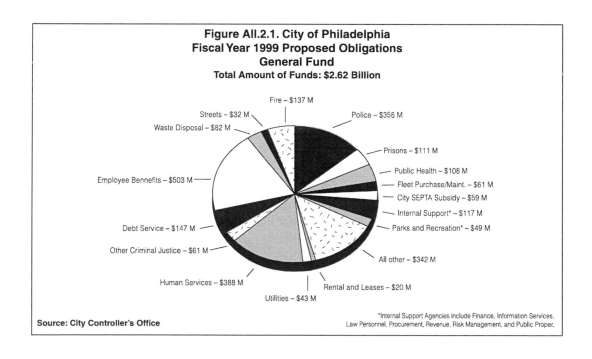

**Figure AII.2.1. City of Philadelphia
Fiscal Year 1999 Proposed Obligations
General Fund**
Total Amount of Funds: $2.62 Billion

Fire – $137 M

Streets – $32 M

Waste Disposal – $82 M

Employee Bennefits – $503 M

Debt Service – $147 M

Other Criminal Justice – $61 M

Human Services – $388 M

Utilities – $43 M

Rental and Leases – $20 M

All other – $342 M

Parks and Recreation* – $49 M

Internal Support* – $117 M

City SEPTA Subsidy – $59 M

Fleet Purchase/Maint. – $61 M

Public Health – $108 M

Prisons – $111 M

Police – $358 M

Source: City Controller's Office

*Internal Support Agencies include Finance, Information Services,
Law Personnel, Procurement, Revenue, Risk Management, and Public Proper.

Table AII.1. City of Philadelphia—Fiscal Year 2004 (July 2003–June 2004)

General Fund (and Other Notable Funds) Summary by Agency, General Fund (and Other Notable Funds) Full-Time Positions

Agency	Actual FY 2004 Expenses*	Actual FY 2004 Positions*
Art Museum Subsidy	$2,250,000	-
Atwater Kent Museum Subsidy	291,396	6
Auditing Department (City Controller's Office)	7,626,341	123
Board of Building Standards	100,182	2
Board of Licenses & Inspections Review	194,434	3
Board of Revision of Taxes	7,888,037	137
Camp William Penn	410,482	4
Capital Program Office	2,327,899	22
City Commissioners	8,815,391	86
City Council	13,343,596	199
City Planning Commission	3,345,688	52
City Representative / Commerce Department	7,801,634	17
Commerce (SEPTA Subsidy)**	54,872,735	-
City Treasurer	735,383	12
Civic Center	233,662	3
Civil Service Commission	128,145	2
Clerk of Quarter Sessions	4,618,161	114
Community College Subsidy	22,467,924	-
Convention Center Advance	31,995,000	-
Debt Service (Sinking Fund)	164,513,811	-
District Attorney	30,471,079	436
Fairmount Park Commission	15,675,340	200
Finance Department	22,599,197	148
Finance (Contribution to School District/Tax Cuts)	36,159,200	-
Finance (Employee Benefits)	598,934,181	-
Fire Department	172,029,888	2,330
First Judicial District	114,877,267	2,039
Fleet Management Office	45,882,277	351
Free Library of Philadelphia	36,120,784	669
Hero Scholarship Awards	2,400	-
Historical Commission	257,683	5
Human Relations Commission	2,280,007	40
Human Services Department	585,442,072	1,833
Law Department	16,904,545	191
Legal Services (Including Defender's Association)	33,359,468	-
Licenses and Inspections Department	24,251,382	379
Managing Director's Office	14,717,928	85
Mayor's Office	3,803,276	48
Mayor's Office of Community Services	820,627	21
Mayor's Office of Labor Relations	461,128	7
Mayor's Office of Information Services	12,760,943	108
Mayor's Scholarships	199,944	-
Office of Housing and Community Development	604,895	5
Office of Emergency Shelter and Services	15,341,940	66
Personnel Department	4,838,129	82
Police Department	499,624,278	7,688
Prisons System	184,859,362	2,007
Procurement Department	5,216,584	68
Public Health Department	115,887,471	690
Public Property Department	104,820,501	197
Records Department	8,512,093	78
Recreation Department	41,490,756	514
Refunds	51,455	-
Register of Wills	3,161,674	66
Revenue Department	16,987,794	256
Sheriff's Office	14,515,026	262
Streets Department	129,341,005	1,950
Tax Reform Commission	352,475	1
Witness Fees	127,344	-
Zoning Board of Adjustments	470,783	6
Total General Fund †	**$ 3,248,174,131**	**23,608**
City Water Department	216,086,188	1,795
School District of Philadelphia (Budget for 2003-2004 School Year)	3,147,600,000	22,057
Total General Fund, Water Department, and School District	**$6,609,860,319**	**47,460**

Source: City Controller's Office

*Note that budgets and positions include only those operations and employees funded from the General Fund; additional agency programs and personnel may be funded from different sources.

** As of FY 2005, the SEPTA subsidy is funded through the Public Property Department.

†Sum of components does not add to total due to rounding.

Table AII.1.1. City of Philadelphia—Fiscal Year 1999 (July 1998–June 1999)		
General Fund (and Other Notable Funds) Summary by Agency, General Fund (and Other Notable Funds) Full-Time Positions		
Agency	Budgeted FY 1999 Expenses*	Budgeted FY 1999 Positions*
Art Museum Subsidy	$2,250,000	-
Atwater Kent Museum Subsidy	200,000	6
Auditing Department (City Controller's Office)	6,756,627	137
Board of Building Standards	111,114	2
Board of Licenses & Inspections Review	198,580	3
Board of Revision of Taxes	7,463,347	157
Camp William Penn	318,666	3
Capital Program Office	2,409,635	22
City Commissioners	8,004,956	84
City Council	10,413,126	211
City Planning Commission	2,469,937	45
Commerce Department	42,831,253	27
Commerce (Economic Stimulus)	38,852,420	-
City Treasurer	935,847	17
Civic Center	358,302	3
Civil Service Commission	151,193	3
Clerk of Quarter Sessions	4,016,920	122
Community College Subsidy	18,267,924	-
Convention Center Subsidy	29,264,528	-
Debt Service (Sinking Fund)	146,551,323	-
District Attorney	23,251,943	422
Fairmount Park Commission	12,753,280	225
Finance Department	15,058,271	155
Finance (Risk Management Division)	1,482,418	27
Finance (Contribution to School District/Tax Cuts)	38,852,420	-
Finance (Employee Benefits)	502,513,453	-
Fire Department	137,464,663	2,489
First Judicial District**	-	-
Fleet Management Office	39,716,455	488
Fleet Management (Vehicle Purchases)	21,018,750	-
Free Library of Philadelphia	31,915,410	698
Hero Scholarship Awards	36,575	-
Historical Commission	253,842	5
Human Relations Commission	2,104,869	46
Human Services Department	388,242,647	1,707
Indemnities	34,134,644	-
Labor Relations, Mayor's Office of	470,164	7
Law Department	13,364,599	244
Legal Services (Including Defender's Association)	24,100,000	-
Licenses and Inspections Department	18,425,353	458
Licenses and Inspections (Demolitions)	10,827,743	-
Managing Director's Office	6,510,975	77
Mayor's Office	2,252,162	44
Mayor's Office of Community Services	1,045,981	27
Mayor's Scholarships	200,000	-
Mayor's Office of Information Services	12,252,349	155
Office of Housing and Community Development	4,130,742	9
Office of Emergency Shelter Services	12,629,219	81
Personnel Department	5,223,822	102
Police Department	347,526,756	7,858
Police Department (Crime Bill Match)	10,793,371	-
Prisons System	93,870,050	1,985
Prisons System (Health Services)	18,552,877	-
Procurement Department	4,474,752	75
Public Health Department	108,534,941	934
Public Property Department	47,272,163	246
Public Property Department (SEPTA Subsidy)	59,343,000	-
Public Property Department (Space Rental)	20,013,000	-
Public Property Department (Utilities)	30,350,000	-
Public Property Department (Telecommunications)	12,235,000	-
Records Department	4,274,912	98
Recreation Department	29,741,862	514
Recreation Department (Stadium Complex)	3,817,538	30
Refunds	876,272	-
Register of Wills	2,627,521	70
Revenue Department	17,213,399	338
Sheriff's Office	9,593,205	252
Streets Department	32,010,633	750
Streets Department (Sanitation Division)	82,448,439	1,430
Witness Fees	239,365	-
Zoning Board of Adjustments	469,496	6
Total General Fund	**$ 2,618,337,000** †	**22,894**
City Water Department	83,664,127	2,015
School District of Philadelphia (Budget for 1998–1999 School Year)	1,728,104,000	25,369
Total General Fund, Water Department, and School District	**$4,430,105,127**	**50,278**

Source: City Controller's Office

*Note that budgets and positions include only those operations and employees funded from the General Fund; additional agency programs and personnel may be funded from different sources.
**The lack of funding for the First Judicial District anticipated assumption of Court costs and personnel by the Commonwealth of Pennsylvania. The City transferred funds from other agencies to fund court operations when Commonwealth funding did not materialize. The First Judicial District employs approximately 2,100 positions.
†Sum of components does not add to total due to rounding.

THE OFFICES, DEPARTMENTS, BOARDS, COMMISSIONS, AND OTHER AGENCIES OF THE PHILADELPHIA GOVERNMENT

CITY ELECTED OFFICIALS

Mayor of the City of Philadelphia

The Mayor, as Chief Executive Officer of the City of Philadelphia, is elected by the citizens to a four-year term. The Mayor is not eligible for election for more than two successive terms. The Mayor's responsibilities include: shaping and controlling fiscal policies; initiating legislation; keeping the public advised on the operation of the government; reviewing and planning governmental operations; and directing the efforts of the city government in operations to make the city a better place for its inhabitants.

City Council

City Council is the unicameral legislative body of the Philadelphia city government. While subject to certain limitations in the Home Rule Charter, Council has the power to legislate all municipal matters. The execution of the legislative function is mainly performed by enacting and amending ordinances. Council enacts ordinances dealing with a wide scope of city matters, such as public health, public safety, zoning, budgeting, building and housing, and the regulation of business, trades, and professions.

To aid in the performance of its legislative functions, Council conducts investigations and inquiries into those matters requiring its attention. These investigations are authorized by resolutions which need not be submitted to the Mayor for approval as is the requirement for ordinances. Council has no direct voice in the establishment of positions or the appointment of officers in the Mayor's administration, except for the City Solicitor and Public Advocate, the appointment of which require confirmation by City Council. Council's investigatory power is important since it is the principal means for the legislative body to check on the administrative operations.

Council has 17 seats. Ten members are elected from each of the city's 10 Council districts and seven members are elected from the city at large. Council members serve a four-year term concurrent with the Mayor's.

The Council elects a President from among its members. Council employees, with the exception of the Chief Clerk (who is selected by the entire Council) and the staff of the individual council members, are appointed by the Council President. All Council employees are exempt from civil service regulations.

The City Controller and the Auditing Department

The Office of the City Controller (Auditing Department) was established by the 1951 Home Rule Charter as the sole auditing agency of Philadelphia City government. This role was expanded in 1965, making the City Controller the auditor for the School District of Philadelphia. The citizens of Philadelphia elect the City Controller to a four-year term midway between the elections of the Mayor and City Council. The Controller heads the Auditing Department, which has broad authority and responsibility for protecting the public's interest in the handling of the City's money. Most of the Controller's functions are defined in the Philadelphia Home Rule Charter. However, certain acts of the State Legislature add to the Controller's powers and duties, particularly in the areas of debt management, real estate bail approval, housing, and employee pension funds.

In its post-audit capacity, the Controller's Office performs annual financial and/or performance audits of every city office, department, board, and commission and, to the extent necessary, any agency receiving appropriations from the city. The Controller's Office also performs an annual financial audit and other reviews of the School District of Philadelphia and special audits whenever the Controller deems them necessary, or as requested by the Mayor. In its pre-audit capacity, the Controller's Office verifies and approves all expenditures of the city.

THE MAYOR'S CABINET AND THE AGENCIES REPORTING TO CABINET MEMBERS

The City Solicitor and the Law Department

The Law Department is the legal advisor to the Mayor, City Council, and all agencies of city government in civil matters. The Home Rule Charter mandates that the City Solicitor shall be a lawyer admitted to practice before the Supreme Court of Pennsylvania and shall have at least five years experience in active practice of the law. The City Solicitor is appointed by the Mayor, with the advice and consent of a majority of the members of the City Council. The functions of the department include: furnishing legal advice; representing the city in litigation; preparing or approving contracts and bonds; investigating alleged violations of statutes and ordinances; and drafting ordinances.

The City Representative (Director of Commerce) and the Department of Commerce

The Office of the City Representative and the Director of Commerce were created by the Home Rule Charter. The Charter provides that the mayorally appointed City Representative shall have the following powers and duties: giving wide publicity to any items of interest reflecting the accomplishments of the city and its inhabitants and the growth and development of its commerce and industry; acting as ceremonial representative of the city and the Mayor; and serving as the Director of Commerce.

The Charter provides that the Department of Commerce shall have the following powers and duties: promoting and developing the city's commerce and industry and encouraging the increased use of port and airport facilities; maintaining and operating the city's port and airport facilities; and, when authorized by City Council, acquiring or constructing additional facilities. Many of the Department's economic development activities are carried out through contracts with various quasi-public agencies.

The Commerce Department's Division of Aviation operates Philadelphia International Airport and Northeast Philadelphia Airport. The Director of Aviation is responsible for the operations of the Division of Aviation. The powers and duties of the Department of Commerce with regard to the two airports include: maintenance, improvement, repair, and operation.

The Director of Finance

The Office of the Director of Finance was created by the Home Rule Charter to give the Mayor and the city government an officer responsible for the financial, accounting, and budgeting functions of the executive branch. The Director of Finance is appointed by the Mayor from among three persons whose names are submitted to the Mayor by a Finance Panel convened for nominating purposes. The powers and duties of the Office of the Director of Finance include: maintaining separate accounts for each city appropriation; devising, after consultation with the City Controller, a uniform system of accounting for all agencies or individuals receiving city appropriations; supervising the detailed accounting records maintained by city agencies; supervising the accounting for all moneys received and receivable by the city; and issuing an annual report within 120 days after the close of each fiscal year.

The Revenue Department

The Revenue Department is the agency charged with the receipt and collection of taxes, license fees, and other moneys due the city. The Director of Finance, with the approval of the Mayor, appoints the Revenue Commissioner. The powers and duties of the Department include: billing and collecting all real estate and personal property taxes, penalties, and interest due to the city; collecting income and other taxes which are due the city; reading water meters, issuing bills for water and sewer charges, and collecting these charges; and collecting license fees.

The Procurement Department

The Procurement Department is the city's central purchasing agency, procuring goods and services for all agencies supported by funds from the city treasury. The Director of Finance, with the approval of the Mayor, appoints the Procurement Commissioner. The Home Rule Charter requires Procurement to secure competitive bids and to award purchases or contracts to the lowest responsible bidder. The powers and duties of the Procurement Department, as established by the Home Rule Charter, include: maintaining written specifications for all standard items purchased; maintaining adequate product standards for the economic and efficient purchase, storing and distributing materials, supplies, and equipment commonly used by city departments and agencies; furnishing, by contract or otherwise, all printing, binding, engraving, and publication services required by the city; awarding all contracts for utility services, concessions, and pubic works projects; arranging for the disposal of surplus and unserviceable personal property; and maintaining records for all personal property owned by the city.

The City Treasurer

The City Treasurer is the official custodian of all city cash and securities. The Finance Director, with the approval of the Mayor, appoints the City Treasurer. The powers and duties of the City Treasurer are: to receive from the Department of Revenue a report of all money collected for daily deposit with the banks designated by City Council; to disburse funds upon the order of the City Controller and to oversee the distribution of all checks drawn; to reconcile the city's bank accounts; to generate reports on cash receipts, deposits, transfers, withdrawals, and securities owned and held by the city (excluding Departmental Custodial Accounts); to invest all money in excess of immediate requirements in banks or securities to produce investment income; and to perform all cash and debt management functions of the city.

The Managing Director

The Managing Director is appointed by the Mayor for a four-year term, but can be removed from office by the Mayor through a formal process outlined in the City Charter. The Managing Director is charged with supervising the departments of the city and their related boards and commissions that render municipal services to the public. The Managing Director appoints, with the approval of the Mayor, the heads of all such departments. The Managing Director's Office is responsible for monitoring various projects and reviewing new proposals for improving city operations.

The Fire Department

Under the Philadelphia Home Rule Charter, the Fire Department was organized as a separate department reporting to, and under the supervision of, the City's Managing Director's Office. The Department is headed by a Fire Commissioner, appointed by the Managing Director with approval of the Mayor. The Department is charged with protecting public safety by responding quickly and professionally to emergencies and by promoting sound emergency prevention measures. This mandate encompasses all traditional firefighting functions, including: suppressing fires throughout the city; investigating the origins of fires; educating the public about fire prevention;

operating the Fire Communications Center within the city's "911" system; and training future firefighters through the Fire Academy. The Department's mandate also includes: delivering emergency medical services (EMS); regulating all public and private ambulance services within the city; and enforcing state and federal hazardous materials regulations. The Fire Department operates 66 facilities, protecting a city of roughly 600,000 housing units.

The Department of Human Services

The Department of Human Services (DHS) traces its origins to the Department of Public Welfare under the Charter of 1919. With the adoption of the 1951 Charter it was established as a department under the Managing Director with the sole duty of carrying out public welfare functions. In 1988, as a result of the Mayor's Executive Orders, two of these welfare functions, Prisons and Services to the Homeless and Adults, were transferred from DHS and established as separate offices reporting directly to the Managing Director. The Managing Director, with approval of the Mayor, appoints the Human Services Commissioner. Powers and duties of DHS include: receiving, caring for, and placing children who are dependent, mentally challenged, neglected, incorrigible, and delinquent, as well as adults who are mentally challenged, aged, infirm, and destitute, whose support is paid for out of the city treasury or from other funds administered by the city. Additionally, DHS is responsible for investigating from time to time the manner in which those placed are being cared for; approving or disapproving billings to the city for maintenance of city residents in state institutions or in private facilities and transmitting to the Revenue Department amounts due the city for care and placement; and supervising the reformatory and the home for the indigent, including determination of capacity, type, and proportion of persons to be received therein.

The Department of Licenses and Inspections

The Department of Licenses and Inspections was established by the Home Rule Charter to enforce laws and regulations regarding building safety, to control the issuance and revocation of city licenses, to test or examine license applicants, and to inspect properties subject to laws enforced by the city. The Department is headed by a Commissioner, appointed by the Managing Director with approval of the Mayor. The Department is responsible for the issuance of licenses and the performance of inspections functions within Philadelphia.

The Police Department

The Police Department is the city's chief law enforcement agency. The Department has the responsibility for preserving public peace, preventing and detecting crime, policing streets and highways, and aiding in the administration and enforcement of state laws and city ordinances within the City of Philadelphia. The Department is headed by a Police Commissioner, appointed by the Managing Director with approval of the Mayor. The powers and duties of the Department include: preserving the public peace; preventing and detecting crime; policing the streets and highways; enforcing relevant traffic statutes, ordinances, and regulations; training, equipping, maintaining, supervising, and disciplining the Philadelphia Police; and operating a police signal system. In 1998, a force of approximately 6,900 uniformed officers protected the city's population and property. For 2004, the uniformed force remains at approximately the same level, and declined to roughly 6,600 by the end of fiscal year 2005.

The Department of Public Health

The Department of Public Health (DPH) is authorized by the City Charter and charged with responsibility for preserving and improving the health of citizens by supplying an accessible, comprehensive system of health care. The Department is headed by a Public Health Commissioner, appointed by the Managing Director with approval of the Mayor. The Department has the following specific functions: administration and enforcement of statutes, ordinances, and regulations relating to public health hazards; the pursuit of occupations affecting public health, and pests, including animal, insect and plant life; institution and conduct of public health programs, medical research, and public education in all matters concerning public health; establishment, maintenance and operation of health centers, stations, clinics, and other health facilities; and compilation, analysis, maintenance, and reporting of statistics and data concerning births, still-births, and deaths. The Public Health Commissioner is also an ex officio member of the Board of Health, which sets policy directives for the Department. The Board of Health is assisted in its policy-making role by two other specialized boards: the Air Pollution Control Board and the Mental Health and Mental Retardation Advisory Board. In 1998, the Department of Public Health operated 22 facilities to serve Philadelphia's residents. As of 2005, the Department operates 20 facilities to serve the City's population of less than 1.5 million.

The Department of Public Property

The Department of Public Property was created by the Home Rule Charter. The Department is headed by a Public Property Commissioner, appointed by the Managing Director with approval of the Mayor. Within the scope of its functions under the Charter, the Department of Public Property exercises the following powers and performs the following duties: supervising the construction, maintenance, and repair of, city facilities; providing telephone service for city facilities; maintaining and assigning city vehicles (now delegated to the Office of Fleet Management); supervising the operation of leases of city transit facilities; and supervising the leases of city gas, electric, and steam facilities.

The Department of Records

The Department of Records was created by the Home Rule Charter. The Department is headed by a Records Commissioner, appointed by the Managing Director with approval of the Mayor. Within the scope of its functions under the Charter, the Department of Records exercises the powers and performs the duties pertaining to the creation, maintenance for public use, retention, and disposition of city records. In 1953, the duties of the former Office of the Recorder of Deeds were merged with those of the Department of Records. The Department of Records is charged with: making rules embodying standards and procedures for record keeping and records systems for all departments, boards, commissions, and agencies; recording all legal documents, maintaining real property data base records, maintaining city tax maps, collecting city and state realty transfer taxes, collecting various fees, and providing copies of police and fire reports; managing citywide acquisition of reprographic and filing equipment, conducting records management studies, creating and managing citywide records retention schedules, designing and controlling forms citywide, managing city archives, and managing the city's records center; and microfilming city records, creating and maintaining photo records of city activities, providing official city identification cards, providing duplicating services, and producing engineering size reproductions.

The Department of Recreation

The Department of Recreation is vested by the Home Rule Charter with the operation and management of all city recreational facilities other than those operated by the Fairmount Park Commission. The Department's duty is to formulate and conduct a comprehensive and coordinated program of cultural and physical-recreation activities. The Recreation Department is responsible for the maintenance, repair, and improvement of all recreation facilities. The Department designs, plans, and oversees the construction of recreation facilities. Additionally, the Department is responsible for operating city historical sites not otherwise entrusted, and for planning the acquisition of buildings and grounds of historical significance. The Managing

Director, with approval of the Mayor, appoints the Recreation Commissioner. The following boards or agencies receive city appropriations through the Department of Recreation: Board of Trustees of the American Flag House and Betsy Ross Memorial; Philadelphia Museum of Art; Board of Trustees of the Atwater Kent Museum (the Philadelphia history museum); and Board of Trustees of Camp William Penn (a camp run by the Recreation Department for city youth). In 2005, the Department of Recreation operated 197 playgrounds and recreation centers, and hundreds of other facilities including neighborhood parks, war memorials, pools, ice rinks and breezeways.

The Department of Streets

The Department of Streets was created by the Home Rule Charter to be responsible for all functions relating to city Streets. The Streets Commissioner, appointed by the city's Managing Director with the approval of the Mayor, directs the Department. Powers and duties of the Department of Streets include: designing, constructing, repairing, and maintaining city streets, roads, and drives in Fairmount Park; locating, designing, installing, repairing, maintaining, and operating equipment for lighting city streets; cleaning and sanding city streets, removing and disposing of ashes, garbage and refuse, removing and disposing of ice and snow from city streets, and administering and enforcing statues, ordinances, and regulations for maintaining the cleanliness of city streets; making regulations governing traffic and parking as authorized by statue or ordinance; and performing all surveying functions of the city. The Department of Streets is responsible for building and maintaining over 2,000 miles of streets in the City of Philadelphia.

The Water Department

The Water Department traces its roots to the origins of Philadelphia's public water system in the early 1800s. With the adoption of the Home Rule Charter, the Water Department was organized to furnish the city with an adequate water supply. The Managing Director, with approval of the Mayor, appoints the Water Commissioner. The Department's responsibilities include: operating and maintaining the city's water-supply and storm water system, including construction, maintenance, repair, and improvement of water supply facilities; operating and maintaining the city's sewage system and wastewater treatment plants; investigating and adopting methods for improving the quality of the water supply; and fixing and regulating rates and charges for supplying water and sewage disposal services. In 2005, the Water Department operated 57 facilities to serve the city's over 1.4 million residents.

The Office of Emergency Shelter and Services

The Office of Emergency Shelter and Services (OESS) was established in 1988 by Executive Order to deliver services to the city's homeless population. These services encompass prevention efforts, shelter care, comprehensive case management, and referral services to a variety of assistance programs dealing with problems such as substance abuse, mental-health ailments, and life-skill deficiencies. Services can range from providing one night of shelter to victims of fire to year-round housing for chronically needy individuals. Many of the services are provided by third parties with which OESS contracts. The overall goal of OESS is to help individuals and families move toward independent living and self-sufficiency in permanent housing.

The Philadelphia Prisons

The Philadelphia Prisons was established as a separate agency, reporting directly to the Managing Director, by Executive Order in 1988. Prior to 1988, the agency's functions were vested in the Department of Human Services. The Philadelphia Prisons system is subject to administration by a Board of Trustees, whose members include the Commissioner of Human Services (ex officio) and six citizens appointed by the Mayor. The Philadelphia Prisons: supervise all city prison institutions; determine the capacity of each institution and the type of persons to be admitted; recommend standards and methods helpful in prison government and administration to the Prison Board of Trustees; establish and maintain industries for the purpose of compensable employment for all physically capable persons sentenced to City prison institutions; arrange compensable employment for inmates at work within or upon the grounds of any city institution as may be necessary for its maintenance; transfer to the city or other public agencies, by sale or otherwise, articles manufactured or produced in prison institutions which cannot be used therein; and require each institution to keep proper records of the labor performed by its inmates, of the compensation paid to them, of the articles manufactured or produced, and of their disposition. In 1998, the Philadelphia Prisons operated a prison system serving approximately 5,600 inmates. In 2005, that number had grown to over 8,000 inmates.

NOTABLE BOARDS AND COMMISSIONS CREATED OR PLACED IN CITY DEPARTMENTS

Office of Administrative Review

The Office of Administrative Review — originally created as the Tax Review Board in the Home Rule Charter — is the official agency of the City of Philadelphia to which taxpayers may appeal decisions made by the City's Revenue Department concerning their tax liability. The agency consists of five members appointed by the Mayor for terms of six years. At least one member must be an accountant and one a lawyer. None of the members can be an officer or an employee of the legislative or executive branch of the Philadelphia government or of any governmental agency that receives an appropriation from the City. An administrator, who is appointed by the Mayor, oversees and directs the Office of Administrative Review. The powers and duties of the Office include the following: reviewing and deciding on appeals for the assessment of taxes for wage-earners and businesses, excessive water and sewer charges, and license and inspection nuisance abatement fees; determining appeals filed for interest and penalties on delinquent taxes; approving or modifying petitions for refunds and offers in compromise which have been granted by the Revenue Department; and hearing petitions resulting from the denial of refunds by the Revenue Department.

The Fairmount Park Commission

In 1867, the Pennsylvania General Assembly authorized the city to purchase land for Fairmount Park in order to preserve the purity of the city's water supply and provide a place of public enjoyment for the people of Philadelphia. The Fairmount Park Commission was established to protect the city's water supply that same year. In 1951, the Fairmount Park Commission was incorporated as a part of the Philadelphia city government with the adoption of the Philadelphia Home Rule Charter. The Fairmount Park Commission has 16 members, of whom 10 are citizens appointed for five-year terms by the Board of Judges of the Court of Common Pleas of Philadelphia. The remaining six are ex officio members and include the Mayor, the President of City Council, the Commissioner of Public Property, the Recreation Commissioner, the Water Commissioner, and the Chief Engineer and Surveyor of the Department of Streets. A Director, appointed by the Fairmount Park Commission, supervises park administration.

Fairmount Park's mission is to provide a major urban park system for Philadelphia residents and visitors with a variety of landscaping ranging from large wilderness areas to highly structured activity areas; provide sufficient maintenance so that all Park areas may be enjoyed according to their intended uses; provide sufficient program leadership and design for meaningful Park activities; and provide a Park tree maintenance program to preserve existing trees and remove those considered dangerous. The Fairmount System comprises approximately 8,700 acres of parkland — more than 10 percent of the city's total land area.

The Board of Revision of Taxes

The Board of Revision of Taxes is an independent seven-member board, appointed by the Board of Judges of the Philadelphia Common Pleas Court. Created by the Pennsylvania State Legislature, the Board is required to make annual assessments of real estate values that serve as a basis for Philadelphia's property taxes. The Board of Revision of Taxes also hears appeals regarding assessment valuations.

The Board of City Trusts

The Board of City Trusts comprises 12 members appointed by the Philadelphia Court of Common Pleas to unpaid, life-long terms. Created to oversee the Stephen Girard Estate, the Board manages and administers all money and property left in trust to the City of Philadelphia. Consisting of over 100 separate gifts valued in excess of $400 million, the Board distributes funds each year in support of the schools, parks, maintenance of Independence Hall, and other causes or organizations.

THE INDEPENDENT OFFICES, BOARDS AND COMMISSIONS

The City Planning Commission

The City Planning Commission is an independent agency of the City of Philadelphia created to guide the physical development of the city. It consists of three ex officio members, including the Managing Director, Director of Finance, and the City Representative, as well as six members appointed by the Mayor. To assure adequate civic representation, the Home Rule Charter stipulates that at least five of the appointed members hold no other public office, position, or employment. An Executive Director, who is appointed by and serves at the pleasure of the City Planning Commission, directs the efforts of the Commission. Powers and duties of the City Planning Commission include the preparation of: a "comprehensive plan" and its modifications, showing the present city and its planned future development; the capital budget and capital program (the city's six-year plan for capital expenditures which includes the actual capital budget for the current fiscal year); proposed zoning ordinances and amendments; and regulations governing the subdivision of land. The City Planning Commission may also advise City Council and the Mayor on proposed legislation affecting the capital programs, plans of streets, zoning ordinances, the "physical development plan," and the acquisition or sale of city-owned real estate. In accordance with state and federal laws and regulations, the Planning Commission must review certain legislation affecting development plans.

The Commission on Human Relations

The Commission on Human Relations was established by the Home Rule Charter and mandated to enforce the Philadelphia Fair Practices Ordinance, which prohibits discrimination in the areas of employment, public accommodations, and housing because of race, color, gender, religion, sexual orientation, and certain other rights. Nine Commissioners are appointed by the Mayor to oversee operations of the Commission on Human Relations. A Fair Housing Commission, created by the Philadelphia Code, is empowered to hold hearings and conduct investigations in connection with any unfair rental practice upon complaint or upon its own initiative. Five Commissioners appointed by the Mayor direct the efforts of the Fair Housing Commission. As of June 1993, the Fair Housing Commission was merged into the Commission on Human Relations. The two independent Commissions now direct a central staff. An Executive Director, appointed by the Mayor, directs the combined Commission on Human Relations/Fair Housing Commission.

The Historical Commission

The Historical Commission is charged with the designation of historical buildings, structures, sites, and objects within the city, as well as the review and approval of permits to alter or demolish historic structures within the delineated boundaries of historic districts. The Commission also maintains an inventory of historic sites within Philadelphia, recommending to the Mayor and City Council the best use of gifts, grants, and appropriations to promote their preservation. It consists of the President of City Council, the Director of Commerce, the Commissioner of Public Property, the Commissioner of Licenses and Inspections, the Chair of the City Planning Commission, the Director of Housing, or the designees of the aforementioned offices. An additional eight members, consisting of at least one historical preservation architect, historian, architectural historian, real estate developer, representative of a Community Development Corporation, and representative of a community organization, comprise the whole of the Commission.

The Board of Trustees of the Free Library of Philadelphia

The Free Library of Philadelphia, initially established through private donations, was incorporated and granted a charter in 1891. The Board of Trustees of the Free Library of Philadelphia was established in 1894 to enable the Library to receive appropriations from the City. A President/Director, who is appointed by and serves at the discretion of the Board of Trustees, oversees and directs Library operations. The Library's purpose is to provide all segments of the population of Philadelphia with a comprehensive collection of recorded knowledge, ideas, artistic expression, and information. The Library seeks to assure ease of access to its materials and to provide programs that stimulate the awareness and use of its resources. In 1998, the Free Library of Philadelphia operated 54 facilities, lending over 6.5 million items to the public. In 2004, the Library had a circulation of over 6.2 million items through its 55 locations.

The Board of Pensions and Retirement

The Board of Pensions and Retirement is an independent board of the City of Philadelphia created by the Philadelphia Home Rule Charter to maintain a comprehensive, fair, and actuarially sound pension and retirement system covering all officers and employees of the city. The Board of Pensions and Retirement consists of nine members. The permanent members include the Director of Finance, Managing Director, City Controller, City Solicitor, and Personnel Director. To ensure adequate representation of covered employees, four other persons are elected by city employees to serve on the Board. An Executive Director, who is appointed by and serves at the pleasure of the Board, oversees and directs Board operations.

The Board formally approves all benefit applications, but its major role is that of "trustee," to ensure that the pension and retirement system remains actuarially and financially sound for current and future benefit recipients. The Board, with the assistance of its professional consultants, develops the policies and strategies that will enable the Board to successfully execute its fiduciary obligations. All major decisions with regard to the Board of Pension and Retirement's investment portfolio are subject to approval by the Board based upon the recommendations of its investment consultants and the Board's Chief Investment Officer. The investment policy developed by the Board provides the framework for the investment of funds. However, the manner in which the Board invests its funds is constrained by legal statutes.

The Tax Reform Commission

Established by amendment to the Philadelphia Home Rule Charter in 2002, the Tax Reform Commission (TRC) was formulated to conduct a comprehensive analysis of and make recommendations concerning reforms to the tax structure and all taxes imposed on Philadelphia's citizens and businesses, including those instituted by the Commonwealth of Pennsylvania. The TRC was also charged to review programs that utilize tax abatements or exemptions, including Tax

Incremental Financing and Keystone Opportunity Zones. The TRC submitted its final report to the Mayor and City Council in 2003 and was subsequently disbanded, though the Charter allows it to be reconstituted at a later date. The TRC comprises four Mayoral appointments, four appointments of the City Council President, one appointment of the City Controller, and one by each of the following: the President of the African-American Chamber of Commerce, the President of the Hispanic Chamber of Commerce, the Greater Philadelphia Chamber of Commerce, the Greater Northeast Chamber of Commerce, the CEO of Greater Philadelphia First, and the Executive Director of the Northern Philadelphia Chamber of Commerce.

The Civil Service Commission and Personnel Office

The Civil Service Commission, established by the City Charter, consists of three members appointed by the Mayor. Its principal responsibilities include: serving as an appellate tribunal for employee appeals; ruling on proposed civil service regulations and modifications of city employee classification and pay plans; ruling on requested exemptions from civil service and the city's residency policy; and advising the Mayor and Personnel Director (whom it appoints) on human resource management issues.

The Personnel Office, also established by the City Charter, serves a dual function. The agency is the Mayor's principal advisor and interpreter for human resource management policy. It also serves as the centralized technical and support staff for human resource management within the city government. The Office is headed by the Personnel Director who is appointed by the Civil Service Commission. In its support capacity, the Personnel Office assists other city agencies in such matters as recruiting, identifying qualified job candidates, classifying departmental jobs, determining appropriate job pay rates, and training employees. It administers employee benefit, labor relation, and equal opportunity programs, and maintains a centralized human resource system that provides an employment history of all city employees.

THE OFFICES OF THE MAYOR

The Insurance Public Advocate / Office of Consumer Affairs

The Office of Consumer Affairs (OCA) was created by executive order in 2003. The mission of the OCA is to receive complaints of consumer abuse and unfair commercial practices, working with the city's Law Department to identify significant complaints and referring those to the appropriate authorities for investigation. The OCA also studies issues related to insurance rates, utility rates, consumer prices and practices in Philadelphia.

The Insurance Public Advocate was established by Home Rule Charter amendment in 2003. Appointed by the Mayor with the advice and consent of City Council, it represents the interests of Philadelphia insurance consumers, investigates rate disparities and unlawful practices in the market, and pursues appropriate remedies. The Insurance Public Advocate also is charged with stimulating the competitiveness of the local insurance market and lobbying for the creation of an Insurance Consumer Bill of Rights.

The Accessibility Compliance Office

The Accessibility Compliance Office (ACO) was established to ensure Philadelphia's compliance with the laws governing the City's relationship with people with disabilities, including the American with Disabilities Act and the Fair Housing Act. The ACO is responsible for coordinating barrier removal efforts, formulating polices on accessibility concerns and responding to reasonable accommodation requests.

The Mayor's Office of Community Services

The Mayor's Office of Community Services (MOCS) was created to ameliorate poverty conditions in Philadelphia. The Mayor appoints the Executive Director of MOCS. As a community action agency, MOCS provides a variety of programs that address the needs of income-eligible clients. Services provided include: addressing issues through programs in the areas of neighborhood structure, homelessness, youth initiatives, and senior citizen programs; funding of community-based programs; and addressing issues concerning nutrition, prenatal care, emergency responses for family, illiteracy, unemployment, training, economic development, and housing.

The Office of Fleet Management

The Office of Fleet Management (OFM) was created by Executive Order in 1993. A Fleet Manager is appointed by the Mayor to direct the efforts of the Office. OFM is responsible for the purchase, maintenance, repair, and disposal of all city vehicles, and the establishment and maintenance of a vehicle management information system.

The Office of Housing and Community Development

The Office of Housing and Community Development (OHCD) was created in 1974 to develop comprehensive strategies and programs for creating viable urban neighborhoods. The agency's director is appointed by and represents the Mayor in the management and execution of city housing policy and community development issues. The agency accomplishes its mission through the coordination of programs for housing, economic development, site improvements, and community planning. Designed to benefit low- and moderate-income Philadelphians, these programs are funded annually through the Federal Government's Community Development Block Grant. The agency's duties include: responsibility for the administration of contracts with public agencies, such as the Redevelopment Authority, Philadelphia Housing Development Corporation, and subrecipient non-profit organizations; and preparing various government reports, such as the Grantee Performance Report and, most important, the annual Final Statement and Plan Report which represents the OHCD's plan and corresponding budget for community development activities.

The Mayor's Office of Information Services

The Mayor's Office of Information Services was originally created as The Philadelphia Computing Center via Executive Order in 1986. The name was changed to the Mayor's Office of Information Services in 1993. A Chief Information Officer is appointed by the Mayor and is responsible for the Office's operations in fulfilling its mission to provide effective and efficient information and communication systems and services to all branches of local government.

The Office of Risk Management

The Office of Risk Management was created by Executive Order in 1993. The Office of Risk Management reports to the Director of Finance and is charged with reducing the financial impact of claims, lawsuits, and employee injuries to the city; reducing the frequency and severity of these events through the application of professional risk-management techniques; and providing a safe environment for employees to work and the public to enjoy.

The Office of Labor Relations

The Office of Labor Relations was created by Executive Order in 1996 to engage in, on behalf of the city, negotiation and administration of collective bargaining agreements concerning all aspects of labor relations with the recognized labor organizations representing Civil Service employees of Philadelphia. Organized under the Office of the Mayor, the agency also advises and consults with the Mayor regarding dispute management between the city and labor organizations, including grievances and arbitration.

The Capital Program Office

The Capital Program Office (CPO) was created by Executive Order in 1996. The agency is administered by the Capital Program Director who is appointed by the Mayor. The CPO performs two primary functions, oversight of the citywide capital program and project management for the city's capital projects. CPO also performs preliminary studies and surveys to allow the most efficient use of space earmarked for the physical improvement of capital projects.

THE FORMER COUNTY OFFICERS

The District Attorney

The District Attorney was originally created as a county office. Although the office is not mentioned in the Home Rule Charter, the District Attorney's Office became part of City government with the 1951 City-County Consolidation Amendment to the Pennsylvania Constitution. In addition, a 1963 amendment to the First Class City Home Rule Act gave City Council the power to pass legislation with regard to operations of the District Attorney's Office. These enactments were further enabled by the 1965 City-County Consolidation Ordinance of City Council. The District Attorney is elected every four years by the citizens of Philadelphia at an election held midway between the elections of the Mayor and City Council. The Office of the District Attorney of the City and County of Philadelphia prosecutes trial- and appellate-level litigation of all criminal and some ancillary civil matters that arise within its jurisdiction. The District Attorney represents the citizenry of Philadelphia and the Commonwealth of Pennsylvania in criminal proceedings throughout the Philadelphia and Commonwealth court systems.

The City Commissioners

The City Commissioners' Office was originally created as a county office. Although not mentioned in the Philadelphia Home Rule Charter, the City Commissioners' Office became part of city government through the 1951 City-County Consolidation Amendment to the Pennsylvania Constitution. In addition, a 1963 amendment to the First Class City Home Rule Act gave City Council the power to pass legislation with regard to operations of the City Commissioners' Office. These enactments were further enabled by the 1965 City-County Consolidation Ordinance of City Council. Three City Commissioners are elected every four years — along with the Mayor and members of City Council — by the citizens of the City and County of Philadelphia and are responsible for voter registration and conducting elections.

The Clerk of Quarter Sessions

The powers, functions, and duties of the Clerk of Quarter Sessions are prescribed by state statutes and the local ordinances of the Philadelphia City Council. The citizens of the City and County of Philadelphia elect the Clerk of Quarter Sessions every four years along with the Mayor and members of City Council. Under current laws, the Clerk of Quarter Sessions serves the Criminal Courts of Common Pleas and Municipal Courts, as well as the Juvenile Division of Family Court. Agency clerks record, index, and file all bills of information and transcripts of Municipal Court. The agency's clerks also post to dockets; take bail imposed by judges; enter judgments upon bail forfeitures; issue bench warrants; collect fines and costs imposed by the courts; record on bills of information or criminal transcripts the decisions of the courts; issue commitments or discharges for defendants; and, when necessary, answer inquiries from prisoners, attorneys, and judges. The Clerk's office also expedites matters such as petitions for writs of habeas corpus, appeals from convictions, issuance of private detective licenses, and other miscellaneous matters. In serving the Juvenile Division of Family Court, the Clerk of Quarter Sessions handles all matters relative to court case files, including sending subpoenas to witnesses and notifying attorneys of case dates and activities.

The Register of Wills

The Register of Wills was originally designated as a county office. Although not mentioned in the Philadelphia Home Rule Charter, the Register of Wills became part of city government through the 1951 City-County Consolidation Amendment to the Pennsylvania Constitution. The Register of Wills is elected every four years — along with the Mayor and members of City Council — by the citizens of the City and County of Philadelphia, and has the responsibility to probate wills (A probate is official proof of an instrument offered as the last will and testament of a deceased person); grant letters testamentary appointing executors of wills; and letters of administration appointing administrators of estates of persons who died without leaving a will; and approve and file the accounts of executors and administrators. The Register's Office records all wills, accounts, inventories, and appraisals of estates. In a separate capacity, the Register also serves as Clerk of the Orphans Court Division of the Common Pleas Court. As Clerk of Orphans Court, the Register supervises the Marriage License Bureau and keeps a record of Orphans Court proceedings.

The Sheriff

The Office of the Sheriff was created as a county office. Although not mentioned in the Philadelphia Home Rule Charter, the Sheriff's Office became part of city government through the 1951 City-County Consolidation Amendment to the Pennsylvania Constitution. In addition, a 1963 amendment to the First Class City Home Rule Act gave City Council the power to pass legislation with regard to operations of the Sheriff. These enactments were further enabled by the 1965 City-County Consolidation Ordinance of City Council. Citizens of the City and County of Philadelphia elect a Sheriff every four years — along with the Mayor and members of City Council. Powers and duties of the Sheriff's office include: transporting and escorting prisoners to and from Philadelphia courtrooms; providing courtroom security for Municipal and Common Pleas Courts; conducting real and personal property sales, as well as collecting and disbursing both fees and funds related to such activities; and serving and executing writs and warrants and enforcing injunctions.

COURTS IN PHILADELPHIA

The First Judicial District of the Commonwealth of Pennsylvania

The court system in Philadelphia originates from various Commonwealth of Pennsylvania laws. Common Pleas and Municipal Courts were established by the Pennsylvania Constitution of 1968 and Judiciary Act of 1976. Philadelphia Traffic Court is authorized and established under the Constitution of Pennsylvania and the Judicial Code. These Courts are part of the state's unified judicial system and comprise Pennsylvania's First Judicial District.

Common Pleas and Municipal Courts

Common Pleas Court, the court of general trial jurisdiction in Philadelphia, shares a limited portion of its jurisdiction with the Municipal Court. It has three divisions: Trial Division — responsible for the bulk of traditional civil and criminal cases; Family Court Division — responsible for domestic relations matters (divorce, custody, and support) and juvenile cases (delinquency, dependency, and adoptions); and Orphans' Court Division — mainly responsible for cases involving estates (including estates of deceased persons and the mentally disabled) and wills and trusts of minors.

Municipal Court's major judicial areas include: exclusive jurisdiction in trying adult criminal cases carrying a maximum sentence of five years; conducting preliminary hearings in adult criminal matters; concurrent jurisdiction with the Court of Common Pleas in small claims cases involving $10,000 or less; landlord and tenant matters and rental values of any amount under the Landlord and Tenant Act; and code-enforcement cases which include up to $15,000 in real estate and school tax cases.

Judges of the Common Pleas Court serve 10-year terms; judges of the Municipal Court serve six-year terms. Voters of the City elect the judges at-large for their initial term. For every subsequent term, judges campaign for re-election on a Retention Ballot.

Traffic Court

Traffic Court's primary function is to adjudicate traffic violations. An ancillary function is the collection and remittance to the City and Commonwealth of fines and costs resulting from adjudicating traffic violations. The Judicial Code grants the court exclusive jurisdiction in all prosecutions for summary offenses arising under the Pennsylvania Motor Vehicle Code, and any related City Ordinance, committed within the limits of the City. Traffic Court judges are elected by the public for six-year terms.

PUBLIC EDUCATION IN PHILADELPHIA

The School District of Philadelphia

The School District is a political subdivision of the Commonwealth created to assist in the administration of the General Assembly's duties under the Constitution of the Commonwealth to "provide for the maintenance and support of a thorough and efficient system of public education to serve the needs of the Commonwealth." The School District of Philadelphia is a separate and independent Home Rule School District of the first class, established by the 1965 Educational Supplement to Philadelphia Home Rule Charter. The District is the largest in the Commonwealth of Pennsylvania, serving approximately 190,000 students, and providing indirect funding for about an additional 22,000 in Charter Schools. In 1998, the District served 215,000 students. The boundaries of the School District are coterminous with the boundaries of the City of Philadelphia.

The School District is governed by the School Reform Commission (SRC), which is empowered with the same authority and duties of the former Board of Education, and was also been granted new abilities. The Commission consists of five members, with four, including the chairman, appointed by the Governor of Pennsylvania. The remaining member is appointed by the Mayor of Philadelphia. At least three commissioners must reside within Philadelphia.

Each commissioner is subject to term limits of three, four, or five years, depending on the nature of their appointment. The duties of the SRC include formulation of educational policy; the adoption of the annual operating budget, capital program, and capital budget; the creation of the annual request to the Mayor and City Council for authority to levy certain taxes; and the incurrence of indebtedness of the School District. The Commission also possesses the authority to suspend many of the requirements of Pennsylvania's Public School Code and regulations of the State Board of Education. The School Reform Commission can only be dissolved by Pennsylvania's Secretary of Education upon the recommendation of a majority of the Commission.

The SRC appoints a Chief Executive Officer of Schools as the chief administrative officer and chief instructional officer of the SRC and the School District. Subject to the policies and direction of the Commission, the CEO is responsible for the execution of all actions of the Commission, the administration and operation of the public school system, and oversight for all matters pertaining to instruction.

NOTABLE MUNICIPAL AUTHORITIES

Hospitals and Higher Education Authority

The Hospitals and Higher Education Facilities Authority was created in 1974 to provide funds through the issuance of revenue or special obligation bonds and notes to assist nonprofit hospitals, nonprofit religious or hospital-affiliated sub-acute care facilities, non-profit nursing homes, and higher education facilities in projects determined to be primarily for the health and safety of the citizens of the Philadelphia area. A five-member board appointed by the Mayor and approved by two-thirds of City Council administers the Authority. The city does not designate management of the Authority, nor does the city have the ability to significantly influence operations. The city does not subsidize the operations of the Authority and does not guarantee its debt service.

PHILADELPHIA MUNICIPAL AUTHORITY

The Philadelphia Municipal Authority was established in 1976 and is governed by a five-member board appointed by the Mayor and approved by two-thirds of City Council. The Authority was established to issue tax-exempt bonds for the acquisition and use of certain equipment and facilities for the city.

NOTABLE STATE AUTHORITIES

Pennsylvania Intergovernmental Cooperation Authority

The Pennsylvania Intergovernmental Cooperation Authority (PICA) was organized in 1991 and exists under and by virtue of the Pennsylvania Intergovernmental Cooperation Authority Act for Cities of the First Class. Pursuant to the Act, the Authority was established to provide financial assistance to cities of the first class in the Commonwealth of Pennsylvania. PICA has the power to issue bonds and grant or lend the proceeds thereof to the city. PICA also has the power, in its oversight capacity, to exercise certain advisory and review powers with respect to the city's financial affairs, including the power to review and approve five-year financial plans prepared at least annually by the city, and to certify noncompliance by the city with its current five-year financial plan (which would require the Secretary of the Budget of the Commonwealth to cause certain Commonwealth payments due to the city to be withheld). The Authority is administered by a five-member governing Board appointed by the Governor of Pennsylvania, the President pro tempore of the Pennsylvania Senate, the Minority Leader of the Pennsylvania Senate, the Speaker of the Pennsylvania House of Representatives, and the Minority Leader of the Pennsylvania House of Representatives each appointing one voting member of the Board.

Philadelphia Authority for Industrial Development

The Philadelphia Authority for Industrial Development (PAID) was established in 1967 to serve as the financing arm of the Philadelphia Industrial Development Corporation, which serves as the official industrial development agency for the city. The Authority issues revenue bonds to help private companies pay for property acquisition, facility expansion, facility renovation, capital equipment purchases, and pollution-control device development. A five-member Board appointed by the Mayor governs PAID.

Philadelphia Housing Authority

The Philadelphia Housing Authority (PHA) was established in 1937 to provide low-cost housing and other social services to the residents of the city. The Authority manages conventional public-housing developments as well as scattered-site housing, and supervises the federal Housing Choice Voucher Program, formerly known as Section 8 housing subsidy, within the city. The Mayor and City Controller each appoint two board members who, together, select a fifth board member to create a five-member Board to govern PHA.

Philadelphia Parking Authority

The Philadelphia Parking Authority (PPA) was established in 1950 to construct, own, lease, and manage off-street parking facilities. The Authority now also coordinates on-street parking on behalf of the City. An eleven-member Board governs PPA, the majority of members are appointed by the Governor.

Redevelopment Authority

The Redevelopment Authority (RDA) of the City of Philadelphia was established in 1945 to rehabilitate blighted sections of the city. The Authority has the power to issue bonds and to acquire and sell real estate through the use of eminent domain (a power denied to the city by the legislation enabling the creation of the City's Home Rule Charter). A five-member Board appointed by the Mayor governs the RDA.

Southeastern Pennsylvania Transportation Authority

The Southeastern Pennsylvania Transportation Authority (SEPTA) was established in 1964 to develop and maintain a coordinated public transportation system in the five-county Southeastern Pennsylvania region. The Authority is governed by a 15-member Board appointed by the five Southeastern Pennsylvania counties (two appointees from each county appointed by the County Commissioners or County Councils of each county and the Mayor of Philadelphia); the Governor of Pennsylvania (one appointment); and the President Pro Tempore of the Pennsylvania Senate, the Minority Leader of the Pennsylvania Senate, the Speaker of the Pennsylvania House of Representatives, and the Minority Leader of the Pennsylvania House of Representatives (one appointment from each).

Delaware River Port Authority

The Delaware River Port Authority (DRPA) was established in 1951 by the states of Pennsylvania and New Jersey to maintain and operate river crossings between Philadelphia and Delaware County and points in New Jersey. The Authority is also responsible for the maintenance and operation of a bi-state rapid transit system and for promotion of commerce on the Delaware River. The Commission is governed by a 16-member Board comprising ex officio members and gubernatorially appointed members from both Pennsylvania and New Jersey.

NOTABLE QUASI-GOVERNMENTAL ENTITIES

Delaware Valley Regional Planning Commission

The Delaware Valley Regional Planning Commission (DVRPC) was established in 1965 as an interstate, intercounty, and intercity agency to provide comprehensive, coordinated planning for the orderly growth and development of the bi-state Philadelphia region. The Commission is governed by an 18-member board with one member appointed by the member cities (Philadelphia and Chester in Pennsylvania, Camden and Trenton in New Jersey); counties (Bucks, Chester, Delaware, and Montgomery in Pennsylvania, Camden, Burlington, Gloucester, and Mercer in New Jersey), and states (Pennsylvania and New Jersey); as well as the Pennsylvania and New Jersey Departments of Transportation, the New Jersey Department of Community Affairs, and the Governor of Pennsylvania's Policy Office.

Philadelphia Facilities Management Corporation

The Philadelphia Facilities Management Corporation (PFMC) was established in 1972 to provide management services on a non-profit basis for the collection of assets comprising the Philadelphia Gas Works. Since 1972, the city has engaged PFMC to run the city-owned gas utility. A seven-member Board appointed by the Mayor governs the Corporation. Since 2000, regulatory control of the Philadephia Gas Works has been the purview of the Pennsylvania Public Utility Commission.

Philadelphia Commercial Development Corporation

The Philadelphia Commercial Development Corporation (PCDC) was established in 1974 to promote small-business development in the city by offering loans as well as technical and management assistance. A 25-member Board selected by previous board members governs the Corporation.

Philadelphia Housing Development Corporation

The Philadelphia Housing Development Corporation (PHDC) was established in 1956 to promote the development of low-cost housing within the city through the use of a revolving loan fund originally established with a $2 million grant from the city. A 35-member Board governs PHDC with 25 members appointed by the city and the remaining 10 designated by virtue of their city position.

Philadelphia Industrial Development Corporation

The Philadelphia Industrial Development Corporation (PIDC) was established in 1956 as the city's official industrial development corporation to encourage commercial and industrial development throughout the city. The agency acquires, develops, improves, maintains, operates, and disposes of property to foster economic development. The agency is governed by a 30-member Board with eight members selected by the city's Chamber of Commerce, seven ex officio city officials including the Mayor and the President of City Council, and 15 members selected jointly by the city and the Chamber of Commerce.

Figure AII.3. Organizational Chart of the City of Philadelphia Government

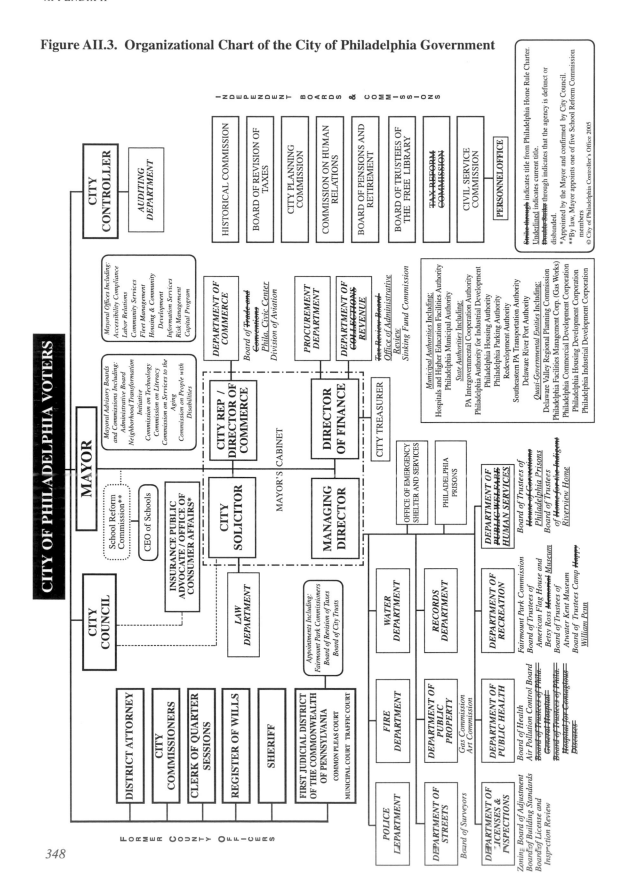

APPENDIX III
TAXATION IN PHILADELPHIA

BACKGROUND

Locally collected city and school district taxes in Philadelphia generated more than $2.72 billion in fiscal year 2004 to help fund approximately $5 billion in annual general and educational services. This is a significant increase over the tax collections and obligations in 1999, when *Philadelphia: A New Urban Direction* was first published. In fiscal year 1999, the city raised $2.62 billion from local taxes to support roughly $4 billion in general and educational expenses. In fiscal year 2004, obligations were greater than annual revenues. In fiscal year 2004 (July 1, 2003 through June 30, 2004), the City of Philadelphia spent more than $3.2 billion dollars to meet General Fund obligations, as compared to $2.6 billion in fiscal year in 1999. During the 2004 school year, the School District of Philadelphia spent more than $2.1 billion dollars to finance its Operating Budget. The City of Philadelphia contributed more than $2.06 billion in locally generated tax revenues (approximately 67 percent of city General Fund budget expenditures) to fund city operations and more than $658.4 million in locally generated tax revenues to fund School District operations. Figures AIII.1 and AIII.2 show 1999 and 2004 revenues and revenue sources for the City and School District. (See Appendix AII for more detailed information on expenditures in Philadelphia.)

With broad taxing authority from the state, the City of Philadelphia may levy a range of taxes, but must follow state Constitutional constraints that taxes upon the same class of subjects within a jurisdiction must be uniform. While the School Reform Commission sets the School District budget, Philadelphia's City Council levies all local taxes (school taxes are collected by the city's Department of Revenue and remitted to the District). Notable exceptions are the city Sales Tax, which is collected by the Commonwealth of Pennsylvania and remitted to the city, and the Public Utility Realty Tax, which is collected by the Commonwealth and remitted to the School District. Philadelphia taxes are described below. Amounts collected (actual fiscal year 2004 collections for city revenues and school year 2004 for District revenues) are listed with each tax. A Valet Parking Tax, set at 15 percent, and a Billboard Excise Tax, set at 7.0 percent, were enacted at the end of Fiscal Year 2005. No annualized collection data is yet available.

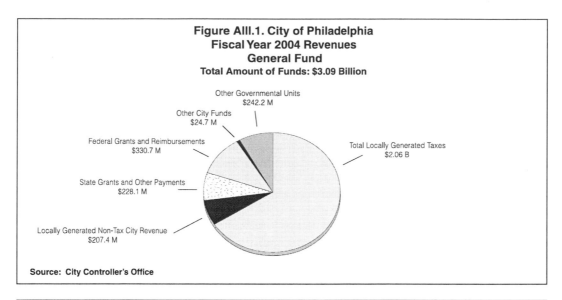

Figure AIII.1. City of Philadelphia
Fiscal Year 2004 Revenues
General Fund
Total Amount of Funds: $3.09 Billion

Other Governmental Units
$242.2 M

Other City Funds
$24.7 M

Federal Grants and Reimbursements
$330.7 M

State Grants and Other Payments
$228.1 M

Total Locally Generated Taxes
$2.06 B

Locally Generated Non-Tax City Revenue
$207.4 M

Source: City Controller's Office

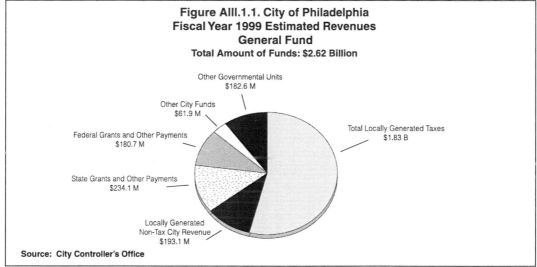

Figure AIII.1.1. City of Philadelphia
Fiscal Year 1999 Estimated Revenues
General Fund
Total Amount of Funds: $2.62 Billion

Other Governmental Units
$182.6 M

Other City Funds
$61.9 M

Federal Grants and Other Payments
$180.7 M

State Grants and Other Payments
$234.1 M

Total Locally Generated Taxes
$1.83 B

Locally Generated
Non-Tax City Revenue
$193.1 M

Source: City Controller's Office

Major City of Philadelphia and School District of Philadelphia Taxes

Taxes Based on Real Estate Assessments

Real Estate Tax (City and School)

- City — $377.7 million in fiscal year 2004, 12.21 percent of city's fiscal year 2004 General Fund
- School District — $513.5 million in school year 2004, 24.03 percent of General Fund portion of the School District's school year 2004 Operating Budget

The Real Estate Tax is levied on the assessed value (32 percent of fair market value) as certified by the Board of Revision of Taxes. The 2004 city rate of taxation was 34.74 mills on assessed value. For the School District, the tax on real estate in Philadelphia was 47.90 mills on assessed value. An increase in the millage that accrues to the School District accompanied the formation of the School Reform Commission. The total rate of taxation, including both the city

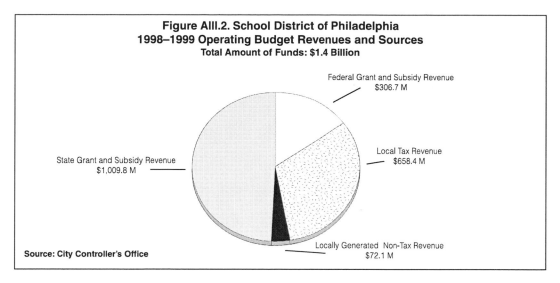

Figure AIII.2. School District of Philadelphia
1998–1999 Operating Budget Revenues and Sources
Total Amount of Funds: $1.4 Billion

Federal Grant and Subsidy Revenue
$306.7 M

Local Tax Revenue
$658.4 M

State Grant and Subsidy Revenue
$1,009.8 M

Locally Generated Non-Tax Revenue
$72.1 M

Source: City Controller's Office

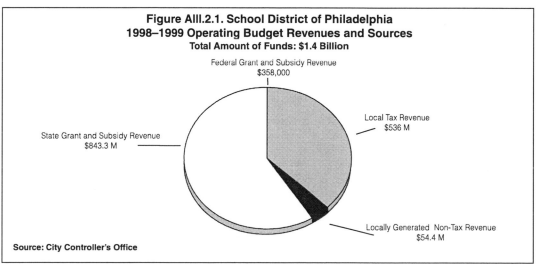

Figure AIII.2.1. School District of Philadelphia
1998–1999 Operating Budget Revenues and Sources
Total Amount of Funds: $1.4 Billion

Federal Grant and Subsidy Revenue
$358,000

Local Tax Revenue
$536 M

State Grant and Subsidy Revenue
$843.3 M

Locally Generated Non-Tax Revenue
$54.4 M

Source: City Controller's Office

and School District portions of the Real Estate Tax (by law, the School District receives 57 percent of Real Estate Tax Collections), is 82.64 mills (8.264 percent) on assessed value. As of 2005, discussions continued on moving towards full valuation, taxing at 100 percent of fair market value rather than 32 percent, to simplify the calculation of tax payments and overcome past inequalities. To avoid a revenue windfall for the city and School District, tax rates would have to be dramatically lowered.

School Use and Occupancy Tax

• School District — $96.2 million in school year 2004, 4.5 percent of General Fund portion of the School District's school year 2004 Operating Budget

Originally authorized in 1970, this tax is levied on the use or occupancy of real estate within Philadelphia for the purpose of carrying on any business, trade, occupation, profession, vocation, or any other commercial or industrial activity. The rate of taxation as of 2004 was a maximum of $4.62 per $100 of assessed value of real estate.

BUSINESS TAXES

Business Privilege Tax (City Gross Receipts Component)

• City — $102.8 million in calendar year 2003

This tax is levied on gross receipts of businesses carrying on or exercising for profit any trade, business, profession, vocation, or commercial activity in Philadelphia. The rate of taxation in 2004 was .2100 percent of annual gross receipts, following annual rate reductions in fiscal years 1996 through 2004. Further reductions are legislated to lower the tax rate to .1500 percent of gross receipts in fiscal year 2008.

Business Privilege Tax (City Net Income Component)

• City — $182.6 million in calendar year 2003

Originally authorized in 1984, this tax is levied on the net income of businesses carrying on or exercising for profit any trade, business, profession, vocation, or commercial activity in Philadelphia. The tax rate is set at 6.5 percent of annual net income.

OTHER TAXES

City Wage and Net Profits Tax

• City — $1.05 billion in fiscal year 2004, 33.95 percent of city's fiscal year 2004 General Fund

Originally authorized as a short-term measure in 1932, this tax continues today and is levied on salaries, wages, commissions, and other compensation earned by residents of Philadelphia; on salaries, wages, commissions, and other compensation earned by non-residents of Philadelphia for work done or services performed or rendered in Philadelphia; on net profits attributable to business conducted in the City of Philadelphia; and on net profits earned by Philadelphia residents conducted in or outside Philadelphia. (Persons subject to the Net Profits portion of the tax deduct from the tax due, an amount equal to 60 percent of the Business Privilege Tax on the Net Income portion of the Business Privilege Tax paid by that person.) The Pennsylvania Intergovernmental Cooperation Authority collects a 1.5 percent tax on the wages and net profits of Philadelphia residents (this is a portion of — not an addition to — the city's 4.3310-percent tax) for the purposes of servicing debt. However, a portion of this amount is refunded to the city's General Fund as "revenue from other governments." The rate of taxation as of 2004 was 4.4625 percent of wages, earnings, and net profits for Philadelphia residents and 3.8801 percent of wages, earnings, and net profits for non-residents after reductions in fiscal years 1996 through 2004. Further reductions are legislated through 2015, reducing both the resident and non-resident tax rate to 3.25 percent of wages, earnings, and net profits. Beginning in calendar year 2009, the tax rate applied to "Very Low Income" residents and non-residents shall be one-half of one percent less than the current resident and non-resident tax rates. As of January of 2014, the "Very Low Income" resident Wage Tax rate will be zero, and the non-resident "Very Low Income" will be reduced to .9127 percent.

Additional Wage Tax rate reductions are scheduled to occur as a result of a redistribution of state tax revenues from slots facilities. The enabling legislation for gaming in the Commonwealth envisions that a portion of the taxes on these facilities will be used to offset local revenue losses as a result of Wage Tax rate reduction in Philadelphia. Philadelphia's receipt of these funds is contingent upon the city continuing planned rate reductions, in addition to the steeper cuts made possible from the receipt of gaming revenues until 2010. The gaming-funded Wage Tax rate reductions can spur economic development without reducing revenues received by the City of Philadelphia from this source. The share of the funds that will be available from the Commonwealth for Philadelphia cannot yet be determined as fewer than expected taxing jurisdictions have opted to participate in the revenue sharing. There are ongoing discussions about altering the mechanism for disbursement of gaming revenues to local taxing jurisdictions for tax reduction. Furthermore, the amount of revenues will also be dependent upon the timing and success of the introduction of this industry into the Commonwealth.

City Sales Tax

- City — $108.0 million in fiscal year 2004, 3.49 percent of city's fiscal year 2004 General Fund

Originally authorized in 1991, this tax is levied on the sale at retail of tangible personal property or services. The 2004 rate of taxation is 1.0 percent of the retail purchase price on top of a 6.0-percent state Sales Tax.

City Realty Transfer Tax

- City — $141.3 million in fiscal year 2004, 4.57 percent of city's fiscal year 2004 General Fund

This tax is levied on the value of real estate sold in Philadelphia. The 2004 rate of taxation is 3.0 percent of the value of the real estate sold on top of a 1.0-percent state Realty Transfer Tax.

City Parking Tax

- City — $42.5 million in fiscal year 2004, 1.37 percent of city's fiscal year 2004 General Fund

This tax is levied on every person parking or storing a motor vehicle in or on any parking facility in the city. The rate of taxation is 15.0 percent of the amount charged for parking. Beginning in fiscal year 2005, this tax will be extended to include valet parking transactions.

Liquor Sales Tax

- School District — $33.1 million in school year 2004, 1.55 percent of General Fund portion of the School District's school year 2004 Operating Budget

Originally authorized by a City Council ordinance in 1995, this tax is levied on the sale — at retail — of liquor, malt, and brewed beverages. The 2004 rate of taxation is 10.0 percent of the sale price.

Hotel Tax

- City — $25.2 million in fiscal year 2004, 0.81 percent of city's fiscal year 2004 General Fund

This tax is levied on rental of hotel rooms in the city. The current rate of taxation is 6.0 percent of the cost to rent a hotel room in Philadelphia on top of a 6.0 percent state Hotel Tax and a 1.0 percent Hotel Occupancy Tax imposed by the city in a move analogous to the 1.0 percent increase in the city Sales Tax.

School (Non-Business) Income Tax

- School District — $14.6 million in school year 2004, 0.68 percent of General Fund portion of the School District's school year 2004 Operating Budget

Originally authorized by a City Council ordinance in 1967, this tax is levied on the non-business income of Philadelphia residents. The tax is applied to income such as the income from dividends or the interest on securities. State enabling legislation for the School Income Tax rate requires that the tax rate on unearned income be no higher than the rate for unearned income. As a result, the rate is linked to the resident Wage Tax rate, set at 4.3310 percent on the non-business income of residents for 2006. As with the Wage Tax, the School Income tax rate will decrease with the legislated declines in the wage tax.

City Amusement Tax

• City — $18.3 million in fiscal year 2004, 0.59 percent of city's fiscal year 1998 General Fund

This tax is levied on the admission charges to theatrical, performance, sporting, and entertainment events. The 2004 rate of taxation is 5.0 percent of the price of event admission.

Outdoor Advertising Tax

• City — $0 million in fiscal year 2004, collections to commence in fiscal year 2005.

This tax is levied on the purchase or rental of outdoor advertising space. The 2005 rate of taxation is 7.0 percent of the purchase price of advertising space. The Outdoor Advertising Tax is budgeted to collect $4 million in fiscal year 2005, the first year that it will be collected.

Public Utility Realty Tax

• School District — $1.1 million in school year 2004, 0.05 percent of School District's fiscal year 2004 Operating Budget

Originally authorized by the Pennsylvania General Assembly in 1970, this tax was levied on the realty of various public utilities located throughout Pennsylvania and distributed to local jurisdictions based on local tax effort. The state modified the PURTA statute in 1999, exempting land and improvements indispensable to the generation of electricity from the PURTA tax base and instead applying them to the local real estate tax.

APPENDIX IV
DESCRIPTION OF THE REMI MODEL

THE REMI MODEL

In brief, the Regional Economic Models Inc. (REMI) Economic-Demographic Forecasting Simulation 172 Sector M (REMI model) is a mathematical representation of the entire regional economy, which provides detailed forecasts through the year 2015 for a wide range of data series. This includes information on retail prices by detailed commodity, wages, and other business costs by detailed industry; employment by industry and occupation; and population by detailed cohort. In 1997, The City Controller's Office, jointly with the City's Office of the Director of Finance, purchased the REMI model to assist with forecasting and policy evaluation. The REMI model is used extensively throughout this publication. As an econometric model, it demonstrates the effects of one or more economic variables on other variables such as employment and population in the system. The behavioral relationships used in the model were estimated using large data sets for all regions of the United States. The REMI model was then calibrated to Philadelphia using local data from a variety of government agencies. Using these parameter estimates and local data series, a baseline forecast of the City and suburban economies is generated for 172 industrial sectors, 94 occupations, 25 final demand sectors, and 202 age/gender population cohorts.

Although there are hundreds of equations and thousands of variables included in the model, REMI can be separated into five fundamental blocks that capture the endogenous linkages in the model illustrated in Figure AIV.1. Most interactions flow both ways, reflecting the simultaneous nature of the economy. Block 1, representing the output in the economy, is the foundation block for the REMI model. It reflects the basic accounting identity taken from the national income and product accounts, stating that all the output produced in Philadelphia is a function of personal consumption, government demand, export demand, and local investment activity.

Changes in output from Block 1 combine with the direction of worker productivity (output per employee) influence the demand for labor in Block 2. In turn, labor productivity is influenced by relative factor costs in Block 4.

Labor supply is a function of population flows determined by a general cohort algorithm and net migration flows to the City. Labor demand and labor supply in Block 3 interact to determine wage levels. Combined with other factor costs, wages determine the relative production costs and profitability of local industry represented in Block 4. In turn, relative profitability influences market share in Block 5, which feeds back into the local output demand in the area in Block 1. For a detailed description of the components in each major block of the model, see Treyz et. al., 1992.

The structure of the REMI model is based on economic assumptions that are widely accepted by economists. The key theoretical assumptions that represent the foundation (structure) of the model include:

1. Businesses are motivated by profits and individuals are motivated by the desire to maximize their well-being (utility);
2. Firms and industries are interconnected in predictable ways over time; and
3. Firms change the relative inputs into production based on the relative cost changes.

These basic assumptions produce the familiar upward slope to the various market supply curves and the traditional downward slope to demand. Since there is a national structure to the model, differences in the economic experience of a particular geographic area do not stem from differences in behavior. Rather, they differ according to their particular economic structure. This allows users to circumvent the paucity-of-local-data problem frequently encountered in forecasting local economies, since the availability of national data and empirically determined parameter estimates allows estimation and forecast of local data series that were previously unavailable.

Again, the objective of this effort is to capture long-term structural changes. Short-term cyclical fluctuations could alter the forecast level during any given period over the forecast horizon. Thus, stronger-than-expected growth in the U.S. economy will likely lead to stronger local growth and vice versa. For a more in-depth description of the REMI model refer to "The REMI Economic-Demographic Forecasting and Simulation Model," by Treyz, Rickman and Shao.

Figure AIV.1. Endogenous Linkages in the REMI Model
Reprinted with permission from Regional Economic Models, Inc.

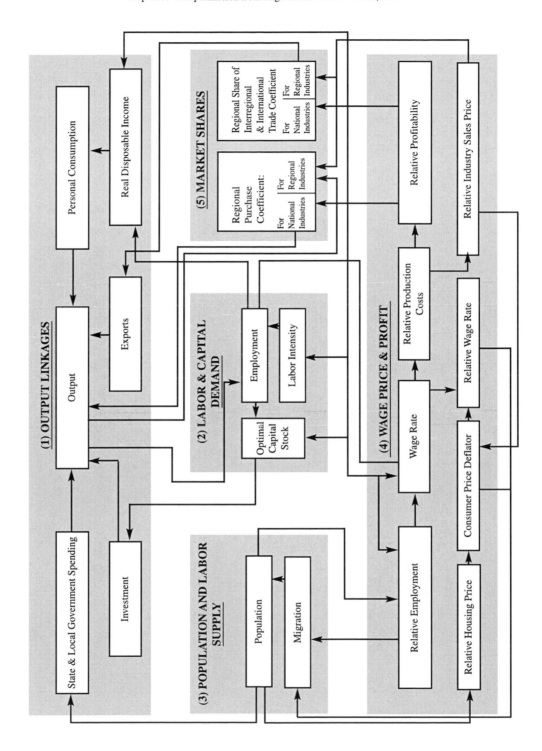

SELECTED BIBLIOGRAPHY

Adams, Carolyn et. al. Philadelphia: Neighborhoods, Divisions, and Conflict in a Postindustrial City. Philadelphia: Temple University Press (1991).

Advisory Commission on Intergovernmental Relations. Bankruptcies, Defaults, and Other Local Government Financial Emergencies. Washington D.C.: U.S. Government Printing Office (1985).

Advisory Commission on Intergovernmental Relations. Significant Features of Fiscal Federalism: Budget Processes and Tax Systems. Washington D.C.: U.S. Government Printing Office (1995).

Ammerman, Peggy. "Sharing the wealth: Taking GIS data to the public," American City & County, October, 1997, 25-32.

Anderson, Curt. "New for '99: Some can tell the taxman to charge it," Philadelphia Inquirer, August 21, 1998. p C1.

Ashenfelter, O, et. al. Contract Form and Procurement Costs: The Impact of Compulsory Multiple Contractor Laws in Construction. Cambridge, MA: National Bureau of Economic Research, Inc. (February 1997).

Barnard, J. L. and Evans, J. C. Citizenship in Philadelphia (1919)
<http://www.libertynet.org/ardenpop/appcitiz.html>.

Barry, Herbert, and Sullivan, Dan. "Effects Of Lower Tax On Buildings Than Land In Pittsburgh." Pittsburgh: University of Pittsburgh (August 1992).

Bartik, Timothy J. Who Benefits From State and Local Economic Development Policies? Kalamazoo: W. E. Upjohn Institute for Employment Research (1991).

Bartlett, Randall. The Crisis of American Cities. London: M. E Sharpe Inc. (1998).

Bartelt, David W. and Shlay, Ann B., "Housing Philadelphia: Low and Moderate Income Home Ownership — Opportunities and Constraints." Philadelphia (December 1995).

Bellush, J., and Netzer, D. Urban Politics: New York Style. London: M. E. Sharpe, Inc. (1990).

Benson, D., et. al. "Performance Budgeting, the Milwaukee Experience." Working Paper Presented at 17th Annual APPAM Research Conference. Milwaukee (1995).

Boston Municipal Research Bureau. Securing Boston's Financial Health: A Blueprint for Boston's Future. Boston: John Hancock Mutual Life Insurance Company (September 1993).

Braddock, David. "The Use of Regional Economic Models in Conducting Net Present Value Analysis of Development Programs." International Journal of Public Administration (18[1] 1995), 59-81.

Brandenburg, Aliki. The Story of William Penn. New Jersey: Prentice-Hall, Inc. (1964).

Bradley, Ann. "New Teachers Are Hot Commodity," Education Week, September 9, 1998. p. 1.

Brecher, C., and Horton, R.D., eds. Setting Municipal Priorities, 1990. New York: New York University Press (1989).

Breckenfeld, Gurney. "Higher Taxes That Promote Development." Fortune (August 1983), 68-71.

Brizius, Jack. "Deciding for Investment." Washington D.C.: The Alliance for Redesigning Government (1994).

Bureau of Recreation and Conservation of the Pennsylvania Department of Community Affairs. Local Government Recreation Services Survey: Summary of Findings. Harrisburg (March 1990).

Calthorpe, Peter. The Next American Metropolis: Ecology, Community, and the American Dream. New York: Princeton Agricultural Press (1993).

Carlin, Gerald A. "Highways and Education: The Road to Productivity?" Business Review (September/October 1993), 21–30.

Carlino, Gerald, and Sill, Keith. "Regional Economies: Separating Trends from Cycles." Business Review (May/June 1997), 19–31.

Carlino, Gerald A. "Trends in Metropolitan Employment Growth." Business Review (July/August 1998), 13-22. Chicago: Nelson-Hall Publishers (1990).

Citizens Budget Commission. "Fiscal Problems of the Two New Yorks: Size, Nature, and Possible Solutions." New York (May 1991).

Citizens Budget Commission. "Political Leadership in the Two New Yorks: Fiscal Policy in the 1990s." New York (June 1993).

Citizens Committee on Public Education in Philadelphia. Report of the Governance Committee. Philadelphia (1975).

City Charter Revision Commission. Report of the City Charter Revision Commission. Philadelphia (1973).

City of Auburn Finance Department. "User Fee Study." Auburn (June 1991).

City of Philadelphia Department of Records City Archives. Charter of the City of Philadelphia 1701. Philadelphia.

City of Philadelphia Office of Housing and Community Development and University of Pennsylvania Department of City Policy and Neighborhood Strategies Studio. "Southwest Center City Directory of Vacant Lots." Philadelphia (1998).

City of Philadelphia Office of Housing and Community Development and University of Pennsylvania Department of City Policy and Neighborhood Strategies Studio. "Southwest Center City Directory of Vacant Houses." Philadelphia (1998).

City of Philadelphia Office of Housing and Community Development. "Neighborhood Transformations: The Implementation of Philadelphia's Community Development Policy." Philadelphia (1997).

City of Philadelphia Office of Housing and Community Development. "Vacant Property Prescriptions: A Reinvestment Strategy." Philadelphia (July 1995).

City of Philadelphia Office of Housing and Community Development. "Home in North Philadelphia." Philadelphia (July 1993).

City of Philadelphia Office of Housing and Community Development. "Learning from Yorktown." Philadelphia (June 1996).

City of Philadelphia Office of the City Controller. Controller's Mid-Year Economic Survey 1998–1999. (1998).

City of Philadelphia Office of the City Controller. 1994 Mid-Year Economic and Financial Report. Philadelphia (1994).

City of Philadelphia Office of the City Controller. 1995 Mid-Year Economic and Financial Report. Philadelphia (1995).

City of Philadelphia Office of the City Controller. 1996 Mid-Year Economic and Financial Report. Philadelphia (1996).

City of Philadelphia Office of the City Controller. 1996–1997 Mid-Year Economic and Financial Update. Philadelphia (1996).

City of Philadelphia Office of the City Controller. 1997 Mid-Year Economic and Financial Report. Philadelphia (1997).

City of Philadelphia Office of the City Controller. 1997–1998 Mid-Year Special Report on the Philadelphia School District. Philadelphia (1998).

City of Philadelphia Office of the City Controller. 1998 City of Philadelphia Economic Update. Philadelphia (1998).

City of Philadelphia Office of the City Controller. 9-1-1 Emergency System Audit. Philadelphia (1994).

City of Philadelphia Office of the City Controller. Department of Licenses and Inspections Auditor's Report Fiscal 1996. Philadelphia (1997).

City of Philadelphia Office of the City Controller. Department of Revenue Tax Enforcement Performance Audit. Philadelphia (1998).

City of Philadelphia Office of the City Controller. Fire Department Performance Audit. Philadelphia (1997).

City of Philadelphia Office of the City Controller. School District of Philadelphia Performance Audit. Philadelphia (1997).

City of Philadelphia Office of the Mayor. "Philadelphia 2000: Working for the Future." Philadelphia (1994).

City of Philadelphia Office of the Mayor. City of Philadelphia Five-Year Financial Plan. Philadelphia (January 1998).

City of Philadelphia Office of the Mayor. Mayor's Report on City Services. Philadelphia (November 1996).

City of Philadelphia Office of the Mayor. Mayor's Report on City Services. Philadelphia (December 1997).

City of Philadelphia. Home Rule Charter. Philadelphia (1951).

City of Philadelphia. The Philadelphia Code. Philadelphia.

City of Tilburg. The Netherlands. The Tilburg Model. Tilburg.

City of Tilburg. The Netherlands. Pop Proces, The Tilburg Experience. Tilburg.

City of Tilburg. The Netherlands. Tilburg, Modern Industrial City. Tilburg.

Civic Federation, The. "From Privatization to Innovation: A Study of 16 U.S. Cities." Chicago (February 1996).

Cohen, B. A., et. al. "Mean Streets: Pedestrian Safety and Reform of the Nation's Transportation Law." Washington D.C.: The Environmental Working Group (1997).

Committee of Seventy. Charter Revision: A Review. Philadelphia (1979).

Committee of Seventy. Economic Development Governance Study. Philadelphia (1982).

Committee of Seventy. Governance Matters: School Reform for the Urban District. Philadelphia (1997).

Committee of Seventy. Housing Governance Study. Philadelphia (1982).

Committee of Seventy. Judicial Selection Governance Study. Philadelphia (1983).

Committee of Seventy. Municipal Utilities Governance Study. Philadelphia (1985).

Committee of Seventy. No School Today. Philadelphia (1981).

Committee of Seventy. Personnel Practices Governance Study. Philadelphia (June 1986).

Committee of Seventy. Philadelphia Police Department Governance Study. Philadelphia: Morrison Press (1998).

Committee of Seventy. Ports Governance Study. Philadelphia (1980).

Committee of Seventy. The Charter: A History. Philadelphia (1980).

Committee of Seventy. Transportation Governance Study. Philadelphia (1981).

Coolidge, Susan. A Short History of the City of Philadelphia, From Its Foundation to the Present Time (1880) <http://www.libertynet.org/ardenpop/appshort.html>.

Cord, Steven. "Land Tax: The Hard Evidence." Columbia: School of Economic and Financial Studies (1989).

Cord, Steven. "The Impact of a Building-to-Land Tax Shift on Homeowners and Other Property Owners in Philadelphia." Indiana: Center for the Study of Economics (1982).

Crone, Theodore M. "Where Have All the Factory Jobs Gone—and Why?" Business Review (May/June 1997), 3-18.

Crone, Theodore M., and Babyak, Kevin J. "Looking Ahead: Leading Indexes for Pennsylvania and New Jersey." Business Review (May/June 1996), 3-14.

Daniel, Kermit. "Fiscal and Political Implications of the Concentration of Immigration." Research Impact Paper # 1. Philadelphia: Department of Public Policy and Management, The Wharton School, University of Pennsylvania (October 1994).

Delaware Valley Regional Planning Commission. "Delaware Valley Data: Employment 1970–1994." Philadelphia (February 1997).

Delaware Valley Regional Planning Commission. "Direction 2020." Executive Summary (May 1995).

Delaware Valley Regional Planning Commission. "Employment Change By County: 1973–1993." From U.S. Bureau of Economic Analysis. Philadelphia (October 1995).

Delaware Valley Regional Planning Commission. "Estimated Population Change By County: 1990–1996." From U.S. Bureau of the Census. Philadelphia (June 1997).

Delaware Valley Regional Planning Commission. "Journey-to-Work: Trends in the Delaware Valley Region, 1970–1990." Report No. 5 (June 1993).

Delaware Valley Regional Planning Commission. "Policies for the 21st Century." Report No. 2 (May 1993).

Delaware Valley Regional Planning Commission. "Rating the Region: The State of the Delaware Valley." Report No. 1 (May 1993).

Delaware Valley Regional Planning Commission. "Year 2020 Comprehensive Plan for the Delaware Valley" (1996).

Delaware Valley Regional Planning Commission. "Year 2020 County and Municipal Interim Population and Employment Forecasts." Report No. 8 (June 1993).

Delaware Valley Regional Planning Commission. "Year 2020 Land Use and Transportation Plan for the Delaware Valley Region" (February 1998).

Delaware Valley Regional Planning Commission. "Year 2020 Municipal Forecasts of Occupied Housing Units, Vehicle Availability and Employed Residents." Report No. 15 (June 1994).

Dilanian, Ken. "Pa. signs deal with Microsoft," *Philadelphia Inquirer*, July 14, 1998, p. 1.

Drennan, Matthew P. Modeling Metropolitan Economies for Forecasting and Policy Analysis. New York: New York University Press (1985).

Dunlap, David W. "Rethinking a City's Street Furniture," *New York Times*, January 18, 1998, p. 1.

Durning, Alan T. The Car and the City. Seattle: Northwest Environment (1996).

Eggers, W. D., et. al. Privatization '98: 12th Annual Report on Privatization. California: Reason Public Policy Institute (1996).

Eggers, William D. Cutting Local Government Costs through Competition and Privatization. California: California Chamber of Commerce (1997).

Eggers, William D., and O'Leary, John. Revolution at the Roots: Making Our Government Smaller, Better, and Closer to Home. New York: The Free Press (1995).

Fazlollah, M., Matza, M., and McCoy, C. "How to Cut City's Crime Rate: Don't Report It." *Philadelphia Inquirer*, November 1, 1998, p. 1.

Federal Writers' Project of the Works Progress Administration for the Commonwealth of Pennsylvania, The, The WPA Guide to Philadelphia. Preface by E. Digby Baltzell. Introduction by Richard J. Webster. Philadelphia: The University of Pennsylvania Press (1998).

Fisher, Peter S., and Peters, Alan H. Industrial Incentives: Competition Among American States and Cities. Kalamazoo: W.E. Upjohn Institute for Employment Research (1998).

Flaherty, John, and Lusht, Kenneth. "Site Value Taxation, Land Values, and Development Patterns." State College: The Mary Jean & Frank P. Smeal College of Business Administration, Pennsylvania State University (October 1996).

Fuchs, Ester R. Mayors and Money: Fiscal Policy in New York and Chicago (American Politics and Political Economy). Chicago: University of Chicago Press (1992).

Fuchs, Ester R. "The Permanent Urban Fiscal Crisis." From: Breaking Away, The Future of Cities Julia Vitullo-Martin, ed. New York: Twentieth Century Fund Press (1996).

Gallery, John Andrew. Philadelphia Architecture: A Guide to the City, 2nd ed. Philadelphia: The Foundation for Architecture (1994).

Garvin, Alexander. The American City: What Works, What Doesn't. New York: McGraw-Hill Companies, Inc. (1996).

Greater Philadelphia First. An Economic Development Strategy for the Greater Philadelphia Region. Philadelphia (May 1995).

Grimes, D., Fulton, G, and Bonardelli, M. "Evaluating Alternative Regional Planning Models: Comment." Growth and Change (Fall 1992), 516-520.

Guinther, John. Direction of Cities. Foreword by Edmund N. Bacon. New York: Penguin Books USA Inc. (1996).

Gyourko, J., and Summers, A. A. "Paying for the Poor: A New Strategy for Handling the Urban Burden." Draft for the Policy Brief of the Brookings Institution. Philadelphia: The Wharton School, University of Pennsylvania (November 1996).

Gyourko, J., and Summers, A. A. "Working Towards a New Urban Strategy for America's Large Cities: The Role of an Urban Audit." Research Impact Paper # 7. Philadelphia: The Wharton Real Estate Center, The Wharton School, University of Pennsylvania (February 1995).

Halbfinger, David M. "As Surveillance Cameras Peer, Some Wonder if They Also Pry," *New York Times*, February 22, 1998, p. 1.

Hanushek, Erik A. "Making America's Schools Work: This Time Money Is Not the Answer." The Brookings Review (Fall 1994), 10-13.

Harris, Blake. "How to Finance 'Service to the Citizen' Projects," <http://www.govtech.net/publication/servicecitizen/financing.shtm>.

Hatry, Harry P. "Tracking the Quality of Services." Handbook of Public Administration; 2nd ed. (1996), 537–554.

Hatry, H., Gerhart, C., and Marshall, M. "Eleven Ways to Make Performance Measurement More Useful to Public Managers." Public Management (September 1994), vol. 76-9, s15-s18.

Hershberg, Theodore. "Regional Cooperation: Strategies and Incentives for Global Competitiveness and Urban Reform." *National Civic Review* (Spring-Summer 1996), 25-30.

Hershberg, Theodore. "The Case for Regional Cooperation." *The Regionalist* (Fall 1995), vol. 1-3, 13-32.

Herson, Lawrence J.R., and Bolland, John M. The Urban Web: Politics, Policy, and Theory. Chicago: Nelson Hall Publishers (1990).

Hilke, John. Cost Savings From Privatization: A Compilation of Study Findings. Los Angeles (March 1993).

Hill, Paul T., and Celio, Mary Beth. Fixing Urban Schools. Washington D.C.: Brookings Institute Press (1998).

Hotchkin, Rev. S. F. Penn's Green Country Town (1903) <http://www.libertynet.org/ardenpop/appgreen.html>.

Hughes, J. W., and Seneca, J. J., "Anatomy of a Business Cycle: The Final Report Card." Issue Paper No. 16. New Brunswick: Edward J. Bloustein School of Planning and Public Policy, Rutgers University (1997).

Hughes, J. W., and Seneca, J. J., "Long Term Regional Momentum: Employment and Income Dimensions." Issue Paper No. 15. New Brunswick: Edward J. Bloustein School of Planning and Public Policy, Rutgers University (1997).

Hurt, Harry III. "Parks brought to you by...," *U.S. News & World Report*, August 11, 1997, 42-45.

Inman, R., Craig, S., and Luce, T. "The Fiscal Future for American Cities: Lessons from Three Cities." Research Impact Paper # 4. Philadelphia: The Wharton Real Estate Center, The Wharton School, University of Pennsylvania (December 1994).

Inman, Robert P. "How to Have a Fiscal Crisis: Lessons from Philadelphia." *The American Economic Review* (May 1995), vol. 85, 378–383.

Inman, Robert P. "Can Philadelphia Escape Its Fiscal Crisis with Another Tax Increase?" *Business Review* (September–October 1992), 6–21.

Integrity and Accountability Office. Philadelphia Police Department, Second Report. Philadelphia (September 1998).

International Personnel Management Association. "1997 Personnel Program Inventory." Alexandria (May 1997).

International Personnel Management Association. "Alternative Work Schedules." Alexandria (1992).

International Personnel Management Association. "Personnel Practices: Telecommuting." Alexandria (January 1998).

International Personnel Management Association. "Personnel Practices: Residency Requirements." Alexandria (December 1997).

International Personnel Management Association. "Personnel Practices: Alternative Work Schedules." Alexandria (February 1995).

Jakubowski, Lara, and Summers, Anita A. "The Fiscal Burden of Unreimbursed Poverty Expenditures in the City of Philadelphia: 1985–1995." Working Paper #238. Philadelphia: Department of Public Policy and Management, The Wharton School, University of Pennsylvania (September 1995).

– "...Just Don't Call 911 to Order a Pizza," *Governing*, March 1996, 17.

Klinger, D.E., and Lynn, D. B. "Beyond Civil Service: The Changing Face of Public Personnel Management." Public Personnel Management (Summer 1997), vol. 26-2, 157-173.

Ladd, Helen F., and Yinger, John. America's Ailing Cities: Fiscal Health and the Design of Urban Policy. Baltimore: The Johns Hopkins University Press (1989).

Lang, Richard W. "City Problems and Suburban Reactions." *Business Review* (September–October 1992), 3-5.

Lemov, Penelope. "Balancing the Budget with Billboards and Souvenirs," *Governing*, October 1994, 46-50.

Luce, Thomas F., and Summers, Anita A. Local Fiscal Issues in the Philadelphia Metropolitan Area. Philadelphia: The University of Pennsylvania Press (1987).

Lynch, Michael, W. "Public-Private Partners that Work," *Investor's Business Daily*, June 11, 1998.

Mahtesian, Charles "Handing the Schools to City Hall," *Governing*, October 1996, 36-40.

Mayor Stephen Goldsmith. The Twenty-First Century City: Resurrecting Urban America. Washington D.C.: Regnery Publishing, Inc. (1997).

McQuown, Lynn S. The Pennsylvania Manual. Harrisburg: Commonwealth of Pennsylvania Department of General Services (1995).

Mezzacappa, Dale. "Under a cloud of despair, he ended a life of promise." *Philadelphia Inquirer*, July, 19, 1996, p. B1.

Murawski, John. "Citizens can swipe away taxes, fees," *Philadelphia Inquirer*, August 8, 1997, p. B1.

Multnomah County Library. "The Official Website for Entrepreneurial Libraries," <http://www.multnomah.lib.or.us/lib/entre>.

National Academy of Public Administration. A Competency Model for Human Resource Professionals. Washington D.C. (June 1996).

National Academy of Public Administration. Managing Succession and Developing Leadership: Growing the Next Generation of Public Service Leaders. Washington D.C. (August 1997).

National Academy of Public Administration. Measuring Results: Successful Human Resources Management. Washington D.C. (August 1997).

National Academy of Public Administration. Work/Life Programs: Helping Managers, Helping Employees. Washington D.C. (January 1998).

National League of Cities. "All in it Together: Cities, Suburbs, and Local Economic Regions." Washington D.C. (February 1993).

National League of Cities. "City Distress, Metropolitan Disparities and Economic Growth." Washington D.C. (September 1992).

New York State Financial Control Board. Other Ways of Doing Business: Fiscal Comparisons of Major U.S. Cities. New York (March 1994).

New York State Financial Control Board. Structural Balance. New York (July 1992).

Norquist, John O. The Wealth of the Cities: Revitalizing the Centers of American Life. Reading: Addison-Wesley (1998).

Nye, B. A., et. al. The Lasting Benefits Study: A Continuing Analysis of the Effect of Small Class Size in Kindergarten Through Third Grade on Student Achievement Test Scores in Subsequent Grade Levels. Nashville: Tennessee State University (1994).

Oldenburg, Don. "Rent-free for life," *Preservation*, September/October 1998, 12-13.

Olson, Lynn. "Keeping Tabs on Quality." *Education Week* (January 1997), 7-49.

Oregon Progress Board. "Growth and Livable Communities." Salem (December 1992).

Orfield, Myron. "Philadelphia Metropolitics: A Regional Agenda for Community and Stability." Report to the Pennsylvania Environmental Council. Philadelphia (March 1997).

Orfield, Myron. Metropolitics: A Regional Agenda for Community and Stability. Washington, D.C.: Brookings Institution Press. (1997).

Osborne, David, and Gaebler, Ted. Reinventing Government. New York: Addison-Wesley Publishing Company, Inc. (1992).

Osborne, David, and Plastrik, Peter. Banishing Bureaucracy: The Five Strategies for Reinventing Government. New York: Addison-Wesley Publishing Company, Inc. (1997).

Pack, J. R. "The Impacts of Concentrated Urban Poverty on City Government Expenditures." Research Impact Paper #6. Philadelphia: Department of Public Policy and Management, The Wharton School, University of Pennsylvania (January 1995).

– "The Paper Prohibition," Governing, November 1997, 58.

Pate-Bain, H., Achilles, C.M., Boyd-Zaharias, J., and McKenna, B. "Class Size Does Make a Difference." Phi Delta Kappan (November 1992).

Pennsylvania Department of Labor and Industry. "Employment Outlook in Pennsylvania Industries and Occupations: Estimated 1990 and Projected 2000 Employment." Harrisburg (January 1996).

Pennsylvania Economy League, Inc. "A Review of Philadelphia's Authorities." Report No. 566. Philadelphia (October 1989).

Pennsylvania Economy League, Inc. "Building a World-Class Workforce: The Key to a Competitive Greater Philadelphia." Report No. 686. Philadelphia (October 1996).

Pennsylvania Economy League, Inc. "Citizen's Guide to the Philadelphia Budget." Report No. 644. Philadelphia (1993).

Pennsylvania Economy League, Inc. "Contracting Out Services in Philadelphia." Report No. 582. Philadelphia (November 1990).

Pennsylvania Economy League, Inc. "Fiscal Crises and Remedies: A Comparative Study of Philadelphia and Other Large Jurisdictions, with Emphasis on Fiscal Supervision Agencies." Report No. 596. Philadelphia (April 1991).

Pennsylvania Economy League, Inc. "Governance, Performance, and Children Achieving in The Philadelphia School District." Report No. 678/P-303. Philadelphia (1995).

Pennsylvania Economy League, Inc. "Greater Philadelphia's Challenge: Capitalizing on Change in the Regional Health Care Economy." Report No. 683. (February 1996).

Pennsylvania Economy League, Inc. "Greater Philadelphia's Competitive Edge: The Nonprofit Culture Industry and its Economic Value to the Region." Philadelphia (September 1998).

Pennsylvania Economy League, Inc. "History and Features of Philadelphia Government." Report No. 631. Philadelphia (1992).

Pennsylvania Economy League, Inc. "Performance Measurement of Municipal Services: How Are America's Cities Measuring Up?" Philadelphia (September 1995).

Pennsylvania Economy League, Inc. "Philadelphia Government." Report No. 421. Philadelphia (1980).

Pennsylvania Economy League, Inc. "Philadelphia Private Sector Employment Trends: Are There Any Growth Industries?" Report No. 649. Philadelphia (July 1993).

Pennsylvania Economy League, Inc. "Productivity Scorecards for Philadelphia Municipal Services." Report No. 523. Philadelphia (December 1987).

Pennsylvania Economy League, Inc. "Survey of the Costs Associated with Illegal Dumping in Philadelphia." Report No. 677/P-601. Philadelphia (June 1995).

Pennsylvania Economy League, Inc. "The Philadelphia Gas Works: Governing for Performance." Report No. 681/P-302a. Philadelphia (December 1995).

Pennsylvania Intergovernmental Cooperation Authority. "Revenue Stress in the City of Philadelphia." (1996).

Perlman, Ellen. "Disability Dilemmas," Governing, April 1998, 30-33.

Philadelphia Campaign for Public Education and the Partnership for Reform. "A Citizen's Guide to the Philadelphia School Budget." Philadelphia (1998).

Philadelphia City Planning Commission. "Recreation Facilities Study." Philadelphia (1992).

Philadelphia City Planning Commission. "Vacant Land in Philadelphia: A Report on Vacant Land Management and Neighborhood Restructuring." (June 1995).

Philadelphia City Planning Commission. Destination Philadelphia. Philadelphia (February 1993).

Philadelphia Education Summit. "Common Ground: Beyond the Politics of Education." Philadelphia (1998).

Philadelphia Independent Charter Commission. Briefing Materials. Philadelphia (1994).

Philadelphia Independent Charter Commission. Educational Materials. Philadelphia (1994).

Philadelphia Independent Charter Commission. Final Recommendations of the Philadelphia Independent Charter Commission As of March 18, 1994: Non-charter Language. Philadelphia (1994).

Philadelphia Independent Charter Commission. Report to the Voters. Philadelphia (April 1994).

Philadelphia Police Study Task Force. "Philadelphia and its Police: Toward a New Partnership." Philadelphia (1987).

Popovich, M. G., ed. Creating High Performance Government Organizations. San Francisco: Jossey-Bass Publishers (1998).

Porter, Michael E. "The Competitive Advantage of the Inner City." *Harvard Business Review* (May-June 1995), 55-71.

Preservation Alliance for Greater Philadelphia. The Economic Benefits of Preserving Philadelphia's Past. Philadelphia (1998).

Rendell, Edward G. "The New Urban Agenda." Philadelphia (1994).

Retting, R. A., and Greene, M. A. "Influence of Traffic Signal Timing on Red-Light Running and Potential Vehicle Conflicts at Urban Intersections." *Transportation Research Record* (1996), 1–6.

Retting, R. A., Williams, A. F., and Ulmer, R.G. "Prevalence and Characteristics of Red Light Running Crashes in the United States." Arlington: Insurance Institute for Highway Safety (March 1998).

Retting, R. A., et. al. "Evolution of Red Light Camera Enforcement in Oxnard, California." Arlington: Insurance Institute for Highway Safety (March 1998).

Retting, R. A., Williams, A. F., and Greene, M. A. "Red Light Running and Sensible Countermeasures: Summary of Research Findings." Arlington: Insurance Institute for Highway Safety (April 1996).

Retting, Richard A., and Williams, Allan F. "Characteristics of Red Light Violators: Results of a Field Investigation." *Journal of Safety Research* (Spring 1997), vol. 27-1, 9-15.

Rifkin, Jeremy. The End of Work: The Decline of the Global Labor Force and the Dawn of the Post-Market Era. Foreword by Robert L. Heilbroner. New York: The Putnam Publishing Group (1995).

Rybczynski, Witold. "Downsizing Cities." Research Impact Paper #5. Philadelphia: Graduate School of Fine Arts/ Real Estate Department. Philadelphia: The Wharton School, University of Pennsylvania (December 1994).

Sandro, Phillip H. "Jobs and Buy Local Programs: Expected Employment Effects of Public-Sector Import-Substitution in Chicago," *International Journal of Public Administration*. Volume 18(1) (1995), 199-225.

Schuster, Karolyn. "Exclusive Brand Contracts," *Food Management*, February 1998, 34-44.

Sharp, Elaine B. Urban Politics and Administration: From Service Delivery to Economic Development. New York: Longman (1991).

Siegel, Fred. The Future Once Happened Here: New York, D.C., L.A., and the Fate of America's Big Cities. New York: The Free Press (1997).

Stull, William J., and Madden, Janice F. Post-Industrial Philadelphia: Structural Changes in the Metropolitan Economy. Philadelphia: University of Pennsylvania Press (1990).

Suellentrop, Chris. "This Government Brought to You By...," *Governing*, November 1998, 43-44.

Summers, Anita A. "Major Regionalization Efforts Between Cities and Suburbs in the United States." Working Paper #246. Philadelphia: The Wharton School, University of Pennsylvania (March 1997).

Tannenwald, Robert. "State business tax climate: how should it be measured and how important is it?" *New England Economic Review*, Jan-Feb 1996, 23.

Tideman, N., and Johnson, C. "A Statistical Analysis of Property Taxes in Pennsylvania." Cambridge: Lincoln Institute of Land Policy (1995).

Tideman, N., and Plassmann, F. "The Impact of Two-Rate Property Taxes on Construction in Pennsylvania." Virginia: Virginia Polytechnic Institute and State University (October 1995).

Toll, J. B., and Gillam, M. S., eds., Invisible Philadelphia: Community through Volunteer Organizations. Philadelphia: Atwater Kent Museum (1995).

Tracy, R. C., and Jean, E. P. "Measuring Government Performance: Experimenting with Service Efforts and Accomplishments Reporting in Portland, Oregon." *Government Finance Review* (December 1993), 11-14.

Treyz, George I. Regional Economic Modeling: A Systematic Approach to Economic Forecasting and Policy Analysis. Boston: Kluwer Academic Publishers (1993).

Treyz, G., Rickman, D., and Shao, G. "The REMI Economic-Demographic Forecasting and Simulation Model." International Regional Science Review (vol. 14, no. 3, 1992), 221-253.

U.S. Conference of Mayors. "Best Practices Center." Washington D.C. (January 1998).

U.S. Department of Housing and Urban Development. "The State of the Cities: 1998." Washington D.C. (1998).

U.S. Department of Housing and Urban Development. "The State of the Cities." (June 1997).

U.S. General Accounting Office. Experiences of Other Cities and Their Oversight Boards. Washington D.C.: U.S. Government Printing Office (1995).

U.S. General Accounting Office. Privatization: Questions State and Local Decisionmakers Used When Considering Privatization Options. Washington D.C.: U.S. Government Printing Office (1998).

U.S. of Mayors, prepared under the leadership of Ernest N. Morial and Marion Barry, Jr. Rebuilding America's Cities. Cambridge: Ballinger Publishing Company (1986).

Useem, Elizabeth L. Renewing Schools: A Report on the Cluster Initiative in Philadelphia. Philadelphia: The Philadelphia Partnership for Education (1994).

Useem, E., Buchanan, J., Meyers, E., and Maule-Schmidt, J. "Urban Teacher Curriculum and Systemic Change." Philadelphia: Philadelphia Education Fund (1995).

Vitullo-Martin, Julia, ed., Breaking Away, The Future of Cities. New York: Twentieth Century Fund Press (1996).

Voith, Richard. "City and Suburban Growth: Substitutes or Complements." *Business Review* (September/October 1992), 24-33.

Voith, Richard. "Commuter Rail Ridership: The Long and the Short Haul." *Business Review* (November/December 1987), 13-23.

Voith, Richard. "The Downtown Parking Syndrome: Does Curing the Illness Kill the Patient?" *Business Review* (January/February 1998), 3-14.

Voith, Richard. "Public Transit: Realizing its Potential." *Business Review* (September/October 1994), 15-23.

Voith, Richard. "The Suburban Housing Market." *Business Review* (November/December 1996), 13-24.

Walters, Jonathan. Measuring Up: Governing's Guide to Performance Measurement for Geniuses [and Other Public Managers]. Washington D.C.: Governing Books (1998).

Weigley, R.F. et. al. Philadelphia: A 300-Year History. New York: W. W. Norton & Company (1982).

SUBJECT INDEX

ABOUT THE CITY CONTROLLER

Jonathan A. Saidel has been re-elected to his fourth consecutive four-year term as Philadelphia's City Controller. Jonathan is a graduate of Temple University and the Delaware Law School of Widener College. He is an attorney and certified public accountant in the Commonwealth of Pennsylvania and is admitted to practice before the Supreme Court of Pennsylvania, United States Tax Court, and the United States District Court for the Eastern District of Pennsylvania. Jonathan serves as a Lecturer at the University of Pennsylvania's Fels Center of Government. He also serves as Adjunct Professor in the Master's Program at Saint Joseph's University and teaches Government Finance in the MBA Program at Drexel University. In the past, he has been an Adjunct Lecturer of Taxes and Accounting at Temple University and an Adjunct Professor in the Master's Program at Saint Joseph's University. He has been honored as "Controller of the Year" from the PA City Controllers Association, by the State of Israel, the Philadelphia Police and Fire Departments, Vietnam Veterans, and many other outstanding organizations.

ABOUT THE AUTHORS

Brett Mandel currently serves as the Executive Director of Philadelphia Forward, a non-profit citizen's organization dedicated to building a constituency for change to promote positive policies for Philadelphia. Previously, he served as Director, Financial and Policy Analysis, in the City of Philadelphia Office of the Controller where he directed the efforts of the Financial and Policy Analysis Unit and oversaw consideration of a wide variety of issue areas relating to municipal governance, budgetary policy, and municipal government operations. Prior to joining the Controller's Office, Brett was an Associate with the Pennsylvania Economy League and Assistant to the Policy Director of the Philadelphia Independent Charter Commission. Brett received his B.A. from Hamilton College and his M.G.A. from the Fels Center of Government of the University of Pennsylvania. Brett is the author of *Minor Players, Major Dreams* (University of Nebraska Press, 1997) and *Is This Heaven? The Magic Of The Field Of Dreams* (Diamond Communications (Rowman & Littlefield Publishing Group, 2002).

Kevin Babyak currently serves as the Chief Statistician for Marketing Systems Group (MSG). In that role he is responsible for creating quantitative based solutions for clients in the public and private sectors. Prior to joining MSG, Kevin served as Assistant City Controller for the City of Philadelphia. Prior to joining the Controller's Office, Kevin was an Economic Research Analyst with the Federal Reserve Bank of Philadelphia and an Economist with the U.S. Department of Labor, Bureau of Labor Statistics. Kevin received his B.A. from Temple University and his M.S. in Economics from Lehigh University. Kevin's model methodology for his Leading Index Model for Pennsylvania and New Jersey was published in the May-June 1996 issue of Business Review.

David Volpe currently serves as Managing Director and a Partner with Emerald Asset Management. Prior to joining Emerald Asset Management, David served as First Deputy City Controller for the City of Philadelphia. In addition to administering operations of the Controller's Office, David was also the Chief Investment Officer of the Philadelphia Gas Works Retirement Reserve. Prior to joining the Controller's Office, David was a Senior Budget Analyst with the Pennsylvania Senate Appropriations Committee and the comptroller of a large non-profit organization in the Philadelphia area. David received his B.S. degree from Potsdam College and his M.A. in finance from the Pennsylvania State University.

ABOUT THE AUTHORS OF THE SECOND EDITION

Marisa G. Waxman currently serves as Director of the Financial and Policy Analysis in Philadelphia's Office of the City Controller. Prior to joining the Controller's Office, Marisa was Director of Marketing for an energy and telecommunications provider. Marisa received her B.A. degree from the University of Pennsylvania and her Master of City Planning from the Graduate School of Fine Arts at the University of Pennsylvania.

Tony Di Martino currently serves as Assistant City Controller for the City of Philadelphia. Tony is life long Philadelphian and has been employed by the City for over 28 years. He has been a member of the City Controller's award winning Financial Policy and Analysis Unit for over ten years. Tony received a B.S. in accounting from La Salle College. He was a contributor to the City Controller's *Tax Structure Analysis Report*, as well as the first edition of *Philadelphia: A New Urban Direction*.

ABOUT THE CITY CONTROLLER'S OFFICE

The City of Philadelphia, Office of the City Controller was established by the 1951 Home Rule Charter as the sole auditing agency of Philadelphia City Government. This role was expanded in 1965, making the City Controller also the auditor for the School District of Philadelphia. The City Controller is elected to a four-year term midway between the elections of the Mayor and City Council, to encourage a measure of independence from the officials whose expenditures the Controller's Office must audit. The Controller heads the Auditing Department, which has broad authority and responsibility for protecting the public's interest in the handling of the City's money.

In recent years, the work of the Controller's Office has resulted in hundreds of million of dollars in cost-saving recommendations, many of which have been implemented by the current and past city administrations. The City Controller's Office has received numerous awards and commendations for its audits and other publications.